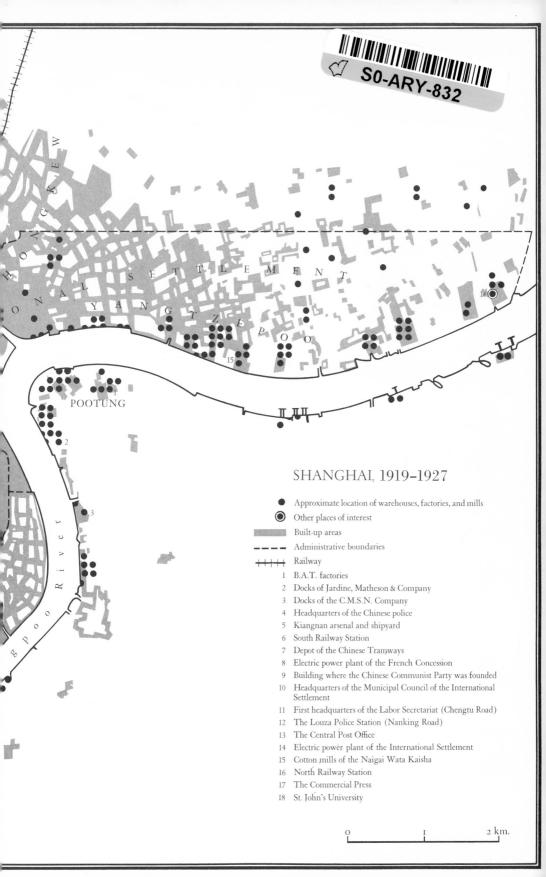

SHANGHAI, 1919–1927

●   Approximate location of warehouses, factories, and mills
◉   Other places of interest
▬   Built-up areas
- - -   Administrative boundaries
+++++   Railway

1   B.A.T. factories
2   Docks of Jardine, Matheson & Company
3   Docks of the C.M.S.N. Company
4   Headquarters of the Chinese police
5   Kiangnan arsenal and shipyard
6   South Railway Station
7   Depot of the Chinese Tramways
8   Electric power plant of the French Concession
9   Building where the Chinese Communist Party was founded
10   Headquarters of the Municipal Council of the International Settlement
11   First headquarters of the Labor Secretariat (Chengtu Road)
12   The Louza Police Station (Nanking Road)
13   The Central Post Office
14   Electric power plant of the International Settlement
15   Cotton mills of the Naigai Wata Kaisha
16   North Railway Station
17   The Commercial Press
18   St. John's University

HONGKEW

NATIONAL SETTLEMENT

YANGTZEPOO

POOTUNG

Poo River

THE CHINESE LABOR MOVEMENT
1919–1927

JEAN CHESNEAUX

THE CHINESE LABOR MOVEMENT
1919–1927

Translated from the French by H. M. Wright

1968
Stanford University Press
Stanford, California

The Chinese Labor Movement, 1919–1927 was originally published in French in 1962 under the title *Le mouvement ouvrier chinois de 1919 à 1927.*

Stanford University Press
Stanford, California
© 1968 by the Board of Trustees of the
Leland Stanford Junior University
Printed in the United States of America
L.C. 68-17136

Foreword

Professor Chesneaux's masterly study is one of the very few seminal works on the history of China in the twentieth century, and a pioneering probe into the vast unexplored realm of twentieth-century Chinese social history. Thus far, research on modern China has been focused primarily on leading personalities and ideologies, partly because the sources for such studies are more readily available but mainly because of a widespread, often unconscious, assumption that the Chinese people have had little to do with the making of their history. In particular, the modern industrial labor force has been seen as trivial or non-existent, an artifact of Comintern strategy rather than an important social element in its own right.

In this volume, Professor Chesneaux gives us a well-documented picture of the Chinese industrial working class in the crucial years 1919–27. He describes the origins of this class, its components, its living and working conditions, and its rapidly expanding social and political role. He demonstrates that despite the minuscule number of industrial workers in the population as a whole, they were strategically so placed that in the key areas of concentration they had by 1925 become a dominant revolutionary force. One of the special merits of the book is the meticulous attention given to geographic variations, which are considerable in a country the size of China. Its wealth of information on conditions in the various industrial regions is worth the attention of all scholars interested in the social history of modern China.

Formidable as the author's data are, they do not prevent the emergence of a vivid picture of actual working-class life and of the enormous and accelerating changes in that life during the 1920's. Indeed, there is no piling up of facts out of context but rather the creation of a context from a skilled analysis of the available facts. Where the evidence is inconclusive but suggestive, the author says so. Where he finds the evidence conclusive, he makes his case with eloquence but always supplies sufficient information—if not in the text, in the Notes—to allow the critical reader to reach his own conclusions.

Though clearly a Marxist, Professor Chesneaux is no dogmatist bent on forcing his data into preconceived molds. He uses Marxism to formulate questions about social change, not to answer them. The result is a well-written, startlingly fresh view of China in the 1920's—not only an important new book in a field in which first-class work is still quite rare, but important in a new way.

In conclusion, a word of tribute to the late Hope Wright, the translator of this volume, to whom our profession owes a debt of gratitude. For many years, Mrs. Wright, herself a skilled writer and widely read in Chinese history and literature, was the main translator into English of important French and German scholarly works on China. Her translations, at once faithful to the original and to the rhythms and idioms of English, are on the shelves of every American university library and every American student of China. In recent years, as she met more American scholars at her home in London and on the continent, she expressed an interest in visiting the United States. In one of her last letters, she wrote: "The spark has crossed the Atlantic." She did not live to cross it herself, but with her translation of this book she sent another spark across.

MARY CLABAUGH WRIGHT

Preface

A special feature of our times is the way social studies of all kinds tend more and more to adopt a global frame of reference. Historians, geographers, economists, and sociologists used to confine their research to western Europe; but the profound social and political changes that have taken place in Asia, Africa, and Latin America have impelled scholars to extend their research to these areas. Equipped with the social scientist's methods and tools of research, scholars can establish important new perspectives in a field like Oriental studies, which was formerly concerned exclusively with describing and analyzing the ancient civilizations of Asia as if they existed in a vacuum. At the same time, training in Oriental studies makes it possible to use original sources, and thus to study the contemporary problems of Asia from the inside; otherwise all that can be done is to examine the political, cultural, and commercial relations of these countries with the West. This study of the Chinese labor movement from 1919 to 1927 is an attempt to give our knowledge of contemporary China a firm documentary basis.

The need to link traditional sinology with modern social history seemed to me so essential that it was worth all the risks and difficulties involved. That formidable difficulties exist cannot be denied. Since a historian's work is as good as the sources he uses, the main difficulty lies in the inadequacy of the available documentation. In the first place, there are some sources that are now inaccessible and seem likely to remain so for a long time. I refer to sources such as the archives of the big foreign enterprises in China, including those of the Kailan Mining Administration (K.M.A.), the British and American Tobacco Company, and the French Tramways in Shanghai; and, to a lesser extent, the archives of the foreign civil authorities in China. With the kind permission of the People's City Government of Shanghai, I was able to consult the Daily Reports of the Commissioner of the Shanghai Municipal Police; but I searched in vain for the archives of the Mixed Court of the International Settlement, which, judging from the extracts on arrests occasionally published in the *North China Herald,* would be of considerable interest for the study of social conflicts and labor activities. Secondly, such documentation as is available is extremely unreliable, and sometimes even contradictory, especially as far as figures are concerned. I have not tried to minimize the problems involved in the collection of material for Chapter II, which attempts to estimate the size of the Chinese proletariat in 1919 or at least to assemble the available data. In 1919 there was no organization in China capable of giving reliable annual figures on economic growth or on the number of enterprises and of workers employed in them. As will be seen, the figures given by the Ministry of Agriculture and Commerce (Nung-shang-pu) are unreliable; and there are no reliable statistics on wages, cost of living, or monetary values. All that can be given are partial and approximate estimates, which, in view of the importance of data of this kind for the history of the labor movement, are rather less than adequate.

I met with the opposite kind of difficulty when I was preparing the results of my research for publication. This arose from the wealth of historical materials published in People's China since 1958, especially those regarding social and political matters. The insistence during the past few years that intellectuals do manual work brought many university lecturers and students into the factories, and this resulted in the publication of a large number of monographs based both on factory archives (in firms that had been Chinese-owned) and on interviews with old workers. Chinese historians have also published a vast amount of material (press extracts, pamphlets, personal memoirs, etc.) concerning episodes such as the May Fourth Movement and areas such as Hunan. Because my research ended in 1960 and my thesis was submitted in the spring of 1961, I was able to use only a very small part of this material, which grows in volume every year and is likely to go on growing, so that it is impossible to keep one's published results entirely up to date.

Nevertheless, there was already a considerable amount of available source material, both in Chinese and in English and Russian. This being the case, I have had to confine bibliographical references to a choice of material dictated largely by circumstances. The four months I spent in China, thanks to the aid extended by the Chinese People's Association for Cultural Relations with Foreign Countries and to the help of the Centre National de la Recherche Scientifique, enabled me to collect much valuable material, but not enough to offset the heavy dependence upon Western sources. I was able to read through all the issues of three important labor periodicals: *Chung-kuo kung-jen* ("The Chinese Worker"), *Lao-tung-chieh* ("The World of Labor"), and *Hsiang-tao* ("The Guide"); but I have not seen the other labor journals of the period and know of them only through the catalogues that have recently been published in Peking. I have been able to make use of practically all the available material in Paris, London, and Geneva; thus the Bibliography contains many books of comparatively minor importance, while really important books such as Ts'ai Ho-sen's on the history of opportunism in China or Ch'ü Ch'iu-pai's on the history of the Chinese labor movement (both in Chinese) are omitted simply because I have not had access to them. Similarly, I was not in a position to consult many works in Russian, and the very few references to Russian-language sources and to the work of Soviet historians does less than justice to the large amount of work in Russian on Chinese history, the extent of which can be judged from Skachkov's bibliography. I was also unable to make use of any Japanese material.

A historian is dependent not only on his sources, but also on work done by forerunners and contemporaries in fields adjacent to his own particular field of research, and in this respect the task of the Western historian of modern China is not made any easier by the generally low level of present-day Western research on this subject. In order to place the Chinese labor movement within its historical context, I have found it necessary to write an introductory chapter on the social and political situation in China around 1919. In later chapters I have had to be content with making brief references to the historical context based on secondary sources and often on mere conjecture, since there are as yet no good general studies on subjects such as the student movement, the peasant movement, the crisis in Chinese industry, the relations between the national bourgeoisie and the Kuomintang, warlordism and provincialism, or the policies of the Comintern with regard to China. Doubtless many of the conjectures on which references of this kind are based will prove to be unfounded when historical research has advanced in this field.

The fact that the Chinese labor movement became a social and political force in its own right at such a late date means that its historian need not go back very far into the past. Although the working class had had a certain amount of historical experience before 1919 (see Chapter VI), its activities had until then been episodic and unorganized, so that it seemed logical to concentrate on the period following the May Fourth Movement. Because this period is a mere thirty-five to forty years ago, one cannot expect to find the same wealth of material that is available to historians of the Taiping or of the reforms of K'ang Yu-wei. On the other hand, it is still possible to talk with people who actually took part in the events of the time, and the interviews I had in 1957 with 32 elderly Chinese workers, almost all of whom had witnessed the activities of the labor movement from 1919 to 1927, were of very great value, more perhaps because of the light thrown on the social environment than on the actual political events.

From another point of view, the question arises as to how far a French historian, interested in one aspect of the social history of modern China, is capable of studying it. Is he too far "distanced," geographically, to be able to do so? Is the stranger from a distant country at an advantage or a disadvantage? Some sociologists have stressed the advantages of the "stranger factor," which enabled visitors such as Arthur Young and Alexis de Tocqueville to seize upon the salient features of the societies they suddenly found themselves in contact with. For my part, I feel that it is more important to stress the advantages of the "inhabitant factor," which confers on the inhabitants of a country the advantages, so essential for any scientific analysis in depth, of lifelong familiarity with the ways of the people of that country, a familiarity built up in each individual from birth onward. Nevertheless, these advantages do not in any way mean that the inhabitants of a country have a monopoly on its history.

Thus there seems no reason to suppose that a Western student would be any less capable of conducting serious research on Chinese social history than a Far Eastern historian would be of conducting research on the French Revolution. It is true that the Western historian cannot hope to be in command of the wealth of information and the subtlety of analysis displayed by Chinese historians in their studies of their own country. But a French historian's study of the Chinese labor movement can perhaps do two things that the Chinese historians cannot do: first, it can contribute toward freeing French historical writing from the European frame of reference to which it has been so long confined; and second, it can provide data for comparative studies on the role of the labor movement in modern times.

This study is only a first step in this direction. It attempts to do no more than open the way to the creation of a French school of modern sinological studies that will eventually, at a higher scientific level and in new historical conditions, produce work that will carry on the traditional French interest in Far Eastern studies that dates back to the Encyclopedists or even earlier. I only hope that this work, despite its imperfections, will induce others to follow the path of this first experiment, and that it will persuade French experts in the various social sciences to take a greater interest in the study of modern China.

Finally, I wish to extend my thanks to Professor Braudel, President of the VIᵉ Section of the Ecole Pratique des Hautes Etudes, to whose encouragement and practical assistance I am indebted for being able to complete the present work. I also wish to express special thanks for the splendid work done by the cartographers of the VIᵉ Section, which has made it possible to provide the various maps and charts included in the text and the appendixes. This study owes its existence largely to the perspicacious advice given by M. le doyen Renouvin to a young graduate who was still uncertain of the path he should follow, and whom he directed toward the study of contemporary China; and it also benefited from advice given by M. Labrousse, Professor at the Sorbonne. My task was greatly facilitated by the trouble taken by the various librarians in Paris, London, Geneva, Moscow, and Peking. The list of their names is too long for me to be able to thank them all personally here. But special mention must be made of the assistance given in China by the Chinese People's Association for Cultural Relations with Foreign Countries, by the History of Trade Unions Department of the Central School for Cadres of the All-China General Union, by the Labor History Committee of the Shanghai General Union, by the Archives Department of the People's City Government of Shanghai, and by the local trade union branch of the Tangshan (ex-K.M.A.) miners; and of the assistance given in Geneva by the I.L.O. library, and in

London by librarians of the Foreign Office, Chatham House (Royal Institute of International Affairs), and the London School of Economics.

Note to the American Edition

I wish to express my gratitude to Stanford University Press for providing the opportunity of making this book known to the English-speaking public.

I should also like once again to stress the point that the present work was first published in March 1962, and that it contains no references to books and articles published since then, with the exception of the book on Feng Yü-hsiang by James Sheridan, which has been added to the Bibliography of this edition. All of the maps and four of the charts in the original edition, which were drawn by M. Bertin, head of the Laboratoire de Cartographie of the Ecole Pratique des Hautes Etudes, and his assistants, have been redrawn for this edition by cartographers working with the art department of Stanford University Press. The endpaper map of Shanghai was originally based on the Feetham Report (see Bibliography, pp. 541–62). Eight charts in the original edition have been converted to tables.

One further point: in France two theses have to be submitted for the attainment of the Doctorat d'Etat. The present book was the main thesis submitted; the supplementary thesis is entitled *Les syndicats chinois, 1919–1927* (Paris and The Hague, 1965). It is a companion volume to the present work, a sort of "Research Guide." It contains an annotated list of some five hundred trade unions, with their names in Chinese characters; a collection of 31 labor movement documents (mostly rare and unpublished) in the original Chinese, with translations and comments; and a list of 30 labor periodicals of the time with comments. I hope it is not presumptuous of me to suggest that serious scholars should refer to the "Research Guide."

The English version of this book is heavily indebted to the skill, care, and deep understanding of the late Hope Wright. A gifted writer herself, Mrs. Wright put aside her own manuscript on James Joyce to devote all her energy to this translation, which must remain, sadly and unexpectedly, her final achievement. Only a few months before her death, we spent a happy week together in London going over the translation in detail. Now, less than a year later, it is my sad duty to pay a last tribute to a modest, hardworking, and cultured friend.

J.C.

Contents

Contents

Illustrations

Maps

Charts

PART I

The Working Class in 1919

CHAPTER I

The Social and Political Situation

The May Fourth Movement, with its student demonstrations and its workers' strikes, is the point of departure for this study, but first a short account must be given of the social, political, and economic situation in China at the time the Movement began. The main feature of the situation was the dominant position of the Great Powers and the foreign business interests in China. Whether this situation is described as an attack on China's "territorial and administrative integrity," in the cautious phrase of the Chinese delegates to the Washington Conference of 1922,[1] or as a "triple oppression, political, economic, and ethnic" by the Powers, reducing China to the condition of a "sub-colony," in the words of Sun Yat-sen in his "Three People's Principles,"[2] or as the spread of imperialism in colonies and semi-colonies, which is how the first Chinese Marxists, following Lenin's classic thesis, saw it in 1919–20—the fact was still the same.

After the opening up of China in the period 1838–60 came the "breakup" of 1896–98, when the Powers embarked upon what amounted to the territorial dismemberment of China, the extent of which was barely disguised by the wide variety of legal formulas used—concessions, settlements, leased territories, railroad zones enjoying special status, colonial territories.

Concessions and settlements[3] were districts in certain of the ports that had been declared "open" for foreign trade, where the Powers had their own municipal administration and where they administered justice, maintained a police force, and levied taxes. In 1919 there were thirty of these concessions[4]— fewer than the number of Treaty Ports. A few were administered jointly by several of the Powers, as in Shanghai and Hsiamen (Amoy), but most by only one of the Powers: six by Great Britain (in Canton, Hankow, Chinkiang, Kiukiang, Tientsin, and Newchwang), four by France (in Shanghai, Canton, Hankow, and Tientsin), and four by Japan. Tientsin had the largest number of separately controlled concessions. In addition to the British, French, Japanese, Italian, and Belgian concessions, there were those of Germany and Austria-Hungary, which had been taken over by the Japanese in 1914 and which were reoccupied by the Chinese when they entered the war against these Central European powers in 1917, and there was the Russian concession, the rights to which were officially renounced by the Soviet Union in 1919.[5]

The most important Western enclave was the International Settlement of Shanghai, where only non-Chinese ratepayers, numbering a few thousand among a population that in 1919 had reached nearly 700,000,[6] were entitled to vote in the Municipal Council elections, or to vote on bylaws introduced by the Council, or on its annual budget, despite the fact that rates and taxes hit all the residents in the Settlement equally hard. The Municipal Council was really a government in miniature, with departments for public works, finance, police, and electricity supply; and, as will later be shown, it employed thousands of Chinese workers as well as workers of many other nationalities. Its police force consisted of the Shanghai Municipal Police, in which the officers were British and the other ranks recruited from Sikhs, Chinese, and White Russians, and the "Volunteers," composed of residents who could be mobilized at short notice. In addition, the Powers had the latitude, if not the actual right, to supplement these forces by stationing contingents of infantry or marines in the Settlement; and in crises such as that of 1927, they brought in large numbers of them. The administration of justice in cases involving Chinese residents in the International Settlement or foreigners not included in the extraterritoriality laws was carried out by a Mixed Court, composed of a Chinese judge and a foreign assessor of the same nationality as the plaintiff. It applied Chinese law, but was under the control of the Municipal Council, which from 1911 on made the appointments to the bench (including its Chinese members), and which, through its police and its prisons, was responsible for carrying out the sentences passed.[7]

The "leased territories" were military bases for which the Great Powers had obtained occupation rights at the time of the breakup in 1896–98, as much to keep watch over each other as to protect their own industrial and financial interests on Chinese soil. The Liaotung peninsula, originally granted to Russia, had since 1905 been occupied by the Japanese, who also occupied Tsingtao, having evicted the Germans at the beginning of the First World War. France occupied the Bay of Kwangchow, at the entry to the Gulf of Tonkin, and Great Britain occupied Weihaiwei, which lies on the other side of the Pohai Gulf, opposite Port Arthur. Great Britain, taking further advantage of the "breakup," had also "leased" the district of Kowloon, on the mainland opposite Hong Kong, as an extension of her territory on the island.[8] China retained nothing more than a purely theoretical sovereignty over all these territories.

The island of Hong Kong ceased to belong to China in the middle of the nineteenth century, when it became a British Crown Colony.[9] Authority was held by the Governor, who was assisted by a Legislative Council and by an Executive Council mainly composed of men in high official positions, including after 1913 a "Secretary for Chinese Affairs," who had the special task of dealing with the problems arising from the existence of a large Chinese population in the colony.[10] Strictly speaking, Hong Kong should not be included in a study of the Chinese Republic, since it was not within China's boundaries. Nevertheless, material concerning the colony has been included because of the close ties that both the labor movement and the Chinese bourgeoisie there maintained with their counterparts in Canton.

The virtual dismemberment of China was further accelerated by the existence of a number of areas that might be called "special status areas." One of these was the Legation Quarter in Peking, which the Powers had occupied by force during the "eight nations expedition" at the time of the Boxer Rebellion. It was surrounded by a zone where the Chinese were forbidden to erect any buildings, and the Powers enjoyed the further right to establish garrisons along the communication route between the capital and the sea.[11] Other areas of this kind were those through which railways had been built by foreign companies such as the Sino-Russian North Manchuria Railway Company, the Japanese South Manchuria Railway Company, and the French Yunnan Railway Company. Agreements made at the time of the breakup authorized these companies to exercise a kind of state control over the territory along the railroad, in which they collected taxes and had their own postal communications and armed patrols.[12] In July 1917 the Governor-General of Kwantung, who was the commander of the Japanese armed forces on the Liaotung peninsula, was authorized to "take charge of the protection and supervision of the railway lines in South Manchuria."[13] Similarly the area in the Tangshan neighborhood containing the coalfields exploited by the Sino-British Kailan Mining Administration (K.M.A.) was to all intents and purposes a foreign enclave, policed by the K.M.A.'s armed police force. In times of unrest, the police were reinforced by British marines, who could be brought in to the coalfields.[14] Finally, the inland waterways might also be regarded as "special status areas"[15] to the extent that foreign shipping and even (on the Yangtze) gunboats made free use of them and were thus able to transport troops to the interior or carry out the classic "gunboat policy" adopted in the nineteenth century.[16] This, at least, was the accepted practice, although China had never signed a treaty giving official consent.[17]

In addition to carving up China's territory, the Powers had also encroached upon the Chinese state by taking over some of its functions either wholly or partially, and by exercising direct or indirect control in certain spheres. One of the earliest rights arrogated was that of extraterritoriality, or, as it is sometimes called, exterritoriality.[18] This enabled nationals of the Treaty Powers to escape the jurisdiction of the ordinary Chinese courts. If they were involved in a case in which the opposing party was Chinese or of a different foreign nationality, or if the charge was a criminal one, their case was tried in the consular courts established by the Powers in the main Treaty Ports.[19] A further encroachment was the appointment of a French director-general to take control of the state-owned Chinese postal services, according to an agreement made at the time of the breakup, with foreigners occupying the posts of provincial superintendents.[20] In addition, the Powers established their own post offices in the main cities, administered directly by them and available for public use.[21] They also controlled broadcasting stations in Shanghai and other big cities.[22]

Chinese state finances also had gradually come under foreign control. The Nanking Treaty of 1842 imposed a 5 per cent limit on the rate of customs duty, and the Taiping Rebellion gave the Powers the opportunity of taking over control of customs. A General Inspectorate of Customs was created, which had a purely nominal allegiance first to the Imperial government and then to the various republican governments after 1912, and in which the chief posts were all filled by foreigners.[23] After the fall of the Empire, the Powers tightened their control by introducing a system whereby all the revenue collected by the customs inspectors was paid to "custodian banks" (the Hongkong and Shanghai Banking Corporation, the Yokohama Specie Bank, the Banque de l'Indochine, etc.), and used to pay off the interest on various Chinese loans and other financial obligations. Only the surplus that remained was put at the disposal of the Chinese government, and then only by decision of the diplomatic corps in Peking.[24] The same system was adopted for the revenue from the Chinese salt tax after the Chinese government was forced to relinquish control of it in 1913.[25] This gradual extension of foreign control over China's finances went hand in hand with the growth of her financial obligations to the Powers during the last years of the Empire and the first of the Republic. In addition to the indemnities imposed on China after her defeat by Japan in 1895, and by all the Powers in 1901, there were loans contracted to pay off the indemnities, loans that in theory at least were supposed to enable her to develop her railways and her mines, and, finally, loans that Chinese governments periodically tried to raise from new sources to meet general expenditures. It would be out of place here to go into the details of the Chinese debt;[26] all that need be said is that the burden it imposed on successive Chinese governments[27] laid them open to the domination of the Powers every bit as much as the clauses of the unequal treaties.

The rapid growth of the Chinese debt from the time of the breakup was, however, only one of the ways in which the Chinese economy was dominated by foreign interests. The amount of foreign investment in China, according to the only study of any depth so far made on this subject, reached a total equivalent to 1,610,000,000 American dollars in 1914, Great Britain's share being 607 million, Japan's 219 million, Germany's 263 million, Russia's 269 million, France's 171 million, and the United States' 49 million, and other countries' 32 million. Probably the figures for 1919 were much the same, except for an increase in Japan's investment.[28] The various foreign interests were then still distributed according to the pattern of the "spheres of influence" into which China was divided at the time of the breakup. French interests, apart from a few medium- or small-scale enterprises in cities like Tientsin and

Shanghai (where there was a French tramway company), were concentrated in the three provinces bordering on French Indochina; British interests settled in the Middle and Lower Yangtze regions (cotton mills, the British and American Tobacco Company's factories, shipping companies, etc.) and in the North China Plain (the K.M.A. mines and the mines of the Peking Syndicate in Honan); and Japanese concerns were established in Shanghai (the Naigai Wata Kaisha cotton mills), in the Northeast (the S.M.R. Company), in Fushun (coalfields), in Tientsin, and, after 1914, in Shantung, where they had ousted the former German enterprises.[29]

Foreign investment, apart from that in trade as such, had since the nineteenth century been placed mainly in light industries (such as cotton, tobacco, and matches), in mining, in the processing of materials for export (vegetable oils, powdered eggs, bales of raw wool and cotton), in modern transport (especially shipping—Mitsui, Mitsubishi, Butterfield & Swire, and Jardine, Matheson & Company), and in public utilities (telecommunications, public transport, water, electricity).[30] Another factor contributing to foreign domination of China's economy was the deficit in her balance of trade. At the time of the Opium War the balance of trade was in China's favor, but the situation was gradually reversed between 1880 and 1890. The amount by which imports exceeded exports had reached the figure of 320 million yuan by 1914, and rose to 424 million in 1918, despite a temporary improvement during the First World War.[31]

The penetration of China by the Powers also occurred in the spheres of culture and religion, especially after the breakup. Very few foreign residents made any serious attempt to familiarize themselves with the Chinese language or with Chinese civilization. Most of them, especially the businessmen in the Treaty Ports, learned only enough of pidgin Chinese to speak to their domestic servants, their rickshaw men, and the foremen and clerks who transmitted their orders. On the other hand, many Western newspapers and periodicals—most of them in English—were published in China.[32] These contributed to the colonial character of life in the big ports, but, with the exception of *Millard's Review of the Far East*,[33] they did not have much impact on the Chinese bourgeoisie. What did have an impact, however, was the foreign universities and colleges, which were essentially designed to cater to the Chinese, with the barely disguised intention of training a new generation of leaders in politics and industry who would be willing to cooperate in maintaining the dominance of the Powers in China.[34] Most of them were run by Catholic or Protestant missions, as were the foreign hospitals scattered here and there throughout China; and the missionaries, except for a few progressive Protestants, usually felt that the future of their work depended on the continued presence of the Powers.[35]

In 1919, the dominance of the Western Powers and Japan over China was summed up in the minds of the Chinese by the term "unequal treaties," although in fact most of the rights arrogated by the Powers did not have even the slender legal basis provided by these treaties that had been forced upon China by military intervention.[36] Meanwhile the balance of forces within the major power bloc had been profoundly altered by the First World War. In 1914 Japan had taken over all the German possessions and settlements in China. The rights of Germany and Austria-Hungary on Chinese soil—extraterritoriality, consular jurisdiction, a share in the Boxer indemnities, etc.— were canceled when China entered the war on the side of the Allies in 1917.[37] The Russian rights, however, continued to be enjoyed by the Tsarist ambassador in Peking, who stayed on there and continued to be recognized as ambassador by the diplomatic corps and by the Chinese government after the Russian October Revolution in 1917.[38] After 1917, the railway in Northeast China, which until then had been run by a Russian company directly controlled by the Tsarist government, remained under the control of the company's managing director, General Dmitri Horvath, with the assistance, beginning in February 1919, of an interallied commission.[39] By this time the other Powers in China had ceased to regard Russia as a partner. Instead, they cast covetous eyes on Russian territory, and both France and Japan urged that a large-scale armed attack be launched against the Soviet Union from Vladivostok, which since June 1918 had been occupied by the Allies. In pursuit of their aims, both these powers supported the moves of Admiral Alexander Kolchak and his like in Siberia; but the British and the Americans were reluctant about supporting this policy of armed intervention, and did so for a short time only.[40] Thus the Bolshevik Revolution accentuated the internal tensions that had been developing within the Power bloc during the First World War. Already in 1915 Japan, taking advantage of the temporary withdrawal of Great Britain from the Far East, had presented her Twenty-one Demands to Yuan Shih-k'ai, which were aimed at making the whole of China into a Japanese protectorate, thus ensuring a special position for Japan at the expense of her rivals.[41]

By 1919, with the Powers concerned reduced in number, these dissensions had become all the more acute. The dissension did not, however, in any way alter the Powers' common determination to hold on to their rights and privileges in China; and their solidarity in this respect found expression in the diplomatic corps in Peking, which, because it was the dispenser of the customs and salt tax surpluses, had in fact, if not by right, a great deal of say in the management of China's affairs, or at least of all affairs controlled by the Peking government. Indeed, it held the power of life and death over each successive Chinese government, since all were dependent upon its generosity for their capacity to survive. The policy consistently adopted by the diplomatic corps was to try to keep the Peking government in power and to maintain control over the various militarist factions that one after another constituted that government by dangling over them the bait of the surpluses.[42] At the same time it refused to grant any portion of the customs revenue to the dissident governments in the South, except during a brief period between 1918 and 1920.[43]

Social and Economic Structure

The gradual penetration of the Powers beginning in the middle of the nineteenth century had deeply disturbed not only the Chinese economy, but also Chinese social organization. After the breakup in 1896–98, the old four-class social hierarchy of scholar-officials (*shih*), peasants (*nung*), artisans (*kung*), and merchants (*shang*), which was the keystone of the classic Confucian concept of social order, was completely upset by the new economic relationships that arose mainly in the towns, and by the violent crisis that shook rural China.

At the time the May Fourth Movement began, capitalist production and capitalist relations of production already held an important place in the Chinese economy. According to the figures given by the Nung-shang-pu (Ministry of Agriculture and Commerce) for Chinese capital investment in 1919, 204 million yuan were invested in banks (169 million in small banks and the traditional money-changing shops, and the remaining 35 million in the big modern banks), 108 million in industry, 22 million in trade, and 21 million in transport.[44] There was already a very active commercial bourgeoisie,[45] and according to its historians, a "golden age" had dawned with the removal of Western competitors from the markets of the Far East during the First World War, despite the fact that Japanese competitors also took advantage of the new situation and increased their hold more rapidly than ever.[46] Between 1914 and 1918 the number of spindles in Chinese-owned cotton mills increased from 160,000 to 216,000 in Shanghai, from 45,000 to 59,000 in Wusih, and from 40,000 to 61,000 in Nantung; the number of Chinese-owned tobacco factories in Shanghai rose from two to nine, and of reeling machines in the Shanghai silk factories from 14,000 to 18,000.[47] An indication of the increasing activity of the commercial bourgeoisie is given by the rise in the number of chambers of commerce. There were 794, with a membership of 196,336, in 1912; after the fall of the Empire, they increased rapidly until in 1915 there were 1,262, with a membership of 245,728.[48]

However, certain difficulties hampered the progress of the part of the bourgeoisie concerned with modern economic development. Not only did it have to face unfair competition from the foreign interests in China, but it had not yet fully integrated the various elements of which it was composed. Its history went back to the eighteenth century or even earlier, when it first began to show vigorous signs of life; and the Western impact at the time of the Opium War had given it a new impetus. Yet even when it had become a capitalist bourgeoisie, it was still composed of such heterogeneous elements as the traditional wholesalers engaged mainly in trading tea or salt; the compradores,[49] whose fortunes had been made in the service of the big Western firms and banking concerns; and those members of the Confucianist bureaucracy and gentry who at the end of the nineteenth century had been bold enough to sponsor and subsidize the first modern Chinese-owned enterprises.[50]

Typical examples of the first group are Fang Chiao-po and Sung Han-chang, both leading members of the Chinese Chamber of Commerce in Shanghai.[51] Fang was the grandson of a Chekiang merchant who dealt in silk and tea,[52] and Sung was the son of a Fukien salt merchant.[53] There was as yet no clearly drawn line between the commercial bourgeoisie with interests in modern industry, and wholesalers as such; and membership in the Chamber of Commerce was accorded equally to the representatives of traditional merchant associations such as the powerful tea and silk guilds, or the "Canton Guild" and "Ningpo Guild" (hui-kuan)* in Shanghai,[54] and to the representatives of the bankers and the cotton-mill owners.[55] Membership was also open to the big compradores, despite their being so closely associated, both politically and financially, with the Great Powers. In Shanghai, Yü Hsia-ch'ing had close associations with Japanese interests,[56] and Ch'en Lien-po, one of the head compradores of the powerful Hongkong and Shanghai Banking Corporation, was at the same time president of the Canton Chamber of Commerce.[57] The third group, the scholar-official element, was still present to the extent that the leading Chinese-owned shipping company, the China Merchant Steam Navigation Company (C.M.S.N. Company or Chao shang-chü), and the Anyuan collieries were still financed and managed by descendants of the two high officials who had founded them, Li Hung-chang and Sheng Hsuan-huai.[58] This group also had a distinguished representative in the person of Chang Ch'ien, who in 1919, despite his continuing ties with the rural gentry and former ruling class, was still honored for having been a promoter of modern industry in his native town of Nantung during the last years of the Empire.[59]

The competition that this heterogeneous group of Chinese capitalists faced from their foreign rivals was unfair on several counts. First, Chinese goods were subject to the likin (li-ch'in), the tax imposed on the internal circulation of merchandise, from which foreign goods were exempt according to the terms of the nineteenth-century treaties;[60] and the likin was apt to be increased from one journey to the next as the need for funds grew among the civil or military governments concerned.[61] Second, protectionist measures were ruled out because the Nanking Treaty stipulated that the tariff rate could not exceed 5 per cent. Third, most Chinese-owned enterprises suffered from chronic undercapitalization, largely as a result of the inexperience of entrepreneurs and of weaknesses in management; and this put the enterprises at the mercy of the first sign of a slump or the slightest rise in the price of

---

* See pp. 430–35 for definitions and characters of Chinese terms used in the text.

raw materials.[62] Most of them were small- or medium-scale concerns,[63] and they lacked the support of an effective banking system such as that enjoyed by British and Japanese firms in China from the end of the nineteenth century.[64] Moreover, even when Chinese firms did attempt, despite these drawbacks, to compete in sectors of industry where foreign competition was strong, they had to import their machinery from abroad, since the machine-tool industry was practically nonexistent in China. They were dependent for sources of energy on the British and the Japanese, who owned the big modern collieries in Chihli, Honan, and the Northeast, and the big electric power plants in Shanghai and the Northeast;[65] and they had to rely mainly on foreign shipping for distribution of their products because most of the tonnage using Chinese ports, including the Yangtze ports, was under foreign flags.[66] The progress made by Chinese capitalist enterprises during the First World War was not sufficient to free them from this basic dependence on the foreign interests.

Along with the new class of industrialists that arose in China in the early twentieth century, there grew up a new working class, most of whose members were employed not by native capitalist enterprise but by foreign firms. We shall return to this subject later. Still another new class in Chinese society in 1919 was the modern intelligentsia, which, although it had many close ties with the bourgeoisie, was nevertheless a highly distinct social group. It was the product of the modern system of education that during the last years of the Manchu dynasty had gradually replaced the old Confucian system with universities, technical colleges, and middle schools.[67] Teachers, many of whom belonged to local or provincial associations, were an active group within its ranks,[68] and so were journalists. (In 1919 there were nearly nine hundred different newspapers and periodicals in existence.)[69] Owing to the existence of the new universities and technical colleges, the number of students had greatly increased, especially in the big cities. In 1915, according to the Peking government, China had 129,739 "new-style" educational establishments, from elementary schools to universities, with a total of 4,294,251 students, 198,976 teachers, and 235,372 graduate students.[70] The young people educated in these schools were to show a lively concern for China's national interests on May 4, 1919, and on many later occasions as well.[71]

Numerically speaking, however, these new social classes—industrialists, industrial workers, intelligentsia—formed only a tiny minority of China's vast population of between four and five hundred million.[72] Not only in the countryside, but also in the towns, with all their petty traders and small craft workshops, precapitalist economic relations still predominated; and small-scale precapitalist forms of production, which were almost universal in agriculture, still formed a large proportion of industrial production as well. It is impossible to estimate just what this proportion was, since the goods supplied by village weavers, semi-peasant miners working with pick and basket, and manufacturers of bamboo articles or of salted and dried foodstuffs, were all for local household consumption. However, the 1918 figures for coal production issued by the Nung-shang-pu, giving 7.3 million tons produced by the traditional methods as against 2.5 million tons produced by Chinese-owned modern mines and 8,600,000 tons by foreign-owned mines, provide some indication.[73] In general, market relations were typical of a subsistence economy, being confined to a single district or, occasionally, to a province; and regional variations in the relation between prices and wages, in weights and measures,[74] and in currency[75] show that in 1919 there was as yet no unified national market.

Yet the lives of the vast majority whose economic activities belonged to the China of the past had been deeply disturbed. Both craftsmen and petty traders found less demand for their services, and could no longer rely on the protection formerly given them by their guilds.[76] Ordinary townspeople were hard hit by the steady rise in prices that had started after the Revolution of 1911 and had been especially marked during the years of the First World War. In 1919, the wholesale price index in Shanghai was 230.7, taking 1914 as 100;[77] and on the same basis, the retail price index in Canton was 136.4.[78]

The peasants were even worse off. They were still completely subjected to the rural gentry (*shen-shih*), who combined the functions of landlord, local administrator, and, until a few years earlier, upholder and dispenser of the official Confucian ideology, so that, with the scholar-officials, they formed "a ruling class of Siamese twins."[79] Chinese historians and politicians of today use the terms "feudal" and "semi-feudal" to describe rural China in the early part of the twentieth century.[80] These terms are not strictly applicable in the medieval European sense, over two thousand years having passed since serfdom had legal status and fiefs were conferred in China. But at least these terms have the advantage of indicating the extent of the peasants' economic subjection to the gentry. To argue against their use by stressing the prevalence of "dwarf" holdings supporting an entire household,[81] or by quoting statistics showing that about half the rural population were peasant owners, the rest being either part owners or tenants,[82] does not alter this fact.

The rent paid by tenant-farmers, whether in money or in kind, might be either a fixed amount or one calculated in proportion to the harvest, but in any case it always came to more than half the harvest. In addition they had to fulfill all sorts of obligations decreed by custom: "presents" to the landlord or his overseer, days of corvée labor, and various other tokens of fealty.[83] In northern Kiangsu, for instance, tenants had to put in a full day's work on the landlord's fields two or three times a month as well as supplying the manor with a bushel of grain and pots of fat, and they had to pay for using his oven and his mill. They also brought their disputes to him to be settled.[84] Peasant proprietors fared little better. The gentry lent them money at a very high rate of interest, and often it was the big landowners who collected the taxes on behalf of the district authorities. Some of these landowners were village potentates who wielded a great deal of influence at the district magistrate's *yamen* (court). Such men did not hesitate to inflict all sorts of exactions on the small peasants,[85] especially in areas where they had official permission to maintain their own private armies.[86]

The agelong sufferings of the Chinese peasant were greatly aggravated in the early twentieth century, and especially during the First World War. Ultimately the peasant had to bear the whole burden of the land tax, whether paid by small peasant proprietors or gentry landowners; and the burden increased steadily both before and after the Revolution of 1911. In the first place, the financial needs of the Chinese state were growing; there were foreign loans to repay, a large army to support, and the problem of maintaining a modern civil service that still clung to the wasteful and inefficient traditions of the old scholar-officials.[87] In addition, land rents had risen, particularly in areas around the big modern towns, where a market economy was developing and where landlords, who had taken to living in town, wanted more money for luxuries. In a village in the vicinity of Tientsin where for generations the rent had stood at one yuan per *mou* (about one-sixth of an English acre), it rose in 1907 to three yuan, and in 1913 to six yuan.[88] It is true that the market price of agricultural products[89] and of land[90] also rose during the same period; but the great mass of the peasantry derived little benefit from these price rises.

Another factor contributing to the peasants' worsening situation was the decline of rural industries. Cotton- and silk-weaving and the manufacture of bamboo articles and pottery had always provided a substantial secondary source of income in the peasant economy, whether carried out as a spare-time occupation or as a full-time one catering to a local or even a wider market. No detailed work has yet been done on this important topic, but it seems that at the turn of the century rural industries were badly hit by foreign competition. Sales dropped in the towns and even in the villages, especially in the Lower Yangtze region, with the introduction of imported goods and of goods manufactured in the modern factories that had been established in China both by Chinese and by foreigners.[91]

All this led to ever greater poverty among the peasants, and to their increasing subjection to their landlords and village moneylenders. The practice of demanding rent deposits—that is, requiring any peasant who wished to rent land to pay a large sum in cash—became more widespread.[92] Land ownership, especially in the vicinity of the big cities and the new economic centers, became more and more concentrated in the hands of the gentry and the big moneylenders at the expense of the small peasant proprietor. In 1919 peasant proprietors formed about 50 per cent of the total population of China, but the proportion was as low as 32 per cent in Chekiang and Kiangsu[93] and 43.5 per cent in Kwangtung.[94] A detailed statistical study of Kunshan and Nantung, two rural districts (*hsien*) in the Lower Yangtze region, made around 1925 and covering the years 1905, 1914, and 1924, provides concrete evidence,

TABLE 1

Economic Pressures on the Peasantry, 1905–24

(As illustrated by data from two hsien)

Category	Kunshan hsien			Nantung hsien		
	1905	1914	1924	1905	1914	1924
Percentage of cases in which rent deposits were demanded	25.5%	40.0%	61.8%	72.9%	76.7%	88.1%
Percentage of landholders who were:						
Owners	26.0%	11.7%	8.3%	20.2%	15.8%	13.0%
Part-tenants	16.6	16.6	14.1	22.9	22.7	22.6
Tenants	57.4	71.7	77.6	56.9	61.5	64.4
Average size of farms (in *mou*) held by:						
Owners	24.6	24.3	23.2	18.8	15.0	11.8
Part-tenants	23.4	20.5	16.9	18.6	14.8	11.0
Tenants	23.1	14.5	9.4	16.6	12.8	10.0
Price per *mou* of medium-quality land (in yuan)	16.36	30.91	60.45	28.06	29.24	67.96
Rent paid per *mou* for medium-quality land (in yuan)	—	—	—	1.31	2.06	3.14
Price per *picul* of polished rice (in yuan)	2.84	4.45	8.42	4.80	6.72	10.94

at least so far as these particular districts are concerned, of the extent to which the condition of the peasantry deteriorated during this period.[95] (See Table 1.)

The resulting social crisis placed the peasants at the mercy of such natural calamities as the drought of 1920–21 in North China, which claimed millions of victims.[96] Every time the harvest was bad, a wave of poor peasants poured into the industrial towns,[97] the ports, and the mines; others migrated to the colonial territories in Southeast Asia[98] and to the Northeastern provinces, which had only been open to Chinese emigrants since the last decades of the nineteenth century. It is estimated that 342,000 emigrants entered Manchuria by land or by sea in 1923, the first year for which the South Manchuria Railway published immigration statistics.[99]

But some peasants chose to stay on and fight, and there was a marked increase in the activities of the traditional secret societies around 1920. In Szechwan, for instance, bands of rebels led by Taoist priests who preached the "Great Peace" (*T'ai-p'ing*) attacked Wanhsien in March 1921;[100] and in western Hupeh a sect arose that worshipped a "living god" supposedly personified in the two peasants who led it.[101] Many of the rebels in this grass-roots revolt against the established order were simply bands of outlaws (*t'u-fei*), which had been growing in number, especially since the death of Yuan Shih-k'ai.[102] Thus in 1919 the impoverished Chinese peasant was still expressing his resentment and his will to resist in traditional ways; and, for reasons that are not yet fully understood, peasant resistance was far less effective than it had been during the unrest that swept the countryside between 1850 and 1870. At the time when the May Fourth Movement began, the peasant movement was in the trough of the wave. It did not reach Taiping heights until 1925–27; and even then the peasants did not display the capacity for political struggle that was later so notable.

The transitional nature of the Chinese economy and Chinese society at the time the May Fourth Movement began was clearly reflected in Chinese social habits and customs. The term "republican era" (*min-kuo*) had been used in official documents since January 1912, yet the traditional lunar festivals were still pivotal points in social life. The New Year was still celebrated around the beginning of February, the Dragon Boat Festival in the fifth "moon," and the Midsummer Festival in the eighth.[103] The customs of the past still predominated in private life and family relationships—not only in the countryside, but to a large extent in the towns as well. The extended family (*ta-chia-t'ing*) was still in existence, and the father of the family maintained his authority over his wife and children. In social and business relations, personal influence and private connections counted as much as ever; intermediaries were still used in various transactions in order to save "face" for the parties concerned; and handsome presents in cash or in kind were still bestowed on those whose support or good offices were sought.[104] Only a small minority among intellectuals and members of the Westernized bourgeoisie favored such ideas as the liberty of the individual or the equality of the sexes, and attacked the customs of the past.[105]

Political Structure

In 1919 China was a republic, but the machinery of state was much the same as it had been during the last years of the Manchu dynasty. There were nine ministries in the central government, the most important for the history of the labor movement being the Ministry of Agriculture and Commerce (Nung-shang-pu), which was responsible for matters concerning industry and labor; the Ministry of Communications (Chiao-t'ung-pu), which supervised all the railways except the foreign-owned lines, notably those in the Northeast and in Yunnan; and the War and Finance Ministries (Lu-chün-pu and Ts'ai-cheng-pu), which were responsible for the arsenals, the armaments and munitions factories, the state printing works, and the mints, and hence for the employees of these establishments.[106] The most inclusive unit of local government was at the provincial level, the provinces consisting of the eighteen traditional ones plus Sinkiang and the three northeastern provinces of Fengtien, Chihli, and Heilungkiang. In 1914 each province had been subdivided into "circuits" (*tao*), replacing the former prefectures and sub-prefectures; and these were further divided into districts (hsien).[107]

The balance of social forces was as little altered as the political structure. The machinery of state was still in the hands of the conservative elements— the rural gentry, former officials of the Imperial regime, military leaders, and the moderates among the big bourgeoisie—whose power had never been seriously challenged in either the town or the countryside. The central government was just as authoritarian as it had been under the Manchus. Among other things, it continued Yuan Shih-k'ai's policy of suspending the liberal measures introduced by the 1912 Constitution, including freedom of assembly, with the result that by 1919 the many political parties that had flourished at the time of the republican revolution had either completely disappeared or been forced underground. All that remained were a number of militarist political factions and civilian cliques that could scarcely be called political parties; they were simply rival groups struggling to gain control of the Peking government, which was by now a republican government in name only.[108]

The most important of these groups were the Anfu faction (named after the street in Peking where its headquarters were situated), led by Marshal Tuan Ch'i-jui, who had close ties with Japan; the Chihli faction, which was associated with British and American interests; and the Fengtien faction, whose leader, General Chang Tso-lin, was master of the three northeastern provinces. Among the civilian groups, the most influential were the "Communications Clique," led by the banker Liang Shih-i, formerly secretary to the presidency of the Republic under Yuan Shih-k'ai, and the "Research Clique," to which the followers of the earlier reformer Liang Ch'i-ch'ao belonged.[109] In 1919 the Anfu faction, in association with the Communications Clique, held power in Peking. The faction had removed General Feng Kuo-chang, leader of the Chihli faction, as President of the Republic, and had installed the colorless Hsü Shih-ch'ang, a former high official and associate of Yuan Shih-k'ai. It held a majority in what was known as the "Anfu Parliament," which it had won in the elections held in 1918 after it had brought down the "Old Parliament" of 1913; and although Tuan Ch'i-jui had now resigned as premier, he had done so only in order to bring more of his lower-ranking colleagues into the cabinet.[110] Tuan's position was fairly secure because of the large loan he had received from Japan in 1918 (the Nishihara loan), ostensibly for use in the Chinese war effort. He also had the army well in hand and could count on the support of most of the provincial governors.[111] His political outlook can be gauged by the fact that in September 1918 he declared the birthday of Confucius a national holiday,[112] which amounted to bringing back the political ethic of submission to the established order on which the domination of the shen-shih had been based for centuries.

The military had been steadily gaining influence since 1912, and indeed throughout the last decades of the Empire. The position held at the Manchu court in the 1870's by the high officials who had defeated the Taiping rebels, the defeat of K'ang Yu-wei and his civilian reformers in 1898, the victory of Yuan Shih-k'ai and his followers over the left-wing republicans in 1912, and the success that the republicans in turn enjoyed when they set up the military government of 1917–18 in Canton, all go to show that only parties or factions backed by armed force could hope to get into power.[113] After the breakdown of centralized control following the death of Yuan Shih-k'ai, provincial government was taken out of the hands of civilians by military governors (*tu-chün*),[114] who created for themselves what were virtually autonomous principalities. These "warlords," as they began to be called, regarded their fiefs simply as a means to enrich themselves. They extorted money from the chambers of commerce,[115] encouraged the cultivation of opium,[116] engaged in a large-scale contraband trade in arms,[117] and formed well-equipped provincial armies whose loyalty was dependent on receiving regular pay.[118]

This centrifugal tendency was already apparent in 1919, and it was to lead eventually to the state of chaos that existed in 1922–25. With the breakdown of the Imperial bureaucratic system, the political functions of the rural gentry took on the same local character as their exploitative economic activities. They were now employed by provincial governments to fill posts such as that of "circuit administrator" (*tao-yin*) or district magistrate (*chih-shih*).[119] They were generally on good terms with the warlords, many of whom came from their ranks although others were soldiers of fortune who owed their positions to the Revolution of 1911.[120] A favorite slogan among provincial moderates at that time, "Protect the neighborhood and maintain order among the people" (*pao-ching an-min*),[121] expressed at once the desire of the military governors to maintain their power and the anxiety of the rural gentry to take local precautions against possible uprisings by discontented peasants.

There was close collaboration between the warlords and the rural gentry in the provincial assemblies that had been created by the Manchu government just before its fall, dissolved by Yuan Shih-k'ai in 1914, and then re-formed after his death;[122] and these assemblies displayed marked particularist tendencies on a number of occasions during the years immediately after the First World War.[123] The same tendencies were displayed by the nascent commercial bourgeoisie in the interior provinces, showing how closely linked it still was with conservative elements. Many factories and mines opened at this time bore names with a provincial flavor, like the Pao-chin ("Protection of Shansi") collieries in Pingting,[124] the Yü-feng ("Prosperity of Honan") cotton mills in Chengchow, and the Lu-feng ("Prosperity of Shantung") cotton mills in Tsinan.[125]

Thus in 1919 China was governed by militarists and civilians who perpetuated the policies of Yuan Shih-k'ai, with the full support of the gentry and of the scholar-officials of the former regime. They also had the backing of the Treaty Powers, who still, as in the times of Yuan Shih-k'ai, favored a "strong man" in Peking, a government that would maintain order and guarantee their rights and privileges.[126] Japan gave direct support to the Anfu faction and the Communications Clique by providing large subsidies, as well as "advisers" such as Sakatani Yoshirō for financial affairs, Ariga Nagao for political affairs, and Aoki Shūzō for military affairs.[127]

The conservatives in power were not, however, without their opponents, and although the opposing forces were scattered and unsure of themselves, they were by no means negligible. Among these opposing forces, the traditional secret societies—the Triad in the South, the Ko-lao-hui in the Middle Yangtze region, the Green and Red Gangs in Shanghai, the Red Swords of Honan, and many others—were in a class by themselves.[128] They, too, operated on a purely regional basis. It was mainly the poor peasants that came under their influence,[129] but the riffraff of the big cities also supplied recruits, notably for the Green and Red Gangs of Shanghai.[130] This form of opposition was, however, marginal, despite the mass support it enjoyed. It was a kind of medieval survival, and as such irrelevant to the problems facing the Chinese in 1919.

The opposition offered by the radical intelligentsia was a very different affair and struck an entirely new note both because of its aims and because of its social origins. In 1919, the journal *Hsin-ch'ing-nien* ("New Youth"), founded in 1915 by a group of Peking professors and students, had begun to set the trend in all of China's political and intellectual centers—notably Shanghai, Wuhan, Changsha, and Canton. Its leading writers were unanimous in attacking old customs and beliefs, in advocating the use of the vernacular (*pai-hua*) in journalism and literature instead of the outdated literary language (*wen-yen*), and in calling for the emancipation of women and the promotion of modern scientific studies.[131] But they were less than unanimous in their political views. Li Ta-chao and his disciple Mao Tse-tung were already looking toward the Soviet Union for inspiration.[132] Ch'en Tu-hsiu shared their Marxist inclinations, but was at the same time deeply influenced by France and the ideas of the French Revolution, to the point of giving his journal, *Hsin-ch'ing-nien,* the French subtitle *La Jeunesse.* On the other hand, the sympathies of Hu Shih, one of the advocates of literary reform, went rather toward the English-speaking world,[133] as did those of another section of the new intelligentsia, the Chinese Protestants who were active in the Y.M.C.A. Yü Jih-chang (David Yui), the general secretary of the Chinese Y.M.C.A. and a leading figure among the moderate Shanghai bourgeoisie, was appointed China's "civic delegate" to the Washington Conference in 1921, which he attended in company with the official delegates of the Peking government.[134]

Chinese businessmen were another group who opposed the regime in 1919. Bitterly disappointed by the failure of the republican revolution,[135] but at the same time encouraged by the economic progress made during the First World War, they wanted to see China reunified and the militarist factions that fought for power in Peking removed. Meanwhile they set about advancing their own projects, and by early 1919 they had formed a number of associations for "industrial advancement" in Shanghai, and a Society for the Study of Mechanics in Canton.[136] They were becoming acutely aware of China's subjection to Japan and the Western Powers, and harbored fond memories of the anti-Japanese boycott of 1915[137] and of the campaign to encourage home industry.[138] By way of protesting Yuan Shih-kai's acceptance of Japan's Twenty-one Demands in 1915, nationalists declared May 7 and 9 Days of National Humiliation.[139] In the spring of 1918 student demonstrations, prefiguring those of May 1919, were held in protest against the financial agreements made between Tuan Ch'i-jui and the Japanese government, and a press campaign to the same effect was launched.[140] By the beginning of 1919, sufficient pressure had been brought to bear on the delegates of the Peking government at the Versailles Peace Conference to make them present a long memorandum demanding renunciation by the Powers of their spheres of influence in China, the withdrawal of foreign troops and police from Chinese soil, the closing of foreign post offices, the abolition of consular jurisdiction and extraterritoriality, the restitution of leased territories, concessions, and settlements, and the return of customs control to China.[141]

Despite all this, the attitude of the bourgeoisie as a whole toward the West and toward the conservatives at home was less clear-cut than might appear. They were opposed to the West, but at the same time profoundly attracted by what they knew of it from the many compradores among them, and also from those who had been to Western universities and those who had been converted to Christianity.[142] *The Chinese Social and Political Review,* an English-language Peking publication for the cultured bourgeoisie, came out the same year *Hsin-ch'ing-nien* began its campaign for the use of pai-hua. The American liberal journal *Weekly Review of the Far East* (soon renamed *China Weekly Review*) was also favorite reading among the bourgeoisie.[143] A pro-Western attitude was already evident in 1912, when the Nanking government showed no signs of questioning the rights enjoyed by the Powers in China, but merely assured them of its goodwill.[144] To be sure, this attitude gave way to bitter disillusionment the following year, when the Powers granted large subsidies to Yuan Shih-k'ai after having withheld the customs surplus from the Provisional Government. Nevertheless, in 1919 the bourgeoisie were still sympathetic toward the West, if only because Westernization meant to them economic and political progress and a means of getting rid of the conservative forces. They wanted to learn about Western science,[145] they wanted to adopt Western methods of parliamentary government, and they still hoped—particularly those in the South—to restore the Constitution of 1912.

The Chinese bourgeoisie's attitudes toward the conservatives were complicated by the fact that there was no clear dividing line between the two groups. Many of the bourgeoisie's most illustrious members had been scholar-officials under the old regime, and others gave highly valued political services to the militarist factions in the North. Notable examples are the banker Liang Shih-i and the industrialist Chang Ch'ien, both of whom held a number of ministerial posts—often important ones—from 1913 on.[146]

There was a similar ambivalence in the attitude and political activities of Sun Yat-sen around 1919. At this time his prestige stood high owing to his thirty years of revolutionary activity, his short spell as President, and his stand against Yuan Shih-k'ai.[147] He had a political organization to support him, the Chinese Revolutionary Party (Chung-hua ko-ming-tang), which in October 1919 readopted the name Kuomintang, under which it had operated in 1912–13. He had gathered around him a brilliant team of politicians, among them Liao Chung-k'ai, a member of the overseas Chinese bourgeoisie; Hu Han-min, who came of a Cantonese shen-shih family and had been governor of his native province immediately following the Revolution of 1911; and Wang Ching-wei, an intellectual who had lived for long periods in Japan and the West.[148]

Along with the new bourgeoisie, who put their entire trust in him,[149] Sun believed that Western parliamentary democracy was the system of government that would best ensure China's revival and future development, and he had taken pains to indoctrinate his countrymen by publishing his *Introduction to Democracy* in 1917.[150] This belief led him to demand the restoration, in its entirety, of the republican Constitution of 1912;[151] he also drew up a grandiose "Industrial Plan," published in 1919, which called for the construction of 126,000 miles of railroads, several big modern ports, and many new factories.[152] He took part in forming the dissident Canton government of 1917–18, which was a federation of six of the southern provinces, in order to carry out these aims. But like all the political moves made by the bourgeoisie, this one was full of contradictions. The Canton government claimed to be safeguarding the Constitution, and it had summoned to Canton all the members of the "Old Parliament" of 1913 that had been dissolved in June 1917.[153] Furthermore, it had pledged itself to advancing the economic development of Kwangtung, and, as a symbolic gesture indicating a break with the past in the interests of urban expansion, it had demolished the old city wall of Canton.[154] Yet it had to rely for its main support on the military governors of the southern provinces and on the moderates among the gentry, whose opposition to the Anfu faction was inspired by personal quarrels rather than by any desire for political progress.

At the beginning of 1918, Sun Yat-sen resigned in discouragement from his position as Grand Marshal, to which he had been elected the year before, and departed for Shanghai. In his telegram of resignation he declared that "even under the banner of the protection of the constitution, the militarists would not obey the law or public opinion."[155] He was, however, elected by the parliament as a member of the seven-man committee formed when the Canton military government was reorganized in May 1918, but he declined to serve. The conduct of affairs in the South was now in the hands of local warlords such as Lu Jung-t'ing, tu-chün of Kwangsi and leader of the Black Flag secret society,[156] and T'ang Chi-yao of Yunnan, and of moderates such as the members of the "Political Study Group." The only member of the seven-man committee who might be regarded as in any way sympathetic to Sun's ideas was the venerable Wu T'ing-fang, a diplomat of the old school who had been a member of the Provisional Government.[157] Thus this rival government was almost as closely linked with the conservatives, the warlords, and the rural gentry as the one whose power it was disputing, and the discussions between them in Shanghai in February 1919, which very soon broke down, were little more than an attempt to reach a compromise made by men with very much the same point of view.[158] The Southern government no longer offered an alternative policy, for either internal or external affairs, to that adopted by the majority of Chinese politicians since the fall of the Manchu Empire.

The Need for Unity

In 1919, what most struck both Chinese and foreign observers was the state of disintegration, or of near chaos, that China was in. Sun Yat-sen spoke of "loose sand,"[159] and the "old China hands" kept pointing out what was wrong with China.[160] After the collapse of the centralized bureaucratic system, there was no disguising the particularist nature of the Chinese economy; and the development of a unified national market was further hindered by the uneven geographical distribution of Western economic undertakings, which contributed to the unequal development of the various regions.

The same particularist, or polycentric, tendencies were apparent in the political structure. It was on a provincial or regional basis that the anti-Manchu revolutionary groups had been organized,[161] and on which the centrifugal forces represented by the warlords were now operating. The southern and central provinces were the main ones involved in the republican Revolution of 1911, and it was largely the lack of support for it north of the Yangtze that enabled Yuan Shih-k'ai to come to power in 1912. Again, it was six of the southern provinces that formed the dissident "constitutionalist" government of 1917–18.

Particularism was also fostered by the wide diversity of vernaculars spoken, especially in the areas south of the Yangtze.[162] Fukienese, Cantonese, Hakka, and the Wu dialects of the Lower Yangtze were different languages—mutually unintelligible without a knowledge of the Chinese script, requiring many years of study. It should, however, be noted that although all these particularist tendencies may, in the short run, have worked in favor of the warlords, in the long run they were of help to the progressive forces, making it possible for Canton to become a revolutionary base and later for Kiangsi to become the area where the "Chinese Soviets" and the autonomous zones of the anti-Japanese guerrillas could be established.

Yet despite all this, nationalist sentiments and hopes for national unity were still evident in the many addresses and resolutions sent by associations of intellectuals and by chambers of commerce to the conference held in February 1919 at which delegates from the Peking and Canton governments discussed the reunification of the country.[163] The hopes for unity were even more forcefully demonstrated by the activities of the May Fourth Movement.

That China in 1919 was still far from achieving national unity was, however, only too apparent. It was a jumble of contrasts, as the most cursory glance at the various forms of production, ways of thought, or political organizations shows. Anachronistic features such as secret societies and the feudal corvée system existed side by side with such innovations as the Y.M.C.A. and the steamship. The introduction of the telegraph and of daily newspapers had made it possible for ideas to circulate with great rapidity, and for millions of people to be mobilized into action within a few days, as happened on May 4, 1919, and on May 31, 1925. Yet the marketing of goods was still as troublesome and as short-range an operation as it was in Europe before the Industrial Revolution. These contrasts were reflected in the social composition of the working class and in the general development of the labor movement. China's economic organization lagged behind the development of its political and ideological superstructure, and this discrepancy was one of the main causes of the failure of the 1911 revolution; it also contributed toward diminishing the effect of the mass movements during the period we are concerned with, movements that, as we shall see, met with setbacks in spite of their broad base.

The explanation for all this lies in two basic anachronisms in Chinese society—one dating from a few score years back, the other centuries old—namely, the domination of the Treaty Powers and the continuing power of a ruling class based on the exploitation of the peasant. These were the two big problems the Chinese revolution was up against, and they still awaited a solution in 1919. The Chinese people had, indeed, already attempted to prevent the further economic and political penetration of the Powers, and to overthrow the anachronistic rule of both the shen-shih and the successive central governments that represented them. But so far the two problems had been dealt with separately. The Boxer Rebellion was directed against the Foreign Powers, but not against the conservatives; the reformers of 1898, like the republican revolutionaries of 1911, maintained a conciliatory attitude toward the big foreign interests, and were more or less resigned to accepting the unequal treaties. What was entirely new about the May Fourth Movement was that it tackled both these vital problems at the same time.

This raises the question of leadership. Up until 1919, the peasantry, the bourgeoisie, and the new intelligentsia had each tried and failed to solve one or the other of the two basic problems. The peasants, under the Taipings, had tried in vain to overthrow the Manchu dynasty and the power of the shen-shih, and to create a new Chinese state half on modern lines and half derived from the old traditions of primitive communism. They had failed again in the Nien Rebellion against the Imperial government and in the Boxer Rebellion against foreign penetration. The bourgeoisie and the new intelligentsia had in turn been defeated in 1898 and again in 1911. In 1919 the profound changes of attitude that had taken place, already apparent in the enthusiasm with which the news of the fall of the Empire was received and in the indignation aroused in 1915 by the acceptance of the Twenty-one Demands, had set a movement on foot that was in search of leadership. The failure first of the peasantry and then of the bourgeoisie as leaders of the Chinese revolution had left the field open for a new claimant—the working class.

This study of the Chinese labor movement from 1919 to 1927 will show the manner in which the working class made its entry into the Chinese social and political scene, the stages the movement went through, and the methods adopted. "Labor movement" is here used to refer to all those activities of the working class that made a creative contribution to the history of the times. Being part of that history, they must be studied in the context of other changes that were taking place in China during the same period. The contribution of the labor movement includes the efforts made by the workers to alter the balance of economic forces in their favor, with either short-term or long-term aims in view; their collective participation in national and international political struggles; their creation of their own organizations, whether friendly societies, trade unions, or political parties; and finally the elaboration, assimilation, and propagation of a working-class ideology.

The big strikes and workers' demonstrations of the May Fourth Movement that occurred in May and June 1919 have been taken as the starting point of this study, and April 1927 has been chosen as the terminal point, because it was then that the sudden break occurred between the labor organizations and the right wing of the Kuomintang after they had won a common victory. But before discussing these eight years of labor struggles, we must first consider the nature of the Chinese working class in 1919. The rest of Part I will be devoted to a review of its size, its social origins, the methods of recruitment employed, its working conditions and rates of pay, its standard of living, and its history as a class.

CHAPTER II

Size and Distribution of the Working Class

In this chapter I shall try to make some assessment of the size of the Chinese working-class population in 1919, but first I must define what is meant by "working class" in this context. I have discarded as inadequate two common definitions—the first based on the criterion of technical skill, which restricts application of the term to workers employed in modern mechanized industrial enterprises, and the other on the criterion of the scale of the enterprise, which was used in certain Chinese investigations of the time;[1] for no history of the Chinese labor movement would be complete that excludes such jobs as mining and dockwork, where little mechanization had been introduced, or small-scale enterprises such as printing plants and the mechanical workshops of Shanghai and Canton. Even before 1919, miners and dockers had engaged in strikes and achieved some degree of organization; and in 1919–20 the mechanics and the printers were the first to form trade unions that to some extent broke away from the guild traditions of the past.

A definition based on economic criteria seems to me far more satisfactory, because it includes all the categories of workers who actively and consistently supported the labor movement during the period under review. Thus the workers regarded here as belonging to the working class include all those wage earners in large- and medium-scale capitalist production and in the closely associated transport industry who no longer owned the instruments of production or the products of their labor, and who were in complete subjection to their employers. No matter whether they were workers in the fully mech-anized cotton mills or miners still for the most part using primitive techniques, seamen on steamship lines or dockers, railwaymen or street-porters, these were the workers who made the history of the labor movement. Also to be included are the employees of various municipal enterprises, such as telecommuni-cations, water supply, and public transport, and also rickshaw coolies, despite the individual nature of their occupation.

Not to be included, however, are wage earners in petty urban trades (bar-bers, tailors, launderers) and in craft industries (makers of baskets, brushes, and bamboo articles), or shophands and building workers, in spite of the fact that their social status was much the same as that of the industrial and trans-port workers. It is true that many of them, especially in Shanghai, took part in the great strike waves of May 4, 1919, and May 30, 1925, and that they often came out on strike at the same time as their fellow workers in the big modern factories or in smaller industrial enterprises. But because they were involved in a system of production or of services that belonged to the past, they tended to look toward the past, and were not really part of the new forces in Chinese society. They were allies of the labor movement rather than an integral part of it.

Two other categories of workers are not included in the term "working class" as understood here, namely, those employed in work done in the home in urban and in rural areas. This was a marginal form of capitalist industrial production that cannot be disregarded in the history of the Chinese labor movement. From a strictly economic point of view, it was closely connected with large-scale urban industry; but as far as the labor movement was concerned, the protests of these workers were always somewhat subdued. Yet in urban areas workers of this kind sometimes formed a very large proportion of the working population;[2] in Shanghai and Tientsin, for instance, a great deal of work was done in the home in connection with the knitting industry and in the manufacture and labeling of match boxes.[3] In rural areas, this form of production was becoming popular with Chinese merchants, particularly those engaged in the textile industry;[4] and a large number of rural workers in the villages of Chihli, Chekiang, and Kwangtung were thus employed. Both urban and rural workers of this kind suffered from direct exploitation by capitalist industry in the towns, but because they were so widely dispersed, they were unable to play any decisive part in the labor movement, and this is why I have not included them.

To assess the size of this arbitrarily defined working class during the period immediately following the First World War is no easy matter. No complete census of the Chinese working class exists for this period. In Peking the Nung-shang-pu (Ministry of Agriculture and Commerce), which was responsible for industrial matters and the employment of labor, published annual statistics of the number of workers, arranged according to industries, until 1920. (See Table 2.)[5] But the figures only cover Chinese-owned enterprises and are thus of limited value for certain important sectors, such as the mining and cotton industries. Moreover, after 1915 they ceased to be even comparatively complete, for after Yuan Shih-k'ai's unsuccessful attempt to restore the monarchy a growing number of provinces were cut off from the capital because of the activities of rival provincial governors, and they were no longer included in the statistics. This explains the fact that, apart from a few exceptions noted in Table 2, the Nung-shang-pu figures for the years 1916–20 are lower than those for 1915. In 1920 the fighting between the warlords increased to such an extent that the publication of statistics ceased altogether. These figures have the further drawback of being based on a population that includes all workers employed in enterprises with more than seven employees. Many of these enter-

TABLE 2

NUMBER OF WORKERS IN CHINESE-OWNED ENTERPRISES IN 1915, AND IN SOME CASES DURING THE BEST YEAR BETWEEN 1915 AND 1920[a]

Industries	Enterprises	Workers (1915)	Workers (best year between 1915 and 1920)	
Textile				
Silk (reeling factories)	654	121,055		
Raw cotton	85	324		
Cotton (reeling factories)	35	42,953	43,825	(1918)
Cotton thread	56	834		
Embroidery	23	2,455		
Weaving	3,599	111,120	148,894	(1916)
Knitting	85	5,562	20,031	(1919)
Garment-making	541	8,840	9,458	(1916)
Dyeing	289	8,523		
Total	5,367	301,666		
Chemical				
Ceramics, bricks, etc.	1,809	42,892		
Paper	2,364	32,155		
Oil pressing	1,523	18,740	19,026	(1916)
Lacquer-work	94	1,125		
Matches	94	12,318	16,846	(1916)
Medicines	91	1,979		
Soap	34	383	2,120	(1917)
Leather and hides	249	5,185		
Candles	179	1,816		
Paints	26	735		
Dyes	59	809		
Lacquer varnish	2	18		
Other	66	1,624		
Total	6,590	119,779		
Metallurgical				
Engineering	111	5,175		
Shipbuilding and vehicles	146	1,893	4,672	(1916)
Tools	179	2,536		
Metallurgy	1,265	16,361		
Total	1,701	25,965		
Food				
Yeast	1,801	20,755	25,579	(1918)
Sugar	830	13,438		
Tobacco	694	12,783	15,519	(1917)
Drinks	10	180		
Tea	553	85,993		

TABLE 2 (cont'd)

Industries	Enterprises	Workers (1915)	Workers (best year between 1915 and 1920)	
Food (*cont'd*)				
Cakes	242	2,599		
Canned goods	8	232		
Rice husking	325	5,527	8,028	(1918)
Meat and fish	9	128		
Other	636	10,045		
Total	5,108	151,680		
Miscellaneous				
Printing	480	4,727		
Paper articles	205	4,450		
Bamboo and wooden articles ...	641	9,993		
Straw hats	70	1,112		
Leather articles, furs, etc.	244	3,188	4,605	(1918)
Jade, bone, ivory	48	507	2,300	(1918)
Other	283	11,108		
Total	1,971	35,085		
Special				
Electricity	10	565	1,391	(1918)
Metal refining	337	12,490		
Waterworks	1	38		
Total	348	13,093		
Grand Total[b]	20,645	647,268		

[a] Nung-shang-pu figures.

[b] This total fell to 575,864 in 1916, 555,592 in 1917, 488,605 in 1918, and 410,279 in 1919, although this was a time when Chinese-owned industry was expanding rapidly. This shows how the statistics became more and more incomplete.

prises must have been no more than small workshops employing craftsmen or part-time peasant employees, as seems clear from the figures given of 85,993 workers in the tea industry and 42,892 in the ceramics and pottery industry, which obviously exceed the number of workers in both industries employed in modern factories.

In addition to the Nung-shang-pu statistics, there are four individual assessments which do not have the same illusory precision, but which are nevertheless worth taking into consideration. (See Table 3.) The first was made by the Japanese writer Nishikawa Kiishi in 1923;[6] the second, which dates from the same year and which, as the similarity of most of the figures indicates,

TABLE 3

VARIOUS ESTIMATES OF THE NUMBER OF CHINESE WORKERS AROUND 1923–27

Industries	Nishikawa Kiishi (1923)	Sen Katayama (1923)	Su Chao-cheng (1927)	American consuls (1923)
Cotton	160,000	100,000	280,000	75,000
Silk	130,000	130,000	160,000	142,000
Knitting, hosiery, etc.	—	—	—	12,000
Flour mills	15,000	18,000	—	15,000
Dried eggs	15,000	15,000	—	—
Tobacco	100,000	100,000	40,000	15,000
Matches	90,000	90,000	—	10,000
Leather	20,000	20,000	—	6,800
Shipbuilding	25,000	25,000	—	182
Metallurgy	200,000	200,000	50,000	12,000
Cement	25,000	25,000	—	15,000[a]
Printing	80,000	80,000	50,000	4,400
Electricity	100,000	100,000	80,000	—
Warehouses, docks, etc.	500,000	500,000	300,000	—
Seamen	60,000	90,000	160,000	—
Postal service, etc.	—	40,000	90,000	—
Miners	420,000	420,000	540,000	—

[a] This figure includes brickworks.

clearly derives from the first, was the work of the Japanese Trade Union leader Sen Katayama;[7] the third, made later, was included in the report submitted by the trade union leader Su Chao-cheng to the Fourth National Labor Congress in 1927;[8] and the fourth, which is more detailed but less reliable, and is included in Table 3 only to show the divergence between the various assessments, is based on American consulate reports and was published in 1923 by the American Bureau of Labor.[9] All four date from later than 1919, the year that is here in question; and during the intervening period there was, despite several setbacks, continuous industrial development in China, especially in foreign-owned concerns,[10] so that the figures in Table 3, which, except for those in the fourth column, include foreign-owned enterprises, are probably higher than those for 1919. But they provide a frame of reference.

There are many inconsistencies in the data contained in Tables 2 and 3. The information is full of gaps, and the headings sometimes vague or ambiguous. For instance, the Nung-shang-pu figures show a large number of workers employed in the manufacture of yeast, which was a craft industry, but do not have a separate heading for albumen (powdered egg) factories, flour mills, or cement works, despite the importance of these three modern industries. They are probably included under the heading "Other" in the Chemical and Food Industries sections. As for the figures shown in these tables for the workers in the electrical and metallurgical industries, they vary so widely that little reliance can be placed upon them. This, then, is all that there is to go on in the way of general statistical information, and the only way to supplement this information is to examine whatever data are available for each sector of industry.

Annual censuses of employees such as those that are available for railwaymen and postal workers are extremely rare, as are careful estimates based on direct enquiries such as exist for carpetmakers, iron-miners, and iron-smelters. Some of the annual censuses date from later than 1919, but in the case of the cottonworkers an estimate for 1919 can be made on the supposition that the ratio of workers to spindles remained constant, because the number of spindles in use each year is known. In certain other industries the annual total production figure is known, but the number of workers employed is supplied for only a few of the enterprises concerned. In these cases, an estimate can be made for the industry as a whole based on the relation between number of workers employed and annual production figures in these particular enterprises. This is the manner in which the figures for the coal-mining industry have been arrived at. Finally, all the information available for some industries consists of a list of factories, for only some of which the number of workers is known. Here, any attempt to arrive at an estimated figure is so risky that in several cases I have simply abstained from giving one.

A further difficulty arises from the fact that, judging from the absurdly high figure of 11,132,290 workers employed in the Three Northeastern Provinces in 1926 given by a Japanese survey that lists 685 enterprises,[11] some of the available surveys lump together handicraft workers and even perhaps agricultural laborers with industrial workers. Methods of recruitment and conditions of employment—especially the *pao-kung* (contract-labor) system about which more will be said later[12]—were such as to preclude any hope of someday arriving at more precise figures. Even the K.M.A., which was as modern an enterprise as any, never knew exactly how many men it employed, because it hired them through the *pao-kung-t'ou* or other suppliers of labor; and even when workers were directly employed by the management, as was the case with the women employees of the Shanghai silk factories, their numbers often varied from day to day.[13] The only industries in which nothing but industrial workers were employed were the railways, the cement works, the electric power plants, and the shipyards. Most of the other modern industries included marginal forms of employment such as seasonal work, work done in the home, work done in rural areas on the "putting-out" system, and work done by handicraftsmen.

Despite all these reservations, an attempt must nevertheless be made to take each branch of industry separately and make a rough assessment of the number of workers employed, and, when possible, to ascertain the nationality of the employers and the geographical location of the enterprises concerned. This will reveal two facts of great importance in the history of the Chinese labor movement, namely, that a large proportion of the Chinese proletariat was directly employed in foreign-owned large-scale industrial enterprises, and that it was very unevenly distributed throughout China as a whole.[14]

The Textile Industry

Cotton. This industry made rapid progress in China from the time when the first modern Chinese-owned cotton mill was established in Shanghai around 1880 under the sponsorship of Li Hung-chang.[15] Given the facts that in 1925 it employed about 210,000 people[16] and that the number of spindles then in use was about twice the number in use in 1919,[17] the number of workers employed in 1919 can be estimated at 100,000. Again on the basis of the number of spindles in use, it can be estimated that over 60,000 worked in Chinese mills, over 20,000 in Japanese mills, and 16,500 in British mills.[18]

Most of these cotton mills, and hence most of the cottonworkers, were in Shanghai and the Yangtze estuary region, where machines and raw materials were accessible, capital and labor in plentiful supply, and an area of large-scale cotton cultivation nearby. Three-quarters of the Chinese, most of the Japanese, and all of the British spindles were concentrated in Shanghai itself,[19] but the new Chinese capitalist enterprise had established mills in Wusih, Soochow, and Chinkiang in the Yangtze estuary region, and another group known as the T'ung-ch'ung-hai cotton mills with a mill on the north bank of the river at Nantung, one in Haimen, and one on the island of Ch'ung-ming. The Ningpo and Hangchow mills in Chekiang can also be included in this cotton-mill area.

The other two centers of the modern cotton industry, of more recent origin and with fewer mills, were the Treaty Ports of Tsingtao and Tientsin, and the two provincial capitals in Central China, Wuhan and Changsha. In the first, all the mills were owned by the Japanese except for one that was Chinese-owned; in the second, the mills were Chinese-owned and dated from the time when the first attempts at industrialization were made under government sponsorship. They were still under provincial government ownership in 1919.[20] Foreign investment in this region was represented by only one Japanese mill, and that was under construction in Hankow.[21]

Silk. At the end of the nineteenth century modern factory methods of spinning and weaving silk began to compete in Shanghai and Canton with the older handicraft methods used throughout the silk-producing areas of the country.[22] The number of factories increased considerably during the First World War.

Here again the number of workers can be estimated only by inference. The only exact figures known for 1919 are those of the number of reeling machines (*ch'e*) in use, and the difficulty of estimating the number of workers employed is increased by the fact that, with the type of machine used in the Yangtze region, an average of 2.5 to 3 workers were employed for each machine, whereas with the simpler type used in Kwangtung there was scarcely ever more than one worker for each machine.[23] With this difference taken into account, on the basis of the figure of 160,000 ch'e in use in 1919 (135,000 in Kwangtung, 23,000 in Shanghai and Wusih, 4,000 in Szechwan),[24] the estimated number of workers is 200,000 (140,000 in Kwangtung, 45,000 in Shanghai, and 10,000 in Wusih).[25]

In the Chinese silk industry the process of modernization and mechanization was a very gradual one. Every type of enterprise existed, ranging from the very small-scale urban and rural workshops to the modern reeling factories in the suburbs of Shanghai. It is therefore much more difficult to assess the proportion of industrial workers than in the case of the modern cotton industry, with its big mills in the Treaty Ports, which had almost no links with the manufacturing methods of the past. Probably the figure given for the number of ch'e on which the above estimates are based includes, at least for Kwangtung, a large number of machines used by handicraft workers.[26] This margin of error is, however, to some extent corrected by the fact that the figure given by the same source for Shantung, the fourth of the silk-industry areas in China, where there were already a large number of modern reeling factories, is obviously too low.[27] Nevertheless my estimated figure of 200,000 is too high; but it is impossible to assess with any accuracy how many handicraft workers employed in the workshops in the South are included in it.[28]

As regards silk-weaving, the figures are very incomplete, and again no differentiation is made between industrial and handicraft workers.[29] Perhaps about ten thousand workers were employed in the modern factories.

Because of the simpler techniques involved, the long tradition behind it, and the extent of the internal market, the silk industry remained in Chinese hands to a far greater extent than the cotton industry; but in Shanghai there were a number of silk factories in the working-class suburb of Chapei belonging to Italian, French, British, and American firms, in which perhaps fifteen to twenty thousand workers were employed.[30]

Carpet-making. During the First World War the ancient Chinese handicraft of carpet-making became transformed into a partially modernized export industry to supply Western countries cut off from their usual source of supply, the Middle East. American firms, soon followed by Chinese entrepreneurs, established large factories in Peking and Tientsin, supplied by wool from Mongolia.[31] There were about seven hundred looms in Tientsin in 1919, operated by nearly three thousand workers.[32] In Peking, a survey made in 1923 gives a figure of 206 factories employing about six thousand workers.[33] The total number of workers in the industry, including those employed in the few small carpet factories in Shanghai, was little more than ten thousand.[34]

A wool industry began to flourish just before the outbreak of the First World War, but never came to anything, except for a few workshops in Tientsin and the big Japanese woolen factory in Mukden.[35] Probably only a few thousand workers were employed in it.

Hosiery, Garment-making, etc. In the Treaty Ports, the adoption of Western habits, and in particular of Western-style clothing, had led to the establishment of a sizable number of small and medium-sized factories producing hosiery, stockings, knitted goods, and towels. It is difficult to estimate the number of workers employed by these factories because, as a result of the small size of the machines used, marginal forms of employment were a feature of this industry.[36] An estimated figure of twenty thousand, in Shanghai, Tientsin, and Wuhan, may be given.[37]

Garment-making was still almost exclusively a handicraft industry, except for the big state factories in Tientsin and Peking making army uniforms and blankets,[38] which employed a further four thousand workers.

Food Industries

Flour Milling. This was one of the industries that profited most from the temporary absence of Westerners in the markets of the Far East during the First World War. China exported four times as much flour in 1920 as in 1914,[39] and during this period the number of flour mills increased from 75 to 117.[40] Each modern flour mill can be estimated to have employed on average a hundred workers,[41] which brings the total figure to at least twelve thousand.[42]

These mills were located in wheat-growing areas, 46 of them in the Three Northeastern Provinces, and 30 in the region of Shanghai. Nearly 20 in all, including the largest, belonged to foreign firms, mainly Japanese.[43] But in the wheat-growing area of North China, flour milling, even in Tientsin, remained a handicraft industry.[44]

Vegetable Oils. Both edible and industrial oils are included under this heading. Production by hydraulic machinery made considerable progress after the First World War.[45] The raw materials consisted of soya, sesame, peanuts, cottonseed, and other oil-bearing plants, all of which were widely cultivated.

The Nung-shang-pu figure for 1915 is 18,000 workers in over 1,500 oil mills. Clearly this figure includes handicraft workers, but the increase in the number of modern oil mills in 1919 would probably bring the total of industrial workers for 1919 to about the same figure. The Nung-shang-pu survey covers only Chinese-owned mills. The foreign-owned mills in Shanghai, Tsingtao, and the ports in the Northeast numbered about one hundred,[46] and taking an average of 150 workers per mill,[47] the total figure approximates to that of the number of workers employed in Chinese-owned mills. The Wuhan region was a third center, coming after Shanghai and the Northeast (Dairen, Newchwang, and Antung) in importance.[48]

Albumen, Husked Rice, Sugar, etc. German and British firms first established powdered egg (dried albumen) factories in China at the beginning of the twentieth century,[49] and their number increased steadily in response to the growing demand for this product on the world market.[50] An incomplete list for the year 1920 gives the names of 22 Chinese-owned and 21 foreign-owned factories situated in the main Treaty Ports.[51] The figure of 15,000 workers employed that Sen Katayama gives is probably approximately correct, since some of these firms employed over a thousand workers.[52]

Although the production of sugar for daily consumption remained a handicraft industry, several modern sugar factories had been opened by Japanese and Russian firms in Manchuria, where sugar beet was cultivated, and by British firms in Hong Kong, in the vicinity of sugarcane cultivation. They catered exclusively to Western or Westernized clients in China, and probably did not employ more than a few thousand workers.[53]

Of the workers in the many saltworks and salt mines in China, probably only a minority were industrial as distinct from handicraft workers. Included in this minority were the 600 workers employed in the modern Chiu-ta salt refinery in Tangku, the outer harbor of Tientsin; they were the subject some years later of a valuable sociological study to which frequent reference will be made.[54] It is impossible to arrive at an exact figure. The same problem arises with the husked-rice and tea industries, about which all that is known is that there were a few factories, apart from those in which handicraft methods were used, that were equipped with modern machinery.[55]

Canneries, breweries, and distilleries had already appeared before the First World War, and increased in number as demand grew among Western or Westernized clients in the Treaty Ports. In 1920 there were about twenty meat or vegetable canneries, mainly Chinese-owned, in the large cities in the South, and about fifty breweries, vodka distilleries, and carbonated water factories, mainly foreign-owned, in the main Treaty Ports,[56] but the number of workers employed cannot have been large.[57]

New Industries

Tobacco. In China, as in other countries in Asia and Africa, cigarette smoking was one of the habits acquired through contact with the West, and it was becoming increasingly popular. At first cigarettes were imported from Europe and the United States, but even before 1914 they were being manufactured cheaply in China in modern factories, the most important of which belonged to the British and American Tobacco (B.A.T.) Company, the Japanese Toa ("East Asia") Company, and the big Cantonese firm Nanyang hsiung-ti (South Seas Brothers).[58]

The figure given by the Nung-shang-pu for factories owned by Chinese in 1917 seems very low, since the Nanyang factory in Shanghai employed eight thousand workers just after the First World War, and this firm also owned large factories in Canton and Hong Kong.[59] An incomplete list given by the *China Year Book* for 1920[60] gives the names of 12 other large Chinese-owned modern factories and of 17 foreign-owned factories, three of which belonged to the B.A.T. Company (in Shanghai, Hankow, and Mukden) and three to the Toa Company (in Tientsin, Mukden, and Newchwang). The number of workers employed by the B.A.T. Company alone must have approached 25,000,[61] and the total number of men and women workers employed in Chinese- and foreign-owned tobacco factories cannot have been much below fifty thousand.[62]

Matches. Just after the First World War there were about a hundred match factories in various parts of China, the main centers being Kwangtung, Shanghai, Tientsin, and the Northeast.[63] Japanese factories predominated in the last three centers. The figure of 40,000 men and women employed in this industry is probably not an overestimate, since many factories employed several hundred workers and some over a thousand.[64] The Nung-shang-pu figure of 17,000 for 1916 covers only Chinese-owned factories, and there was certainly an increase in production after this date.

Ceramics and Glass Manufacture. A number of modern factories, Japanese-owned in the Northeast and for the most part Chinese-owned elsewhere, had recently been established, although the handicraft and semi-handicraft industry, such as the famous Kingtehchen workshops in Kiangsu, continued to supply the major part of the consumer market. The employees of the modern factories cannot have exceeded a few thousand.[65]

Soap, Paper, Leather, Hides, etc. Of the 50 modern soap factories that existed in the large cities in 1919, 15 belonged to foreign firms, some of them large concerns such as China Soap in Shanghai and a company in Mukden belonging to the Mitsui group.[66] Most of them were medium-sized or small concerns.[67] The total number of workers employed, allowing an average of 100 per factory, was perhaps about five thousand.

Similarly, there were probably no more than a few thousand workers employed in the modern papermaking and leather and hide industries. An incomplete list for 1921 gives the names of 14 paper works and 28 tanneries,[68] all of them fairly small concerns.[69]

Basic Industries

Metallurgy. The only two centers of heavy industry in China were those in the Northeast and in Hupeh. The number of workers manning the blast furnaces of Penhsihi and Anshan, owned by the Japanese South Manchuria Railway Company, may be estimated at around five thousand,[70] and those working at the furnaces in Tayeh and Hanyang, which belonged, at least nominally, to the Chinese companies Hanyehping and Yangtze Engineering Works, may be estimated at around twenty-three thousand.[71]

Mechanical workshops, small foundries, and small metalworks covered a much wider area, and their dispersal makes it difficult to form an exact estimate of their number. Figures of a slightly later date give, for instance, 2,920 workers in 17 workshops in Tsingtao,[72] 703 in 8 workshops in Tientsin,[73] and 9,250 in 98 workshops in Shanghai.[74] A similar proportion were employed in the other big cities in China, for example Canton, where the workers in the numerous small mechanical workshops on Honam island, to the south of the city, formed one of the earliest and most vigorous of the modern Chinese trade unions.[75] The total number for 1919 is perhaps around twenty thousand.

Shipyards and Arsenals. The Chinese-owned commercial shipyards, like the Army arsenals, were state enterprises dating from the end of the nineteenth century, and were still owned by the state.[76] The total number of workers employed in them in 1924 was around twenty thousand,[77] concentrated in several large concerns such as the arsenals of Tehsien (in Shantung) and of Hanyang, and the shipyards at Kiangnan (near Shanghai) and at Fuchow, one of the earliest modern enterprises in China. In addition, Japanese and British merchant shipping activities in the Far East had led to the establishment of about fifteen shipyards, including the Japanese yards at Antung, Dairen, and Tientsin and the British yards at Shanghai, Amoy, Tientsin, and Hong Kong.[78] These were vast concerns, each employing a thousand or several thousand workers, amounting to a total that cannot have been less than forty-five thousand.

Cement Works. The cement industry, technologically dependent on access to supplies of coal dust, was already before 1914 located in the ports and industrial centers that were near coal mines.[79] The big Chinese-owned cement works at Canton, Tayeh, and Tangshan, the Japanese-owned cement works at Dairen, and the British-owned cement works at Macao and Kowloon, must together have employed from five to six thousand workers, according to estimates made from the available figures.[80]

Electric Power Plants. Small or medium-sized generating stations existed in all the Treaty Ports and in most of the other big cities.[81] The biggest were those run by one or the other of the Foreign Powers in the various concessions or other special-status areas.[82] All the Chinese-owned plants were very small, except for the one in Canton owned by the provincial government.[83] The figure of 68 generating stations given by the *China Year Book* for 1920 would certainly account for a larger number of electrical workers than the 1,391 listed by the Nung-shang-pu, but could not possibly account for the figure of 100,000 given by Nishikawa Kiishi for 1923.

Bricks and Tiles. Although this branch of industry was still mainly a rural handicraft industry,[84] about fifty quite large brickworks had been operating for several years in the vicinity of large cities and industrial centers, mainly in North China and mostly owned by Japanese and Western firms.[85] Each employed several hundred workers, and the total number was probably from fifteen to twenty thousand.[86]

Soda and Other Chemical Products.   There were scarcely more than twenty or so modern factories for chemical products, most of them Japanese,[87] and they were concentrated in industrial centers within the Japanese sphere of influence (Tsingtao, Mukden, Dairen). The total number of workers employed, though higher than the figure of 809 given by the Nung-shang-pu for 1915, must nevertheless have been very small.

Other Industries

Printing.   This industry, which had a far longer tradition in China than in Europe, remained for obvious reasons mainly in Chinese hands, but both Catholic and Protestant missions, as well as several Japanese firms, had printing presses in China using Chinese characters. In addition there were the printing presses for the Western newspapers and periodicals published in some of the big cities.[88]

Some of the Chinese-owned printing plants were very large concerns, such as those belonging to the Commercial Press, which, from the beginning of the twentieth century, had pioneered the movement to popularize formal learning, and which had branches in Shanghai, Peking, and Hong Kong. Of secondary importance were the printing plants belonging to a Shanghai firm called "China Bookshop,"[89] and the state-owned printing plants under the Ministry of Finance. Including all the smaller printing plants, the total number of workers employed can be estimated at thirty thousand, if the figure of 11,000 for the Shanghai agglomeration alone, given by the survey conducted by the review *Hsin-ch'ing-nien* in 1920, can be regarded as reliable.[90]

Woolen and Cotton Yarn.   Industrial processing of woolen and cotton yarn for export was almost exclusively in the hands of several large British firms such as Jardine, Matheson & Company and Mackenzie & Company,[91] which owned factories equipped with hydraulic machinery and had long commanded the Chinese export trade. Their factories were mainly in Shanghai, Tientsin, and Hankow, and employed about twenty-five thousand workers.[92]

Mints.   These were nominally under the Ministry of Finance (Ts'ai-cheng-pu), but in the provinces they were in fact under the control of the warlords. In 1924, according to the Ts'ai-cheng-pu figures, the mints of Wuchang, Nanking, and Hangchow alone employed about four thousand workers.[93] To these must be added the number of workers employed in other important provincial capitals, such as Changsha.[94]

Mining

Coal Mines.   After the opening up in 1878 of the Kaiping collieries under the sponsorship of Li Hung-chang,[95] a large number of modern coal mines under Chinese, Japanese, and British ownership were opened up in North,

Northeast, and Central China. Although no figures are available for the number of workers employed in 1919, there are quite reliable figures for the amount of coal produced.[96] Moreover, for the six mines for which the number of workers employed is also known (those at Fushun and Penhsihi in the Northeast, at Tzechwan and Fangtze in Shantung, at Kiaotso in Honan, and at Pingting in Shansi) it is possible to arrive at an estimated figure of an average annual output of 100,000 tons per 1,350 workers.[97]

This figure enables a rough estimate to be made of the number of workers employed in the other mines, on the basis of their annual production figure; and including the known figure for the six mines above mentioned and the estimated figure for the other 13 mines or groups of mines, the estimated total comes to around 180,000. (See Table 4.)

This figure is probably below that of the actual number of miners employed in modernized mines, because although five of the six mines that served as a basis for the estimated figure of 180,000 were foreign-owned, the sixth was Chinese-owned, and Chinese-owned mines, which were less mechanized and less efficiently run, tended to employ a proportionately higher number of workers.

Metal Ore Mines.   The Japanese iron mines at Anshan and Penhsihi, which supplied the blast furnaces in that area, and the Chinese iron mines at Tayeh, which supplied the Hanyang blast furnaces, employed little more than six thousand workers.[98] The Shantung iron mines (at Chinlingchen) and those in Anhwei (at Taiping and Fanchang), which supplied the export trade controlled more or less directly by Japanese interests, probably employed even fewer workers.[99]

As regards modernized mines producing nonferrous metals, the only ones of any importance were the lead mine at Shuikowshan and the antimony mines at Sinhwa and Pantzu, all in Hunan. The Shuikowshan mine, which was owned by the provincial government, employed about six thousand workers in 1925.[100]

A large number of unmechanized or semi-mechanized mines continued to exist in various other parts of China, producing gold in Manchuria, iron in Central China, copper and tin in Yunnan, and manganese in areas south of the Yangtze. But the tens of thousands of workers employed in these mines should be classed as peasants rather than as industrial workers, since many of them were employed on a part-time basis. This is the case also with many of the salt miners and quarrymen, and with the coal miners employed in mines where old-fashioned methods (known as *t'u-fa*, "local methods") were still used.[101]

Of the 200,000 or so miners, over half—about 115,000 coal miners and seven to eight thousand iron miners—worked in foreign-owned mines, all of which, except for the Kailan and Pingsiang mines, were situated at some distance from, or on the fringe of, the main industrial centers. Thus the miners did

TABLE 4

NUMBER OF WORKERS EMPLOYED IN MODERN COAL MINES AROUND 1920

Site of mine	Company	Known numbers of workers	Annual production in tons[a]	Estimated numbers of workers
Fushun (Fengtien)	S.M.R. (Japanese)	38,600 in 1920[b]	3,000,000 (100,000 per 1,300 men)	—
Penhsihi (Fengtien)	S.M.R. (Japanese)	5,500 in 1920[c]	400,000 (100,000 per 1,400 men)	—
Kiaotso (Honan)	Peking Syndicate (British)	9,000 in 1920[d]	560,000 (100,000 per 1,600 men)	—
Tzechwan and Fangtze (Shantung)	Lu-ta (Japanese control)	7,000 in 1912[e]	600,000 (100,000 per 1,170 men)	—
Tangshan (Chihli)	K.M.A. (British)	25,000 in 1920[f]	4,400,000 (100,000 per 570 men)	—
		50,000 in 1922[g]	(100,000 per 1,100 men)	—
Pingting (Shansi)	Pao-chin Co. (Chinese)	2,000 in 1919[h]	200,000 (100,000 per 1,000 men)	—
Chalainor (Heilungkiang)	A White Russian group?	—	200,000 in 1920	2,700
Various mines in Fengtien	S.M.R. (Japanese)	—	200,000 in 1919	2,700
Tsingsing (Chihli)	Chinese state (German-owned before 1914)	—	580,000	7,800
Lincheng (Chihli)	Chinese state (Belgian-owned until 1919)	—	180,000	2,400
Mentowkow (Chihli)	Sino-British	—	150,000	2,000
Toli and Choukoutien (Chihli)	Chinese	—	550,000	7,500
Various mines in Chihli	Chinese	—	240,000	3,250
Kiaotso (Honan)	Chungyuan (Chinese)	—	830,000	11,200

Table 4 (cont'd)

Site of mine	Company	Known numbers of workers	Annual production in tons[a]	Estimated numbers of workers
Anyang (Honan)	Liu-ho-kou (Chinese)	—	190,000	2,550
Poshan (Shantung)	Chinese	—	300,000	4,050
Ihsien (Shantung)	Chunghsing (Chinese)	—	570,000	7,700
Pingsiang (Kiangsi)	Hanyehping (Chinese)	—	800,000	10,800
Kiawang (Kiangsu)	Chinese	—	140,000	1,900
Total known number of mineworkers		112,000	—	—
Total estimated number		—	—	66,550
Combined total of workers..		178,550		

[a] *China Year Book,* 1923, pp. 115ff.   [b] *Nien-chien* [138] I, 202.   [c] *Ibid.,* I, 98.   [d] *China Year Book,* 1921, p. 193.   [e] *Ibid.,* 1916, p. 65.   [f] *Chinese Economic Bulletin,* 7.i.22.   [g] *Chien-shih* [165], p. 79.   [h] *Nien-chien* [138] I, 205.

not play the leading part in the Chinese labor movement that their numbers, their local concentration, and their direct subjection to foreign employers might lead one to expect.

Transport

Railways. According to the official statistics, the state railways had 73,651 employees in 1919,[102] and the same source indicates that there were in addition about 45,000 employees on the foreign-owned railways, namely the Chinese Eastern Railway (C.E.R.), which came under joint Russian and international control in 1919,[103] the Japanese-owned South Manchuria Railway, the French Railway in Yunnan, and the British section of the Canton-Kowloon line. These figures include the workers in the repair shops, the chief of which were those at Changsintien, to the south of Peking, and at Kiangan, to the north of Hankow, at either end of the so-called "Ching-Han" line between Peking and Hankow; and those at Tangshan on the "Ching-Feng" (Peking-Mukden) line, at Szefang, and at Sinho on the northern section of the Canton-Hankow line. All these repair shops were from the very beginning active centers of the Chinese labor movement.[104]

The railway system in China was still very patchy and disconnected. There were very few links between the main north-south lines (S.M.R., Ching-Feng, Ching-Han, Tientsin-Pukow or "Chin-P'u," Tsingtao-Tsinan or "Chiao-Chi"); and the local or branch lines, such as the Shihchiachwang-Taiyuan or "Cheng-T'ai" line, the Chuchow-Pingsiang line, the Tangshan branch of the Ching-Feng line, and the Poshan branch of the Chiao-Chi line, were mainly designed to serve the mining centers.[105] The east-west "Lunghai" line across the Great Plain had just been begun. It ran eastwards as far as Huchow on the Chin-P'u line, and did not yet reach further west than a little beyond Loyang. South of the Yangtze the railway "system" consisted of only a few separate stretches of railroad: the Yunnan line, terminating at Haiphong, which was really an extension of economic enterprise in Indochina; the northern section of the Hankow-Canton line (known as "Yueh-Han"), which terminated in Hunan; the Shanghai-Nanking ("Hu-Ning") and Shanghai-Hangchow lines; and the Nanchang-Kiukiang provincial line. Only in the region of Canton did anything that could be described as a system exist, consisting of the three lines converging on that city, the Canton-Sanshui, Canton-Süchow (that is, the southern section of the Canton-Hankow line), and Canton-Kowloon lines (the last had both Chinese and British ownership).

Postal and Telecommunications Services. The postal services in China were still under foreign control of a kind similar to that exercised over the customs office. In 1919 the number of employees was 28,298.[106] In addition there were several thousand employees in the various private telegraph and telephone companies, either Chinese or foreign, operating in the main ports.

Seamen. No other figures exist except those already quoted: Sen Katayama's figure of 90,000, and Su Chao-cheng's of 160,000.[107] Teng Chung-hsia's estimate for 1924 is 150,000.[108] The tonnage figure for ships using Chinese waters is much lower for 1919 than for 1924;[109] so on this basis, if Teng's estimate is anywhere near correct, it can be inferred that in 1919 there were around 115,000 seamen. From the tonnage figures, it would appear that only 25 per cent of them—that is, about thirty thousand—served under the Chinese flag.

Dockers, Street-porters, etc. The abundance of cheap unskilled labor in China, which will be discussed later at some length, meant that it was uneconomical to use mechanized transport for moving goods about in the main centers of production and transit. The long lines of coolies loading and unloading trains and ships without any cranes to aid them was a sight that struck all foreign travelers. But here again nothing but somewhat arbitrary estimates of their actual number exist. These are estimates from various sources for various individual cities: 12,800 dockers and unskilled laborers in Dairen, 5,000 in Tientsin, and 4,000 in Hankow in 1925,[110] 47,000 in Shanghai, 3,000 in Nanking, and 4,000 in Wusih in 1920.[111] These estimates, which are often inconsistent and do not cover all the big ports,[112] refer to dockworkers only, and do not include coolies employed elsewhere. Physical strength was the only requirement for this type of work; yet there was a high degree of specialization among these unskilled workers. There were distinct categories of dockers and porters according to the techniques they employed: those who worked in pairs carrying goods on a bamboo pole, those who roped their load on to their backs, those who bore a flexible pole loaded at either end on their shoulders, and those who pushed a wheelbarrow or hauled a string of small handcarts. There was seldom any changing from one category to another.[113]

One of the most highly specialized categories of all was the turbulent army of rickshaw men, who, despite the growth of public transport, still provided the main means of transport in most of the big cities. An incomplete list includes, for instance, the figures of 55,000 for Peking, 50,000 for Shanghai, and 8,000 for Canton.[114]

In all, it is impossible to give more than a very rough estimate of the total number of these various types of coolies, and the figure of 300,000 advanced by Su Chao-cheng for 1927 (see Table 3) seems reasonable, if perhaps on the low side. Out of this total, it is very difficult to assess the proportion of unskilled labor employed by foreign firms. In the case of the dockers, the tonnage figures indicate that it may have amounted to as much as 75 per cent. On the other hand, almost all the rickshaw men worked for Chinese employers, but many were under the administrative control of various Settlement authorities, with whom they often came into conflict.

Municipal Transport and Other Municipal Services. Foreign tramway companies operated in most of the Treaty Ports—French and British ones in Shanghai, a Belgian one in Tientsin, Japanese ones in Dairen and Mukden, and a British one in Hong Kong.[115] There were also Chinese bus companies in all the big cities on the coast and in the interior.

Water supply in all the big cities was in the hands of private companies, either foreign-owned (as in the French Concession in Shanghai) or Chinese-owned, the only exception being the supply provided by the Municipal Council of the International Settlement in Shanghai.

The number of workers employed in the various municipal services (including removal of nightsoil and other public services) provided in the International Settlement was about forty-four hundred.[116] It is quite impossible to assess the number of municipal employees in China as a whole, or even in the big modern cities.

Distribution of the Working Class

If the figures arrived at for all the various categories of workers examined above are brought together, the total comes to 1,489,000. It must once more be stressed that this is no more than a rough estimate, especially since not even approximate figures have been advanced for a number of light industries. (For instance, in Table 5 no mention is made of workers in mechanized rice-husking factories, breweries and distilleries, salt refineries, wool spinning and

TABLE 5

Number of Chinese Workers Around 1919

Industries	Total number of workers	In Chinese enterprises	In foreign enterprises
Cotton	100,000	62,000	38,000
Silk	200,000	180,000	20,000
Carpets	10,000	7,000	3,000
Hosiery, etc.	25,000	20,000	5,000
Flour mills	12,000	8,000	4,000
Oil mills	30,000	15,000	15,000
Dried eggs	15,000	10,000	5,000
Sugar	3,000	—	3,000
Tobacco	50,000	20,000	30,000
Matches	40,000	30,000	10,000
Soap, candles, etc.	5,000	3,000	2,000
Metallurgy	45,000	40,000	5,000
Shipbuilding, arsenals	45,000	20,000	25,000
Cement	6,000	3,000	3,000
Bricks and tiles	15,000	5,000	10,000
Printing	30,000	20,000	10,000
Processing of wool, cotton	25,000	—	25,000
Minting	5,000	5,000	—
Coal mines	180,000	60,000	120,000
Metal ore mines	25,000	17,000	8,000
Railways	120,000	74,000	46,000
Postal service	28,000	—	28,000
Telecommunications	10,000	5,000	5,000
Ocean transport	115,000	30,000	85,000
Dock loading, etc.	200,000	50,000	150,000
Rickshaws	150,000	150,000	—
Total	1,489,000	834,000	655,000

weaving, ceramics, glass, papermaking, or leather and hides; nor are electrical workers or employees in public transport and other municipal services included.)

What we are concerned with, then, is over one and a half million industrial workers in all,[117] nearly half of whom were employed in foreign-owned enterprises. On the basis of the figures given in Table 5, the proportion is 44 per cent, but in fact it was probably less, because many of the light industries and municipal services (e.g. rice-husking, glass manufacture, municipal transport) excluded from the table for lack of adequate data were Chinese-owned. There will be further discussion on the importance for the Chinese labor movement of this group of workers employed by foreign firms, who, apart from the fact that there were so many of them, could bring extra weight to bear because the firms that employed them were concentrated in certain areas, advanced technologically, and predominantly in heavy industry. But the majority of the Chinese proletariat, whether employed by foreigners or not, worked in light industry and transport. Workers in these categories account for 78 per cent of the total in Table 5, and formed in fact an even higher proportion, since the industries and services omitted from the table almost all come under these two categories. This is another factor of importance in the history of the Chinese labor movement.

As for the geographical distribution of the Chinese proletariat,* there were six clearly defined regions in which it was located: the Shanghai area and the Yangtze estuary; Canton and its hinterland together with Hong Kong; the provinces of Hupeh and Hunan in Central China; the central lowlands of Shantung; the northeastern borders of Chihli; and the southern section of the northeast plain. In these six regions were concentrated 100 per cent of the foreign and 95 per cent of the Chinese cotton spindles, 100 per cent of the foreign and 98 per cent of the modern Chinese silk-reeling factories, 100 per cent of the foreign and 75 per cent of the Chinese flour mills, 100 per cent of the foreign and the great majority of the Chinese oil mills, 75 per cent of the albumen factories, 100 per cent of the tobacco factories, 100 per cent of the blast furnaces, 93 per cent of the foreign and 90 per cent of the Chinese shipyards, 100 per cent of the cement works, 95 per cent of the foreign-owned modern brickworks and 83 per cent of the Chinese brickworks, 100 per cent of the woolen and cotton yarn factories, 84 per cent of the foreign coal mines (but only 16 per cent of the Chinese), and finally, 100 per cent of the foreign and 70 per cent of the Chinese metal ore mines.[118] These percentages show that there was a greater concentration of foreign enterprises within these six regions than of Chinese enterprises.

It might be useful to cast a glance at the character of each region. Without any question the most important of them, both because of its position in general and because of the size of its working-class population, was the Shanghai and Lower Yangtze region. Shanghai was at once a great trading center and a center for light industry, and this determined the nature of the employment available. Its dockers and porters, seamen and boatmen, shipyard workers, warehousemen, tanners, and workers in the factories that processed hides and cotton yarn, were gradually joined by the workers in the cotton mills, the silk factories, the flour and oil mills, and the match and tobacco factories. In addition, since Shanghai was the main intellectual center in China, it contained a great many printing companies, both Chinese and foreign, from the vast establishments of the Commercial Press to little workshops of all kinds.

The presence of a large industrial proletariat affected the very layout of the city.[119] Before the arrival of the foreigners it had been a small place of minor

---

* See maps in Appendix A, pp. 415–26. The first of the two series shows the geographic distribution of each industry, and the second the industries in each of the main economic regions.

importance. The old town survived, in the city of 1919, as the "Southern District" (*Nanshih*), with its old-style streets enclosed within an ancient crenellated wall. The big modern firms had sprung up in two main centers: on the banks of the Whangpoo, and on those of Soochow Creek. Going up river, there were first the cotton mills, the docks, and the warehouses of the Yangtzepoo district, within the territory of the International Settlement; the main electricity generating station was also in this district, supplying power and light to a large number of enterprises on Chinese territory as well as to the Settlement. On the same side of the river, beyond the "Bund" with its palatial office buildings, were further industrial enterprises in the Southern District, the main ones being the Kangnan shipyards and docks. In Pootung, on the other side of the river, there was a large industrial area containing cotton mills and tobacco factories (including the factory of the British and American Tobacco Company), which continued without a break, up and down river, and included the wharves and warehouses belonging to all the firms with big names in the business world of the Far East: Mitsui, Jardine, Matheson & Company, Standard Oil, K.M.A., the China Merchant Steam Navigation Company, etc.

Although Soochow Creek was silting up and becoming less and less navigable, its banks had been chosen as the site for a large number of modern factories since the beginning of the twentieth century. Its south bank lay within the territory of the International Settlement. On its north bank lay the Chinese districts: Hongkew, with its cotton mills and silk factories; Chapei, in which silk factories, printing shops, and the main railway station, the North Station, were situated; and Hsiaoshatu and Tsaokiatu, with their cotton mills, hosiery factories, and flour and oil mills.

In all, the number of male and female industrial and transport workers in Shanghai was probably about 300,000, if an estimate made in 1920 can be relied upon.[120] To these must be added the several tens of thousands of workers employed in the secondary industrial centers of the Lower Yangtze region, where after 1900 a large number of mills and factories had been established under the stimulus, and after the pattern, of Shanghai's development. Cotton mills, steam-powered silk-reeling factories, and modern oil and flour mills had transformed the towns of Wusih,[121] Chinkiang,[122] and Soochow, which had formerly been centers of handicraft industries, and had even penetrated as far as the cities of Nantung,[123] Chungming, and Haimen on the north bank of the river.

Trade and the silk industry were the main activities in the Canton–Hong Kong region. The importance of silk-reeling and silk-weaving in Canton and its surrounding districts (e.g. Shunteh, Fatchan, Kongmoon, and Namhoi) has already been mentioned. Otherwise there was very little in the way of industrial enterprise in Canton, apart from the electricity generating station, the provincial cement works, and the railway workshops belonging to the lines operating within the region. Craft industries and workshops predominated, as exemplified by the small mechanical workshops on the island of Honam.

Hong Kong, being the main British trading center in the Far East, contained huge repair yards belonging to Butterfield & Swire (the Taikoo docks), W. S. Bailey & Co., and other firms. Because of its urban development and the availability of large amounts of British and Chinese capital, it had attracted entrepreneurs, and there were printing plants, match factories, and a tobacco factory of the Nanyang Company, and also a large cement works belonging to the Green Island Company (which owned another in Macao), situated in the suburb of Kowloon, on the mainland.

The nucleus of a working-class population in this second region had been in existence longer than that of the Shanghai region, but was very much smaller in size. According to Teng Chung-hsia's estimate for 1926, there were at that time scarcely as many as fifty-five thousand workers employed in capitalist industrial enterprises in the Canton region, even including those which were not fully mechanized.[124] To these must be added the workers employed in the silk factories of the region, those employed in the modern enterprises in Hong Kong, and also most of the Chinese seamen, who, although they were seldom resident, generally came from either Canton or Hong Kong. But the total figure cannot have been more than 200,000.

The industrial region of Hupeh and Hunan was dominated by the Han-yehping Company, a vast industrial combine which owned the Pingsiang collieries, the Tayeh iron mines, and the Hanyang steelworks. The coal from Pingsiang was sent by rail to Wuchang and then ferried across to the other side of the Yangtze; the Tayeh iron-ore and smelting works, which was linked by a short railway to the river, then transported it by coal barge to the railhead. Teng Chung-hsia, who when working at the Hanyehping founded the first big industrial union in the history of the Chinese labor movement,[125] estimated the number of employees, including miners, metalworkers, seamen, dockers, and porters, at nearly 100,000.

Heavy industry prevailed in the Hupeh-Hunan region, other enterprises being the lead mine at Sinhwa, the antimony mine at Shuikowshan, the cement works at Tayeh, the state arsenal at Wuchang, the railway workshops of the northern section of the Canton-Hankow line at Sinho and Hsükiapeng, and the railway workshop at Kiangan, the southern terminus of the Ching-Han line. But some light industry, using the agricultural produce of the region, existed in Wuhan and Changsha, where there were Chinese and Japanese cotton mills, and also oil mills, flour mills, tobacco factories (including a big branch of the B.A.T.), and British cotton-processing factories.[126]

The Shantung region was at one time in the German sphere of influence, but after 1914 it was under Japanese control. Foreign interests predominated in its industrial development, which had affected Tsinan, the ancient capital of the province. The Chiao-Chi railway formed the central axis of the region, and the industries consisted of a cotton mill, flour mills, oil mills, brickworks, cement works, and chemicals and match factories (mostly Japanese) at Tsingtao and its industrial suburb Szefang; mines at Poshan, Tzechwan, Fangtze, and Chinlingchen; flour mills, albumen factories, tobacco factories, and railway workshops at Tsinan; and a state arsenal at Tehsien.

In Chihli there was no manufacturing tradition such as existed in Hunan, Kiangsu, and Kwangtung. The industrialization of its northeastern corner was almost exclusively due to the opening up of Tientsin to foreign trade and the exploitation of the coal mines in the Tangshan area. A large number of Chinese, Japanese, and British enterprises were concentrated in Tientsin: cotton mills, flour mills, oil mills, powdered egg factories, tobacco factories, shipyards, wool-processing factories, and carpet factories. In addition there were the numerous Chinese and foreign printing plants in Peking and Tientsin, and the salt and soda works at Tangku. Tangshan, as well as being the administrative center of the K.M.A., also had the main railway workshop of the Ching-Feng line, a cement works, potteries, and oil mills.[127]

In the Northeast, the sixth region with a large working-class population, there was still less of a link with the industrial traditions of the past. It was the region from which the Manchus originally came, but it had been opened to substantial Chinese immigration for only about twenty years.[128] Industrial development was almost exclusively confined to the areas in the vicinity of the two big railway lines, the Chinese Eastern Railway and the South Manchuria Railway;[129] and foreign capital investment—Russian in the north and Japanese in the south—predominated.[130] The only exception was Newchwang (Yingkow), which became a Treaty Port in 1860. Even before 1914, Chinese merchant capital had established silk factories and oil mills there, which however were finding it more and more difficult to compete with rival Japanese concerns in Dairen and Antung. All the most important firms throughout the south of Manchuria, apart from the B.A.T. factory at Mukden, were Japanese: oil mills, match factories, and brickworks at Mukden and Dairen, and blast furnaces at Anshan and Penhsihi.

The vast majority of the Chinese proletariat was concentrated in these six regions. The rest consisted of the workers in the silk and cotton industries in Chekiang, in the silk and printing industries in Szechwan, in the flour mills scattered among various medium-sized towns in the Yangtze valley and the Great Plain, in the canneries and the arsenal in Fuchow, and in the small match factories dispersed among several of the urban centers in Central China, as well as the miners in several modern collieries in Chihli, Honan, Shantung, and Kiangsu. These workers amounted in all to no more than fifty to seventy-five thousand. Thus in the main, the Chinese working class was concentrated in several big centers with high population density; but these centers were far apart from each other, and the groups of workers found it difficult to communicate with one another.

These working-class nuclei were, of course, only a minute fraction of the vast population of China—not as much as 0.5 per cent.[131] Yet because the working class was concentrated in these big industrial centers, it was able to bring much more weight to bear than its actual size in relation to the total population would warrant. The lack of exact figures makes it impossible to estimate the percentage of the working-class population in relation to the total population of the six industrial regions. In Shanghai, if we accept the figures of 300,000 male and female workers given by *Hsin-ch'ing-nien* and 1,538,000 total population given by the Chinese Post Office,[132] we can put the working-class population at perhaps 20 per cent of the total population of the greater urban area. These basic facts about the situation of the working class— its absolute numerical weakness in relation to the population of the country as a whole, and the weight it could bring to bear within the limited areas where its forces were concentrated—are essential to any understanding of the Chinese labor movement.

CHAPTER III

Social Origins and Recruitment of Industrial Workers

Peasant Workers

In the years immediately following the First World War, almost all Chinese industrial and transport workers were former peasants who had recently moved to the towns. They were not yet accustomed to their new environment, and still retained close links with the country. The absence of documentation on internal migration in China at that time makes it impossible to prove this statement,[1] but there is evidence of various kinds to support it.

For instance, a number of investigations were carried out into the former occupation of given groups of workers, and all except one show that the majority were of peasant origin. (See Table 6.)

The same result was shown by an investigation carried out in 1929 among three hundred workers in the Tientsin carpet factories. Unfortunately this investigation—the only one of its kind—concerned a somewhat marginal industry.[2] Most of the workers came from hsien in the purely rural areas of the province; indeed it was the hsien farthest from the railways and least affected by the development of a market economy that supplied the largest contingents: Tsaokiang 37 workers, Shulu 36, and Shenhsien 29. (See Map 1.)

TABLE 6
PROPORTION OF WORKERS OF PEASANT ORIGIN

Survey	Year	Workers of peasant origin	Percentage
189 Shanghai printing workers[a]	1935	151	79%
985 li-kung mine workers in the Chunghsing coal mine[b]	1931	503	52
1,025 wai-kung mine workers[c]	1931	768	75
51 Shanghai rickshaw men[d]	1934	36	71
100 Dairen dockers[e]	1925	69	69
86 Chiu-ta salt workers[f]	1926	51	59.3
50 workers in the soda factory at Tangku[g]..	1926	22	44

[a] Gear [67]. [b] Lin Hsiu-chuan [73]. For the terms li-kung and wai-kung, see p. 58. [c] Ibid.
[d] Municipal Gazette, 13.ii.34. [e] MDN, 6.iii.25. [f] Lin Sung-ho [74], p. 53. [g] Ibid., p. 100.

The workers in the Shanghai cotton mills were also peasants, coming from the villages of Kiangsu.[3] An enquiry carried out by the Shanghai Y.W.C.A. among the women employed in the silk-reeling factories of Wusih[4] shows that 50 per cent of them came from the villages around Lake T'ai and 30 per cent from the poverty-stricken areas north of the Yangtze (Chiang-pei, known as "Kompo" or "Supo" in local dialects). A circular issued by the Hong Kong Seamen's Union to its members just before the great strike of 1922 declared: "We seamen have left our villages and our village wells to risk our lives working at sea."[5]

Many of the Chinese trade union leaders at this time were also of peasant origin. For example, Jen Shu-te, who in 1922 collaborated with Mao Tse-

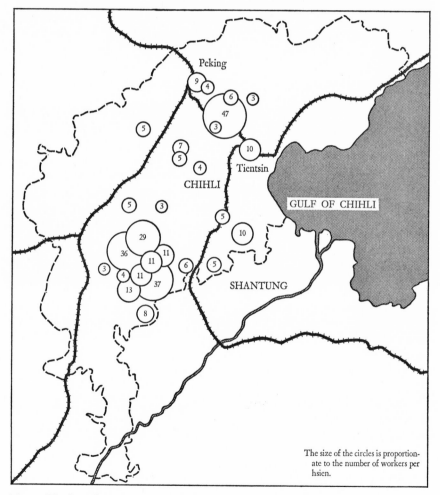

Map 1. Districts of Origin of 300 Tientsin Carpet Factory Workers in 1929.

tung in organizing a strike of building workers in Changsha,[6] Wang Cheng, a plate-layer on the Hankow-Chuchow railway who became an engine-driver and the leader of the railwaymen's union on this line,[7] and T'ang Shou-i, a miner and active trade unionist in the Hanyehping Company,[8] were all peasants from Hunan. Su Chao-cheng, founder of the Hong Kong Seamen's Union, who at Wuhan in 1927 became the first Minister of Labor in China's history, was a peasant from Kwangtung,[9] as was Ch'en Ch'üan, another seaman, who in 1926 represented the Canton–Hong Kong Strike Committee at the International Congress in Brussels.[10] Lun K'o-chung, founder of the railwaymen's union on the Chiao-Chi line in 1924, was a peasant from Shantung.[11] Many more such examples could be quoted.[12]

The peasants who left the land under pressure of the agrarian crisis were all either agricultural laborers or small peasant proprietors who could no longer get a living from their farms.[13] The Kompo area of Kiangsu province, lying north of the Yangtze, where life was extremely hard,[14] formed a reservoir of labor that supplied Shanghai, Wusih, and other industrial centers in the Yangtze estuary with a constant stream of workers. Many of the cotton and silk workers,[15] the rickshaw men,[16] and the dockers came from there. The poor peasants from the overpopulated areas of Shantung provided a similar supply for the mines, factories, and railways in the North and the Northeast.[17]

At times of famine or unrest, this migration of population from the country to the towns became intensified. The great famine in Chihli in 1920–21[18] brought large numbers of refugees (*tsai-min*) to the industrial centers and into the cotton mills of Tientsin[19] and the Japanese enterprises in Manchuria. The number of workers sent to the Fushun mines by Japanese recruiting agents in Shantung and Chihli rose from 10,874 in 1918 to 16,516 in 1920.[20] Similarly, in Fukien around 1924–25 the spread of banditry and the general insecurity brought many peasants to Fuchow, where they were ready to take on any kind of work, even pulling rickshaws.[21]

These peasants joined the working class with comparative ease and rapidity, but this was because of the very low degree of skill required. (This important point will be dealt with in detail later.) Despite this rapid integration, workers of peasant origin did not break their ties with the land. On the contrary, many of them (e.g., 420 out of the 556 workers employed in the Chiu-ta salt refinery in Tangku)[22] had left their families behind and sent them monthly remittances out of their savings.[23] Absenteeism in the factories usually increased during the summer harvest. Attendance at a Tientsin cotton mill in 1928 fell in July to 88.15 per cent of the total number employed, as against 93.76 per cent in January.[24] The same fluctuations occurred among the rickshaw men of Shanghai, where the hiring companies were able to dispose of all their vehicles during the winter months, whereas in summer many of their coolie clients hired themselves out as harvest laborers in the surrounding countryside.[25] It was the same with the antimony miners of Hunan, who are said to have found it more remunerative to do harvest work in summer,[26] the iron miners of Chinlingchen in Shantung,[27] and the workers in the match factories of Tientsin.[28] In fact, it was not unusual for factories to close down altogether at times when agricultural work was at its peak. The Hankow rice-husking factories closed during the season when the rice was transplanted,[29] and the Harbin oil mills during July and August.[30] There were even a few enterprises that combined industrial and agricultural work, such as a Peking carpet factory, situated on the outskirts of the city, that owned a large amount of land upon which the workers were employed during slack periods.[31]

Another indication of the links maintained by workers with their native villages is the way in which travel expenses featured in workers' budgets, in so far as this can be ascertained by the few surveys available. According to a survey conducted by the Y.M.C.A. in 1922, these formed 6 per cent of the monthly outlay of coolies (i.e. 0.71 yuan), and 11 per cent of that of skilled workers (i.e. 2.12 yuan).[32] In both cases, this item came fourth after food, clothing, and rent. These were quite large amounts, even though they probably included the expenses of daily transport, which were unavoidable for even the very poorest in a vast metropolis like Shanghai.[33] But equally large amounts were spent on travel by the workers in the Chiu-ta salt refinery, situated in a much smaller town; and here the percentage increased in inverse ratio to the wage-scale, which suggests that it was the less skilled workers that were least acclimatized to town life.[34] One of the earliest demands of the railwaymen, already met in 1918 by a regulation issued by the Ministry of Communications,[35] was for free travel or travel at reduced rates on the railways. This journeying between place of work and home village did not escape the attention of trade union leaders, who were quick to see the advantage that could be derived from it; and at the Second National Labor Congress (1925) a resolution was passed calling for an alliance between workers and peasants, and urging workers who returned to their villages to carry out propaganda among the peasants and help them form militant peasant unions.[36]

Workers who failed to adapt to factory life frequently gave up their factory jobs and returned to their home villages. Of the workers who annually left the Chiu-ta salt refinery, 60 per cent returned to farming.[37] Return to the village was also frequent during prolonged strikes; when the Hong Kong mechanics obtained their 32 per cent wage increase in April 1920, they did not return to work until the thousands of strikers who had gone to the rural areas of Kwangtung came back to the island.[38] The same happened with the strikers at the San-hsin cotton mill in Shanghai in February 1922,[39] and when in April 1925 the workers in the Japanese cotton factories in Tsingtao went on strike, the silk factories took the precaution of sending their women employees back to their villages with fares paid.[40]

The question of where workers chose to be buried is one upon which no documentation exists. But the fact that the railways granted free transport for the coffins of their employees presumably indicates that this was to enable the coffins to be taken to the native district of the deceased.[41] We know how the Chinese cherish their ancestral graves and how every corner of Chinese soil is scattered with grave-mounds. We would have an interesting indication of the extent to which the workers had broken with their rural origins if we knew what proportion of them still made the last journey of all to their native village, and how many were simply buried in the towns.

Other Recruiting Sources

Although the working class was primarily drawn from the peasantry, two other social groups provided some of its members: the skilled craftsmen and the populace of the towns.

It is very difficult to ascertain the extent to which modern industry absorbed the handicraft workers of the traditional craft industries. No study of the craft industries in modern times has yet been made, and all that can be said is that a map of the traditional crafts and manufactures still flourishing at the beginning of the twentieth century would probably bear little resemblance to the modern industrial map with its six regions discussed above. With a few exceptions, such as the spinning and weaving industries in Soochow and Hangchow, the rice-husking industry in Wuhan, the flour mills of Tientsin and Wuhan, and the silk factories of Kwangtung, the process of industrialization in China was not an extension of earlier craft industries, but had been introduced from abroad in peripheral areas such as the Treaty Ports and the foreign railway and mining concessions. There was scarcely ever any direct opportunity for modern industries to absorb the surplus labor made available by the crisis in the craft industries caused by competition with factory goods, because hundreds of miles usually separated the one from the other.[42] Therefore old-style craftsmen were of minor importance in the Chinese working class.[43]

The new industries, being situated in areas which had no traditions of manufacture, were forced to adopt systems of production that enabled them to make do with an unskilled labor force of peasant origin. Nevertheless they still required a minimum of skilled workers, and the only way to get them was to bring them from other, and often distant, areas. These migrant workers, although relatively few in number, were quite an important element of the working class. They provided a good many proletarian leaders, and helped to give the working class a unified, national character. On the other hand, they tended to arouse regional rivalries, often to the displeasure of the unions.

Sometimes these migrations of skilled labor merely extended traditional practices or perpetuated local specialization in a particular trade. When the

Chiu-ta refinery was established, all the carpenters employed came from Shen-hsien, a small market town in Chihli famed for its carpentry.[44] Again, the workers in the Japanese slaughterhouses in Tsingtao were all Muslims from western Shantung who traditionally specialized in this occupation;[45] those in the Shanghai ink factories all came from the hsien of Wuyuan in Anhwei, which had long monopolized the manufacture of ink;[46] and those in the Shanghai carpet factories came from Peking or Tientsin, which were older carpet-making centers than Shanghai.[47]

Another reason for this migration of skilled labor was that sometimes entrepreneurs liked to bring skilled workers from their own province with them when opening factories elsewhere. This was true of the Cantonese merchant capitalists who played an important part in the industrialization of North China at the beginning of the twentieth century;[48] many of the skilled mechanics in the new factories, the mines, and the railway workshops there were Cantonese.[49] Similarly, the British brought Cantonese skilled workers from Hong Kong with them when they opened railway workshops on the Peking-Mukden line and started other industries in Tangshan.[50]

In general, however, migration of skilled labor simply followed the normal path of a movement from earlier to more recent industrial areas. After the Nanking Treaty and the opening up of China, it was in the southern ports—Canton, Ningpo, Fuchow, and Shanghai—that Chinese workers first became acquainted with Western industrial techniques, particularly in ship engineering. Consequently it was mechanics from Canton and Ningpo that were brought to staff the antimony mines of Sinhwa in Hunan, the steelworks of Hanyang, and the German collieries in Shantung, at the turn of the twentieth century.[51] Similarly, it was workers from Ningpo that Chang Ch'ien recruited when he founded the Nantung engineering works in 1905.[52] And when at the beginning of the century the French-owned Peking-Hankow railway was opened, a number of mechanics were recruited in Fuchow, where nearly fifty years before a modern arsenal had been established with the technical assistance of French naval officers.[53] Likewise, when the Tientsin cotton mills were opened shortly after the First World War, the skilled workers were recruited from Shanghai, one of the earliest centers of the modern cotton industry.[54]

Another source of recruitment for industrial manpower was the urban populace, consisting of the many different categories of poor people in the towns, some of whom had recently left their villages. (Others had done so generations before, in order to try to make a living out of the gentry, the wealthy merchants, and the officials in the towns.) After the Nanking Treaty their numbers swelled rapidly in the Treaty Ports, long before industrialization had begun in earnest.[55] When it did begin, shophands, street vendors whose entire stock-in-trade consisted of the few articles they had on display, soldiers dismissed from the army, peddlers, coolies who hired themselves out by the day for any kind of work that was going, nightwatchmen, boatmen, scavengers, domestic servants in wealthy households—everyone in fact who had no steady occupation and who faced the constant threat of unemployment—tried to find a steadier, although not necessarily a better-paying, job in modern industry or transport.[56] This phenomenon is illustrated by the surveys shown in the table below.

TABLE 7

PROPORTION OF WORKERS OF URBAN ORIGIN

Survey	Year	Workers of urban origin	Percentage
51 Shanghai rickshaw men[a]	1934	12	24%
86 Chiu-ta salt workers[b]	1926	25	29
50 workers in the soda factory at Tangku[c] ..	1926	12	24
100 Dairen dockers[d]	1925	27	27

[a] *Municipal Gazette*, 13.ii.34.   [b] Lin Sung-ho [74], p. 53.   [c] *Ibid.*, p. 100.   [d] *MDN*, 6.iii.25.

In Shanghai these dregs of the urban populace were especially numerous, and they gave the working class in that city a character of its own. Their tendency toward semi-clandestine forms of organization such as the *pang-hui* or brotherhoods (some of which included the very lowest of the *Lumpenproletariat*), or bands of thugs like the famous Red and Green Gangs,[57] held back the development of true industrial trade unionism in Shanghai, and it was not until after the great strike of June 1925 that unions gained a firm hold there.

Methods of Recruitment

There were during this period three main methods of recruitment of industrial workers. Apprenticeship under contract was one—a method found in almost all precapitalist societies where industry is organized in corporations of small producers. It survived in a debased form in certain sectors of modern industry in China. Another method was recruitment by "labor contractors," or *pao-kung-t'ou,* who had the workers completely in their power. This form of recruitment was particularly prevalent in Shanghai, but was found in many other parts of the country as well. The third was the method typical of capitalist production with its free labor market, consisting of free hiring of labor. But this third form was very far from being the predominant method, and when it did occur, the workers were usually signed on through an intermediary, such as a foreman, who made a profit on the deal.

It was natural enough that the customary guild apprenticeship system[58] should be carried on in partially mechanized concerns such as small mechanized workshops, weaving establishments, carpet factories, and dye-works; but the position of the apprentices was very different from the traditional one. According to a report on a visit in 1923 to a Peking carpet factory where 120 workmen were employed, this was the situation there:

> Only 40 were what might be called journeymen; 80 were lads serving a three years' apprenticeship, during which they received little beyond their food and lodging. These apprentices all came some hundreds of miles from a neighbouring province and were entirely in the hands of the employer. It is quite clear that unless the industry extends with phenomenal rapidity, this must prove a blind-alley occupation for a large proportion of them. Indeed many are being turned away on the completion of their apprenticeship, and are obliged to take up unskilled labour, such as pulling rickshaws.[59]

This description could in the main apply to all concerns where apprentices were employed. The apprenticeship contract (*i-t'u ho-t'ung*) laid down very strict conditions. The apprentice's family had to produce a "guarantor" (*pao-jen*),[60] and for a period of three years, or sometimes four, as in the mechanical workshops and leather workshops of Tientsin,[61] he received merely nominal payment, amounting to no more than board and lodging. The employers' associations, which were what remained of the old mixed guilds, included the obligations of apprentices in their rules. In the weaving establishments of Tientsin, for instance,[62] apprenticeship lasted for three years and four months (three years and one festival), and the only holidays the apprentice had were the Dragon Boat Festival in the fifth moon, the Moon Festival, and New Year; he was not allowed to leave the workshop at any other time, except on the occasion of deaths or marriages in his family; and there was a written agreement that if he left before his contract had expired, his family would have to pay six yuan per month toward the expenses his master had incurred.

The other side of the bargain—namely, that after this period of semi-slavery the apprentice could count on qualifying as a skilled worker and on employment as such within the trade—had, however, disappeared completely. Like the factory described above, all other similar factories and workshops had so many "apprentices" that most of them could not hope ever to become a skilled worker certain of finding a steady job. (This is confirmed by the figures shown in Table 8.)

The report on the carpet factories of Peking quoted above reveals that 78 of them employed nothing but apprentices, which shows that apprenticeship had become entirely divorced from its former function. It had become nothing more than the misuse of an ancient custom to provide an excuse for the employment of child labor, which was more or less unpaid yet kept completely submissive by means of the customary apprenticeship contract. In Chekiang,

TABLE 8

Proportion of Apprentices in Several Factories

Survey	Total number employed	Adult workers	Apprentices
Peking carpet factories in 1923[a]....	6,834	1,768	5,066 (74%)
Tientsin weavers in 1930[b]	7,873	2,756	5,117 (65%)
Tientsin hosiery knitting workers[c]..	1,610	451	1,159 (72%)
Tientsin engineering workshops[d]...	742	332	410 (55%)

[a] Chu and Blaisdell [59], p. 34.   [b] Fong [64].   [c] Fong [63].   [d] Nien-chien [138] I, 582.

with its strong craft traditions in weaving, apprenticeship survived in the semi-modernized workshops only in this debased form, with long-term contracts, low pay, and no guarantee of subsequent employment.[63]

In order to obtain a low-paid and submissive labor force, some of the big new industrial enterprises in Chihli, the Middle Yangtze valley, and the Canton–Hong Kong area also made use of the old apprenticeship system. The Tientsin cotton mills, for instance, employed a large number of children under the name of "apprentice labor" (yang-ch'eng-kung), some of whom were classed as Category A workers (chia-kung), who had the right to visit their families. The remaining Category B workers (i-kung) came from hsien in the rural areas of Chihli or from even further afield. They were under a much stricter contract, were clothed in blue, and were given board and lodging but practically no wages.[64] They were recruited by agents sent by the companies into the villages for this special purpose, who assured families that signed a contract that the work would not be hard, that two hours of schooling and one of physical training would be given daily, and that not only traveling expenses and board and lodging would be paid, but also a tidy sum of pocket money.[65] Unfortunately, these apprentices were very badly treated as soon as they entered the mill. Many of them died and were buried in a special workers' cemetery a few miles away from the mill.[66] The same was true of the Tangshan cotton mill opened in 1922, where "apprentices" of this kind formed a third of the workers employed,[67] the match factories of Tientsin and Peking,[68] the glass works of Hong Kong and Peking,[69] the railway workshops of the Ching-Han line,[70] the silk-reeling factories of Wusih,[71] the cotton mills of Hankow,[72] and many other concerns. In all of them, children were simply used in the same way as any other type of worker employed in modernized production processes, forming part of day and night shifts (pan) without regard to their age or their supposed thirst to acquire technical skill.[73]

Although this pseudo-apprenticeship system was widely adopted by industrial enterprises in areas such as Chihli, Central China, and the South, where manufacturing traditions were strong and old social customs still survived, no need seems to have been felt in Shanghai to use it as a disguise for the employment of child labor, except in a few small concerns such as dye-works and canneries,[74] and in the printing industry.[75] Other industries employed children quite openly and blatantly. Owing to a lack of adequate documentation, it is impossible to say why this should have been so or to give a fuller description of the use of child labor in each of the industrial regions.

The Shanghai textile industry, on the other hand, was the classic example of an industry in which the pao-kung or contract-labor system operated, although the system was also widespread in other regions and other branches of industry. The details varied, but the main feature of the system was that the labor force was recruited by the owner or the manager of an enterprise through an intermediary, who was given full or partial authority over the workers he recruited throughout their term of employment, and upon whom they were completely dependent for payment of wages and arrangements about working conditions.

A typical example of how the system affected the women employed in the British and Japanese cotton mills in Shanghai is afforded by the experience of one of them as described in an interview.[76] Her mother, a widow living in a village in the Kompo, signed a written contract presented by the recruiting agent (*lao-pan*) whereby the daughter, then aged thirteen, was engaged to work for three years without wages, but with board and lodging and clothing provided by the lao-pan. The lao-pan, whose traveling expenses were paid by a Japanese mill, also visited the neighboring rural districts, where he gave enthusiastic descriptions of factory work in Shanghai. He brought back with him fifty young girls from these hsien and as many again from his own native village. These girls had to work twelve hours a day in the mill, and had to go on foot to and from work. They were lodged in premises provided by the lao-pan, where they were under constant surveillance by his cook and other domestic servants. For three whole years they were thus entirely cut off from the outside world, with no means of communication with their families. They had only two days' holiday in the year, both at the lunar New Year; and if they were absent through illness, their "time" was prolonged accordingly.

This was the situation of the majority of the female employees in the Shanghai cotton mills, although there were slight variations here and there.[77] Sometimes the terms "pao-fan-tso" and "pao-kung-t'ou" were used for the recruiting agent instead of "lao-pan"; and in some cases the girls' wages were paid directly to him by the management, while in others he made a deduction from their earnings. When he received the whole sum, he was often obligated to pay a certain amount to the family of the girl worker, either in a lump sum when the contract was signed or by installments at the beginning of each year.[78]

The pao-kung system was in use in most of the modern mines, but here the recruiting agents, known as "pao-kung-t'ou," "pa-t'ou," or "tsu-chang,"[79]

were also involved in the production side of the industry, being responsible
to the management for a fixed amount of coal output. They themselves organized the work with the assistance of their own foremen and overseers. According to Torgasheff, the main feature of the pao-kung system was simply
the transfer of all responsibility for the workers to the labor contractors, who
made a fat profit out of it.[80]

Some of these labor contractors engaged in competition on a very small
scale; in 1931, for instance, the Chunghsing coal mine had dealings with 26
separate contractors, each employing from 150 to 300 miners.[81] Others were
in really big business, with a whole hierarchy of managers, assistant managers,
foremen, and assistant foremen, down to the basic units consisting of shifts
of a score or so of men. These contractors were well able to deal with the mine
owners on more or less equal terms.[82] In 1930, contractors of this kind could
earn several tens of thousands of yuan a year in North China.[83]

Usually the labor contractors provided board and lodging for the miners,
and received from the company the total amount of wages in proportion to
the amount of coal extracted, from which, before paying the miners their
share, the contractors deducted a recruitment commission plus their expenses
for board and lodging. They also lent money to the miners at exorbitant rates,
and ran small shops, opium dens, and gambling houses,[84] all of which helped
to trap the miners into a position of indebtedness from which there was little
chance of escaping.

In the mines, contract labor was known as *wai-kung,* or "external labor,"
as against *li-kung,* "internal labor" (also known as *ku-kung,* "hired labor"),
the latter consisting of workers employed directly by the company.[85] It is very
difficult to know what the proportion of miners recruited on the contract-
labor system was because of the very nature of the system. In 1928, the manager of a Chinese-owned coal mine in Shantung, when asked by an investi-
gator how many men were employed,[86] first gave the figure of 5,000; when
it was objected that this hardly tallied with the high output of the mine, he
admitted that there were 17,000 contract-labor men as well, but said that
"they are no concern of ours; we do not pay them directly, and do not know
the exact number of men working for contractors." It is, however, certain that
the number of wai-kung greatly exceeded the number of li-kung, sometimes
reaching as much as 75 or 80 per cent of the total number of employees.[87] As
will be shown later, the li-kung were usually the more skilled workers, such
as carpenters, mechanics, and pit workers.[88]

A similar form of contract labor was that found among the seamen of Canton and Hong Kong and commonly employed by the British and Japanese
shipping companies whose ships docked at the ports of South China. The
seamen were recruited by agents known as *hsi-ma-sha* (the Cantonese version
of the English word "shipmaster"), who ran what might be described as employment agencies.[89] They demanded a down payment (perhaps ten yuan)

from seamen who made use of their services, and a pledge that they would receive part of the seamen's wages, sometimes as much as half, over a fixed period (six months, a year, or even more). Some of them even had an agreement with a shipping company that the amount of the seamen's wages owed to them should be paid to them directly.

Contract labor was also the rule among the dockers in the big ports and the coolies in big cities where there was large-scale transportation of goods.[90] Some of these dockers and coolies formed gangs (*pang*) of about a hundred, and all dealings were conducted by the head of the gang; but the rest were completely dependent on powerful contract-labor agencies, and a whole hierarchy of middlemen (*ta-pao, erh-pao, san-pao,* etc.—that is, first, second, and third contractor) each took his cut from the sum originally intended as payment for the work done.[91] As in the mines, these contractors bore full responsibility not only for recruitment, but also for the amount of work done. Those who operated in a small way came to agreements with each other to prevent competition. In Nanking the heads of the pang of basket-carrier coolies divided up the town into sectors, and raised complaints against each other if any trespassing occurred;[92] and in Hong Kong the contractors who supplied coolies for coaling the ships that docked there joined together to form a powerful employers' guild (*hang*), with which the shipping companies dealt directly.[93]

Contract labor was widely employed in many other branches of modern transport and industry. The Municipal Public Works Department in the International Settlement of Shanghai often had to resort to it, although the annual reports record the poor work done by the men thus recruited.[94] The French Tramway Company in Shanghai also recruited some of its employees in this way,[95] as did the B.A.T. Company for the packaging of cigarettes by hand (whereas the workers tending the machines were directly employed by the company).[96] Similarly on the railways, the tracklayers and gangers, who were the least skilled of the workers employed, were recruited through pao-kung.[97]

Is it possible to build up from these various pieces of information an overall picture of the industries and the regions where contract labor was employed? It seems clear that the system was most common in those enterprises or sectors of enterprises in which only a low degree of skill was required. On the railways, gangers were recruited by it but engineers or workshop mechanics were not, and most mine workers were recruited by it but not the skilled li-kung. But, as with the apprenticeship system, less tangible factors, connected with local customs rather than with economic matters, seem to have played a part in determining the geographical distribution of the system. How else can it be explained that the modern cotton mills in Tientsin employed *yang-ch'eng-kung,* child labor disguised as "industrial apprentices," and almost never used the contract-labor system, whereas in the Shanghai mills the latter was widely used and the former unknown? The contracting system, in turn, seems to have been unknown in the Shanghai silk-reeling factories, even for women employees, who were just as unskilled as the workers in the cotton mills and who came usually from the same poverty-stricken areas of northern Kiangsu.

The only way to find out more about the distribution of the pao-kung system and to discover the extent to which it was determined by social customs would be to go into the history of its origins, which is beyond the scope of this work. None of the historians of late-nineteenth-century China has made a study of this kind, but if one existed, it would doubtless find a link between this form of recruitment and the way in which the new Western enterprises in China—factories, mines, railways, and shipping companies—were run. The Westerners, ignorant of the customs and even of the language of the country, may have thought that the easiest way of solving the problems involved in the employment of labor was to hand over all responsibility to Chinese intermediaries. A detailed study of the beginnings of foreign enterprise would probably show that the pao-kung-t'ou (usually translated as "contractors" in the English documentary material), to whom Western firms resorted more and more as their requirements for Chinese labor increased, were in league with the compradores employed by the banks and the commercial firms since the time of the Opium Wars. There are even indications that occasionally the contractor and the compradore were the same person, especially in British firms.[98]

This, however, is by no means the whole story of the origins of the contract-labor system, for it is linked not only with the practices adopted by Western firms established abroad, but also with methods used in precapitalist China that were still employed at the beginning of the twentieth century in several of the small-scale traditional manufacturing industries for which there were no problems of acclimatization to a strange environment. For instance the workers in the small Tientsin flour mills were recruited by agencies (*kuan-tien*) that provided them with board and lodging in exchange for a regular deduction from their wages as soon as work was found for them, and with lodging, but not board, during periods of unemployment.[99] In Changsha carpenters, bricklayers, masons, stonemasons, and other building workers were employed through contractors,[100] who each disposed of several hundred and sometimes several thousand men and often supplied their clients through a subcontractor. It was the same with the tin miners of Kokiu in Yunnan, who in the twentieth century were still using very archaic methods in surroundings where old social customs were quite unchanged. The mine owners sent recruiting agents into all the rural hsien of Hunan and even to Kweichow, each of whom had to bring back about fifty men, who remained entirely under the agent's control.[101] The mines were more like prison camps, within which the miners worked under armed guards. Similarly, the owners of the old-style coal mines in Shansi sent their agents to recruit all the riffraff and unemployed in the towns, tempting them with fine promises and then keeping them under armed guard in a condition of semi-slavery until the winter. These miners were known as *mai-shen-kung* ("workers who have sold their bodies") or as *ssu-kung* ("dead labor"), as opposed to *huo-kung* ("living" or in other words "free" labor).[102] Thus the pao-kung system had deep roots in Chinese feudal society, despite the fact that its most spectacular development occurred in large-scale foreign-owned capitalist industry at the beginning of the twentieth century.

A further hint that the system had links with old social customs is provided by the fact that a similar system was used for seasonal agricultural work. Every spring landless peasants and rural vagabonds formed themselves into gangs under the leadership of a head coolie, who alone had the right to hire out the gang and to whom the employer paid the wages, only a part of which reached the men under his control.[103] In view of the fact that so many of the new industrial workers were, as we have seen, recent immigrants from the country to the towns, it would be particularly interesting to follow up this question of the rural origins of the contract-labor system. Apparently many of the labor contractors were themselves of peasant origin, and enjoyed the encouragement and active support of the rural gentry and the big landowners when they came to recruit workers in the villages.[104] This would indicate that the adoption of the system for the recruitment of industrial workers was simply an extension of earlier semi-feudal methods of exploitation of labor still used in the Chinese countryside during the period in question; but this hypothesis would have to be supported by a study of how the system operated at its starting point in the village as well as at its culmination in modern industry.

Just as little is known about the development of the contract-labor system during the twentieth century as about its origins, and only by careful study of the remaining archives in Chinese of the firms involved will more detailed information be obtained. It remained the chief form of recruitment until the *chieh-fang* (Liberation) of 1949. Still, under the combined effects of policy changes on the part of employers and of progress made by the labor movement, it underwent continuous changes, advances, and retreats. The changes of policy on the part of employers were no doubt due to their conflicting desires to extend the field in which the system operated for reasons of convenience,[105] and to restrict it in order to raise productivity.[106] The labor movement, for its part, never ceased to bring pressure to bear for the abolition of the system, and, as will be seen, during the peak periods of the workers' struggle such as the strike waves of 1921–22 and 1925–26, appreciable and sometimes permanent results were achieved in this respect.

However complex the problems of social history raised by the pao-kung system may be (and perhaps a comparative study would help to throw light on them),[107] the fact remains that the system itself had a marked effect on the position of the worker during the period under review, and accounts for the vagueness of the data relating both to wages and to the number of workers employed. It acted both as a stimulus and as a brake at the time when the Chinese labor movement began to be of importance on a national and international scale. The trade unions wanted it abolished, not so much because they wanted to see a comparatively free labor market as because they themselves hoped to take the place of the labor contractors and to enjoy a monopoly, recognized by the employers, over the hiring of labor such as that obtained by the Hong Kong Seamen's Union after the big 1922 strike. On the other hand, the semi-slavery to which many of the workers recruited by the system were condemned accounted for their inability to make a stand for better conditions, and also accounted for the general weakness of union organization in many branches of industry.

Finally there remain the large number of workers recruited more or less freely from the labor market and paid directly by the employers. Sometimes factories found it necessary to organize systematic recruitment of free labor, and they sent agents into the rural areas charged with the task of bringing back the workers required. This happened when firms wanted to expand rapidly, or when they thought it preferable to go further afield in order to find workers in rural areas who would supposedly be more amenable to discipline. When the Yü-yuan cotton mill in Tientsin opened in 1919, it got its workers from Honan, paying all their traveling expenses;[108] and in 1920 a Shanghai cotton mill mounted a big publicity campaign to attract women employees from Hunan, offering them a fixed wage of eight yuan a month, guaranteed for three years.[109] Similarly, the Hanyehping Company sent agents (known as "buttymen" in pidgin) to recruit new workers in the rural districts of southern Hunan.[110]

This was the procedure usually adopted by the Japanese companies in Northeast China. They opened agencies in Chihli and Shantung that engaged coolies on the spot and organized travel arrangements. Recruits for the Pen-hsihi mines were made at the rate of over a hundred a day in the ports of Dairen and Newchwang during the peak immigration season,[111] and the South Manchuria Railway issued tickets covering the sea voyage and the journey by rail from Tientsin, Tsingtao, and Chefoo to the main stations on their network.[112] Since, however, most of the workers in the Northeast were either temporary or seasonal immigrants, they can only be regarded as marginal members of the Chinese working class; and the fluctuation in their numbers is reflected in the figures of arrivals and departures of immigrants published by the S.M.R. from 1923 onward, although they represent the total number and not merely the number of those employed in industry. The figures for 1923 are 342,033 arrivals and 240,565 departures, and for 1926, 572,648 arrivals and 323,566 departures.[113]

Most of the free labor was, however, recruited locally from the great mass of the unemployed, or of the semi-employed with no stable occupation, that swarmed about in all the big industrial centers, consisting either of peasants who had left the land or of the urban poor. The total absence of statistics concerning unemployment and underemployment, and of organizations from whose records statistics might be established, makes it impossible to arrive at any exact figure, but all contemporary observers and surveys stress the existence of a large "reserve army" of industrial workers.[114] To find workers, all that was necessary was to dip into this huge reservoir, perhaps in the random manner adopted by the Hua-hsing cotton mill in Tientsin, where, in 1928, an employee used to throw a number of bamboo slips, corresponding to the number of vacancies, in front of the closed gates every morning, and then let in only those who by hook or by crook had managed to grab hold of one of these precious objects.[115] In some of the smaller Chinese firms where traditional attitudes concerning family and personal relationships remained and importance was still attached to protection, recommendations, and *mien-tzu wen-t'i* ("questions of face"), employment was obtained through a relation or friend of the employer or the manager, or through a comrade already employed there. In the Tientsin carpet factory, which was the subject of a survey made in 1929, 165 of the 354 workers employed had been signed on because they were relations or friends of workers already employed in the factory, and 71 through introductions by a relation or friend of the employer.[116]

There were a few employment agencies that acted as intermediaries between employers and employees without maintaining any subsequent control over the workers such as that exercised by the various kinds of labor contractors. In Hong Kong, for instance, there were employment agencies for seamen, run either by private firms (*chün-chu-kuan*) or by the seamen's friendly societies (*hsiung-ti-kuan*).[117] In either case, a seaman seeking employment registered his name, paid a regular subscription,[118] and was lodged until he embarked; but once engaged, he became a completely independent wage earner, unlike his comrades recruited by the shipmasters.

The vast majority of free recruits, however, were hired by the man who was in direct control of the factory floor and their direct superior in the hierarchy—that is, the foreman (*kung-t'ou*) or overseer (*ch'a-t'ou*) or "number one" (in pidgin, *na-mo-wen*). This powerful person never consented to take anyone on unless he received down payment of a large commission, often amounting to as much as two weeks' or even a month's wages.[119] Sometimes a worker was introduced to the foreman by one of those professional go-betweens (*chung-chien-jen*) who intervened on so many occasions in Chinese society. This particular species was picturesquely described by the workers as the *ch'iao-liang* (the "bridge beam").[120] Trouble always arose if a worker happened to be dismissed a few days after he had paid the usual bribe to the foreman. In April 1924, the Mixed Court of Shanghai imposed a fine of five yuan on a foreman of the Gas Company of the International Settlement for having refused to refund the five yuan paid him by a worker whom he had dismissed a few days after signing him on, and whom he had had beaten up by his henchmen.[121]

It was by no means rare for the foreman, upon whose goodwill the workers depended for their continued employment in the factory, to exact from them in return a variety of gifts and services, and sometimes even a percentage of their wages.[122] Thus the distinction between free and contract labor was not as sharp as might at first appear, since free labor had no defense against the greed of the intermediaries without whom no work could be obtained. Another instance of parasitical profiteering in the employment of labor, which has been justly viewed as a minor form of the pao-kung system,[123] was the practice of "substitute" labor prevalent in the silk factories of Canton, whereby a male or female regular employee arranged to have his or her work done by a substitute, who received only part of the wage paid to the regular employee.[124]

Thus most of the workers hired as free labor found themselves in just as precarious a position as the others, being under constant threat of arbitrary dismissal by foremen or overseers, from which there was no appeal. Only a small minority of them, either because of superior skill or because of personal contacts, could feel relatively secure in their jobs. These were the workers known as ch'ang-kung ("permanent workers") or cheng-shih-kung ("regular workers"), or, in the mines, li-kung,[125] as against lin-shih-kung ("temporary workers"). They were better paid, and also enjoyed various benefits such as medical care and workers' compensation. In theory, skill was the only criterion for inclusion in the category of permanent worker with its accompanying benefits; but a card or certificate for this category could easily be bought from an obliging foreman, and this sort of deal was common practice in the K.M.A. mines, where the overseers sold li-kung ("internal worker") cards to the "external workers" who wanted to escape from the control of the contractors.[126]

In direct contrast to all this, stability of employment was the rule in the traditional craft workshops. Here it was only during the New Year Festival that the employers, who at this season published their accounts and settled with their debtors and creditors, could dismiss their employees or engage new workers. This practice seems to have survived at least in the small and medium-sized modern Chinese-owned enterprises.[127]

Workers' Ages and Provincial Origins

In the 1920's, the Chinese proletariat consisted mainly of young workers, a result not only of the prevalence of recruitment by industrial apprenticeship or by the contract-labor system, but also of the peasant origin of many of the workers. Naturally it was the young people, being freer of attachments of various kinds, that left the villages in search of work in the new industrial enterprises.

The thirteen items in Table 9, taken from a wide variety of regions and of industries, show how low the average age of Chinese workers was, even in industries such as the mines, the railways, and the rickshaw trade, in which there was almost no employment of child labor. In the textile factories of Shanghai, Hangchow, Tsingtao, and Tientsin, where a large proportion of child labor was employed, the average age was below twenty. The figures for the distribution of age groups in the population of Kiangsu shown in Table 9 are not entirely reliable, but they nevertheless contrast strikingly with the figures for workers listed there and are a good indication of the extreme youthfulness of the Chinese proletariat.[128]

Another feature of the Chinese proletariat in the 1920's was the wide va-

TABLE 9

DISTRIBUTION OF THE CHINESE PROLETARIAT BY AGE GROUP
(Based on representative industries)

Group involved	Under 15	15–20	20–25	25–30	30–35	35–40	40–45	45–50	Over 50
Total population of Kiangsu in 1920 ..	20.0%	7.2%	8.0%	8.5%	8.8%	8.6%	7.9%	6.8%	24.2%
Chunghsing mines, 1931[a]									
223 mechanics	—	1.3	13.0	24.2	14.8	17.9	8.2	7.2	13.4
199 electricians	—	2.0	11.6	30.7	22.1	17.1	7.5	4.5	4.5
563 *li-kung* miners ..	—	2.1	11.4	21.7	16.0	20.1	10.8	9.2	8.7
1,023 *wai-kung* miners	—	5.2	18.2	24.0	19.1	16.4	10.3	5.2	1.6
Hangchow textile workers[b]									
147 men	1.4	4.8	13.2	20.0	20.0	16.5	12.4	6.9	4.8
115 women	7.4	77.0	11.1	4.5	—	—	—	—	—
Cotton mill workers[c]									
1,916 workers in a Japanese mill in Shanghai	23.0	36.1	19.9	12.1	7.3 for both		1.2 for both		0.4
1,263 workers in a Japanese mill in Tsingtao	6.6	59.8	23.5	5.6	2.7	—	—	—	—
504 workers in a Chinese mill in Tsingtao	21.2	40.8	16.8	6.9	5.9	2.2	3.0	1.8	1.2
3,891 workers in a Chinese mill in Tientsin	11.5	33.0	26.4	14.4	5.7	3.7	2.5	1.8	1.0
1,000 Peking rickshaw men[d]	1.7	11.3	16.1	14.9	15.5	13.6	11.5	7.5	7.9
Workers in the Chiu-ta salt refinery, 1926[e] .	—	5.0	30.0	25.0	21.0	15.0	3.0	1.0	—
10,532 employees of the Ching-Feng r'way[f].	—	3.7	18.7	19.4	16.1	14.0	11.5	7.6	9.0

[a] Lin Hsiu-chuan [73]. [b] *CEJ*, Mar. 1931. [c] Fong [252], pp. 116ff. [d] *CEM*, June 1926. [e] *Nien-chien* [138] I, 381. [f] *Ibid.*, p. 383.

riety in provincial origins of workers in any one area of enterprise. This was the result of the combined effects of the migration of skilled labor, the systematic recruitment of both free and contract labor in distant areas, and the spontaneous movement from country to town that brought the surplus peasant population into the big industrial centers. The nine items in Table 10 clearly display the wide geographic distribution of the areas of recruitment.

TABLE 10

Workers' Places of Origin

	Number and percentage of workers from:			
Group involved	The town	Other parts of the province	Neighboring provinces	Other provinces
3,958 workers in a Tientsin cotton mill[a]	987 24.9%	2155 53.3%	702 18.9%	114 2.9%
354 workers in a Tientsin carpet factory[b]	10 2.8%	327 92.5%	15 4.2%	2 0.5%
88 workers in a Tientsin flour mill[c]	5 5.7%	47 53.4%	36 40.9%	— —
317 Tientsin weavers[d]	12 3.8%	244 77.0%	60 18.9%	1 0.3%
85 Shanghai postal workers[e] ..	11 12.9%	53 62.4%	19 22.4%	2 2.3%
1,924 workers in a Japanese cotton mill in Shanghai[f] ...	231 12.1%	1371 71.2%	239 12.4%	83 4.3%
100 Yangtzepoo workers[g]	12 12.0%	45 45.0%	35 35.0%	8 8.0%
979 Chunghsing miners[h]	— —	686 70.0%	161 16.5%	132 13.5%
239 Tsaokiatu workers[i]	— —	156 65.4%	63 26.3%	20 8.3%

[a] Fong [252], p. 115.   [b] Fong [65].   [c] Fong [62].   [d] Fong [64].   [e] CEJ, Sept. 1930.
[f] Fong [252], p. 115.   [g] Ibid.   [h] Lin Hsiu-chuan [73].   [i] Yang and Tao [81], p. 26.

TABLE 11

Provincial Origin of Husbands and Wives in 230 Working-Class Families in Shanghai

Women → Men ↓	Kiangsu	Chekiang	Anhwei	Hupeh	Hunan	Shantung	Chihli	Unmarried	Unknown	Total
Kiangsu	119	1	1					10	25	156
Chekiang	3	4						1	7	15
Anhwei	2		29					4	3	38
Hupeh				3	1			1	2	7
Hunan					5			1	1	7
Shantung						5				5
Yunnan							1			1
Unknown									1	1
Total	124	5	30	3	6	5	1	17	39	230

The majority of workers came from hsien in the rural areas of the province where the enterprise that employed them was situated; a substantial minority came from neighboring provinces or even farther afield; and only a minute proportion were drawn from the population of the industrial center itself.

Further evidence of the mingling of workers from different provinces is provided by the figures giving the provincial origins of the Chinese residents in the International Settlement of Shanghai in 1920, shown on Map 2. They apply, of course, to all Chinese residents, and not merely to the working class, yet it is significant that natives of Kiangsu amount to only 42.8 per cent of the total number of residents; and, although the municipal statistics do not go into this kind of detail, probably very few Chinese residents there were actually born in the hsien of Shanghai itself. For the rest, it can be seen that substantial minorities came not only from Chekiang, but from Kwangtung, from Hupeh, and even from Chihli. Maps 3, 4, and 5 show the provincial origins of smaller and more homogeneous groups and display the same variety. Map 3 shows that, although most of the workers in this cotton mill came, as was normal, from Kiangsu, and particularly from the Kompo in the

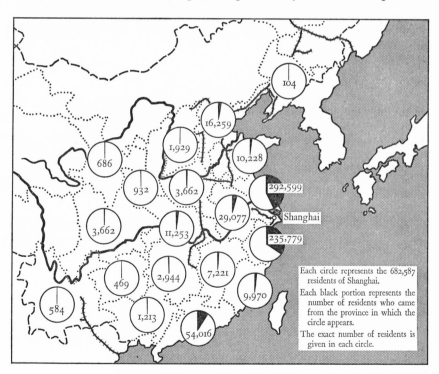

Map 2. Provincial Origins of Chinese Residents in the International Settlement of Shanghai in 1920 (taken from *SMCR*, 1920).

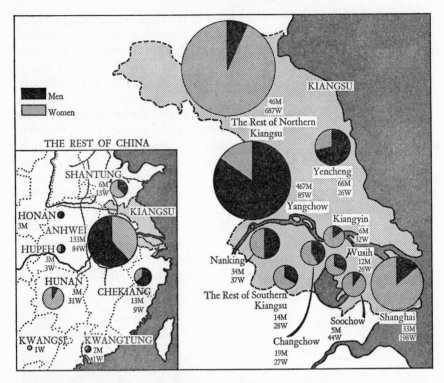

Map 3. Native Provinces or Districts of 2,197 Workers in a Japanese Cotton Mill in Shanghai (*Nien-chien* [158] I, 360–62).

The figures supplied have been broken down by major districts for Kiangsu province only; for the rest, figures are given only for northern and southern parts of the provinces. Note that there were many more women than men from the Kompo and the districts around Lake T'ai.

north of the province, there were also quite large groups from Anhwei, Shantung, and Hunan; Map 4 shows that 36 of the railwaymen killed in the massacre of February 7, 1923, came from Hupeh, where the railhead of the Ching-Han line was situated, and especially from the rural hsien of Siaokan and Hwangpei (populous districts to the north of the Yangtze), but that 19 came from four other provinces, including a large group from Fukien (where, as we know, the Fuchow arsenal supplied a number of skilled workers for the Ching-Han line). Map 5 shows that less than 10 per cent of the presidents of the Shanghai trade unions in 1925 were natives of the city itself, that many of them came from small country towns on the Yangtze estuary or from Chekiang, and that quite a number came from Anhwei, Hupeh, Canton, and Tientsin.

Although this coming together of workers from different provinces helped to strengthen the national character of the working class, it also fostered regional or provincial rivalries within a given industrial center or enterprise, and rival groups or cliques were formed that sometimes engendered very bitter feelings, which in the South were further exacerbated by language differences. It will be shown later how provincial loyalties affected both the attitude toward strikes and the forms of labor organizations. That they also affected private life is shown by an investigation carried out in 1928 into the provincial origins of 230 married couples among the working-class families of the Tsaokiatu district of Shanghai, which provides evidence of the predominance of marriages between people from the same province and of the infrequency of marriages between people from different provinces, whether the workers concerned came from Kiangsu, Hunan, Shantung, or Anhwei.[129] (See Table 11, p. 66.)

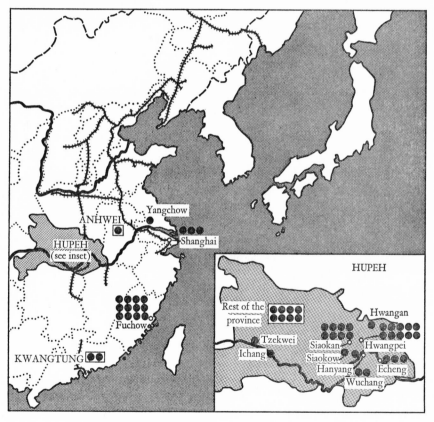

Map 4. Native Provinces or Districts of 55 Railwaymen of the Kiangan Railway Station Who Were Victims of the Massacre of February 7, 1923 (*CTSTL*, 1955, No. 1).

Each dot represents one railwayman. In cases where only the province of origin, but not the exact district, is known, the dot or dots are framed.

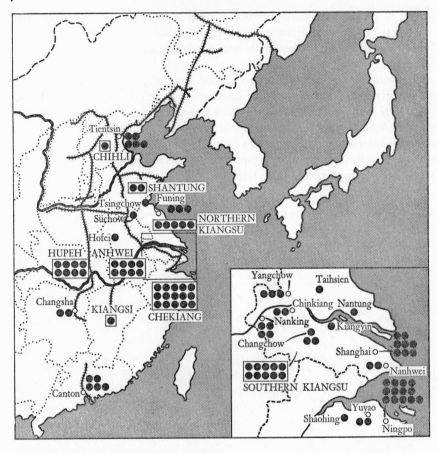

Map 5. Native Provinces of 109 Presidents of Unions Affiliated with the Shanghai General Union in 1925 (listed in T'ang Hai, *Lao-tung wen-t'i* [164], pp. 510–20).

As in Map 4, the frames indicate cases where only the province, and not the district, of origin is known.

All these divisions and inequalities due to differences in social or provincial origin or in methods of recruitment soon vanished, however, in the face of the shared hardships of working-class life. Because of the merciless effects of long working hours, frequent accidents, brutal treatment by foremen, and strict discipline enforced by overseers—in short, because of working conditions in modern industry—all the disparate elements joined to form a genuine and united proletariat.

CHAPTER IV

Working Conditions

The long hours and infrequent holidays that made life so hard for English and French industrial workers in the mid-nineteenth century were still a feature of industrial work in China in the 1920's.

Two twelve-hour shifts were worked in many of the modern mines and factories. This was common practice in the big cotton mills of Shanghai,[1] Tientsin, Tsingtao, and Wusih;[2] but in the silk factories, although the hours were long, no night work was done, except in a few in Shanghai and Tsingtao.[3] The practice was common also in flour mills,[4] factories producing foodstuffs,[5] tobacco factories (for instance, the Nanyang factories in Shanghai),[6] and small mechanical workshops such as the Kuangming electrical equipment works in Shanghai.[7] The mines that adopted it included those at Chinling-chen, Fangtze, and Tzechwan in Shantung, at Anshan and Fushun in the Northeast, at Pingsiang in Kiangsi, and at Tsingsing in Chihli.[8]

Thus night work was done not only in large-scale mechanized industry, but also in an industry such as tobacco processing, in which most of the work was done by hand and there was no cause for concern about rapid depreciation of fixed capital. Shortly after the First World War, night work began to be introduced in semi-modernized industries and even in the crafts—for instance, in a paper works in Hangchow,[9] small foundries and forges in Tientsin,[10] a printing plant in Peking,[11] and slipper factories and coal yards in Peking.[12]

A few electricity plants,[13] the waterworks,[14] and certain hardware factories[15] operated on three eight-hour shifts. This might appear to be less hard on the workers, but in fact it often resulted in longer working hours, for in order to earn more, workers tried to work either two consecutive shifts or every second shift. This was common practice in the K.M.A. mines, where the three-shift system operated;[16] and in a Harbin flour mill all the workers did eight hours one day and sixteen the next.[17]

No statistics are available to permit any assessment of the extent of night work on either the two-shift or the three-shift system, and such information as exists must be used cautiously.[18] But as far as can be ascertained, night work seems to have been usual in the modernized mines and in the cotton mills, but less common in other branches of industry. A long working day seems to have been the more general rule, although its length varied considerably among branches of industry, regions, individual enterprises, and different kinds of work within a given enterprise.

Often the working day lasted for as long as twelve hours or even more, as in the silk factories of Shanghai, where work began at six or even five o'clock in the morning, and did not end until five or six o'clock in the evening;[19] or in the British and American Tobacco factory in Pootung, where the hours were from 7 A.M. until 7 P.M.[20] In the 23 Tientsin textile factories investigated in 1925, the average working day was 11 hours 55 minutes, with the employees at one mill working as long as 15 hours and those at two others for 14 hours.[21] Twelve to fourteen hours were worked in the silk factories of Shantung and Szechwan,[22] and in the match factories of Tientsin, Tsingtao, Tsinan, and Peking.[23] In the Peking carpet industry, according to the survey of 1923,[24] the working day was just as long: 14 hours in 19 factories, 13 in 83, 12 in 21, with only three factories working for ten hours or less.

Slightly shorter hours seem to have been worked in printing plants, mechanical workshops, shipyards, railways, and railway workshops. In 1920 the Commercial Press's printing plant in Shanghai had a nine-hour day;[25] in 1926 its workers in Tientsin worked nine to ten hours,[26] and in Peking ten to eleven hours.[27] The hours varied from nine to twelve in the mechanical workshops of Tientsin, Dairen, and Mukden,[28] and seldom exceeded nine in the shipyards and arsenals of Shanghai and Hong Kong.[29] They were much the same on the main railway lines—ten hours, for instance, in the Tangshan workshop, the principal one on the Ching-Feng line.[30] The conclusion to be drawn from these figures seems to be that the higher the degree of skill required, the shorter the working hours; this is confirmed by the difference in the number of hours worked by skilled and unskilled workers in the Chiu-ta salt refinery, the first working ten and the second twelve hours.[31]

Thus except in a few special cases, the number of hours worked per day was seldom less than ten, and often as much as twelve or more. From this must be deducted the time allotted for the midday meal (although of course this does not apply to the night shifts, which usually worked without a break). Sometimes an hour's break was allowed, as in some printing works,[32] some of the silk factories in Shanghai,[33] and the B.A.T. Company's Pootung factory;[34] and sometimes only a half-hour's break, as in a Japanese sugar refinery in Shanghai.[35] As often as not, however, and especially in the cotton mills, the workers heated up their food as best they could and swallowed it hastily without pausing in their work at the machines.[36]

No distinction can be made between Chinese and foreign-owned firms with regard to hours of work. The Commercial Press and the shipyards of Butterfield & Swire were among the most liberal in this respect, whereas a 14-hour day was worked both in the weaving mills of the British Ewo Company of

Shanghai[37] and the Japanese match factories,[38] and in the Chinese rice-husking factories in Hankow[39] and the Chinese carpet factories in Peking.

Monthly or even annual holidays were rare in China, and a weekly day of rest was unknown, there being no religious sanction for it such as existed in Islamic countries or in European Christendom in the Middle Ages. The only holidays were the widely spaced ones connected with the lunar calendar, the three most important being the New Year, the Dragon Boat Festival on the fifth day of the fifth moon, and the mid-autumn or Moon Festival on the fourteenth day of the eighth moon.[40] Around 1920 these traditional holidays, the dates of which often varied from province to province according to local custom, were still usually the only ones observed, not only in the old craft workshops, but also in most industrial enterprises. This applies, for instance, to the Japanese mines in the Northeast,[41] and to the Chiu-ta salt refinery, which gave its workers 5½ days off at the New Year and 1½ days at the festivals in the fifth and eighth moons.[42] The Peking carpet factories gave ten days off for the first festival and three days for each of the other two.[43]

It was exceptional to give a weekly day of rest in Chinese or even in Western enterprises. The custom was observed in several railway workshops,[44] in the Commercial Press in Shanghai and Peking,[45] in the Edison factory for electrical equipment in Shanghai (which was under American ownership),[46] and in the postal service.[47]

It was more usual, although by no means the general rule, to give a day off every fortnight, as in several silk factories and cotton mills in Shanghai,[48] and in most of the railway workshops and depots.[49] In the Hankow cotton mills, days off were given when the machines were stopped for maintenance purposes, which happened every ten days.[50]

The workers, however, did not derive the expected benefit from the holidays officially granted to them, because they had to spend most of them doing various domestic and other chores for the foremen and overseers, to whom even "free" workers were bound by almost feudal ties entailing certain purely customary, but nevertheless binding, obligations.[51] Thus the kindly intentions of some firms went entirely amiss. When the trade unions came to demand a weekly day of rest, they at the same time stipulated that "private work" (*ssu-kung*) done for foremen must be abolished.[52]

Female and Child Labor

Another typical feature of Chinese industry at this time was the sizable proportion of female and child labor employed. Women and children were paid at lower rates than men, but they had to endure the same long hours and harsh treatment.

Female and child labor was especially prevalent in the textile industry, and

TABLE 12

PROPORTION OF CHILD LABOR IN VARIOUS SHANGHAI FACTORIES

Industries	Men		Women		Boys under 12		Girls under 12	
Silk								
39 Chinese factories ...	2,274	9.6%	17,895	74.5%	105	0.4%	3,461	15.5%
27 foreign factories ...	797	3.5%	12,458	55.5%	1,364	6.1%	8,566	34.9%
6 Italian factories	203	3.4%	3,160	48.2%	440	7.0%	2,620	41.4%
5 French factories	219	3.9%	2,650	48.4%	372	6.8%	2,227	40.9%
9 British factories	235	3.4%	3,618	52.6%	552	8.1%	2,469	35.9%
7 American factories ..	140	3.1%	3,050	68.6%	—	—	1,250	28.1%
Cotton								
18 Chinese mills	8,682	26.9%	19,822	62.8%	1,005	2.9%	2,610	6.4%
24 Japanese and								
British mills	15,048	26.1%	38,157	65.9%	1,615	2.8%	2,690	5.2%
Various (hosiery, knitting, stockings, etc.)								
9 factories	1,259	48.2%	1,211	46.5%	56	2.1%	84	3.2%

in particular that of Shanghai, as is shown above in Table 12. (The figures are taken from a list of the principal industrial enterprises in that city made in 1923–24.)[53]

The table shows that the proportion of female and child labor employed in the foreign-owned silk factories was higher than in Chinese-owned silk factories, whereas in the cotton mills no such difference existed. In both industries, the working conditions of women and children were equally deplorable, and although the employers were not always very loquacious on that subject,[54] there is a certain amount of firsthand evidence that recalls the celebrated reports of the British factory inspectors, or of Dr. Villermé concerning the Rouen district, dating from nearly a hundred years earlier.

Evidence of this kind is provided by the investigations of the Child Labor Commission set up by the Shanghai Municipal Council in 1923.[55] Mrs. McGillivray, a member of the Commission, described the horror she felt at the sight of the children they saw working in the mills. She felt certain that most of them were no more than ten years old, and perhaps even less. They all struck her as being physically underdeveloped, and almost all were in a wretched state of health, some having running sores on their legs or scabs covering their heads. All the children seemed exhausted; many were terrified when spoken to, and some even ran away. It was hard to get a smile out of any of them. Their food was kept in wicker bowls or old tin cans on the floor, placed underneath the basins of boiling water with no attempt to cover it up. Sometimes babies lay sleeping on the floor, looked after by tiny children; and occasionally there was a chicken or two nearby as well. No seats of any kind were provided in the first two silk factories visited.[56]

Further evidence of this kind is provided by Colonel L'Estrange Malone.[57] After visiting some Shanghai silk factories in 1926, he reported that many of the children could not have been more than seven years old, and some were probably younger. He described the work they had to do, which consisted of moving the cocoons about in the steaming basins of boiling water, often scalding themselves while doing so, and then handing the moistened cocoons to the women workers who spun the thread. The atmosphere in which these children had to work was suffocating, since there was no ventilation system for dispersing the steam or introducing any fresh air. In summer it must have been quite unendurable. All the women workers were covered with sweat, and the stench coming from the dead cocoons piled up on the floor made the atmosphere still more unendurable.

The employment of female and child labor was not, however, peculiar to the Shanghai textile industry. It also predominated in the Kwangtung silk factories,[58] the clothing factories of Canton,[59] the silk and cotton factories of Wusih,[60] and the cotton mills of Wuhan,[61] as well as those of Tientsin, where, as already mentioned, the pseudo-apprenticeship system was so much to the fore. Women and children were also extensively employed in knitting, hosiery, embroidery, and the manufacture of hairnets.[62] Some of this work was done in huge modern factories or in small workshops; the rest took the marginal form mentioned earlier of machine work done in the home in either urban or rural areas. Pseudo-apprenticeship was also, as we know, a feature of the carpet industry.

The tobacco and match factories were another sector in which the employment of female and child labor predominated. In Shanghai, according to an incomplete list of 1923, 69 per cent of the employees in four Chinese tobacco factories were women, and in seven foreign (mostly Japanese) factories 62.7 per cent of the employees were women and 7.3 per cent children.[63] A simple method adopted at some of the B.A.T. factories for preventing the entry of girls considered too young for factory work was to place a horizontal wooden bar across the gates so that those able to pass under it could be eliminated.[64] In the match factories the proportion of women and children employed was perhaps even higher. In the Tientsin factories, for instance, women and girls were classed as wai-kung ("external labor") and were far more numerous[65] than the li-kung ("internal labor"), which consisted of boy pseudo-apprentices and skilled adult men and benefited from higher wages and better working conditions. Many of the wai-kung worked at home making boxes, sticking on labels, etc.

A third group of industries featuring large-scale employment of female and child labor consisted of factories for the handling and processing of a number of products for the export trade. In 1925, 68.7 per cent of the employees of five foreign firms dealing in the cleaning and packaging of raw cotton, wool, and hides were women,[66] and out of the total of 9,000 employed by the three British press-packing factories in Hankow, 6,000 were women.[67] It was the same in Tientsin, where the work of cleaning raw cotton and wool, and of shelling, peeling, or otherwise preparing nuts—especially peanuts—and oilbearing seeds, was almost exclusively done by women. Much of this work was seasonal, and depended upon bulk arrivals of export crops after they had been harvested.[68]

It thus appears that women and children were employed in sectors of industry where only a low degree of skill was required, or where the work was seasonal or could easily be done in the home, or lastly where the work was traditionally women's work in pre-industrial times, as with spinning and weaving.[69] Although women and children usually received very much lower wages than men, there was no difference in their hours of work, and in the cotton mills and other big modern enterprises women and children were included in the two twelve-hour shifts just as the men were.[70] When they were paid at piecework rates, as in the match factories, their hours might be even longer.[71] Virtually nothing was done for their social welfare—there was neither maternity leave for women nor reduced hours for children. Among the few rare exceptions were the evening classes and elementary schools run by the Commercial Press.[72] The proposed labor legislation of 1923, which required, among other things, leave with pay for women in childbirth and shorter hours for children, never came into force.[73]

Accidents and Health Problems

Other features of industrial work in China in the 1920's were the frequent occurrence of accidents, the widespread incidence of occupational diseases, and the general low standard of health among the workers, all of which are reminiscent of working-class conditions of a century ago.

Mining disasters and various kinds of accidents to miners seem to have been particularly frequent and serious in the big foreign mines in China at this time. In the Japanese collieries of Fushun there were 1,247 casualties in 1911, 1,864 in 1912, and 3,184 in 1913.[74] In 1917 the Oyama pit disaster claimed over a thousand victims,[75] and in 1919 fifty men were killed and 4,539 injured at this pit.[76] In the Penhsihi mines, during the same year, 242 men are recorded as killed or unaccounted for, 253 as seriously injured, and 2,162 as slightly injured.[77] In an accident that occurred in a Japanese mine near Mukden in January of that year, 250 men were killed or unaccounted for.[78] The explosion in the K.M.A. Tangshan mines that occurred on October 14, 1920, and claimed over 400 victims, was caused, according to the company's official report, either by the use of open lamps by the miners, or by the miners' having opened their regulation safety lamps to light their cigarettes. In an editorial on the disaster, the liberal American journal *China Weekly Review* described these allegations as patently absurd. It reported that, according to information supplied by the miners' families, the miners had warned the British engineers of the first signs of firedamp, and the engineers, instead of giving the order to stop work, merely told them to turn down their lamps and carry on. The editorial concluded by saying that, according to information received, firedamp often explodes, not only in contact with an open flame, but also in contact with light. Thus the order given by the foreign engineers quite deliberately sent 400 or so coolies to their death, which amounted to "cold-blooded murder."[79] In March 1924, 53 Tangshan miners were buried by a roof that caved in on them.[80] But accidents of this magnitude were just as common in the modern Chinese-owned mines, as is shown by the figures of 400 dead and 200 injured in the Chunghsing mines in 1915,[81] or of 75 dead in the Fangtze mines in 1924.[82] The safety regulations laid down by some of the companies do not seem to have been observed very carefully.[83]

The big industrial concerns in the cities had just as bad a record. A survey of industrial accidents carried out in 1928[84] reports that out of a thousand accidents in the 26 factories investigated, employing a total of 18,748 workers, 79 were fatal. The survey also indicates that in some factories the accident rate was extremely high: 137 accidents, including 35 deaths, in a Hankow factory employing 1,300 workers, and 111 accidents, including nine deaths, in a Pootung flour mill employing 890 workers. In 1924 over a hundred workers died in a fire at a Shanghai silk factory.[85] In the same year a report by Dr. Decker of the missionary Industrial Hospital in Pootung was published, showing that of the approximately eight hundred workers hospitalized there during the year, most of whom were employed in the cotton mills of the district, 20 per cent of the men, 29 per cent of the children, and 44 per cent of the women were permanently injured; that more than half the accidents incurred by women and children affected the upper limbs, 95 per cent of the injuries being to the hand; and that eye injuries were very frequent among workers tending looms, owing to their being hit in the eye by the pointed shuttle as they bent over their work.[86]

Although the difficulties the peasants had in adapting to modern techniques in the newly opened factories may have been a subsidiary cause of these frequent accidents, the main cause seems to have been the inadequacy, or quite simply the absence, of safety precautions. For instance, the machine belts had no protective casing, so that in 1921 a fourteen-year-old girl was killed in a Shanghai cotton mill in an attempt to get hold of a bit of rope that had got entangled in her machine; at the inquest held by the Mixed Court, a police inspector stated that "the machinery was all of the latest pattern," but that there was "no covering to protect the workers."[87] The fatal accidents described by H. D. Lamson in the investigation quoted above include such flagrant examples of the lack of safety precautions as the fall of a huge iron girder that crushed the head of a worker, the collapse of a machine on top of the man repairing it, and the case of a foundry worker who lost his footing and was scalded to death in molten metal.[88] In 1933, rather later than the period here under review, a fire broke out on the ground floor of a boot and shoe factory, probably caused by faulty electric wiring. The fumes from the spirit used in the processing of the rubber caught fire, and the flames spread rapidly to the wooden floorboards of the first floor, which had no emergency exit and where women worked with other inflammable materials. There were 81 deaths.[89]

Other accidents were caused by the strain and physical exhaustion suffered by factory hands as a result of undernourishment and long hours made longer by the distances between their place of work and their living quarters. Many accidents in the cotton mills occurred toward the end of the day shift, but they happened most often at night.[90] In a survey conducted in 1931, a woman worker is reported as saying that she much preferred farm work to factory work, because when she worked on the farm, although she might be physically exhausted, her mind remained clear; whereas in the factory the noise of the machines and the monotony of the work made her dizzy.[91]

Despite the prevalence of industrial accidents, the compensation provided for the victims was ludicrously inadequate and seldom compulsory. The families of the victims of the explosion at the Tangshan mines in 1920 each received 60 yuan, representing about four months' wages. Chinese progressives pointed out that this figure was well below the value of each of the 60 mules that also perished in the disaster.[92] In the lead and zinc mines of Shuikowshan in Hunan, compensation rates were 30 yuan for a fatal accident and 15 cents to injured workers for each day lost.[93] At the Pingting collieries the rate for a fatal accident was 45 yuan,[94] and in the Shanghai cotton mills 10 to 15 yuan.[95] Only a very few enterprises, including the Japanese collieries of Penhsihi and Fushun, the Commercial Press, a certain number of Shanghai cotton mills, and the railways, had a fixed scale of compensation for accidents according to the seriousness of the accident, the seniority of the victim, and the importance of his work.[96]

In some sectors of industry a very high proportion of workers were affected by occupational diseases that were neither diagnosed nor treated systematically, and against which no preventive measures were taken in the sense of altering the industrial processes that caused them. In the match factories, for instance, white phosphorus, which causes necrosis of the jaw, continued to be used instead of red phosphorus because its price was lower,[97] despite the fact that its use had been prohibited in most European countries since the end of the nineteenth century. The same indifference is seen in the high incidence of inflammation of the tissues caused by constant contact with salt in the Chiu-ta salt refinery and the soda works attached to it,[98] of trachoma in carpet factories,[99] and of lead poisoning among printers. In an investigation of the last disease made in 1929, it was pointed out that the methods of handling the lead and the lack of ventilation in the workshops caused contamination of the air and of food and drink taken while at work.[100] An investigation of the Pingsiang coal mines in Hunan carried out in 1914 found that 81.6 per cent of the surface miners and 90.2 per cent of the pit workers suffered from intestinal worms (ankylostomosis) caused by prolonged contact with earth infected by them.[101]

Finally, account must be taken of the general physical effects of bad working conditions. In addition to the fatigue and wear-and-tear caused by long hours, undernourishment, the gobbling of cold meals so that machines could be tended uninterruptedly,[102] and bad ventilation,[103] many factory workers also suffered from the ill effects of having begun work at far too early an age. Endemic tuberculosis seems to have claimed a particularly high proportion of victims. Out of the 880 workers from the Yangtzepoo cotton mills examined by Dr. Decker in 1924, 6 per cent of the men were found to be tubercular, 14 per cent of the women, and 22 per cent of the children.[104] Similar ravages were observed among the Changsha printers[105] and among the workers in the Chefoo silk-reeling factories, where they worked naked to the waist in steam-filled rooms from which, even during the hard Shantung winter, they had to emerge, without taking time to put anything extra on, to fetch the baskets of cocoons from the courtyards.[106] Skin troubles and gastrointestinal and other complaints were equally frequent, according to the few available investigations.[107]

The paucity of detailed information concerning the health of workers, which forces one to refer over and over again to the same two or three sources, merely goes to show how inadequate the medical services provided for industrial workers were. In 1919 very few employers provided hospitals or dispensaries for their employees, and during the following years the number established was very small.

Management and Discipline

The strictness of factory discipline and the disagreements that arose between workers and management were just as great a cause for dissatisfaction among workers during this period as the long hours and all the other conditions detrimental to health.

In the foreign-owned enterprises, foreigners were employed in the upper and middle managerial ranks and also often were foremen and overseers. The Japanese staffed the management of their cotton mills and mines in Northeast China with their own countrymen.[108] Sikhs, originally brought over from northern India by British firms and British civil and military authorities, were also much sought after by Chinese and Japanese firms because of their strong physique combined with their amenability to discipline.[109] White Russians who had recently emigrated from eastern Siberia were also often employed in minor managerial posts and as factory overseers, especially by French firms.[110] The engineers and the occupants of top managerial positions on the railways owned by the various Foreign Powers tended to be of the same nationality as the owners, so that most of them were either French or Belgian on the Ching-Han, Lunghai, and Cheng-T'ai lines, British on the Canton-Hankow line, and British or German on the Tientsin-Pukow line, even after these lines had come under the Chiao-t'ung-pu.[111] Similarly the upper and middle managerial posts in the postal service were still filled by Frenchmen, Englishmen, and Japanese even after the Washington Conference had officially put an end to international control of the Chinese Post Office.[112]

Disputes frequently arose between Chinese workers and these foreigners supervising them, whose material circumstances were much better than theirs and whose authoritarian attitude was often tinged with racial prejudice.[113] Altercations and brawls were common and sometimes ended in murder, as in several incidents between Sikh overseers and Chinese workers.[114] More than once strikes were held in order to get a hated Sikh or Japanese dismissed or otherwise punished for cruel treatment of workers.[115] There was also sharp antagonism between the workers and the foreign engineers on the railways, which led to several strikes.[116]

Relations between the workers and their Chinese foremen and overseers were not much better, even in the case of free labor, which did not have to endure the slavery of the pao-kung system. As we have seen, foremen and overseers wielded absolute power over the engagement and dismissal of workers, and many strikes were called in order to obtain a guarantee from the management that foremen would not dismiss men without a valid reason. Most enterprises had a system of fines, which gave added power to those in control of the workers, as did frequent administration of corporal punishment (by means sometimes of the cangue and sometimes of strokes with a cane or a bamboo rod) in both foreign and Chinese factories.[117] In 1923 the women employees in a silk factory sent a letter to the press complaining that at the least sign of slowness or clumsiness they were whipped, or had boiling water poured on their hands, or were branded with a hot coal.[118] In the big factories the foremen even had their own gangs of henchmen who were told to beat up any headstrong characters at the factory gates. An example of this is the case of the foreman of the Gas Company that came before the Mixed Court in Shanghai.[119]

Regional rivalries sometimes further envenomed relations between workers and the lower-ranking managerial staff. In the Japanese cotton mills of Shanghai, for instance, most of the workers came from the Kompo, while the foremen and overseers were often men whom the Japanese had brought from Shantung, in the Japanese sphere of influence. Shantung people are known for their heavy build and physical strength, and these men treated the workers under them very roughly, so that rows would occur. These sometimes turned into pitched battles in which numbers were killed and wounded and much damage was done, as in June 1926 in No. 4 mill of the Naigai Wata Kaisha.[120]

Yet strangely enough the constant resentment felt by workers toward foremen, which was daily reinforced by all the chores they had to do for them, did not exclude a certain sense of loyalty. However harsh and despotic the kung-t'ou, or foreman, might be, he was accepted as simply something that had to be put up with in factory life. So long as the labor movement lacked the strength or the will to change the whole system of employment, these foremen were the only channels through which jobs could be obtained. Moreover, should a foreman himself be dismissed by the management, his successor would immediately bring in his own men, engaged either on the recommendation of friends and relatives or because of some "question of face," to replace the existing employees. There thus arose a degree of solidarity between the exploiters and the exploited that alone can explain such apparently uncharacteristic incidents, on occasions when foremen were threatened with dismissal, as the strike in the Chunghua match factory in Tientsin in 1926,[121] or the attack a Chinese foreman was able to organize against the manager and his Sikh guards in an American carpet factory there in 1927.[122] This paradoxical solidarity was further strengthened by the fact that a foreman often engaged men from his own village or hsien, although here a fear of reprisals sometimes led to the kind of forced loyalty that brought 1,400 bricklayers out on strike in Dairen in August 1919 in protest against the dismissal of 19 foremen who came from the same district.[123] This type of loyalty also explains the existence of unions controlled by foremen.

The foremen were responsible for maintaining factory discipline, which in itself was another cause for discontent and resentment among workers. Factory regulations, judging from those mentioned in strike demands, appear to have had three main aims: to maintain the quality of output,[124] to prevent delinquency, and to keep a strict control over each individual worker. It was with the second purpose in view that rules were made restricting the comings and goings of workers, obliging them to take their meals at the factory,[125] and forbidding their wives and children to visit them at the place where they worked in the factory.[126] For the same reason workers were often searched, either in the factory or as they left.[127] Identity controls, such as fingerprints,[128] identity discs,[129] numbers marked on the chest,[130] or identity cards,[131] were introduced only gradually, and seem to have been politically motivated rather than instituted for the purpose of raising output or keeping the labor force in order. These measures were apparently part of the efforts made during the revolutionary upsurge of 1925-27 to hamper the activities of "propagandists of unwholesome ideas," to use the expression adopted by Japanese employers in the Northeast.[132]

Training Programs and Levels of Skill

There are three other characteristic features of industrial work in China at this time which, although the workers may not have been as aware of them as they were aware of long hours and bad relations with management, are nevertheless just as important as any of those already mentioned in arriving at an understanding of the special nature of the Chinese labor movement. These are: the low level of skill required, the concentration of labor in large enterprises, and the high rate of labor turnover.

The Chinese worker's lack of skill and the low output per head that resulted from it were favorite themes of foreign employers in China;[133] but there are no reliable data to go on, and on this subject as on so many others, any conclusions drawn can only be based on fragmentary pieces of information and on guesswork. Such information as is available, however, leaves no doubt whatsoever about the overwhelming preponderance of unskilled labor.

In Tientsin, for instance, the B.A.T. factory, according to an estimate made in 1926,[134] employed only 350 men regarded as "skilled," as against over 2,000 women and children; the Tan-hua cigarette factory employed 200 skilled men along with 300 unskilled men and 1,500 women and children; and the Yü-yuan cotton mill had only 2,000 skilled men, brought from Shanghai and Wuhan, as against 4,400 unskilled workers (600 of whom were women, and 100 children).

In Shanghai, only 5 per cent of the employees in the silk-reeling factories were skilled workers, all of them men. They were known as "officers," and consisted of clerks, foremen, and workers employed in the weighing and transporting of the cocoons and in machinery maintenance. For the rest, 60 per cent were silk-reelers, who might be regarded as semiskilled, and 35 per cent were women and girls who were quite unskilled, and whose work consisted of cleaning and soaking the cocoons and then unrolling them over bowls of boiling water.[135]

In the Chunghsing collieries, to take but one further example, there were, in 1925, 212 mechanics, 234 electricians, and 913 semiskilled pit workers, all directly employed, as against several thousand unskilled workers recruited by the contract-labor system.[136] Generally speaking, in the mines the dividing line between free and contract labor seems to have been that between skilled and unskilled workers.[137]

This low standard of skill, which is in no way incompatible with the traditional manual dexterity of Chinese artisans and workers, is a complex socioeconomic phenomenon, raising problems that go beyond the scope of the present work. The only way to find an explanation for it would be to make a detailed examination of the conditions in which industrialization took place. Account would have to be taken of the abundant supply of cheap labor, the low rate of fixed capital investment to which Western firms preferred to confine themselves, the long hours of work, and the rapid rate of labor turnover.[138] Here all that need be done is to stress its importance. It had widely varying effects on the progress of the labor movement. On the one hand, because the great majority of the workers were unskilled, there was little rivalry between different categories of workers or between different degrees of skill; thus industrial trade unions could be formed with comparative ease. On the other hand, workers with no special skill could easily be replaced, since all the employers had to do was to dip into the limitless reserves of labor provided by the unemployed and the underemployed among the urban populace and the peasants who had left the land. Many a strike was easily broken by the immediate signing on of hundreds and thousands of new workers just as capable of turning out the mediocre quality of work expected of them. The strikes that lasted longest were those held by skilled workers such as printers, railwaymen, and mechanics.

Employers do not seem to have taken much trouble to organize training for their workers in order to raise the level of their skill. As we have seen, no attempts at training were made in the pseudo-apprenticeship system used in some of the big modern factories. The only industries in which proper technical training was given were those in which it was indispensable, as in printing plants and on the railways. The Commercial Press in Shanghai, for instance, offered a fairly complete course of technical training,[139] and in 1925 6.6 per cent of the railwaymen on the Ching-Feng line, 10.8 per cent of those on the Ching-Han line, 8.9 per cent of those on the Chin-P'u line, and 7.3 per cent of those on the Ching-Sui line were taking continuation courses.[140]

Distribution of Workers

The concentration of the major proportion of workers in a number of large or very large enterprises is the second of these last three features of industrial work in China that require to be stressed. Here again only a generalization is possible because there are no exact figures to go on. For what it is worth, there is a list of enterprises compiled in 1914 from a number of incomplete lists, and therefore itself incomplete, which contains 85 enterprises employing between five hundred and a thousand workers, and 67, including mines and railway workshops, employing over a thousand.[141] The only comparable list is one made in 1923 by the Child Labor Commission set up by the Shanghai Municipal Council that comprises the factories situated within the International Settlement and a number of those in Chapei and Pootung, although it omits such places as the Commercial Press printing plant in Chapei.[142] At 57 of these factories, between five hundred and a thousand workers were employed, and 49 others each had over a thousand employees. This seems to confirm my generalization that a large proportion of the working class was concentrated in large-scale enterprises; and both these lists further show that the biggest concentration of workers was in the cotton mills, the silk factories, and other textile plants, in the heavy industries and the shipyards, and in the mines. (See Table 13.) It was within these industries, to which of course must be added the docks and the transport industry, that in 1919 and even earlier the greater part of labor movement activities in forming unions and organizing strikes took place.

Another thing that emerges from the two lists is that among the larger

TABLE 13

Large-Scale Industrial Enterprises

Enterprises	1914 Census (All of China)		1923 Census (Shanghai)	
	500–1,000 workers	Over 1,000 workers	500–1,000 workers	Over 1,000 workers
Cotton mills	6	23	4	33
Silk factories	59	15	41	11
Various textile mills	6	1	2	1
Tobacco, matches	1	4	2	3
Metallurgy, shipbuilding, etc.	6	8	2	1
Mines	2	12	—	—
Various	5	4	6	—
Total	85	67	57	49

enterprises there was little difference between Chinese- and foreign-owned ones in either number or size, especially in the case of those employing over a thousand workers. In the 1914 list, the number of large-scale enterprises for the whole of China breaks down to 40 Chinese enterprises employing a total of 82,615 workers, and 27 foreign enterprises employing a total of 100,427 workers; in the 1923 list the comparable figures (for Shanghai only) are 15 Chinese enterprises employing a total of 42,702 workers, and 34 foreign enterprises employing a total of 76,382 workers.

Although there are no exact figures on which to base an estimate, the average size of foreign-owned industrial concerns must have been quite large, since few of them were small-scale concerns.[143] In addition, they included those enterprises or groups of enterprises in which there was the highest concentration of workers, such as the K.M.A. Tangshan mines and the Fushun mines, each employing about fifty thousand miners, and the Naigai Wata Kaisha group of cotton mills in Shanghai, employing approximately twenty-five thousand workers.

In contrast, although there were huge Chinese-owned enterprises such as cotton mills in Shanghai, the Hanyehping Company, the Nanyang tobacco factories, and the Commercial Press, a great deal of Chinese capital was invested in concerns on a smaller scale, such as the mechanical workshops of Canton, Tientsin, and Shanghai,[144] and many small printing plants, flour mills, oil-pressing mills, and textile workshops. (See Table 14.)

It would be rash to attempt to assess the exact percentage of workers employed in the larger enterprises. In Shanghai, according to the 1923 list, the figure for the number of workers in factories with over five hundred employees is 157,464, which is more than half the working-class population of the city insofar as it can be estimated for this period.[145] Concentration must have

TABLE 14

NUMBER OF WORKERS EMPLOYED IN SMALL TEXTILE WORKSHOPS IN
PEKING AND TIENTSIN

Survey	Number of Workshops			
	Less than 20 workers	20–40 workers	40–100 workers	Over 100 workers
404 rayon- and cotton-weaving workshops in Tientsin in 1928[a]	279	95	27	3
206 Peking carpet workshops[b]	105	57	32	12
303 Tientsin carpet workshops in 1929[c]	152	70	59	22
149 Tientsin hosiery workshops in 1929[d]	135	11	3	—

[a] Fong [64].　[b] Chu and Blaisdell [59].　[c] Fong [65].　[d] Fong [63].

been still more intense in the Northeast industrial region, where big Japanese enterprises predominated. The effect of this high concentration of the working-class population within a small number of enterprises, added to the effects of the concentration of industry within several specific geographical areas, was that the Chinese industrial proletariat was able to acquire a unity and vigor as a class that was scarcely to be expected in view of its numerical weakness and its youth.

High Rate of Turnover

Finally, the mobility of the Chinese proletariat must be taken into account as an influence on the form the labor movement took. Workers frequently moved from one enterprise to another and from one region to another, as a few individual examples will show. Take the case of two workers, Lim Chou and Lok Shoo-yung, who in the spring of 1926 came up before the Mixed Court in Shanghai on a charge of having murdered a foreman who in 1925 had tried to break the strike at the waterworks. Lim had come from Canton to Shanghai in 1918; after working in several Japanese metalworks there, he had gone to Hankow in 1920, and then returned to Shanghai in 1924 to take up a job in the waterworks. Lok had been an apprentice smith in Hankow from 1919 to 1922, had then been employed as a smith in the Northeast by the S.M.R. from 1922 to 1925, and after 1925 had carried on the same trade in Shanghai.[146] Again, the railwayman Yü Mo-huai, one of the strike leaders in the Shanghai insurrection of 1927, had been successively employed as a steward on a river steamer on the Yangtze, as a mechanic in a public service company, and as a railwayman on the Shanghai-Nanking line.[147] Many other examples could be quoted.[148] The militants of the trade union movement took advantage of this situation; without incurring any suspicions, they moved easily from one end of China to the other, taking on successive jobs as miners, railwaymen, or factory workers according to the exigencies of the labor movement in any one particular sector of industry.[149]

One result of this mobility, however, was that workers did not stay long on the average in any one enterprise but were constantly going to and fro between one place and another; and this led to absenteeism and to variations in the numbers employed during any one year. In a Japanese cotton mill in Shanghai, 2,150 workers left and 2,417 entered the mill between November 1923 and October 1924, the greatest number of changes taking place in March, when there were 342 departures and 278 new arrivals.[150] Similarly, out of a total of 9,932 workers employed in 26 factories in the Northeast during 1925, there were 5,143 departures, amounting to 51.7 per cent of the total.[151]

An investigation into the reasons why the 2,150 workers left the Japanese cotton mill in Shanghai in 1923–24 shows that 257 of them quit to return home, 168 "for domestic reasons," 129 because of a marriage or a birth, and 33 because they were dissatisfied, while 280 were dismissed because their work was found to be unsatisfactory, 105 on the grounds of not having worked hard enough, 91 for having disobeyed rules and regulations, and 605 for excessive wastage of materials—to mention only some of the reasons.[152] This seems to indicate that the high rate of turnover was not due merely to the fact that many of the workers were peasants who had only recently come to the towns, but also reflects their difficulty in adapting to industrial work and to factory life.

Conditions in Old-Style Industries

Was working in the big capitalist industrial enterprises any worse or any better than working in what remained in the 1920's of the old forms of small-scale industry such as the craft workshops and the mines where "indigenous methods" (*t'u-fa*) were used? Superficially, working conditions in these pre-capitalist enterprises were just as bad as those in the modern factories, and the descriptions of both by visiting observers are equally unfavorable:

> Some of the match factories and carpet factories, the ceramics and glass works, and the old-style silk and cotton factories could well have served as an inspiration for even Dante's descriptions of the infernal regions. Pale, sickly creatures move around there in almost total darkness, amidst indescribable filth, and breathing an atmosphere that is insupportable to anyone coming in from outside. At ten o'clock at night, or sometimes even later, they are still at work, and the feeble light of a few oil lamps lends the factories a still more sinister aspect. A few breaks are taken to snatch some food while still at work, or to eat a meal in a courtyard covered with excrement and filth of all kinds. When the time to stop work finally comes, these miserable creatures doss down in any place they can find—the lucky ones on bales of waste material or in the attics if there are any, and the rest on the workshop floor, like chained dogs....[153]

Similarly, the investigators who visited the old-style Peking carpet factories in 1922–23 were struck by the filth and the disorder, the darkness, the bad air, and the complete lack of sanitary measures.[154] The apprentices had to sleep and prepare their frugal meals in these appalling surroundings. Working conditions in the old-style mines were just as primitive and as unbearable. For instance, at the Mentowkow mines near Peking the pit workers often stayed for eighteen hours on end in the galleries hauling coal in wicker baskets. Ventilation was introduced by the simple expedient of lighting a fire at the far end of the gallery, except at times when there was a deep frost.[155]

Nevertheless, comparisons between the old-style and the modern enterprises must not be confined to questions of hours of work, the physical demands made on workers, or sanitary conditions. Without in any way wishing to idealize the old-style enterprises, it must nevertheless be said that in them class distinctions were less sharp, working conditions less inhumane, discipline less severe, and output demands less rigorous. In a small workshop, the distance between employer and worker was not so very great, and every worker could hope to become someday or other a small producer.[156] But for the worker in large-scale modern industry, employed in some concern with vast technological and financial resources that only made him more aware of his own insignificance, and working side by side with hundreds or thousands of others in the same position as he, the only hope for the future lay in the betterment of his class as a whole.

CHAPTER V

Wages and Living Standards

Although payment for industrial work in the form of wages was introduced in some manufacturing centers in China as early as the seventeenth and eighteenth centuries,[1] it was still far from universal in the 1920's. The forms it then took varied widely within the same region, the same branch of industry, or even the same enterprise, but seldom consisted of a simple, direct cash payment.

It was common practice to pay piece rates to some workers and time rates to others. Piece rates were usual in the tobacco and match factories,[2] but also quite common in the cotton factories, the weaving mills, and the hosiery and knitting factories.[3] Time rates on the other hand were the most usual, if not the only, form of payment in the mechanical workshops, the shipyards and repair yards, and the flour mills and oil-pressing mills; printing plants made almost equal use of both.[4] There is very little documentation on this question, but piece rates seem to have been the lot of the least skilled and lowest paid workers. Thus in the Shanghai silk-reeling factories,[5] the women who cleaned and sorted the cocoons were engaged and dismissed according to each day's needs and were paid piece rates, whereas the reelers and their assistants, who had more regular employment, were paid by the day. Similarly, in the Fushun mines[6] the carpenters, mechanics, and pit workers were paid time rates, while coolies were paid piece rates—that is, the few coolies who were directly employed by the company and not by the contractors.[7]

Among the workers who were paid time rates, some were paid by the day and others by the month. This was an important distinction compounded by a corresponding difference in the kinds of currency used: workers for daily wages were paid in copper, and those paid by the month received silver. Here again it was the degree of skill that determined the category. In the Shanghai silk factories, for instance, all the men were paid by the month and bore the title of "officers," whether they did manual work such as weighing the cocoons, packaging the silk, or maintaining the machinery (in which case they were known as "military officers"), or whether they belonged to the administrative and managerial staff ("civil officers"). The women, however, even if skilled, were paid by the day.[8] Among the workers in the cotton mills who were paid time rates, only the mechanics and foremen were paid monthly.[9]

Another distinction—one that was peculiar to China, and very widespread there—was that between direct and indirect payment of wages. Indirect payment occurred when the workers' wages were paid to an intermediary, who then gave them only a part of the money he had received on their behalf. This was the contract-labor system already discussed in connection with the recruitment of workers and their working conditions. In some places the system in use was pao-kung, or contract labor proper, as in the K.M.A. mines, where the labor contractor entered into a direct contract with the company to extract a certain amount of coal; in others it was like the one in use in the Shanghai cotton mills, where the pao-fan-tso, or supplier of labor, recruited the workers and had their wages paid to him without his necessarily taking any responsibility for the work done. However, in both systems the major part of the sum paid in wages was absorbed by the intermediary or intermediaries, and managements were usually no more aware of the amount the workers actually received in wages than of the exact number of workers employed. The amount deducted from the wages by the contractor was always large,[10] and it became even larger if there were several middlemen between the employing firm and the workers, as was the case with the dockers.[11] The contractors, in addition to making a regular deduction from the wages, also made a profit on the food sold to workers and on the lodgings when these were provided. They made an even larger profit from lending money in advance against wages not yet paid.[12] They profited also from financial transactions involving conversion of the silver dollars they received from the company as a lump-sum payment of wages into the depreciated and unstable copper currency that they paid to the workers.[13] (If the amount came to over one yuan, the yuan was paid in silver and the rest in copper currency.)[14] Another procedure they often adopted was to pay out wages only once a week or once a fortnight, even though they received the money daily from the company. This was very profitable during periods of depreciation, and in any case allowed plenty of opportunity for profitable moneylending.[15] They used many other tricks for increasing their profits, such as pretending that the difficulties encountered in extracting the coal were greater than they actually were so as to be able to claim a supplementary bonus, receiving pay for nonexistent workers, or misrepresenting the amount of coal supplied according to their contract with the company.[16] All in all, the margin of profit enjoyed by the contractors was considerable, despite the fact that they had certain commitments, such as having to share with the company the costs of compensation for accidents.[17]

The pao-kung system was the most important and the most widespread form of indirect payment of wages, but it was not the only one. Since the straightforward purchase of labor power had not yet completely replaced earlier practices, which often entailed ties of personal allegiance, there were still anomalies in the wage structure. A typical example is provided by the arrangements for the supply of steam in the Shanghai silk factories.[18] The men employed on this task were regarded as belonging to the silk-reeling plant, and they received, for instance, the same monthly "cocoon bonus" as the other skilled workers. But they were recruited, controlled, and paid by the contractor who supplied the boilers, who was known as the *lao-kuei* ("old devil"). He contracted to supply the factory with the mechanical energy required and the steam needed for the preparation of the cocoons at a fixed price that included all expenses except the supply of coal, which was provided by the factory. But often a contractor made a deal with more than one silk factory, in which case he resorted to the use of a subcontractor known as *erh-kuei* ("second devil"). Another example of indirect payment is the method by which the Shanghai rickshaw men were paid.[19] Here again one middleman or more came between the owners of the vehicles and the coolies who pulled them.

A different kind of anomaly in the labor system was the way in which some of the workers employed in modern industry retained something of the economic independence enjoyed by the craftsmen of former times. For instance, it is reported that in 1920 the miners in the lead and antimony mines of Shuikowshan in Hunan still owned their own lamps, and still had to provide their own lamp oil and explosives; still, the Mines Department of the Hunan provincial government, which owned the mines, supplied the hammers, picks, and other tools, and paid the miners a monthly wage.[20]

Other examples of survivals from the precapitalist era are the supplementary benefits either in money or in kind that were enjoyed by a large number of workers under the guise of traditional privileges. In some modern enterprises the workers had either free board or free lodging, and sometimes both. Benefits of this kind were often extended to the more skilled workers such as the carpenters and the pit workers in the Fushun mines,[21] the "officers" of the Shanghai silk factories,[22] the workers in the Wuhu machine shops,[23] the mechanics employed in the Chihli flour mills,[24] the adult men employed in the Shanghai match factories[25] and in the Nanking towel factories,[26] and the skilled workers in a Japanese cement works in Shantung.[27] In all such cases, the workers that benefited were already better paid than the average worker, and the main idea seems to have been to preserve for skilled workers the comfortable position enjoyed by the journeymen of the old craft guilds. But on the other hand, it was sometimes the lowest paid and the least privileged categories of workers that were given board and lodging, so the companies could avoid having to pay them more than a purely nominal wage. This was the case, as we have seen, with the children hired under the "apprenticeship" system in the match factories, cotton mills, and carpet factories of Peking and Tientsin. It also applies to the coolies working in the rice-husking factories of Hankow and its surrounding neighborhood in 1924; for work that demanded sheer physical strength, they received a few copper cash plus three meals per day consisting of rice and vegetables to which meat was added twice a month.[28]

Other benefits, consisting of payments in kind over and above the basic wage, were probably also survivals of old craft customs. Thus, for example, workers in the silk-reeling factories were allowed to sweep up the silk waste and either sell it or make it up into quilted garments;[29] women employed in the Shanghai stocking factories could take away a few pairs for their own use;[30] and Chiu-ta salt refinery workers who had families received free salt to the amount of one catty each per month for husband and wife and half a catty for other members of the family.[31] But ancient customs tended to give way before the commercialization introduced by the development of a market economy, and after the First World War these payments in kind were gradually replaced by cash bonuses, which, however, remained distinct from the wage as such, thus preserving something of their former character. The silk factories took to selling the waste to manufacturers of winter clothing, but paid their male skilled workers a "cocoon bonus" prorated to the wage scale,[32] and some factories paid their workers a bonus instead of the meals they had formerly provided.[33]

In the old craft workshops employers had the right to dismiss their employees and the obligation to settle their accounts at the end of the lunar year. It was also customary to pay the employees an annual bonus at this time, and around 1920 this practice was still widespread. It was retained, for instance, in the modern potteries in Peking[34] and in some of the Shanghai cotton mills.[35] At the Chiu-ta salt refinery it took an even more traditional form, consisting of the gift of "two suits of clothing and some edibles," but in 1927 this was commuted to a cash bonus of nine yuan.[36] In the numerous modern enterprises where this lunar New Year bonus was distributed,[37] the old names for it were retained—*hung-li* ("red earnings," red being the color of festivals and widely used in those days in connection with gifts, greeting cards, and such) or *hua-li* ("earnings for festive spending").

In general the practice of paying bonuses over and above the basic wage was very widespread in Chinese industry in the 1920's, and although some of them, as we have just seen, were commutations of traditional payments in kind, others were innovations brought about by the particular way in which large-scale modern industry operated. For instance bonuses were introduced to combat absenteeism and to encourage workers to stay on in their jobs. Bonuses of this kind were distributed in the Harbin flour mills and oil-pressing mills to workers who had been employed for at least three years,[38] and in the Chefoo silk factories to those who had worked for a month without a single day's absence.[39] At the Chiu-ta salt refinery, every worker who had not been absent for more than a month was entitled to an extra month's pay at the end of the year.[40] The general term for these various efficiency bonuses was *shen-kung* ("extension of wages"). The widespread adoption of the practice provides further indication of the high degree of mobility of Chinese labor at this time.[41]

Another type of incentive bonus, designed to raise productivity, was the kind of payment-for-results system adopted by a Japanese cotton mill in Yangtze-poo, where each worker producing more than 126 balls of cotton per day got a 10 per cent increase in wages.[42] Many other Japanese factories in Shanghai paid a bonus to workers who exceeded the accepted output norm,[43] and in Tientsin the employees of the French Tramway Company received a bonus if their daily receipts exceeded a certain amount.[44] Incentive bonuses of this kind were also paid to the "industrial apprentices" in the Tientsin match factories and knitting factories to induce them to work harder.[45] Sometimes bonuses were paid to counteract a temporary rise in the cost of living, and remained separate from wages so long as the firms concerned maintained the hope of being able to abolish them at the next seasonal fall in prices. The history of the Chinese labor movement provides many examples of strike waves that succeeded in obtaining cost-of-living bonuses, notably during the rice crisis in Shanghai in the spring of 1920. Fluctuations in the price of rice several times caused big Shanghai firms such as the British and American Tobacco Company, the Commercial Press, and the Japanese cotton mills to institute a sliding scale of food bonuses in relation to the retail price of rice.[46]

Payments for overtime were, however, seldom made, if only because in most industries the working day was already so long that the question of overtime never arose. The only occasions when bonuses of this kind were paid occurred in industries where a high degree of skill was required, in which case, as we have seen, the working hours were shorter. Thus in the Kiangnan shipyards in Shanghai, those working two hours overtime at night in 1920 were paid at the rate of a third or a half of the average daily wage.[47]

In all, the various bonuses and supplements came to quite a sizable proportion of the total amount of remuneration. At the Chiu-ta salt refinery the annual bonus, the monthly efficiency bonus, the productivity bonus for those who had a claim to it (it was calculated according to the amount of salt produced), the money paid in commutation of the traditional gifts, and the overtime bonus if there was any, together amounted to, on the average, 31.1 per cent of the total annual earnings of the workers.[48]

Finally, this brief survey of the extra payments over and above wages would be incomplete without mention of the various illicit means by which workers sought to supplement their earnings in industries that provided such opportunities. This was a form of delinquency that arose from the wretched poverty of most Chinese workers, and it should be judged from a social rather than from a moral point of view.[49] Sometimes workers removed electric light bulbs from the galleries of the mines;[50] seamen smuggled in arms and ammunition, and stowaways as well, on merchant ships in South China;[51] workers slashed machine belts to make leather soles for shoes;[52] and along the railroad tracks it was a common sight to see women and children—despite the risk of accidents and the prohibitions against the practice—picking up, one by one, cinders that were not quite burned out and pieces of coal that had fallen from the tenders.[53] The high incidence of practices of this kind in the cotton mills led to an insistence on the part of the managements that workers be systematically searched at the mill gates, and to a prohibition against children's bringing food to parents working in the mills.[54]

Deductions from wages were no less numerous and varied than supplementary payments. The most common deductions were the many fines exacted—as frequent a feature of factory regulations as corporal punishment. In general workers were fined for any material damage caused, or for infringements of factory discipline such as sleeping while on duty[55] or smoking.[56] In the silk factories they were fined for bad workmanship, such as breaking the thread or spinning the wrong thickness.[57] And on the tramways, fines were exacted for admitting passengers who did not pay their fares.[58]

Another common practice was that of holding back part of a worker's wages until, during a given period, he had given satisfaction in his work. This took various forms. The Shanghai Post Office, for instance, retained one yuan from the wages of each of its employees as a guarantee of good conduct;[59] and in 1922 the Ministry of Communications instituted a compulsory savings scheme for the railwaymen (1 per cent on a wage of 20 yuan per month, 2 per cent on a wage of 50 yuan, and so forth), the total amount saved being repayable only in the case of an accident, at death, or on retirement.[60] The Tientsin master masons withheld 5 to 10 per cent of their employees' wages until the job they were doing was completed,[61] and in some of the Shanghai silk factories half of each worker's wages was withheld over a period of two months, out of which confiscations were made for the least infringement of factory discipline, or for such things as absenteeism or bad workmanship.[62]

The "gifts" and customary services exacted by foremen[63] might perhaps be regarded as a survival from a precapitalist economy, but as far as their actual effect on wages was concerned they come under the category of deductions. On every possible occasion—the lunar festivals, or family celebrations such as a birth, a birthday, or a wedding—foremen and overseers demanded gifts from the workers under them, and often quite costly ones. They also often insisted on having work done for them in their gardens, or on having their houses swept and their washing done, or their children looked after, all without payment; and they held such a position of power that no one dared to refuse to fulfill these almost feudal exactions and obligations.[64]

There were two additional factors responsible for reducing the amount of pay the workers actually kept; neither was directly due to actions taken by the employer, but they nevertheless seriously affected the workers' standard of living. The first of these consisted of the exactions demanded by gangsters (*liu-mang*), who operated mainly in the suburbs of Shanghai. Information on this subject, whether from Western or Chinese sources, is hard to come by, but there can be little doubt that criminal gangs recruited from the riffraff of the town were able to control certain districts, and that they derived a considerable income from the thousands or tens of thousands of workers who passed through "their" territory. Having their own bands of armed henchmen, they had the workers completely at their mercy, and met with no opposition from the police or from the labor contractors, with whom they were often in league. They were especially powerful in the western districts of Shanghai, which were not under the control of the police of the International Settlement and where many cotton mills were situated. Not only did they exact a toll from the workers who passed along streets they controlled, but they demanded gifts at the traditional festivals and did not hesitate to indulge in a bit of kidnapping for ransom, or to exploit the charms of pretty young women workers.[65] All in all, factory workers had to pay a heavy price to these gangsters, and rickshaw men too were exposed to their operations. The gangsters would seize a vehicle in passage containing a client and his luggage and only hand it back on payment of a ransom, or they would hire a rickshaw and get the coolie to take them to some isolated spot where by prearrangement accomplices were waiting to attack the coolie, beat him up, and rob him of his earnings.[66]

The second factor contributing toward lessening the amount in the pay packet was the instability of the Chinese currency—another reflection of the troubled state of Chinese society and the Chinese economy. This was something from which the labor contractors made a fat profit. It has already been mentioned that, owing to the depreciation of small silver coins in relation to the yuan and the still greater depreciation of copper coinage, two systems of payment of wages were in use: the *ta-yang* system, whereby wages were calculated in "big money," and the *hsiao-yang* or "small money" system. In the first, the amount of wages due to a worker was reckoned up at the end of a week or a fortnight; he was paid in actual dollars for every 100 cents he had earned, and the rest in small coins. In the second, the total amount, even if it came to several yuan, was paid in small silver or even in copper coins.[67] The hsiao-yang system, which was less advantageous for the workers, was the one most commonly in use, and often strikes were held solely in order to obtain a fairer method of calculating wages, especially after the depreciation of copper coinage became more acute in 1922–23.

During the period with which we are concerned there was considerable variation in the wage rate from one industry to another, from one region to another, and from one type of job to another. Table 15, despite the fragmentary and contradictory nature of the data, reveals these inequalities. Because of the disparities in pay, the unions and the labor movement in general were unable to pursue a unified policy with regard to wages. In the disintegrated state of the Chinese economy, the only way to deal with the wage question was to make empirical decisions on the spot.

Although the figures in Table 15 are unreliable, especially for the industries in which the contract-labor system is known to have predominated, they do at least indicate that there were considerable regional differences in nominal wages. In general, wages seem to have been higher in the South than in the North: a carpenter earned 0.43 to 0.87 yuan in Shameen and 0.10 to 0.30 yuan in Shansi; a railway laborer 0.58 yuan in Kwangtung and 0.17 to 0.42 yuan in Shantung. They also seem to have been higher on the coast, especially in Shanghai and Canton, than in the interior. The differences in wage rates between the various branches of industry are no less striking, with laborers and porters lowest in the scale, followed by the female and male employees in the silk-reeling factories and cotton mills, then by the miners, and lastly by the metalworkers.[68] Similar grading is found in later documents, such as a survey carried out by a Shanghai union in 1927, which shows that at that time the lowest paid workers were the women employees in the silk factories (6 to 10 yuan a month), next the dockers (9 yuan), followed by the workers in the cotton mills (12 yuan), those in the tobacco factories (15 to 20 yuan), the printing workers (20 to 30 yuan), the Post Office employees and the railwaymen (25 yuan), and finally the mechanics and electricians (30 yuan).[69]

There was also considerable variation in wage rates within a given enterprise, and the high wages of some skilled workers only emphasize how low the rate of payment was for the great mass of the unskilled. This is brought out by the figures in Table 15 for the Shanghai cotton mill, or for the Tzechwan or K.M.A. mines. In the Shanghai silk factories a few years later, the women employed in cleaning the cocoons earned 9 cents a day, those moistening them over bowls of boiling water 36 cents, the sorters and reelers (also women) 65 to 70 cents, and the men known as "officers" one to one and a half yuan.[70] Similarly, in the flour mill at Tsangchow in Chihli, in 1926, unskilled workers earned 10 yuan per month and mechanics 30 yuan, a difference that was accentuated by the fact that both categories of workers were given board and lodging by the firm.[71]

Further variations in wage rates were due to differences in the nationality, the sex, or the age of the workers concerned. In Dairen in 1920, Japanese workers were paid 2 yen a day and the Chinese 0.80 yen for the same work;[72] and in Mukden in 1922, Japanese unskilled glassworkers received 2.50 yen and Chinese 1.20.[73] Women always received lower rates than men, as is apparent in a survey conducted by a Shanghai newspaper in 1920, which shows that the women's average wage in the woolen factories there was 0.19 cents as against 0.40 for the men, in the match factories 0.15 cents as against 0.25, in the tobacco factories 0.22 as against 0.70, in the cotton weaving mills 0.18 as against 0.45, and so on.[74] It must, of course, be remembered that in the tobacco factories, for example, the women usually did less skilled work than the men, and allowance must be made for this in considering the above figures, which give only the average wage. Nevertheless a substantial difference in

TABLE 15
Wage Rates in China Around 1920

Industry (1919 unless otherwise indicated)	Wage rate in yuan (daily wage unless otherwise indicated)	Price of 1 picul of poor-quality cereal in 1920[a]
Shanghai:[b]		
coolies	0.22–0.45	9.23 yuan (rice)
skilled mechanics	4–10 (mo.)	
electricians	4.92–7.89 (mo.)	
Shanghai (1920):[c]		
silk: men	0.65	
women	0.35	
cotton: men	0.91	
women	0.45	
matches: men	0.45	9.23 yuan (rice)
women	0.25	
printing: men	0.46	
women	0.27	
A Shanghai cotton mill:[d]		
cleaning cotton	0.30	
reeling: men	0.30–0.44	
women	0.22–0.29	
children	0.18	
weaving (women)	0.15	9.23 yuan (rice)
mechanics	17–22 (mo.)	
forewoman	0.55	
Ssufang cotton mills (Tsingtao):[e]		
reeling	0.20–0.42	
combing	0.20–0.28	5.49 yuan (millet)
Shantung dried egg factory:[f]		
skilled men	12–15 (mo.)	
women	0.15	5.49 yuan (millet)
coolies	0.30	
Miscellaneous:[g]		
Peking carpenters	0.57	7.70 yuan (millet)
Taiyuan carpenters	0.10–0.30	
Nanking railway laborers	0.50–0.65	
Nanking railway mechanics	0.67–1.00	Figures missing for others
Amoy carpenters	0.43–0.87	in this group
Chiao-Chi railway line:[h]		
station employees	0.47–1.80	
engine-drivers	0.45–0.41	5.49 yuan (millet)
mechanics	0.29–0.48	
laborers	0.18–0.42	

TABLE 15 (cont'd)

Industry (1919 unless otherwise indicated)	Wage rate in yuan (daily wage unless otherwise indicated)	Price of 1 picul of poor-quality cereal in 1920[a]
Canton-Kowloon line:[i]		
laborers	0.60	
carpenters	0.73	
stokers	9 (mo.)	Figures missing
mechanics	0.78	
Fuchow (1921):[j]		
unskilled men	0.30–0.40	
unskilled women	0.25	8.13 yuan (rice)
mechanics	7.30 (mo.)	
printers in Western firms	4–9 (mo.)	
Chunghsing miners:[k]		
semiskilled	27.79 (mo.)	Figures missing
unskilled	7.65 (mo.)	
K.M.A. miners:[l]		
surface workers	0.20–0.25	
pit workers	0.25–0.30	7.38 yuan (millet) in
skilled electricians	1.00–1.85	Tientsin
electricians' mates	0.15–0.25	
Tzechwan miners:[m]		
pit workers	0.28–0.85	
sorters	0.22–0.55	Figures missing
carpenters	0.18–0.76	
laborers	0.16–0.47	

[a] *Nien-chien* [138] I, 67. These prices are given only in order to indicate the variation in the real value of wages from one province to another; they do not represent exact figures.   [b] Trade report, 1919 [19], pp. 52ff.   [c] *Nien-chien* [138] I, 47.   [d] *Ibid.*, p. 21.   [e] *Ibid.*, p. 227. [f] *Ibid.*, p. 262.   [g] *MLR*, Aug. 1921.   [h] *Nien-chien* [138] I, 299.   [i] *Ibid.*, p. 56.   [j] *TIB* No. 75, 30.x.22.   [k] Lin Hsiu-chuan [73].   [l] *Nien-chien* [138] I, 278.   [m] *Ibid.*, p. 285.

rates existed. Children of both sexes also received very much lower rates, even apart from such extremes as the merely nominal wages paid to industrial apprentices.

Inadequacy of Workers' Income

What was the purchasing power of these wages? The only information available about this is what can be gathered from a few individual reports and approximate estimates which, although they cannot make up for the lack of proper statistics, give a clear enough indication of the desperate situation of

TABLE 16

RELATION OF WAGES TO COST OF LIVING AROUND 1920–25

Category of workers	Monthly income (in yuan)	Monthly expenditure (in yuan)
Hong Kong seamen in 1922[a] ...22 (average)		30 (for support of family of four)
Shanghai workers in 1922[b] .....6–12 (for unskilled workers)		Minimum living wage: 11.85 (single man) 21.34 (family of four)
Pootung workers in 1923[c] 6–10		Minimum living wage: 8 (single man) 16–20 (family of four)
Tsinan workers in 1925[d] ....7.50 (average)		Cost of living: 7.50 (single man) 15 (family of four)

[a] Figures for the seamen taken from demands presented by the union before the 1922 strike (*SCMP*, 2.xii.21).   [b] Figures from an I.L.O. report (*ILR*, July 1923).   [c] Child Labor Commission, *Minutes* [17], 6.vii.23.   [d] *CEB*, 22.viii.25.

the workers. (See Table 16.) All the data in Table 16 lead to the same conclusion: workers and their families simply did not have enough to live on. The writers of the *International Labor Review* article quoted in the table estimated that 40 per cent of the Shanghai workers were more or less permanently short of money; and all they could do was to borrow from moneylenders, as several investigations made at the time show. Seventeen per cent of the 100 printing workers' families interviewed in Shanghai in 1930,[75] 29 per cent of the 85 postal workers' families also interviewed in Shanghai in 1930,[76] and a very large number of the 230 families in the working-class district of Tsaokiatu surveyed in 1928,[77] all said they were in debt and having to pay high rates of interest. In the Tsaokiatu survey, the rate of interest was said to be 5 per cent per month, or 60 per cent per year. The families with the lowest incomes seem to have been the most heavily in debt. The industrial commissioner of Kiangsu province estimated that in 1920 workers earning 15 yuan a month were on the average 4 yuan in debt, those earning 20 yuan 3.50 yuan in debt, and those earning 25 yuan 1.50 yuan in debt.[78] The same inverse ratio is reported for the workers in the Chiu-ta salt refinery: 12 out of 22 families earning 130 to 180 yuan a year, 8 out of 21 earning 180 to 230 yuan a year, and so on, were in debt.[79] Even the very poor who came from the Kompo to find work in Shanghai as porters borrowed money to build their mud and wattle huts along the banks of the Whangpoo and its tributaries.[80] A hut cost from 12 to 30 yuan, and they borrowed either from friends at the rate of 10 copper cash per month on every yuan (or about 50 per cent per year), or from professional moneylenders at the rate of 10 silver cents on every yuan (or about 120 per cent per year).

TABLE 17
WORKING-CLASS FAMILY BUDGETS

Group involved	Average monthly income (in yuan)	Percentage of income spent on:				
		Food	Rent	Clothes	Heat and light	Other
Shanghai workers, 1920[a]...............	15.0	63.1	15.7	10.6	—	10.6*
Shanghai working-class families, 1925[b]..	21.0	64.4	9.5	7.1	9.5	9.5
Shanghai skilled workers, 1925[c].........	38.5	42.0	14.0	11.0	7.0	26.0
Shanghai unskilled workers, 1925[d]......	21.7	52.0	13.0	10.0	9.0	16.0
Shanghai workers, 1927[e]...............	19.5	53.8	15.4	15.4	9.5	5.9
Peking workers, 1922[f]	—	73.6	11.1	6.6	—	8.7*
113 Peking working-class families, 1926[g].	17.6	58.2	9.4	4.6	11.8	16.0
48 Peking working-class families, 1926[h]..	16.9	72.0	7.3	6.6	11.1	3.0
Dairen dockers, 1924[i]..................	19.0	56.5	16.9	9.8	16.0	0.8
86 unmarried workers at the Chiu-ta refinery, 1926[j]	12.4	62.7	—	15.2	—	22.1
61 working-class families at Chiu-ta, 1926[k]	22.0	55.7	7.1	9.5	8.1	19.6
Coolies, 1927[l]	—	75.0	8.0	9.0	5.0	3.0
Industrial workers, 1927[m]..............	—	65.0	13.0	7.0	15.0	—

* Includes heat and light. [a] *CWR*, 30.xx.22. [b] *NCH*, 4.ix.26. [c] *TSTL*, 1954, No. 4.
[d] *Ibid.* [e] *Nien-chien* [138] I, 161. [f] Tao [78], Appendix. [g] Gamble, *AAAPS*, Nov.
1930. [h] *Nien-chien* [138] I, 163–64. [i] *MDN*, 10.x.24. [j] Lin Sung-ho [74], p. 61.
[k] *Ibid.* [l] *PPW*, 1.x.27. [m] *Ibid.*

The examples of family budgets given by several surveys and investigations further emphasize the acute poverty of the workers. All these budgets are characterized by the high proportion spent on food, which almost always came to more than half the total amount of expenditure and sometimes to as much as two-thirds or even three-quarters. (See Table 17.) In a few particular instances figures are available showing variations in expenditure in relation to actual, and not average, incomes, such as the figures shown in Table 18. It can be seen that, contrary to Ernst Engel's First Law concerning the decrease in the amount spent on food in ratio to an increase in the wage rate, the tendency here was the very reverse. The figures demonstrate, in fact, that Engel's laws apply only to societies in which a certain minimum standard of living has been achieved, and we can safely assume that in China, during the period in question, the "threshold of application" had not yet been reached even by the highest paid categories included in Table 18.

The amount spent by workers on food, even if it was a large proportion of their incomes, did no more than provide them with a diet that was monotonous, of poor quality, and lacking in nutritive value. Often the daily diet con-

TABLE 18

VARIATIONS IN THE PERCENTAGE OF INCOME SPENT ON FOOD AROUND 1925

Income	Percentage spent on food
48 working-class families in Peking[a]	
Under 70 yuan per half year	67.0%
70–110	70.7
110–50	72.8
150–90	70.4
86 unmarried workers at the Chiu-ta salt refinery[b]	
115–40 yuan per year	61.8
140–65	63.2
165–90	62.1
190–215	70.2
215–40	62.2
240–65	68.9

[a] *Nien-chien* [138] I, 164.   [b] Lin Sung-ho [74], p. 61.

sisted simply of a few bowls of rice (in South and Central China) and some soup and cooked vegetables.[81] The workers in the Peking carpet factories, according to a survey made in 1923,[82] had only two meals a day, consisting of corn bread, onions, and soup, or of noodles, pickled vegetables, and soup; they had meat only once a month. In the Chiu-ta salt refinery the daily diet of an ordinary worker was restricted to three *man-t'ou* (steamed wheat rolls), three pieces of corn bread, three bowls of millet porridge, and three dough-nuts.[83] The survey conducted in 1928 among 230 workers' families in Tsao-kiatu[84] shows that on an average reckoning of 4.7 persons per family, each family consumed 90 *tou* (about 14½ cwt.) of rice per year, and 45 catties (52 pounds) of wheat, and that 53.2 per cent of their expenditure on food was on cereals, while 7.6 per cent of the expenditure on vegetables was on soya bean products (either beans as such, bean sprouts, or *tou-fu,* a fermented paste made from soya), and 10.9 per cent on green vegetables, such as Chinese cabbage, spinach, celery, and on other vegetables pickled in vinegar. Each of these 230 families consumed an average of 35 pounds of meat per year (mainly pork, but also chicken), representing 7 per cent of the total expenditure on food. Another important item was edible oils and fats; miscellaneous items such as eggs (92 per family per year), condiments, a little sugar, a few watermelons, and seeds and nuts at New Year, accounted for 14.3 per cent of the total. But all these are merely average figures calculated over a range of family incomes of which the lowest was under 20 yuan and the highest over 50 yuan. A sep-arate survey of the lowest income levels would reveal an even more meager diet.

The inadequacy of the workers' diets was studied from a medical point of view in a survey conducted around 1935 by a Shanghai missionary organization, the Henry Lester Institute for Medical Research, and no doubt its conclusions are applicable to the earlier period. It showed that a worker, even if he ate a little pork at the midday meal, which would place him well above the average, consumed no more than 2,660 calories per day, of which 75.1 per cent was provided by carbohydrates, 15.4 per cent by fats, and 9.5 per cent by proteins. The calorie deficiency was therefore qualitative as well as quantitative, since the accepted norm is 3,000 to 4,000 calories per day, 45 per cent of which should be provided by fats and proteins. Moreover, in the cases examined, 70 per cent were deficient in Vitamin A, 80 per cent in Vitamin B, and 40 per cent in Vitamin C.[85]

The circumstances in which workers' food was supplied and consumed varied greatly. Sometimes food was brought in from outside and eaten in the factory,[86] and sometimes, as we have seen, it was supplied by the firm as part of the workers' remuneration. There seem to have been very few workers' canteens where everyone paid for his own meals,[87] but occasionally workers paid a cook to prepare meals for them.[88] Married workers usually took the evening meal at home, whereas unmarried men had to make do with what they could get from street vendors. According to one report,[89] they could often be seen buying very meager quantities of food from these peddlers—perhaps half a boiled egg, a pot of hot water, a dash of sauce, half a dozen dried shrimps. Meals could also be taken in one of a number of cheap restaurants, the unsavoriness of which may be judged from recommendations concerning them made in 1923 by the Shanghai Y.M.C.A. These included suggestions that the rice used should not be of such old stock as to be uneatable, that the vegetables should be washed before being cooked and the bowls washed after use, that garbage should be removed daily, that food should be protected from flies, and that the floor should be swept at least once a month.[90] There were also basement boardinghouses for unmarried men. A typical one in Shanghai charged 4 yuan a month for feeding and lodging two laborers using the same pallet bed alternately night and day.[91]

Living quarters for workers in the big centers of mining and heavy industry were probably worse still, whether they were rented houses, dormitories, boardinghouses, dwellings provided by the firms, or huts and shelters of various kinds. A common type of housing consisted of rows of houses of the traditional kind, built of bricks or pounded earth with tile roofs and having a tap at one end of each row.[92] The houses might have either one or two stories, but the one-story houses often had matting stretched over poles on top to house a second family. The furniture was extremely sparse: a small clay stove, a few planks to serve as benches, some tables and beds. In a report on his visit to Shanghai in 1922, Dr. Sherwood Eddy, an internationally known member of the Y.M.C.A., described a room measuring ten square feet, devoid of furniture, in which six persons slept, and a dwelling in which every room was divided up into small cubicles, each of which was let at a rent of one yuan a month or even more, and one of which housed six persons.[93]

The impression of extreme overcrowding conveyed by various accounts and surveys is confirmed by the few investigations in which figures are given. One made in Shanghai in 1930 reports that the average number of rooms per family occupied by the 100 families investigated was 1.26, and that 30 of these families did not have even one whole room to themselves.[94] Of the 230 families investigated by S. Yang and L. K. Tao, 62.6 per cent lived in one room or less, and each room was occupied by an average of 3.29 persons.[95] The lower the family's income, the more cramped were its living conditions. The average number of rooms occupied by the families of workers at the Chiu-ta salt refinery ranged from 1.18 for those earning less than 180 yuan per year to 1.6 for those earning between 230 and 280 yuan, and on up.[96] But a point that must be taken into account, to which I shall return later, is that the average size of the family rose in relation to higher income, and this tended to keep the level of overcrowding constant, as is shown by the figures given by Yang and Tao for the 230 families they investigated.[97] (See Table 19.)

Whatever the shortcomings of the rented houses may have been, only the higher paid workers seem to have been able to afford them because of the excessive rents charged.[98] In 1926 the price of the very smallest type of house in Shanghai was 700 yuan (the value of land, even in the suburbs, having already reached 4 yuan per mou), and landlords, hoping to make a profit of not less than 15 per cent, often demanded a rent of as much as 100 yuan per year. Even if several families were crowded together into one house, the rent for each came to several yuan a month, which was far beyond the means of many families.

Dormitories and boardinghouses were mainly occupied by unmarried men. Here the best a worker could hope for was to have a lower bunk and a shelf on which to put his personal belongings. Often twelve or fifteen had to share

TABLE 19

HOUSING CONDITIONS IN SHANGHAI AROUND 1930

(Survey of 230 working-class families)

Monthly income (in yuan)	Number of rooms per family	Number of persons per room
Under 20	1.04	3.33
20–29	1.19	3.35
30–39	1.52	2.00
40–49	2.00	3.08
50 and over	2.6	3.58

a room, had to rise and go to bed at fixed times, and enjoyed no personal comfort whatsoever.[99] The dormitories in which the labor contractors lodged the peasants they had recruited were a still more uncomfortable version of this type of lodging. When companies provided dwellings for their workers, they did so both because they required a permanent labor force and because they wanted to be able to maintain strict control over it. Some enterprises, such as the Naigai Wata Kaisha in Shanghai,[100] the silk factories in Wusih,[101] the K.M.A. in Tangshan, and the S.M.R. in Anshan,[102] built houses which they then rented out to their workers. Others built cantonments in an area enclosed by a fortified wall guarded by their own private police, so that the workers could not come and go as they pleased. Japanese firms seem to have had a particular liking for this system, which was used for the miners in the Northeast[103] and for the dockers and porters employed in Dairen and on the S.M.R.[104] The Japanese owners of a Tsingtao silk factory built a huge encampment in 1924 that consisted of a number of small houses for workers with families and twelve two-story twenty-room buildings, with each room lodging twelve unmarried workers.[105] The Chinese-owned Yü-yuan cotton mill in Tientsin built a workers' village, also surrounded by a wall, near the mill.[106]

The various dwellings provided by companies, whether dormitories or houses for families, were not better than other types of accommodation. The dormitories were overcrowded and badly kept, and the houses were rented at a rate that obliged the families occupying them to sublet or to share their already overcrowded living quarters, just as in other rented houses. In Wusih, each four-room house provided by the silk factories was usually occupied by six families,[107] and in Hong Kong, a large room rented out in 1924 at 18 yuan a month by the Taikoo shipyard—that is, by the British firm of Butterfield & Swire—had to be divided up by the original occupants by means of matting partitions and sublet at four to five yuan per subdivision.[108] In all, although the houses provided by the companies, in Shanghai at least, were of better quality than those rented out by private owners, being built of either brick or wood, with glazed windows, electric lights, and so on, the overcrowding in them was even worse than in other types of accommodation. According to the findings of the American sociologist H. D. Lamson in 1932,[109] the average amount of space occupied by each of the 221 families housed by the Naigai Wata Kaisha in Shanghai was 0.94 of one room; 108 families had one room each, and 73 half a room.[110]

Some firms, however, offered a very different type of accommodation consisting simply of free floor space on the premises, as had been the custom in the old craft workshops. In many small workshops where no nightwork was done, such as the mechanical workshops in the big cities[111] and the carpet factories of Peking and Tientsin,[112] the workers laid their mattresses on the floor of the workshop at nighttime and in the morning rolled them up and stored them in some convenient corner. Similarly, many of the rickshaw men of Peking had no other lodging than the place where they kept their vehicles at night.[113]

Finally, a large number of the industrial proletariat led a kind of marginal existence, finding whatever shelter they could. In Shanghai this consisted of either unused boats on the creeks of the Whangpoo, or huts made of boards, reeds, or any old odds and ends of junk, iron sheets, or kerosene cans.[114] These huts had an average area of about 10 by 12 feet, and were sometimes shared by two families, with a piece of matting hung on bamboo poles to divide the hut into two rooms. As mud built up round the huts, the floor became lower than ground level, and every time it rained water poured in, bringing with it all sorts of filth. Probably several hundred thousand people lived this way, many of them the very poor from the Kompo. According to an official report made by the Shanghai Municipal Council in 1926, there were 14,394 of these hut dwellers in the Yangtzepoo district alone,[115] and there were even more in Chinese territory outside the settlements. Not all of them were semi-employed or coolies working by the day; some had steady jobs as factory workers, dockers, rickshaw men, or municipal employees.

Even with miserable dwellings such as these huts, speculators lost no chance of making a profit out of them. Some of the occupants were simply squatters, but most paid at least a ground rent, even if they owned and had themselves built their huts (which cost an average of 10 yuan). The rent for a ready-built hut was 50 cents to 1 yuan a month, and the ground rent per hut was usually 1 yuan, and sometimes 2 or 3 yuan. Thomas Tchou reports one case in which half a mou of land was rented to 21 families at 200 yuan a year for a stipulated period of five years, the full five years' rent having to be paid in advance in case the tenants departed before the period expired, although the landlord could give notice whenever he chose.[116] And here, as elsewhere, there was overcrowding. H. D. Lamson reports that there were 5.4 persons per hut in a group of 23 huts in Yangtzepoo;[117] and the sanitary conditions were even worse than in the ordinary houses in the town. There was also a constant danger of fire[118] and a constant fear of eviction, for with the rise in the value of land in Shanghai after the First World War[119] the owners of the land on which the huts were built took to evicting the occupants, who then moved to the outskirts. However, their very presence there raised the value of the land where they had squatted once again, thus bringing about a renewed threat of eviction. For instance, the Hongkew district to the north of the International Settlement was more or less uninhabited in 1920, when all it contained was a few houses of traditional design, a few straw huts built by coolies from the Kompo along the banks of the Soochow Creek, and for the rest vast stretches of marshy land. But between 1920 and 1927 about thirty factories were built there, and the gradually increasing number of straw huts erected there slowly gave ground to this new development.[120]

Although these huts were mainly typical of the Shanghai outskirts, dwellings of a similar kind were to be found in other industrial centers in China. In Tientsin, for instance, employees of the Ching-Feng railway lived in sheds near the station,[121] and workers in the factory making army uniforms lived in mud huts on the banks of the canal.[122]

Whatever the type of accommodation—whether rented houses or company dwellings, dormitories for unmarried men or straw huts—all of it had the drawbacks of overcrowding, insecurity of tenure because of either high rents or the threat of eviction, and a total lack of comfort and hygiene. There was the further drawback that, except for the company dwellings built in the immediate vicinity of the mills or the mines, workers' housing tended to be scattered at considerable distances from the place of work. Family budgets had such a narrow margin that most workers with families could not afford to live in the factory area and had to find cheaper accommodations elsewhere, entailing daily journeys of one, two, or even three hours.[123] The workers often traveled on foot, but if the distance was too great they had to go by bus or tram. This accounts for the large proportions of Shanghai family budgets spent for travel, as much as 4, 6, or even 11 per cent of total expenditures.[124]

Thus in many Chinese cities, large industrial and working-class districts sprang up that lacked both the Chinese urban traditions of gracious living and fine architecture, and the modern comforts and advances in technology achieved by Western civilization. In the new districts, factory buildings and working-class housing alike were jerry-built, and the roads muddy and badly lit. In Shanghai a sharp contrast to the ultramodern office buildings of the "Bund," the luxurious residences in the French Concession, the bright lights of the big modern shops along Nanking Road, and the picturesque elegance of the pagodas in the "Southern District," was offered by the working-class districts of Yangtzepoo, Pootung, Chapei, Tsaokiatu, and Hsiaoshatu, which were not very different from poor districts everywhere—in Saint-Etienne, Glasgow, Anzin, or the London East End.

Segregated working-class districts of this kind, which further increased the social isolation of the workers, were to be found in other industrial centers in China. In Tsingtao the cotton mills and railway workshops were situated in the northern district of Szefang,[125] and in Tientsin all the big cotton mills and modern factories, with their concomitant wretched housing, were concentrated in the Hopei ("north of the river") district, formerly the territory of the Austro-Hungarian and Russian concessions;[126] and dozens of the Harbin flour mills and oil-pressing mills were located in the outlying working-class districts of Pachan, Hsiangfang, and Liang-t'ai-hsiao-chan.[127]

Social and Cultural Life

In this precarious existence led by the workers in the big cities, what opportunities did they have for social and cultural activities, and to what extent were

TABLE 20

Monthly Variations in the Number of Workers Employed in Selected Enterprises
(Using an index of 100 for the month of January)

	Jan.	Feb.	Mar.	Apr.	May	June	July	Aug.	Sept.	Oct.	Nov.	Dec.
Coolies of the Works Department of the International Settlement, 1920[a]	100	88	110	137	150	142	157	154	133	140	132	103
Employees in the Pao-chin coal mine, 1920[b]	100	49	40	55	74	60	84	89	69	103	109	116
Monthly entries and departures in a Shanghai cotton mill, 1923[c]	100	77	273	170	199	155	147	186	129	175	255	146
Arrivals in the Penhsihi mines, 1926[d]	100	44	135	161	105	64	114	105	44	92	95	—

[a] SMCR, 1920.   [b] Nien-chien [138] I, 370.   [c] Ibid.   [d] Ibid., p. 373.

they able to enjoy a normal family life? The Chinese working class could hardly be said to have broken with the age-old folk traditions of the country. Workers still celebrated the festivals of the lunar calendar with all the accompanying ritual of firecrackers, specially baked cakes, and such, still observed the customary marriage and funeral ceremonies with their picturesque processions, and still kept up the rites of ancestor worship.[128] The lunar New Year, which fell in February, continued to be observed as a holiday even in modern foreign-owned firms. Indeed, February was the month when, as can be seen in Table 20, the number of workers employed was at its lowest, and when there was a general slowing down in the number of coolies seeking work in mills and factories or in the mines of the Northeast.[129]

Something of the old religious customs survived in some working-class homes despite their poverty. A scroll representing Kuan-yin or some other deity of the syncretic peasant cults would hang on the back wall of the main or only room; on the left wall (the side of honor) were "parallel sentences" presented by relatives or friends, and on the right wall there might be a few cheap pictures bought from a peddler, representing scenes from a play or a well-known novel. (The scrolls and pictures usually cost only a few copper cash.) At the back of the room there might be a table or a shelf bearing candles or sticks of incense to be lit on the first and fifteenth of every moon.[130]

Again, in the few enterprises where hours of work and holidays permitted, groups of amateur players continued to take a keen interest in their national opera and folk dances. In 1925 the workers of the Chiu-ta salt refinery still kept up the lion dance, the dragon-lantern dance, and other traditional amusements of the Chihli peasants, from whose ranks they had recently emerged.[131]

Nevertheless folk traditions and old customs were undoubtedly disappearing among the workers in the big centers of modern industry. Judging from family budgets, in which social and cultural expenses were very small items, this must have been largely due to low wages, the high cost of living, and the constant fear of unemployment.[132] There was practically nothing to spare out of a meager wage for celebrating, however cheaply, weddings and funerals in the old style, or for entertaining guests at festival times, or for a few amusements. Expenditure on wine and tobacco, which was an individual rather than a social matter and quite consistent with the routine of factory life, was slightly higher; but many workers had to do without them altogether. What shows even more convincingly how workers had absolutely no money to spare is the complete absence of tea as an item in the budgets of more than a third of the families investigated, even though tea was the national beverage par excellence in China and an indispensable accompaniment to all social occasions. Most workers had to be content with buying cups of hot water from street vendors, or perhaps on special occasions a bowl of tea from the local tea vendor. The budgets of the lowest paid workers show, of course, the smallest amounts spent on amusements or social items, the only exception being

TABLE 21

PERCENTAGES OF INCOME SPENT ON AMUSEMENTS AND SOCIAL ACTIVITIES

(Surveys of the poorest families around 1930)

Families surveyed	Social expenses	Amuse-ments	Tobacco and wine	Weddings, funerals, etc.	Religion
230 families in Tsaokiatu[a]					
All 230 families	2.60%	2.82%	3.20%	2.95%	0.70%
Families earning:					
under 20 yuan per month	1.60	0.09	3.70	2.50	0.39
20–30 yuan per month	2.40	0.23	3.60	1.62	0.62
61 families at the Chiu-ta salt refinery[b]					
All 61 families[c]	3.86	0.20	1.74	6.08	0.45
Families earning:					
130–80 yuan per year	3.40	0.05	1.08	0.37	0.25
180–230 yuan per year	5.00	0.32	1.77	4.40	0.34

[a] Yang and Tao [81], statistical tables.   [b] Lin Sung-ho [74], p. 83.   [c] Incomes ranging from 130 to 430 yuan per year.

amounts spent on wine and tobacco, which were more or less constant whatever the wage rate. The most striking feature of Table 21 is the very low amount spent on items for religious ceremonies. The surveys show that a large number of families dispensed with them altogether: this was the case, for instance, with 63 per cent of 100 Yangtzepoo families, two-thirds of 85 Shanghai postal workers' families, and 32 per cent of 100 families of printing workers in the Commercial Press in Shanghai.

The fact that expenditure on wine and tobacco remained more or less constant indicates that poverty alone cannot account for this break with the customs of the past, but any attempt to discover what the deeper reasons may have been would entail a detailed examination of such characteristics of working-class life as the long hours, the dispersed housing away from the factory area, the new technical skills, and the changes in social structure. This kind of study would go beyond the scope of an introduction to a history of the Chinese labor movement, but it should be noted here that a number of technological, social, and even political factors led to the decline of traditional customs among industrial workers. Lin Sung-ho remarked on the decline of the theatrical performances staged by the Chiu-ta workers: "Owing to the unsettled social and political conditions in these years, workers are not as enthusiastic for these shows as they used to be."[133] All the more striking is the contrast afforded by the craftsmen of the old type of guild in Peking, where modern industry had hardly penetrated at all; in 1925 these workers continued to conduct their traditional ceremonies.[134]

The working class was, in fact, a new kind of class, already alien to China's former mental universe and capable of behaving very differently from other social classes, especially the peasantry, from which it had so recently emerged. Despite the long hours of work and the low wages, new interests and new traditions gradually began to replace the customs of former days. Although the lunar New Year festival continued to be observed, dates of quite another kind began, as we shall see, to acquire a growing importance for the great mass of workers throughout China—dates such as International Labor Day on May 1, and other anniversaries of the workers' struggle. Little by little a new calendar of traditional working-class festivals became established, gaining additions as contacts increased between Chinese workers and the international labor movement and as the workers' struggle in China itself progressed.

Workers, despite their lack of funds and of leisure, showed a much greater interest in acquiring a modern education and training than in upholding ancient traditions. The rate of illiteracy was not extremely high; for example, illiterates amounted to 60 per cent of the men employed in a Shanghai cotton mill in 1924,[135] 58 per cent of the men and boys from the 230 families in Tsaokiatu surveyed in 1930,[136] and 77 per cent of the Chiu-ta workers in 1925–26.[137] Naturally illiteracy was higher among women: 85 per cent in the Shanghai cotton mill and 98 per cent among the Tsaokiatu families were illiterate. Life in a big city like Shanghai, the pressure of the political situation (which was felt more directly there than elsewhere), and factory work all contributed during the 1920's toward arousing a desire for education among workers such as had never been felt by the peasants in former times. Moreover, the success of the campaign for the adoption of *pai-hua* as the written language[138] meant that learning to read was no longer a matter of almost insuperable difficulty. Thus the workers' education movement in China between 1919 and 1927 was not merely something in which reformist organizations took an interest; it was also a basic concern of the revolutionary trade unions, and at the same time it provided a convenient screen for other activities.

Family Life

The family life of workers was another thing that set them apart from other classes. In the traditional extended family (*ta-chia-t'ing*), several generations lived together, people married young, few remained unmarried, there were many children, and women had no independence whatsoever. However, in the 1920's this type of family was rapidly disappearing among the working class.[139] According to two surveys, the first conducted in 1929 among men employed in a Tientsin weaving mill and the second in 1930 among women employed in a Shanghai cotton mill, most of the men and women under twenty were unmarried, and there was even quite a substantial minority of unmarried men over thirty. (See Table 22.)

TABLE 22

PERCENTAGE OF MARRIED WORKERS AROUND 1930

Age group	317 Tientsin weavers (men)[a]	70 cotton mill workers in Shanghai (women)[b]
15–19 years	19.2%	11.54%
20–24 years	42.4	57.14
25–29 years	65	81.82
30–34 years	73.3	100

[a] Fong [64].   [b] Lamson, CEJ, Oct. 1931.

TABLE 23

SIZE OF WORKING-CLASS FAMILIES AROUND 1930

Families surveyed	Avg. no. of persons per family	Trade
262 Hangchow families[a]	4.44	Probably cotton mill workers
230 Shanghai families[b]	4.76	Cotton mill workers
100 Commercial Press families[c]	4.42	Printing workers
100 Yangtzepoo families[d]	4.11	Probably cotton mill workers
85 Shanghai postal workers' families[e]	5.20	Postal workers
1,125 Wuhan families[f]	3.23	Various
1,484 Nanking families[g]	3.68	Various
65 Nanking families[h]	4.90	Arsenal workers, railwaymen, weavers
61 families at the Chiu-ta salt refinery[i]	3.72	Salt refinery workers

[a] CEJ, March 1931.   [b] Yang and Tao [81], p. 24.   [c] CEJ, Sept. 1930.   [d] CEJ, Aug. 1930.
[e] Ibid.   [f] CEJ, March 1931.   [g] Ibid.   [h] CEJ, Sept. 1931.   [i] Lin Sung-ho [74], p. 71.

However, the most remarkable feature of this tendency to marry later was the way in which many women workers chose to do so, despite the fact that it was customary for daughters to accept passively the marriage arrangements made for them by their parents at whatever age the parents decided upon. And the parents of these girls seem to have approved, or at least accepted, their decisions, judging from remarks quoted by one survey: "Girls, nowadays, marry later than they used to.... Since they earn money, we do not insist on their marrying early."[140] Some of the women silk workers in the Canton region, whose work had made them economically independent, formed groups known as *pu-lo-chia* ("women refusing to marry"). These women were so determined not to marry that they were prepared if necessary to refund, out of their own pockets, the bride-price to the husbands chosen for them. They were known for their spirit of independence, and were regarded by employers as difficult to manage.[141] However, when a woman factory worker did marry, she was, in the words of a sociologist who in 1935 investigated women employees in Shanghai and Wusih, "a new kind of wife."[142] She no longer gave blind obedience to her mother-in-law, and there was also a change in her relations with her husband. Out of 60 women employees interviewed, 23 had more power than their husbands, 8 had equal power, 12 were consulted by their husbands in all matters, and only 16 showed, like old-fashioned wives, the docility required by the Confucian moral code.[143]

The small size of the working-class family is another indication of the decline of the traditional extended family. Children were few, and there was no room in the home for the aged or for older or unemployed members of the same generation, whose presence would have been an insupportable burden. All the available sources agree that the working-class family was simply the conjugal family with two or three children. Table 23 shows that the more skilled workers had larger families than the unskilled. The few surveys concerning the size of families in relation to the wage rate confirm that the poorest

TABLE 24

RELATION OF FAMILY SIZE TO INCOME
(Working-class families around 1930)

Income	Average number of persons per family
230 Tsaokiatu families[a]	
Under 20 yuan per month	3.45
20–29	3.79
30–39	4.98
40–49	6.03
50 and over	7.76
100 Yangtzepoo families[b]	
160–299 yuan per year	2.70
300–499	3.70
500–699	5.28
700–899	4.14
900–1,099	7.50
1,100 and over	9.00
48 Peking families[c]	
Under 70 yuan per half year	3.67
70–109	4.18
110–49	5.36
150–90	5.67

[a] Yang and Tao [81], p. 24.   [b] *CEJ*, Aug. 1930.   [c] Tao [76], p. 37.

TABLE 25

NUMBER OF WAGE EARNERS IN WORKING-CLASS FAMILIES

Families surveyed	Number of persons	Number and percentage of workers	Average number of wage earners per family
21 Shanghai families[a]	97	58 (59.7%)	2.76
100 Yangtzepoo families[b]	411	211 (51%)	2.11
230 Shanghai families[c]	1,097	538 (49%)	2.32
61 Chiu-ta families[d]	227	108 (47.6%)	1.77

[a] CEJ, Nov. 1930.   [b] CEJ, Aug. 1930.   [c] Yang and Tao [81], p. 36.   [d] Lin Sung-ho [74], p. 72.

families had the smallest number of children, no doubt because of a higher infant mortality rate. (See Table 24.)

The splitting up of the family into those who remained in the country and those who sought employment in the towns was a further factor in the disappearance of the extended family. Sometimes it was the wives and daughters who got jobs in the towns in the silk, cotton, match, or tobacco factories, either as independent workers or under the control of a labor contractor, and at other times it was the men who went, leaving their families behind and sending them small monthly remittances. Out of 500 workers at the Chiu-ta salt refinery, 210 sent remittances in 1925, and 123 in 1926. The sums they sent were quite large—on the average, 23 yuan per worker per year in 1925, and 39 yuan in 1926.[144] But the lower-paid workers could not keep up their remittances for long, and at Chiu-ta the number of workers' families residing in Tangku increased, in 1926, from 70 to 136.[145] Poverty tended to make families move from the country to the town; thus in Shanghai, it was the lowest paid workers, particularly those who came from the Kompo, who customarily brought their families with them. Only those workers who had some means and the prospect of a comparatively steady job could be sure of being able to maintain wives and children left behind in the village, or could at least hope to make a substantial contribution toward their livelihood.[146]

A further change in family life came about when a growing number of women and children went out to work because the father of the family did not earn enough to keep them all. According to several surveys on this point, there were almost always more than two wage earners in each family—that is, half or over half the average number of persons in the family. (See Table 25.) All the changes leading to the weakening of family ties, together with the fact that half or over half the members of every family were thrown upon the labor market, contributed to the mobility, the rootlessness, and the dynamism of the Chinese working class.

CHAPTER VI

Political Experience of the Working Class

"China was not present at the recent International Labour Conference for the simple reason that she has no labour problems." The British Board of Trade official who made this statement in 1919 may perhaps be thought to have come to a somewhat hasty conclusion.[1] Certainly the role of the working class in China at that time was not yet as prominent as that of the industrial proletariat in the West after the middle of the nineteenth century. Nevertheless it already had traditions of labor organization, of strike action, and of participation in the political life of the country that were by no means negligible, and it is worth investigating in some detail the extent of political experience it had at its command.

The oldest traditions of the new working class were those it had inherited from the guilds, and although it was chiefly among the skilled workers and the coolies drawn from the urban populace that these traditions were kept alive, they were important enough among the main body of workers to warrant a brief discussion. The guilds (*kung-so*), some of which were centuries old, had always been, and still were at the beginning of the twentieth century, characterized by the fact that they exercised a rudimentary type of economic control.[2] They kept strict control over such aspects of production as fixing the quality of wool or silk to be used by the weavers; or they issued prohibitions such as that against barbers drinking alcoholic beverages or eating onions and garlic.[3] If necessary, they took precautions to preserve the secret of certain processes, and they specified conditions to be complied with in the exercise of any particular trade. It was laid down, for instance, that anyone wishing to open a workshop must first have completed his apprenticeship, and must then obtain the permission of the guild and pay the required dues. (These were sometimes very high: 20 yuan in 1920 for Hankow dyers, 200 taels for jade carvers in Canton.)[4] The guilds also fixed the prices of goods, which, with commodities such as rice that underwent short-term fluctuations, might be changed from day to day; and they exercised a strict control over the labor market, not only by deciding upon the amount to be paid in wages and the number of hours to be worked, but also by managing the apprenticeship system. No one could practice a trade without first having served as apprentice to a master for a period that varied in general from three to five years but was always strictly stipulated in the rules of each guild. Each apprentice had to have a guarantor (*pao-jen*), who had to sign a certificate of guarantee (*pao-tan*); and the guild in question had to supply the guarantor with a letter of acceptance (*chih-ku-shu*) containing the guild rules concerning apprenticeship, which was to be handed to the owner of the workshop in which the apprentice was employed. There were guilds in which masters were not required to obtain the guild's formal acceptance of an apprentice, but even so, no master would take one on unless he had a genuine vacancy. During the period of apprenticeship the apprentices were required to give complete obedience to their masters, and guild rules were greatly influenced by the Confucian traditions of respect for the established order and of submissiveness toward elders and betters.[5] The young apprentices were given board and lodging, and received over and above this only a very modest sum of pocket money. They could not leave their masters before the expiry of the apprenticeship period. The conclusion of the period may not have been marked by the execution of a "chef-d'oeuvre," as was the custom in France in the old days, but it was at least celebrated by an official initiation ceremony.

The guild was by definition and in fact a mixed organization, a community of small-scale producers who were chiefly concerned to keep prices stabilized. The master craftsmen (*ta-shih-fu, ku-chu*), the journeymen (*erh-shih-fu, huo-yu*), and, on a temporary basis, the apprentices (*t'u-ti, i-t'u*), all belonged to it. The journeymen and other workers had full rights of membership and enjoyed the various benefits, such as sickness compensation and financial assistance with the expenses of family funerals or children's education. It was, however, the master craftsmen who ran the guilds, for although the entire membership was supposed to elect (usually annually) the governing board, it was in fact only the well-to-do employers who were chosen. These boards consisted of a manager known as the *chih-nien* ("in charge for the year") and a number of other officers, usually twelve or a multiple of twelve, so that they could officiate in rotation during the twelve-month lunar year without any of them having his normal professional activities disturbed for too long. The board dealt with the regulation of prices and wages and with all the other guild activities, and it was also responsible for maintaining discipline. It sent inspectors to workshops and shops, and inflicted the various penalties, ranging from corporal punishment and fines to the extreme penalty of temporary or final exclusion from the guild, which amounted to a prohibition against continuing to practice the trade in question. The rules seldom insisted upon compulsory membership, but the pressure of custom was such that no one dreamt of not belonging to, and enjoying the support of, the guild concerned with his particular trade. Another function of the board was to arbitrate disputes, whether these were between master craftsmen or, as was more often the case, between masters and journeymen. Most guilds even included in their rules a prohibition against guild members taking cases before the ordinary civil courts before having exhausted the opportunities for arbitration offered by the guild. The board also managed the guild finances. Income was derived from entry fees, subscriptions (usually annual, but occasionally monthly), fines, taxes on the sale of workshops, and revenue from investments in land or from capital lent out at interest; expenditure was mainly on benefit payments, management expenses, and the annual celebration of the guild festival.

Obviously, in a system of this kind, the interests of the journeymen were very far from coinciding with those of the masters, and disputes over wages were by no means rare. In the case of the shoemakers and the jade workers in Peking, a wage dispute in 1885 even attained the proportions of a strike.[6] Nevertheless, the main feature of the guilds seems to have been the loyalty felt by all members toward each other. These trade loyalties, partly customary and partly due to economic pressures, were reflected in the religious cults maintained by the guilds. Each had its patron saint or "ancestral master" (*chu-shih*), who was supposed to have been the original teacher of the techniques of the trade. Most of these patron saints were either gods of Taoist folk tradition or mythical emperors; but some were historical personages who had become mythologized. Among the latter were Lu-pan, the god of the carpenters, masons, and all other building workers, who is supposed to have lived in Shantung in the fifth century B.C. and to have been clever enough to have constructed a bird that flew into the heavens and a wooden ladder that rose up into the air at his command; or Sun Pin, a hero of the Warring States period, who is alleged to have invented shoes that hid the fact that his feet had been cut off by his enemies, and who was the patron saint of cobblers and shoemakers; or Lo-tsu, the patron saint of the barbers, who in the Ming period was said to have protected his master, the emperor, against the Mongol invaders by providing him with the effective disguise of an altered hair style. Some guilds had their own temples for the worship of their patron saints, which were kept up at their expense.[7] Others merely hired a Taoist temple in the town at certain periods of the year. But whatever the circumstances, every guild held an annual celebration for its own patron saint, on which occasion no work was done. At this time a banquet was held for all members, and the annual general meeting, at which the board was elected and all accounts settled, took place. The celebrations ended with a theatrical performance of a ritual character.

Guild rules were another important factor in contributing to a strong sense of internal solidarity. In later years it had become usual to have them in writing, and they were revised or added to as the need arose.[8] They contained in full detail all regulations concerning apprenticeship, the conditions to be complied with for the practice of the trade in question, the techniques to be employed, the methods for selecting the governing bodies, and the powers enjoyed by them.[9] The economic and customary ties by which the members of a guild were bound, and which found direct expression in the guild rules, were further reinforced by the widespread practice of the guilds' providing board and lodging for the apprentices and journeymen employed in a master's workshop.

On the other hand, there was strict demarcation between one trade and another, and the fact that some guilds in the same line of business shared the same chu-shih did little to alter this. Carpenters, joiners, masons, and workers in bamboo all worshipped Lu-pan; Ts'ai-shen was the patron saint of all types of engravers and lithographers, Sun Pin for makers of clogs, slippers, boots, and other footwear, and Ko for dyers, painters, and makers of incense sticks and so on. Yet the degree of demarcation was such that in Shanghai in 1921, for instance, there were as many as eight separate carpenters' guilds, each representing either a separate stage of carpentry work or the various provincial origins of the journeymen.[10] In Peking in 1927 there were still separate shoemakers' guilds for makers of riding boots, of ordinary shoes, of padded slippers, of shoelaces, of soles, and of shoehorns.[11] The same high degree of specialization was to be found in the famous "seventy-two" guilds of Canton,[12] and in the Hong Kong guilds.[13] Demarcation disputes frequently arose between the related guilds, and the tradition of specialization in the form in which it was inherited by workers in modern industry became a considerable obstacle—especially in Canton—to the organization of unions on an industrial rather than a trade basis.

A further complication in the structure of the guild system was the question of regionalism. In every big town, the ink-makers were all natives of Wuyuan hsien in Anhwei,[14] and the water carriers in all the towns in North China were recruited from the robust Shantung peasants.[15] Within the same trade, craftsmen from a particular region sometimes formed their own guild. In Shanghai there were, in addition to the local carpenters' guild, guilds for carpenters from Ningpo,[16] Soochow, and Canton.[17] There was always fierce competition between them. In 1902, for instance, the Ningpo carpenters employed in the shipyard of Farnham & Company refused to support a strike held by their Cantonese fellow workers in order to obtain a raise in wages.[18] Among the Shanghai incense manufacturers there was the same kind of discord between the local craftsmen's guild and the one to which craftsmen from other parts of the country belonged.[19] Guild rules did little to lessen provincial rivalries or preserve the unity of the trade as a whole. The Peking fur guild was an exception. It had a rule whereby natives of Chihli, Shansi, and Shantung must each constitute not less than one quarter and not more than one third of the governing board, the 48 members of which were divided into twelve committees which took charge in turn by monthly rotation. These committees had to include a native of each of the three provinces, the fourth member being chosen from natives of other regions.[20] Most guilds refused to admit members from other provinces; the Hunanese dyers, for instance, were not even allowed to pay the standard fee of 16 yuan for permission to work within other guilds.[21] This strongly provincial character of the guilds is worth noting, because it reflects the regional character of the Chinese economy and of Chinese society up until the twentieth century.

The strength of provincial feeling was also evidenced by the existence of many regional "guilds" (*hui-kuan,* "society offices," or *t'ung-hsiang-hui,* "same-district societies") in all the big cities. Provincial origin, without distinction of class or occupation, was the basis of membership, and members ranged from wealthy notables and businessmen to skilled craftsmen and even porters and coolies.[22] Some of them, such as the Canton and Ningpo Guilds in Shanghai, were essentially bourgeois in character, and wielded a great deal of power both socially and politically by guaranteeing the credentials of their members in intercity business transactions, providing storage for goods, offering hospitality to visitors, and taking part in local affairs. They had great influence also among workers and coolies, who applied to them for funds in an emergency, for help in transporting a relative's coffin back to the home village, or for the support of their influential fellow provincials when in difficulty with the authorities or in search of employment. These regional "friendly societies" used to seize every opportunity of acting as mediators in strikes, and continued to do so in many industrial disputes after 1919, especially in Shanghai.

Like the guilds, the friendly societies were properly constituted organizations with rules, funds, boards of management, premises,[23] and archives. Regional associations of a very different kind were the "mutuals" (*pang, pangk'ou,* or *pang-hui*) formed by coolies, street-porters, and the semi-employed in the big cities.[24] These groups—exclusively plebeian and proletarian in membership—were much smaller than the others and had no elaborate internal organization. A pang simply consisted of several score, or at the most several hundred, unskilled workers who had clubbed together in order to find employment and to escape from the feeling of isolation resulting from barriers of language or dialect.[25] The leader or *t'ou-mu* ("head") was the man who, perhaps to further his own interests, had got together a group from his own district and formed a pang, and it was he who conducted negotiations for hiring it out. Possibly this was an early form of the pao-kung system. All that was required for a t'ou-mu to become a pao-t'ou was that he should make a profit on negotiating employment for his out-of-work comrades.

Another traditional form of organization was the secret society. No systematic survey of Chinese secret societies in modern times has yet been made, but there are indications that until the First World War they still had some influence among craftsmen and even more among the urban populace. The Hsiao-tao-hui ("Small Knife Society"), affiliated with the Triad, which in 1853 had succeeded in gaining temporary control of the old walled city in Shanghai, had many seamen, boatmen, and dockhands among its members,[26] and in Hong Kong the Triad itself was influential enough to organize a strike in 1884 that affected the principal trades on the island (and especially in the port) in protest against Admiral Courbet's attack on Taiwan and Fuchow.[27] Two big secret societies more specifically connected with the world of labor were those known as the Green Gang (*Ch'ing-pang*) and the Red Gang (*Hung-pang*).[28] The Green Gang was formed at the beginning of the eighteenth century among the sailors, dockers, and coolies employed in the transport of rice from the provinces to the capital along the Grand Canal. It was originally a huge trade association controlling the hiring of labor and the coordination of the transport system, and is said to have had as many as 200,000 members or men under its control. The Red Gang on the other hand was a political organization formed in the seventeenth century for the purpose of getting rid of the Manchu invaders and restoring the legitimate Ming dynasty. By the beginning of the twentieth century both organizations still preserved their hierarchical structure, their rites of initiation, and their discipline, but their aims were very different from the original ones. Traffic on the Grand Canal had fallen off rapidly ever since the opening of the sea route for the transport of rice from the Yangtze estuary to Tientsin in 1903; and the restoration of the Ming dynasty was becoming less and less probable. That both the Green and Red Gangs did still concern themselves with labor questions is shown by the part they played in organizing or supporting strikes,[29] and this is admitted by the founders of trade unionism;[30] but by 1919 they were much more in the nature of gangs of racketeers run for the profit of the gang leaders, and they lost none of the opportunities provided by a big metropolis like Shanghai for indulging in lucrative illicit practices such as gunrunning, traffic in drugs, prostitution, and various forms of extortion.[31]

All the traditional forms of labor organizations or associations to which workers belonged, whether guilds, friendly societies, pang, or secret societies, were however on the decline in 1919. This was true especially of the guilds, which were beginning to split up into separate organizations for employers and employees. This had happened with the Peking cosmetics guild, the Hangchow incense guild,[32] the dyers and weavers of Hunan,[33] and the tilers, carpenters, and stonemasons of Fuchow.[34] In Hong Kong the splitting up of mixed guilds was still further advanced.[35] Moreover, owing to the development of a market economy and of capitalist free enterprise, master craftsmen no longer felt the same loyalty toward each other, and in guilds such as the Peking carpet guild, which was in competition with American carpet factories recently established in North China, they tended to disregard fixed prices and go over the head of the guild to deal directly with foreign buyers.[36] Nevertheless, in many urban districts, whether old-style like the *hu-t'ung* (alleys) of Peking,[37] or new, such as the Shanghai concessions,[38] the old corporate guilds were still very active in 1919. Despite the fact that the majority of the workers in modern industry and transport were of peasant origin rather than skilled craftsmen, guild traditions were still strong enough to have a profound influence on the Chinese labor movement during its early stages, and they bequeathed to it such features as demarcation of trades, mixed associations of employers and employees, and provincial or local particularism.

Guilds and the Beginnings of Trade Unions

To what extent had the new industrial and transport workers actually been members of guilds prior to 1919? It seems that many of the skilled workers—especially mechanics, carpenters, and weavers—had been taken on by the new mechanized enterprises after receiving their training, and often after being employed, in the old craft industries; hence they were at first content to continue as individual members of the guilds to which they belonged.[39] This was the case with the weavers and printers employed in modern enterprises in Hang-chow,[40] and the carpenters employed in the Chinese and British shipyards in Shanghai.[41] Similarly, in Shanghai the mechanics employed in the tramways, the railways, the waterworks, and various mills and factories were still, in 1919–20, members of the old Metalworkers Guild, to which the employers and journeymen in the craft workshops belonged.[42] Wage earners in large-scale capitalist industry who kept their memberships in the guilds—which were originally designed to protect the interests of small-scale mercantile-capitalist production—must have experienced enormous difficulties; but the extent of this can only be guessed at since there is no documentation on the subject. Apparently an effort was at first made by the guilds concerned to protect their economic rights, and more particularly to gain some control over the hiring of their skilled members by modern enterprises.[43] But by this time probably the only reason why workers, especially Shanghai workers, still subscribed to a guild was because of the benefits they could get from it.

Although some members of the working class of 1919 still belonged to the traditional guilds, others belonged to the new organizations that had been formed for the purpose of promoting Chinese, as apart from foreign, industrial development. These organizations had sprung up during the last years of the Empire, when, after K'ang Yu-wei's first attempts at industrialization, development had reached a point at which the entrepreneurs hoped to be able to canvass the support of employees as well as of employers. In a sense, these organizations were simply an extension of the old idea that in the guilds, masters and journeymen must stand together to protect the craft as a whole. The fact that most Chinese capitalists were able to promote only small or medium-sized concerns facilitated the formation of associations in which both the employers and the employees in modern industry took part. One of the earliest of these mixed associations was one with the significant title of "The Society for the Study of Mechanics," founded in Canton in 1909, which formed the nucleus of what would later be known as the Canton Mechanics' Union.[44] It drew its membership from the small employers and skilled workers of Canton and other parts of Kwangtung and also from those of the Chinese communities of Southeast Asia, especially that of Singapore. The purpose in forming it was to provide a skilled labor force for all the Chinese enterprises in the region employing mechanics or metalworkers by giving its members a proper training provided by lectures, evening classes, and qualifying examinations at various stages of training. In 1912 it established its headquarters on the island of Honam, south of Canton, where there were a number of small Chinese mechanical workshops; and in 1918 it amalgamated with a Hong Kong mechanics' guild and adopted the title of "General Association of Chinese Mechanics," while still retaining its mixed membership of both employers and employees.

There was a brief flowering of similar mixed associations during the first months after the founding of the Republic in 1912, when Chinese capitalists, hoping for new advances in industrialization, thought it advisable to obtain the cooperation of the workers. Most of these associations were founded by employers, but had names indicating that employees would play an important part in them.[45] For instance, according to the Shanghai press, a Silkworkers' Friendly Society was formed in April 1912 by the silk merchant Wu Chü-t'ing, supported by a number of women workers; and in May 1912, an intellectual named Yü Hui-min founded a Shipyard Workers' Alliance in the Kiangnan arsenal that announced its purposes in a manifesto calling for collaboration between employers and workers. But most of these organizations were swept away in the reaction of 1913–14.

With the temporary withdrawal of Western competitors during the First World War, Chinese capitalists were able to compensate for the political defeats of the preceding years by achieving successes in the field of light industry, and this new wave of industrial expansion brought renewed attempts to obtain the cooperation of the workers along the lines of what had been done in Canton and Shanghai in 1912. In 1918–19, just before the May Fourth Movement, there appeared in Shanghai a number of "semi-working-class" associations with names that clearly indicated the purpose behind them: for instance, the Industrial Society of China (founded in February 1919),[46] the Chinese National Industrial Federation,[47] and the Society for the Study of Industry and Commerce.[48]

There was yet another type of mixed association that appeared during the years immediately preceding 1919 which, because it was confined to one particular trade or one particular concern, shows how the old guild traditions still remained very much alive within the context of modern industry. One example is the Federated Friendly Society of Pharmacists, founded in Shanghai in January 1918, to which both employers and employees belonged and which in 1920 was one of the seven organizations that supported the first celebration of May Day in the city.[49] The year before, the Commercial Press had founded a Friendly Society of Common Virtue, which was open to both management and workers, and which, as well as providing its members with reading rooms and recreation rooms, also provided courses in technical training, thus perhaps revealing its underlying purpose.[50] According to a Shanghai newspaper report of 1919, there was also a mixed association for the rickshaw trade, open to coolies, to hirers of rickshaws, and also to the owners, who had no doubt been behind the formation of the association.[51]

Nevertheless, in the years leading up to May 4, 1919, the trend toward the formation of separate working-class organizations was already perceptible, just at the time when the journeymen of the old craft guilds were beginning to form their own organizations; and it was mainly among the skilled workers that genuine working-class organizations first appeared. There is said to have been a Postal Workers' Club in Canton as early as 1906,[52] and a Foundry Federation formed by the Hanyang metalworkers in 1913.[53] In 1918 the Hunanese Printers' Union was formed in Changsha, which provides a clear example of how industrial and handicraft workers were moving in the same direction, for it included workers in all branches of the trade. This was perhaps the first working-class association to use the term *kung-hui* ("trade union") in its title.[54] It was formed after a strike for higher wages had been held, and resulted from an amalgamation of the lithographers' association and an association of printing workers that had been in existence since 1913. A strike was also the occasion for the formation of a "Society for the Well-being of the Rickshaw Men of the Hankow Concessions" at Wuhan in June 1912, the dispute being with the British firms (*hang*) that owned the vehicles.[55]

As a rule, however, these first genuine working-class organizations were not much concerned with strike action. As far as one can judge, most of them were in the nature of friendly societies, with the main stress on leisure occupations, mutual aid, and educational activities. A club was formed in Tangshan at the beginning of the twentieth century that was open to the K.M.A. miners, the railwaymen and other workers employed at the local depot of the Ching-Feng line, and the workers in the cement works; it provided facilities for reading, making music, and attending lectures. However, in 1905 a dispute broke out between the workers of local origin and the Cantonese workers who had been brought from Hong Kong by the British mining and railway firms, and the Cantonese broke away and formed their own club.[56] Shortly after the republican revolution several mutual aid societies were formed among the railwaymen in Central China. One was started by an engineer on the western section of the Lunghai line in March 1921,[57] and another was formed at about the same time in Nanking by the railwaymen of the southern (British-owned) section of the Chin-P'u line. The rules of the second were published in a Shanghai newspaper in April 1912.[58] They stressed members' obligations concerning mutual aid and solidarity, urged them to work hard and to look upon each other as equals, and stipulated that all dealings with the management of the railway must be conducted through the society's president and vice-presidents. A mutual aid society was also formed among the workers of the

Chiu-ta salt refinery.[59] But prior to 1919 it was above all among the seamen that mutual aid societies flourished, and these might well be regarded as the precursors of industrial unionism. The Seamen's Mutual Benefit Society that was formed in 1914 among Chinese seamen on oceangoing vessels had certain political aims to which I shall return later, but it was also a philanthropic association which later moved its headquarters to Hong Kong, where it was legally registered under the name of "Seamen's Philanthropic Society."[60] This was the direct forerunner of the Hong Kong Seamen's Union that declared the big 1922 strike. Attempts were made in Shanghai in 1912 to organize the seamen there,[61] and at the time the May Fourth Movement began, two mutual benefit societies existed:[62] the Yen-ying Society, formed in 1914 among ships' stokers and mechanics, and the Chün-an Seamen's Guild, to which Ningpo seamen had belonged since 1918. Despite the trade demarcation of the first and the purely regional character of the second, both provided a starting point for industrial unionism among the seamen in the port of Shanghai.

It would be interesting to know which of the sectors of industry gave rise to the type of labor organization that emphasized mutual aid, and which to the type of mixed association connected with "industrial advance." Unfortunately documentation for the early stages of the labor movement is scanty compared with that for the 1919–27 period; but judging from the examples provided by the railways, the Hanyang steelworks, the K.M.A. mines, and the seamen, it would appear that enterprises run by the state or by foreign firms offered the best opportunities for the formation of the first type, whereas the ground was well prepared in Chinese-owned firms for the second type to flourish.

In general, all these early labor organizations and mixed associations bore the marks of the past. From the craft guilds they inherited not only the tradition of mixed membership, but also, even when separate workers' associations had been formed, the old tendencies toward demarcation of trades and regional distinctions, as exemplified by those of the Tangshan workers and the Shanghai seamen. They were also strongly influenced by the moralistic attitudes and terminology of Confucianism. This is noticeable in the frequent use of terms such as *chün-an* ("equality and peace"), *t'ung-i* ("the common good"), and *t'ung-jen* ("common virtue") in the names of these associations.

None of the early labor organizations, with the possible exception of the Hunanese printers' and the Hankow rickshaw men's associations, could be regarded as genuine trade unions organized on a class basis and pursuing clearly formulated objectives; and up until 1919 the number of workers belonging to them or influenced by them was probably very small. No detailed study has been made of the social origins of their members, but it is more than likely that the great mass of the peasants who had recently come into the factories and the mines not only were not members, but had never even heard of them. A mass meeting such as that held in Shanghai on July 7, 1912, by the

Shipyard Workers' Alliance, which was attended by over 800 workers,[63] was an isolated phenomenon. Probably the only form of organization known to the factory workers, dockers, railwaymen, and miners whose trades were not catered to by the guilds—especially as regards the unskilled and the semi-skilled among them—was the pang, the same elementary type of association recruited on a regional basis to which, as we have seen, laborers in the towns belonged long before industrialization began. Prior to 1919, pang for natives of Hupeh, Anhwei, the Kompo, Changchow, and Nanking existed in the Japanese cotton mills of Shanghai,[64] and workers in the Shanghai silk-weaving mills were divided into four pang-k'ou: those of Tungyang and Shenghsien (two districts in Chekiang which had traditions of weaving), and those of Hangchow and Soochow, both ancient centers of the silk-weaving industry,[65] these being the four areas from which most of the workers came when the modern silk industry was established in Shanghai. The Ching-Han railway-men[66] and the Anyuan miners[67] were also divided into regional pang. The workers, and especially the women workers, in the B.A.T. factories in Shang-hai formed groups of a still more elementary type, known as *shih-ti-mei* ("ten brothers and sisters"). Peasants who had been abruptly transplanted into fac-tory surroundings formed these cells spontaneously in order to protect them-selves against the inhuman atmosphere of the big factories.[68]

It was also among the unskilled workers who had recently migrated from the villages and who were unacquainted with the crafts and customs of the guilds that the secret societies obtained most of their recruits—the Green and Red Gangs in Shanghai, and the Lao-chün Society among the tin miners of Szechwan,[69] the workers in the Hanyang arsenal,[70] and the Lunghai rail-waymen.[71] The Hung-ch'iang-hui ("Red Swords Society") of Honan, which was essentially a peasant organization, also found supporters among the Lung-hai railwaymen,[72] as did the Ko-lao-hui ("Society of Seniors and Elders") among the pang formed by the coolies of the Middle Yangtze region.[73]

Government Policies on Trade Unions

The youth and inexperience of the Chinese proletariat partly accounted for the difficulties encountered in trying to form labor organizations, but an added difficulty was the severity of official regulations concerning labor activities. In this respect, there was little to choose between the various Chinese govern-ments, whether Imperial or Republican, and the various authorities established *de jure* or *de facto* by the Foreign Powers on Chinese soil.

Until the Revolution of 1911, the only associations recognized by the Impe-rial government were the traditional guilds (kung-so) and regional societies (hui-kuan). A tolerant attitude seems to have been adopted toward a few of the other types of association (for instance, repressive measures never seem to have been taken against the Tangshan Workers' Club), but the groups mostly led a precarious existence, constantly under the threat of being classed as secret societies or political conspiracies.[74]

For a brief period, the republican revolution brought much greater freedom of action for labor organizations as well as for political factions and parties. Article 6 of the provisional constitution of March 1912 granted the right of association,[75] and we have already seen that a large number of working-class or semi-working-class organizations profited from the new, more liberal measures, particularly in Central China. But this was no more than a lull in the storm, and was accepted with bad grace by Yuan Shih-k'ai and the conservatives. Soon after the assassination of Sung Chiao-jen and the defeat of the "second revolution," repression began. Already in 1912, Article 224 of the provisional penal code imposed severe sanctions on strike leaders: a fine of 300 yuan and fourth-degree detention.[76] In 1914, Section 1 of the law relating to the preservation of public order gave full powers to local authorities to provide police control of workers' meetings, and Section 22 prohibited such meetings altogether if they were likely to lead to a strike, a collective stoppage of work, or wage demands.[77] In 1913 all existing labor organizations, whether political or merely trade associations, were dissolved by government order,[78] and on several occasions, especially under Yuan's dictatorship, strikes were suppressed by the brutal expedient of executing the leaders.[79] The legislation for the mines promulgated by Yuan in March 1914[80] also comes within the general category of repressive measures. It included a provision for a "work book," to be given by the management to every worker that had left the mine, in which the length of time he had been employed, his good and his bad points, and the reason for his departure were to be entered. After Yuan Shih-k'ai's death, all these various laws and regulations (except the last mentioned, which was probably never applied anyway) remained in full force throughout China, and apparently it was still only the traditional organizations such as the guilds and the associations that had sprung directly from them, together with the mutual aid societies and the associations for industrial expansion, none of which were at all militant, that escaped dissolution.

The restoration of the 1912 Constitution in South China in 1917 meant that in principle the right of association was reestablished there, although in fact the right was more or less nominal and was sometimes not recognized. Nevertheless, the situation seems to have been favorable for the development of labor organizations in Canton.[81] However, since industrialization had not advanced very far in the area under the control of the southern government, it was the craft guilds and the trade associations descended from them, rather than trade unionism proper, that benefited most from the greater freedom they now enjoyed.

In those parts of Chinese territory under the control of the Western Powers or of Japan, there was just as little opportunity for labor organizations to develop as in the rest of the country. At the time of the breakup, the agreements regarding railway and mining concessions that were concluded between the Chinese government and the foreign companies concerned included clauses providing for the repression of any labor unrest that might arise. The Franco-Chinese agreements of 1902 and 1903 relating to Yunnan provided for strict control over the Chinese labor force employed and the right of the Syndicat du Yunnan to have its own police force in the mines.[82] Similar clauses appeared in the agreement of 1898 between the Chinese government and the Peking Syndicate, and in that of 1900 with the Schantung Berg-baugesellschaft.[83] The presence in the Treaty Ports and in the Tientsin-Peking area of contingents of foreign infantry and marines enabled the foreign companies—invoking, if necessary, Article 224 of the 1912 Code—to intervene effectively in any labor dispute, especially in the big mining centers. In 1921 and 1922, for instance, British marines took part in repressing the K.M.A. strikes.[84]

In principle, Chinese law was in force within concession territory; so the Land Regulations of the International Settlement of Shanghai referred explicitly to the laws of 1912 and 1914 prohibiting all meetings and publications likely to disturb public order.[85] In the International Settlement a strict watch was kept on any signs of trade union activities, as was noted in the Municipal Gazette in 1920;[86] and when workers' demonstrations were held, the municipal police did not hesitate to intervene just as rapidly and as roughly as any warlord in the interior. On one occasion in April 1917, they fired shots from their revolvers at a meeting of rickshaw men who were protesting against a traffic regulation; one of the demonstrators was killed and the rest were dispersed by a Sikh cavalry charge.[87] The municipal police could be hired by any individual requiring their services at rates that were scaled according to a racial hierarchy.[88]

Cases concerning working-class activities in the International Settlement usually fell within the jurisdiction of the Mixed Court, and in cases involving a national of one of the Treaty Powers, the non-Chinese assessor was automatically chosen from among magistrates of the same nationality.[89] Thus, any foreign firm that was plaintiff in a case concerning a strike, or concerning a person judged to be an "intimidator," had on the bench a fellow countryman whose support could be relied upon. Throughout the 1919–27 period the Mixed Court made full use of Yuan Shih-k'ai's repressive laws, which it considered to be still in force,[90] in order to repress the labor movement not only within Settlement territory but in the whole of the Shanghai urban area, and its role in doing so was an important one.

To some extent, Chinese labor organizations were able to establish themselves on concession territory simply because of the divided responsibility for the administration of the Shanghai urban area as a whole and for the preservation of law and order within it.[91] But owing to cooperation between the Chinese and the concession authorities on repressive measures against the labor movement, the concessions, far from being a haven of peace and tolerance as they have sometimes been depicted, were no more than a temporary refuge. During the 1919–27 period, many militant trade unionists arrested by the municipal police were handed over to the local Chinese authorities.[92]

The only place where the Chinese labor movement enjoyed, at least for the time being, relative security was the island of Hong Kong and its mainland dependent territories, where Chinese associations had a higher status than in China proper. The Hong Kong government regularly published a list of those which were considered to be legal,[93] and also banned those which were thought to have "aims incompatible with the maintenance of peace and order in the colony."[94] But recognition was the rule, and prohibition the exception. There was also no law against strikes, in contrast to China proper. This was a question upon which the British authorities, acting through the Secretary for Chinese Affairs, remained faithful to their empirical traditions. Although it cannot by any means be said that the Hong Kong government was a model of goodwill toward the world of labor during the postwar period,[95] it is nevertheless true that the labor movement of South China, at least during its early stages, did find some degree of freedom of action in the colony. On the other hand, it also came under the moderating influence of the craft guilds and the compradore bourgeoisie there.[96]

Nature and Frequency of Strikes, 1895–1918

Despite the inadequacy of labor organizations and the severity shown by both Chinese and foreign authorities, there had been strikes and movements of protest in China since the end of the nineteenth century. A very incomplete list puts the number of strikes held between 1895 and the end of 1918 as high as 152.[97]

Most of the strikes were a rudimentary form of economic strike held in protest against low wages or against attempts to reduce wages still further. Out of a list of 72 strikes held between 1895 and 1913,[98] 22 were for wage demands, one was in protest against the substitution of piece rates for time rates, and 15 were in protest against reduction of wages, mainly in the Shanghai silk-reeling factories, which were affected by the slump in the Chinese silk industry. Reduction of wages was also the cause of the strikes in the B.A.T. factories in Pootung in 1916 and 1917.[99] Other strikes were held in protest against measures introduced by the management that added to the hardships of factory life. Instances are the Kiangnan arsenal strikes of 1883 and 1890 in protest against longer hours,[100] the strike held in the Shanghai silk factories in 1909 for the same reason,[101] and the 1918 strike in a Japanese cotton mill in Pootung in protest against an increase in the number of mechanical looms each woman worker had to tend.[102] Disputes with Chinese overseers over the introduction of new regulations and complaints about ill-treatment were further causes of strike action, the latter giving rise to 12 strikes between 1895 and 1914.[103] Bad relations between workers and foreign overseers or engineers were yet another, as in the Kaiping mines strike in 1891, caused by a dispute with a British engineer;[104] the strike in the Pingsiang-Anyuan mines in 1915, when allegations were made that a German engineer was inciting the foremen to ill-treat the workers;[105] and the Shanghai rickshaw men's strike in 1911 after one of them had been beaten up by the British police of the International Settlement.[106]

As a rule, strike action was spontaneous, and not something decided upon or terminated by an organization. Occasionally the press, or upholders of traditional attitudes, discovered "leaders" supposedly belonging to secret societies. A man named Liu, who belonged to the Lao-chün Society, was supposed to have started the strike in the Hanyang arsenal in 1913,[107] the Red Gang to have been behind the Pingsiang miners' strike in 1915,[108] and the Green Gang to have directed the Shanghai carpenters' strike (including those employed in modern industry) in 1918.[109] The frequent occurrence of what was known as *ta-ch'ang* ("hitting at the factories") is only one indication of the spontaneous nature of many of these strikes. In April 1905 the mechanics employed in a Japanese cotton mill in Yangtzepoo went on strike in protest against the brutal methods of a Chinese member of the management. The strike soon spread to the rest of the 2,000 employees, and when they were suddenly let loose, the violence that ensued resulted in smashed windows and much damage to furniture and machinery.[110] Riots of this kind also occurred during a strike in a Hankow modern dye-works in 1909, one in a Shanghai silk factory in 1910, and one held in several Japanese cotton mills in Shanghai in 1911. In the last two cases, they were caused by the resentment aroused by the arrests of strike leaders and the penalties inflicted upon them.[111]

This Luddite element in the early stages of the Chinese labor movement was probably due to the fact that there was as yet no sharp dividing line between industrial workers on the one hand and peasants and handicraft workers on the other, so that manifestations of class solidarity on the part of the first still bore traces of the deep-seated hostility toward machines and modern industrial techniques felt by the other two social classes. It is worth noting that it was the skilled craftsmen employed in the Hankow dye-works who launched the strike held in 1909;[112] and in 1905-6, the destruction of recently installed mechanical looms in the textile center of Hsinan, to the west of Canton, was the result of attacks carried out by women weavers from the neighboring villages.[113] There are also reports of physical damage in the Anhwei mines in 1898, and in the Pingsiang mines in 1905, when the workers, in addition to destroying installations in the mines, attacked and wrecked the dwellings of foreign engineers.[114] The Shanghai rickshaw men's strike in 1918 is an even clearer example of the hatred manual laborers harbored against modern techniques that threatened their livelihood. During the strike, large bands of rickshaw coolies attacked the depots of the tramway company, destroying eleven streetcars and wrecking the workshops,[115] because they suspected that the company was behind the recently introduced police control of their vehicles, which had resulted in one of them having his license withdrawn.

It should also be noted that, as far as can be judged, acts of ta-ch'ang seem mainly to have been directed against foreign enterprises established in China, although they are known to have occurred also in both private and state-owned Chinese enterprises. This suggests a link between the early stages of the labor movement and the anti-Western mass movements at the end of the nineteenth century, when machine-wrecking activities, such as the attacks made by the Boxers on the telegraph system of North China, took place; and such a link further suggests that the Luddite trends in the Chinese labor movement were not merely expressions of protest against the new machines that were ruining the traditional economy, as was the case with Luddism in the West at the beginning of the nineteenth century. They were also politically motivated, and were an extension into the twentieth century of earlier manifestations of anti-foreign feelings.

Although a strong sense of working-class solidarity was sometimes displayed during the early efforts at strike action, as is shown by some of the incidents of ta-ch'ang referred to, the Chinese labor movement was nevertheless still as much divided by regional and provincial rivalries as the guilds had been. Often when strikes were held by one regional group of workers, the rest of the workers concerned would refuse to take part. It was only the Cantonese carpenters that went on strike in the Hanyang arsenal in 1896;[116] and when the Shanghai carpenters declared a general carpenters' strike in November 1912, the Wenchow men carried on with their work.[117] Naturally the employers were able to make good use of these rivalries. In Shanghai, they got Ningpo carpenters to replace the Cantonese carpenters when they went on strike in 1911, and at a lower wage rate (0.60 yuan instead of 0.73). The situation was reversed when the Shanghai shipping companies broke the strike of their Ningpo crews in 1914 by employing Cantonese seamen.[118]

Almost all the early strikes met with defeat, whether the issue was one of wages, hours, or ill-treatment of workers. Only nine in the list of 72 strikes between 1895 and 1913 are known to have succeeded, while 38 are either known or presumed to have failed, and the results of the remaining 25 are unknown.[119] Failure was as much due to repression by employers and even more by government as to the inexperience of the strikers or the persistence of regional rivalries. In 17 cases the strike leaders were immediately arrested, and there were nine arrests in the Yingkow oil-pressing mill in 1899, and nine also in the Shanghai silk factories in 1911.[120] In state enterprises such as arsenals, mines, and public services, it was not the police but the army that intervened and carried out a summary execution of the strike leaders. The 1913 strike in the Hanyang arsenal in protest against payment of wages in depreci-ated paper money lasted only a few hours, because Li Yuan-hung, formerly head of the 1911 Provisional Government and subsequently Governor of Hupeh, brought in his troops and had the strike leaders executed. The strikes of the Peking postal workers in 1913 and that of the Pingsiang-Anyuan min-ers in 1915 were ended in the same manner.[121]

Another matter of interest regarding these early strikes is their distribution according to region, branch of industry, and nationality of employers. The main center was the light industry of Shanghai, but other regions, including remote Szechwan and the Northeast region, which had only just begun to be industrialized, were affected to a greater degree than might be expected. (See Map 6.) With regard to branches of industry, strike action occurred to a considerable extent in the mines, the metallurgical industries, and munici-pal services, but it took place chiefly in the textile industry.[122] As to the nation-ality of employers, 25 of the 72 strikes in question were held in enterprises that were either wholly or partially foreign-owned, 35 in private Chinese-owned enterprises, and 14 in enterprises owned by provincial governments or by the state. Clearly the entire working class was on the move.[123]

There were four peak periods of strike action prior to 1919: 1898-99 (10

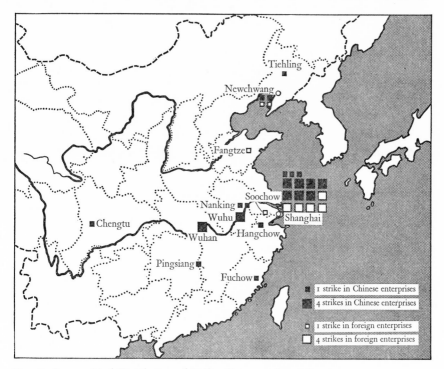

Map 6. Geographical Distribution of Strikes Between 1895 and 1913.

strikes), 1904–6 (15 strikes), 1909–13 (38 strikes), and 1917–19 (46 strikes). (See Table 26.) This shows that even at this early stage of spontaneous and rudimentary strike action, the Chinese labor movement was already very much in tune with political developments in the country. The first peak period, when strikes were held in the big foreign-owned cotton mills and silk-reeling factories of Shanghai and in the Anhwei mines and the Fuchow arsenal, corresponds with the breakup of 1898, K'ang Yu-wei's efforts, and the beginning of the Boxer Rebellion. During the years 1904–6, there was an upsurge of nationalism throughout the whole of Asia, which in China was expressed by the foundation of the T'ung-meng-hui, the anti-American boycott of 1905, and the anti-Manchu rising in Hunan; and it was also during these years that intensified strike action affected not only the Shanghai textile industry, but also the Chengtu arsenal, the Hangchow mint, and the Pingsiang oil-pressing mills. The third peak period, with strikes against the Shanghai silk factories and other enterprises in the city, the Anhwei mines, and (twice) the Hanyang arsenal, came immediately before and during the Revolution of 1911.

The fourth peak period, lasting from 1917 to 1919, merits closer attention, because it clearly indicates that the May Fourth Movement was not something that suddenly came out of the blue, but rather was preceded by a whole series of economic strikes that prepared the Chinese working class for their mass entry upon the political scene. The deterioration in the economic situation of the workers at the end of the First World War was the main cause of the increase in strikes during this period. Another contributory factor was the decline in the power of the central government after Yuan Shih-k'ai's death, which made brutal repression less likely. Although the war years had been a "golden age" for Chinese capitalists, temporarily rid of their Western competitors, they had only made conditions worse for the Chinese proletariat, who had to contend with longer hours, attempts to reduce wages, and a rise in unemployment in the industries dominated by foreign enterprise, which were limping along at a very slow pace.[124] Moreover, as elsewhere in the world,

TABLE 26
Annual Number of Strikes, 1895–1913

Year	Strikes	Year	Strikes	Year	Strikes
1895	2	1902	2	1908	1
1896	0	1903	2	1909	8
1897	0	1904	4	1910	5
1898	5	1905	7	1911	12
1899	5	1906	4	1912	4
1900	1	1907	1	1913	8
1901	1				

prices had risen sharply in China since 1914.[125] In South China, for instance, the price of rice had soared from 5.60 yuan per picul in July 1918 to 10.50 yuan in April 1919.[126]

The growing depreciation of copper currency had a further adverse effect on wages. In Shanghai the silver yuan was worth 130 copper cash in 1913 and 136 in 1919;[127] in Hankow, it was worth 130–40 in 1917, and 138–47 in 1919;[128] and in Shansi, 70 in 1912, 140 in 1915, and 170 in 1920.[129] But wages had not kept pace with this double trend of rising prices and depreciated currency. In Canton, official figures for 1919 show that the wage index was only 106.9 in relation to 100 for 1913.[130] In the spring of 1919 the manager of the Shanghai branch of the Ewo company (a subsidiary of Jardine, Matheson & Company) stated that "the rise in the cost of living will make it necessary for us to review the wage scale for native employees."[131]

The strikes during the wave of strike actions that immediately preceded the May Fourth Movement were still of an elementary economic kind. Fifteen of the 25 declared in 1918 had no aim other than to obtain higher wages or to maintain the existing wage rates, and most of the others were simply the result of bad relations with overseers and management or of dissatisfaction with factory regulations.[132] Action was chiefly centered in Shanghai, where the women employees in the Japanese Jih-hua cotton mill in Pootung went out four times in 1918.[133] But strikes were also held in other parts of China: by the telegraphers[134] and the Ningpo boatmen[135] of Canton, printing workers in Dairen,[136] and weavers in Hangchow.[137] There were also many handicraft workers' strikes, such as those of the Hangchow writing-brush makers,[138] the Soochow tailors,[139] and the Shanghai carpenters,[140] all of which were due to the rise in prices. All these examples are further indications of the worsening situation of the workers.

The strikes of 1917–19 seem to have been much more successful than those of earlier periods, and to have lasted longer (an average of 8.27 days for the 15 for which the duration is known).[141] A survey of those held in Shanghai alone shows that in 1918, 12 of the 19 of which the outcome is known succeeded in having all demands met, and five achieved partial success.[142] And it is perhaps significant that at the beginning of 1919 the big foreign cotton mills in Shanghai found themselves forced to increase the number of their workers by 12–15 per cent.[143]

Influence of the Bourgeoisie and the Intelligentsia

The amount of political experience that the Chinese working class of 1919 had at its command consisted in the main of the experience gained by individual workers who had participated in national politics, since hitherto the working class as a whole had not yet taken action on its own behalf, but had merely provided support for movements directed by other social classes.

Nevertheless, there are plenty of examples of workers' participation in the popular movements of resistance to Western economic and military penetration of China at the end of the nineteenth and the beginning of the twentieth century. The dockers and other Chinese workers of Hong Kong went on strike in September 1884 to protest the arrival of a French ship, *La Galissonière*, that had taken part in Admiral Courbet's attack on Fuchow and now hoped to have repairs made in the British colony. The strike began in the shipyards, but soon spread to the dockers, the coaling-coolies, and the hotel employees, so that the French ship was finally forced to leave and have its repairs made in Japan. In early October, after the Hong Kong government had arrested about a dozen of the dockers, the strike turned into something more in the nature of a riot, in which the Triad society seems to have played a very active part.[144] During the anti-American boycott of 1905 held in protest against the immigration laws prohibiting the entry of Chinese workers into the United States, the dockers of Canton came out in support,[145] as did the workers of Shanghai, Nanking, and Wuhan.[146] The anti-Japanese boycott of 1915, in protest against the Twenty-one Demands, was supported by the dockers of Shanghai as well as by the workers and other employees of the Japanese firms in Changsha; and it is reported that on this occasion workers contributed, even if only in minute amounts, to the funds raised for "national salvation."[147] Nationalist feelings were also to the fore in the strike held in the Hua-hsin cotton mill in Shanghai in 1905 to protest the handing over of the mill to Japan by its owner, Sheng Hsuan-huai, although doubtless the prospect of a resulting reduction in the number of employees also played a part.[148]

With the possible exception of the last example, all these efforts on the part of the proletariat to support nationalist causes were, however, made on behalf of movements led by members of other social classes—specifically, the commercial bourgeoisie and the intelligentsia. A good example is the "Lao-hsi-k'ai affair" in 1916.[149] Lao-hsi-k'ai was a district in Tientsin adjoining the French Concession upon which the French had long cast a covetous eye. On October 20, 1916, French police and troops took it over, arresting nine Chinese policemen in the process. Thereupon a Society for the Preservation of National Rights was formed in Tientsin, in which both merchants and students were very active, and which, at a general meeting held on October 23, decided to submit a demand to the central government asking it to break off commercial relations with France and to prohibit further employment of Chinese workers in French enterprises and the payment of wages in French currency. On November 2, a few days after a student demonstration, about 1,600 workers employed in French enterprises went on strike, all of whom, however, were employed in small concerns such as foundry workshops and rickshaw-rental firms. The strike, which was accompanied by a boycott of French goods, was actively supported by the Chinese Chamber of Commerce in Tientsin and by other groups formed by the local bourgeoisie, who distributed funds and allocations of coal and rice to the strikers. Messages of solidarity came from the Chinese Chambers of Commerce in Kalgan, Hangchow, and Chengtu, from the provincial assemblies of Chekiang and Fukien, and from numerous organizations and notables. The end came when, at the end of November, a Franco-Chinese agreement set up joint control of Lao-hsi-k'ai, operating very much in France's favor.

This incident can be singled out as a forerunner of the big strikes held in Shanghai in June and July of 1925, not only because it provides an early example of common action taken by the workers and the bourgeoisie against the Treaty Powers, but also because the strikers formed a *kung-t'uan* ("workers' corps"), consisting of delegates from the various associations that had gone on strike. This group, which met daily and carried out the distribution of funds, provided an organized, independent leadership similar to that in Shanghai in 1925 and in Canton in 1925–26.

The working class of 1919 also had quite a long tradition of revolutionary struggle against the former Manchu regime and its militarist successors. In 1895, 40 seamen on the *T'ai-an* were arrested for taking part in the abortive attack by the Hsing-chung-hui on the yamen in Canton,[150] and in 1906 approximately three thousand of the Pingsiang, Liuyang, and Liying miners, who were in liaison with the T'ung-meng-hui, rose against the Manchu dynasty in the name of the Republic and of liberty and equality.[151] In 1911 many members of the T'ung-meng-hui were of working-class origin,[152] some of them being tracklayers employed in constructing the Szechwan-Hupeh line[153] and others railwaymen on the Shanghai-Hangchow and Shanghai-Nanking lines.[154] During the republican revolution, the Swatow seamen and dockers,[155] the Hanyang arsenal workers, and the railwaymen of Central China[156] all took part in the fighting against the army and the police of the Manchu government. After the defeat of the "second revolution" of 1913, it was among the workers that Sun Yat-sen recruited some of the most militant members of his new Chung-hua ko-ming-tang ("Chinese Revolutionary Party"), a secret organization with a program that broke completely with the moderate aims of the Kuomintang in 1912 and prepared to adopt extreme methods. Sun counted on the seamen on the big oceangoing vessels to maintain his contacts with wealthy overseas Chinese merchants, and organized a special Overseas Communications Department of the Lien-i-hui ("Society for Justice") which he placed in the charge of Ch'en Ping-sheng, one of his political associates.[157] Soon after, this department was transformed into a seamen's mutual benefit society with its headquarters in Hong Kong,[158] which, however, still retained close relations with Sun Yat-sen's entourage. This seems to have been the time at which Sun's party, aware of its numerical weakness, began to try to gain recruits from the working class, especially in Shanghai.[159] The anti-monarchical "Movement for the Protection of the Country" (Hu-kuo yun-tung) of 1915–16 also found support among the workers, and accounted for the inclusion of political as well as economic demands in the strike held in 1916 by the printing workers employed by the Finance Ministry of the Peking government.[160]

An examination of the various political factions—they can scarcely be called political parties—that sprang up from 1912 onward[161] shows that they at least claim to have had a certain amount of working-class support. Claims of this kind were made by T'an Jen-feng's Liberal Party, by Ch'en Ch'i-mei's Society for the Promotion of Labor,[162] and particularly by Chiang K'ang-hu's Socialist Party. The last, which was mainly concerned with winning seats in the elections and which had some success in the 1913 elections,[163] seems to have enjoyed a certain amount of support from the first railwaymen's organizations formed at this time on the lines in Central and North China,[164] and it published a weekly newspaper.[165] But it disappeared completely after Yuan Shih-k'ai seized dictatorial powers.

After Yuan's death, political factions and organizations began to spring up again, and once again a number of individuals with political ambitions looked toward the labor movement as a fruitful field of action. In Shanghai a student named Hua Hung-t'u founded a Chinese Workers' and Peasants' Federation in 1916,[166] and in 1918–19 Tai Chi-t'ao, an intellectual who was a close friend of Sun Yat-sen, ran a "People's Rights Daily" that called for the formation of a Labor Party.[167] It was, however, chiefly in Canton that Laborism flourished, after the establishment there of the dissident Constitutionalist Military Government in 1917. In that same year an Overseas Chinese Industrial Federation was formed, one of its founders being Hsieh Ying-po, a former member of the old Parliament who had spent several years in the United States after Yuan Shih-k'ai's coup, and had even been a member of the American Socialist Party.[168] This was the Federation that first celebrated Labor Day in China by holding a public meeting attended by about a thousand people in the "Eastern Garden" (Tung-yuan) in Canton on May 1, 1919.[169]

The very existence of these various political organizations shows how important the labor movement had become as a factor in Chinese political life after the Revolution of 1911, and how politicians were beginning to feel that it might be well to gain its support. But, from what little is known of their activities, their political and economic aims, and the social origins and political views of their leaders, they must be regarded not as genuine working-class organizations, but rather as "laborite" groups aimed at using the support of the labor movement in order to further the interests and the muddled aims of other social classes—mainly the Chinese capitalists and petty bourgeoisie. They were as far from being working-class political parties as the mixed associations for "industrial advance" were from being genuine trade unions recruited on a class basis.

Does this mean that in 1919 there was as yet no political organization designed primarily to further the interests of the proletariat as such and launch it upon the political scene? At least there were certain preliminary trends in this direction, such as the Labor Party (Kung-tang), the activities of the anarchists, and the beginnings of Marxist influence.

The Labor Party merits closer attention than any of the other political organizations mentioned above. It was founded in December 1911 by Hsü Ch'i-wen, an intellectual who had been an active member of the T'ung-meng-hui, and Chu Chih-yao, an industrialist who was its first president. In a curious way, it combined the characteristics of a mixed association with those of a specifically working-class one, and if it had not been dissolved, it would no doubt have foundered because of this contradiction.[170] Superficially it resembled the many associations for economic advance that appeared at this time, for the aims expressed in the first two clauses of its statutes were the promotion of China's industrialization and better technical training for workers; and in the manifesto it published on May 1, 1913, shortly before its dissolution, an appeal was made for the formation of cooperatives and the creation of savings banks. The Hunan branch had, in fact, already established a workers' bank, and also a masons' cooperative following upon a masons' strike, while the Shanghai branch had set up a metal workshop. But at the same time the Labor Party presented itself as an organization for the defense of working-class interests, prepared to take part on the side of the workers in the political struggles of the day. Clause 3 of its statutes called for a "lessening of the sufferings of the workers," and Clause 4 for the formation of a workers' corps (*kung-t'uan*) for use in strikes or in political struggle against either civil or warlord governments. Two other clauses advocated the introduction of labor legislation, and recognition of the principle of workers' unity without regard to trade or regional distinctions.[171] In practice, the Labor Party seems to have actively supported, or even organized, strikes such as that of the Shanghai smelters in July 1912, and that of the handicraft workers employed in the manufacture of soya paste. Its leaders also tried to found a workers' hospital and an employment agency, sent a telegram expressing solidarity with the strikers at the Hanyang arsenal in 1913, and in February of that year sent a delegation to the newly elected Parliament with demands for a weekly day of rest, a guaranteed minimum wage, and workers' insurance.

The Labor Party was also the first organization in the history of the Chinese labor movement to operate on what might be called a national scale. It had over 70 local branches, most of them in the Yangtze valley, and representatives of every sector of industry sat on its committees along with the regular committee members. At the National Conference it held in Nanking in November 1912, party membership was said to have reached the figure (no doubt exaggerated) of 400,000.[172] The Hunan and Tangshan branches seem to have been fairly effective. The latter was under the control of the Cantonese in the town, whose efforts in creating a mutual benefit society have already been mentioned, and who, before the republican revolution, had formed workers' associations in support of constitutional reform.[173] The party was banned in May 1913, after its co-founder, Hsü Ch'i-wen, had been arrested and executed for his attempt, with workers' support, to seize the Kiangnan arsenal during the "second revolution." But the Tangshan branch survived for several years, pursuing activities of mutual aid and training.[174]

The anarchist movement, promoted by intellectuals who had returned from France and who were familiar with the ideas of Bakunin and Kropotkin, published several periodicals during 1912, including *Min-sheng* ("The Voice of the People") in Canton,[175] and it undoubtedly had a considerable amount of support among the working class prior to 1919. In Shanghai another anarchist periodical entitled *Lao-tung* ("Labor") came out in 1918, but published only five issues. Its editor was Wu Chih-hui, an intellectual who had spent some time in Paris, and who in 1908 had published an anarchist journal there in Chinese, *Hsin-shih-chi* ("New Century").[176] *Lao-tung* gave prominence to the ideas of Proudhon and Tolstoy, and also featured articles on the Russian October Revolution and on Leninism which, with certain small reservations, were favorably received. It urged workers to celebrate May Day and expounded its significance, and called for a general strike and for a take-over of the factories by the producers. It also expressed support for current Shanghai strikes, such as those of the rickshaw men (including support for the attack on the tramways depots) and the carpenters. It declared itself in favor of the idea of a working-class party (kung-tang), but held that the time was not yet ripe for forming one.[177] In Hunan, at the time when Mao Tse-tung was starting his political career, anarchist ideas were widely held,[178] and in Canton they had penetrated to certain sections of the working class, being upheld in particular by barbers' assistants and teahouse employees.[179] In South China there was even an official Anarchist Party founded by Liu Shih-fu shortly after the Revolution of 1911.[180]

Marxist influence began to be discernible among Chinese intellectual radicals soon after the Russian October Revolution; it was conveyed by articles such as those of Li Ta-chao and Ch'en Tu-hsiu in *Hsin-ch'ing-nien*. Even before 1919 the Chinese exponents of Marxism had taken a practical interest in their country's working class—this class whose important political future they now read in the predictions of their new masters, Marx and Engels. Li Ta-chao was apparently already in contact with the short-lived Socialist Party of Chiang K'ang-hu in 1912.[181] At the beginning of 1919 he had an article published in the Peking daily *Ch'en-pao* on the need for workers' education, and another—an indignant report on the conditions of the Tangshan miners, which he described as "worse than those of mules"—in his own review, *Mei-chou p'ing-lun* ("The Weekly Critic"); and he wrote the editorial for the May 1, 1919, issue of *Ch'en-pao,* which was devoted entirely to Labor Day.[182] The general interest in working-class problems evinced by the entire radical intelligentsia between 1917 and 1919[183] must certainly have been partly responsible for the adoption of Marxist views by the working class, but it is difficult to make any accurate assessment of the extent to which Marxism was a really decisive influence on the May Fourth Movement.[184]

Contacts with Foreign Labor Movements

What did the Chinese working class of 1919 know about the labor movement in the rest of the world? What contacts had it had with ideas and labor organizations in the big industrialized countries, or with international labor organizations? This is a question about which one can only hazard some guesses.

By 1912, the permanent headquarters of the Second International had already made some contacts in China, for instance through members of the American Socialist Party residing in Shanghai. The Brussels office was also in direct contact with Sun Yat-sen, and even sent out a circular to its branches after the republican revolution urging them to pay more attention to affairs in China.[185] But it seems only to have been with certain circles of young intellectuals, and not with members of the working class, that contact was made.

The geographical proximity of Russia and the predominance of Communist influence in the Chinese labor movement throughout the whole of the following period are two arguments in favor of supposing that any outside relations established by the Chinese working class are likely to have been with the October revolutionaries and the recently formed Soviet government. If direct relations were established between the Chinese working class and the Soviet revolutionaries, there are two obvious channels through which contact might have been made: the Chinese workers employed in Russia, and the Russian workers employed on the Tsarist-Russian railways in Northeast China.

The number of Chinese workers employed in Russia, although not as great as the number that went to France at the end of the First World War, probably amounted to several tens of thousands.[186] Apparently some of them took active parts in the civil war there on the side of the Red Army,[187] and in January 1919 a Chinese Workingmen's Association was formed,[188] which Lenin himself regarded as important enough to require his attendance at one of its meetings in that same year.[189] This was probably the association to which the Chinese delegates at the First Congress of the Communist International belonged, since they were said to be representing a Chinese Socialist Workers' Party, and, according to Chicherin, were workers living in Russia.[190] Most of the Chinese workers in Russia returned to their own country during 1919 and 1920, and both the Chinese government and the Western press in China began to spread alarmist reports that, since they must all be well indoctrinated, they would start a Bolshevik revolution in China at the earliest opportunity.[191] Some of them no doubt had been strongly influenced by Russian Communism, and some may even have actually taken part in the revolution.

In June 1920, a Third All-Russian Congress of Chinese Workers was addressed by Bukharin; and at the Second Congress of the Communist International held later in the month, the delegates, after listening to speeches by Kalinin, Chicherin, and Voznesensky, adopted resolutions concerning Chinese workers in Russia, including one dealing with their evacuation from Russia to their homeland.[192] But it is extremely difficult to find out what part was actually played by these workers after their return. Many of them must have talked with other Chinese workers about the events they had witnessed,[193] and some may well have played an active part in starting the Communist movement in China. Yang Ming-ch'ai, for instance, who had worked in Moscow, acted as interpreter to Voitinsky, one of the first Soviet emissaries to visit China, during the winter of 1919–20.[194] However, the only way to assess the extent of the influence they brought to bear would be to make a detailed study of the leaders and active members of the Chinese labor movment at this time and find out how many of them were drawn from the ranks of workers who had returned from Russia.

Between 1917 and 1919 the Chinese employed by the Tsarist-Russian railways, mines, and factories in Manchuria worked side by side with Russians whose outlook and organizations were under strong Bolshevik influence. During this period, despite the fact that White Russians were still in control of the area, several strikes were held in which both Chinese and Russian workers took part, such as the strike in Harbin in May 1918 following upon the murder of a schoolteacher by the henchmen of Ataman Semenov.[195] In August 1917, and again in September 1918, the employees of the Chinese Eastern (Trans-Manchurian) Railway went on strike for higher wages.[196] The main feature of these strikes was the solidarity that seems to have existed between Russian and Chinese strikers.[197] This was true also of a strike held in August 1919 in protest against payment in the depreciated ruble paper currency issued by the Whites, during which there was what amounted to armed combat between soldiers and workers leading to the proclamation of martial law. It is hard to believe that the Chinese workers who took part in these semi-revolutionary strikes were not influenced by their Russian comrades and by their Bolshevik sympathies; but here again there are very few hard facts to support the supposition that Bolshevik influence was transmitted through this channel.[198]

The same difficulty makes it impossible to assess accurately the extent to which the Chinese workers in France (of whom there were nearly 200,000 from 1916 onward)[199] served as a channel of communication between the Chinese labor movement in its early stages and the international labor movement. The numbers involved during that period would surely lead one to suppose that contact of some kind must have been established. The workers concerned were peasants and skilled craftsmen, mostly from Chihli and Shantung, who had been posted to provide personnel for private firms in France working for the War Ministry—companies such as Schneider, Delaunay-Belleville, Forges et Chantiers de la Méditerranée—or for French state enterprises (arsenals, munitions factories), or for the camps, depots, commissariats, and engineer corps of the French army, and also of the American and British armies in France. There were, in all, 87 camps of Chinese workers under French control, seven under British, and twelve under American. In all these camps there was a great deal of discontent about regulations and working conditions, and in 1917 and 1918 a number of strikes and demonstrations were held, some of which became violent and a few of which came very near to being riots. Ch'en Ta reports 13 strikes, six cases of collective insubordination, and three of mutiny.[200] (See Map 7.) After the strike at the Roanne military arsenal in November 1916, the entire corps of Chinese workers employed there was dismissed; and in September 1917, the Chinese coolies employed at Dunkirk refused to dig front-line trenches, insisting that they had been engaged on the understanding that they would not be employed in military operations. Armed with picks and bricks, they put up quite a fight against the

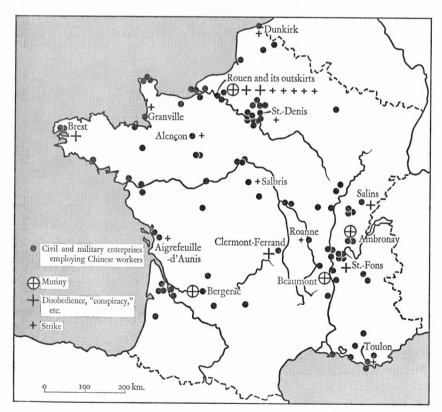

Map 7. Labor Agitation among Chinese Workers in France, 1916–18.

troops that tried to get them to dig the trenches. It was in order to counteract this growing discontent that the Allies called in the Y.M.C.A. in 1918;[201] the Y.M.C.A. proceeded to publish a magazine in Chinese for workers in the camps, organize chess clubs and theater clubs, give lectures, and campaign against gambling and the use of narcotics.

All the Chinese workers who had served with the British and American armies returned to their own country at the end of the war, and so did many of those who had worked in French factories and army services. Their return caused something of a stir in China. For instance, in March 1919 the nine hundred workers brought back on the *André Lebon* marched down the Avenue Joffre in the heart of the French Concession of Shanghai.[202] But was the actual role they played in subsequent events as important as a spectacular demonstration of this kind would lead one to expect? Some writers thought that it was, saluting these returned workers as "the stormy petrel of the Chinese labor world,"[203] or as forming "a solid and energetic nucleus" in the new Chinese labor organizations.[204] Most of them, however, were simply peasants who had managed to save enough from the meager wages and allowances they had received in France[205] to enable them to realize the cherished ambition of every Chinese peasant—namely, to buy a little land—and these returned to their native villages.[206] Others among these returned workers no doubt sank immediately into the lower depths of city life and joined the ranks of the underemployed.[207] The association that was formed in September 1919 among the returned workers who were better off remained very much on the fringe of the Chinese labor movement.[208] Must one therefore exclude the hypothesis that a certain amount of influence was exerted by workers who may well have been in contact with minority groups of the Socialist Party and the C.G.T. in France, and who may have witnessed or taken part in the strikes held there at the end of the war? Here again only after a detailed study of individual cases can any assessment be made of the extent of the influence they exerted. Certainly some Western employers in China at the time did not doubt that it existed.[209]

There is much less doubt about the political and ideological influence exerted by the "worker-students" who went to France in order to widen their political horizons and to acquaint themselves with modern industrialized society. Under the guidance of the educator Ts'ai Yuan-p'ei, the first "Work and Study Groups" were formed in Paris as early as 1915 and 1916.[210] These activities were expanded during the summer of 1918, and it was then that Ts'ai Ho-sen, the future leader of the Chinese Communist Party, and Mao Tse-tung formed an organization for sending young Hunanese to France for "work and study." Those in this second wave of Chinese visitors to France were initiated into Marxism, and from 1916 on, they spread propaganda among the Chinese workers who had remained in France to work in private French firms. On their return to China, the students played an important part in the formation and growth of the Chinese Communist Party in 1920–25.[211]

To give a complete account of possible channels of contact between the Chinese working class of 1919 and the international labor movement one would have to look in other directions as well. In Japan, for instance, a socialist and trade union movement of considerable size had flourished since before the First World War and may have exerted some influence in China through the many Japanese workers and overseers in the Northeast, especially in Dairen and Tsingtao.[212] Great Britain has to be considered also, since the workers of Hong Kong, especially the seamen, had at least indirect contact with the British;[213] and the Chinese students and intellectuals who went to the U.S. must be noted as well.[214] But none of these various contacts seems to have had any decisive influence on the Chinese labor movement. At the very most, they were a subsidiary factor, occasionally an important one but usually of very minor importance. The sudden upsurge of the Chinese labor movement in 1921–23 was due primarily to internal developments within the Chinese working class itself. This process of development was precipitated by the one outside influence that really did play a decisive role, namely that of the Soviet revolution mediated by Chinese radical intellectuals. It was to the sound of its salvos that Marxism and Communism began to penetrate China prior to 1919.

CONCLUSION TO PART I

To sum up, then, the Chinese working class of 1919 was in many respects similar to the proletariat of all the other countries that, one after another, had followed Britain and France along the path of the industrial revolution. It was directly involved in the economic system and the advanced techniques introduced by industrialization. It was also highly concentrated within a few regions that were centers of development for modern industry, and again, within these regions, in vast enterprises employing hundreds, thousands, or tens of thousands of both male and female workers—such places as the Shanghai cotton mills and silk-reeling factories, the Tangshan mines, the Tientsin tobacco and match factories, the railways, and the merchant shipping lines.

Unlike the craftsmen of former times, the new industrial workers were no longer the owners of the instruments of production or of the product of their labor. All they had to sell was their own physical strength; and the permanent presence of a large labor reserve, consisting of peasants who had had to leave the land because of the agrarian crisis and of the unemployed in the cities, had an adverse effect on working conditions. As a result, they had to endure long hours, the imposition of corporal punishment and fines, deplorable health and safety conditions, and the strict discipline of foremen and overseers, in return for a wage that was barely sufficient—and in some cases simply insufficient—to keep them from starvation. It was the workers who had to shoulder the weight of the whole capitalist system of production.

The Chinese industrial proletariat was able, like that of other countries in recent times, to make a sudden and disturbing entry upon the political scene, its numerical weakness being more than compensated for by its high degree of geographical and industrial concentration and by its direct involvement with the most advanced sectors of the Chinese economy, which were the sectors that were of vital importance, both financially and politically, to those who wielded power in China. This made the activities of the proletariat as a group extremely effective, and even its poverty left it with "nothing to lose but its chains." Finally, since the only way Chinese industrial workers could earn their living was by the sale of their labor power, they were in no position to derive any advantage from the economic situation or to make profits at the expense of another social class. Everything therefore contributed to make them a revolutionary class par excellence.

Thus the Chinese industrial proletariat in the twenties was completely differentiated, because of its new economic status, from the social classes from which it had been recruited: the poor peasants, the skilled craftsmen, and the urban populace. It had undergone a qualitative change. Common experience of industrial work had welded its composite elements together to form a new social force that was quite alien to older Chinese traditions.

Unique Features of the Chinese Proletariat

Although the Chinese proletariat was similar to that in other countries, it nevertheless had certain distinctive features. For one thing, it was a new movement composed of young members. In 1919 most industrial enterprises had been in existence for less than 15 years, and very few of the workers were second-generation workers.[215] The labor movement was thus gravely lacking in experience and tradition, and had no memories to serve as inspiration such as the peasants had in the Taiping or French workers in the Commune.

This young proletariat was still in the process of forming. Its lower ranks were swollen with marginal elements that were as yet barely differentiated from the urban populace and the peasantry and not yet acclimatized to industrial work or fully class-conscious; and the low degree of skill required by the industries, as well as the manner in which the industrial enterprises of the time had to operate, further contributed to this hypertrophy of its more unstable elements. On the other hand, it lacked, in its upper ranks, the kind of labor elite that was becoming important in the industrialized countries in the West, but which in China either had atrophied or had not yet developed. Skilled workers such as the mechanics in the big modern enterprises or certain categories of printers were the exception rather than the rule. This lack of a labor elite was due in part to the very nature of the Chinese proletariat, but also to the fact that in China, contrary to what had happened in the West, the employers had made no efforts to extend the internal market for the consumer goods produced by raising the purchasing power of the workers. Chinese employers might occasionally have thought of paying higher wages,[216] but they were not in a position to do so because of the permanent disadvantages they suffered vis-à-vis their foreign competitors, and also because of the restricted and unstable nature of the internal market. Very few foreign employers had any intention of following such a wage policy.[217] Indeed, British and Japanese industrialists, backed by the big banks in Hong Kong, London, and Tokyo, remained quite indifferent toward the economic development of China as a whole, and with regard to the question of wages usually contented themselves with remarks such as "The workers are not interested in working shorter hours because they do not know what to do with their time outside working hours," or "If women's wages are raised, their husbands will refuse to work," or "The Chinese worker is happy and the children sing on their way to work."[218]

All these features peculiar to the Chinese proletariat—its youth, its instability, its swollen lower ranks, and its lack of a fully developed labor elite— were a direct consequence of the historical situation in which it had arisen, and of the social and political circumstances in which it now operated.

It was steeped in the customs of former days. There was no free labor market properly speaking. Precapitalist labor relations still predominated, as shown by the preponderance of practices such as the contract-labor (pao-kung) and industrial apprenticeship systems, and the persistence of customary ties between free labor and foremen. The corporate traditions of the guilds and the regional loyalties—which were inherited from the times when capitalist production had not yet supplanted small-scale mercantilist enterprise, and a national market had not yet come into being—were still very much alive. Finally, the proletariat was still in the main up against the same opponents it had had to face during the imperial regime. The militarists and the rural gentry still dominated the central and provincial governments, which employed large numbers of workers, including railwaymen, arsenal employees, miners, and workers employed in the enterprises owned by the Hunan provincial government.[219] And in general, throughout the whole of Chinese territory, except for the concessions and the foreign special status areas, the labor movement came up against legislation and a state system that were still semi-feudal. Because the state lacked experience in handling the threat presented by the labor movement the workers were able to make rapid advances in 1921–23, but in the end they came up against brute force, as they had in the time of Yuan Shih-k'ai.

At the same time, the new Chinese proletariat had to cope with the fact that it belonged to a "semi-colonial" country already deeply penetrated by foreign interests. Almost half the workers were employed by foreign firms and had to deal with foreign managers, as on the railways and in the Post Office, or else, like the rickshaw men in the concessions, they were under the control of foreign administrative authorities and police. Moreover, within certain limited but highly industrialized areas such as the International Settlement of Shanghai, the territory controlled by the S.M.R., and the Wuhan concessions, these foreign administrative authorities proved themselves to be determined opponents of strikes and of militant trade unionism, and were all the more formidable because they had at their disposal their own armed forces and repressive mechanisms (such as the Mixed Court of Shanghai), as well as long experience acquired in dealing with the working class in their own countries. (This was especially true in the case of the British and the Japanese.) For all sections of the proletariat that, one way and another, came into conflict with the foreigners, the economic struggle immediately became tied up with the nationalist struggle. On the other hand, the very presence of the Foreign Powers, with their armed forces and their administrative machinery, appreciably affected the "natural" play of political forces in China, since in the big industrial centers the proletariat had to deal not only with the feudal gentry and the compradore bourgeoisie, but also with this other, and often more powerful and more experienced, opponent. This was a situation that did not exactly increase the chances of success for the labor movement, so long, at least, as revolutionary strategy was based on the belief that control of the big urban centers was the main and immediate objective and the peasants a mere "rearguard" in the fight.[220]

Nevertheless, although the Chinese working class of 1919 had a triple burden to bear—capitalist exploitation, a semi-feudal system of government, and domination by the Foreign Powers—it enjoyed one advantage: the fact that the whole body of employers was deeply divided within itself. The labor movement lost no opportunity of exploiting these divisions.

Conditions of employment, and even more, relations between capital and labor, varied greatly as between the foreign-owned, the state-owned, and the Chinese privately owned sectors of industry. The pao-kung system, for instance, was much more widespread in state- or foreign-owned enterprises, whereas even in the larger enterprises in the Chinese private sector something remained of the customary ties found in the guilds. Working conditions were probably worse in the foreign-owned enterprises, where the relentless rhythms of modern mechanized industry swept away the fairly free and easy atmosphere and the tolerant attitude toward hours of work and speed of production that characterized even some of the modern Chinese enterprises. Moreover, the foreign enterprises, with their high concentration of capital and machinery that enabled them to pursue coherent and vigorous policies,[221] were backed by the political and military strength of the Foreign Powers in China.[222] The privately owned Chinese enterprises, on the other hand, offered the area of least resistance in the employers' front, since they were weakest in financial resources and thus least able to stand out against a prolonged strike, and could not always be certain of the support of the police or of the armies of the war-lords, with whom they were not on good terms. Relations were good between the foreigners and the Chinese authorities, and they often acted together to counteract advances made by the labor movement;[223] but the situation was very different for the Chinese private employers, who were opposed, politically and economically, both to the foreigners and to the forces of the old order. These contradictions were severe enough to make them try to avoid becoming involved in labor conflicts that did not directly concern them, and even at times express open sympathy with the cause of the workers.[224]

The survival of these archaic features differentiated the Chinese industrial proletariat from its mid-nineteenth-century Western counterpart. Their inter-action with the forces of modern development created a situation as complex and unique as that of China as a whole.

Concentration in Major Industrial Regions

As we have seen, the Chinese working class of 1919 was split up into several big population clusters that were hundreds of miles apart from each other, and the six main industrial regions varied widely in such matters as the balance between light and heavy industry, the proportion of women and children employed, the stability of the labor force, the extent of working-class experi-ence in social and political struggles, and the relations between labor and the various sectors of Chinese and foreign capital. There were thus marked re-gional differences, in 1919, within the Chinese working class as a whole.

In the Northeast, where mining and heavy industry predominated, a neg-ligible amount of female and child labor was employed in the big Japanese enterprises, and the workers were for the most part simply temporary mi-grants. This was a region that had not begun to be industrialized until the very end of the nineteenth century, where there was very little Chinese capital investment and no guild traditions among the workers, and where there was no intelligentsia to help in the formation of labor organizations. The workers had no experience of strike action or political struggle; yet it was these inex-perienced and unseasoned workers who found themselves in conflict with Japanese authorities and employers.

The Chihli region, on the other hand, was one where light industry pre-dominated, and where many women and children were employed in the textile mills and the tobacco and match factories; but it was also one in which miners and railwaymen were the most active participants in the labor move-ment. Craft traditions were not strong here, and many of the workers were scarcely differentiated from the peasants in the surrounding villages. Nor was there much Chinese capitalist investment in this region, which until the nine-teenth century had lagged far behind the southeastern provinces in economic development. But the proximity of Peking, the foremost intellectual and university center in China, meant that there was a constant supply of young and ardent sympathizers ready to help in organizing trade unions. Peking was, however, also the seat of the central government, and therefore a place that all the rival military factions wished to capture; thus the city was well guarded by a large concentration of the Chinese armed forces as well as by contingents of the armed forces of the Foreign Powers, who were authorized to station them in the surrounding neighborhood. The labor movement had, therefore, just as little chance of developing here as in the Northeast.

In Shantung, where the mines and the railways were as important as the light industries of Tsinan, Tsingtao, and Chefoo, the situation of the working class was more or less the same as in Chihli, except that probably less female and child labor was employed. Japan, established in the province since 1914, held the same dominant position here as it did in the Northeast, and Chinese capitalist investment was of very minor importance.

All three of these regions differed from each other in a number of respects; but all of them, in 1919, were regions where the labor movement had so far been unable to make any impact, apart from a few exceptions such as the Tangshan Workers' Club, because the workers there all lacked craft traditions and were inexperienced both in industrial techniques and in methods of labor organizing. It will subsequently be seen that this backwardness of the northern regions was never really overcome, except in the case of the railwaymen.

It was in the three southern regions (those of Hupeh-Hunan, Shanghai, and Canton–Hong Kong) that the labor movement made the most notable advance from 1919 onward. Here, from the time of the republican revolution or even before, the first labor organizations were formed, the first strikes were held, the first labor martyrs fell, and for the first time the workers became politically motivated. But here, too, there were marked regional differences in the situation of the workers and in the success of the labor movement.

The Shanghai and lower Yangtze region, China's main industrial center, was one where light industry predominated and where much use was made of female and child labor in the cotton mills and the silk-reeling, tobacco, and match factories. Shanghai itself was as lacking in craft traditions as the Northeast, since in 1842 it had been no more than a large village. Its working-class population was drawn from all over the country, and, being very mixed, afforded plenty of opportunity for regional rivalries. Because it was far larger than the working-class population of any other city in China, it had great potential strength, but it was difficult to organize, not only because of its size, but also because of the complex administrative system of the Shanghai metropolitan area. It was not until the mass struggles of 1925–26 that the trade unions here really began to solve their problems of organization.

Shanghai was where Chinese capitalist enterprise was at its most vigorous, and its entrepreneurs tried to gain support among the working class for their industrial and political ventures; it was also an important intellectual center, full of lively students who were already deeply influenced by new ideas and ready to play an active part in social struggles. But it was at the same time the place where the big foreign financial interests were centered and the principal military base of the Foreign Powers in China, so that labor unrest was more swiftly dealt with than elsewhere, either directly by the foreigners or through the medium of the compradore bourgeoisie, as in the summer of 1925 and the spring of 1927. Because Shanghai was the main working-class center, the main center of the Chinese bourgeoisie, and the main base of the foreigners, the fate of mass movements there decided their fate on a national scale, at least during the period when the struggle was centered in the cities. It is significant that the period studied here begins with the Shanghai workers' strikes in June 1919, which were decisive for the May Fourth Movement, and ends with the attack on the Shanghai trade union militias that brought about the break between the labor movement and the right wing of the Kuomintang.

Four main features distinguished the Hunan-Hupeh region: it was one of the earliest industrial centers in China, dating from the time when Chang Chih-tung was viceroy at the end of the nineteenth century; it had a balance between light and heavy industry that was quite exceptional at that time; it contained a much larger number of enterprises owned by the state or by the provincial government than existed anywhere else; and it was farther away than the other regions from the main bases of the Foreign Powers. It was a region where more men were employed than women and children, where Chinese capitalist enterprise was very active, and where the old scholar-official traditions of Hunan survived in a large and influential intelligentsia who took part in provincial affairs. It was here that the labor movement had its first outstanding successes in organizing trade unions and strikes, and where it withdrew after the setback in the spring of 1927 in order to reorganize its forces.

The last of the six regions, Kwangtung, had a number of distinguishing characteristics. Here modern industry was far less developed than elsewhere. Small workshops and semi-modernized factories predominated, and guild traditions were probably stronger than anywhere else in the whole of China. Furthermore, there was very little foreign capital investment in this region, apart of course from Hong Kong, with which the Cantonese bourgeoisie had close ties. There was less employment of female and child labor than in Shanghai. Although the Cantonese working class proved better able to organize itself than that of any other region, this was because of its guild traditions, which for many years provided an obstacle to the unity of the labor movement in general.

Thus in each of these industrial regions in China, the chances of success, and the factors accounting for the failures of the labor movement, were different, and one of the outstanding features of the workers' struggles during the period in question was the way they took on a different character, and had a different timing, in each of the six regions. It was only at a much later date—and even then incompletely—that the labor movement achieved some degree of national unity.

But these regional differences must not be allowed to overshadow the fact that the Chinese working class, despite its youth and its unstable character, was by 1919 already united by the hardships endured in common by all its members, and was preparing to play a leading part in the political and economic struggles that shook Chinese society between 1919 and 1927.

PART II

The Rise of the Labor Movement
1919–1924

CHAPTER VII

The May Fourth Movement and After

When, on May 4, 1919, news reached Peking of the Versailles Peace Conference proposal that the former German bases and rights in Shantung be handed over to Japan, it so shocked the students at the capital and Chinese public opinion as a whole that a wave of political agitation was started that swept the entire country on a scale never known before.[1] Three thousand students demonstrated in front of the T'ien-an Gate, demanding that the Chinese delegation refuse to sign the treaty and calling for the return of Tsingtao to China, the abolition of the Twenty-one Demands, the boycott of Japanese goods, and the resignation of the pro-Japanese ministers in Tuan Ch'i-jui's cabinet. They beat up Chang Tsung-hsiang, a former Chinese ambassador to Japan, and set fire to the house of the notoriously pro-Japanese Minister of Communications, Ts'ao Ju-lin.

The "May Fourth Movement" spread rapidly, affecting students, intellectuals, politicians, and businessmen in all the provinces of China. The "Shantung Question" crystallized the nationalist sentiments that for the past few years had been finding more and more vociferous expression among members of the Chinese bourgeoisie as their hostility increased toward the militarist and conservative forces in power after Yuan Shih-k'ai's coup in 1913. Students' strikes and demonstrations became widespread. Chambers of commerce, educational and industrial associations, provincial assemblies, and regional friendly societies (hui-kuan) made their position clear by communications to the press, telegrams sent to Paris or Versailles, and public meetings; and in all these communications they all reiterated the demands made by the students of Peking. In Shanghai a meeting was held on May 7, called by 57 associations and groups of various kinds.[2] Nor was this sudden and unprecedented outburst of activity on a national scale restricted to merely academic protests; a systematic boycott of Japanese goods was proposed, since patriotic support for the integrity of national territory was, for the Chinese bourgeoisie, a matter of direct self-interest. In the middle of May organization of the boycott was started in the main ports[3] with the participation of the "Groups of Ten for National Salvation,"[4] an organization that had sprung up spontaneously, and one in which students played a very active part. Members of these groups swore an oath declaring not only that they would themselves refrain from using Japanese goods, but that they would also try to persuade others to do the same and, if necessary, would engage in direct action in the docks and the shops.

Even at this initial stage of the movement quite a large number of workers took part in both the demonstrations and the boycott. In Peking, a big meeting of workers who were natives of Shantung was held on May 11; and in Tsinan many workers attended an open-air meeting of protest on May 22.[5] In Nanchang, a meeting held on May 9, attended by several thousand people including a large number of workers, gave its support to the idea of a workers' strike and the closing of shops.[6] Dockers and rickshaw men were of course among the first to be involved in the anti-Japanese movement, and the dockers refused to handle Japanese goods,[7] just as the Hangchow rickshaw men refused, on May 25, to transport Japanese nationals.[8] In addition, many workers —notably those in Changsintien—joined the "Groups of Ten" and swore the oath;[9] and in Hunan nearly four hundred such groups combined to form a provincial federation.[10]

Nevertheless, the Peking government did not allow itself to become intimidated. It retained in office Ts'ao, Chang, and a third pro-Japanese minister who had handed in his resignation shortly after May 4; and it arrested the most active among the students, as well as leaders of radical opinion in the universities such as Ch'en Tu-hsiu. As a result, the movement entered a new phase at the beginning of June, marked not only by a further spread of demonstrations and of the boycott, but also by the outbreak of workers' and tradesmen's strikes. When the news reached Shanghai that four hundred Peking students had been imprisoned, tens of thousands came out on strike there during the days following June 6, and Chinese shops in the concessions and the Chinese districts were closed.[11]

The Shanghai strikes affected the cotton mills of Yangtzepoo, the Kiangnan arsenal, a number of foundries and mechanical workshops, the docks (where both dockers and seamen came out), the Shanghai-Nanking and Shanghai-Hangchow railway lines, telegraph and telephone companies, the foreign and Chinese-owned tramways, the waterworks, the Commercial Press, the B.A.T. factories, and the storage depots of Standard Oil and of the East Asia Company. Many of the craft guilds also took part, including those of the blacksmiths, the weavers, the tinsmiths, the painters, and the building workers.[12]

At first glance, these strikes give the impression of having been sudden and spontaneous. In each concern, they were initiated by the zealous few who persuaded the rest to follow suit. The French Tramways strike was decided upon at a meeting held in the offices of the company, and that of the printers of Chinese newspapers was planned at secret meetings held in neighboring tea-houses.[13] The strike at the Heng-feng cotton mill in Yangtzepoo followed a mass meeting held on June 6, at which it was decided to boycott Japanese goods and to appoint a delegate to represent the employees if necessity arose.[14] Similarly, the seamen met at the offices of the mutual aid society of the Chün-an Seamen's Guild and drew up a communication to the press announcing that they were going on strike.[15]

Closer scrutiny reveals, however, that behind these strikes, which were without precedent in Shanghai's history, lay the beginnings, at least, of concerted organized action. The traditional craft guilds organized or supported strikes not only in workrooms or shops where craftsmen were employed,[16] but also in modern enterprises where the skilled workers were members of a guild. The Metalworkers' Guild organized the strikes in the waterworks, the railways, and the Chinese Tramways.[17] A mixed organization known as the Association for the Advance of Young Workers launched the Commercial Press strike, and also organized teams of young workers to disseminate propaganda in the streets of Chapei.[18] Even the secret societies—the Green and Red Gangs—declared themselves in favor of the strikes, and threatened nonstriking members with reprisals.[19]

The Labor Party (Kung-tang), which had recently reappeared in Shanghai after its dissolution in 1913, published an appeal to workers urging them to form "workers' groups," either large or small, in preparation for a mass parade. This appeal was signed not only by two of the party leaders, but also by eleven craftsmen of various kinds, two dockers, two rickshaw coolies, and workers employed in the metallurgical, tobacco, cotton, and silk-reeling industries.[20] The many semi-working-class associations for "industrial advance" that had recently been formed in Shanghai, such as the Society for the Study of Industry and Commerce[21] and the Industrial Federation,[22] also came out in favor of the strikes; and the Industrial Society, which had already signed the appeal made at the meeting on May 7 called by 57 organizations, convened a workers' meeting on June 11, which was chaired by one of its leaders, Wu Ts'an-huang, and which debated the idea of extending the boycott, appealed for financial aid for the strikers from the guilds and the chambers of commerce, and reaffirmed the nationalist aims of the strikes.[23]

Yet all of this organized action, except perhaps that of the Kung-tang, was carried out by organizations that despite their influential position among the working class were primarily representative of other social classes; indeed it seems quite clear that, although at times working-class participation in the May Fourth Movement may have been a spontaneous affair, it was in the main mobilized, just as proletarian political activities in the preceding period had been, in support of the interests of these other social classes. The working class was not yet, and could not yet have been, in a position to organize in defense of its own interests and to deal with its allies on equal terms.

When the All-China Industrial Federation was formed in Shanghai on June 5 in protest against the arrest of the Peking students, the active groups were those of the merchants, journalists, and students, with labor organizations playing a very minor role.[24] Further confirmation of the subordinate role of the workers is provided by the slogan written on the banner carried through the streets by the young workers of the Commercial Press: "We comrades from the world of labor want to march in step with the merchants and the students."[25] *Hou-tun* ("rearguard") was an expression often applied to the workers who took part in the May Fourth Movement.[26] The employers, who were behind all the activities of the organizations for "industrial advance" and of the guilds, seem to have taken every measure to ensure that the role of the proletariat remained subordinate. This intent is evident in the words of declaration issued by the Metalworkers' Guild on June 11 that launched the strikes in the various modern enterprises where the guild's members were employed: "The workers form the rearguard of the merchants and the students, but let us maintain public order and avoid the outbreak of disturbances."[27] The workers themselves, in their strike communiqués and at meetings held in June, merely reiterated the demands already formulated in May by the Chinese bourgeoisie, namely, the return of Shantung to China, the dismissal of the pro-Japanese ministers, and the boycott of Japanese goods, to which, since June 6, had been added the demand that the imprisoned students be released.[28] They apparently never reached the point of making either economic or political demands affecting the proletariat as such.[29]

The Shanghai workers' strikes ended on June 12, immediately upon the Peking government's dismissal of the three pro-Japanese ministers whom the students had attacked on the very first day of the movement. These strikes were the most important but not the only contribution made by the Chinese working class during this great wave of national indignation. The railwaymen of Changsintien and Tangshan also organized demonstrations and took part in the anti-Japanese boycott.[30] On June 1 the coolies and street-porters of Canton had taken part in the destruction of stocks of Japanese goods,[31] and on June 10 several workers' and merchants' organizations met together at the Canton offices of the Overseas Chinese Industrial Federation to organize a campaign in support of "national products" (*kuo-huo*).[32] The dockers of Amoy, the rickshaw men of Nanking and Tientsin, and the dockers and seamen of Kiukiang refused to transport Japanese nationals or goods.[33] On June 10 there were strikes in the Hangchow factories and among the Tangshan miners.[34] On June 14 a meeting was held in Tsinan at which a decision was reached to call a strike in the Japanese-owned enterprises there;[35] and on June 25 there was a mass parade in Changsha in which organizations such as the federated printers' union, formed several months earlier, took part.[36]

What was entirely new about the May Fourth Movement was that for the first time in the history of modern China certain sections of the bourgeoisie, the intellectuals, the craftsmen, and the industrial proletariat all joined together to take common action in protest against China's subjection to the Foreign Powers. This was the first time such a protest had been made, and also the first time a stand had been made against the conservative forces that had been in power since 1913. Thus the "Shantung Question" and the dismissal of the three ministers possessed a wider significance; and there can be no doubt that the participation of the workers in the May Fourth Movement (and in particular, the wave of strikes in June, however minor a role they may have played in the movement as a whole) contributed considerably toward forcing the Peking government to give way more quickly than it would have if it had merely had to contend with students' demonstrations. Not only

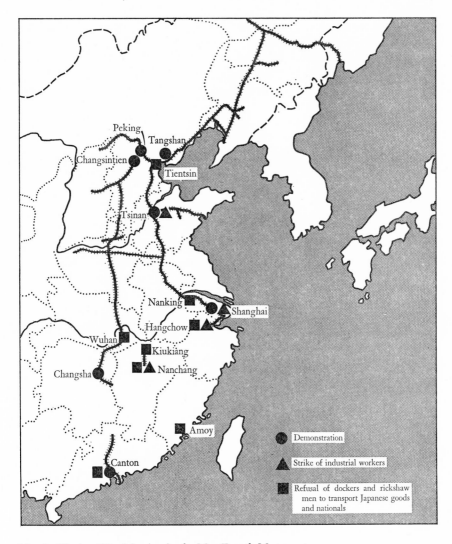

Map 8. Workers' Participation in the May Fourth Movement.

were the ministers dismissed, but the Chinese delegation at the Versailles Conference refused to sign the treaty. It is true that for the time being nothing further was achieved. The liquidation of the conservatives and the restoration of China as a sovereign power had to wait until 1924–25, when the Shanghai and Canton strikes took place after the Kuomintang had been reorganized and an alliance had been formed between the working class, the national bourgeoisie, the craftsmen and petty traders, and the intelligentsia. But the events of May 4, 1919, and the workers' strikes and demonstrations that followed (see Map 8), were by no means simply an episode without further consequence for the labor movement, for not only did the struggle become wider in the ensuing months and years, but there was also a steady growth of organizations—especially in Shanghai—relying partly, or wholly, on workers' support.

The Strike Wave of 1919–21

From June 1919 to July 1921, when with the founding of the Communist Party a new stage was reached in the Chinese labor movement, the wave of economic strikes that had begun to gather momentum in 1917–18 became more widespread and grew in intensity, affecting all regions and all branches of industry.[37] In Shanghai it affected the Chinese and Japanese cotton mills and other Japanese textile factories, metallurgical works, the B.A.T. factories, the dockers of Pootung and Yangtzepoo, the silk-reeling factories, and the French tramways. In the South it involved the mechanics of Canton and Hong Kong, the railwaymen of Kwangtung, the Hong Kong printers, the Canton telephone employees, and the coal-transport coolies; and in North and Central China, the K.M.A. miners, the railwaymen of Nanking, the metalworkers of the Hanyehping Company, the postal workers of Dairen, and the rickshaw men of Hankow.[38]

Most of these strikes were of an elementary economic kind, the same protests against the high cost of living as had been made in 1917–18. Of the 46 strikes mentioned in 1920 by Ch'en Ta, 36 were for a raise in wages or against a reduction in wages.[39] If the figures for the number of strikes per month in Shanghai are compared with those for the rise in the price of rice, it can be seen that these strikes were held simply in order to get enough to eat. The next most important cause of strikes was conflict between workers and management, which accounted for the K.M.A. miners' strike in May 1921, that of the railwaymen on the southern section of the Chin-P'u line in June 1921,[40] and the B.A.T. strike in July 1921.[41] Sometimes a strike was held to protest oppressive factory regulations, as in the B.A.T. factory in 1920,[42] or, more rarely, in demand for an eight-hour day, as in the case of the Hong Kong printers[43] and the Canton mechanics[44] in the spring of 1921.

The strikes of 1919–21, especially those held in protest against low wages and the high cost of living, were to some extent successful. Wages increased appreciably during this period: by 10 to 15 per cent in the cotton mills of Shanghai,[45] 10 to 40 per cent among the mechanics of Canton,[46] and 20 per cent in the French Tramway Company of Shanghai.[47] A typical instance of the effectiveness of these strikes is afforded by what happened in the spring of 1920 in Shanghai, when an abrupt rise in the price of rice, due to a bad harvest in the Lower Yangtze valley and subsequent speculation, evoked a wave of protest. In December 1919 rice was 7.40 yuan a picul, and the price rose to 8.80 in March 1920, 9.00 in May, 10.40 in June, and 14.00 in July.[48] A series of strikes broke out in the Shanghai silk factories, cotton mills, and metalworks, and also among craftsmen; and by the end of June there were 8,800 out on strike in the International Settlement.[49] A raise in wages of from 10 to 20 per cent was then fairly generally granted, and the bigger firms made their own arrangements for the supply of rice to their employees. The Nanyang tobacco company imported rice at its own expense from South China;[50] and the Pootung shipyards paid half the agreed increase in wages in rice.[51]

The raise in wages was clearly the result of the strike wave of 1919–21 and of the militancy so often shown by the workers; but no doubt the relative shortage of labor at the time, at least in Shanghai, helped the strikers to press home their demands. Not only had Western firms resumed their activities in China after the end of the First World War, but Chinese industrialists, who had come into their own during the war, were continuing to expand theirs. In the Yangtze valley, for instance, 53 factories of various kinds, 16 cotton mills, and 26 electricity plants had sprung up between 1919 and 1920;[52] and in Shanghai 42 new factories, 16 of which belonged to the textile industry, were built in 1921.[53] Despite the fact that there was always a certain amount of underemployment, it was not always easy to recruit the labor required for this or that particular factory. This began to create some uneasiness among foreign business circles in Shanghai, which was reflected in an editorial of their principal organ, the *North China Herald,* complaining of the difficulties of finding labor in Shanghai just at a time when business was booming and expressing the hope that the city would soon become again "the happy hunting ground for casual labour."[54]

Another feature of the 1919–21 strikes was that most of them were spontaneous, suddenly decided upon at the prodding of a few of the more determined workers. When the employees of the French Tramway Company of Shanghai went on strike in March 1921, they handed in a long list of demands that had been worked out at meetings held in teahouses in the neighborhood, as well as asking for a raise in wages.[55] And spontaneous action of this kind, as soon as victories were won, seemed to spread from one factory, or one region, to another. Thus in January 1920, strikers at a Japanese cotton mill in Shanghai demanded an annual bonus (hua-li) because it had recently been obtained by the workers in British-owned mills;[56] and the strike of the Tangshan miners in June 1920, the immediate cause of which was the rise in prices in Chihli and the hardships of the pao-kung system,[57] was in part a consequence of the benefits obtained by the Shanghai strikers during the rice crisis, and of the increase in wages won by the Hong Kong mechanics, both of which were explicitly referred to by the miners in their petitions.

While some of these spontaneous strikes were carried out in an orderly manner, such as the one held by the French Tramways employees in Shanghai, others were accompanied by the violence that had often characterized labor conflicts during the closing years of the Empire. In July 1920, during the rice crisis in Shanghai, women strikers from the Chapei silk-reeling factories entered a plant in Hongkew, persuaded nearly seven hundred women employees there to cease work, and set about cutting the thread on the reeling machines.[58] Similar disorders accompanied a strike held in a Yangtzepoo cotton mill in May 1920, when the electric power was cut off and machine belts were ripped.[59] In Soochow there were outbreaks of violence in June 1920 that were even more akin to classical Luddism, for here weavers who had been refused a raise in wages attacked the factory belonging to the president of the mixed satin-weavers' guild to which they belonged, and smashed the machines.[60] A further indication of the unbridled nature of these strikes of 1919–21 was the violent treatment handed out by strikers to workers who refused to take part in a strike. During this period, the Mixed Court of the International Settlement of Shanghai frequently tried and sentenced "intimidators" accused of forcing their fellow workers to go on strike. Twenty-six cases of this kind are recorded for June 1921, when strikes were held by the waterworks employees, the scavengers of the French Concession, and the masons and carpenters.[61] The same aggressiveness was shown by workers on occasions when violence broke out in clashes with the police. When the Hankow rickshaw men went on strike in the spring of 1921 to protest an increase in the charges for the rental of their vehicles, the police arrested several of them, and then fired into the crowd that met to protest these arrests, wounding several of the protesters. Such a serious view was taken of this incident that the foreign consuls of Hankow, the Chamber of Commerce, the local Y.M.C.A., and the Chinese civil authorities all offered to mediate in the dispute, and succeeded in postponing the increase in charges that had caused the strike.[62] Another violent clash with the police occurred in July 1921, on the occasion of a strike at the Shanghai B.A.T. factory caused by the unpopularity of a British supervisor.[63]

Not all of these strikes, however, were spontaneous; some were the result of organized action. In Shanghai, the strike held in September 1920 by the Cantonese carpenters employed in the small workshops in the docks, the shipyards, and boat repair yards such as those in the Kiangnan docks, was launched by the mixed guild to which these Cantonese carpenters belonged, and was supported by all the guild members, but not by any other carpenters;[64] and the jobs, at least for the duration of the strike, were soon filled by men from Ningpo, the eternal rivals of the Cantonese. The Canton region, where guild traditions were particularly strong, was, however, the main area of organized action during the 1919–21 strike wave, in contrast to the generally spontaneous nature of the strikes in Central and North China. In April 1920, the strike of the Hong Kong mechanics, who were demanding a 40 per cent increase in wages, quickly spread to the British ship repair firms, the transport workers, the telecommunications services, and the metalworkers, and soon there were nine thousand strikers on the island, involving 26 enterprises; and since all the strikers were skilled workers, it was impossible to replace them at short notice. The strikers were led, encouraged, lodged, and taken care of by the trade association of their fellow mechanics in Canton, and on April 19 they obtained 20 to 32.5 per cent raises in wages through the mediation of the British authorities, who, in the circumstances, displayed a commendably moderate, if cautious, attitude.[65] This success emboldened the Canton mechanics to take an independent stand against their employers, who still belonged to the same association they belonged to.[66] In the following year they in turn demanded a raise in wages, and in the manifesto addressed to their employers, they also raised the questions of the eight-hour day and of workers' insurance.[67] These demands were at first refused, but on June 9 the strikers won substantial concessions: 10 to 40 per cent raises in wages, a nine-hour day, and double pay for nightwork.[68] The spectacular successes of the mechanics gave encouragement not only to various craft guilds in Canton and Hong Kong, which in their turn obtained considerable wage increases,[69] but also to other sectors of industry. The Hong Kong printing workers' guild, for instance, after a strike in the spring of 1921, obtained a reduction in hours and a raise in wages,[70] and here again the strikers took refuge in Canton. Solidarity was thus established between the workers in the British colony and those of the big neighboring Chinese city, and this remained an outstanding feature of the labor movement in this region during the ensuing years.

Growth of Labor Organizations, 1919–21

The first stage of the May Fourth Movement was characterized not only by the spread of strike action, but also by the growth of working-class or semi-working-class organizations. The movement had brought Chinese capital and labor together in a common patriotic cause, namely, the struggle against the economic and political penetration of China by Japan, and against the conservatives who furthered it; and Chinese capitalists, all of them small-scale operators, together with the intelligentsia, were deeply impressed by the scope of the movement and by the strength displayed by the workers. They hoped that it might be possible to steer the forces of the labor movement at this early stage along the lines already followed by Chinese capitalist enterprise during

the early stages of industrialization, when the interests of employers and employees were at one. But now the prospects seemed much less rosy, especially
since the renewal of competition from the big industrialized countries of the
West had begun to dim the "golden age" of 1914–18.

Nevertheless, semi-working-class organizations for "industrial advance,"
similar to those that had appeared earlier, continued to multiply after May 4,
especially in Shanghai, which had been the main theater of strike action in
the spring of 1919 and was also the main base of Chinese capitalist enterprise.
The summer of 1919 saw the formation of the Society for the Promotion of
Industry,[71] the General Society of Chinese Trade Unions,[72] the All-China Society for Industrial Advance,[73] and the Returned Laborers' Association for
workers who had been in France.[74] At the end of 1919, the Chinese Labor
Federation was started;[75] the Shanghai Workers' and Merchants' Friendly
Society appeared in August 1920;[76] and the Shanghai Employees' and Workers' Club was founded in the following year.[77] All these seem to have been
mixed associations, open to employers, workers, management, technical advisers, and others interested in the problems of industrialization; and the term
kung-chieh ("industrial world") often occurs in their names, purposely used
in order to suggest class collaboration. Although the leader of the Labor Federation was an electrician—a Protestant named Li Heng-lin[78]—most of the
leaders were members of the middle class, such as the Cantonese merchant
Lu Wei-ch'ang of the Society for Industrial Advance,[79] the former student
Huang Chieh-min of the Industrial Society,[80] the industrialist T'ung Li-chang
of the Workers' and Merchants' Friendly Society,[81] and the journalist Hsia
Ch'i-feng of the Returned Laborers' Association.[82]

One of the main aims of these organizations was to develop small-scale
industry as part of the campaign launched soon after May 4 for the use of
"national products" (*kuo-huo*) instead of Japanese goods. The slogan of the
second meeting of the General Society, for instance, was "Industrial expansion and support for national products" (*k'uo-chan kung-yeh, t'i-ch'ang kuo-
huo*),[83] and in the summer of 1919 this Society worked out a plan for setting
up factories for making buttons and straw hats.[84] In July 1919 the Society for
the Promotion of Industry proposed setting up a model factory for the manufacture of textile goods with a share capital of 5,000 shares at the modest price
of 5 yuan per share.[85] In projects such as these, special opportunities were given
to workers returned from France, who were expected to provide skilled labor.
The association to which these men belonged planned to open a factory in
Hankow at the beginning of 1920 for the employment of its members.[86] But
the founders of these organizations hoped to solve the question of labor supply
chiefly by improving the technical skills and the general level of education of
workers, and they announced plans for evening classes, training courses, and
journals and pamphlets in elementary pai-hua,[87] which probably never got
beyond the planning stage. This concern to provide instruction was very much
in line with Confucian tradition, as reflected, for instance, in the motto "Virtue

and knowledge" (*tao-te yü chih-shih*) adopted by the Society for Industrial Advance.[88] This moral tone was of course further strengthened by the Protestant influence as represented by the Y.M.C.A., which had been so active in the workers' camps in France and which kept in touch with the Returned Laborers' Association in Shanghai;[89] the Y.M.C.A. rules, for example, contained clauses prohibiting members of the organization from gambling or frequenting prostitutes.[90]

Another feature of these organizations was that, in addition to forming projects for industrial development and technical training, they worked at promoting the interests of the workers. They had plans for founding workers' hospitals, savings banks, and benefit systems,[91] and they supported demands for higher wages, reduction in hours,[92] and the right to strike and to hold meetings.[93] In all of this they were drawing their inspiration, of course, from the labor legislation of the industrialized countries in the West.[94] The extent of Western influence in these circles of small Chinese industrialists can be gauged by the prestige enjoyed there by the International Labor Organization, which the Industrial Society, at the end of 1919, urged the Peking government to join[95] and which the Society for Industrial Advance saw as "a new dawn for China."[96] Another favorite theme of these mixed associations was "the sacred nature of work," a phrase much used in China in 1917–18[97] and often accompanied by a metaphorical comment on the fact that the character for "work" (*kung*) consisted of a vertical stroke joining two horizontal strokes which were said to represent Heaven and Earth, or spirit and matter.[98] There was also talk of the need to arouse "working-class consciousness,"[99] and it is significant that some of the associations, despite their mixed character, described themselves as trade unions (kung-hui).[100]

In the wake of these semi-working-class associations with their wide basis of recruitment, there appeared in 1919–20 several organizations in which membership was more strictly according to trade, such as the Electrical Industries Federation, formed in July 1919,[101] the Industrial Federation of Boathands and Warehousemen, formed in February 1920,[102] and no doubt others as well. But these were not really trade unions. The Electrical Industries Federation was more in the nature of a guild, and its members were employed in very different types of enterprise (tramways, telephone and telegraph services, silk-reeling factories, and workshops for electrical goods).[103] Membership in the Boathands and Warehousemen's Federation was confined to Cantonese employed as stewards, mechanics, and dockers.[104] Moreover, both these associations still had a mixed membership, as is indicated by the description "Industrial Federation" (*kung-chieh lien-ho-hui*), and owners of small electrical firms,[105] boatswain's mates, and warehouse foremen[106] were very active in them.

These "pre-trade-union" associations, of which there are other examples,[107] used the same phrases and had the same aims as the associations for the promotion of industry,[108] and, like them, hoped that the I.L.O. would intervene in China.[109] Both types of association were very active and eager to draw the attention of the press and of the public at large,[110] and both wanted to extend their influence beyond Shanghai. They made frequent use of the terms *Chung-hua* ("Chinese"—with a patriotic connotation) and *Ch'üan-kuo* ("All-China"—with a geographic connotation) in their official titles. In March 1920 the Society for the Promotion of Industry established a branch at Yangchow, the Lower Yangtze textile center, and delegates from Peking and Tientsin attended the Society's first anniversary celebrations.[111] Tientsin electrical workers sent a delegate to the inaugural meeting of the Electrical Industries Federation.[112] All these associations took part in the Labor Day celebrations on May 1, 1920, in order to show how representative of the labor movement they were and to gain support among the working class.

Seven organizations sponsored these first May Day celebrations in Shanghai,[113] four being of the semi-working-class type of association for industrial advance that had been so active since 1918–19—namely, the Industrial Society, the Society for Industrial Advance, the General Society of Trade Unions, and the Society for the Promotion of Industry. Two others, closely linked with the four, were industrial federations, one for electrical workers and the other for boatmen and warehousemen.[114] The seventh was a trade association with mixed membership, founded in 1918 and known as the Pharmacists' Friendly Society. On the day fixed for the celebrations the police prohibited all public demonstrations, and the participants held a meeting at a sportsground. The speeches made by Li Heng-lin and other leaders, the banners placed in the hall, as well as editorials on the event in progressive Shanghai newspapers such as *Shen-pao* and *Min-kuo jih-pao,* all reflected the conciliatory and reformist tendencies already noted as being characteristic of these associations. The *Min-kuo jih-pao,* for instance, declared that "The May Day celebrations are being carried out in a happy, harmonious, and orderly way." At the commemorative meeting the themes of the sanctity of labor and of the promotion of workers' interests were raised once again, and hopes were again expressed that the I.L.O. resolution on the eight-hour day adopted by the Washington Conference would be applied to China, although no one advocated more than cautious and gradual steps in this direction. It is an astonishing fact that during these May Day celebrations not a single gesture was made signifying solidarity with, or encouragement of, the strike wave that was beginning to rouse the Shanghai proletariat, hard hit by the rise in the price of rice.[115]

The ideas spread by these semi-working-class associations in 1919 and 1920 almost certainly bore fruit in the circles touched by them. An interesting indication of this is that in May 1920 the shareholders of the Commercial Press decided to create a special fund for subsidizing evening classes, a dispensary, and recreation facilities on the firm's premises, and for paying old age and maternity allowances.[116] Another indication is that the strikes that were held from the middle of 1920 on, although they were still spontaneous rather than organized by associations, nevertheless made much wider and more diversified demands—probably as a result of the associations' propaganda—and were no longer simply protests against hunger and poverty. When the French Tramways' employees went on strike in the spring of 1921, in addition to asking for higher wages they presented demands for payment of medical expenses during sickness, a revision of the system of fines, and an eight-hour day—[117] evidence that the new ideas were gradually filtering down.

None of this amounted to very much, however. The propaganda of the semi-working-class associations may have added to the effect of the strikes and may have widened the demands of the strikers, but their activities were far from being those of a genuine trade union, and, as has been seen, they had no sympathy for militant action. They might adopt positions favorable to the proletariat, as on the question of the eight-hour day, or celebrate May Day, but their main objective was still the development of small-scale national industry in China. Their failure during the next few years marked the end of their forlorn hope of uniting the bourgeoisie and the working class in a common effort to industrialize in a China still dominated by militarists and conservatives and by the vested interests of the Foreign Powers.

It was clearly these associations without any definite class basis that came under attack in the inaugural manifesto of the Shanghai Mechanics' Union, in which five types of association were listed as being the very opposite of the Union's aims. These five types were "capitalists' associations," associations supported by regional friendly societies (hui-kuan), "politicians' associations," "mixed associations" (that is, with both employers and workers as members), and "associations concerned with publicity." "We hope," declared the manifesto, "that our association will not be in the hands either of capitalists or of politicians and that there will be no discrimination according to province, but that it will include all mechanics, and no one else."[118] This new Shanghai union still retained certain features inherited from the past. It had a trade rather than an industrial basis, since it included mechanics employed in all types of enterprise, even if there was only a handful of them, as in the cotton mills; it continued to support the old apprenticeship system as a protection against the risks of unemployment; and it gave primary emphasis to training and mutual aid. But its subscription was fixed at 4 copper cash per month, and it had authentic working-class leaders such as Li Chung, a worker in the Shanghai arsenal. "We are workingmen dressed in workingmen's clothes," declared its members in December 1920, when discussing the dangers of the capitalist "running dogs" (*tsou-kou*) who might attempt to gain control of their organization.[119] A printing workers' union formed in Shanghai in March 1921 seems to have had the same exclusively proletarian character.[120]

Canton shared with Shanghai the distinction of being the working-class center where union organization had advanced furthest since May 4. There were probably over a hundred unions there, including no doubt some catering to craftsmen or to commercial employees.[121] A similar development had taken place in Hong Kong, to such an extent that in June 1920 the Hong Kong government made the registration of unions and guilds compulsory, whereas before it had been optional.[122] In the latter half of the year, 81 associations complied with the registration order.[123]

The Canton Mechanics' Union, which originated near the end of the Empire, held a position of paramount importance in the working-class world of South China. In 1919 it still preserved its mixed character; but in 1921 the employer-members—owners of small mechanical workshops in the Canton region, who in 1920 had supported the vigorous campaign of the association against the big British firms of Hong Kong—refused to give their employees the raise in wages that the Hong Kong mechanics had won through striking. In April 1921, therefore, the Canton Mechanics' Maintenance Society was formed, organized as a purely working-class organization. It absorbed a number of workers' clubs that had sprung up in 1920 among the Cantonese railwaymen and telephone employees and among workers in various factories in the region; these afforded the mechanics practical examples of the kind of independent workers' organization they wanted to found.[124] The important victories gained in the strike launched by the new union in June 1921, following upon those of the Hong Kong strike of the year before, greatly increased the prestige of the Canton mechanics in South China and in the country as a whole.[125] But the union—which now fully merited that title—still maintained a very moderate attitude, despite having broken away from the employers. It continued to be interested in technical training, recreational facilities, and mutual aid, rather than in militant action,[126] and even the strike of June 1921 was entered into halfheartedly. "We have no desire that peace should be disturbed," the union declared when it presented its demands on May 26, "and if we should be unfortunate enough to create a disturbance, we hope that the distress caused will be forgiven by all our relatives."[127] It also remained a union with membership based exclusively on mechanical skills, and thus included among its membership railwaymen of the Kwangtung lines, employees of provincial government enterprises such as the arsenal, workmen in the small Chinese mechanical workshops of the region, and mechanics in the big British firms of Hong Kong.

The Seamen's Union, which had its headquarters in Hong Kong, where it had registered under the name of General Industrial Federation of Chinese Seamen,[128] was beginning to adopt a much more radical attitude than the Mechanics' Union. Originally it had been concerned primarily with mutual aid, but later had agitated against the labor contractors, and on various occasions had attempted to have seamen reinstated after dismissal. Now, however, it contained a number of very militant members, such as Su Chao-cheng and Lin Wei-min,[129] who had joined the Communist Party and who later turned the union into a genuinely revolutionary organization.

The Ching-yuan guild of printing workers, which in March 1921 led a strike in Hong Kong that lasted for several weeks, was really an early form of industrial union, including in its membership compositors, printers, binders, and type-carvers.[130] Like the Mechanics' and Seamen's Unions, it covered both Hong Kong and Canton, providing another instance of how the links between the big working-class centers in the South (of which Macao, too, was one) overrode political boundaries. These links meant that the workers of Hong Kong and Macao had a place of refuge when they were on strike, and that the Cantonese workers did not have to fear recruitment of strikebreakers from the neighboring colonial territories.

Although the trade union movement in South China was remarkable for its cohesion, discipline, high level of organization,[131] and dissemination of propaganda for such "new" demands as the eight-hour day,[132] it was nevertheless still characterized by a somewhat narrow outlook regarding trade demarcation, which was perpetuated by the constant threat of unemployment. The Canton labor movement seems not to have had the advantage of a shortage of labor as the movement in Shanghai did. In Canton there were, for instance, nearly 20,000 seamen out of work, to give but one example;[133] and it was the presence of this labor reserve that explains the harsh treatment given by union members to nonmembers in the various enterprises.[134]

The development of trade unionism in South China was facilitated by the political situation that had existed there since the formation of the dissident "Constitutionalist" government in 1917. Both the traditional guilds and the new unions were on excellent terms with the Constitutionalist leaders, chief of whom, after the departure of Sun Yat-sen in 1918, was the venerable Wu T'ing-fang. He was in sharp conflict with two fellow members of the government, Lu Jung-t'ing and Mo Jung-hsin, both of the Kwangsi militarist faction; and in July 1919, when the troubles that started on May 4 had not yet calmed down and the anti-Japanese boycott was in full swing, a political crisis arose in Canton in which the working class gave active support to the Constitutionalists. The cause of the crisis was the nomination of Wu T'ing-fang, who came from an old Cantonese family, as civil governor of Kwangtung. His nomination was supported by the local chambers of commerce and by all representative bodies in the province, but was opposed by the Kwangsi group.[135] On July 11, 1919, the merchants of Canton went on strike, supported by the Mechanics' Union (still at that time a mixed one) and by other labor organizations. On the 13th, the workers at the electric power plant cut off the city's supply and the telephone employees went on strike, soon followed by the railwaymen of the three Cantonese lines.[136] This whole movement of protest, which was led by the Kuomintang militant Hsieh Ying-po and by the mechanics' leader Huang Huan-t'ing, had an expressly particularist character. During a meeting held by the mechanics the cry was raised: "Canton for the Cantonese!"[137] and bourgeoisie, craftsmen, intellectuals, and industrial workers alike were all determined to prevent the Kwangsi militarists from seizing control of their province. But the Kwangsi group was still in a strong enough position to have Huang Huan-t'ing arrested and about fifty people executed, and they remained in control of Canton after Wu T'ing-fang had withdrawn his candidacy, after which the movement gradually died down.

The labor organizations again gave their support to the Constitutionalists and the Kuomintang at the end of the following year, when Cantonese troops under General Ch'en Chiung-ming finally succeeded in getting rid of the Kwangsi faction. Ch'en's slogan: "Let the Cantonese govern Canton!" (*Yueh-jen chih Yueh*) was popular not only with the Cantonese bourgeoisie, but also with the guilds and the unions. The Mechanics' Union declared a strike in October 1920, the railways ceased to function,[138] thus hindering the movements of the Kwangsi troops, and the Canton printing workers also went on strike.[139] Sun Yat-sen and Ch'en Chiung-ming triumphed at the beginning of 1921, and the effective contribution made toward this victory by the Cantonese working class was given formal recognition during the festivities held to celebrate the return of Sun and his election on May 5 as President of the new Southern Constitutionalist government. At this time he accorded the labor organizations, who took an active part in the celebrations, an official audience.[140] In exchange for their support, the new government abolished the anti-labor laws of Yuan Shih-k'ai, and even gave the unions official representation in the new municipal council of Canton, under Sun K'o, by appointing three trade unionists to its advisory council.[141] In January 1921 a government Department of Labor was created at the instigation of Sun Yat-sen,[142] and, as a further sign of his interest in the workers, on April 17, 1921, he addressed a public meeting presided over by Huang Huan-t'ing that was attended by 3,000 Cantonese workers.[143] May Day celebrations, which in 1920, when the Kwangsi faction was still in power, had been restricted to a procession and a public meeting,[144] were much more elaborate in 1921, and included several public meetings and a grand lantern parade organized by the guilds and unions.[145] A number of minor details further emphasize the good relations between Sun Yat-sen's government in South China and the Cantonese labor movement; for instance, among the holidays granted to the mechanics as a result of their strike in June 1921, "Constitutionalist" ones such as October 10 (commemorating the 1911 rising) and May 5 (the day when Sun Yat-sen became President of the Southern government) figured as well as traditional holidays such as the lunar New Year and Arbor Day.[146]

Thus during 1920–21 certain sections of the Canton labor movement came to be closely associated with Sun Yat-sen and the Kuomintang, mainly through the activities of men like Hsieh Ying-po, Huang Huan-t'ing, and the leader of the Seamen's Union, Ch'en Ping-sheng, who tried to combine politics with trade unionism. At the beginning of 1921 Hsieh Ying-po formed a workers' mutual benefit society, open to party members only.[147] In other parts of China too the Kuomintang seems at this time to have made a determined effort to create groups of workers faithful to the "three principles," such as those among the railwaymen of the Hsükiapeng depot and on the Yueh-Han and Chin-P'u lines.[148] A similar venture was the Shantung Reading Society, formed by the committee of the Tsinan party branch at the beginning of 1921 with the aim of organizing unions in the Tsinan cotton mill, the arsenal, and several printing works.[149]

Next to Shanghai and Canton, Hunan was the place where trade union organization had advanced furthest since May 4, but it is rather difficult to assess the exact nature of the labor organizations that were formed. In the case, for instance, of the Mechanical Society of the Chinese Union of Hunan, which was formed in November 1920 and which featured in its program higher wages, reduced hours, and a raising of the level of training,[150] it is hard to tell whether it was a genuine working-class organization or simply a tool in the hands of local politicians.[151] Nor is it any easier to discover to what extent the Hunan Workingmen's Association, created at the end of 1920, was really representative of the industrial workers in the province. It was founded by two young workers named Huang Ai and P'ang Jen-ch'üan, who, while attending training courses in Changsha, had been won over to anarchist ideas.[152] Its program included a combination of social and patriotic aims: the raising of the workers' standard of living, the reunification of the country, and the restoration of national honor.[153] Among the organs of management listed in its rules, there came, next to eight committees for propaganda, finance, and so on, each with its own chairman, a body of 28 delegates representing the 14 most important trades belonging to the association, including miners, metalworkers, electrical workers, foundrymen, and weavers, but also painters, embroiderers, and building workers, which leads one to suppose that industrial and handicraft workers were on an equal footing as members.[154] By December 1920 the association seems to have had a membership of over 2,000 and already to have opened a school for workers. But its working-class character is put in doubt by a letter to the Shanghai newspaper *Lao-tung-chieh* from a worker in an antimony foundry in which he stated that the foundry employers made their workers join the association and then got themselves elected as "union advisers."[155]

Nevertheless, in March 1921 the Hunan Workingmen's Association took an active part in the labor unrest that broke out in Changsha when news was received that in the city's cotton mill, formerly owned by the provincial government but sold in 1920 to merchants from Hupeh, Hunanese workers were to be replaced by workers from Wuhan and Shanghai.[156] The students, the chambers of commerce, and groups of intellectuals started a movement of agitation that culminated in a huge mass procession largely organized by the Association.[157] When they reached the mill, the demonstrators declared it to be "the property of the thirty million Hunanese," invaded it, forced the manager to resign, and obtained a promise that the workers from Hupeh would be sent home and that in the future only Hunanese would be employed. Taking advantage of the stimulus this gave to the labor movement, the Workingmen's Association then organized May Day celebrations in Changsha, during which a big public meeting, attended by 5,000 workers, was held to discuss both future safeguards for the mill and the question of the eight-hour day.[158]

From this it can be seen that in Hunan the labor movement was as particularist in outlook as in Kwangtung, and here too it was the local political situation that accounted for this trend. The new warlord of Hunan, Chao Heng-t'i, who had come to power after the fall of the Anfu faction in 1920, was trying to consolidate his position by playing up provincial autonomy. In this he was of course supported by the conservative Hunanese gentry, but at the same time he was trying to enlist the support of more progressive elements by promises that his government would grant civil liberties, including even the right to form trade unions.[159] No doubt he had not been entirely unsympathetic toward the protests in March and the Changsha May Day celebrations, and this probably accounted for the tolerant attitude displayed by the authorities toward the labor movement.

In the remaining areas of China there is little to record concerning labor activities, except for occasional, poorly documented attempts at union organization in Nanchang,[160] Chengtu,[161] Chungking (among the printing workers),[162] and Hangchow,[163] and May Day celebrations in Tientsin and Wuhan.[164] This is due not only to the fact that the bulk of the documentation for this study concerns Shanghai and Canton, but also to the fact that the provinces in Central and North China were under the heavy hand of warlord governments; this is undoubtedly the main reason why it was impossible for an awakening to take place in these areas on the scale of what occurred in Canton, Shanghai, and to some extent Hunan. The victory of the allied Chihli and Fengtien factions, led by Wu P'ei-fu and Chang Tso-lin, in June and July of 1920,[165] which resulted in the fall of Tuan Ch'i-jui and the Anfu government, was merely an interlude in the interminable feuds between the rival warlords, and did not in any way change the fundamentally authoritarian and conservative character of the Peking government and its dependent provincial governments. At the most, the new rulers of China made a few ineffectual gestures of appeasement toward the proletariat in order to create a different public image from that of the much detested Anfu faction; but the very fact that they did so is an indication of the growing importance of the labor movement in Chinese political life. The Peking government made a show of concern after the big mining disaster in the British-owned Tangshan collieries in October 1920, and it demanded that better safety precautions be introduced for the K.M.A. miners;[166] and when in May 1921 the Tangshan miners went on strike, General Yang I-te, one of Wu P'ei-fu's lieutenants who was then Chief of Police in Chihli, intervened as mediator. He announced to the workers that he wanted to protect their interests, but that they must realize that the foreigners were helping economic advance in China.[167] Similarly, members of the Peking "Communications Clique," who during the past few years had made the railway network of North China into a private fief of their own and were now allies of Chang Tso-lin, tried to conciliate the railwaymen by introducing training courses and by promoting a measure designed to improve working conditions.[168] But these were merely demagogic gestures without any real significance.

Founding of the CCP

The spreading wave of spontaneous economic strikes, and the growth of labor organizations of unspecified political allegiance, many of which were still controlled by non-proletarian elements, were not the only results of the May Fourth Movement. Its main effect was to fuse the labor movement and the current of Marxist thought that first appeared in 1918 among certain circles of the radical intelligentsia, and that led to the founding of the Chinese Communist Party in July 1921.

During 1919 and 1920 the Marxist ideology increased its hold upon Chinese intellectuals and became much more widespread than it had been in 1918. It was adopted by teachers with well-established moral authority such as Li Ta-chao and Ch'en Tu-hsiu, as well as by the younger generation, of which Mao Tse-tung was one of the most active members.[169] *Hsin-ch'ing-nien*, in which Li Ta-chao published his epoch-making articles on "My Marxist Point of View" in the fall of 1919, was the main organ of these progressive intellectuals; but there were other periodicals, founded shortly after May 4, in which the ideas of Marx and Lenin figured predominantly, and which exerted considerable influence. These included *Hsiang-chiang p'ing-lun* ("Hunan Critic"), founded by Mao Tse-tung in Changsha in July 1919 and suppressed by the authorities after the appearance of a few numbers; *Mei-chou p'ing-lun* ("Weekly Critic"), published in Peking by Li Ta-chao; and *Hsing-ch'i p'ing-lun* ("Weekly Critic"), a Shanghai paper.[170]

It was only gradually that men like Ch'en Tu-hsiu and Li Ta-chao were able to accept the ideas of historical and dialectical materialism, the class struggle, imperialism, and the transition from capitalism to socialism.[171] But by 1920 their convictions were already firm enough to allow them to become deeply involved in the famous controversy about "isms" and "problems" (*chu-i* and *wen-t'i*). This was started by Hu Shih, who was one of the pioneers of the literary reform movement, but whose already moderate political views had become strengthened by his recent contacts with John Dewey and Bertrand Russell. He launched it with his empiricist and pragmatic slogan "More study of problems, less talk of 'isms,'" to which Li Ta-chao made a vigorous reply.[172] The Marxists also crossed swords with the supporters of

Western anarchism, of Tolstoyan moralism, and of the "model village" type of utopianism found in Japan.[173] This battle of ideas occurred in 1920, mainly in Peking, and gave rise to the first publication in Chinese of such texts as the *Communist Manifesto* and *Socialism: Utopian and Scientific*. *Hsin-ch'ing-nien* had already brought out a special number on Marxism in 1919.[174]

In 1920 the spread of Marxism was further fostered by the formation of study societies such as the Hupeh Reading Society for the Enlightenment of the Masses, and the New Studies Society in Canton.[175] In Hunan, a People's Study Society was formed in 1918 and took an active part in the May Fourth Movement, and it was followed by the Study of Literature Society created in 1920 by Mao Tse-tung for the express purpose of spreading socialist propaganda. Mao also formed a Russian Affairs Study Group in August 1920, aimed not merely at providing information about the U.S.S.R., but also at encouraging the study and active support of its ideology.[176] This last venture shows the extent to which the early Chinese Marxists were able to take advantage of the wide interest aroused in China in the new Soviet government[177] as a result of its renunciation, on July 25, 1919, of all rights and interests formerly enjoyed by the Tsarist regime (including extraterritoriality and concessions), its return to China of the Russian share of the Boxer Indemnity, and its offer to sign new treaties on an equal basis.[178]

Marxism is a doctrine of action, so already in 1920 Marxists were planning to organize themselves in order to be able to take part directly in the social and political struggle. Small "Communist groups" began to be formed from May 1920 on, first in Shanghai, then in Peking, Changsha, Hankow, Tsinan, Tientsin, Hangchow, and Canton, and *Hsin-ch'ing-nien* became their official organ.[179] And it was in 1920 that the Comintern sent Voitinsky to China, who, visiting first Peking and then Shanghai, made contact with Li Ta-chao and Ch'en Tu-hsiu and other members of the radical intelligentsia, including Sun Yat-sen's friend Tai Chi-t'ao. His presence helped their efforts at organization.[180] At the end of 1920, branches of the Socialist Youth Corps of China had been formed in most of the big cities,[181] and during this same period Communist groups of Overseas Chinese in Japan and France were created, among which the Paris group already showed signs of becoming the seedbed that would eventually produce such outstanding politicians and statesmen as Chou En-lai, Li Fu-ch'un, Li Li-san, and Ts'ai Ho-sen.[182] In China, the best organized and most active of the Communist groups seems to have been the one in Shanghai. It already contained within it the future central committee of the Communist Party, and in addition to starting authorized organizations such as the Sino-Russian News Agency and a school for foreign languages,[183] it had started publication in November 1920 of a clandestine monthly called *Kung-ch'an-tang* ("The Communist"), which devoted much of its space to Marxist theory and the activities of the Third International.[184] Apparently it was the Shanghai group that took the initiative in forming similar groups in the other big cities, including the Canton group. In the spring of 1921, Ch'en Tu-hsiu was called to Canton by the Constitutionalist government to become chief of the education board.[185]

The Marxist doctrine of the revolutionary role of the proletariat provided a theoretical basis for the alliance that had been cemented between members of the left-wing intelligentsia and the working class during the patriotic strike wave of May and June in 1919, the mass demonstrations held to mark its anniversary in May 1920, and the anti-Japanese boycott, which lasted through 1920.[186] Similarly, Marxist theory strengthened and gave direction to the interest left-wing intellectuals had been taking in labor problems since May 4. Another thing that helped to bring these intellectuals closer to the working class was that they had been just as much affected by the rise in prices. Thus Peking teachers, who, because of the incompetence of the warlord government, often had to go for months on end without having their salaries paid, were sometimes forced to go on strike along with workers hit by the high cost of living.[187]

The May 1920 number of *Hsin-ch'ing-nien,* prepared with the help of correspondents from all parts of China, was devoted entirely to labor problems, and its success is striking evidence of the new awareness on the part of left-wing intellectuals of the growing national importance of the proletariat. Li Ta-chao contributed a long article on the history of May Day, in which he stressed how vital it was for the international labor movement to win an eight-hour day.[188] That year's May Day was celebrated at Peking University by a big meeting attended, symbolically enough, by professors, students, and workers and domestics employed by the university, at which the students, giving a new content to an old popular custom, distributed loaves decorated with the four characters *lao-kung shen-sheng,* "Work is sacred."[189]

The Communist groups were every bit as interested in spreading Marxism among the proletariat as they were in awakening Chinese intellectuals to an awareness of labor problems. In January 1921 two members of the Shanghai group, Li Han-chün and Yü Hsiu-sung, started a Labor Movement Committee,[190] which distributed Socialist brochures in numbers sufficient to draw the attention of the police of the International Settlement and to cause disquiet among foreign journalists in China.[191] A little later, Li Ch'i-han, a militant Communist of Hunanese origin, organized an extramural workers' school in the working-class suburb of Hsiaoshatu, right in the midst of the Western-owned cotton mills of Shanghai, which attempted to provide not only general education, but also political indoctrination.[192] By means of contacts established through a woman worker who attended this school, Li Ch'i-han was able to gain the acceptance of the Green Gang secret society, and thus to establish relations with workers in the Chinese tobacco factories and silk factories in Pootung and Chapei.[193]

In August 1920 the Shanghai group started publication of a weekly named

Lao-tung-chieh ("The World of Labor"); 23 issues appeared between then and January 1921.[194] It featured discussions on Marxist theory, such as one on the theory of value and one on the theory of wages.[195] During the rice-crisis strikes in the spring and summer of 1920 the weekly reminded its readers that the question here was a matter not of lowering the price of rice, since this would hit the peasants, who were the natural allies of the proletariat; but rather of raising wages.[196] Judging by the readers' letters published in the paper, such as those from a worker in the Yangtzepoo cotton mill, from a Nanking rickshaw man, from a worker in the Hunan arsenal, and from a Tangshan miner, it appears to have had a wide distribution, not confined merely to Shanghai working-class circles.[197]

In the rest of China small Communist groups were working along the same lines. In Peking, Teng Chung-hsia and Li Ta-chao published *Lao-tung-yin* ("The Voice of Labor"), six issues of which came out between November and December 1920;[198] and the group in Canton published *Lao-tung-che* ("The Worker"), which lasted from October 1920 until January 1921, and *Lao-tung yü fu-nü* ("Women at Work") from February to April 1921.[199] These papers discussed the Marxist theory of the class struggle, and, like *Lao-tung-chieh,* featured articles concerning the local proletariat—for instance, on the situation of the Tangshan miners, or on the preparations for forming a trade union for the printing workers of Canton.[200] In January 1920 Teng Chung-hsia left Peking to take up work at the railway depot of Changsintien, a town which was one of the main industrial centers of Chihli. There, with the help of several Peking students, he organized evening classes,[201] which were the starting point of what in the following year became something like a trade union.[202] In Hunan, Mao founded branches of the Socialist Youth Corps in the main working-class centers: the Anyuan and Pingsiang collieries,[203] the Shuikowshan mines, and the Sinho railway workshops.[204]

None of these efforts was more than a first feeler put out by the Chinese Communists in the direction of the industrial proletariat. They were not yet quite clear in their own minds about the exact dividing line between Marxism-Leninism and other currents of revolutionary thought. Most of the contributors to *Lao-tung-chieh* were Marxists, but the journal also published an article by the anarchist Huang Ai on the founding of his Hunan Workingmen's Association;[205] and one has the feeling that there were different shades of opinion within the small Communist groups. The Shanghai group, for example, contained moderates like Li Han-chün, who wanted to undertake only "legal" activities,[206] and reformers like Chou Fu-hai, who believed in Laborism of the English variety;[207] and, at least when it was first started, it included among its members young radical intellectuals of the Kuomintang like Tai Chi-t'ao and Shao Li-tzu.[208] The Peking and Canton groups too probably at one time had some anarchist members.[209] Certainly the first number of *Lao-tung-che* of Canton carried an article by the anarchist Huang Chien-sheng on "the real labor movement," in which anarchist and syndicalist views on the use of the general strike and the role of the trade unions in the revolutionary struggle were discussed.[210]

In January 1921 *Lao-tung-chieh* was discontinued, and the only Communist journal remaining was the monthly *Kung-ch'an-tang* ("The Communist"), which had much closer links with the Third International but gave far less space to local labor problems and to Chinese affairs in general.[211] This change of policy probably reflects the hesitations and differences of opinion that were still in evidence after the founding of the Communist Party later in the year.

During 1920–21 the small Communist groups succeeded in gaining a firm footing in working-class circles. The Shanghai group, as well as pursuing its own activities, followed a policy of attending the public meetings held by the various semi-working-class organizations for "industrial advance," which apparently attracted a working-class audience. Ch'en Tu-hsiu, Chang Kuo-t'ao, and other Communist intellectuals spoke at meetings of the Industrial Society, the Electrical Industries Federation, and the Boathands' and Warehousemen's Federation, exalting the role of the workers in the modern world,[212] and urging their hearers to create "a country of workers" and not "a country of capitalists."[213] Communist intellectuals sometimes even accepted leading positions in these organizations.[214] Their policy of cooperation was carried furthest in their relations with the Workers' and Merchants' Friendly Society, with which, in the fall of 1920, the Communist group jointly published a weekly for shophands, *Shang-hai huo-yu* ("The Shanghai Shophand").[215] This cooperation between Communists and petty capitalists, foreshadowing political alignments in 1924–27 and 1948–56, was openly displayed on May 1, 1921, when Labor Day was celebrated under the joint direction of the Communist Li Ch'i-han and the small industrialist T'ung Li-chang, leader of the Workers' and Merchants' Friendly Society. They held meetings on the Society's premises to make plans for the celebrations, and they organized a procession in Chapei,[216] during which students distributed leaflets in buses and trams and along Nanking Road.[217]

In 1919–20 it was not unusual for Communist intellectuals to come across prominent members of the Kuomintang within the organizations for "industrial advance." Shanghai was full of them now that the Kwangsi militarist clique had taken over in Canton, and they too were hoping to gain influence among the working class. In August 1919, Liao Chung-k'ai came to convey greetings to the Society for Industrial Advance,[218] and in the spring of 1920, Tai Chi-t'ao and other friends of Sun Yat-sen were present at the inaugural meeting of the Boathands' and Warehousemen's Federation.[219] Another old associate of Sun Yat-sen, Ts'ao Ya-po, helped to found the Industrial Society of China in 1919, and in 1920 presented the report on the first year's activities at the annual general meeting of the Society.[220]

The militants of the small Communist groups did not, however, confine their activities to running journals for workers, organizing clubs and evening classes, and collaborating with the associations for industrial advance. They were also endeavoring to hasten the development of the class struggle and to form class organizations. The Shanghai group does not seem actually to have been able to organize any strikes, but it gave active support to the strike action over the rice crisis in 1920.[221] Also *Lao-tung-chieh* devoted a lot of space to trade union questions, and from the start issued constant warnings against unions that included employers in their membership and against those run by rapacious foremen or ambitious politicians for their own ends.[222] It published letters such as those by the metalworker Li Chung, who in September 1920 declared himself in favor of genuine working-class trade unions.[223] In fact, in the fall of 1920, Li Chung helped to found the Shanghai Mechanics' Union, which can be regarded as the city's first proletarian organization.[224] Its formation was undoubtedly a result of the activities of the Shanghai Communist group, and Ch'en Tu-hsiu himself collaborated with Li Chung in drawing up its rules.[225] In Shanghai, as in Canton and Changsha, it was the mechanics employed in modern industry who at this time showed the greatest capacity for organization on a class basis; but since, unlike Canton, Shanghai was a center where large-scale industrial enterprises predominated, and since Marxist influence was stronger there, the Shanghai mechanics naturally tended to adopt a more radical position than their Cantonese comrades, who were still much influenced by the guild traditions of the small workshops.

In Hankow, it was the Communists who were behind the strike of the rickshaw men,[226] and in Hunan, Mao Tse-tung and comrades of his such as Ho Shu-heng[227] made appeals in the press, or through the Hunan Students' Federation, for the formation of trade unions on a class basis. At the end of 1920 they made contact with the Hunan Workingmen's Association, and seem to have persuaded its leaders, Huang and P'ang, to join the Changsha branch of the Socialist Youth Corps.[228] The small Communist group in Canton seems to have been less effective than the others, partly because of the vigorous trade union movement led by moderates with the support of the Constitutionalist government, and perhaps also because of uncertainties in the political attitudes of some members of the group.[229] Nevertheless, Communist influence made itself sufficiently felt to arouse disquiet among "laborite" politicians such as Hsieh Ying-po, who probably founded his mutual benefit society at the beginning of 1921 in order to counteract it.[230] On the outskirts of Peking, however, attempts to organize the workers seem to have been more successful. The workers' school founded by Teng Chung-hsia in the railway workshop of Changsintien acquired a more pronounced proletarian character during 1920;[231] several foremen who had tried to infiltrate it were thrown out, and the workers formed a Workers' Club (*kung-jen chü-lo-pu*) with activities comprising recreation, training, and political education. It was this club that organized a May Day procession over a thousand strong in Changsintien in

1921, and that decided to form a proper railwaymen's union—an example soon followed in the other depots and stations of the Ching-Han line.[232]

There was an extremely active Communist group among the Overseas Chinese in France, whose numbers, depleted after many of them returned to China in 1920–21, had again increased with the arrival of the young "worker-students" and also of a number of unemployed who had left China in search of work. These last were very militant at this time, taking part, for instance, in the Paris gas workers' strike in April 1920, and starting agitation in Caen in July 1921 that ended in a lockout.[233] They formed a union of their own with a very militant program and a membership of several thousand.[234] The Overseas Chinese in France came under the influence of all sorts of new ideas, particularly anarchist ones. It was in order to counteract this anarchist influence that Ts'ai Ho-sen, who at this time seems to have been the most active member of the Paris Communist group, founded mutual aid societies for the worker-students, and also Marxist study circles,[235] in which Chou En-lai, Li Fu-ch'un, and many other future leaders of the Chinese revolution received their political education.[236]

Growth of Class Consciousness

Thus the May Fourth Movement had opened up quite new perspectives for the Chinese labor movement. To be sure, some of the hopes it had given rise to among the intellectuals, the national bourgeoisie, and even the industrial proletariat were rather ambiguous and confused, especially the hope entertained in the spring of 1919 that it would be possible to maintain a class alliance in the interests of "national salvation" and "industrial advance." When the semi-working-class organizations, controlled mainly by small-scale capitalists, took the initiative in organizing the first May Day celebrations in Shanghai in 1920, it did not occur to them that what they were doing went directly against their own aims for China's industrial development—on the contrary, they thought they were furthering them. And in the ideological ferment that began on May 4, the working class was subjected to the influence of a great variety of new ideas—those of the anarchists, the Kuomintang, the associations for industrial advance—as well as to the influence of the traditional guilds. Chinese Marxists were not yet in a position to counteract these influences; indeed, they were themselves not yet quite clear about their own views.

Nevertheless, the two intervening years between May 4 and the foundation of the Chinese Communist Party saw a marked increase in labor agitation. In May and June 1919 the working class became conscious of its strength and learned to use this strength in the defense of its own interests; and some of the strikes, such as those of the Canton and Hong Kong mechanics, had repercussions throughout the country. It was during these two years that genuine working-class organizations, such as the Hong Kong Seamen's Union, the Shanghai Mechanics' Union, and the Changsintien Railwaymen's Union, either came into being or were consolidated, that the class-conscious demand for the eight-hour day became a popular cry throughout the Chinese labor movement, and that May Day celebrations became general in all parts of China, from Peking to Canton.

Certainly this new class consciousness displayed varying degrees of aggressiveness. For every one worker who might agree with the sentiments expressed by Li Chung in his letter to *Lao-tung-chieh* in the fall of 1920—a letter in which he pointed to the example of Russia, proclaimed his belief in the future of socialism, and declared himself in favor of proletarian trade unions—[237] there were many who, like a printing worker whose letter appeared in *Hsin-ch'ing-nien* in May 1920,[238] continued to believe that the best way to relieve the sufferings of the working class was "to raise the educational and moral standards." But both attitudes displayed a real capacity for reflection on the situation of the working class as a whole, and for an earnest search for a solution of its problems.

It was this steady development of class consciousness that was the main contribution of the small Communist groups in their efforts, during 1920–21, to bring Marxism to the masses. Their efforts reached a more advanced stage with the foundation of the Chinese Communist Party in July 1921.

CHAPTER VIII

The First Big Wave of Labor Struggles

The Chinese Communist Party was founded in July 1921, in a Chinese school in the French Concession of Shanghai. It was there, at least, that the opening meetings of the first conference were held. On the fourth day, however, the premises were raided by the police, and the delegates were dispersed. The conference was reconvened at Southern Lake in Chekiang in order to get the final resolutions adopted.[1] Twelve (or thirteen) Communists, representing seven of the eight small Communist groups already in existence,[2] were present, as well as one foreign visitor, the Comintern emissary Hendricus Sneevliet, known as "Maring."

The delegates, representing the 57 members who then constituted the total strength of the party, were all intellectuals, including Li Ta, Li Han-chün, and Chou Fu-hai from Shanghai, Mao Tse-tung and Ho Shu-heng from Hunan, Tung Pi-wu from Hupeh, Ch'en Kung-po from Canton, and Chang Kuo-t'ao from Peking. (Their distinguished elders, Li Ta-chao and Ch'en Tu-hsiu, had been prevented from coming, but Maring had had previous talks with them.) Nevertheless, it is surely legitimate to regard the founding of the Chinese Communist Party as a decisive stage in the development of the Chinese labor movement.

It is significant that the place chosen was Shanghai, the main industrial and working-class center in China, rather than Peking, the ancient cultural center where the literary renaissance of 1915 and the great patriotic May Fourth Movement had begun, or Canton, to which Sun Yat-sen had returned a few months earlier, and which was still the main base of the progressive political forces. It should also be remembered that the twelve or thirteen intellectuals who founded the Communist Party had all had real experience in the labor movement through the work they had done among the proletariat as members of the small Communist groups, and were thus to some extent entitled to speak in the name of the workers in the cotton mills of Shanghai, the railwaymen of Changsintien, the rickshaw men of Wuhan, and the printing workers of Changsha. If it is true that, as one eyewitness testifies,[3] the Comintern emissary Maring was accompanied by a Soviet worker named Lizonsky, who, as a delegate of the Red International of Labor Unions, gave a report on the aims and activities of this organization at the first meeting of the conference, then we have further confirmation that the main aim of the conference was to defend the interests of the working class.

However that may be, the discussions at the conference were devoted largely to the Chinese labor movement, which came second on the agenda after the drawing up of the party rules. This was of course to be expected in a party accepting the Marxist theory of the dictatorship of the proletariat, to which reference was made in the final resolution. It was decided, contrary to the views of moderate Marxists like Li Han-chün who wanted to keep to "legal" activities, that the main operations of the party should be clandestine, but that an open organization under the party's control should be formed for the purpose of stirring up labor unrest and using propaganda to encourage the formation of trade unions. This became known as the Chinese Labor Organizations Secretariat.[4] From the very first, the Communist Party considered itself to be the party of the working class and intended to act as such. Identification with the workers was facilitated by the fact that it was a party which, although launched by Chinese radical intellectuals, had no social-democratic traditions behind it like its Western prototypes. It was not the result of a schism in a social-democratic party, but of the belated introduction of Marxism in its Leninist form into China at the time (or, as Mao Tse-tung later put it, "under the salvos") of the Soviet revolution, and there were no entrenched positions for it to come up against such as Communist parties in the West had to contend with after the schisms of 1920.[5]

The Labor Secretariat was formed during the first days of July—that is, about the same time as the conference was held. Its manifesto,[6] after reiterating the Marxist denunciation of capitalist exploitation of the proletariat, was critical of existing Chinese labor organizations, and called upon the workers to organize themselves on an industrial basis. It was signed by Chang T'e-li, the pseudonym adopted by Chang Kuo-t'ao, who had come from Peking to attend the conference and who was put in charge of the new organization.[7] He had previously taken part in the first Communist attempts in 1920 to organize the Changsintien railwaymen.[8] Li Ch'i-han, a Hunanese student who had had his first taste of battle among the workers in the Western-owned cotton mills of Shanghai,[9] was appointed as his assistant. The Secretariat had its premises at 19 Chengtu Road in the International Settlement, and soon had correspondents in Wuhan, Peking, Tsinan, and Changsha.[10] It published a journal called *Lao-tung chou-pao* ("Labor Weekly"), and the premises in Chengtu Road soon became a center of labor activities. In January 1922, Li Ch'i-han held a commemoration meeting there on the anniversary of the deaths of Karl Liebknecht and Rosa Luxemburg,[11] and in February 1922 he held another meeting for the workers from a score of printing plants for the purpose of forming a compositors' union.[12]

From the summer of 1921 on, the Labor Secretariat concentrated on encouraging strike action and union organization. In Shanghai it helped to organize several of the strikes that broke out during the fall, especially the strike in the B.A.T. factory in Pootung.[13] The Wuhan branch, in which the lawyer Shih Yang was particularly active,[14] was behind the strike on the northern section of the Yueh-Han railway in October 1921[15] and the Hankow rickshaw men's strike in December.[16] Shih Yang had been acting as legal adviser to the Hankow rickshaw coolies in their disputes with the *hang* (the firms who owned the vehicles), and had helped them form their own union; it was this union that actually directed the December strike and succeeded in getting the announced rise in the charges for the hire of vehicles postponed. The Secretariat supported the strike by collecting donations from sympathizers in other industrial centers in China.[17] The strike was a complete success, and the two coolies who had been arrested during its course by the police of the French Concession were released.

On the railways north of the Yangtze, the Secretariat continued with the work of forming workers' clubs in the main stations of the Ching-Han line; and on the Lunghai line Communist militants collaborated with the Lao-chün Society, the traditional organization to which railwaymen on this line belonged,[18] in organizing the big strike in the fall of 1921, which was another complete success.[19] During the course of the winter, the Lao-chün Society was transformed into the Lunghai General Union,[20] with which the Secretariat maintained good relations despite the fact that it apparently remained largely under the control of the foremen who had been to some extent responsible for the grievances that had brought on the strike in the fall.[21]

It was, however, in Hunan that, from the time the Secretariat was founded, the Communist militants connected with it took the most vigorous action. Mao Tse-tung himself took command of the operations, assisted by students such as Kuo Liang, Liu Shao-ch'i, Li Li-san (who had returned from France at the beginning of 1922), and Chiang Hsien-yun.[22] The first thing they did was to organize evening classes and extramural schools for the railwaymen and miners of the province, an undertaking that provided these young intellectuals with a good opportunity of making contact with the workers and of getting to know about their problems, while at the same time widening the workers' horizons.[23] Among the schools founded was the school for the Pingsiang and Anyuan miners, founded by Li Li-san in January 1922.[24] Kuo Liang helped with the successful Changsha rickshaw men's strike at the end of 1921,[25] and the Changsha printing workers' strike in April 1922 was directed by the printing workers' union founded earlier by Mao.[26]

Nevertheless, the main labor organization in the province was still the Hunan Workingmen's Association, in which, ever since its foundation in 1920, the leading spirits had been young anarchists like Huang Ai and P'ang Jen-ch'üan. During the second half of 1921, Mao and the other members of the Changsha branch of the Labor Secretariat tried to maintain the policy of cooperation with it that had been attempted before the Communist Party was founded, but they criticized it for its timidity in taking strike action, its neglect of financial problems (particularly the failure to accumulate strike funds), the laxity of its rules (which permitted workers and students to join on equal terms), and its failure to plan for industrial unionism.[27] But at the end of 1921 they persuaded several of the leaders of the association, including Huang and P'ang, to become members of the Socialist Youth Corps, an organization closely linked with the Communist Party;[28] and relations remained good enough to enable Mao Tse-tung to make a week's tour of the Anyuan collieries, the main working-class center in the region, in the fall of 1921 in the company of Huang and P'ang and other members of the association.[29] The Secretariat's influence can also be detected in the general tenor of *Lao-kung chou-k'an* ("The Work-ingmen's Weekly"), which the association began publishing in October 1921.[30] It is true that anarchist and syndicalist views were expressed in this journal, and that the general strike was still regarded as the most effective weapon; but now a more definite appeal was made for labor unity, organization on an in-dustrial basis was advocated, and the customary pang vigorously attacked. The association gave just as vigorous support as the Secretariat to the strikes that took place in Hunan in the fall of 1921.

Tragic events, however, soon put an end to all this. On December 31, 1921, a strike broke out at the provincial cotton mill in Changsha—the same mill where mass protests had resulted in the expulsion of Hupeh merchants and workers in the preceding spring.[31] The strike was initially a protest against a reduction in the traditional gratuities at the lunar New Year, to which were added demands concerning wages and working conditions. It became very violent, with recourse to ta-ch'ang, when windows were broken and machinery wrecked. On January 17 the strikers sent Huang and P'ang as their delegates to see Chao Heng-t'i, the governor of the province, whose autonomist policy had led him to make certain approaches to labor circles. Most of the strikers' demands were granted, but Chao immediately had Huang and P'ang executed in front of one of the gates of the city, and the Hunan Workingmen's Associa-tion was dissolved and its publications suppressed. These brutal measures gave rise to protests, the raising of funds, and various gestures of sympathy in all the main working-class areas in China.[32] It is clear from this response that by the beginning of 1922, the sense of interprovincial working-class solidarity was sharpening.

The Hong Kong Seamen's Strike

This working-class solidarity was to be still more clearly demonstrated sev-eral weeks later during the big seamen's strike in Hong Kong. The main cause of the strike was the growing disparity between prices and wages starting at the end of the First World War;[33] this disparity was particularly apparent to men whose sea voyages brought them constantly into contact with other countries and made them aware of the worldwide strike wave of 1920–21. Additional grievances were the hardships endured by Chinese seamen in recruitment and working conditions, which compared most unfavorably with those enjoyed by white seamen on oceangoing ships. The recent victories gained by the Hong Kong mechanics in 1920 and the Canton mechanics in 1921, and the 40 per cent raise in wages obtained in December by the printing workers of Canton—all as a result of strike action—[34] encouraged the seamen to employ the same means, especially now that they had a proper trade union, the General Industrial Federation of Chinese Seamen, which a few months earlier had replaced their mutual benefit societies.[35]

The president of the seamen's union was Ch'en Ping-sheng, who was a prominent member of the Kuomintang rather than an active trade unionist.[36] But more aggressive members, such as Su Chao-cheng and Lin Wei-min,[37] were already coming to the fore, and preparations for the strike were under way in the summer of 1921. Internal organization was strengthened by the formation of a "committee for wage readjustments" and of various special departments (for propaganda, pickets, and so on); and a propaganda campaign was launched to make the hardships of the Chinese seamen better known in the South. A list of demands was worked out, which included demands for 10 to 50 per cent raises in wages, and for the right of the union to deal directly in the signing on of seamen, thus eliminating the hsi-ma-sha, and to have a delegate present when contracts of employment were signed. The first presentation of these demands in September 1921 met with no response,[38] and a further demand for a raise in wages made in November produced no result either.[39] A third demand, presented on January 12, 1922, was in the nature of an ultimatum, and the strike was declared the following morning. A first contingent of about two thousand seamen left the port for Canton, where the strikers established their headquarters; and a picket system was organized so that crews could be contacted as soon as their ships berthed,[40] when they immediately joined the strike; by the end of the first week 6,500 men were out.[41]

During the first stage, the number of men on strike steadily increased until, by the end of January, nearly thirty thousand men were out[42] and 151 ships, with a tonnage of 231,000, were immobilized.[43] The strike not only affected the big shipping companies, but upset the whole economic life of the island. The shortage of raw materials and food very soon made itself felt, and prices rose, the situation being further aggravated by the refusal of the coolies of Canton, out of sympathy with the strike, to load the ships sent from Hong Kong to obtain supplies.[44] The Hong Kong government, through the Secretary for Chinese Affairs, Halifax, made enormous efforts to bring about a settlement, and these efforts were actively supported by all members of the compradore bourgeoisie of Hong Kong, who were also directly affected by the strike. From January 17–28, a series of negotiations took place between the seamen on the one hand, and Halifax and the shipping companies on the other. The shipping companies were not prepared to grant more than 17.5 to 25 per cent raises in wages, and this stand was supported by Halifax. But the seamen insisted upon raises of 20 to 40 per cent according to categories, and proposed that an arbitration committee be set up composed of representatives of the Canton government, the British consulate in Canton, the Western shipping companies, and the union to discuss not only a raise in wages but also the reinstatement of strikers without penalties and the whole question of recruitment.[45] Canton was suggested as the place where the committee should meet.

On January 29, however, the various guilds of the coolies and dockhands of Hong Kong declared a sympathy strike, and the response was good, despite the fact that these guilds were highly demarcated and that foremen and recruiting agents exercised a lot of power in them.[46] The Hong Kong government, which had proclaimed martial law on January 16,[47] now tried to break the strike by attacking the leading organizations. The Seamen's Union was declared illegal, its premises closed, its papers seized, and its leaders arrested,[48] and on February 8 the dockhands' guilds were also dissolved;[49] in addition, the police intensified their surveillance of the most active members of the Seamen's Union.[50] These repressive measures were accompanied by a certain amount of pressure brought to bear on the strikers by the Chinese Chambers of Commerce of Hong Kong and by various Chinese bourgeois groups such as the Tung-hua hospital foundation.[51] But the seamen stuck to the demands made in January, to which was now added the demand to have their union reopened under its own name and not under a new one, as proposed by Halifax in order to "save face" for his government. There was an attempt to introduce another form of pressure by the recruitment of strikebreakers (hsin-kung, "new labor") from Ningpo, the Philippines, and the East Indies to replace the Hong Kong men at a wage of 1.50 yuan a day plus food,[52] as against the 20 yuan per month average wage for seamen prior to the strike, and the even lower wage for coolies. But the counter-propaganda of the union, together with the committees for seamen's aid which were formed in Shanghai, largely nullified these attempts, and in February the strike continued to spread. By February 10 there were fully forty thousand strikers,[53] and by February 15 280,000 tons of shipping were immobilized.[54]

The prolongation and spread of the strike were made possible only by strong internal organization and by the support received from outside. The spearhead of the attack was formed by the body of strikers who remained in Hong Kong working underground from February 1 on; but the central direction had been in Canton since January, where it benefited from the tolerant attitude of the Southern government; and local branches had been established in Swatow and Wuchow, the other two main ports of Kwangtung.[55] The vital problem was the question of financing the strike—that is, of providing subsistence for the strikers. For this purpose a strike fund had been accumulated over a long period, which was said to amount to 200,000 yuan in January,[56] although this figure is no doubt exaggerated. The Canton government regularly made a substantial contribution, amounting in all to 100,000 yuan, according to a figure given at the time.[57] It was thus possible to transport the strikers to Canton and lodge them there with the help of the local unions and guilds.[58]

Outside support was very important: there was first of all the action of the seamen in other ports, without which it would have been impossible to prevent the strike's being broken by the employment of hsin-kung. Already in January the Wuchow and Swatow seamen went on strike, urged to do so by the local branches of the union, and Hong Kong men were lodged in both ports.[59] Indications of solidarity also came from the Chinese seamen in Siam, the Philippines, Yokohama, and Calcutta.[60] But the deciding factor was the support given in Shanghai. Since it was the largest port in South China and indeed in the whole of the Far East, it should have been easy to recruit labor among the large number of underemployed there with which to replace the strikers and thus break the strike. The seamen's guilds and the militants of the Labor Secretariat in Shanghai were alerted to this danger by the Seamen's Union in Canton, and took due precautions. A committee of support for the strikers was formed at the offices of the Secretariat,[61] and was run chiefly by the former seaman Ch'ien Chiao-yü, now president of the Chün-an Seamen's Guild, and the Communist Li Ch'i-han. Both were arrested at the end of January for attempted interference with the activities of a Chinese labor-recruiting organization, but were quickly released and subsequently succeeded in dissuading most of the hsin-kung who had been recruited from leaving for Hong Kong.[62]

The help given by the Canton trade associations was no less important, because it provided the Hong Kong strikers with a nearby base to which they could withdraw. Canton mechanics, railwaymen, and craftsmen all gave hospitality to the strikers.[63] Testimonies of solidarity came also from other industrial regions of China—for example, from the railwaymen on the Yueh-Han line and from the Hankow rickshaw men.[64] The Labor Secretariat formed a committee of support among the railwaymen on the Ching-Han line.[65]

What precisely was the attitude of the Constitutionalist government in Canton? Officially, the financial aid it provided was supposed to be no more than a loan, and it kept to its principle of nonintervention in the strike,[66] confining itself to offering its services for mediation between the two parties.[67] But there is no doubt that certain government circles supported the cause of the strikers, and that the political climate in Canton was largely favorable to them.[68] Does this mean that there was a certain duplicity in the Southern government's attitude? It was probably more a question of disagreement among its members over the course to be adopted. Progressive members of the Kuomintang, such as Liao Chung-k'ai,[69] serving as deputy for Sun Yat-sen, who at the time was conducting military operations on the northern frontiers of Kwangtung, were certainly in favor of giving substantial aid to the strikers. Ch'en Chiung-ming and the moderates among the Cantonese gentry, thanks to whom the Kuomintang had been able to return to Canton in the fall of 1920, were probably more hesitant, for, although during Ch'en's campaign in Kwangsi the year before they had come to realize the importance of working-class opinion in Cantonese affairs[70] and wanted to remain on good terms with labor circles, they must nevertheless have found it difficult to feel entirely in sympathy with the strikers in view of their conservative attitude in general and their friendship with Chinese and British businessmen in Hong Kong.[71] Altogether, the Canton government does not seem to have gone beyond a display of benevolent neutrality, and it declined to take any direct action on behalf of the strikers; as the strike continued into February, it came to adopt the attitude of the Chinese bourgeoisie of Hong Kong in trying to make the strikers accept a compromise.[72]

The situation in Hong Kong became more serious, however, when on February 26 all the Chinese workers in the colony came out on a sympathy strike, despite the fact that this was equivalent to a declaration of war.[73] By the beginning of March the number of strikers had reached the figure of 120,000, and they included everyone from vegetable sellers to tramway employees, from basketmakers to electricians, and even domestic servants.[74] An exodus to Canton took place immediately, during which violence broke out when, on March 3, the British police post in Sha-t'ien, a suburb of Hong Kong, opened fire on strikers who were making their way on foot to their point of embarkation.[75] The life of the colony then became completely disorganized, and the Seamen's Union seized the opportunity to bring the strike to a successful conclusion. Its delegates arrived in Hong Kong on the evening of March 3, and after final talks, an agreement was signed at 5 A.M., granting raises of 15 to 30 per cent in wages,[76] and in addition promises for the abolition of recruitment by the hsi-ma-sha. On March 6 the order for the dissolution of the Seamen's Union and the three transport guilds was annulled, and the following day all of them were formally reinstalled in their premises and the arrested members were released.[77] It was a considerable victory for the strikers, both from an economic and from a psychological point of view.

The seamen's strike cost the private shipping companies and the Hong Kong government itself a great deal of money,[78] and gave a solemn warning to all Western employers in China—a warning commented on in a letter sent at the end of March by the Commissioner of Police of the International Settlement of Shanghai to the secretary of the Municipal Council;[79] but more important still, the strike gave a tremendous stimulus to the whole Chinese labor movement. Its immediate effect was to encourage a big wave of economic strikes in South and Central China during the spring and summer of 1922,[80] but it also helped Sun Yat-sen and the Kuomintang see the importance and the potential strength of the labor movement, and thus prepared the way for the policy of cooperation between the Kuomintang and the Communists that was initiated in 1924. Perhaps most important of all, it was "the first strike in China to place class solidarity on a national basis,"[81] while at the same time being the first direct attack made by the Chinese working class on the big foreign interests. It is true that at first the strike was no more than a local affair with aims confined to economic and trade union matters, and that the political aims of the strikers were always far behind those of the Labor Secretariat, which played no part in starting it. But by its very extent, and because of the repercussions it aroused, it made the work of the Secretariat among the masses very much easier, and prepared the way for the first All-China Labor Congress.

The All-China Labor Congress

It was during April 1922 that the Labor Secretariat took the initiative in convoking an "All-China Labor Congress" to be held in Canton, open to all labor organizations in China. According to the letter of invitation, its purpose was "to strengthen the unity of the world of labor, discuss how to improve the standard of living, and examine the various suggestions put forward by delegates."[82] The date was fixed for May 1 in honor of Labor Day, and the letter of invitation was distributed to the Chinese press[83] as well as sent directly to all those concerned.

The Labor Secretariat was far from exercising the same influence in Canton as it did in the factories of Shanghai and Central China and among the railwaymen in the North, but the Congress had to be held there because it was the only place on Chinese territory where the organizers could hope for an attitude of benevolent neutrality on the part of the authorities. The Southern government, especially since the seamen's strike, had expressly adopted a policy of tolerance toward the labor movement. Article 224 of Yuan Shih-k'ai's criminal code had been annulled as well as other legal measures for the suppression of strikes,[84] and members of the government openly expressed their support of trade unions.[85] The Congress opened on May 1, attended by 160 delegates from twelve cities representing a hundred trade associations with a total membership of about 300,000.[86] Most of the delegates came from Cantonese organizations, but about forty were sent by workers' groups in Central and North China, and although they were in a minority, they seem to have been the main influence at the Congress. Among the non-Cantonese groups were several in close touch with the Labor Secretariat, such as the Changsintien railwaymen's club, the Hankow rickshaw men's union, and the Pootung textile workers' union.[87] Other older organizations were just as genuinely working-class in character, such as the Shanghai seamen's mutual benefit society, the Tangshan Workers' Club, the printing workers' club, the Shanghai Mechanics' Union, and the Hong Kong Seamen's Union. There were still others that only partially represented the working class, such as the associations for "industrial advance."

Although neither the proceedings of the Congress nor a full text of its decisions has survived,[88] it appears that during the four days of the meetings clashes of opinion occurred between Communists, anarchists (still strong in the Canton area), those with rather narrow syndicalist views, and those whose political sympathies were with the Kuomintang. As soon as the Congress opened there was a dispute about the chairmanship, which was finally conferred on Hsieh Ying-po, a friend of Sun Yat-sen.[89] Examination of the resolutions carried reveals the same conflict of opinion.[90] There was of course no great difficulty for either the left or the right wing of the Congress in accepting a declaration in favor of the eight-hour day, a proposal for standardization of union flags and hymns, a decision to commemorate annually the massacre of Sha-t'ien and the death of the two Hunanese, Huang and P'ang, and the convocation of a second congress to be held in Wuhan in 1923. But three of the decisions were much more in line with the policy pursued by the Labor Secretariat in its attempts to tighten union discipline and bring about greater militancy in the labor movement. The three resolutions in question were a special one on solidarity during strikes (up to and including a general strike), one in favor of the principle of industrial rather than trade unions, and one severely condemning demagogic and parasitic elements in the labor movements, picturesquely described as "the ghosts that aid the tiger."[91] A similar tendency was shown in the resolution put forward by the Hankow rickshaw men's union concerning the formation of a national union for their trade, which would be the first Chinese industrial union to cover the whole country.[92] On the other hand, the decision to assign to the Labor Secretariat the function of a coordinating body until such time as a proper all-China trade union organization could be formed must surely have been a compromise, falling short of the initial aims of the Secretariat. This would explain Teng Chung-hsia's criticism of the decisions made at the Congress as being either "half-hearted" or "too technical." Still less in line with the Labor Secretariat's aims was the resolution proposed by the Hunanese railwaymen of Hsükiapeng prohibiting trade unions from engaging in political activities: "the labor movement at its present stage is an economic movement only and is not concerned with political matters."[93] The fact that this resolution came from Hunanese workers clearly shows that the anarchist influence was still strong in that province, despite the work done by Mao Tse-tung and other cadres of the local branch of the Secretariat.

The Labor Secretariat and the Communist Party had had high hopes for the Congress, to which, for instance, a special May 1 number of *Hsien-ch'ü* ("The Pioneer"), the weekly of the Socialist Youth Corps, was devoted. The issue contained an article by Ch'en Tu-hsiu calling for an awakening of interest in trade unions, and another by Li Ta expressing the hope that the Congress would without delay form a national labor organization, get rid of regionalist views,[94] dissipate the workers' fears of socialism, and obtain labor legislation. An article by Ts'ai Ho-sen stressed the point that the final aim was socialism and that the daily economic fight was necessary but not enough.

The Congress of May 1922 certainly fell far short of this ambitious program.

But with all its high hopes and its shortcomings, it marks an important stage in the history of the Chinese labor movement.[95] For the first time the regional barriers really came down, and the labor organizations of the entire country made contact with each other. Naturally the Secretariat came up against divergent political trends and could not always get its point of view accepted.[96]

Nevertheless, new ideas such as the prime importance of industrial unions, class solidarity, and the eight-hour day had never before been so widely diffused. The principle of having an all-China labor organization was accepted, and was to be put into practice three years later, again in Canton. Men already experienced in the labor movement asserted themselves as leaders at the Congress, including the intellectual Teng Chung-hsia, who founded the railwaymen's club in Changsintien, the student Li Ch'i-han, who ran the Labor Secretariat in Shanghai, the Cantonese seaman Su Chao-cheng, who was one of the leaders of the big February strike, and the Shanghai seaman Chu Pao-t'ing,[97] who in February had taken part in the action to prevent the recruitment of hsin-kung in Shanghai. Although the Labor Secretariat had not yet organized the whole labor movement on the lines of the theory of class struggle that it was preaching, it had at least established contacts during the Congress and gained experience that was to be of great value during the following months. The very success of the Congress gave the Labor Secretariat a prestige that considerably facilitated the expansion of its activities during the rest of the year.

Secretariat Activities During 1922

The period of nine months between the Canton Congress and the massacre of the Ching-Han railwaymen on February 7, 1923, was in fact the time when the influence of the Secretariat reached its height. In June its offices were transferred from Shanghai to Peking, apparently as much because of difficulties encountered with the police of the International Settlement[98] as from geographical considerations. But the Secretariat had very little influence in South China, and was influential only here and there in the Lower Yangtze region. Its strength lay in Hunan, Hupeh, and the railways and mines in the North; thus the northern capital—despite its outlying situation—proved to be a better headquarters than the great metropolis on the east coast because the network of railways converging on Peking was strategically superior to Shanghai's maritime and riverine system of communications. According to Teng Chung-hsia, who seems to have been largely responsible for the transfer, the railways provided the framework for the Secretariat's activities.[99] The Peking office embarked upon a period of intense activity, remaining constantly in touch with its branches in Shanghai, Wuhan, Tsinan, and Hunan, sending cadres to places where strikes had broken out in order to give support, organizing collections for strikers, and keeping the public informed both through its own publications[100] and with the help of the progressive press.

It was in Hupeh, and still more in Hunan, that this activity produced the best results, probably because it was here that the general situation was more favorable than anywhere else for the growth of workers' struggles and labor organizations along the lines laid down at the Congress. The importance of heavy industry in these two provinces gave the proletariat there, concentrated in several large-scale enterprises, a capacity for exerting pressure far greater than that of the workers in the mills and factories of Shanghai or the mechanical workshops of Canton. The proletariat of Central China was more stable as a class, since the enterprises there dated from the end of the nineteenth century and contained a larger proportion of adult men than elsewhere. And there were hardly any guild traditions as in Canton, or any superficially zealous semi-working-class and "laborite" organizations of the Shanghai type, to stand in the way of revolutionary trade unionism. The field was wide open.

On May 1, 1922, Liu Shao-ch'i and Li Li-san started a workers' club at the Anyuan collieries that was virtually a trade union, solidly based on "delegates of tens," "delegates of hundreds," and "general delegates," which by the end of the year had a membership of over ten thousand.[101] It ran a mutual benefit system, a consumers' cooperative, educational and recreational facilities, and a library; and in addition it handled the workers' grievances, most notably in the big strike in September.

Workers' clubs of a similar type were started during the succeeding months among the railwaymen on the northern section of the Yueh-Han line. Shih Yang took the initiative in the stations of Hupeh,[102] and Kuo Liang in those of Hunan—at Yochow, Sinho, and Hsükiapeng.[103] In September these station clubs were amalgamated into one general club for the whole line,[104] which in November became a full-fledged union. A manifesto was issued calling for a strengthening of workers' solidarity and the overthrow of the forces of oppression.[105]

During 1922, clubs were formed among the metalworkers of Hupeh (at the Tayeh foundry and the blast furnaces and steel works of the Yangtze Engineering Works), again on the initiative of the militants of the Secretariat.[106] The workers themselves took the initiative at the lead mines of Shuikowshan: hearing of the successes gained by their Anyuan comrades in their September strike, they sent one of their men there—the mechanic Liu Tung-hsuan—who made contact with Li Li-san and returned to Shuikowshan accompanied by the student Chiang Hsien-yun, who had been delegated by the Secretariat as a helper. In October a club was formed at the mine.[107]

The name "workers' club" (*kung-jen chü-lo-pu*) was the usual cover for these efforts to organize the workers, which extended also to the printing workers and rickshaw men of Changsha[108] and the employees in the Wuhan powdered-egg, cotton-baling, and tobacco factories.[109] It is interesting to note that the same term had been employed at Changsintien at the beginning of 1921 and also, during the same period, by the Cantonese mechanics, when they were trying to create their own labor organizations as distinct from the mixed associations in which the employers were fellow members. The term "chü-lo-pu" was a neologism, being simply the phoneticization of the word "club." But it is doubtful whether Teng Chung-hsia is justified in attributing a new connotation to it.[110] He held that it was a more class-conscious term than "kung-hui" (trade union), which had been contaminated by the use made of it by nonproletarian elements who wanted to gain influence among the working class. There certainly were cases where the term "kung-hui" had fallen into a certain disrepute, while on the other hand the term "chü-lo-pu" was retained by the Anyuan miners even when their organization was at the very height of its power. But the distinction between the two terms was far from being either rigorous or general; as often as not, the club—as among the railwaymen—was merely a stage in the formation of a genuine union. The word "chü-lo-pu" had the additional advantage of being more innocuous in the eyes of the authorities.

The formation of all these clubs and unions within the main branches of industry in Hunan and Hupeh was not carried out without encountering some resistance, especially from managements, since provincial or state enterprises were of much greater importance in this region than private firms. In October 1922 the foremen and labor contractors at the Anyuan collieries tried to get the employees to join a *yu-lo-pu* ("recreation section"), which they started in competition with the club, and it is said that they even planned to have Li Li-san assassinated.[111] The foremen on the Yueh-Han line also tried to provide a counter-attraction to the clubs by forming "workers' study centers" (*kung-jen yen-chiu-so*)[112] and regional friendly societies.[113]

But opposition of this kind did not stop the Secretariat from pursuing its efforts to organize on a wider basis, setting up groups either by industry or by region rather than clubs in separate enterprises. In Hupeh a "Federation of Workers' Groups" was formed at the end of the summer with its headquarters in Wuhan; over 20 unions and clubs were affiliated with it, representing a membership of about forty thousand.[114] It first appeared in public in the procession on October 10, 1922, the anniversary of the founding of the Chinese Republic; its delegates marched bearing banners demanding the improvement of the workers' lot.[115] In Hunan a similar federation was formed on November 1, with Mao Tse-tung as its secretary-general. It included members of the former anarchist Workingmen's Association, dissolved in January 1922, and of groups connected with the Labor Secretariat, such as the miners' clubs of Anyuan and Shuikowshan.[116] Finally, the existence of the big Hanyehping combine in this region provided the Secretariat with the opportunity to attempt for the first time in China to form a widely based industrial union. In December 1922 the Hanyehping General Union was founded, which combined clubs and unions of the Anyuan mines, the Tayeh mines and foundries, the Hanyang steelworks, and the Yangtze canal boats.[117]

The Secretariat's underlying aim in founding all these clubs and unions in

Hupeh and Hunan was to advance the class struggle, and this soon found expression in extensive strike action organized by most of them. In July strikes broke out at the Hanyang steelworks and the provincial textile factories in Wuchang, in August at the Hanyang arsenal, in September on the northern section of the Yueh-Han line and in the Anyuan collieries, the Yangtze Engineering Works, and the water and electricity works in Wuhan, and in October at the B.A.T. factory in Hankow and the mines at Shuikowshan.[118] This was not simply a series of isolated strikes, but rather a coherent and coordinated strike wave. The strikes at the Yangtze Engineering Works and the Anyuan collieries were declared upon receipt of the news that the Yueh-Han railwaymen were coming out,[119] and the Shuikowshan strike was the first public action taken by a club that had just been formed with the help of the Anyuan miners.[120]

These strikes differed from the spontaneous strikes of the preceding period not only because they were led by responsible organizations enjoying the confidence of the workers, but also because the demands presented were quite extensive. The demands (and the Anyuan miners presented as many as 27) were not confined to the question of higher wages, but included ones for compensation for sickness, injury, and death (at Anyuan, Shuikowshan, and the Yangtze Engineering Works), for a share in the profits (at Shuikowshan), and for the abolition of "private labor" (ssu-kung) done for overseers and foremen. Most of these demands were met. The Hanyang steelworkers obtained a 20 per cent raise in wages in July, and in September Liu Shao-ch'i and Li Li-san succeeded in getting the Hanyehping Company to accede to most of the demands presented by the Anyuan miners, including a complete revision of the pao-kung system of recruitment. A fixed scale was established that did not allow overseers to take more than 15 per cent or foremen more than 5 per cent of the total wages, the workers being assured of the rest.[121]

The strikes were primarily union strikes, not only in the sense that the unions and the workers' clubs were the real instigators and also negotiated settlement in the name of all the employees,[122] but also because the strikes were held in order to force government authorities and employers to grant official recognition to the unions and clubs,[123] or to protest if a club or union had been closed down,[124] or to ask that they be subsidized.[125] Here again most of these demands were met, and these labor organizations, like the regional and industrial unions that superseded them at the end of 1922, became quite powerful local bodies, particularly in the case of the Anyuan club.

However, because almost all these strikes took place in either provincial or state enterprises, or in a company such as the Hanyehping that was closely connected with the government, the various government authorities concerned did offer a certain amount of opposition. Sometimes they even went so far as to use armed force, as at Yochow during the Yueh-Han railway strike in September. On this occasion, when a troop of soldiers found workers lying down on the rails, ten workers were killed, twenty wounded, and many drowned in the nearby river into which they had leaped for safety.[126] Force was used also during the Hanyang arsenal strike in August,[127] and the Anyuan collieries strike in September.[128] This was a foretaste of what was to happen in February 1923, when the conservative forces in Central China tried to crush the sudden upsurge of labor agitation.

Because of both the extent of the strike wave and the importance of the work done by the Secretariat in building up union organization there, Hupeh and Hunan must certainly be regarded as the area where the labor movement was most vigorous and made the most progress during the summer and fall of 1922, and all the more so if the efforts made to establish links with rural workers are taken into account—something quite exceptional in the Chinese labor movement at that time. Kuo Liang, who collaborated with Mao Tse-tung in running the Provincial Federation of Hunan, was sent by Mao in 1922 to organize the rural potters in the villages of his native district, T'ung-kuan. A little later he founded there a union for rural craftsmen, the inauguration of which in March 1923 was attended by delegates of the Anyuan and Shui-kowshan miners and of the Changsha trade unions.[129] Similarly, the Shui-kowshan strike in October 1922 was actively supported by the peasants in the neighborhood, who gave hospitality to the strikers, supplied them with food, and took part with them in the festivities held to celebrate their victory.[130] There were the beginnings here of something unusual in any labor movement, which, if developed, could have altered entirely the events of the following years.[131]

The same twofold task of organizing unions and strikes was carried out by the Labor Secretariat during 1922 on the railways north of the Yangtze, despite a number of difficulties, such as survivals of trade and regional rivalries, the influence of foremen, and the intrigues of politicians at the capital. Although the railwaymen had no craft traditions, they nevertheless had trade rivalries, being divided into track workers, train crews, and railway workshop employees. The foremen wielded a great deal of power, and sometimes, as on the Lunghai line, succeeded in organizing unions that they could control and use in their machinations against the management.[132] As for the politicians: they consisted of Liang Shih-i and Yeh Kung-ch'o of the "Communications Clique," who had managed to stay in power in Peking after the fall of their allies, the Anfu faction, in 1920 because they also had the support of the Fengtien faction. They had made the railways of North China into their own personal fief, and they sought to maintain a certain amount of influence among the employees.

When in spring 1922 Wu P'ei-fu and the Chihli faction triumphed over their Fengtien rivals, and Liang Shih-i's group, deprived of its militarist protectors, was eliminated,[133] Li Ta-chao, who at that time was working hard among the railwaymen for the Secretariat,[134] decided that it might be possible to come to some sort of an understanding with the Chihli faction or even obtain their co-operation. Wu P'ei-fu had made adroit use of his victory in 1920 over the corrupt and much hated Anfu faction, which swung Chinese public opinion over to his side, and he had further increased his popularity by playing up the notorious connections of his other opponents, the Fengtien faction and the Communications Clique, with Japan. He posed as a militarist who supported social and political progress and China's territorial integrity. The "protection of labor" (*pao-hu lao-tung*) was one of the four points of his political program, and he took care to make propagandist gestures in the direction of the work-ers.[135] But the Communications Clique still had some influence among the railwaymen[136] that could prove dangerous in the event of a military crisis, so the support of the Communists was essential if this threat was to be averted. The Labor Secretariat for its part felt that the rivalries between the conservative factions offered a good opportunity for putting the organization of the rail-waymen on a solid foundation. Li Ta-chao had a meeting with one of Wu P'ei-fu's lieutenants, and an agreement was reached whereby six members of the Communist Party were appointed as "secret inspectors" by the Peking gov-ernment and authorized to circulate freely throughout the network with all expenses paid.[137] If Li Ta-chao pursued this policy because of certain illusions he may have had regarding the genuineness of Wu P'ei-fu's goodwill toward the labor movement, the bloody events of February 1923 were soon to disillusion him. (He was later criticized as having been opportunist.)[138]

However, the policy had the immediate effect of enabling the Labor Secre-tariat to make good progress in 1922.[139] By the end of the year it was in control of the whole Ching-Han network, with workers' clubs in 16 stations, and of the Cheng-T'ai network; and it had clubs in the four main stations of the Ching-Feng line at the Great Wall end (Tangshan, Shanhaikwan, Tientsin, and Fengtai), at the Pukow, Tsinan, and Puchen stations on the Chin-P'u line, in the train-crew and workshop sections of the Ching-Sui line, and at Loyang on the Lunghai line. It was only on the Chin-P'u and to a lesser ex-tent on the Lunghai line that the unions controlled by foremen were still strong.[140] The Communications Clique had completely lost its hold on the Ching-Han line, and all it had left was a form of guild among the track work-ers on the Ching-Sui line.[141]

During the latter part of 1922 these railwaymen's clubs, like the Hupeh and Hunan clubs, launched a series of successful strikes: in August on the south-ern section of the Ching-Han and on the Ching-Sui, and then at Changsintien; in September at Shanhaikwan; in October at Tangshan and among the train crews on the Ching-Sui line (but not in the other sections); and in December on the Cheng-T'ai line.[142] Like the strikes in Central China, these railway strikes were much more sophisticated than the elementary spontaneous pro-tests of the preceding years. They raised not only the question of wages, but also that of control over the signing on of labor and of the pao-kung system (at Tangshan), and of recreational facilities and the provision of restrooms for the workers (at Changsintien). Discipline was strictly maintained by pickets organized by the unions, as at Changsintien in August, when the strikers invaded the workshops. Recognition of the clubs as representative bodies of the railwaymen was obtained at Changsintien, Shanhaikwan, and Tangshan and on the Ching-Sui line (although here only the train crews were represented). By the end of 1922 the railwaymen were well enough organized, and the successes won by the strikes sufficient, to allow the Labor Secretariat to begin planning a big national federation for this branch of industry. A preparatory commission was set up in Peking,[143] and contacts followed up throughout the winter; but "February Seventh" put an end to all these hopes.

In the other branches of industry in North and Northeast China the Secretariat was not nearly so successful. It cannot be credited with having founded a single important union there during 1922, and the fact that the miners of Kiaotso in Honan joined the Ching-Han railwaymen's union, the collieries there being served by a branch of the Ching-Han line, is indicative of this failure.[144] Mines and factories in North China did, it is true, take part in the big strike wave during the summer, but the Secretariat only came in after the strikes had been declared, instead of taking the initiative. This is what happened, for instance, when close to fifty thousand miners of the British K.M.A. came out in October 1922.[145]

The aims of the K.M.A. strike, which was launched on October 23, were to obtain higher wages, an annual New Year bonus equivalent to one month's wages, payment by the company of medical expenses, and an increase in the amount of compensation paid for the death of an employee which would bring it to the equivalent of five years' wages. Several days after the strike began, additional demands were made for official recognition of the union, which had been spontaneously formed a short time before, and for its right to exercise control over the hiring and dismissal of workers. The strike was apparently initiated by the skilled Cantonese mechanics employed at the mine,[146] and following the example set by the Hong Kong seamen, they immediately set up a strike committee, pickets, and special departments dealing with finance, propaganda, and so on. But the political situation here was not the same as in South China, and very soon British marines, the mine's private police force, and forces under the command of Yang I-te, one of Wu P'ei-fu's lieutenants and Chief of Police of Chihli, combined in taking action to suppress the strike. Yang I-te's participation in this operation represented simply a continuation of the alliance that had existed since the end of the First World War between the British and the Chihli militarists,[147] which was further strengthened after the Washington Conference.[148] On October 25 several men were killed in a clash between the strikers and the armed forces used against them, the union was dissolved and its leaders arrested, and action was taken against the other groups of Tangshan workers (cement workers and railwaymen) who had shown solidarity with the miners. The strike then went through a crisis in leadership, some members of the committee taking refuge in the countryside while others made off with the funds. Obviously the Southerners, most of them skilled workers, who are credited with having launched the strike, had failed to take the necessary precaution of undertaking a thorough organization of the great mass of the miners, all of whom were unskilled men recruited from the Chihli and Shantung peasantry. As a result of this failure, they had no firmly established leadership hierarchy like that which had led to the successes of the Anyuan miners. The Labor Secretariat sent in some of its cadres as soon as the strike began, but they were arrested along with the local leaders on October 26; and after that, it does not seem to have made any further moves; this inaction was later excused by Teng Chung-hsia, who was in Peking at the time, with the plea that he was then "overwhelmed with work."[149] Nevertheless, solidarity with the K.M.A. strike was expressed on a national scale, and all the more so because, as in Hong Kong, it was directed against the main enemy: British capitalism. Both moral and financial support for the K.M.A. miners was provided not only by workers' groups,[150] but also by the intelligentsia,[151] and even by the commercial bourgeoisie.[152] The large sums collected throughout China, and even as far away as Singapore,[153] enabled the strike to continue for a time, without, however, achieving final success. On November 16 work was resumed on the basis of a uniform 10 per cent raise in wages and a hua-li (New Year bonus) equivalent to two weeks' wages. It was almost a defeat, and showed that the tide was beginning to turn after the great wave of activity in the labor movement during 1922.

In the Shanghai region the tide had begun to turn even earlier. The Labor Secretariat was very active there at the beginning of the year, and in July supported the Yangtze seamen's strike[154] organized by the local branch of the Hong Kong and Canton seamen's union. This local branch had been formed in the spring by the most active members of the existing seamen's mutual benefit societies. One of these was Chu Pao-t'ing, who was helped by "advisers," such as Lin Wei-min, sent by the Hong Kong union.[155] Chu and Lin, both of whom shortly joined the Communist Party, were already in touch with the Labor Secretariat. The success of the strike,[156] which gained for the seamen of Shanghai and the Lower Yangtze the same advantages obtained by their Hong Kong comrades four months earlier, was a recommendation for the idea of widely based industrial unions, which at this time the Secretariat was trying to organize in Shanghai among the postal workers (with whom Li Ch'i-han had made contacts),[157] and among the workers in the Japanese textile factories in Pootung.[158] Li Ch'i-han was one of the leading members of the committee formed to give aid to the workers in these factories when they went on strike in April and May—a committee in which "laborite" organizations such as the Society for Industrial Advance and the Workers' and Merchants' Friendly Society cooperated with the Labor Secretariat.[159] The strikers obtained a raise in wages and recognition of the union by the management.

The labor offensive met, however, with much stronger opposition in Shanghai than it had in South and Central China or on the railways in the North. Neither the authorities, whether those of the International Settlement[160] or the Chinese authorities under General Ho Feng-lin,[161] nor the employers, whether foreign or Chinese, were taken by surprise as those in Hong Kong had been in February; and their methods of dealing with the situation were much superior to those of the government officials and the generals in Hupeh and Hunan. Li Ch'i-han, who had long been under surveillance by the police of the International Settlement,[162] was arrested on June 1 for disturbance of the peace and for his activities in the postal workers' strike. Shortly afterward the Labor Secretariat, which had been functioning openly in the Settlement for a year, was closed down[163] and had to carry on its activities underground, so that during the succeeding months it was no longer able to exert as much influence among the Shanghai workers. Li Ch'i-han was tried by the Mixed Court early in June and sentenced to three months' imprisonment; at the end of his sentence he was handed over by the British police to the mercies of Ho Feng-lin, who kept him prisoner.[164]

This close cooperation between the Settlement authorities and the Chinese police[165] was still in effect in August, when the strike of twenty thousand women employees in the silk-reeling factories of Hongkew and Chapei was broken. This was the first big strike held by women in the history of the Chinese labor movement. The women, exhausted during the height of summer by the damp heat of the steam that rose from the basins of boiling water for softening the cocoons, and working more than 13 hours a day for 40 cents, asked for a reduction in hours and a raise in wages. The Chinese police replied by closing down the "Women Workers' Society for the Promotion of Virtue" (a kind of friendly society), which had initiated the strike, and forced the women to return to work without having achieved anything. The strike leaders were brought before a military tribunal.[166] At the end of September the Pootung textile workers' union was dissolved by the Chinese police, and in November a triple strike—in the Japanese cotton mills, the B.A.T. Company, and the goldsmiths' and silversmiths' workshops (where a club had recently been formed by the Labor Secretariat)—was broken by Ho Feng-lin. Some violent incidents, reaching the point of street fighting and the wrecking of the private houses of some of the engineers, showed that the tradition of ta-ch'ang was still alive among the proletariat of the Shanghai textile industry.[167]

Generally speaking, then, the Labor Secretariat may be said to have made appreciable, if uneven, progress throughout 1922. Its influence remained slight in the South; in Shanghai it lost the ground gained earlier in the year owing to the wave of repression during the summer; and in the mines and factories of the North and Northeast it did little more than make a few short-lived contacts. But in the two big industrial strongholds of Central China, and on the railways of Central and North China, it achieved a really strong position, for in both sectors it succeeded not only in initiating or supporting an imposing series of strikes, but also in spreading among the working class the anti-capitalist and anti-imperialist slogans then being proclaimed by the Red International in Moscow,[168] and in founding a number of unions which may not have lasted long but were extremely vigorous while they lasted.

The rules of these unions founded by the Secretariat were usually drawn up in very great detail, amounting at times to a kind of formalism. The basic organizational structure was three-tiered, quite alien to Chinese guild traditions[169] and probably borrowed directly from the Red International and other Communist organizations. It consisted of a general assembly of delegates, an executive committee empowered to carry out its decisions, and a small permanent central office dealing with matters in hand. Another feature of these unions was their democratic nature. Regarding membership, the rules disallowed any discrimination on the basis of provincial origin, age, sex, or degree of skill, and stipulated only that a new member have two sponsors. Stress was laid on rank-and-file activities in each railway station, each mine pit, and each factory department,[170] and the subscription rate was comparatively low (half a day's wages per month).[171] However, with a few exceptions such as the workers' club at the Anyuan collieries[172] union rules were never really put into effect, and the organizational structure remained "purely academic," according to a contemporary Soviet observer.[173] The clubs and unions run by the Secretariat were, as Teng Chung-hsia admitted,[174] entirely controlled from the top.

Doubtless the lack of leadership within the unions was one reason for the failure to implement the rather elaborate organizational rules. Efforts were made during 1922, especially in Hunan, to appoint working-class union leaders, such as the miners Liu An-i and Hsieh Huai-te, who ran the Anyuan workers' club;[175] the mechanic Liu Tung-hsuan, who helped to found the Shuikowshan club;[176] the seamen Lin Wei-min and Chu Pao-t'ing, through whom the Secretariat made contact with the seamen's unions;[177] and the railwaymen Lin Hsiang-ch'ien, a mechanic from Fukien, and Yang Te-fu, former leader of the Hupeh pang in Chengchow, both of whom helped to found the workers' clubs on the southern section of the Ching-Han line.[178] But in the main, the Secretariat and the unions run by it were led by intellectuals such as Mao Tse-tung, Liu Shao-ch'i, and Li Li-san in Hunan, Li Ch'i-han in Shanghai, Shih Yang in Hupeh, and Li Ta-chao, Teng Chung-hsia, and Chang Kuo-t'ao in Peking, all of whom helped to start the movement; and by student supporters such as Kuo Liang and Chiang Hsien-yun in Hunan,[179] or Lin Yü-nan in Hupeh, the last having forsaken the anarchists to work in the Wuhan branch of the Secretariat.[180]

Many of these older and younger intellectuals actually took jobs in factories

and mines requiring a physical effort for which their Confucian gentry education had done little to equip them.[181] But drive and good intentions were not
enough to make up for the lack of working-class leadership, and many unions
had to make special provision in their rules for "associate members"—that is,
for middle-class sympathizers prepared to undertake the administrative tasks
that most workers were incapable of carrying out for lack of education.[182] Too
often, however, this degenerated into what Teng Chung-hsia called a "dictatorship of the secretariat."[183]

Thus there seems to have been something of a time lag between the upsurge
of labor agitation promoted by the Labor Secretariat in 1922 among large sections of the working class, and the growth of internal strength and cohesion of
the unions it helped to organize.[184] This time lag was not immediately apparent; but the violent shock suffered by the labor movement after the incident of February 1923 shows how real it was, and how vulnerable and easily
shaken the unions were in consequence.

It was precisely in order to compensate for this weakness in internal organization of the unions, and to strengthen adherence to them, that the Labor Secretariat launched a campaign for labor legislation in the summer of 1922,
which at the same time was aimed at awakening the Chinese public to the
distress suffered by Chinese workers. A campaign of this kind had been on
the Secretariat's agenda for the Labor Congress of May 1922;[185] and it became
a feasible proposition when in July the Chihli faction recalled the Old Parliament and the former President of the Republic, Li Yuan-hung, to take over in
Peking,[186] since this gave high hopes that liberal measures, such as those contained in the earlier program put forward by Wu P'ei-fu, would be introduced.[187] The Labor Secretariat thereupon drew up a very full program of labor
legislation containing 19 articles,[188] the most important of which concerned
recognition of the unions, the eight-hour day, union control over the employment of women and children, the introduction of a minimum wage, workers'
participation in several state organizations (not yet created) dealing with labor
problems, and workers' insurance. During August, September, and October,
this program became widely accepted throughout China, both by the organizations connected with the Secretariat and by other labor organizations. Those
of Wuhan, for instance, took up all the 19 points in a petition addressed to
parliament in September;[189] in Changsha a workers' meeting on labor legislation was held,[190] and the Tangshan workers formed a "League for Labor
Legislation."[191] Action of this kind was also taken by the Ching-Han railwaymen in Changsintien[192] and in Chengchow,[193] by some of the trade associations of Canton,[194] by the Shanghai seamen,[195] and by the Shanghai-Nanking
railwaymen.[196] The movement even broadened to the provincial government
level when the women employed in the Shanghai silk-reeling factories, during
their strike in August 1922, appealed—in vain—to the provincial governor of
Kiangsu for a reduction of hours.[197]

As the last example indicates, there was little likelihood of the campaign achieving its objective within the context of warlord-dominated China, although some of the leaders, including Teng Chung-hsia, seem to have nursed illusions about it.[198] Nevertheless the very extent of it helped to raise the prestige of the Secretariat among the workers and among the public at large, and its promoters thought it had been successful in "strengthening the class consciousness of the proletariat."[199]

Thus the Labor Secretariat was the means whereby the Chinese Communist Party was able to take an active part in the labor movement. Although it did not openly or actively support the political program of the party, but rather confined itself to legal and broadly based activities, it spread new ideas about organization and action, such as industrial unionism and the class struggle, even if its approach to the main Marxist themes was a cautious one; and it introduced the publications of the Red International to China. It also provided the labor movement with energetic leaders who helped to raise the level of strike action and to found a large number of clubs and unions. Furthermore, it organized the first big demonstrations of working-class solidarity on a national scale, such as the Canton Congress and the campaign for labor legislation.

It would be wrong to minimize the role of the Secretariat,[200] but equally wrong to regard it as the primary impetus behind strike action and union organization in 1922. The Secretariat itself neither desired to do nor claimed to have done anything more than channel, give leadership to, and broaden the activities of the labor movement; but the movement was far wider than the sphere of action of the Secretariat. The Hong Kong seamen's and the K.M.A. miners' strikes show how determined the Chinese working class was to form its own fighting organizations, and in these instances all the Secretariat did was to support, with greater or less success, strikes and unions that it had played no part in initiating. The unions formed in Shantung in 1922, after the departure of the Japanese, are another example of the strength of this spontaneous movement toward union organization. An "Association of Worker Comrades" was formed in Tsinan, an "Association of Machinist Comrades" in the Fangtze collieries, and in Tsingtao an "Association for the Celebration of Industry," to which skilled workers in the waterworks, the arsenal, the Szefang railway workshops, and a factory for electrical equipment all belonged.[201] The upsurge of the labor movement in 1922 can only be accounted for by the conjunction of the two factors: the organizing activities of the Secretariat with the Communist Party behind it, and the profound unrest among the Chinese proletariat, who had matured since 1919 and were becoming aware of their own strength.

The Secretariat succeeded on the whole in maintaining good relations with other labor organizations that had vaguer or more moderate programs than its own, which had been formed during this upsurge of the labor movement, and it enjoyed their support, as is evidenced by the success of the Canton Congress and of the campaign for labor legislation. Even unions with very different aims, such as those in Shanghai and Canton, did not oppose it.

In Shanghai such semi-working-class or laborite organizations as the Society for Industrial Advance, the Workers' and Merchants' Friendly Society, the Electrical Industries Federation, the Boathands' and Warehousemen's Federation, the All-China Industrial Federation, the Chinese Returned Laborers' Association, and the National Labor Federation (together with many others) remained very active.[202] They were represented, for instance, on the committee to aid the Hong Kong strikers in February 1922,[203] and on the committee that in April and May organized support for the strikers in the Pootung textile factories.[204] They cooperated with the Shanghai office of the Labor Secretariat when it organized the Labor Day celebrations in 1922. At the ceremony on May 1, both Li Ch'i-han of the Secretariat and T'ung Li-chang of the Workers' and Merchants' Friendly Society spoke, as they had done the year before.[205]

The break between these organizations and the Secretariat seems to have taken place at the beginning of July, as soon as measures had been taken against the Secretariat both in the concessions and on Chinese territory. On August 1, 1922, their leaders held a meeting to condemn the activities of the Secretariat, singling out leading Communists such as Ch'en Tu-hsiu for attack and accusing them of exploiting the sufferings of the workers for political ends.[206] From then on, these organizations sought to dissociate themselves from revolutionary activities of any kind and to oppose them. Furthermore, taking advantage of the temporary defeat of such activities in Shanghai, they tried to take the lead in the labor movement there, with the result that the movement was slowed down and diverted from its course. Although these organizations had taken active part in the May Fourth Movement and had collaborated with the Communists in 1920–21, their activities from the end of 1922 revealed a complete change of outlook. In supporting the campaign for labor legislation in September, they insisted on the need to weaken the influence of the Communists, although it was the Communists who had started the campaign.[207] In October they protested an order that the Pootung textile workers' union be dissolved. (This union had been started by the Communists, but the laborite organizations had later infiltrated it.)[208] However, in November the organizations refused to support the big "triple strike" held to protest the action of the police in closing the union.[209] In contrast to the ambitious program for the industrialization of China formulated by these organizations at the end of the First World War and their brave hopes of being able to obtain the cooperation of the proletariat and its political representatives in exchange for social reforms, their aims were now restricted to counteracting Communist influence and directing the labor movement along a path of moderation in both social and political matters.

The leaders of these organizations had already changed their views earlier in 1922; and during 1923–24, when there was an ebb in the labor movement as a whole, their new attitude hardened and they set about creating a number of rather artificially contrived organizations designed to increase their influence and prestige. They hoped they would win the esteem of both the moderates

and the progressives in the city if they helped satisfy the long-standing desire
of the Shanghai proletariat to have its own labor organizations; thus they
formed, for instance, a mutual benefit club in the Nanyang tobacco factory
that had very moderate aims and was on good terms with the management.[210]
They also gained control of the "Women's Society for the Promotion of Virtue," a friendly society for women silkworkers.[211] Hoping to profit from the
regionalist feelings still very much alive among the composite Shanghai proletariat, they formed a workers' association for natives of Anhwei residing in
Shanghai in September,[212] and in October one for Cantonese residing in Shanghai.[213] They also tried to exploit, for their own benefit, the prestige of the
Hunan Workingmen's Association, which had been broken up after the execution of its two leaders, Huang and P'ang, in January 1922; and with the help
of former associates of these two, they set up a "Shanghai Office of the Hunan
Workingmen's Association," which took part in all their activities[214] and was
a constant reminder of the two heroes.

These leaders were quite energetic in organizing the manifold activities of
their organizations, and were very good at seizing every opportunity of being
mentioned in the press or making a personal appearance in public. Among
them were the Hunanese postal worker Hsü Hsi-lin and an employee of the
Nanyang factory named Wang Kuang-hui, both of them survivors of the
Changsha affair who had taken refuge in Shanghai;[215] the tailor Ch'en Kuo-
liang, who already in 1919 was the leader of the General Society of Chinese
Trade Unions,[216] in which capacity he took part in the May Fourth Movement,
and who in 1922 ran the Society for Industrial Advance;[217] the small-scale
entrepreneur T'ung Li-chang, president of the Workers' and Merchants'
Friendly Society, who in 1920 collaborated with the Shanghai Communist
group;[218] Shih Kuan-t'ao, a B.A.T. employee and the president of the National
Labor Federation (N.L.F.);[219] and the bookbinder Wang Kyih-zung,[220] a
leader of the N.L.F. and also of the Society for Industrial Advance, and, as a
native of Anhwei, the founder of the friendly society for natives of that
province.

When the Washington Conference was held at the end of 1921, the chambers
of commerce, the teachers' associations, the provincial assemblies, and the big
progressive newspapers launched a campaign—continuing into early 1922—
against Japan's designs on China.[221] The Chinese bourgeoisie and its spokesmen hoped that this would force the Chinese delegation at the Conference not
only to demand the return of Shantung to China, but also to raise questions
about customs autonomy, extraterritoriality, and in general the rights enjoyed
by Westerners on Chinese soil. As we know, the only satisfaction China obtained, apart from the return of Shantung, was the abolition of foreign post
offices and concessions on a few other minor points, while the questions of
customs and extraterritoriality were referred to international commissions for
study. While the Conference was being held, workers almost everywhere—in

Tientsin,[222] Peking,[223] Changsha,[224] Szechwan[225]—joined in the protests raised by the organizations of the bourgeoisie, but the Labor Secretariat does not seem to have attempted to organize their protests in any systematic way.[226] In Shanghai the semi-working-class organizations played a very active part in this campaign. They organized a procession in Nanshih on December 9, in which several thousand marchers bore white banners (the color of mourning). Significantly enough, one of the slogans was: "There is no need for us to strike."[227] The same cautious line was adopted at another demonstration held by them at the beginning of January for which the directive was: "No strikes, no threats, nothing but the expression of our feelings."[228]

The anniversaries of Sun Yat-sen's appointment as President of the Republic in May and of the Macao affair in June[229] were occasions that were celebrated boisterously by these organizations. When Sun Yat-sen, once more chased from Canton (this time by his former ally Ch'en Chiung-ming), arrived in Shanghai, delegates from all the semi-working-class organizations turned out in full force (T'ung Li-chang, Wang Kuang-hui, Wang Kyih-zung, Mu Chih-ying, Shih Kuan-t'ao, Hsü Hsi-lin, Ch'en Kuo-liang, and about thirty others) and went to greet him ceremoniously at his villa in the rue Molière.[230] They also celebrated the republican festival of October 10th with the same ceremoniousness.[231]

Labor Affairs in Canton, 1922

In Canton the moderate labor organizations, which here were of the kind that preserved the old guild traditions, also continued to dominate the labor movement, despite the vicissitudes of the local political situation. But they were opposed by the anarchist group and by the group consisting of Kuomintang supporters.[232]

Although a few amalgamated groups with a wider basis of membership existed, such as the Mechanics' Union formed in 1921 or, in the craftsman category, the bakers' guild with its six sections (bakers, pastry cooks, cooks, and so forth),[233] demarcation of trades and of categories of trade still predominated. Canton at that time had nearly 200 craft or industrial associations,[234] among which there was a very high degree of specialization: three separate associations for employees in teahouses,[235] three for woodworkers,[236] five for boatmen and boathands of various kinds.[237] There was frequent rivalry between these demarcated associations, and sometimes they even came to blows, as when in March 1922 the sawyers attacked the carpenters with iron bars for refusing to support their strike.[238] The existence in Canton of a provincial federation of trade associations and guilds[239] and in Hong Kong of two separate federations, the General Association of Chinese Workingmen[240] and the General Association of Labor Organizations,[241] all three very loosely organized and without much power, did little to solve the demarcation problem.

Although it was now exceptional to find master craftsmen and journey-men belonging to the same corporation (one exception being the bricklayers' guild),[242] the Cantonese trade associations still bore the marks of the old guild system. One of their main preoccupations was to regulate the labor market for their own exclusive advantage, and to maintain a monopoly over the supply of new recruits:[243] although they did occasionally hold strikes, they much pre-ferred to settle disputes by mediation or conciliation rather than by open con-flict with employers.[244] Another indication of the persistence of the old guild traditions was the occasional unsuccessful attempt on the part of workers in a particular trade to found a cooperative workshop with the support of their guild when they were on strike. This happened in 1921 when workers in the book trade were on strike,[245] and in 1922 during the strikes of restaurant em-ployees and of watchmakers.[246]

The anarchists seem still to have been quite lively here in 1922, and they took active part in the Labor Congress.[247] On that occasion the special May 1 num-ber of the Cantonese review *Lao-tung-hao* ("The Cry of Labor") that was devoted to the Congress contained an article with the significant title: "Direct Action and the General Strike." But anarchism was already on the decline, and gradually disappeared during 1923-24.

Sun Yat-sen and the Kuomintang, on the other hand, received steadily in-creasing political support from the labor movement. Most of the guilds and trade associations, and with them the Kwangtung provincial federation, pre-tended to stand apart from politics, while in fact remaining extremely con-servative; but several organizations actively supported the program of na-tionalism, constitutionalism, and moderate socialism still propounded by Sun Yat-sen in 1922. These included the Mechanics' Union, the mutual benefit society run by Hsieh Ying-po,[248] and the Seamen's Union, the president of which was Ch'en Ping-sheng, an old associate of Sun Yat-sen.

In June 1922, when Ch'en Chiung-ming and his Cantonese troops forced Sun Yat-sen, Liao Chung-k'ai, Hsieh Ying-po, Ch'en Ping-sheng, and all the rest of the Kuomintang group to leave Canton,[249] the conservative elements belonging to the provincial federation began to adopt an independent political line. Ch'en Chiung-ming, in turning against the erstwhile allies whom he had brought back to Canton after his victory over the Kwangsi militarists in 1921, was only acting in accord with the views of the Kwangtung gentry and of the moderates among the bourgeoisie of Canton and Hong Kong, all of whom were disturbed by Sun's plans for military action against the North.[250] When Ch'en staged his coup, all the Canton labor organizations that supported Sun tried to intervene on Sun's behalf. The Mechanics' Union launched a strike at the Canton power plant,[251] and during the following months continued to show their hostility to the new regime.[252] But the leaders of the provincial fed-eration seem to have welcomed the installation of Ch'en's conservative and authoritarian regime; and in June, they offered to mediate between Sun and

Ch'en, while expressing disapproval of the strike launched by the Mechanics' Union at the time of the coup.[253] They also took part in the ceremonies organized by the new Canton government in celebration of the republican festival of October 10th.[254]

In this conflict between the followers of Sun Yat-sen and Ch'en Chiung-ming, the Cantonese Communists seem to have adopted a somewhat ambivalent attitude. Ch'en Kung-po, at that time the chief Communist leader in South China, actually issued the directive: "Unite with Ch'en in order to overthrow Sun."[255] The party leadership quickly condemned this as opportunism, and dismissed Ch'en Kung-po; but this episode did little to strengthen the very feeble influence so far exerted by the Communists in South China.

Ch'en Chiung-ming's policy toward labor from July 1922 on is a fair enough indication of the conservative nature of his regime. The legislative reforms carried through in the spring of 1922 that abolished Yuan Shih-k'ai's anti-strike laws were allowed to stand, but strikes were rigorously controlled.[256] In November a Labor Office was created,[257] composed of employers' delegates, magistrates, and workers' delegates and charged with the task of keeping a watch over the trade associations; its arbitration had to be accepted in all labor disputes.

The Labor Secretariat does not seem to have had much influence in Canton. Its representative there was Feng Chü-p'o,[258] who, together with another militant Communist, T'an P'ing-shan, gained admission to the Mechanics' Union at the end of 1921 and tried to take charge of education; but they were soon thrown out.[259] The attempt made at the beginning of 1922 to create a "Federation of Unions" in opposition to the conservative provincial federation was no more successful.[260] In short, the Secretariat seems to have had less influence in Canton in 1922 than in any other part of China, except for the Northeast. Su Chao-cheng, future president of the All-China General Union, later said that in 1922, after the Hong Kong seamen's strike, he had tried to contact Communists in Canton and could not find any.[261]

Thus, although the labor movement in South China was in the first stage and going well, by the end of 1922 there were no signs of the new turn things had taken in Central China and to some extent in Shanghai. The explanation for this must lie in the nature of Canton's economy and in the fact that its industry consisted of small dispersed units of production. But despite the antiquated conservatism of the trade associations and the political allegiance, mostly because of personal ties, of some of their leaders to Sun Yat-sen, there were already murmurings in the depths that were to lead to the mass movement of the workers of South China in 1924–27. The movement of solidarity with the Hong Kong seamen in February had been supported by the entire working-class population of Canton. In June the Macao affair raised this sense of solidarity to a much higher degree of class consciousness. The affair started with a clash between the Portuguese police and some Chinese workers in Macao who were acting in defense of a woman who had been maltreated by a Goan policeman.[262] On May 29 the police fired on a protest demonstration, killing 40 and wounding 130. The guilds of Macao replied by declaring a general strike, and there was an exodus to the neighboring island of Kungpei (Lappa) which many Chinese in Portuguese territory joined. In Canton, the trade associations and the whole population took up the cudgels for the Macao Chinese; they organized a subscription fund, demanded that the government should take up the matter with the Portuguese authorities, sent provisions and medicines to the refugees in Kungpei, and stocked rice in anticipation of a prolonged conflict. The Portuguese authorities did not in fact give way until February 1923, when they negotiated with the Chinese associations in Macao for a return to work against payment of indemnities to the wounded and the families of the victims of May 29.[263] This episode was not only significant in itself; it also curiously prefigured, even including details of events, the great movement of solidarity that brought the whole of the Cantonese proletariat behind the Chinese strikers on two other islands under foreign control: Shameen in 1924, and Hong Kong in 1925–26.

Chinese Protestant Views on Labor Issues

When faced with the upsurge of the labor movement in 1922, to what extent did employers and government authorities, either Chinese or foreign, reflect upon labor problems and consider adopting the kind of reformist policy that Western governments since the end of the nineteenth century had used to moderate the conflict between capital and labor? Did it never occur to them that it might be possible, and to their own advantage, to adopt such a policy?

As far as one can judge from the negative evidence supplied by the English-language press of Shanghai, Western businessmen there never considered adopting a general reformist policy. The first time any attention was paid to labor problems in these circles was in an editorial of the *China Weekly Review* in the spring of 1922, when the effects of the Hong Kong seamen's strike were still being felt. But the appeal in this editorial for "progressive moves" remained an isolated one.[264] Western employers in Shanghai were more concerned to find more effective methods of repression.[265]

The Chinese Protestants seem to have been the only people to make a serious attempt to grapple with labor problems, possibly because they were anxious to vindicate themselves against accusations made by anti-Christian Chinese intellectuals,[266] but also perhaps because they were coming under pressure from certain Western labor organizations which they had encountered when working in the labor camps in France in 1917–18, and which now felt threatened by the competition offered by a downtrodden and underpaid Chinese labor force. Probably many of these zealous Protestants were unable to distinguish between their sincere desire to improve Chinese labor conditions and their acute anxiety about the "disorders" that might ensue if the rising tide of the labor movement was not stopped.[267]

The Protestants' reflections upon labor problems, which afford a strong contrast to the rather scornful indifference shown by the Catholic missionaries,[268] resulted in a number of practical steps being taken. As early as 1920 and 1921, the Y.M.C.A. introduced "industrial departments" within its organization, and encouraged its local branches to appoint an "industrial secretary," whose job it was to study labor problems in each of the main centers.[269] In May 1922, at a time when the nationalist movement in China was felt to be a threat to the Protestant missions, a meeting was held in Shanghai at which a "National Christian Council of China" was formed, which included representatives of the various denominations of Chinese Protestantism as well as of most of the Western Protestant missions.[270] A report on "the attitude of the Church regarding the industrial and social problems of China" was presented by the missionary F. C. Remer, who was also an economist who held a chair at the St. John University in Shanghai. The report described at length the poverty-stricken situation of the Chinese proletariat.[271] At the meeting—which, it is worth noting, was held at exactly the same time as the Canton Labor Congress —it was decided that efforts should be made to have the norms defined by the I.L.O. at its inaugural meeting in 1919 (concerning the eight-hour day, control over the employment of women and children, and so on) applied to China, and that for a start the following three rules should be put into practice: prohibition of the employment of children under twelve, a weekly day of rest, and improvement of sanitary conditions and safety precautions.

When the world-famous Protestant progressive Dr. Sherwood Eddy visited China during the summer and fall of 1922, further discussions were held on these problems. Dr. Eddy visited many mills and factories, and wrote articles and gave lectures denouncing what he, as a Christian, regarded as the scandalous working conditions existing in China.[272] In December 1922 Dr. Eddy, assisted by Miss Agatha Harrison—an ardent Quaker who two years before had been asked by the Y.M.C.A. to study labor problems in China, and who had devoted herself to making Christians in China aware of the situation of the Chinese proletariat—held a "Conference on Industrial Problems" in Shanghai under the aegis of the National Christian Council, at which it was decided to publish a bulletin and to make approaches to industrialists. An appeal was made to Christian employers urging them at least to introduce a weekly day of rest.[273]

In addition to their study of labor problems and their propaganda work, the Protestant organizations also made some practical attempts to improve working-class social conditions. The Hankow branch of the Y.M.C.A. established an industrial department in the factory district in 1921, which opened its premises to unions wishing to hold meetings there,[274] and even offered to mediate in strikes such as that of the rickshaw men at the end of the year.[275]

The Shanghai Y.M.C.A., in conjunction with the Municipal Council, organized evening courses for postal workers;[276] and another instance of cooperation between employers and the Protestant organizations was the founding of the workers' hospital in Yangtzepoo, which was financed by the cotton mills of the district and staffed by missionaries.[277] The "Yangtzepoo Social Center," founded by Baptist missionaries and partially subsidized by employers, ran a school for two hundred children and in addition gave classes for adults; the fees were from 12 to 20 yuan a year—a sum that only a tiny minority of the better-paid workers could afford.[278]

All these efforts on the part of missionaries did not, however, amount to very much, and the appeals of the National Christian Council fell on deaf ears among employers, even among those Western employers who were so eager to defend "Western Christian civilization" against any new ideology in China, and what is more, even among the small number of Chinese Protestant employers. The example set by the Chinese Christian employers of Chefoo in granting a paid day off on Sundays, and in getting the Chinese Chamber of Commerce in the town to make this a general rule, does not seem to have been followed anywhere else.[279] Almost the only efforts at social welfare made by the big industrial firms in China were the opening of a workers' hospital in Tangshan by the K.M.A.,[280] and the initiation of a reserve fund by the B.A.T. Company after the big strikes in Pootung in the fall of 1922. The fund was made up of annual company payments equal to 5 per cent of the total annual wage bill, and it was used to provide sickness and old age benefits and extra payments when prices were high; only workers who had been employed in the factory for a minimum of five consecutive years were eligible.[281]

Government authorities, both Chinese and foreign, were no more enthusiastic about social reform. Nothing further was done in Peking in the fall of 1922 to carry out the proposals of the Labor Secretariat concerning labor legislation, despite Wu P'ei-fu's promised "protection of labor"; nor did the Shanghai Municipal Council ever seem to have seriously considered doing anything in this direction. The Hong Kong government did, it is true, establish official control over the employment of children under 15, prohibiting employment of children under ten (in some enterprises, of children under 15) and limiting their hours of work to a nine-hour day, with a prohibition against night work and work on Sundays.[282] But this was a measure that did not go very far, and although it was proclaimed as having been introduced out of humanitarian motives, it was probably just as much planned for the sake of gaining popularity.[283]

The Ching-Han Incident

By the beginning of 1923 the Chinese labor movement had lost something of the enthusiasm and the dynamic force that during 1922 had been displayed during the seamen's strike in Hong Kong, the Labor Congress in Canton, the strike wave of the spring and summer, and the campaign for labor legislation. In Shanghai, in the K.M.A. mines, and also in Canton after Ch'en Chiung-ming had come to power, it had suffered a number of setbacks and counter-attacks. But in Hupeh and Hunan, and among the railwaymen in Central and North China, the work of organization undertaken by the Labor Secretariat during the previous eighteen months still remained intact. It was soon to be suddenly jeopardized by the massacre of February 7, 1923.

After the fall of 1922, relations between the labor movement and the war-lord government in Central China had steadily deteriorated. Strikes such as the Changsintien strike in September had hurt Wu P'ei-fu's government finan-cially,[284] and Wu must have had some anxieties about the future in seeing the growing influence of the Communists among the Ching-Han railwaymen. Since the Ching-Han railway was the communications system between the northern capital, the British mines in Honan, the military camps at Paoting and Loyang, and Wuhan (which was the political and economic center of Cen-tral China and the Lower Yangtze region), it was of great strategic importance both to Wu P'ei-fu and his Chihli faction and to the British firms with which they had such close ties. They could not afford to have political unrest among the railwaymen. Wu, who had temporarily given support to the Communists in order to get rid of the pro-Japanese Communications Clique, was by the end of 1922 doing all he could to counteract their influence. Still officially retaining his program of the "protection of labor," he saw to it that employees' clubs and regional friendly societies under his control were formed, and also squads of railwaymen-soldiers,[285] the military nature of which makes it clear that the use of force in the February incident was something that was planned well ahead.[286]

Further, the labor movement in Central China, which during 1922 had mainly come up against state enterprises (the railways, the mines, and the fac-tories and arsenals under provincial government control) or against the Han-yehping combine, which was closely connected with the state, was at the begin-ning of 1923 beginning to come into conflict with Western, and above all with British, firms in Hupeh. In Hankow, strikes held at the British Cigarette Com-pany,[287] the British cotton mills,[288] and the cotton-baling factory of Mackenzie and Company[289] in January gave rise to violent clashes between the strikers and the British police. On several occasions police stations were besieged, and once the Superintendent of Police himself was roughly handled. Over a hun-dred arrests were made, and the British authorities were alarmed enough to mobilize the special constabulary (an armed volunteer force of foreign resi-dents) at the outbreak of each strike. These strikes in British enterprises in Hankow were actively supported by the local unions and by the Hupeh pro-vincial federation. A new feature of them was their pronounced anti-foreign tone, which had been much less noticeable during the strikes of the Hong Kong seamen and the K.M.A. miners. Thus already in January 1923 defense of the workers' immediate material interests was being merged with political action against the Foreign Powers and the rights they enjoyed on Chinese soil. The leaflets distributed during the Hankow strikes and the statements issued by the provincial federation suggested that commercial relations between China and Great Britain be broken off, criticized the British police of Hankow, and attacked the "foreign capitalists" and their compradores.[290] The British firms and authorities, faced with this unexpected attack, temporarily gave ground. The workers arrested were released, Mackenzie and Company and the British Cigarette Company officially recognized the unions in their factories to the extent of agreeing to consult them on a number of questions, and a substantial raise in wages was granted, as well as various bonuses (for night work, the New Year holiday, and so on).[291] But this was no more than a tactical withdrawal, and the government authorities in Central China hastened to calm the anxieties of the British firms there, who, according to the *Central China Post,* were worried about this apparent capitulation to the demands of the "Bolsheviks."[292]

All these latent antagonisms suddenly came into the open at the beginning of February, when the 16 Ching-Han railwaymen's clubs amalgamated to form an official Ching-Han General Union.[293] Talks about the amalgamation had begun in the fall, and a provisional set of rules had been drawn up.[294] The management of the Ching-Han network had been kept informed about this, and granted travel facilities to the delegates of the 16 clubs who were to meet at a conference to be held on February 2 in Chengchow, the center of the network. Members of other railwaymen's unions and of other labor organizations in Central China who had been invited to attend were on their way when, on January 30, Wu P'ei-fu suddenly informed members of the planning committee that he had decided to ban the conference for reasons of "military security," at the same time declaring that he still kept to his "protection of labor" policy. In spite of this, the conference opened at the arranged time and place, declared the union to be founded, and immediately dispersed, although not quickly enough to prevent the police and the army from arresting several of the delegates and pursuing several others. The leadership of the new union responded to this harassment by ordering a general strike, and presented demands for the dismissal of the managing director of the network, the reimbursement of expenses incurred by the union in preparation for the conference, and the removal of police from union premises, as well as for a weekly day of rest with pay and a week's paid holiday at the lunar New Year. The general strike began on February 4 throughout the network; and despite such pressures brought to bear as arrests of leaders, attempts to requisition engineers for military service, and the employment of hsin-kung (strikebreakers), all the personnel held out and refused to go back to work unless ordered to do so by the union, thus demonstrating the extent of the union's authority. After the strike had lasted three days, the Chihli militarists decided to use force, and the troops of Ts'ao

K'un at Changsintien, of Wu P'ei-fu at Chengchow, and of Hsiao Yao-nan, governor of Hupeh, at Kiangan, attacked the strikers, killing 35 of them and seriously wounding many more. Lin Hsiang-ch'ien, branch secretary of the union in the Kiangan depot, was beheaded on the station platform in front of his comrades for having once again refused to give the order to return to work.

Although the onus for the instigation and execution of these brutal measures must be laid on the warlord government in North China, it would seem that the Western authorities in Hankow, who had themselves been under attack from the labor movement during the preceding weeks, also played a part in the affair. It is an established fact that contingents of British marines landed at Hankow on February 8 and took part in the suppression of a sympathy strike declared by the Hupeh provincial federation the day after the massacre. Furthermore, according to reports supplied by union sources, the use of force was decided upon only after consultation with the Western Powers. It seems that a secret meeting was held on the evening of February 6 at the British consulate in Hankow, attended not only by the chief foreign consuls, but also by representatives of the Chinese police and army, of the management of the Ching-Han railway, and of the principal foreign firms of Hankow.[295]

The order to return to work was given on February 9, thus closing the Ching-Han incident. But by this time feelings were running high throughout China. All the Wuhan labor organizations launched sympathy strikes on February 8, which, however, were called off the following day. The railwaymen on the Cheng-T'ai, Chin-P'u, and Ching-Feng lines in North China came out on strike and carried out further demonstrations of protest.[296] In Shanghai, representatives of the moderate labor organizations, such as the Nanyang and B.A.T. workers' clubs, the Anhwei and Canton regional friendly societies, the electrical workers, the seamen, and the Workers' and Merchants' Friendly Society, sent a telegram of protest;[297] and apparently the Mechanics' Union, which was one of the organizations that had remained in touch with the Labor Secretariat, formed a plan for a general strike, which was cut short by General Ho Feng-lin's declaration of martial law on Chinese territory,[298] and by a search of the Mechanics' Union premises by the police of the International Settlement.[299] In addition to the protests and declarations of solidarity from labor organizations came those from the Communist Party,[300] from Sun Yat-sen, from student associations in Wuhan, Peking, and Shanghai, from the Chinese bourgeoisie in Southeast Asia, and from the Hupeh regional friendly societies in Peking, Shanghai, and other cities.[301] The Chamber of Commerce of Changsintien interceded on behalf of eleven union militants who had been arrested, and obtained their release.[302] Thus the incident of February 7 became the occasion for a truly nationwide expression of class consciousness on the part of the Chinese proletariat; and progressives in general became much more outspoken in their criticism of the warlord government and the terroristic methods employed by the tu-chün than they had ever been before.[303]

It was also an occasion that led the leaders of the Chinese labor movement to examine the seriousness of the defeat they had suffered, the possible errors they had made, and the prospects offered by the future. Regarding their immediate situation, the Secretariat was criticized[304] for having entertained certain illusions concerning Wu P'ei-fu, and for failures in union organization such as having done little or no work in the army and having delayed in starting the sympathy strikes of the local unions in Wuhan. They were reprimanded also for not having gained enough influence among the workers in the telecommunications services, with the result that the three main centers of resistance after February 4 (at Changsintien, Chengchow, and Kiangan) were completely cut off from each other.

As for the future, the sudden check to the labor movement caused by the Ching-Han incident meant that some new thinking would have to be done about the balance of social and political forces in China. From this point of view, the incident prepared the way for the new alliances that were to be entered into during the revolution of 1924–27, after a temporary lull in the labor movement.

CHAPTER IX

Two Years of Retreat

In 1923 and 1924 that anachronistic social and political phenomenon, warlordism, was at its height in China. The tu-chün, or warlords—whose rule by force dated back in certain respects to the days of Yuan Shih-k'ai, and even to the times when provincial armies were raised to crush the Taiping—had rapidly increased their power after the First World War, and they now dominated the Chinese political scene. What first enabled them to thrive was the worsening agrarian crisis which drove hundreds of thousands—perhaps even millions—of ruined peasants from their villages, some of whom enrolled, willy-nilly, in local or provincial armies, while others "took to the hills" to join the bands of outlaws connected with the secret societies; still others boarded ships bound for the distant mines and plantations of Southeast Asia. More recently, the position of the warlords had been strengthened still further by the intensification of international rivalries in the Far East following the end of the Anglo-Japanese alliance and the Washington Conference in 1921. The Chinese militarist factions owing loyalty to the French (mainly in the Southwest) and to the Japanese (mainly in the Northeast and on mainland territory opposite Taiwan) were opposed to those who had ties with British and American interests. In 1920–22 the most overt, although not the only, reflection in Chinese politics of these international rivalries was the rivalry, first between the Anfu and Chihli factions, and afterward between the Chihli and Fengtien factions. In 1923–24 warlordism had increased to such an extent that it was now necessary to distinguish between what were usually known as "supertuchun" (whose official title was "Inspector General") and the small fry consisting of provincial or district potentates who were more or less directly linked with one or another of the main factions. There were three such main factions at the time of the February Seventh incident: the Chihli group, which had twice got the better of its pro-Japanese opponents, and now controlled, either directly or through some intermediary, the whole of China from the Great Wall to the Lower and Middle Yangtze valley; the Fengtien group led by Chang Tso-lin, which held the whole of Northeast China; and the Anfu group, which had been dominant from 1916 to 1920, but whose only representative now was Lu Yung-hsiang, the governor of Chekiang, whose territory included Shanghai and its immediate surroundings. Lu's position was secured by the control exercised over this area by his associate, General Ho Feng-lin. Some of the local warlords were direct dependents of the supertuchun. The governors of the Northeast provinces were all Chang Tso-lin's men, while the leaders of the Chihli faction, Wu P'ei-fu and Ts'ao K'un, could count on the loyalty of men such as Yang Sen in Szechwan, Ch'i Hsieh-yuan in the Lower Yangtze valley, Hsiao Yao-nan in Hupeh, Ch'en Chiung-ming in Kwangtung, and the "Christian General" Feng Yü-hsiang, whose treasonable intentions were not yet evident, in Honan. South of the Yangtze and in the Southwest allegiances were less clear-cut and there was a far greater proliferation of petty military leaders, who were endlessly at war with each other. Occasionally, however, a figure of larger stature emerged from their midst, such as Chao Heng-t'i in Hunan and T'ang Chi-yao in Yunnan, the first of whom played a complicated game to further his own interests, while the second pushed his enthusiasm for French influence to the point of having the *Marseillaise* played on the "National Day of Yunnan."[1]

The February Seventh incident was not the first time the warlords had used force against the labor movement; they had already done so during the Yueh-Han railwaymen's and the K.M.A. miners' strikes in 1922, and during the Hanyang arsenal strike in 1915. But until 1923 they had on the whole adopted a tolerant attitude toward the labor movement, and had even on occasion enlisted its support in their intrigues against each other, as Chao Heng-t'i had done in Hunan in 1921, and Wu P'ei-fu on the railways in the North in 1922. After February 7, however, having realized that in the long run the working class might prove as dangerous an enemy as rival warlords, they adopted a policy of putting down all activities of the labor movement by brute force.

From this time on, the army was regularly brought in to break strikes, and strike leaders were often arrested. This happened in Chang Tso-lin's territory (during the strike at the Yingkow oil-pressing mills in April 1923 and that at the Mukden hemp factory in June 1924),[2] in Hsiao Yao-nan's (the Hankow brewery strike in April 1923 and that of the Hankow rickshaw men in September 1924),[3] and in Ch'i Hsieh-yuan's territory (the rickshaw men's strikes in Wuhu in November 1923 and in Soochow in February 1923).[4] Similar incidents took place in Shanghai, where the strikes held in 1924 in the Chapei silk-reeling factories and the Nanyang tobacco factory in Pootung were ruthlessly put down.[5] And at Tientsin, in the very heart of the Chihli faction's territory, a strike held in two Japanese-owned cotton mills ended in army occupation of the mills after what amounted to a pitched battle, in which eight men were killed and more than one million yuan worth of damage was done.[6]

The new repressive policy was also directed against unions and militant members of the working class. Already in the summer of 1922 Ho Feng-lin had declared illegal all labor organizations in Shanghai that showed any radical tendencies, however slight; and in July 1924, when Ho Feng-lin had fled with Lu Yung-hsiang to Japan following their defeat by Ch'i Hsieh-yuan and the take-over of the Shanghai region by Fengtien troops, a similar policy was instituted by the new military commander, who ordered all unions to send their rules to the police for approval under penalty of being banned. In addition, he announced that anyone who, in the name of a union that had already been dissolved or was now banned, incited workers to strike, would be sentenced by martial law.[7] During this same year, Yang Sen, in distant Szechwan, banned the Szechwan General Union, which he suspected of having revolutionary intentions;[8] and in Wuhan, Hsiao Yao-nan arrested those remaining trade union militants who had not been intimidated by the February Seventh incident, and had them deported to the military camp in Loyang, Wu P'ei-fu's main stronghold.[9] Workers became involved in all sorts of absurd situations, as for instance when, in October 1924, the Shanghai police decided to arrest everyone who happened to have been tattooed, on the grounds that tattoo marks were secret signs of membership in a trade union.[10]

There was, however, one warlord who did not at first join the others in adopting a repressive policy after February 7, or at least did so only to a moderate extent. This was Chao Heng-t'i, who was still playing off the main factions against each other and doubtless needed all the support he could get in his own province.[11] But on June 1, 1923, a serious incident occurred in Changsha between Japanese marines and a crowd of demonstrators demanding the return of Port Arthur and Dairen to China. Four Chinese were killed, and when a general strike was declared in protest, Chao changed his tune. He prohibited the anti-Japanese boycott that workers and students were beginning to organize, and banned all the unions that had been formed in Changsha during the preceding year with the help of the Labor Secretariat.[12] He took further measures against the labor movement in 1924, when he broke the strike of the Shuikowshan miners and closed down their club,[13] promulgated a "trade union law" under which the only authorized bodies were guilds directed by employers,[14] and finally attempted to take advantage of the fame that had been attained by the Hunan Workingmen's Association by creating an organization with the same title that was entirely under his control.[15] With the exception of the Canton region, where Sun Yat-sen came to power again in 1923,[16] all the industrial regions of China were subjected to reactionary measures imposed by the warlords; the only working-class organization in these areas that escaped this treatment and that survived through to 1925 was the Anyuan workers' club, owing largely to its isolated situation on the mountain borders between Hunan and Kiangsi.[17]

It was, however, not merely the few labor militants—those who during 1923–24 tried to keep the trade unions operating clandestinely and to launch strikes—that were affected by warlordism, but rather the entire working class. The warlords made prodigious profits from the exactions they imposed, the capital levies they demanded from the bourgeoisie and the chambers of commerce, and their traffic in arms and opium;[18] and they invested these, not only

TABLE 27

NUMBER OF TROOPS TRANSPORTED BY THE RAILWAYS, 1920–25[a]

Line	1920	1921	1922	1923	1924	1925
Ching-Sui	56,506	54,922	17,931	34,824	13,672	122,007
Hu-Ning	6,446	3,460	4,459	2,260	80,893	65,844
Chin-P'u	272,220	75,109	69,858	102,858	760,552	1,291,065
Ching-Feng	199,204	191,116	1,425,348	57,608	2,665,405	1,680,877
Ching-Han	290,788	228,426	196,132	161,242	273,418	662,348

[a] Figures are from *Statistics of Government Railways* [36]. The table shows that all lines were affected by the fall of the Anfu faction in 1920, the Ching-Han and Ching-Feng lines by the Feng-tien-Chihli wars in 1922 and 1924, the Hu-Ning and Chin-P'u lines by the Chekiang-Kiangsu war in 1924, and again all lines by the military operations of 1925.

in land, but also in industrial enterprises, especially in Hupeh, Chihli, and Fengtien, where Chinese capitalist enterprise was almost nonexistent.[19] It is not difficult to imagine what the results of this renewal of the "bureaucratic capitalism" of the 1870–90 period were for the people employed in these enterprises.

Furthermore, in view of the incessant movement of troops necessitated by existing or planned military operations, the warlords were obliged to assume control of the railways. Table 27 shows the steady increase in the number of soldiers transported from 1920 to 1925. This resulted in clashes with railwaymen, which were often violent,[20] irregular payment of wages, lengthening of working hours, and straight requisitioning of labor. Moreover, both Wu P'ei-fu and Chang Tso-lin requisitioned not only dock porters and coolies for service in the transport of their armies,[21] but also factory workers,[22] a move which was highly unpopular among the workers concerned and which was also viewed unfavorably by the industrial enterprises in the war zones, constantly threatened as they were by a labor shortage.[23]

The labor shortage was not the only problem industry had to face as a result of the incessant military operations of the warlords. The supply of raw materials[24] and of fuel[25] was interfered with, so that many factories were unable to maintain their normal rate of production.[26] Some enterprises laid off some of their employees, and others made reductions either in wages or in hours.[27]

The Crisis in Chinese-Owned Industry

Chinese capitalist enterprise was at this time encountering other difficulties, apart from those caused by the renewal of fighting among the warlords, which brought on a deterioration in the situation of the workers. After an unexpected "golden age" during the First World War, Chinese capitalists had not stood up well to the return of Western competitors from 1920 on, and were in addition threatened by the steady growth of Japanese economic penetration of

China. Chinese industrialists, being inexperienced, handicapped by having to pay the likin, and without the banking support enjoyed by their British and Japanese competitors, were at the mercy of the slightest change in the state of the market.[28] There was a crisis in the Chinese-owned cotton mills in 1923–24 because of a rise in the price of raw cotton and a fall in the price of yarn.[29] The flour mills, which had increased in number since 1914, were hit by imports of corn and flour from the United States and Canada, who had turned to the Far East now that the market for army supplies in Europe no longer existed.[30] Oil-pressing mills and the silk industry were also having difficulties, and the Hanyehping blast furnaces, even more vulnerable than light industry, suffered considerable losses as a result of the deal with Japan in 1913, in which Japan got the lion's share of the market.[31]

Thus, in 1923–24 many Chinese-owned private firms had either to cut production or to close down temporarily, and some even went out of business altogether. The Shanghai association of Chinese cotton mill owners had already decided at the end of 1922 to cut production by 25 per cent, thus throwing ten thousand employees out of work;[32] the Tientsin association decided on a 50 per cent cut,[33] and similar cuts were made in mills in Wuhan, Hangchow, Chengchow, and Changsha.[34] Mills in Wuhu, Ningpo, and Wuhan resorted to temporary shutdowns during 1923 and 1924,[35] and quite a large number in various places closed down altogether.[36] The Chinese-owned oil-pressing mills in Dairen cut their production by two thirds in 1924,[37] flour mills in various centers ceased production entirely,[38] and so did several silk factories in Shanghai and Kwangtung.[39] The Hanyang steelworks closed in 1922 and the Yangtze Engineering Works in 1924.[40]

This crisis in Chinese-owned industry hit the working class hard. The resulting unemployment was not the only problem, for wages fell in the enterprises that still kept going, or else output rates were raised to unheard-of heights. In Shanghai the silk-reeling factories reduced wages,[41] and in some cotton mills piece rates were introduced that compared unfavorably with the time rates they replaced;[42] the same was true of the Shunteh silk factories and the Hangchow cotton mills.[43] In other mills the weight of the baskets of cotton on which wage rates were based was raised,[44] a device also used regarding the baskets of ore in a manganese mine.[45] There was also a speeding up of production at the cotton spindles.[46]

The rise in prices, particularly food prices, that occurred at this time affected not only the employees of Chinese-owned enterprises, but the whole of the working population in the towns. A few local surveys that were made give a general idea of this price rise, which affected all areas, though not uniformly. (See Table 28.)

All wages were adversely affected by the depreciation of copper currency that had occurred after the end of the First World War, and this also accentuated the effects of the price rise, for prices (even retail prices) were usually

TABLE 28

PRICE RISES BETWEEN 1919 AND 1925

Region and categories	Prices or price index figures, c. 1919	Prices or price index figures, c. 1925
Canton (Index of 100 in 1913):		
Cereals[a]	132.6 (1919)	132.9 (1925)
General price index[b]	136.4 (1919)	175.6 (1925)
North China (Index of 100 in 1926):		
Food price index[c]	62.44 (1919)	97.18 (1925)
General price index[d]	81.00 (1919)	97.23 (1925)
Chengchow:[e] rice	12 copper cash/pound	28 copper cash/pound
coal	45 copper cash/picul	200 copper cash/picul
flour	2.80 yuan/sack	3.40 yuan/sack
Hankow:[f] rice	19,000 cash/picul (March 1922)	30,000 cash/picul (May 1925)
Shanghai:[g] rice	7.48 yuan/picul (1919)	13 yuan/picul (1925)
Shansi:[h] rice	1,520 cash/bushel	2,040 cash/bushel
corn	848 cash/bushel	1,222 cash/bushel
local cloth	72 cash/foot	134 cash/foot (figures for 1923)
Tsingtao:[i] rice (low quality)	7.18 yuan/picul (1920)	17.21 yuan/picul (1924)

[a] *Nien-chien* [138] I, 146.   [b] *CWR*, 28.i.28.   [c] *Nien-chien* [138] I, 145.   [d] *Ibid.*
[e] *CEB*, 24.x.25.   [f] *CWR*, 18.iii.22 and 16.v.25.   [g] *SMCR*, 1919 and 1925.   [h] *CEB*,
30.viii.24.   [i] *Nien-chien* [138] I, 67.

reckoned in terms of silver currency, whereas the copper cash received in wages were accepted only at their depreciated value.[47] The fall in the value of copper currency was perceptible everywhere, but it varied from region to region. (See Table 29.) There was also a fall in the value of silver cents in relation to the silver one-yuan piece, so that even the wages of those fortunate enough to be paid in silver were affected by currency depreciation.[48] Depreciation was further accelerated by the warlords' habit of minting an excessive number of small coins and of making frequent issues of provincial paper money, a still more depreciated form of currency, in an attempt to meet extravagant expenditures. This became common practice in Hupeh after the Chihli faction put the Anfu faction out of power in 1920,[49] and in Fengtien Chang Tso-lin sent monetary inflation to considerable heights in 1924 and 1925.[50]

According to the very inadequate available information, it would appear that the overall economic situation of Chinese workers in 1923 and 1924 was worse than it had been in 1919, despite the raise in wages gained during the 1922 strikes. The price index in Canton, taking 1913 as 100, rose from 136.4 in

TABLE 29

DEPRECIATION OF COPPER CURRENCY BETWEEN 1919 AND 1925

| Locality | Exchange rate (Copper cents per yuan) | |
	Earlier	Later
Hangchow[a]	132 (Dec. 1918)	197 (March 1925)
Tientsin[b]	137–82 (Dec. 1918)	280 (March 1925)
Canton[c]	136 (1919)	206.4 (Dec. 1924)
Shanghai[d]	136 (1919)	217 (March 1925)
Hankow[e]	138–47 (1919)	209–69 (1924)
Peking[f]	138 (1919)	285.5 (c. 1924)
Shansi[g]	170–80 (1920)	290 (Dec. 1924)
Wuhu[h]	198 (Jan. 1924)	218 (Dec. 1924)

[a] *CEB*, 4.vii.25. [b] *Ibid.* [c] *Ibid.* [d] *Ibid.* [e] Kann [264], p. 537. [f] Meng and Gamble [75], p. 89. [g] *CEB*, 24.xi.25. [h] *RT*, 1924, Wuhu, p. 4.

1919 to 175.6 in 1924, while the corresponding figures for wages are 106.19 and 135.28.[51] Thus the increase in wages fell far below the rise in prices. The average wage of a skilled worker in the Chunghsing collieries in Shantung only rose from 27.12 yuan per month in 1919 to 28.90 in 1925,[52] and that of an unskilled worker in the Shanghai cotton mills rose from 30 silver cents per day in 1920 to 38 cents in 1925;[53] these small increases were more than offset by steep price rises in both Shantung and Kiangsu. In 1925 the Shanghai dockers received only 60 to 100 copper cash per day, which is very little more than their pay rate in 1919.[54]

Such were the effects of warlordism at its height, and of the crisis in Chinese capitalist enterprise. The eventual results were the development of a new political attitude among the bourgeoisie from 1924 on, and improved prospects for the labor movement's political struggle through the Kuomintang's policy of cooperation with the Communists.[55] The immediate result, however, was a serious deterioration in the situation of the workers, one indication of which is that more and more workers in the Chiu-ta salt refinery began having their families live with them because they could no longer afford to send remittances to them in the home village.[56] The lives of workers, not yet rescued from their poverty by the strike wave of 1921–22, were of little account: 100 died early in 1924 in a fire at the Hsiang-ching silk-reeling factory in Shanghai, 75 in an explosion in the Fangtze mine in Shantung, and 53 as the result of a roof collapse in the K.M.A. mines.[57]

Recession of the Strike Waves

Strikes were still held during the difficult years of 1923–24, but the incomplete lists available show that their frequency and scope were much reduced in comparison with the earlier strike wave. (See Table 30.)

During 1921–22 the main battleground had been the railways, the mines, the shipping lines, the cotton mills, and the tobacco factories—all the big enterprises, in fact, whether foreign- or Chinese-owned, employing large numbers of workers. By contrast, in 1923 and 1924 it was Chinese capitalist enterprise that was the main target of attack. The Labor Year Book [138] lists 100 strikes for these two years, only six of which were in foreign enterprises (a British shipyard, several Japanese cotton mills in Shanghai, a cotton-baling factory in Hankow, the Japanese telephone system in Tsingtao, the electric power plant in the International Settlement of Shanghai, and a Japanese cotton mill in Tientsin).[58] No strikes took place in state enterprises—a further indication that the Chinese central and provincial governments were now taking a tougher line toward the labor movement. The remaining 94 strikes were in Chinese-owned private firms—large and small cotton mills, silk-reeling plants and silk-weaving factories, oil-pressing mills, rickshaw rental companies, printing plants, and tobacco factories—because they were now the weak point in the employers' front owing to the economic difficulties of Chinese capitalist enterprise.

The nature of the demands presented, the low level of solidarity and organization, and the frequency of defeat are further signs of regression in the labor movement during 1923–24. Almost all the strikes, like those held up until 1920, were simply elementary protests against low wages and the high cost of living, or against the strictness of factory discipline.[59] Occasionally provincial rivalries caused the dispute,[60] or the old guild mentality brought a reactionary attack against modern technological innovations;[61] but demands for changes in the system (the eight-hour day, paid holidays, workers' insurance, new methods of recruitment),[62] which had been an important feature of the

TABLE 30

Strikes in 1922–24

Area covered[a]	1922	1923	1924
All of China (Chen Ta's figures)[b]	91 strikes	47 strikes	56 strikes
	139,050 strikers	35,385 strikers	61,860 strikers
	(for 30 strikes)	(for 17 strikes)	(for 18 strikes)
All of China (*Nien-chien* figures)[c]	108 strikes	49 strikes	55 strikes
International Settlement and nearby Chinese districts[d]	71 strikes	51 strikes	60 strikes
	66,000 strikers	24,000 strikers	38,000 strikers
	728,000 days	118,000 days	289,000 days
Shanghai cotton mills[e]	14,200 strikers	1,500 strikers	600 strikers

[a] Because none of the surveys from which these figures are taken is exhaustive, regional comparisons within a given year are not necessarily reliable.   [b] Chen Ta, *CEJ*, Oct. 1927.   [c] *Nien-chien* [138] II, 154–282.   [d] Kotenev [156], pp. 10–11.   [e] Fong [252], appendix.

1921–22 strikes as the proletariat grew in maturity, were now almost never made. At the most, workers tried to oppose increases in output norms that the embattled Chinese capitalists had felt were needed,[63] or clung tenaciously to the old hua-li, or bonus system, in the hope that this would compensate for their failure to obtain a raise in wages.[64]

During this period of retreat, almost all the strikes were spontaneous protests, because the remaining authorized labor organizations, such as "workers' clubs" run by employers or semi-working-class associations that wanted to keep on good terms with the authorities, preferred not to become involved, and the militant Communists, now operating clandestinely, were seldom able to take part in them. Thus, in sharp contrast to the earlier chain reactions, in which the successes of the Canton mechanics in 1921 or of the railwaymen of Central China in 1922 brought about a whole wave of strikes, these strikes remained isolated, local, and restricted in nature, and there were now at best only a few partial successes to report. The strike at the Heng-ta cotton mill in Shanghai in March 1923 was a failure, and so were those held in the summer of 1924 by twelve thousand women workers in the Chapei silk-reeling factories (where the only concession obtained was a slight reduction in hours during the hot season and the abolition of certain fines) and at the Nanyang tobacco factory in Pootung.[65] Apart from the fact that the police or the army were often brought in, a general hardening of attitude on the part of Chinese employers, due to their own economic difficulties and also to the political atmosphere that prevailed under the warlord government after the Ching-Han incident, seems to have been responsible for the frequent defeats. The Chinese and Japanese owners of the Dairen oil-pressing mills agreed, after a strike in April 1923, to establish a central register of employees, to fire (and warn each other against) "undesirable elements," to fix a uniform wage rate that was not to be increased even by bonuses and other special allowances, and to refrain from enticing away each other's employees.[66]

Still, at least the sporadic and hazardous strikes held during this period covered a much wider area than ever before. It was in 1923–24 that labor troubles first arose in the huge Japanese enterprises in the Northeast, where there had been scarcely any echo of the 1921–22 strike wave. The peasants from Shantung and Chihli who had gone as seasonal immigrants to work on the S.M.R. or in the Mukden factories and Dairen shipyards were acquiring a new social status of their own, and with it a sharper realization of their problems as a class. "The willingness of Chinese coolies to accept incredibly low wages, as used to be the case, is now a thing of the past," sadly commented one of the main Dairen newspapers after a strike held in the spring of 1923 in a Japanese factory in Mukden.[67] In the spring of 1924 strikes continued to be held throughout the Northeast, including one in a Japanese woolen factory in Dairen, one in a hemp factory in Mukden, and one in the Japanese Toa tobacco factory in Yingkow,[68] all three of which failed because the Japanese employers at each factory retaliated with an immediate lockout. Nevertheless these strikes are an interesting sign of the way the Chinese labor movement was expanding even in the difficult circumstances of early 1924.

The Labor Secretariat in 1923–24

Most of the revolutionary labor organizations started by the Labor Secretariat either disappeared in 1923–24 or else had to restrict their activities owing to the reaction that set in under warlord government. The Secretariat itself was never officially dissolved, but it gradually ceased functioning. Immediately after the Ching-Han incident on February 7 it transferred its headquarters back to Shanghai and did its best to distribute aid to the victims and their families,[69] and also to inform the public about the incident.[70] After that all trace of it is lost. Probably doubts arose within the Communist Party after the arrests of February 1923 as to the immediate prospects of continuing the class struggle, which in 1922 had seemed so rosy.[71] Ch'en Tu-hsiu's thoroughgoing indictment of anarchism and syndicalism, published in the party organ in June 1924, suggests that ideas of this kind may have been entertained, although personal accusations;[72] a certain defeatist tendency seems also to be hinted at in his remark of December 1923 that "the vast majority of Chinese workers neither want to fight nor are able to fight their own class battles."[73] There were others, however, including Teng Chung-hsia, a leading figure in the Labor Secretariat during its great wave of activity in 1922, who vigorously opposed any idea of "liquidation."[74]

Already in 1923 ideas concerning the need for the working class to form an alliance with other social classes were in the air;[75] but significantly enough, the brochure on the Ching-Han incident issued in the spring of 1923 by the Secretariat, of which Teng Chung-hsia himself was probably the author, merely called for a strengthening of genuine working-class organizations, and stressed the need for a working-class political party (in other words, the Communist Party), in order to prevent any further defeats like the defeat of February 7.[76] No mention was made of any prospective new alliances like those reported in the news after the publication of the famous joint statement issued by Adolph Joffe and Sun Yat-sen.[77]

All these doubts and hesitations only added to the difficulties of the clandestine attempts to preserve the labor organizations that had been openly set up by the Secretariat in 1921–22. It was in Hupeh, and even more in Hunan, that the positions gained were most effectively maintained. In Hupeh, where the rickshaw men's union and that of the workers in the cotton-baling factories still survived,[78] the revolutionary strain in the labor movement was strong enough to play a very active part in the anti-Japanese demonstrations held in June 1923 to demand the return of Dairen and Port Arthur to China, and in the boycott that followed;[79] but the provincial federation of unions, formed in Wuhan in 1922, was dissolved after February 7.

The Hunan federation, however, seems to have carried on its activities through 1923 and even in 1924, despite the attacks directed against it by Chao Heng-t'i after June 1, 1923.[80] In 1924 it still had 50,000 members,[81] drawn from the Anyuan workers' club and the unions of the Yueh-Han railwaymen, the mechanics, and the rickshaw men.[82] It ran workers' evening classes, gave aid to the Shuikowshan strikers, and made an appeal to the Hunan provincial assembly to vote for labor legislation.[83] The organization best able to maintain activities at the pitch reached in 1922 was the workers' club of the Anyuan miners, probably because of its remote situation on the borders of Hunan and Kiangsi, beyond the easy reach of the warlords of these two provinces. This club was an important feature in the everyday life of the locality, with its evening classes, its reading rooms, its consumers' cooperatives, its three shops backed by a capital investment of 2,000 yuan, and the two-story building, constructed at its own expense, where it had its offices.[84] It rested upon a solid organization of 1,382 "delegates of tens" and 131 "delegates of hundreds," who, representing individual pits or factories, elected the 51 members of the central council. This system, directly inspired by the Workers' Councils of Soviet Russia, earned the club the name of "Little Moscow." The club was strong enough to insist on being the only intermediary between the management of the mine (that is, the Hanyehping Company) and the workers,[85] thus abolishing completely recruitment of labor by foremen or contractors. It celebrated the 1923 May Day with great ceremony, and received regular visits from top-ranking Communist leaders such as Li Li-san, Liu Shao-ch'i (who was the club's president), and Mao Tse-tung, which shows the importance of this outpost of the revolutionary wing of the labor movement.

The organizations among the railwaymen set up by the Labor Secretariat in 1922 also survived in the form of small clandestine groups on the Ching-Feng, Ching-Han, Yueh-Han, and Cheng-T'ai lines, and in larger groups—some of them containing as many as a thousand or more—on the Chin-P'u line and among the train crews of the Ching-Sui line. A new clandestine union was formed on the Chiao-Chi line.[86] In February 1924 Teng Chung-hsia and other Communist leaders, with support from various quarters, even tried to form a National Union of Railwaymen. They held a meeting in Peking, attended by about twenty delegates, on February 7, the anniversary of the Ching-Han incident, at which they issued a manifesto and drew up rules. Both documents, however, put forward a very moderate program confined to improvement of conditions, workers' unity, and technical training.[87] But the police soon intervened, dispersed the union's provisional committee, and arrested several of its members.[88] Arrests were also made among the Cheng-T'ai and Chiao-Chi railwaymen. Owing to the political situation in the country as a whole, the time was not yet ripe for organizing large industrial unions on a national scale as called for by the resolution adopted at the Congress of May 1922.

The Seamen's Union was another labor organization in which militants had

gained some influence in 1922, although until then the leading role in founding and organizing it had been played by men who appeared to be more concerned about their own political careers than about the labor movement. But
in Canton, and to an even greater extent in Shanghai, seamen such as Su Chao-
cheng, Lin Wei-min, and Chu Pao-t'ing had established contact with the
Labor Secretariat in 1922. They lost ground, however, in 1923–24, and Ch'en
Ping-sheng, the founder of the union, who had ties with moderate Kuomintang circles, came to the fore again after having been removed from the
managing committee in 1922 for a breach of morals. He brought with him
men whose very occupations inclined them to make a profit out of the seamen
rather than to defend their interests, such as Chai Han-ch'i, a maker of coffins
for seamen,[89] or Chu Yao-kuan, who ran a boardinghouse for seamen. The
latter became president of the Shanghai Seamen's Union in May 1924 upon
Ch'en Ping-sheng's return to Canton.[90] Regional quarrels between Cantonese
and Ningpo seamen, rivalries between various mutual benefit societies that
had not become fully integrated within the union, and the lack of any proper
trade union organization—all these helped to make it possible for a few individuals to seize control of the union; and these factors were responsible for its
decline during 1923–24.[91]

In Shanghai, China's main industrial center, where Communist militants
had taken the first steps to join forces with the working class even before their
party had been formed, the ebb in the labor movement was also perceptible.
All that remained of the labor organizations started or supported by the Labor
Secretariat in 1922 were a few mechanics' or goldsmiths' and jewelers' clubs.[92]
Communist cadres, however, despite having no organization behind them,
tried to play a part in strikes such as those held in the summer of 1924 in the
Nanyang factory and in the silk factories.[93] Hsiang Ching-yü, a student who
had recently returned from France, where, as a worker-student, she had encountered Marxist propaganda and had become a member of the Communist
Party, was very active during these two strikes.[94] But since the Shanghai proletariat lacked trade union leaders of working-class origin such as those who
had been trained up among the railwaymen and among the workers of the
Hupeh-Hunan region in 1922, Communists must have found it a tricky business to work among them.

In the other provinces of China isolated attempts were made here and there
to keep labor organizations going along the lines originally laid down by the
Secretariat and the Canton Congress—for instance among the coal miners of
Tzechwan in Shantung province,[95] in Szechwan,[96] and more markedly in
Nanchang, where in 1924 the Communist Chao Hsing-nung organized unions
among the printing workers, the railwaymen on the Nanchang-Kiukiang line,
and the boatmen.[97]

Activities of Moderate Labor Groups

Throughout this period, it was the moderate labor organizations that were in the forefront. In Shanghai, some of those that had appeared during the May Fourth Movement or just after were still in existence. They included groups such as the Workers' and Merchants' Friendly Society or the Society for Industrial Advance[98] that were composed of small employers, management staff, and a few workers without distinction as to trade, as well as others catering more to separate trades, such as the Boathands' and Warehousemen's Federation,[99] various printing workers' associations,[100] the mechanics' and electrical workers' unions, and the workers' clubs for employees of the Nanyang tobacco factory, for the women silkworkers of Chapei, and for the Pootung textile workers.[101] Most, though not all, of these had been formed for the purpose of gaining support among skilled workers, and in 1923–24 the leaders of these organizations tried to gain even wider support by creating regional friendly societies for workers—a formula they had already begun to adopt in 1922—catering to natives of northern Kiangsu (the Kompo), Chekiang, Anhwei, Kwangtung, Szechwan, Hunan, and Hupeh.[102] Some of the trade associations also had regional bases, most of the members of the Boathands' and Warehousemen's Federation being Cantonese,[103] and all those of one of the main printing workers' associations being natives of Chekiang.[104]

All these organizations had for several years had a common outlook, which was fostered by a network of personal ties between them. (The same people held leading positions in several of them.)[105] All of these groups had taken part in the first Labor Day celebrations in Shanghai in May 1920, and all had been equally eager to welcome Sun Yat-sen when he came there at the end of 1922; and after having cooperated with the Communists for a brief period, they all broke with them in the early summer of 1922. They had several times thought of combining to form one inclusive organization. In the spring of 1922 they had formed a joint committee to aid the Pootung strikers, a committee to which the Labor Secretariat also belonged,[106] and during the winter of 1923 they jointly organized aid for the victims of the Ching-Han incident, a number of whom had fled to Shanghai.[107] In 1924, after lengthy discussions, a Federation of Labor Organizations was founded in Shanghai, which secured, as affiliates, about thirty semi-working-class associations and societies for industrial advance, as well as regional societies, trade associations for skilled workers, and clubs run by firms.[108]

The Federation like its affiliated associations, seems to have been on good terms with both Chinese and foreign employers in Shanghai. Some of the affiliated associations were run by small employers, such as T'ung Li-chang of the Workers' and Merchants' Friendly Society and Li Heng-lin of the Electrical Workers' Union.[109] Others, such as the Nanyang club,[110] the China Bookshop club,[111] and the Commercial Press club for young workers, were controlled and subsidized by big firms. Slogans such as "Harmony between capital and labor" and "Mutual aid" figured among those borne by representatives of the Federation during the May Day celebrations in 1924.[112] None of the affiliated associations incorporated any clauses in their rules concerning strike demands or provisions for going on sympathy strike,[113] and the rules of the Federation itself were very lax, having no clause enjoining solidarity between member associations in the event of labor disputes.[114] Indeed the "Society for Workers' Moral Improvement," a mutual aid club run by Mrs. Mu Chih-ying, who was a leading figure in the Federation, actually tried to curb the strike of the women silkworkers of Chapei in the summer of 1924,[115] and the same attitude was adopted by the Nanyang workers' club during the strike held in September.[116] When these moderate labor organizations did present demands, they did so always with great circumspection and apparent regret, as when the rickshaw men of the International Settlement of Shanghai, protesting in October 1924 against the rise in charges for the hire of their vehicles, explained their grievances to the secretary of the Municipal Council.[117] The main emphasis was on mutual aid, technical training, and recreational activities. The first thing the Federation did when it came into being in the spring of 1924 was to form plans for a workers' savings bank;[118] the Boathands' and Warehousemen's Federation ran a life insurance fund;[119] and the Mechanics' Union, which had originally been genuinely working-class in character and had supported the Labor Secretariat at the 1922 Congress, but which since then, through lack of funds, had fallen into line with the Cantonese mechanics' union,[120] drew up a new set of rules aimed simply at improving morals and skills.[121] The rules of the Electrical Workers' Union recommended negotiation in the event of disputes with employers, and included proposals for periods of training abroad, the organization of exhibitions, and the awarding of medals to workers who invented new technological processes, while also containing clauses stipulating that no member should either recommend or employ nonmembers (thus indicating the mixed character of this association), and that members who had found employment through the union should contribute a month's wages.[122]

These organizations prided themselves on their political impartiality: e.g., at the beginning of 1924 they sent a telegram of condolence to the Soviet government on the death of Lenin, and also one of congratulation to Ramsay MacDonald on becoming the British Prime Minister.[123] Nevertheless they were strongly opposed to the Communists and to Communist sympathizers in the labor movement, and were even accused by the latter of going to the length of denouncing them to the police.[124] The antagonism between the two sides came out sharply during the strikes in the summer of 1924, which one side tried to curb and the other secretly supported.[125] It was also reflected in slogans such as "Let us ask for bread only, and leave politics alone," or "All we need is unions, we do not need political parties," displayed by the Federation at the May Day celebrations in May 1924.[126] In fact, behind the Federation's supposed impartiality, a strong leaning toward the Kuomintang right wing in Shanghai was easily discernible,[127] an inclination that did not in any way prevent its being on good terms with the local Chinese military authorities.[128] Since General Ho Feng-lin, like his chief Lu Yung-hsiang, was a member of the dwindling Anfu faction, he was probably not displeased by the intense hostility shown by the Federation and its member associations toward the Chihli faction, which had put the Anfu group out of power in 1920;[129] and his granting of permission to hold May Day celebrations in 1923 and 1924 was doubtless motivated as much by political reasons as by any hopes he may have entertained that these associations might help to keep the Shanghai workers under control. The Nanyang club and the Workers' and Merchants' Friendly Society were particularly conspicuous in the public ceremonies held by the associations on May 1, 1923,[130] and on May Day 1924 the newly formed Federation figured prominently. Taking their stand by the side of its leaders were Wang Ching-wei, representing the Kuomintang; the Japanese Susuki, representing the Amsterdam International Federation of Trade Unions; and Dame Adelaide Anderson, a British expert on labor problems, whose presence reflected hopes held at the time for carrying out social reforms in the Western manner.[131]

To what extent were these moderate labor organizations representative of the Shanghai working class, and how much working-class support did they enjoy? A few of them, among them the seamen's,[132] printing workers',[133] and mechanics' unions, were undoubtedly genuine mass organizations, at present deflected along a reformist path because of the personal predilections of their leaders, but ready to fight on behalf of the Shanghai proletariat as a whole when the hour of battle came in 1925. But most of the associations affiliated with the Federation had never been more than groups used by persons who were anxious to obtain control over the Shanghai working class and were now able to profit from the temporary eclipse of the Communists. The presence in Shanghai of militant members of the Hunan Workingmen's Association such as Wang Kuang-hui and Shen Hsiao-ts'en, who had escaped in the spring of 1922 when repression set in after the execution of Huang and P'ang, and of railwaymen like Yang Te-fu and Kuo Chi-sheng, who had escaped after the Ching-Han massacre in the spring of 1923,[134] provided the moderates with an opportunity for carrying out a cunning maneuver to extend their influence. Taking advantage of the emotions aroused among the Shanghai workers by the bloodshed of January 17, 1922, and of February 7, 1923, they encouraged the creation of a "Shanghai Office of the Hunan Workingmen's

Association" and of a "Shanghai Office of the Ching-Han General Union."
The prestige of these famous names admirably suited their demagogic purposes, and the refugees for their part fell in with the plan. A few of the refugees
may have been guilty of dubious conduct,[135] but for the most part their personal integrity seems to have been above suspicion. Nevertheless, cut off as
they were from the environment where they had risen to positions of responsibility among the newly awakened miners and railwaymen of Central China,
and finding themselves suddenly transplanted into the highly competitive and
rather artificial world of the "poster unions" of Shanghai, they soon became
absorbed by it and caught up in its fierce internal squabbles;[136] and while they
were careful to preserve appearances, for instance by solemnly observing every
anniversary of the deaths of Huang and P'ang,[137] they became in fact scarcely
distinguishable from all the other leaders of the moderate labor organizations,
such as T'ung Li-chang, Mu Chih-ying, and Li Heng-lin.

A good indication of the real nature of the associations affiliated with the
Federation is provided by the clauses in their rules concerning relations between the rank and file and the leadership, which—unlike the rules of the
unions formed by the Labor Secretariat in 1922, when a successful effort had
been made to introduce representation of the rank and file—provided only for
a general assembly for the election of leaders that would have very little effective control over the leaders' activities. Almost no provision was made for
rank-and-file units in factories and workshops,[138] and even where such units
existed, they had no representation as such in the general assembly.[139]

A complete survey of the organizations with some influence among the
working class of Shanghai should include the secret societies that flourished
in the Shanghai underworld. While there is no doubt that they existed, references to them in contemporary documents are so rare and so brief that the
merest mention of them must suffice. The Green Gang in particular seems to
have had a good deal of influence among the urban populace as a whole and
especially the great mass of unskilled workers, and made use of tattoo marks,
secret signs of recognition, and ritual observances to maintain its hold over
certain sections of the proletariat.[140] Its underground activities and its capacity
to spring suddenly into action were displayed during periods of crisis or of
revolutionary activity, especially during the summer of 1925 and the spring
of 1927.

It was in Shanghai that the activity of reformist and moderate labor organizations during the period of retreat in the labor movement was most noticeable, and it is Shanghai for which we have the most impressive documentation. But the same trend seems to have prevailed in the other parts of China
where the warlords were in power.[141] In Wuhan, for instance, there existed a
provincial federation of pronouncedly moderate character, whose links with
the federation established by the Labor Secretariat in 1922 are difficult to
trace.[142] Sun Yat-sen criticized it for its apolitical attitude in a famous passage

of his "Three People's Principles."[143] In the remote Northeast, where the first stirrings of labor unrest were taking place, such unions as are known to have existed—for example those of the printing workers and tramwaymen in Dairen,[144] and of the Harbin railwaymen[145]—were not at all militant. In the spring of 1925 the Federation of Shanghai Labor Organizations was beginning to contact reformist circles in other industrial centers of China and was hoping to form a national federation with the same outlook as its own.[146] These hopes were dashed by a sudden violent renewal of activity in the labor movement.

Government Attempts at Social Reform

Throughout the history of the labor movement, periods of retreat in the movement coincided with government attempts at social reform, and the years 1923–24 were no exception. In reaction to the emotion aroused in all circles in China by the Ching-Han incident, President Li Yuan-hung issued a decree on February 22 ordering labor legislation to be drawn up.[147] On March 29, 1923, the Nung-shang-pu promulgated a provisional Factory Law.[148] The law, which applied to all enterprises employing more than a hundred workers regardless of the nationality of the owners, as well as to enterprises classified as dangerous or unhealthy, prohibited the employment of girls under twelve and of boys under ten, limited the hours of work for children and laid down a minimum amount of time off for adults, prohibited deductions from wages, provided for the payment of grants on dismissal or death and urged firms to introduce life insurance plans, granted maternity leave for women workers, and prohibited the employment of women on dangerous work. No mention was made of the basic question of the pao-kung system, and there was no limitation on hours of work for adults. In May there followed four decrees on work in the mines,[149] laying down regulations for conditions of employment and dismissal, for the work of women and children, for hours of work for adults, and for certain compulsory safety precautions and hygiene measures. A few timid clauses attempted to reduce the power of foremen and pao-kung-t'ou; thus one clause stipulated that a pao-kung-t'ou must not have more than 200 miners under his control, another that he must sell them articles for current consumption at cost price, and a third that wages must be paid in cash and not in vouchers for the canteen or shop.

The Peking government had further plans in the spring of 1923 to introduce trade union legislation that would make unions legal on the condition that their activities be confined to social matters, mutual aid, and improvement of the standard of living, and further, that their rules be submitted for government inspection together with full information about membership and leadership. Should a union take part in anti-government activities, disturb public order, or act against the "interests of the nation," it would automatically be dissolved. A draft bill to this effect, which would have put severe limitations on the labor movement's sphere of action, was submitted to parliament by the government on April 18, 1923,[150] but it never got beyond the draft stage. The matter was brought up a second time at the beginning of 1924, but again without results.[151]

A few of the provincial governors also took up the question of labor legislation. In June 1923 the governor of Kiangsu ordered the introduction of a nine-hour day and one day off per week,[152] and in 1924 the governor of Shantung issued regulations concerning the employment and dismissal of workers.[153] The trouble with all these attempts at legislation, whether national or provincial, was that they contained no provision for enforcing the regulations. It is difficult to avoid receiving the impression that they were devised simply to create a good public image rather than to effectively relieve the sufferings of the workers. The special departments created at this time in various ministries, such as the department for the control of labor at the Nung-shang-pu,[154] the department for the protection of industry at the Ministry of Home Affairs,[155] and the Labor Department of the Chiao-t'ung-pu,[156] were equally ineffective.

Thus it is hardly surprising that all these labor laws, which, with the exception of the regulations for mines introduced by Yuan Shih-k'ai, were the first in China's social history, remained a dead letter. In July 1923, for instance, the women workers in the Chapei silk-reeling factories had to protest, by means of pamphlets and street demonstrations, against the nonapplication of the governor of Kiangsu's order concerning hours of work, the long hours being all the more insupportable during the stifling heat of the Shanghai summer;[157] and the reports of the British consuls in China sent to the Foreign Office in 1924, following the campaign conducted by the left wing of the labor movement against bad working conditions in British-owned factories in China, all stressed the fact that the Chinese-owned factories were just as guilty in failing to apply the 1923 regulations as foreign-owned factories were.[158]

The I.L.O.'s activities with regard to China in 1923–24 were not of very much account either. The Chinese government displayed a very faint interest in the Geneva organization, and sent only some diplomats posted in Berne as its representatives at the annual International Labor Conferences, which was as good as not being represented at all.[159] Its only positive action was to send to Geneva the text of the 1923 provisional legislation[160] and to attempt to prohibit the use of white phosphorus in the manufacture of matches in conformity with a resolution adopted by the I.L.O.[161] The I.L.O. for its part showed an equal lack of interest, and its efforts were confined to sending Paul Henry to China in 1924 on an unofficial mission of investigation[162] and to conducting an intermittent correspondence with Peking on the possibility of inducing the Treaty Powers to apply the norms laid down by the Washington

Conference regarding the eight-hour day, the weekly day of rest, and so forth.[163]

Still more indicative of the ineffectiveness of attempts at reform in China was the affair of the Child Labor Commission set up in 1923–24 by the Municipal Council of the International Settlement of Shanghai.[164] At the end of 1922 and the beginning of 1923 a propaganda campaign against the employment of children in the factories of the International Settlement was waged by Protestant circles in Shanghai, and especially by the Y.W.C.A. and various other English-speaking women's groups. Public meetings were held, letters exchanged with associations of Chinese and Western employers, and approaches made to the Municipal Council. In the spring of 1923, shortly after the Ching-Han incident and the promulgation of the provisional labor laws by the Peking government, the municipality decided to set up an official commission of investigation charged with presenting its findings to the Municipal Council. The commission was composed of representatives of the chief industrial firms in Shanghai (Jardine, Matheson & Company, Naigai Wata Kaisha, Mu Ou-ch'u), and a number of prominent women, both Chinese and foreign. The women included Dame Adelaide Anderson, a former factory inspector in the United Kingdom; Miss Agatha Harrison, the secretary of the Y.W.C.A.; and Sung Mei-ling, the sister-in-law of Sun Yat-sen. It set to work immediately, and held 33 meetings, sent out questionnaires, and visited factories. It sent in its report in July 1924.[165] The report was very moderate in tone, and included only a very small part of the material contained in the minutes of the meetings.[166] Its final recommendations were that employment of children under ten should be prohibited, that hours of work for children of 10 to 14 years of age should not exceed twelve, that within a specified period the employment of children on night work should be abolished, and that children under 14 should have 24 hours' rest each week and should not be employed on dangerous or exhausting work. It also recommended that persons contravening regulations be sentenced to imprisonment, and that a corps of factory inspectors be formed. In all, the recommendations, except for the last two points, were far less stringent than the Chinese regulations of 1923.

It was on the basis of these recommendations that the Shanghai Municipal Council decided, at the beginning of 1925, to submit a bylaw regulating child labor to a meeting of ratepayers of the International Settlement for their vote, according to custom. But the meeting held for this purpose on April 15 was not attended by the necessary quorum of one third; only 622 Japanese and Western ratepayers out of a total of 2,743 had troubled to turn up.[167] The matter was complicated by the fact that other bylaws were presented at the same meeting by the Municipal Council, dealing with an increase in wharfage dues and the tightening of controls over publication of printed matter. Many of the voters knew how unpopular these measures were among the Chinese inhabitants of the Settlement.[168] On June 2 a second meeting was held with no better results (only 725 persons attended). But two days before that the British police had fired upon a crowd assembled in Nanking Road, thus starting the biggest strike wave in Shanghai's history. The way toward the emancipation of the workers was decidedly not to be that of a cautious and gradual carrying out of reforms in the English manner.

CONCLUSION TO PART II

I have chosen the fall of 1924 as the time when the period of retreat in the labor movement ended because it was not until then that, with the movement for the restoration of the trade unions, activities were renewed that paved the way for the great social and political struggles of the summer of 1925. But a profound alteration in the balance of forces in Chinese politics and society, of which the revival of activity in the labor movement was a reflection, had already taken place in January 1924, when the Kuomintang Congress was held and cooperation with the Communist Party decided upon. Thus the closing date of the first period of labor struggles is less clearly defined than its opening date in May 1919. Another point that underlines the dangers of adopting too strict a "periodization" for this stage of the Chinese labor movement is that in Canton, after Sun Yat-sen returned to power in 1923, the situation of the labor movement was very different from that in the rest of the country under warlord government.

Nevertheless the year 1924, taken as a whole, was a real turning point, and now is the moment to pause and consider the wealth of experience gained by the Chinese labor movement during the four or five years after the beginning of the May Fourth Movement, and the new demands that had been made on it.

This first ground swell of the labor movement was characterized by progress in strike action involving workers in all the industrial regions, in every industry, and in every kind of enterprise, and also by the development of labor organizations that already held a considerable degree of authority. The railwaymen, the miners, and the metalworkers of Central and North China, and the mechanics and seamen in the South, proved themselves to be particularly militant and well disciplined. To the fury of the warlords, who were full of Confucianist contempt for manual labor, and to the astonishment of Western businessmen accustomed to thinking that the Chinese worker was interested only in his bowl of rice, the seamen of Hong Kong and the Ching-Han railwaymen had stood solidly behind their unions when on strike, until the former achieved final victory and the latter had put their lives in jeopardy.

Thus through participation in the strikes, and within the framework of the newly formed labor organizations, the proletariat had developed a sense of class consciousness. Its demands now went beyond a mere concern with basic subsistence requirements, and touched upon questions such as workers' insurance and the pao-kung system of recruitment. The eight-hour day was no longer a phrase known only to a few intellectuals who were familiar with Western ideas, as in 1919, but one that had reached the great mass of the workers. The tradition of celebrating May Day, which from 1920 on was gradually adopted by one after another of all the big working-class centers, was another factor that increased class consciousness. Guilds and regional societies, although they had not yet entirely disappeared, were in retreat before the growth of industrial unionism, especially among the railwaymen, the metalworkers and miners in Central and North China, and the seamen. The Chinese proletariat had demonstrated its cohesion on a national scale by the solidarity shown and the aid given to the victims of Chao Heng-t'i in January 1922, to the Hong Kong seamen during their strike in February–March 1922, to the K.M.A. miners in October 1922, and to the Ching-Han railwaymen in February 1923. Working-class leaders had begun to emerge, especially among the seamen and the railwaymen, and were working together with left-wing intellectuals in a large number of unions. Finally, class consciousness had extended beyond the frontiers of China and acquired international dimensions. The May Day celebrations were part of this wider outlook, and so were the hopes entertained—vainly, as it turned out—by some of the semi-working-class organizations around 1919–20 that the I.L.O. would be of help to China. Meanwhile the Labor Secretariat had formed more solid ties with the Red International, and in general the Chinese proletariat had begun to turn toward Moscow and the international Communist movement.

This development of class consciousness on the part of the Chinese proletariat cannot be viewed purely as a social phenomenon. It was just as much bound up with the political and ideological aspects of the experience acquired during these early years. At the time of May 4 and during the months that followed, the labor movement was still in search of an ideology and had a variety of political views to choose from: those of the anarchists, the Kuomintang Nationalists, the believers in "industrial advance" through an alliance between petty capitalists and the proletariat, and the Marxists, who came last upon the scene. Five years later things were very different. The anarchists had been more or less eliminated. The Shanghai semi-working-class associations for "national salvation" had become mere tools in the hands of ambitious leaders whose program became more and more confined to an aggressive anti-Communism and who were quite cut off from the working masses. The Kuomintang, even in South China, had only had intermittent contact with the labor movement and never thought of it as more than a supporting force. In contrast, the Marxists and the Communists, especially after the Labor Secretariat was formed, had become more and more closely identified with the labor movement. They provided most of its leaders, and were responsible for impressive demonstrations of labor solidarity, such as the first Labor Congress and the campaign in the summer of 1922 for labor legislation. But it must be stressed once again, for the point is an important one, that the Chinese labor movement was in no way something that was created artificially by the Communist Party. If the Communist Party was successful, it was only because the ground was already prepared. Chinese labor had begun to move on its own from the very beginning of the May Fourth Movement. The Hong Kong Seamen's Union is a good example: its president had close ties with the leadership of the Kuomintang, and its most militant rank-and-file members had never had any contacts with the Communist Party.

In 1924 the rapprochement between the labor movement and the Communists was at different stages of advance in the various industrial regions of China. It was in Central China and among the railwaymen in the North that the best results had been obtained by the Labor Secretariat and by the Communist militants who had been assigned by the party to undertake union organization, and it was there that some of the more important positions won had been to some extent held during the period of setbacks. In Canton, on the other hand, the old guild traditions still dominated, sometimes combined, as in the case of the mechanics, with fairly direct links with the Kuomintang. In Shanghai the activities of the Secretariat had been short-lived, and by 1924 there were hardly any organizations left that were under Communist influence; the only ones that could be regarded as genuinely working-class were the seamen's and printing workers' unions, and even they had some of the old corporate tendencies.

As far as the political aspect is concerned, it must be remembered that the class consciousness of the Chinese proletariat developed within a historical context in which the two basic political problems to be faced were the preponderance of large foreign interests and the dominance of the militarists, who kept alive the social forces of the ancien régime.

The working class, especially during the big strike wave of 1922, had fought its own battles against the Hong Kong shipping companies, the Japanese cotton mill owners of Shanghai, and the British owners of industrial concerns in Hankow and Chihli. The rickshaw men, who engaged in militant action in all the Treaty Ports, constantly came into conflict with foreign civilian and military authorities, especially with the Japanese.[169] In the areas controlled in one way or another by foreigners, the labor movement had on many occasions after 1919 come up against foreign authorities, who had put down strikes, arrested militant trade unionists, prohibited demonstrations, and proceeded against labor organizations. The tone of the workers' demands in Hankow in January 1923, just before the February Seventh incident, shows the extent to which the antagonism between the labor movement and the big foreign interests in China had developed.

After 1919 the working class had also fought its own battles against the medieval power wielded by the warlords. The illusions entertained in Changsha in 1921 or in Peking in 1922 regarding warlords no longer existed, for those warlords had turned out to be political tricksters. The incident of February 7, 1923, with its bloodshed, was the most spectacular, but not the only one of its kind in the unequal struggle that ended in universal repression of the labor movement by all the warlord governments, whatever their allegiance, during 1923 and 1924.

Thus the proletariat had continuously carried on and intensified the political fight on two fronts that had been prominent in the May Fourth Movement. But now the proletariat was no longer, as it had been then, an auxiliary force or "rear guard." It was for its own ends, and on its own initiative, that it had resisted the British companies in Hong Kong and confronted the soldiers of Wu P'ei-fu; but being without allies, it had been defeated. It is true that the intelligentsia and the national bourgeoisie, the craftsmen and the petty employees, had none of them been unsympathetic to the struggles that had taken place between 1919 and 1924 against the foreign interests and the warlords. But occasional expressions of sympathy do not provide the same encouragement and support as fighting side by side. In 1924 the main problem facing the labor movement was that of finding another class with sufficiently similar interests to make feasible the formation of an alliance and the creation of a united front. The alliances formed at the Kuomintang Congress in January 1924 were destined to help the working class play a decisive role in the Chinese Revolution of 1924–27.

PART III

The Working Class in the 1924–1927 Revolution

CHAPTER X

The Revival of the Labor Movement

Toward the Formation of a United Front

The "Chinese Revolution of 1924–27" or, as Chinese historians now prefer to call it, the "First Revolutionary Civil War," was heralded by a new alignment of social and political forces which opened up new horizons for the labor movement, enabling it to form new alliances and to show signs of a rapid and vigorous renewal of activities.

In 1924 the twofold dominance of the warlords and the Treaty Powers was an even more prominent feature of the Chinese political scene than it had been in 1919. As already recounted, after the Washington Conference the warlords had increased their hold on power to a disastrous extent, and the Treaty Powers had been steadily strengthening their position since the end of the First World War, despite the renunciation of the "unequal treaties" by the Soviet Union[1] and the decision of the Weimar Republic to accept the loss of its privileges,[2] and despite the growing antagonism between the Anglo-American and Franco-Japanese blocs that had begun even before the Washington Conference. The conference may have been a triumph for the Anglo-American bloc, but it nevertheless safeguarded most of the common interests of the Powers on Chinese soil, and gave China nothing but vague promises, to be fulfilled in the distant future, about such questions as customs control and extraterritoriality.[3]

That the Powers were still as anxious as they had been at the time of the breakup to seize any possible opportunity to further their ambitions was shown by the Lincheng incident in May 1923, when the Tientsin-Pukow express was attacked by bandits in Honan. One European was killed and 36 kidnapped, including the sister-in-law of one of the Rockefellers. The diplomatic corps immediately presented a number of demands that went far beyond the actual needs of the situation, just as the Chefoo Convention in 1876 and the Protocol of 1901 had done. The demands included one for the payment of 100,000 yuan in compensation to each victim, one for China's renunciation of the Washington Conference proposals for abolishing extraterritoriality and the Mixed Court of Shanghai, and one for permanent military control over the Chinese railways by the Powers.[4] Western businessmen called for armed intervention, and asked that the Powers assume direct military control over the whole of China.[5]

The combined domination of the warlords and the Foreign Powers did not, as might have been expected, create friction between them. On the contrary, they gave each other mutual support: the Powers by extending political, financial, and sometimes military aid to one or another of the rival warlords operating within their several spheres of influence,[6] and the successive warlord governments in the North by their docile acceptance of the unequal treaties.[7]

We have seen how the proletariat had already vigorously attacked this twofold domination between 1919 and 1924. Although its victories had been only partial ones and had been won mainly in the economic sphere, the experience gained had been considerable, and there had been a strengthening both of internal organization and of the sense of class consciousness. The proletariat had also increased in numbers, owing to the economic growth that had taken place, especially in foreign and state enterprises. The number of men employed on the state railways had risen from 73,000 in 1919 to 113,000 in 1924,[8] and the number of postal workers from 25,000 to 35,000.[9] The number of spindles in use had more than doubled during these five years, going from 1.8 million to 3.9 million,[10] which, in view of the difficulties encountered by Chinese-owned cotton mills, means that there was a huge increase in the number of workers employed in Japanese-owned mills.[11] Thus, because of its growth in size and political maturity, the Chinese proletariat was now in a far better position than it had been in 1919 to play a leading role in China's social and political struggles. It had shown its strength during the great strike wave of 1922–23, and its close ties with the Communist Party gave it a new authority.[12]

But the growing strength of the working class is not of itself enough to account for the new alignment of forces that took place in 1924–25. Other social strata contributed just as much to it. The national bourgeoisie, the peasants, students and intellectuals, and the petty bourgeoisie were now also more directly opposed to the warlords and conservatives on the one hand and the Treaty Powers on the other than they had been in 1919. For the big Chinese industrialists, the "golden age" of the Great War period was now a distant memory, and we have already seen[13] how, as much because of their own failings as because of foreign competition and the disorders caused by warlordism,[14] their enterprises had declined since 1922–23. Some of their factories were closed, some had slowed down production, and some had increased hours of work or reduced wages;[15] others were in debt to foreign banks or had simply been bought up by foreign competitors.[16] During these trying years, Chinese industrialists had made desperate efforts to unite. Chambers of commerce attempted to join forces, first at the provincial level[17] and then at a national level,[18] and on several occasions they took a stand against the scourge of warlordism and in support of raising China's international status. As soon as a provincial chamber of commerce was formed in Hupeh, it announced its intention to resist the exactions of the warlords;[19] and at the national conference of chambers of commerce held in November 1922, a plan was put forward for the demilitarization of China to be carried out under the control of four civilians; those nominated for the task included the cotton magnate Nieh Ch'i-chieh (C. C. Nieh) and the secretary of the Chinese Y.M.C.A., Yü Jih-chang (David Yui), a leading figure in the Protestant section of the Shanghai bourgeoisie.[20] In their appeals and manifestos, the chambers of commerce often included demands for the restoration of customs control to China and for the abolition of the likin, a tax from which foreign competitors were exempt and which brought in a fat profit for the warlords, but that fell heavily on Chinese industrialists and merchants.[21] Patriotism combined with the defense of business interests led them to demand the early application of the terms of the Washington Treaty concerning the revision of tariffs, which so far had remained empty promises;[22] and they often raised protests against foreign encroachment on the Chinese economy.[23]

The political and administrative problems peculiar to Shanghai meant that the local bourgeoisie came up against the foreign municipal authorities there. Chinese ratepayers paid a higher proportion of the rates than the foreigners, yet they were not entitled to a Municipal Council vote.[24] Galled by this inferior status, several members of the bourgeoisie had formed a Chinese Ratepayers' Association in October 1920 (membership in which was confined to those owning property worth 500 taels or more), and this association obtained permission from the Municipal Council to nominate members of a Chinese Advisory Committee.[25] But this was not enough. The Chinese Ratepayers' Association continued to demand Chinese representation on the Municipal Council, for which they obtained strong support from the combined associations of Shanghai shopkeepers.[26] Further quarrels with the Municipal Council arose in the spring of 1925 over its proposals to increase wharfage dues, control the Chinese press, and construct roads beyond the Settlement boundaries. The unpopularity of these proposals[27] to a large extent explains why the Shanghai bourgeoisie took sides, temporarily at least, with the trade unions after the shootings of May 30, 1925.

In short, on the eve of the May Thirtieth Movement, the bourgeoisie was much more aware than it had been in 1919 of the contradictions that had brought it into opposition both with the forces of the old order and with the Western Powers. "The old idea that businessmen should concern themselves only with their own affairs is no longer valid," wrote one of the chief cotton mill owners, Mu Ou-ch'u (H. Y. Moh), at the end of 1922. After stressing that China must be freed from the "pressure of external forces" and its own "internal troubles," he concluded: "It is the duty of our businessmen to get together and devise every way and means to force our government to improve our internal affairs."[28]

Thus in 1924 the bourgeoisie found itself on the side of the labor movement with regard to the essential questions upon which China's future depended.

The industrialists, when hit by the 1922–23 crisis, had of course at first tried to get out of their difficulties at the expense of the working class by increasing hours, reducing wages, and cutting down production; yet the increasing pressure of foreign competition and the growing disorders caused by warlordism had at the same time forced them to try to win the political support of the labor movement. The new alignment of social and political forces had been foreshadowed during the 1922 strikes, when the chambers of commerce gave financial support to the Hong Kong seamen and the K.M.A. miners, and in February 1923, when various bourgeois organizations expressed their sympathy with the victims of Wu P'ei-fu's attack on the railwaymen. In January 1924 it was to be given open expression in the agreement to cooperate reached between the Kuomintang and the Communist Party.

What the bourgeoisie was primarily after, however, was support. It had every intention of keeping the upper hand,[29] and was determined to maintain the relations of capitalist production that in the economic field inevitably made it the enemy of the class with which it was seeking to form a political alliance. Hence during the great battles of 1925–27 against the Foreign Powers and the warlords, it was as much concerned with surveillance of the labor movement as with encouragement of it; and it was less wholehearted in waging the fight than its working-class allies. Many among its various sections would have been happy to arrive at an honorable compromise with the Great Powers and with the conservatives, especially in the two key areas of Canton and Shanghai, where the compradores and the elements linked with the rural gentry were influential in the chambers of commerce. Thus, although in 1924 the Chinese bourgeoisie as a whole was inclined to favor an alliance with the labor movement, its activities still retained the contradictory character they had had during the May Fourth Movement.

The middle and petty bourgeoisie of the towns, consisting of intellectuals and students, petty traders and craftsmen, civil servants and clerks, also found that by 1925 their antagonism toward the Treaty Powers on the one hand and the warlords on the other had sharpened since 1919. The student groups that were formed in every university in May 1919 had continued their activities, and vigorously supported the campaign for demilitarization, the anti-Japanese demonstrations of 1921–22 following the Washington Conference, and the campaign for the return of Dairen in 1923. On the ideological level, their twofold protest against the foreigners and the conservatives took the form of a violent anti-Christian propaganda campaign (notably during the Protestant Youth Conference held in Peking in 1922), and an intensified attack on the Confucianist morals of former times, particularly in regard to marriage and the family.[30]

Craftsmen and petty traders found that economic conditions had worsened for them owing to their inability to compete with capitalist production, despite the growing practice of doing night work in craft workshops, a practice formerly unknown.[31] Like the industrial workers, craftsmen had been affected by the growing instability of currency and the depreciation of copper coinage[32] that resulted from the incessant fighting between warlords. The many craftsmen's strikes that occurred at this time were put down by the warlords with the same ferocity as was used in suppressing those of the industrial workers,[33] and although some craftsmen may have made a desperate attempt to stand together and keep up old guild practices in order to safeguard employment in their trade,[34] in the end they probably all came to adopt wider views and were ready to cooperate with other social classes instead of relying entirely on their own resources. Many of them did in fact become ardent supporters of the fight being carried forward by the labor movement and the bourgeoisie, and showed themselves to be as capable as they had been during the May Fourth Movement of taking effective action. Cooperation with the labor movement was, indeed, less new for them than it was for the bourgeoisie. Ever since 1919, workingmen in the craft industries had fought side by side with the industrial workers for higher wages (particularly in Shanghai and the South) and had taken part with them in May Day celebrations. They had even at times belonged to the same unions, notably in the provincial federations of Hupeh and Hunan formed in 1922, which included carpenters and masons as well as the miners and metalworkers of the Hanyehping Company in their membership. Petty traders, too, along with student groups, had been brought into close cooperation with the working masses during the anti-Japanese boycotts of 1920 and 1923, especially with the dockers and rickshaw men in the main ports and industrial centers; and during the summer of 1924 the student federations of Peking and Shanghai, together with the labor and merchant organizations of these cities, started agitating anew against the Treaty Powers.[35]

The labor movement found it easier to cooperate with these middle and lower-middle classes than with the upper bourgeoisie, because they were not subject to the same contradictions. Nevertheless, repercussions of these contradictions sometimes disturbed relations between them. For instance, an important section of the intellectuals who had taken part in the May Fourth Movement, and who after 1924 supplied the spokesmen for the right wing of the Kuomintang, had already in 1922 opposed the idea of the "fight against imperialism." Their views were expressed in a review edited by Hu Shih entitled *Nu-li* ("The Effort"). Some of the craftsmen and petty traders were also subject to the influence of the upper bourgeoisie: some belonged to the hui-kuan (the regional friendly societies), others had contracted financial loans that placed them under obligation, and so on.

As for the peasants, they too were in a worse position than in 1919. In addition to suffering from the rise in rents, the ruin of rural industries, and the concentration of landownership—all the long-term results of the penetration of Western capitalism in China—they were suffering from the immediate results of warlordism, which had become accentuated after the death of Yuan Shih-k'ai. Requisitioning, pillage, forced cultivation of opium,[36] and depredations of all kinds[37] were the rule in most provinces.[38] The tax burden had increased, not only because of a rise in the amount of the annual payment, but because of the practice of raising taxes several years in advance.[39] The peasants' usual reaction to this deterioration in their economic situation was the traditional one: they either emigrated to the "South Seas,"[40] joined bands of outlaws,[41] or else took part in the activities of the secret societies, which had grown noticeably stronger between 1920 and 1925.[42] But some of them, especially some of those who lived south of the Yangtze, were beginning to think that it might be possible to attempt a collective defense of their interests. It was in Kwangtung, under the leadership of the militant Communist P'eng P'ai, that the first peasant unions were formed in 1920–21. The immediate aim of these unions was to bring the collective pressure of the middle and poor peasants to bear upon the question of reduction of rents. Unions were subsequently formed in Kiangsu, Hunan, and Chekiang,[43] and by 1923 the peasant unions had a membership of several hundred thousand.[44] The poor and middle peasants, because there were so many of them and because their economic situation was so acute, were capable of supplying firm supporters of the labor movement and of the Nationalist movement as a whole, and ran no danger of having their revolutionary ardor sapped by a spirit of compromise. The labor movement had to some extent realized, prior to 1924, the potential importance of an alliance with the peasants. Already in 1922 the labor legislation program drawn up by the Labor Secretariat included among its 19 points the fixing of price levels for agricultural products by agreement with representatives of the peasants, regulations for working conditions on farms, and control of farm rents. Episodes such as the Shuikowshan strike in the fall of 1922, when the Hunanese peasants extended help to the strikers, had shown that the poor peasants were prepared to take action on the side of the proletariat.[45] Nevertheless there is no doubt that in 1924 the Chinese labor movement, in its fight against its various enemies, failed to make full use of the immense untapped resources represented by the peasantry,[46] and this was a failure that was never rectified during the 1924–27 revolution. What part, indeed, could middle and poor peasants play in a revolutionary strategy based essentially on the action of the industrial proletariat in the big cities? And how could an alliance with the peasantry be reconciled with an alliance with the bourgeoisie, since the latter still had close ties with the rural gentry, who were extremely antagonistic toward the formation of peasant unions? These thorny theoretical and practical problems were not peculiar to China, and the Communist Party's tentative approach to them merely reflected the heated discussions on these questions that were then taking place among all members of the Comintern.[47]

The Kuomintang Congress of January 1924

Although all kinds of difficult problems were raised by the idea of forming a united front composed of all social classes and political parties who were opposed to the Foreign Powers and to the militarists and conservatives, the political situation in China in 1924 made it essential to bring such a united front into being as soon as possible. This was the reason the Kuomintang Congress of January 1924 was held; at this time the party was reorganized and the policy of cooperation with the Chinese Communist Party was officially adopted.

Cooperation between the two parties had been led up to by internal developments in both of them during the past few years. As early as 1920, the Comintern, in its theses on the national and colonial question, had stressed the possibility of forming alliances with the national bourgeoisie in colonial countries or in those subjected to the control of foreign powers,[48] and the extension of an invitation to the Kuomintang as well as to the Chinese Communist Party to send delegates to the Congress of Toilers of the Far East (held in Moscow in January 1922) was a first move in this direction.[49] During the congress, however, frequent disputes arose between the two sets of delegates.[50] The Chinese Communist Party at its second conference discussed the question of cooperation with the national bourgeoisie in rather vague terms, and although mention was made of the Kuomintang, all that was envisaged was support for Sun Yat-sen's party from outside it.[51] At the end of 1922 and the beginning of 1923, however, the Comintern passed resolutions insisting more emphatically on the need for the two parties to come closer together, so long as the Chinese Communists maintained their independence.[52] The bitter defeat of February 1923 proved the Chinese Communists' need for allies, and the growing economic difficulties of the Chinese bourgeoisie in the face of Western and Japanese competition now made the idea of cooperation seem more feasible.[53] Hence, at the third conference of the Chinese Communist Party in June 1923, a proposal that Communists be allowed to become individual members of the Kuomintang was approved, and a call was made to transform the Kuomintang into a "revolutionary alliance" of the four classes opposed to warlordism and foreign penetration of China.[54] The Communist Party was at the same time to maintain its separate existence. This decision was a defeat both for Ch'en Tu-hsiu and other supporters of the "two revolutions" theory, who wanted to leave the first part of the job entirely to the bourgeoisie, and for Chang Kuo-t'ao and other supporters of the "closed door" theory, who wanted to keep the working class in its state of splendid isolation.[55]

Similarly, the new line adopted by Sun Yat-sen was one that had begun to take shape in 1920–21, and that he was now forced into by the pressure of events rather than by any theoretical considerations (though much had been said at the third conference of the Chinese Communist Party about Sun's "objective position" on the revolutionary struggle against the warlords and the Treaty Powers). His personal attitude toward the whole situation is what really counted, because the Kuomintang, despite the reorganization of 1919, had little more than nominal power, and was an organization entirely based on personal loyalty to its leader.[56] The coup brought off by Ch'en Chiung-ming in July 1922 unquestionably afforded Sun Yat-sen as much food for thought as the incident of February 7, 1923, afforded the Communists. Chased once again from Canton, this time by a man in whom for years he had placed great confidence and who had enabled him to return there the year before, he had come to realize that political alliances with the militarists, upon which he had relied since 1917, were not to be depended upon. No less bitter were the disappointments he had suffered, and continued to suffer, at the hands of the Western Powers, who in 1921 and 1922 had refused to grant his government the "customs surplus," yet had bestowed their favors on Ch'en Chiung-ming after he had staged his coup.[57] He had to find new allies, both at home and abroad. He was coming to regard the labor movement, which at the time of the Labor Congress in May 1922 had seemed to him merely a supporting element,[58] as a new force destined to play a unique part in Chinese politics.[59] In 1923 he had learned to appreciate the support of the Canton trade unions in his fight against the warlords in the North and the Western Powers; in October, for instance, they had supported his protest against the scandalous election of Ts'ao K'un to the presidency (when the votes of members of parliament were bought at 5,000 yuan a head), and against the subsequent recognition of Ts'ao by the Powers.[60] They had again given him vigorous support in December, when he tried to appropriate the "customs surplus" from the customs collected in the port of Canton, only to be defeated by a classic display of gunboat politics.[61]

During his stay in Shanghai after once again taking refuge there in August 1922, Sun Yat-sen was already having discussions with Li Ta-chao and other Communists on the prospects of reorganizing the Kuomintang.[62] First Li and then others were admitted as individual members of the Kuomintang without having to give up their membership in the Communist Party.[63] At the same time the ties between Sun and the Soviet Union were strengthened. The first approaches had been made in 1921, when Sun was president of the Canton Republic, in an exchange of letters between him and G. V. Chicherin, the Soviet Commissar for Foreign Affairs,[64] and this was followed by a visit paid to him by Maring, a delegate of the Comintern.[65] Sun had further discussions with Maring in Shanghai in the summer of 1922,[66] and then met Adolf Joffe, an envoy of the Soviet government, who had just been in Peking trying vainly to negotiate a Soviet-Chinese treaty. In January 1923 the famous Sun-Joffe statement was published, affirming the community of views between the two men, and describing China as not yet ripe for Communism. Further direct contacts were established in 1923: in February Sun sent his colleague Liao Chung-k'ai to accompany Joffe on his visit to Tokyo, and during the summer Sun's brother-in-law Chiang Chieh-shih (Chiang Kai-shek) went to Moscow. In the autumn Borodin's political and military mission arrived in Canton.[67]

Thus the Kuomintang Congress in January 1924 was the culmination of a gradual rapprochement.[68] The internal organization of the party was greatly strengthened, modeled upon the Bolshevik Party of the Soviet Union, even to the extent of using the terminology of that party's rules. At the same time, the congress manifesto reaffirmed the Three People's Principles formulated by Sun Yat-sen twenty years before; but now in addition there was a vigorous denunciation of "militarism" and "imperialism" as the two basic causes of China's ills. The congress also reapproved the "three new policies" laid down in Canton at the end of 1923: cooperation between the Kuomintang and the Communist Party, alliance with the Soviet Union, and support for the workers and peasants. Members of the Communist Party and of the Socialist Youth Corps of China were to be admitted as individual members of the Kuomintang, and several Communist leaders, including Li Ta-chao, Mao Tse-tung, Ch'ü Ch'iu-pai, and Chang Kuo-t'ao, became members of the Central Committee. Soviet military and political advisers also attended the congress; and when the news of Lenin's death came, it adjourned as a tribute of mourning and sent a telegram of condolence.[69] Finally, the congress came out in favor of support, including financial aid, for the labor movement and the trade unions, called for labor legislation, and invited workers and peasants to become members of the Kuomintang, assuring them that "from the moment the Kuomintang takes up the fight against the imperialists, the warlords, and the privileged classes, the Nationalist Revolution will at the same time be a revolution for the emancipation of the workers and peasants." Further, the new party rules adopted by the congress included proposals for the setting up of "labor departments" (*kung-jen-pu*) by party committees at all levels; these departments were given the special task of implementing the policy of cooperation with the labor movement.

Shifting Alliances in Canton

The Canton labor movement took a new direction as a result of the Kuomintang Congress of January 1924 and of the profound political changes reflected by it. No new possibilities for action had been opened up in South China by Ch'en Chiung-ming's defeat and the return of Sun Yat-sen at the beginning of 1923, and labor activities there still preserved the same narrow corporate character as before.[70] Moreover the Canton government still kept a strict watch over labor organizations, and even arrested the leaders of the telegraphers' strike in March 1923.[71]

In 1924, however, in accordance with the line adopted at the January congress, the government's attitude toward the labor movement changed, and labor activities were given a new stimulus. Much of this stimulus came from Liao Chung-k'ai, one of Sun Yat-sen's earliest companions and a leader of the left wing of his party. Now, in his double capacity as provincial governor and head of the labor department of the Central Committee,[72] he threw himself wholeheartedly into carrying out the policy of cooperation with the Communist Party, the Soviet Union, and the trade unions, and flew the red flag with hammer and sickle above his yamen.[73] He appointed a Communist, the Cantonese Feng Chü-p'o, as secretary of the labor department of the Central Committee,[74] and saw to it that the 1924 May Day celebrations in Canton were on a very much grander scale than the year before.[75] In 1924, 170,000 workers marched through the streets of Canton,[76] and Sun Yat-sen made a lengthy speech on "the sufferings endured by the workers because of the unequal treaties," in which he stressed the difference in attitude between Chinese and foreign employers, called upon the workers to strengthen their unions and to take part in the revolutionary struggle being waged by the Kuomintang against the Foreign Powers, and expressed the hope that harmonious relations would be established between the workers and the Chinese employers.[77]

A further initiative taken by Liao in May was to form a federation of the unions that supported the new line, as a counterpoise to the provincial federation with its traditional guild outlook. This was the Canton Workers' Delegates' Conference, an organization so centralized that the executive committee had the right to dissolve unions belonging to it as well as the right to declare a general strike.[78] But this new federation did not yet carry much weight, because only about a dozen unions in the more modern sectors of the economy, such as those of the railwaymen, the dockers, the printers, and the rice-huskers, were involved. Most of the other trade associations remained with the old federation, except for the Mechanics' Union, which chose to stay independent. In Hong Kong, an amalgamation of the two federations of trade unions there (the General Association of Chinese Workingmen and the General Association of Labor Organizations) had been proposed by Sun Yat-sen when he passed through on his return to Canton in February 1923,[79] but nothing had come of the proposal so far. The Canton government could, however, count on the support of the second of these federations.[80]

Trade union organization in South China took a new turn with the holding of the first conference of transport workers of the Pacific in Canton in July 1924. The conference was organized by the Red International, and railwaymen from North China and seamen from the Philippines, Java, and Singapore attended, as well as members of the Cantonese unions concerned. There was very little discussion of occupational problems, because these varied too much among countries; but political policies were adopted similar to those advanced at the Kuomintang Congress a short time before.[81]

Nevertheless the trade associations that were not in favor of the new line remained very influential in Canton.[82] The Mechanics' Union sent a delegate to the Workers' Delegates' Conference in May 1924 who tore Liao Chung-k'ai and the entire government apart on the grounds that Chinese employers treated their workers no better than foreign employers did.[83] In December 1923 Sun Yat-sen had approved the appointment as manager of the Canton arsenal of Ma Ch'ao-chün, who was one of the many moderates who were still at that time extremely active in the trade union movement, and who was also one of the leaders of the Mechanics' Union most hostile to the left and most severely criticized by the left.[84] Thus as early as 1923 there were already signs of the split that was to occur in the Canton labor movement during the 1924–27 revolution. Disputes over members became frequent between rival labor organizations,[85] and sometimes broke out into violence, as when an official of the rice porters' union, which had been on strike for two weeks, was murdered on January 30, 1924. (The murderer was never discovered.)[86]

Meanwhile, one sign of the renewal of labor activities in Canton resulting from the Kuomintang Congress in January was the wave of economic strikes in June 1924, which obtained an appreciable raise in wages for a large number of trades.[87] But even more significant was the Shameen affair in July.[88] The island of Shameen, a central part of the city of Canton, contained the French and the British Concessions. When Martial Merlin, the Governor-General of French Indochina, was passing through there in June on his way back from Tokyo, he was assassinated by a Vietnamese belonging to the Nationalist V.N.Q.D.D. party, whereupon new police regulations were introduced for the purpose of maintaining a strict control over the identity of all Chinese entering or leaving the island. On June 16 all the Chinese employed there, whether as domestic servants or in consulates, banks, and the like, went on strike, demanding the abolition of the new restrictions and an apology from the consuls. The strikers, among whom were the Chinese policemen in the concessions, immediately crossed over to the Chinese districts of Canton, where they organized a "People's Association Against the Shameen Regulations." They stationed pickets, gave each striker a strike certificate stamped by the association, and collected large sums of money in Canton for the subsistence of the strikers. Their manifestos, which were drawn up with the help of the Cantonese Communists,[89] show what a long way the labor movement in South China had come since the Hong Kong seamen's strike in 1922. Now, explicit reference was made to the unequal treaties, to incidents such as the Lincheng affair and the Canton customs dispute, and to the "struggle against imperialism" as defined by the Kuomintang Congress in January. On August 13 the consuls were forced to agree to the reinstatement of all the strikers, including the police,[90] and to the abolition of the restrictions introduced in June. This strike was not only a great psychological success in that it encouraged the Canton unions to accept the new Kuomintang policies; it also helped to lay the ground for the grand maneuvers of the Canton–Hong Kong strike of 1925–26 because of the solid organizational work involved.

There was, however, a considerable amount of opposition to the new line that had been adopted in Canton since the January congress. Small employers and the guilds and trade associations that clung to the old traditions were all somewhat disturbed by the new upsurge of activity in the labor movement shown by the May Day celebrations, the Workers' Delegates' Conference, and the Shameen strike. The local bourgeoisie was groaning under the burden of the many taxes imposed on them by Sun Yat-sen[91] in order to meet the expenses of the military operations that had had to be resumed in the spring against the Kwangsi militarists and the remains of Ch'en Chiung-ming's followers, and it was terrified by the prospective cost of the "Northern Punitive Expedition" (pei-fa), plans for which Sun Yat-sen had once again announced. The Cantonese gentry, particularists all, were equally alarmed by Sun's military plans. They disliked the tough Hunanese and Yunnanese mercenaries in whom Sun preferred to place his trust after Ch'en's Cantonese troops had betrayed him, and they were not very enthusiastic either about the products of the Whampoa Military Academy, which had been established in May under the control of the Soviet military advisers. In short, there was already a deterioration in the relations between Sun Yat-sen's circle and large sections of the Cantonese bourgeoisie.[92] The policy of cooperation between the national bourgeoisie and the labor movement was still part of the political program, but locally it was running into serious difficulties, as a result not only of Sun's maladroit financial and military policies but also of the very nature of the Cantonese bourgeoisie, with its conservative outlook, its backward views on economic development, and the ties it still had with the rural gentry of Kwangtung and with the compradore bourgeoisie of Hong Kong. All of this made it extremely suspicious of the two main points in the program: the struggle against the "feudalists" and that against the "imperialists."

Thus, in 1924 the same elements that in 1922 had preferred Ch'en Chiung-ming to Sun Yat-sen were once more inclined to take a stand against Sun. This was certainly the implication of the affair of the Merchants' Volunteers. Already in 1923 the Canton Chamber of Commerce had organized a corps of "Merchant Volunteers," an example that was swiftly followed in other urban centers in the province; and in May 1924 over a hundred such groups, amounting to a total of 100,000 men, were amalgamated.[93] An indication of their ties with the Hong Kong compradores on the one hand and with the local gentry on the other was given by their respective choices for president and vice-president of this amalgamated body. The president was Ch'en Lien-po, head compradore of the Canton branch of the Hongkong and Shanghai Banking Corporation and a British subject, whom the Chinese conservative press had hailed as a kind of Mussolini and for whom they wished an equally rapid rise.[94] The second was Ch'en Kung-shou, a wealthy landowner from the Foshan district.[95] The Volunteers, who made no secret of their dislike of Sun Yat-sen, declared themselves to be "a non-partisan military unit for local self-defense against lawlessness, to preserve peace and order," and complained that "the lawlessness of a certain element" was harming foreign trade.[96] They very soon came into direct conflict with labor organizations linked with the left wing of the Kuomintang,[97] and the Workers' Delegates' Conference, when it first met in May, demanded that they be disbanded.[98] The trial of strength came in August, when the Canton government seized a shipment of arms brought in by a Norwegian ship for delivery to the Volunteers.[99]

There is no need here to go into the details of this affair. The only point of importance that concerns us is the support the labor organizations gave the government in its fight against the Volunteers. The only forces at the disposal of the government were the mercenaries, whose leaders could not be entirely relied upon, and the Whampoa Academy cadets (to whom the confiscated arms had been handed over), who were not yet strong enough to meet a situation of this kind. The government was therefore in crying need of additional military support, and this need was met when the Workers' Delegates' Conference formed a "Labor Organizations' Army" (*Kung-t'uan-chün*), a group sanctioned by Sun Yat-sen and Liao Chung-k'ai.[100] This meant that for the first time the Chinese proletariat had an armed force of its own. Such a force had already been seen as essential by its leaders after the blow delivered by Wu P'ei-fu,[101] and had been foreshadowed by the teams of pickets that had more than once been formed during strikes.[102]

On October 9, after two months of complicated negotiations, the Volunteers demanded that Sun immediately and unconditionally surrender all the arms he had confiscated; but during the procession held in honor of the Nationalist festival the following day, they came up against the troops of the Labor Organizations' Army and were defeated by them. They then tried to snatch a victory by declaring a general strike of merchants; but on October 15 the union militias, the Whampoa cadets, and several army units came into action, and the Volunteers' units were broken, their headquarters occupied, and the shops in which they had tried to take refuge taken by assault.[103] A further contribution to the government's victory was provided by the strike declared by the newspaper printers, who, in addition to asking for a raise in wages, demanded that the daily press (for the most part closely linked with conservative circles) stop supporting the Volunteers.[104]

The Canton government emerged from this trial of strength with its relations with the labor movement very much improved. Despite the pressures brought to bear in favor of a compromise,[105] it had now definitely broken with the conservatives who had supported the Volunteers. These conservatives had consisted in the main of the members of the chambers of commerce, and of the remaining members of the former provincial assembly, with their close ties with the rural gentry.[106] Both these groups were openly opposed to the "three new policies," and especially to collaboration with the Communists,[107] and had simply used the matter of the confiscation of arms as an excuse for attempting to reverse the direction of the Canton government's policy. Ch'en Chiung-ming's renewed attacks on the eastern borders of Kwangtung suggest that there was a concerted plan.[108] The defeat of all these opponents of Sun Yat-sen was at the same time a defeat for Great Britain, whose consul general had sent Sun what amounted to an ultimatum on August 29, threatening "immediate action" if he attacked the Volunteers,[109] and whose gunboats flying the Union Jack had been sent as usual to Cantonese waters.[110] The vigor of Sun's reply, including a regular indictment against Britain for its many interventions in Chinese internal affairs since the time of Yuan Shih-k'ai and before as well, shows that here too a fight to the death had begun between the Canton government and British interests in the Far East.[111] The whole affair threw a sharp light on the thesis of the indivisibility of the fight against the forces of social reaction and the fight against the penetration of the Foreign Powers that had been discussed at the congress in January 1924, and Sun Yat-sen emphasized this in his manifesto of November 13.[112]

Another indication of the Canton government's move to the left after this serious conflict was the way in which the celebration of the October Revolution took on, for the first time, a semi-official character.[113] That the government was genuinely anxious to implement the third of the "new policies" and to support the workers is shown by the promulgation in October of very enlightened trade union laws, in which recognition was given to the unions, and to their rights to conduct collective bargaining with employers, to declare strikes and negotiate their settlement, to own property, and to federate on an industrial basis.[114] When, in October and November of 1924, the unions in the South declared a boycott of the products of the Nanyang Company in sympathy with the large number of workers who had been laid off at the company's Shanghai factory, the Canton government maintained a position of benevolent neutrality, thus showing that it had no hesitation in subordinating the interests of one of the foremost Chinese capitalist enterprises to the interests of the workers, now that it had formed an alliance with the labor movement.[115]

Attitudes Toward the Policy of Cooperation

The policy of cooperation between the Kuomintang and the Communist Party laid down at the congress in January 1924 was taken very seriously by both sides. The policy's chances for success were considerably helped when the Soviet Union and the Peking government signed a treaty on May 31, 1924, thereby making a profound impression on people's minds throughout China.[116] Nevertheless cooperation raised a number of rather tricky problems.

To the Chinese Communists it was clear that the policy of cooperation applied only to the two main objectives: the fight against the feudal rule of the warlords and the fight against the encroachments of the Foreign Powers. It was equally clear to them that it should in no way interfere with the labor movement's freedom of action in other matters, such as its drive to press economic demands on Chinese employers. The best way to support the Chinese bourgeoisie, wrote Ch'en Tu-hsiu in a semi-official article that appeared in June 1924, was to help remove the dual constraint on their progress rather than to restrict the activities of the labor movement. Cooperation between the working class and the bourgeoisie was initiated for the purpose of bringing about the revolution of national liberation and not for reaching compromises in the economic field.[117] The Fourth Communist Party Conference in January 1925 passed a resolution that made it clearer still that there was no incompatibility in pursuing the policy of cooperation while at the same time preserving independence of action for the proletariat in the defense of its own interests. This resolution stressed the need to increase the number of unions in the big industrial centers and the number of Communist Party cells within each enterprise. It distinguished between the left wing of the Kuomintang, consisting of petty bourgeois and working-class elements, and the right wing, composed of compradors and landowners, and stressed the need to support the one and oppose the other while keeping a close watch over the swing of opinion at the center (composed of "national capitalists").[118]

This complex but perfectly viable line met with a good deal of opposition within the Communist Party itself. The "two revolutions" and "closed door" theories, both officially condemned at the Third Conference in 1923, and both of which were against cooperation with the Kuomintang on the grounds that it would interfere with the Communists' freedom of action, still found support. The supporters of the first, including Ch'en Tu-hsiu himself, whose above-mentioned article probably did not express his own personal views, were pessimistic about the future of the Chinese proletariat, or at least about its immediate future. When Ch'en, still feeling the discouragement caused by the defeat of February 7, 1923, wrote that "the vast majority of Chinese workers neither want to fight nor are able to fight their own class battles," he added that "in a country as little industrialized as China, purely economic struggles on the part of the working class are not of much significance," and that "the fight against colonial and semi-colonial rule is a fight for political liberty common to all classes, and is quite distinct from the class struggle of the proletariat."[119] It was in order to counteract this pessimistic attitude that in October 1924 Teng Chung-hsia and Chang Kuo-t'ao started the weekly *Chung-kuo kung-jen* ("The Chinese Worker"),[120] in which precisely the opposite view was often expressed, namely that the working class should not form any alliances with other classes but should go its own way alone.[121] Chang Kuo-t'ao, who, it will be remembered, was the leading supporter of the "closed door" theory at the 1923 conference, contributed to the weekly as one of its editors under the pseudonym of Chang T'e-li. The paper's vigorous attack on the plan for the Northern Expedition, announced by Sun Yat-sen in the autumn of 1924, expressed another of the reservations felt about the policy of cooperation with the Kuomintang.[122]

These reservations were felt by a number of Communist trade union leaders. Their reluctance to form alliances of considerable consequence and their stubborn preference for confining themselves to class-struggle activities were reinforced by the attitude adopted toward them by the moderates of the Kuomintang. Anti-Communist feelings among Kuomintang members did not disappear overnight after the congress of January 1924. The party pinned its hopes on being able to counterbalance Communist influence among the proletariat and thus keep labor agitation within reasonable limits. Hence implementation of the policy of support for the labor movement developed into a fierce struggle to gain influence among the workers, in which the right wing of the Kuomintang obtained valuable support from the deserters from the labor movement and from the upholders of the old corporate traditions, who, as we have seen, had come to the fore again in 1923–24. For example, the committee of the Shanghai branch of the Kuomintang, composed largely of compradores, was on excellent terms with the anti-Communist associations affiliated with the Federation of Labor Organizations.[123] These associations were astute enough to support the political alliance with the Soviet Union in the spring of 1924, but at the same time they attacked "politicians ... who call themselves socialists [but who] take the opportunity of the labour movement ... for enriching themselves."[124] The Communists were not included in their May Day celebrations in 1924, when they were honored by the presence of the Kuomintang veteran Wang Ching-wei.[125] The divergence in views became still more evident during the strike of the Nanyang workers in September 1924, a strike that was supported by the Communists but curbed by the moderate-led workers' club in the factory and by the Federation. The attacks against the strike made by the *Min-kuo jih-pao,* a daily newspaper linked with the Kuomintang and the upper bourgeoisie, led to a lively exchange of charges between it and the Communist Party weekly, *Hsiang-tao.*[126]

This struggle for influence that was being waged between the Kuomintang moderates and the militant Communists was not confined to Shanghai. We have already seen that in Canton, despite the fact that Liao Chung-k'ai had appointed a Communist as secretary of the labor department of the Central Committee of the Kuomintang, the influence of right-wing elements, as represented by the Mechanics' Union, was still strong enough in December 1923 to lead to the appointment of one of their members, Ma Ch'ao-chün, as manager of the arsenal.[127] Similarly, on the Lunghai railway, in Chungking, and in Foshan (a center of the silk industry near Canton), elements linked with the right wing of the Kuomintang made strenuous efforts during 1924 to form unions that would not be under Communist influence, and came up against the Communists in doing so.[128]

In some areas, however, especially in those where the social structure was such that compradore influence had little chance of penetrating, positive results of the agreements reached in January 1924 sometimes materialized. In accordance with the new party rules, all the provincial and local branches of the Kuomintang created labor departments, in which the responsible posts were often given to Communists because of their experience in these matters.[129] For example, in the province of Kiangsi, five out of the seven members of the labor department of the Nanchang branch were Communists, including Chao Hsing-nung, who was responsible for Communist activities throughout the province. Under his guidance, unions were formed among the printers, the railwaymen, and the boatmen.[130]

New Developments in the North

When Feng Yü-hsiang, suddenly turning against the Chihli faction which he had hitherto supported, staged his coup d'état on October 24, 1924, thereby bringing a new government to power in the North, new prospects were opened up for the labor movement and indeed for the entire Nationalist movement.[131] The Chihli faction must have thought that it was just about to triumph, because it had succeeded in chasing Lu Yung-hsiang and Ho Feng-lin, the last two supporters of the Anfu faction, out of the Chekiang and Shanghai areas, and it was preparing for a final attack against its Fengtien opponents in the Northeast. But the about-face of its faithful follower Feng led to the arrest of Ts'ao K'un, the President of the Republic, whereupon Wu P'ei-fu withdrew to the British sphere of influence in the Middle Yangtze area. The central government in Peking was now in the hands of Tuan Ch'i-jui, a veteran of the Anfu faction that had been overthrown in 1920, Chang Tso-lin, master of the Northeast, and Feng Yü-hsiang, a soldier of fortune known to be a Protestant and a sympathizer with the Canton government. Tuan and Chang were both warlords of the old school, but since the summer of 1922 they had had a three-cornered alliance with Sun Yat-sen.[132] Altogether, the Communist trade union leaders were led to believe that the new Northern government was based on such a precarious balance of forces as to suggest that it would have a more favorable attitude toward their activities,[133] and in the fall they launched a "movement for the restoration of the trade unions."

It was among the railwaymen of the North, who had been the avant-garde of the labor movement until the setback of the February Seventh incident, that this movement had its broadest development. Trade union leaders who had been imprisoned were released, including those on the Cheng-T'ai line;[134] dismissed workers were reinstated;[135] old unions were re-formed, and new ones created.[136] In February 1925, on the anniversary of the incident in 1923, the Second National Congress of Railwaymen was held in Chengchow,[137] attended by 45 delegates from a dozen lines—that is, all the Chinese railways except the Shanghai-Nanking and Shanghai-Hangchow lines—and also by trade unionists from Hamburg, Moscow, and Singapore.[138] The congress called for a strengthening of union organization, for the final elimination of the "Communications Clique," which still had influence on certain lines, and for an end to the influence of foremen and to demarcation disputes.[139] It also announced its support for the Nationalist revolution and for the policy of Sun Yat-sen, and gave special attention to the activities of the *kung-tsei* ("labor brigands")—that is, deserters from the revolutionary labor movement who had gone over to the side of the moderate labor organizations as a result of weakness or ambition, or because of the prospects of financial gain. The railwaymen's unions were urged to keep a close watch and to expel anyone suspected of being from the ranks of the kung-tsei.[140]

The movement also had repercussions in the Seamen's Union, which, during the period of retreat, had come under the leadership of men aligned with the moderate associations of Shanghai. Radicals such as Su Chao-cheng and Lin Wei-min once more took over the leadership,[141] and when British firms in Hong Kong queried certain clauses in the 1923 agreement, there was a renewal of strike action there.[142]

Tientsin, the big industrial center of North China, had so far remained outside the sphere of activities of the labor movement and of developments in union organization. This lack of labor activity was due perhaps to its proximity to the capital and to the concentrations of troops in the surrounding neighborhood, and perhaps also to certain features in its social structure.[143] In the fall of 1924, however, the local committee of the Communist Party, using the same tactics that had been used in 1921 in Hunan and Shanghai, instituted workers' evening classes that provided the nucleus of the unions formed at the beginning of 1925 in the cotton mills, in the carpet factories, in the printing works, and among the seamen.[144]

But it was in Shanghai, which the new government in the North decided in January to demilitarize and where the arsenal was dismantled,[145] that the most spectacular result of the "movement to restore the trade unions" occurred, namely the strike in the Japanese cotton mills in February 1925.[146] This strike, which lasted from February 10 to 27 and which involved from thirty to forty thousand people, was at first nothing more than a simple economic strike to protest a number of dismissals, with additional demands for a raise in wages and greater regularity in the payment of wages in silver currency, and for the payment of bonuses for hard work and guarantees against maltreatment by foremen. It was still very much like those sudden outbursts of anger that were a familiar occurrence among the Shanghai textile workers, and there were one or two instances of ta-ch'ang with wrecking of workshops and machinery. But its extent, the rapidity with which it spread, and the discipline shown by the strikers clearly reveal the presence of experienced organizers. At the end of 1924 the Communist Party had re-formed a workers' club that became known as the West Shanghai Workers' Club, with premises in Hsiaoshatu, outside Settlement territory. Its leaders, including the printer Liu Hua[147] and the cotton worker Sun Liang-hui, took over the direction of the strike on February 10. Soon they were joined by two even more experienced cadres, Li Li-san and Teng Chung-hsia, sent by the Central Committee of the Communist Party when the strike began to spread[148] because it seemed to be an excellent opportunity to put into practice the policy of turning the workers' struggle into a direct attack on foreign interests in China, a policy that had been adopted at the Canton Congress and was supported by the Communists. Throughout the strike, mass meetings were held daily, delegates from factories and mills went to the rostrum, and leaflets were distributed. This was a far cry from the spontaneous and unorganized strikes that had taken place in these same mills several years before. The moderate associations of the Federation, well aware of the fact that the balance was tipping over in favor of Communist influence, which for the past two years had been completely absent in the Shanghai labor movement, made every effort to put a stop to the strike. Their leaflets warned the workers against "agitators" and appealed to them to return to work.[149] But the West Shanghai Workers' Club, where Liu Hua held press conferences for Chinese journalists[150] and paid out 20 cents a day to each striker,[151] retained full control.

The strike not only enjoyed the political and financial support of Chinese labor and financial aid from the international labor movement (the Red International contributed 30,000 rubles),[152] but also received wide sympathy from Chinese of all shades of opinion. The Shanghai students offered their services for the collection of funds and for help with the administrative work of the strike committee.[153] Large sums were collected from the Chinese bourgeoisie, whose news publications, such as the *Min-kuo jih-pao,* came out so strongly on the side of the strikers that they were even fined by the Mixed Court. The Chinese municipal authorities, on instructions from the new government in Peking, adopted a comparatively tolerant attitude,[154] and the Workers' Club was able to function in Hsiaoshatu quite openly and without any interference throughout the strike. (The strike occurred mainly on Chinese territory, except for the Yangtzepoo mills.) Even the big compradores of the Shanghai Chinese Chamber of Commerce were acting on the side of the strikers when they offered to mediate on February 26, for this saved the strikers from a humiliating defeat. Work was resumed on February 28 on the promise that all acts of cruelty would in future be punished, that strikers would be reinstated, and that wages would be paid regularly every fortnight.

Although the Japanese cotton mill strike was only partially successful as far as immediate objectives were concerned, it nevertheless marked the end of the long period of inactivity in the Shanghai labor movement and the beginning of the outburst of activity that was to lead to the explosion of May 30. As soon as the strike was over, the Workers' Club became the Shanghai Cotton Mills Union,[155] which, supported by a large number of factory committees and under the guidance of Liu Hua, became quite a powerful body; the Japanese firms had to deal with it unofficially on matters of reinstatement of strikers, wages, and compensation to workers who had been dismissed or ill-treated.[156] The scale upon which workers took part in the May Day celebrations in 1925 and even more in those of May 9 ("Day of Humiliation," the anniversary of the acceptance of the Twenty-one Demands),[157] both organized by the Communists, shows how rapidly the associations of the Federation, which had been so active in 1923–24, had lost influence. On May Day they made a vain attempt to give a new impetus to their activities by reintroducing Chiang K'ang-hu, the founder of the first "Socialist Party" in 1912.[158]

In varying degrees, the strikes that broke out here and there in most parts of China during the winter and into the spring of 1925 show the extent and the vigor of the revival in the labor movement. Although the Chiao-Chi railwaymen's strike in February was mainly a regionalist affair,[159] and the strike in the silk-reeling factories of Chekiang and Kwangtung was a purely economic one in protest against the reduction in wages introduced by Chinese firms in their efforts to meet the crisis,[160] others took on a Nationalist flavor. In January, for instance, the Hankow rickshaw men went on strike as a result of a clash with the British police in which several deaths occurred, and they were supported by several local bourgeois organizations.[161] Again, the Canton-Kowloon rail strike in April was in protest against reductions in wages introduced by a British superintendent.[162] The tendency even spread to the Japanese firms in the distant Northeast,[163] where, for example, the question of equality of treatment for Chinese and Japanese workers was raised during a strike at the Mukden sugar refinery organized by a mutual benefit society that had recently been formed by the workers.[164] But the strike of twelve thousand workers in the Tsingtao cotton mills in April and May 1925 is the best example of the new wave of activity.[165] It was declared by the union that had recently been formed, with the help of the Chiao-Chi railwaymen, among the workers of the Ta-k'ang cotton mill. In order to maintain strict discipline, the strikers were organized into groups of ten, one hundred, and five hundred. The Japanese government sent reinforcements of police to Tsingtao in order to break the strike, but found that the Chinese municipal authorities there were just as reluctant to take action against the strikers as those in Shanghai had been. Finally the Chinese Chamber of Commerce acted as mediator, and the strikers, who had received large sums from local student and other organizations, returned to work on May 10 after being on strike for three weeks, having obtained a large number of the economic demands they had originally presented. But the dispute flared up again when, on May 25, the Chinese authorities finally gave in to Japanese pressure and arrested the union leaders. This provoked a regular riot of the ta-ch'ang type, with the workers occupying the mill and wrecking it. On May 29 the police counterattacked, killing several workers and wounding twenty.[166] When news of this incident reached Shanghai, it added to the feelings aroused by the Nanking Road shootings on May 30.

The change of government in the North in the fall of 1924, in addition to opening up new possibilities for union organization and strike action, provided the labor movement with an opportunity for direct intervention in Chinese politics. On the invitation of Tuan Ch'i-jui and Chang Tso-lin, Sun Yat-sen went to Peking in November to discuss the affairs of the nation.[167] Before leaving Canton, he launched the idea of a National Convention in which all representative bodies in the country, including the trade unions, would take part.[168] Its aims were to be the two basic ones laid down in January: the fight against the Treaty Powers and the liquidation of militarism. But the government in the North was disturbed by the radical program of Sun Yat-sen's convention and suggested instead a much less democratic "Truce Conference," to be attended mainly by important civilians and militarists. The Canton government and the Kuomintang then launched an appeal for "support for the National Convention," which was backed by the Communist Party and the unions under its control. The Communist Party, however, advised the unions to bring forward their own demands as well (restoration of trade unions, right to strike, and so on), without which the idea of the National Convention would be nothing but an "empty slogan."[169] From December to February a propaganda campaign to this effect was organized in various working-class centers—Canton,[170] Shanghai,[171] Kwangsi,[172] and the railways in the North.[173] This effort resulted in a "Conference in Support of the National Convention" held in Peking in March, for which delegates were chosen at workers' meetings.[174] But the death of Sun Yat-sen left the promoters of this campaign without any hope of having their ideas accepted through negotiations with the Peking government, and the Conference dispersed in April.[175]

Thus for the time being, the idea of having the working class exercise its full political rights by taking part in the general management of affairs in China had to be given up. This seems to have given rise to some uncertainties of opinion within the Communist Party. Ch'ü Ch'iu-pai and others continued to demand that priority be given to workers' participation in the revolution of national liberation[176] in accordance with the line adopted in 1924 and confirmed at the Fourth Communist Party Conference, whereas another group still gave preference to the class struggle of the proletariat, their views being given expression in an important article by Chang Kuo-t'ao in the April 1925 number of *Chung-kuo kung-jen*. Chang proposed replacing the "movement for the restoration of the trade unions" and the "movement in support of the National Convention" by a "movement in support of the fight for liberties" (civil liberties, the right to strike, the right to form unions, and so on),[177] which would be directed against both the Settlement authorities and the Peking government, and in which the Cantonese proletariat would take part.

The Second National Labor Congress

In the spring of 1925, the success of the renewal of trade union activities was such as to warrant the convocation of the Second National Labor Congress, scheduled for Canton on May 1. Officially, the initiators of this congress were the four principal left-wing labor organizations then in existence in China: the Canton Workers' Delegates' Conference, the General Union of Railwaymen, the General Union of Seamen, and the Hanyehping General Union.[178] The last, which had been formed in 1922 and which in theory had survived the repression of 1923, was probably in fact no longer operative except for the Pingsiang collieries branch.[179] But the seamen's and railwaymen's unions could lay claim to a long tradition of strike and trade union activities. The Workers' Delegates' Conference in Canton, although of more recent date, had enjoyed great prestige ever since the defeat of the Merchant Volunteers, and possessed the additional advantage of being firmly backed by the left wing of the Kuomintang, in particular by Liao Chung-k'ai. The Communists were extremely active in all four organizations, but they apparently preferred to adopt the procedure of putting the responsibility for the congress on these organizations so as to avoid any harm that might be done to the policy of cooperation with the Kuomintang.[180] The Labor Secretariat, which had organized the 1922 congress and whose direct links with the Communist Party were well known, had never been officially closed down; but its activities had gradually slackened off during 1923-24, and after that ceased altogether.[181]

One hundred sixty-six unions, claiming a membership of 540,000, sent a total of 281 delegates to the Canton Congress on May 1,[182] many of whom had been appointed by rank-and-file organizations, such as those elected by the Shanghai Cotton Mills Union formed after the strike in February.[183] Not only were the numbers taking part in this congress far greater than in 1922 (attended by only 160 delegates representing 300,000 union members), but there was also far greater homogeneity among those attending. The moderate and semi-working-class organizations that had taken part three years before had now completely broken with the left, and refused to attend. The Shanghai Federation went out of its way to denounce this "Bolshevik enterprise."[184] The Canton Mechanics' Union abstained, and the Hong Kong General Association of Labor Organizations sent only observers, and then only at the request of the Seamen's Union.[185] Thus the composition of this congress as compared with that of 1922 reflects the decline in influence of the moderates, the almost complete disappearance of the anarchists, and the growing strength of the organizations that supported the policy jointly adopted by the Communists and the Kuomintang.

With regard to trade union activities, the congress passed two resolutions, one on economic strikes and one on organization.[186] The first listed a number of essential demands (minimum wage, the eight-hour day, abolition of the pao-kung system, protection of women and children, insurance plans); and the second stressed the superiority of industrial unionism and the need for a centralized organization with a strong hierarchical structure stretching from the central committee to the rank-and-file organizations in the factory, the mine pit, and the ship's crew.[187] Three special resolutions called for the speediest possible unification of the labor organizations in Canton, Hong Kong, and Shanghai.

There were serious discussions on the renewed activities of anti-Communist associations, starting around 1923–24. The struggle for influence between these associations and the Communist trade union militants, which began in 1924,[188] had widened by March 1925, when an "All-China Federation of Unions of All Provinces and Districts" was formed in Peking on the initiative of the Shanghai Federation, the Canton Mechanics' Union, and other associations of lesser importance. Sun K'o, the son of Sun Yat-sen and an avowed opponent of all cooperation with the Communists, was invited to attend the inaugural meeting.[189] The Second Labor Congress therefore passed a resolution particularly devoted to the question of the "labor brigands" (kung-tsei), 19 of whom were denounced by name;[190] the resolution included detailed directives on how to counteract their influence. A further resolution was adopted concerning workers' education, with particular reference to those areas where the political situation made any open trade union organization impossible.

The congress also decided to form an "All-China General Union," which had already been envisaged in May 1922. Now a general consensus was obtained for its rules and for the formation of a central committee, which was given extensive power in regard to strikes, intervention in the activities of affiliated organizations, political activities, and relations with the international labor movement. Among the 25 members of this central committee were such labor movement veterans as the seamen Lin Wei-min, who became president, and Su Chao-cheng; Liu Shao-ch'i, who became a vice-president; the railwayman Liu Wen-sung, also a vice-president; Teng Chung-hsia; and the Shanghai cotton worker Sun Liang-hui. The majority of its members were Communists, and the new national organization immediately voted for affiliation with the Red International. The Chinese labor movement had had close relations with the International for several years, and its views and experiences had been propagated by the journal *Chung-kuo kung-jen* from the end of 1924.[191]

The political situation in China also came up for discussion, and one resolution, which went against the old guild traditions, stressed the need for workers to participate in the political struggle for national liberation, which, in view of the "semi-colonial" status of China, was to be regarded as a preliminary stage leading to the proletarian revolution. The text of this resolution displays, however, the hesitancies about alliances with other classes already expressed during the winter in the pages of *Chung-kuo kung-jen*. It indicated that, in view of the "counterrevolutionary" schemes of the upper bourgeoisie, the temporizing of the middle bourgeoisie, and the lack of organization among the petty bourgeoisie and the small producers, it was left to the working class to bring about the defeat of the warlords and the foreign interests and to ensure the success of the "Nationalist Revolution." For this reason, the resolution concluded, their immediate objective must be the attainment of workers' liberties. The same timidity about alliances with other classes was shown in a resolution on cooperation between the proletariat and the peasants. The advisability of an alliance between these two partners in the revolution was solemnly affirmed, but since it was stated that "the towns were the centers of political action and therefore the main centers of the struggle," the alliance appeared to be for the benefit of the workers.[192]

Yet although the congress took a somewhat narrow view of the alliance between workers and peasants, this does not mean that it was not concerned about the subject. A big public meeting was held to which both congress delegates and members of a provincial conference of peasants taking place in Canton during the same week were invited.[193] In February and March 1925 the trade unions and the Kwangtung Peasant Union had fought side by side when both gave assistance to the Whampoa cadets during the "First Eastern Expedition" against the troops of Ch'en Chiung-ming that were still operating on the eastern borders of the province.[194] Memories of these common struggles were still fresh, and the rather hesitant formulations of the congress were probably far from reflecting the potentialities for common action between the peasants and workers that existed at that time.

Thus the Second National Labor Congress, held amid the echoes of May Day celebrations in all the big industrial centers of China,[195] contributed toward strengthening the unity and organizational capacities of the Chinese labor movement, even if it neither gave rise to quite so wide-ranging a discussion of ideas as the first,[196] nor arrived at any very clear decisions about the complex problems of political strategy that faced the unions at that time. Several weeks later, unforeseen incidents suddenly sparked off mass agitation in Shanghai, Canton, and other big cities in China, giving the labor movement important new allies. The organizers of the Canton Congress had perhaps failed to realize the full importance of these allies, but the success of the congress in strengthening the internal organization of the labor movement made it possible for the working class to be, in effect, the leaders of the great revolutionary upsurge in the summer of 1925.

CHAPTER XI

The May Thirtieth Movement

The whole complex of workers', merchants', and students' strikes, of street demonstrations, press campaigns, and political moves of various kinds that took place in Shanghai (for the sake of convenience they will be termed the "May Thirtieth Movement") might be said to be the first dramatic outcome of the new balance of political forces that had begun to emerge at the end of 1923. The May Thirtieth Movement demonstrated the new possibilities that were opened up for the Nationalist movement by the alliance between the Kuomintang and the Communist Party, and it was sustained by the sudden upsurge of labor activities throughout the country that had taken place at the beginning of 1925. It also gave expression to the growing antagonism felt by the national bourgeoisie, the students, and the urban petty bourgeoisie toward the Treaty Powers.

The May Thirtieth Movement was also the outcome of the local situation in Shanghai, where for the previous few weeks there had been a renewal of activities among the bourgeoisie as well as in the labor movement. The upper bourgeoisie, through the medium of the General Chamber of Commerce, had reacted vigorously against the proposed bylaws concerning an increase in wharfage dues, press control over Chinese newspapers published within Settlement territory, and other matters, all of which the Municipal Council of the International Settlement had announced it would put to a vote at a meeting of ratepayers. These influential bourgeois Chinese were backed in their opposition by the shopkeepers' associations (representing petty traders and craftsmen), which registered their protest by means of appeals and demonstrations.[1] The authoritarian attitude of the Municipal Council was thrown into relief by the measures recently taken by the Peking government, especially Peking's transfer of the arsenal installations into private hands, in what appeared to be an attempt to encourage the economic development of Shanghai in accordance with the wishes of the local bourgeoisie.[2]

As for labor agitation, it had continued almost without pause since the February strikes in the Japanese cotton mills, for in the meantime there had been a sharp fall in the value of copper currency,[3] and the wholesale price of rice had risen from 9.20–10.40 yuan (minimum and maximum) in January to 10.30–11.40 in May.[4] The West Shanghai Workers' Club, which had now become the cotton workers' union, took control of the strikes that broke out during May as a result of various incidents in several Japanese cotton mills.[5] (The club's leaders—particularly Liu Hua and Sun Liang-hui—had acquired a great deal of authority since the February strikes.) The club distributed strike certificates to individual workers, organized pickets, and made contact with the shopkeepers' associations for the purpose of creating a strike fund.[6] At the start of these strikes a worker named Ku Cheng-hung was killed by a Japanese foreman during a scuffle that ensued from a typical occurrence of ta-ch'ang, when gates were broken down, machinery wrecked, and so forth. This happened on May 15. The union decided to hold a memorial service in his honor on May 24, with the backing of the student associations, and some five thousand people took part. Meanwhile the cotton mill strike continued to spread.[7] The central committee of the Communist Party discussed the situation on May 28 at an emergency meeting that was made still more tense by the approaching meeting of the Municipal Council, arranged for June 2, at which the new bylaws would be put to a vote. The committee was disturbed also by recent news from Peking that serious incidents had occurred there in a clash between students and police.[8] After what seems to have been a very lively discussion, those in favor of adopting a bold line, led by Ts'ai Ho-sen, overcame the hesitations of Ch'en Tu-hsiu, and it was decided to hold another demonstration for the combined purpose of further commemorating Ku Cheng-hung and of stimulating an all-out fight against the Treaty Powers.[9] The workers' clubs prepared to take part in this demonstration, fixed for May 30, and made approaches to the student associations, calling upon them to "revive the spirit of May 4."[10]

The demonstration took place as planned on the afternoon of May 30 and several thousand people took part. In a clash in Nanking Road with the police of the Louza Police Station, the police inspector, without warning, gave the order to fire in order to free his men from the crowd, with the result that ten people were killed and over fifty injured, most of them workers.[11]

Serious incidents like this had occurred in Shanghai before, for instance during the anti-American boycott in 1905, when this same Louza Police Station had been besieged by the crowd and Sikh police had fired, killing three and wounding large numbers.[12] The victims of the 1905 shootings were, however, quickly forgotten. The repercussions throughout the country of the Nanking Road incident therefore give some indication of the advance in national awareness during the intervening twenty years. Not all these repercussions can be discussed here, since the May Thirtieth Movement involved almost all social strata in the cities and affected foreign as well as internal policy. Discussion will be confined to the part played in the movement by the working class and to the new stimulus labor derived from it.

On the day after the shootings a meeting was held in the offices of the General Chamber of Commerce, in the presence of the acting president, Fang

Chiao-po.[13] It was attended by about fifteen hundred persons, and chaired by a leader of the Students' Federation. Several of the Communist leaders of the Chapei Workers' Club spoke, as did delegates of the shopkeepers' associations. It was decided to hold a general strike of workers, students, and merchants, and to boycott the foreign banks and withdraw sums deposited in them by Chinese. The meeting also demanded that whatever those responsible for the shootings might say, compensation had to be paid to the victims and their families, and that those arrested must be released. Regarding municipal affairs, it called for the withdrawal of the three bylaws recently put before the municipal electors, Chinese control over the Shanghai police, and the removal of foreign ships from the Whangpoo.[14] Further resolutions were along the lines of proposals in the handbills distributed that morning by Liu Hua and the Chapei Workers' Club,[15] demanding the right to strike, improvement of working conditions in the cotton mills, and an end to both the ill-treatment of workers and the employment of foreigners to police them.

On June 1 all work came to a standstill in shops and teaching establishments, and the strike spread rapidly in the factories. The evening before, a new organization called the Shanghai General Union had been formed to take control of the strike. It had direct links with the Communist Party, since its leaders were Li Li-san, Liu Shao-ch'i, Liu Hua, Sun Liang-hui, and the student Yang Chih-hua, who was the wife of Ch'ü Ch'iu-pai.[16] At the General Union's request, meetings of employees in the public utilities and all the big enterprises were held in order to decide upon strike action.[17] By June 4 there were 74,000 strikers,[18] and by June 13 nearly 160,000.[19] The enterprises primarily affected were the Japanese and British firms and the municipal services. The ships in the docks were immobilized and the goods left standing; the telephones ceased to function and foreign newspapers ceased publication; there was nothing but a skeleton staff left at the power station in the International Settlement,[20] and there were even quite a number of defections among the Sikhs of the Municipal Police.[21]

The foreign authorities countered with the use of force. The Volunteers were mobilized, martial law was declared, 26 gunboats were brought up the Whangpoo and marines were landed, and Shanghai University was closed.[22] During the first few days of June many violent incidents occurred in the center of the Settlement, and the police and the Volunteers several times opened fire on the students and workers who were distributing handbills and haranguing the crowd, with as many as sixty people killed and as many again seriously wounded.[23]

The tense situation that now existed in Shanghai merely strengthened the determination of the strikers. On June 7 an action committee was formed at the instigation of the unions, with joint participation of the Shanghai General Union, the Shanghai Students' Federation, the National Students' Federation, and the federated shopkeepers' associations.[24] The General Chamber of Commerce was approached about joining, but refused. The new organization was called the Shanghai Workers', Merchants', and Students' Federation, and its political program, consisting of 17 points, was ratified on June 11 during a demonstration held in Chapei, in which twenty thousand took part.[25] The program, in addition to repeating the demands formulated on May 31 for the settlement of the May 30 incident and for the rights to strike and to form trade unions, went much further and included demands for changes in the status of the International Settlement. In accordance with the often expressed wishes of the local bourgeoisie, it called for the abolition of the Volunteer Corps, freedom of speech, of assembly, and of the press on Settlement territory, the return of the Mixed Court to Chinese control, the right to vote for Chinese ratepayers, the withdrawal of foreign armed forces, and the abolition of extraterritoriality and consular jurisdiction.[26]

In the official title of the new organization the workers took precedence over the other two classes represented on the action committee; but this was not the only indication of the fact that it was indeed the Shanghai working class that played the principal role in the May Thirtieth Movement. For, since the Settlement authorities were not likely to be greatly disturbed by the actions of students and shopkeepers, the success of the movement as a whole depended primarily on whether the workers' strikes were successful or not, and the Shanghai General Union did all it could to ensure that they would be successful.[27]

The General Union that had been formed on May 31 was in firm control of the entire Shanghai proletariat. Its headquarters were in Chapei,[28] but it established branches in the working-class areas of Pootung, Yangtzepoo, Chapei, and Hsiaoshatu[29] so as to be able to deal more efficiently with local matters and in particular with the allocation of strike duties. It encouraged the formation of unions in certain enterprises or trades, such as a union for the employees of the Chinese-owned tramway company[30] and unions for printing and postal workers. In order to counteract the propaganda in Chinese issued by the Municipal Council of the International Settlement,[31] it distributed a bulletin—published several times a week[32]—that provided a supplement to the *Je-hsueh jih-pao* ("Bloodshed Journal") published by the new action committee.[33] It organized pickets (*chiu-ch'a-tui*) at each of its branches and in the principal trade unions, which, although armed only with thick sticks, were given some kind of military training. These pickets kept watch over attempts to hire strikebreakers, and held any such persons in detention at branch headquarters. They also prevented the transportation of Japanese goods, and kept order at workers' meetings, especially when strike funds were being distributed.[34] Altogether, the General Union seems to have established contact with all sections of the Shanghai proletariat from the very beginning of the movement. At its headquarters in Chapei, where already in March and April the indefatigable Liu Hua and his collaborators had tried to show the workers the way forward, hundreds, and sometimes thousands, of strikers arrived to proclaim their support.[35] As the strike wore on, they queued up to show the strike certificates that had been issued to them, which entitled them to a minimum of 20 cents in silver per day.[36]

This touches upon the major problem of how the strike was financed. It is estimated to have cost over a million yuan per month;[37] in order to meet the cost, a strike fund was organized with the help of the students, and contributions were collected in the Chinese-owned factories in Shanghai (where work continued), and throughout the entire country. The extent to which the movement enjoyed popular sympathy can be measured by the millions of small coins collected for the fund.[38] Appeals for sympathy were also made to the international labor movement, and particularly to the Red International via the All-China General Union formed the month before.[39] The Red International proposed to the Amsterdam International that they furnish joint aid, but Amsterdam decided to confine its contribution to a commission of inquiry;[40] its affiliated organizations contributed large sums, however, especially the affiliated Soviet trade unions, which sent 400,000 rubles.[41] Considerable sums were also subscribed not only by the Canton government but also by the warlord government in the North, which was anxious to avoid going against public opinion on this issue.[42] Nevertheless, the major part of the necessary financial aid was supplied by the Chinese bourgeoisie of Shanghai, for whom the movement was doubly beneficial, since it supported their political demands and at the same time, through the strikes, put the foreign enterprises in the city out of action. The General Chamber of Commerce formed a "Committee for Aid and Peace," which collected funds for the strikers independently of those collected by the unions.[43] By June, the expenses of the strike were more or less met, the Committee for Aid and Peace having contributed 470,000 yuan, the General Union having collected, through its own efforts, 350,000 yuan,[44] and the remainder having been advanced by the Chinese banks through the intervention of the chamber of commerce.[45]

There seems, however, to have been little response from the peasants of the Yangtze estuary to the Shanghai strikes, despite repeated appeals made by the unions and the Communist Party for unity between workers and peasants ("of capital importance in the struggle against imperialism," according to a leaflet distributed in June).[46] At the most, attempts seem to have been made to collect provisions and spread propaganda in the villages with the help of strikers who came from the rural districts in the neighborhood of Shanghai and who had returned home at the beginning of June.[47]

Compromises and Strike Settlements

Before long, however, enthusiasm began to wane, and by the end of June cracks were appearing in the common front of those engaged in the struggle to get the Settlement authorities to accept the program laid down on May 31.

The Chamber of Commerce had joined in the movement right from the start, lending its offices for the meeting of May 31 at which the decision had been taken to declare a general strike. Under pressure from the federated shop-keepers' associations, it had approved the decision, and had to a large extent financed the strike; and on June 6 the wealthy Chinese who formed the Advisory Committee of the Municipal Council resigned out of sympathy with the strikers.[48] But Yü Hsia-ch'ing, the president of the chamber of commerce, and other leading compradores had never been wholehearted in their support of the May Thirtieth Movement. Already on May 31 Fang Chiao-po, acting president of the Chamber of Commerce, had assured the Settlement authorities that he was against the strike but that in the circumstances he and his friends had been forced to adopt a favorable attitude toward it.[49] During the following weeks the upper bourgeoisie made every effort to check the movement, attempting for instance to limit the attack to one against Great Britain, instead of raising the whole question of the international status of China, which was what the workers, the students, and the shopkeepers were attempting to do.[50] The real intentions of the Chamber of Commerce became clear when, in the middle of June, it agreed to present only 13 of the 17 demands of the Federation of Workers, Merchants, and Students to the Peking government.[51] The demands omitted were those concerning trade union organization and the right to strike on the one hand, and on the other those concerning Chinese control over the police of the International Settlement and the abolition of extraterritoriality. All the diplomatic corps and the Shanghai Municipal Council had had to do to persuade these tepid revolutionaries to come to a compromise was to dangle in front of them the prospects of returning the Mixed Court to the Chinese, admitting wealthy Chinese to the Municipal Council, and reopening the negotiations on customs control provided for in the Washington Treaty in 1922.[52] Despite sharp criticism from workers and Communists,[53] and hesitations on the part of the shopkeepers, the merchants' strike ended on June 25.[54] But already on June 20 the General Union had held a meeting attended by 130 delegates representing the unions affiliated with it, at which it was decided to continue the struggle in spite of the defection of the merchants.[55]

The Municipal Council, in order to create a rift between the Chinese industrialists and the laboring masses and thereby to consolidate its gains, then did something quite unprecedented: following a suggestion made by the manager of one of the British cotton mills a few days before, it cut off the supply of electricity to Chinese-owned factories on July 6.[56] It was solely to supply power to these factories, where the workers were not on strike, that the Settlement electric power plant, where the workers had gone on strike on the first day of the movement, had been kept in operation. It was hoped that by cutting off the supply the number of people out of work would be increased, thus placing an additional strain on the financial resources of the General Union while at the same time bringing pressure to bear on the bourgeoisie in order to discourage their furnishing further aid to the General Union. It did indeed become more and more difficult to provide for the strikers, whose numbers, although they had fallen to 80,000 on July 1, had risen again to 100,000 by the end of the month;[57] and the cutting off of the supply of electric current did immediately result in the chamber of commerce's dissolving its Committee for Aid and Peace.[58] The Peking government sent another 150,000 yuan,[59] but this was not enough to cover the deficit, nor was there a sufficient return from such expedients as demanding contributions to the strike fund from Chinese newspapers as a form of fine if they had published communications from the Municipal Council[60] or instituting a temporary tax (by agreement with the chamber of commerce) on goods piled up in the foreign warehouses since the beginning of the strike to ensure the removal of those goods.[61] Toward the end of July it was beginning to look as though the working class was becoming dangerously isolated, with a falloff not only of contributors to the strike fund, but of political allies. Even its most ardent allies—the students—were beginning to flag, though at their seventh annual conference they had resolved not to weaken in their fight for the workers' cause but rather to continue helping the unions and spreading propaganda for the strikers.[62] The members of the shopkeepers' associations were also losing their enthusiasm, since they were financially dependent on the Chinese banks and thus affected by the bankers' policy of compromise.[63]

Difficulties were also arising with the Chinese authorities. The unstable coalition that had been established in Peking after the defeat of the Chihli faction in the fall of 1924 had at first shown sympathy toward the strike. Tuan, the head of the Executive, had sent large sums of money, and had even agreed to pass on the watered-down form of the strikers' demands, sent to him by the Shanghai Chamber of Commerce, to the diplomatic corps.[64] This was a gesture he could afford to make, because, like Yü Hsia-ch'ing, he was a friend of Japan, and the moderates had seen to it that Japan was spared the worst of the attack in June in order to ensure that Great Britain bore the brunt of it. The Fengtien military authorities, who at that time administered Shanghai in the name of the Peking government, also showed tolerance in June. The strike organizations were allowed to function more or less without interference on Chinese territory, especially in Chapei,[65] even to the point where the police of the International Settlement complained about an unaccustomed lack of cooperation from the Chinese police.[66] But after the defection of the bourgeoisie in July, when the movement became more of a class struggle, there was a change of attitude. On July 8 the military commander of Shanghai issued a proclamation complaining of the "troublemakers" who claimed to be labor leaders and who disturbed public order; the proclamation went on to order compulsory registration and inspection of all unions formed since May 30 on penalty of dissolution.[67] On July 23 this stiffening of attitude became still more pronounced when the seal was put on the Seamen's Union, the unions in foreign firms, and the Federation of Workers, Merchants, and Students.[68] Yü Hsia-ch'ing, who was anxious to maintain a limited degree of cooperation with the strikers, immediately intervened to request that these organizations be reopened and the arrested leaders released.[69]

As the strike wore on, a certain weariness became noticeable here and there among the strikers.[70] The anti-Communist associations of the Federation of Labor Organizations immediately seized the occasion to distribute leaflets accusing the General Union of prolonging the strike for political purposes, and its leaders of pursuing their own personal ambitions;[71] they even went so far as to try to foment disturbances involving the strikers. It was probably they who staged a demonstration on August 13 in which several hundred dockers protested against the Seamen's Union and about the distribution of strike funds by the General Union.[72] On August 22 several groups of well-armed, well-disciplined men arrived in automobiles at the General Union headquarters in Chapei, where, without even the pretense of using some discontented strikers to camouflage their action, they simply attacked the offices, destroying the furniture and documents, making away with the money, and leaving behind them about a dozen wounded pickets.[73] Chinese opinion ascribed direct responsibility for this raid to Hsü Hsi-lin, Wang Kuang-hui, and other leading figures in the Federation of Labor Organizations.[74]

What with the withdrawal of the bourgeoisie, the hardening of Western attitudes in the International Settlement, the disapproval of the Chinese authorities, and the attacks of the kung-tsei, who were trying to cash in on the weariness of the strikers, the strike leaders realized that they would have to reach a compromise. But they wanted a real compromise, not a capitulation; for after the General Union had gradually been deserted by its allies, it had done a tremendous job of organization during July and August, and had given the working masses of Shanghai a unity and a crusading spirit they had never known before. On July 28 the General Union was able to announce that 117 unions, with a combined membership of 218,000, were affiliated with it.[75] The best organized were those in the cotton mills, the public utilities (waterworks, tramways, power plants, the Post Office, and telecommunications), the docks, the printing works, and foreign-owned enterprises manufacturing foodstuffs and various other products (flour mills, soap works, glass works, tobacco factories, powdered-egg factories, and so forth). All these unions had unwaveringly supported the strike since June 1. The General Union had, however, failed to gain much influence in sectors of industry that had not been directly affected by the May Thirtieth Movement, such as the Chinese-owned silk-reeling factories, the shipyards, the small Chinese-owned mechanical workshops, and the tramways in the French

Concession. Its most striking successes were its innovative attempts to organize the dockers (who until then had only had their traditional pang), the cotton workers (who for many years had been without any proper form of organization and had instead resorted to the use of ta-ch'ang), and the printing workers, whose only form of organization hitherto had been demarcated trade associations. In July a Dockers' Federation was formed,[76] in August the 36 unions that had been formed in the cotton mills in June and July were amalgamated into a General Cotton Mills Union,[77] and the various unions of printing workers employed by newspapers, the Commercial Press, and the China Bookshop, of binders, and of workers in related trades were now all brought into the General Federation of Printing Workers.[78]

The main purpose of this intensive organizing effort was to establish a firm control over the shifting and unstable Shanghai proletariat and make it capable of prolonged, sustained effort, so that it would not have to resort to occasional destructive outbursts of ta-ch'ang as hitherto. The General Union had several times officially condemned such outbursts.[79] It had also attempted, in contrast to policies followed by the Federation of Labor Organizations during 1923–24, to form unions on a mainly industrial basis so as to get rid of the demarcation problems and the regional rivalries that were precisely what the Federation delighted in making use of. The rules of the various unions affiliated with the General Union may have been far from uniform; for instance, those of the China Bookshop union laid stress on matters of general education, mutual aid, and technical training, which had always been given priority among printing workers. But all of them[80] stressed the need for uniting all the different trades employed in one enterprise (for example, the Post Office), or all the trades employed in one industry (for example, printing), the need for having well-organized rank-and-file units in the factories and the public utilities, and the need to maintain strict discipline in the relations between unions in separate enterprises and the industrial unions, and between the industrial unions and the General Union.

In July and August, despite the growing difficulties as the strike wore on, the Shanghai General Union was in fact the spokesman of all the workers in the city. It held press conferences,[81] received with due ceremony the visit of a Soviet trade union delegation,[82] and entered into public discussion with the Peking government on the question of the trade union laws which that government was preparing.[83] It still commanded enough influence to ensure that it would be able to make a retreat in good order.

At the beginning of August, when it had become clear that the May Thirtieth Movement could no longer hope to win, the General Union made public its proposals for reaching a compromise. These included clauses for settling the strike and the incidents that gave rise to it (reinstatement of workers and strike pay amounting to one third of the normal wage, punishment of those responsible for the Nanking Road incident, and compensation for the families of the victims), as well as demands for recognition of the unions affiliated with the General Union as representative spokesmen of the workers, a general 10 per cent raise in wages to be paid only in ta-yang, and guarantees against ill-treatment and unjust dismissal of workers.[84] What this spelled out was that the working class, like the bourgeoisie several weeks earlier, had now abandoned the original political aims of the movement, and instead was pressing only its own economic demands. The Japanese were the first to take steps toward meeting these demands. Their consul general agreed to meet Li Li-san and other representatives of the General Union at the Foreign Affairs Office in Shanghai, in the presence of representatives of the Chinese Chamber of Commerce.[85] Agreement was soon reached concerning compensation for the family of Ku Cheng-hung, the worker whose murder had been the starting point of the whole affair, and on recognition of the unions' right to represent the workers, the prevention of ill-treatment of workers and unjust dismissals, and the payment of wages in ta-yang (with a further promise from the Japanese to consider a possible raise in wages).[86] Nothing was mentioned about strike pay, but the Chamber of Commerce paid out a sum of 260,000 yuan for this purpose.[87] It had learned from the International Settlement authorities that the electricity supply would continue to be cut off until there was a complete return to work, and Chinese industrialists had begged it to intervene. By the end of August work was resumed in the Japanese cotton mills, or at least in those that had their own supplies of electricity,[88] and the Japanese consul general paid out 10,000 yuan to the General Union as compensation for the family of Ku Cheng-hung, through the mediation of the Chinese local authorities.[89] The Japanese shipping companies reached an agreement along similar lines with the Seamen's Union, which thereupon ordered a return to work.[90]

At the same time these negotiations were being carried out with the Japanese,[91] three big economic strikes were declared: that of the postal workers on August 17,[92] one at the Commercial Press on August 22,[93] and another at the China Bookshop on August 29.[94] Was this an adroit move on the part of the General Union to compensate for the failure to obtain the political objectives of the May Thirtieth Movement by switching the energies of the labor movement to the presentation of economic demands?[95] Or was it simply that skilled workers such as the printers and the postal workers (who in addition were still under the burden of foreign control)[96] had been sufficiently stimulated by the class struggle that had been going on in Shanghai since the beginning of June to fight for their own interests? Certainly all three strikes showed how even those sections of the Shanghai proletariat that had been most influenced by the old guild traditions had acquired a new unity and a new class consciousness since the Nanking Road incident. The strikes were directed by the unions in each of the three enterprises concerned, all of which were affiliated with the General Union, whose directives were unanimously accepted by the strikers. The Commercial Press strikers declared, "We ourselves formed the Union; therefore we *are* the Union....We must give it our wholehearted support and obedience."[97] All three strikes succeeded in obtaining official recognition of the unions involved, from the administrative authorities in the case of the Post Office and from the private firms in the other two cases.[98] They also won a large wage increase, and both the Commercial Press and China Bookshop strikers won a reduction in hours. Finally, the Commercial Press workers achieved the abolition of the pao-kung system and the payment of an annual bonus equivalent to one month's wages.

At the end of August, labor agitation spread to the railways in the Shanghai region. Without recourse to a strike, the railwaymen on the Shanghai-Nanking[99] and the Shanghai-Hangchow lines[100] obtained a raise in wages. But this spread of the movement that had begun on May 30 to Chinese-owned private firms and public utilities did not improve relations between the General Union and the Chinese bourgeoisie and authorities in Shanghai. After work was resumed at the electric power plant on September 8,[101] the Fengtien military authorities in Shanghai put an abrupt end to the tolerance they had been showing the labor movement since May 30. The police announced on September 19 that until the trade union legislation promised by the Peking government was promulgated, all labor organizations were illegal; consequently, the General Union was declared to be dissolved, and a warrant was taken out for Li Li-san's arrest.[102] The main unions affiliated with the General Union—the Commercial Press unions, the cotton mill unions, and about fifteen others—were also closed down.[103] The great strike wave had temporarily come to an end. On September 23 the Federation of Workers, Merchants, and Students, which had nominally survived the break in July between the labor movement and the bourgeoisie, was officially dissolved.[104]

At the end of September an agreement similar to that reached in August with the Japanese firms was signed by Yü Hsia-ch'ing on behalf of the Chamber of Commerce, and by the British cotton mills.[105] It included the payment of 3 yuan as strike pay, a promise to pay wages in ta-yang, guarantees against ill-treatment and unjust dismissals, and a possible eventual raise in wages. However, recognition of the unions was postponed, even more definitely than in the Japanese agreement, until such time as the Peking government had promulgated its trade union legislation; and as things were going, this action did not seem likely to be taken in the near future. By the beginning of October, work had been resumed in almost all the enterprises in Shanghai.

Response in Other Parts of China

When news of the Nanking Road incident reached the various provinces of China during the first days in June, it started a movement of solidarity such as had never occurred before, and the movement lasted throughout the summer. I cannot attempt to give a complete account of it here, or to examine in any depth the class relations and political alliances involved. As with the Shanghai movement, discussion will be confined to the part played in it by the working class.[106]

Map 9 shows the extent of working-class participation in the political agitation that took place during the months of June, July, and August in all parts of China. Workers and workers' associations joined with students, merchants, and other representatives of the middle classes to support the Shanghai movement, forming in Wuhan a "Committee of Support for May 30,"[107] in Peking a "Committee of Support for the Workers, Merchants, and Students,"[108] and in Hunan a "Committee for Effacing Shame."[109] Large numbers of workers took part in the widely held demonstrations in order

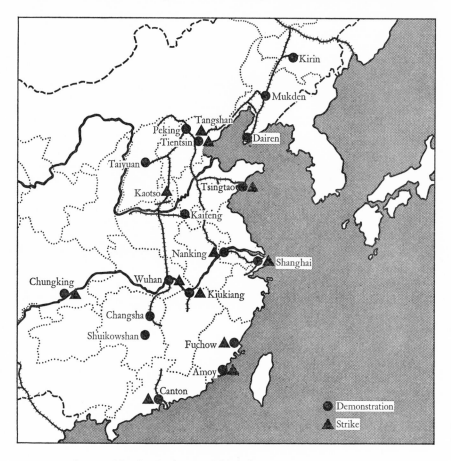

Map 9. Worker Participation in the May Thirtieth Movement.

to assure the Shanghai strikers of the support of the rest of the country, to condemn the actions of the British police of Shanghai, and to demand justice. In Peking a big meeting, attended by over 300,000 people of all kinds, was held on June 10 in front of the T'ien-an Gate, under the chairmanship of Li Yü-ying, an intellectual who was a member of the Central Committee of the Kuomintang. Many railwaymen, printers, rickshaw men, and tramway employees were present.[110] Similar meetings were held in Kirin, Mukden, and Dairen in the Northeast,[111] one at Changsha in Hunan on June 6,[112] one in Tientsin on June 14,[113] one in Shameen on June 6,[114] and others in many other industrial and university centers. In Kiukiang violence broke out during the demonstration held there on June 12, when there was a clash between the crowd and the police of the British Concession, following which the crowd, led by dockers and seamen, set fire to the Bank of Taiwan (Japanese) and attacked the offices of the shipping firms Jardine, Matheson & Company and Naigai Wata Kaisha.[115] It was mainly the students' associations that organized the collection of subscriptions to the fund set up throughout China for the maintenance of the strikers, and that also handled the boycott of foreign goods that had been started in the Yangtze valley; but workers too took part in both these activities. In Wuhan and Changsha the federations of labor organizations, inactive throughout 1923-24, helped the students and the shopkeepers' associations collect funds.[116] The Chiao-Chi railwaymen formed a "Committee in Support of the Shanghai Victims," each contributing a day's wages;[117] and the Dairen printers,[118] the Ching-Han railwaymen, the workers of Harbin,[119] and many others organized collections for the fund. As usual, the rickshaw men and dockers were keen supporters of the boycott of foreign goods and nationals, for instance in Chungking, where the boycott continued until October,[120] in Nanchang,[121] and in Amoy.[122]

Occasionally token protest strikes were held, even in Chinese-owned enterprises. At the time of the big T'ien-an Gate meeting in Peking, work stopped in a number of factories,[123] and in one clothing factory the employing firm reportedly told its employees to stop work, gave them strike pay, and destroyed the British and Japanese sewing machines used in the factory.[124] The Tangshan railwaymen[125] and the antimony miners of Shuikowshan and of Sinhwa in Hunan[126] also stopped work, as did the Chinkiang workers, who met in a violent clash with the British police there.[127]

The movement of solidarity with the Shanghai strikers was more vigorous still in the big foreign enterprises in the interior. Here the workers conducted a direct attack, both political and economic, against Japanese and British interests. During the fall of 1922, strikes had taken place here that were essentially economic in nature, even if sometimes tinged with Nationalist aims. In the summer of 1925, however, strikes were held mainly for political ends, although at the same time the workers employed by foreign firms tried to obtain a substantial improvement in their conditions of employment.

In Nanking, while the rickshaw men were refusing to transport British and Japanese goods and nationals, and the seamen employed by British firms were on strike, the workers in a big British powdered-egg factory, the International Export Company, went on strike on June 8, both to protest the Shanghai incident and to demand a raise in wages, guarantees for stability of employment, and recognition of the union they had just formed.[128] Their demands were met and they returned to work after being out for over a month. But at the end of June, the firm, probably thinking that the slowing down of the Shanghai movement had made trouble much less likely, dismissed several hundred employees. A crowd of workers invaded the factory in retaliation and wrecked the plant and the machinery. The British gunboat *Durban* intervened; several people were killed and many wounded.[129]

In Wuhan, the main industrial center in Central China, there had been a certain amount of labor agitation with a Nationalist flavor in foreign-owned factories in January 1923.[130] This tradition was now revived by demonstrations staged to show solidarity with the Shanghai strikers,[131] despite the fact that there was a great deal of unemployment in the city owing to the influx of peasants who were victims of recent floods[132] and the further fact that the province was still in the hands of a member of the Chihli faction, Hsiao Yao-nan. Instead of using cunning stratagems against the May Thirtieth Movement like the Anfu and Fengtien factions in the North and the East, Hsiao launched a frontal attack on it and aligned himself with the British.[133] A workers' and students' demonstration was planned for June 13, and a general strike for the day after. But on June 10 incidents occurred in the British Concession between the police and the dockers and other employees of the British firm Butterfield & Swire; the next day marines and the civilian volunteers of the concessions fired on the crowds, killing eleven and wounding twenty, mostly workers.[134] Hsiao Yao-nan's police arrested the workers and students who were organizing the strike, thus preventing it from taking place. In Chungking also, workers and employees of British and Japanese firms went out on strike on June 28, but British marines were immediately brought in; two people were killed and a number wounded in their clash with the crowd.[135]

In July the movement spread to other foreign enterprises, such as the mines of the Peking Syndicate at Kiaotso (in Honan), an industrial center that had so far been very little affected by strikes and union organization, probably because of its geographical isolation. Urged by a group of students who came to organize the workers, the miners ceased work on July 7; guards and pickets were organized, and telephone and water lines were cut off. The only thing the European staff at the mine could do was depart for Peking, leaving the miners in charge. Work was not resumed until the end of August, after substantial concessions had been granted.[136] The strikers had enjoyed the protection of the units of Feng Yü-hsiang's People's National Army that were stationed in the area.

In Tsingtao, which was in the hands of Chang Tsung-ch'ang, a ruthless general belonging to the Fengtien faction, it was the Szefang branch of the Chiao-Chi General Union that organized a campaign in June to protest the Shanghai incident. On July 22 the workers in the Japanese cotton mills declared a strike, which Chang broke the next day by bringing his troops into action and making many arrests. Shortly after, the workers' leader Li Wei-nung and the editor of a paper that supported the Nationalist movement, Hu Hsin, were executed.[137]

In Tientsin, too, workers in the Japanese cotton mills came out on strike in August, after a strike by the seamen, dockers, and other employees of the British shipping firms. The Japanese Pao-ch'eng cotton mill was the first to be affected. The strike there passed off without incident, obtaining a raise in wages and a reduction in the number of fines. The union that had recently been formed under Communist influence maintained "revolutionary order" by means of pickets.[138] But when, on August 11, a strike broke out at the Yü-ta silk-reeling factories, where no union had been formed because of the strength of the customary pang, it turned into an unusually violent outburst of ta-ch'ang. The workers, reinforced by peasants from the neighborhood,[139] wrecked the entire factory. Li Ching-lin, who was in command of the Fengtien police in the province, laid siege to the factory and gained possession of it only after a prolonged battle in which 20 workers were killed and 300 wounded. He suspended the cottonworkers' union that had recently been formed and other associations that supported the May Thirtieth Movement (the association of students and the Cantonese Regional Friendly Society), while the police of the French Concession dissolved the printers' and seamen's unions that had been established there.[140]

There were repercussions of the Shanghai incident in many other enterprises in North and Central China. On the South Manchuria Railway, for instance, the leaders of a Chinese union obtained a raise in wages and the same treatment for Chinese as for Japanese workers without going on strike.[141] In the British K.M.A. mines the workers at the Chao-ko-chuang pit made contact in August with the Shanghai General Union, the Tangshan railwaymen's union, and students' associations in the area. As a result, a union was formed which issued an inaugural manifesto[142] that was clear evidence of the influence the events in Shanghai were having and the extent to which the labor and Nationalist movements were merging all over China. It was this union that on September 13 declared another strike of the K.M.A. miners, demanding higher wages and recognition of the union by the mine owners.[143]

These last two examples, together with those of the powdered-egg factory in Nanking and the cotton mills in Tientsin and Tsingtao, show that the May Thirtieth Movement stimulated not only a wave of strikes, but also new efforts to organize the proletariat. During the summer of 1925, advances of this kind were also made in various Chinese-owned private firms and public utilities, though they were not necessarily accompanied by strikes as in the foreign enterprises. A Mechanics Society was formed in Fuchow for skilled workers in the electric power plant, the arsenal, and various other works, its membership totaling over 3,000.[144] The restoration of the railwaymen's unions in the North, begun the previous winter, went ahead; in July the Lunghai and Chin-P'u unions were formed again, and in August the three rival sections of track workers, train crews, and workshop employees on the Ching-Sui line were at last amalgamated.[145] According to the manifesto of the Chin-P'u union, the railwaymen had a dual aim: to fight for the emancipation and the well-being of the workers, and to get rid of the imperialists.[146]

In several of the big cities in the North—Tsinan,[147] Chengchow,[148] and even Tientsin[149]—a few fleeting attempts were made to form "General Unions." These were in fact no more than local or provincial amalgamations of unions that took the name and adopted the line of the powerful organization that since May 31 had been directing the Shanghai labor movement. An attempt of this kind was even made in distant Yunnan in September, but without success.[150]

However various the ways in which the working class took part in the May Thirtieth Movement, it was almost always supported by the students' organizations and by the shopkeepers. In Wuhan, Changsha, Tientsin, Tsingtao, Peking, and all the other big cities, the working class maintained a close association with these two allies in demonstrating solidarity with the Shanghai strikers, while at the same time fighting its own battles. It had also shown itself capable of winning a considerable amount of international support for the Chinese revolution. While the wave of activity that began in May 1919 had passed almost unnoticed by the rest of the world, and that of 1922 had aroused only a faint response, even among members of the extreme left in the West, the Shanghai incident and the political agitation that followed during the summer of 1925 brought expressions of sympathy from all over the world. Not only was sympathy manifested by the Comintern[151] and the Soviet Union, which sent vast sums of money as well as a trade union delegation to China,[152] and by the Overseas Chinese (especially those in the Paris group),[153] who were very active in their support, but campaigns in support of the Shanghai strikers were organized by workers' associations and left-wing intellectuals in the very countries—Great Britain, Japan, France—whose governments were in conflict with the Chinese Nationalist movement. Meetings of solidarity were held in Paris, London, Berlin, and Tokyo, and on June 6 an International Committee of Aid was formed in Berlin, sponsored by Henri Barbusse, Bernard Shaw, Upton Sinclair, Klara Zetkin, Auguste Forel, and other big names among the progressive intelligentsia of the West.[154]

On the other hand, throughout China, as in Shanghai, there was a noticeable lack of peasant support for the May Thirtieth Movement. In the main, and in spite of the fact that its aims were Nationalist ones, the movement was conducted by the industrial proletariat, the students, and the middle and petty bourgeoisie in the towns, and it very rarely affected the countryside. The Hunan Committee for Effacing Shame had branches in 46 rural hsien, many of which were in effect small country towns;[155] and in one rural hsien in Honan the peasants held a meeting to condemn British and Japanese activities in China.[156] But Chinese peasants seldom came into contact with the big foreign interests in China, one of the few exceptions being Honan, where B.A.T. agents collected tobacco crops. Of the two declared objectives of the Nationalist revolution laid down in Canton in 1924—the struggle against the Treaty Powers and the struggle against the conservatives and warlords—it was the second that had the most direct appeal for the peasants;[157] and since the May Thirtieth Movement was aimed primarily at the big foreign interests, it could not hope to gain much support from the peasants. It was only during the Northern Expedition in the following year that they entered the political arena.

The upper bourgeoisie in the interior at first gave wide support to the movement, but as in Shanghai, it soon began to show hesitations, anxieties about the growing labor agitation, and preference for a policy of compromise. In Changsha, the General Chamber of Commerce and the provincial teachers' association, with the full approval of the governor, Chao Heng-t'i, made efforts from the middle of June to curb the activities of the Committee for Effacing Shame.[158] In Wuhan, the General Chamber of Commerce and the General Association of Chinese Commerce (the latter representing the compradores) urged the governor, Hsiao Yao-nan, to prevent the general strike planned for June 10.[159] In Kirin, the Provincial Assembly and the Merchants' Guild got the governor there to prohibit students from collecting contributions for the Shanghai fund on the grounds that their own contributions were sufficient.[160] In Amoy, thanks to the reports of a rather vain and slow-witted British consul, we know in some detail about the deal made between him and the chamber of commerce, the president of which played a double game, informing the consulate of the strikers' intentions and complying with British directives for reducing as much as possible the effects of the boycott.[161]

Finally, to complete this brief sketch of the relation between the industrial proletariat and the other social strata in China during the May Thirtieth Movement, a word should be said about the attitude of the provincial military commanders, all of whom, with one notable exception, adopted the same policy as the commander of the Fengtien troops in the Shanghai area: after a show of tolerance, they soon reverted to the ruthless repressive methods they had begun to use in February 1923. Li Ching-lin in Tientsin and Hsiao Yao-nan in Wuhan collaborated with Western and Japanese authorities in order to repress labor agitation directed against foreign-owned industries. Chang Tsung-ch'ang, who in June had felt he must make a gesture and had sent 2,000 yuan to the Shanghai victims,[162] used force at the end of July to dissolve the organizations in Tsingtao that supported the movement. He even appropriated for his own use the contributions to the Shanghai fund they had recently collected, amounting, appropriately enough, to 2,000 yuan.[163] In Mukden, when the labor organizations there announced their intention to declare a general strike and refused to accept foreign currency and goods or to travel on foreign trains and boats, the military governor, who was a direct subordinate of Chang Tso-lin, put an immediate end to the agitation.[164]

The only area where the military authorities adopted a policy of cooperation instead of repressing the labor movement was the area under the control of the Kuominchun (the "People's National Army"). This was the name adopted by Feng Yü-hsiang's army as a mark of its sympathy with the Canton government after Feng and his army had fallen out with the Anfu and Fengtien factions, whose accomplices Feng and his troops had been in the coup d'état of November 1924.[165] When the Nanking Road incident occurred, Feng declared his sympathy with the Shanghai strikers, issued an appeal to fight against foreign aggression,[166] and published a letter addressed to "the Christians of the world" in which he condemned the behavior of the Western nations in China.[167] In Honan and Suiyuan, the areas under his control, the military government actually encouraged the development of a labor movement after May 30, instead of opposing it as the rulers in Chihli and Shantung did. In August a strike broke out at the Chengchow cotton mill, with the strikers presenting demands not only for higher wages and various forms of compensation, but also for wider benefits: improved conditions for women and children, sickness benefits, and the recognition of the union and its right to control the engagement and dismissal of workers. When, probably at the instigation of the mill owner,[168] armed bands attacked the strikers and destroyed the union headquarters, the Second Army of the Kuominchun helped the workers repulse the attacks and obtain their demands.[169]

The Kuominchun authorities also encouraged the formation of unions on the Lunghai and Ching-Sui lines,[170] and the founding in September of the Honan General Union, with which the unions in the Chengchow, Changteh, and Wei-hui cotton mills, the Kiaotso and Liu-ho-kou mines, the stations on the Lunghai and Ching-Han lines, and the Kaifeng mint and arsenal were affiliated. The number and variety of these unions, including some in state enterprises, show what progress trade unionism had made in this region, which was not highly industrialized, following the takeover by the Kuominchun.[171] The inaugural meeting of the Honan union was held at the Y.M.C.A. headquarters in Chengchow,[172] and was attended by official representatives of the Christian General and by working-class members of the Communist Party such as the railwayman Liu Wen-sung, vice-president of the All-China General Union, who became one of the leaders of the new Honan union.[173] Another example of the sympathetic attitude of the Kuominchun authorities toward the labor movement during the summer of 1925 was the granting of a number of concessions to the workers on the Lunghai line (a ten-hour day, free travel, sickness benefits, free issue of raincoats, travel permits for trade union delegates, and the like).[174] In exchange, the workers, especially the railwaymen, cooperated with Feng's armies by helping to restrict enemy movements.[175] All these developments looked like the first tentative steps toward building up a democratic base in the North that would provide a counterpart to the one in the South, where, starting in June 1925, the big Canton–Hong Kong strike was being held in response to the Nanking Road incident.[176]

General Union Activities after the May 30 Incident

In Shanghai, no sooner had the May Thirtieth activities died down than an intensive wave of strikes began, heralded by the postal and printing workers' strikes in August. It lasted from October 1925 through the winter and the spring, and was still in full swing when the Northern Expedition set forth from Canton in July 1926.

This strike wave grew steadily in intensity throughout the period: 6 strikes in November 1925, 10 in January 1926, 21 in March, 25 in May.[177] In June, when the price of rice suddenly shot up,[178] over a hundred enterprises were affected, many of them textile concerns, and over seventy thousand strikers were involved.[179] Although low wages and bad working conditions were the chief causes of these strikes, the part played by the Shanghai General Union, formed the day after the May 30 incident, made them very different from the spontaneous protests of the earlier period. In spite of frequent attempts to ban it,[180] the General Union managed in the main to hold together the unions that had been formed during the summer in industries, trades, and enterprises. In June 1926, just before the departure of the Northern Expedition, it claimed a membership of 210,000—a figure which, it is true, included a number of craftsmen. While this figure is much the same as the one given at the time of the general strike in July 1925, a detailed comparison of the membership at these two times shows considerable changes during the year's interval between them.[181] The number of dockers had increased appreciably, but membership totals of the unions formed in several

Chinese-owned cotton mills had fallen. In sectors such as public utilities, public transport, and electric power plants, and in printing trades as well, the number of affiliated unions, and even their names, had changed, and not merely the size of the membership.[182] It is therefore not hard to understand why the Shanghai trade union leaders were not yet satisfied with the progress they had made, and thought that union organization in the city still required tightening up if it was to be adequate for the struggles ahead.[183]

In spite, however, of the traditional reluctance of the Shanghai proletariat to submit to strict organization, the General Union and the unions affiliated with it seem to have had considerable authority and prestige. In June 1926, for instance, the cotton mills union was able to force the employers, under threat of a strike declaration by all 36 of the separate factory unions, to reinstate some workers who had been dismissed;[184] and in the same month, the General Union negotiated the settlement of a strike in a hosiery factory, obtaining a reduction of hours and guarantees against ill-treatment and unjust fines and dismissals.[185] The fact that prestige was regarded as important is shown by the frequency with which strikers put forth demands for employers' recognition of unions,[186] for the right to collect union subscriptions,[187] for the right to hold union meetings,[188] and for the protection of union officials, including reinstatement after strikes and release from arrest.[189]

The spread of modern trade unionism does not, of course, mean that older features of the labor movement had been entirely eliminated. Provincial rivalries still arose during the 1925–26 strike wave, and so did outbursts of ta-ch'ang. In June 1926 a violent brawl, in which several people were wounded, broke out in the Naigai No. 5 cotton mill between unskilled workers from the Kompo (in Kiangsu) and workers from Shantung,[190] an occurrence likely to happen in Japanese mills because Shantung men often occupied minor managerial posts such as overseer or "number one." Again, a fight over nothing occurred in March, in Chapei, between several hundred Hupeh boathands and Kompo dock laborers.[191] Machine-wrecking was the reply to the decision of the management of the Nanyang tobacco factory in September to install new machines that would reduce the number of workers employed,[192] and to the refusal of the management of the Naigai No. 4 cotton mill, in June, to comply with the Kompo workers' repeated demands for the dismissal of an overseer who was a native of Anhwei.[193] But incidents of this kind were becoming less frequent, and were officially frowned upon by the General Union, one of its leaders declaring that "destruction of the means of production is unnecessary and even dangerous."[194] The cotton mills union did its best to calm down the conflict between the Kompo and Shantung workers in the Naigai No. 5 mill.[195] On the other hand, the General Union encouraged go-slow tactics (tai-ḳung), a strategy the hot-headed Shanghai proletariat took some time to get used to.[196]

Faced with the powerful organizational apparatus of the General Union, the moderate associations that had been so active in 1922–24 and the Federation of Labor Organizations they had formed, which in the spring of 1924 had made a first attempt to provide central control of the Shanghai labor movement, were now losing ground. But they still tried to put themselves forward as an alternative form of unionism. When, in January 1926, they held their customary ceremonies for the anniversary of the death of the Hunanese anarchists Huang and P'ang, they once again attacked the Communists, accusing them of having betrayed the Shanghai proletariat after May 30, whereas Huang and P'ang were faithful unto death. They also stressed the need to settle differences with employers by negotiation, and apparently felt that sociological studies of labor conditions were of primary importance.[197]

This attempt to take an independent left-wing stand against the General Union failed, however, to disguise the fact that all these associations were becoming more and more closely linked with the Shanghai employers. The friendly society for women employed in the silk-reeling factories, run by Mrs. Mu Chih-ying, had gained so much support since 1923 that silkworkers were prevented from taking part in the May Thirtieth Movement; and when the General Union announced in June 1926 that it proposed to form a General Silk Filatures Union, Mrs. Mu tried to get the workers under her control to go on strike to protest the "violent methods of the General Union." But nearly twenty-five thousand of the women workers declared a counterstrike, demanding that the society controlled by Mrs. Mu in the interests of the employers be closed down. The Chinese police then felt obliged to intervene and put down the counterstrike, their thoughtfulness being duly rewarded by the employer-controlled Silk Guild.[198]

Thus the May Thirtieth Movement brought to an end the fierce struggle to gain influence among the Shanghai proletariat that had been waged for several years between the militant Communists and the kung-tsei associations, the latter groups fostered by the local employers and the right wing of the Kuomintang. The kung-tsei had now suffered complete defeat; even their most ardent supporters realized that the Federation of Labor Organizations, owing to a lack of real working-class support, had been unable to play any part in the Nationalist strikes during the summer of 1925.[199] It had, in fact, opposed them, and had thereby lost all its influence. During these mass struggles, the entire working class had rallied to the support of the General Union, which remained in control of the economic and political struggles of the Shanghai proletariat until April 1927.

The strikes that took place toward the end of 1925 and during the first part of 1926 not only reflected the growing authority of the General Union, but were also characterized by a widening of the demands presented. In addition to the usual demand for higher wages, there were demands for the abolition of fines, the payment of bonuses when no absenteeism had occurred over a given period (*shen-kung*), a reduction in hours, maternity leave for women, the right to take meals during working hours, and the improvement of conditions for young workers and apprentices.[200] The strikes were also directed against the counterattack that seems to have been staged at this time by both foreign and Chinese employers. The employers were encouraged to move against the workers by the tactical withdrawal of the unions after the failure to obtain the political objectives of the May Thirtieth Movement. Thus many strikes, with the support of the General Union and the cotton mills union,[201] stopped attempts to lay off workers, especially in the Japanese mills,[202] and got various identity checks on workers abolished.[203] Others protested the lengthening of hours,[204] the use of efficiency experts,[205] and the installation of machines for recording the rate of output.[206] Another move in the employers' counterattack was to increase the staff employed in the control and supervision of factory work, and many strikes were held to protest the brutal behavior of Chinese, Japanese, White Russian, and Sikh foremen, overseers, "number one" men, and "armed bullies"—as they were called in the English newspapers in Shanghai—engaged to keep order in the factories.[207] The workers demanded their dismissal, sometimes with success, as in January in the Japanese Toa jute factory, in March in the Naigai No. 7 cotton mill, in April in the British Lumber Import-Export Company, in May in the Japanese Kiwa cotton mill and the Swiss A.B.C. printing works, and in June in the B.A.T. Pootung factory, the Naigai No. 13 cotton mill, and the Jih-hua cotton mill.[208] The employers' counterattack did not succeed in breaking the strike wave. Out of the 127 disputes between October 1925 and June 1926 for which the results are known, 82 were either partially or entirely successful.[209]

During this period the same uneasy, knife-edge relations continued between the General Union and the military authorities in the Shanghai region. The Fengtien army, which had occupied the city from the beginning of 1925 and which, after showing a certain amount of tolerance at the time of the May 30 demonstrations, had banned all labor organizations in the middle of September, was evicted a few weeks later by Sun Ch'uan-fang and his army.[210] Sun was a warlord with a reputation for liberal views because of his support for the restoration of the 1912 Constitution in 1922. Formerly a follower of the Chihli faction, he now kept only a nominal allegiance to Wu P'ei-fu. After taking Shanghai, he proclaimed himself Inspector General of the five southeastern provinces, and clearly had every intention of working for his own ends. The leaders of the General Union, Liu Hua, Sun Liang-hui, and Hsiang Ying, thought that this might be an opportunity to gain official sanction for the unions. They offered Sun union support in his fight against his Fengtien opponents, who were still active in the Lower Yangtze region.[211] Sun seems to have been uncertain at first whether to accept this offer, and meanwhile allowed the General Union and its local branches to resume their activities more or less openly. On November 29 the General Union returned officially to its headquarters, and on December 7 it held a meeting in Chapei attended by several thousand. But on December 10 it was once again closed down,[212] Sun having in the end opted for the classic warlord policy of repression. He had got in contact with the compradore section of the big bourgeoisie in Shanghai through its most typical representative, the banker Yü Hsia-ch'ing, whose hostility toward the labor movement had steadily increased ever since May 30 while his ties with the Western authorities in Shanghai had become closer.[213] On December 17 the president of the General Union, the former printing worker Liu Hua, who had been arrested at the end of November by the police of the International Settlement, was turned over by them to Sun Ch'uan-fang's military authorities and was executed—on the insistence of Yü Hsia-ch'ing, according to a tradition in the labor movement.[214] But the Shanghai unions could no longer be broken as easily as this. Although the Chinese police continued to be hostile to the General Union, and in April arrested its new president, Wang Ching-yun, a worker in the Commercial Press and president of the union in that firm,[215] it was nevertheless still influential and active at the beginning of 1926. Its activities were semi-legal rather than clandestine. In January it launched a campaign to help the unemployed,[216] and in February it issued a political manifesto urging the people of Shanghai to cooperate with the Canton government and the People's National Armies in the Northwest, and calling for the convocation of a National Convention.[217] Despite police prohibitions, it celebrated May Day by holding a public meeting;[218] and on May 30 it commemorated the anniversary of the Nanking Road incident at a meeting of several thousand held in Chapei and organized with the help of associations of students and shopkeepers; the Commercial Press and other Chinese-owned enterprises allowed their employees to take time off for the occasion.[219] On July 11, despite new prohibitions against its activities following its support for the strike in the Chapei silk factories at the end of June,[220] the General Union held a conference of delegates from the principal unions affiliated with it, at which a program of minimum economic demands was worked out, including demands for a minimum wage based on the price of rice, a weekly day of rest, a ten-hour day, the abolition of fines, insurance against accidents and illness, and recognition of the right to strike and the right to form trade unions.[221] When the Northern Expedition set out from Canton at the end of July 1926, the Shanghai labor movement was still as strong as ever despite the setbacks of August and September 1925. It was very soon able, in collaboration with the advancing Cantonese armies, to launch the "three armed uprisings," the last of which left the trade unions in control of Shanghai in March 1927.

Crackdowns on Labor in Large Industrial Centers

In the industrial centers in the interior, both Chinese and foreign employers began in the fall to mount an even stronger counterattack than that launched against the Shanghai labor movement. Many workers were laid off, provoking a strike in the B.A.T. Hankow factory and one in a Japanese cotton mill in the same city in February 1926;[222] and as in Shanghai, there was a tendency to mechanize production, probably in order to reduce the risk of strikes rather than for the purely economic purpose of increasing fixed capital investment. Strikes in protest against newly installed machinery broke out in May and June at the B.A.T. Hankow factory,[223] and in April at the Japanese hemp factory in Mukden.[224] Control over workers was tightened also, again for political reasons rather than to decrease labor turnover in the interests of production. The Japanese enterprises in Manchuria gradually adopted the practice of taking the fingerprints of their workers, and this became general at the beginning of 1927.[225] At that former stronghold of the labor movement, the Anyuan mine, the employers' counterattack was more violent still.[226] The economic difficulties of the Hanyehping Company had steadily increased during 1925, and at the time of the May Thirtieth Movement had reached the point where wages had not been paid for four months—which explains why the miners confined themselves to organizing a Committee for Effacing Shame, rather than declaring a sympathy strike as did their comrades at Shuikowshan and other industrial centers in the region. When in September they went on strike to obtain back payment of wages, the manager called in the police and the army, and there were three deaths and 40 arrests. Several thousand workers were laid off and hsin-kung hired to take their place.[227] The Workers' Club, which since 1922 had been the pride of the Chinese labor movement with its twelve thousand members, its seven night schools teaching around two thousand pupils, its twelve reading rooms, its women's education department, and its consumers' cooperative with a capital of 13,000 one-yuan shares, was closed down and its property dispersed or wrecked. In Changsha students demonstrated in protest, and rickshaw men and printers went on a sympathy strike (the city went for four days without newspapers), only to meet with severe repression by Chao Heng-t'i.[228]

The employers' counterattack was accompanied by a renewal of activity on the part of the kung-tsei, the deserters from the labor movement. In Central and North China there were no organizations similar to either the Cantonese guilds or the semi-working-class associations of Shanghai for these opponents of the left-wing unions to join. All they could do was find support as best they could among a very small section of employees—on the railways, for instance—and, for the rest, obtain supporters from the Lumpenproletariat. Only after the warning of the May Thirtieth Movement were efforts apparently made by Chinese and foreign employers and government authorities to create a rival force that would take determined action against the left-wing unions. It seems to have been a force of this kind that carried out an armed attack on the strikers at the Chengchow cotton mill in August 1925; and in Peking a "General Union of Changsintien" was formed, supported by elements of the right wing of the Kuomintang, which had moved further away from the left wing of the party since the summer of 1925.[229] This new organization accused the Communists of being the slaves of Russia and of betraying the workers, and also accused the Kuominchun of collaborating with the Communists.[230] In February it celebrated the anniversary of the Ching-Han massacre in the presence of dignitaries of the Kuomintang right wing, and raised cries of "Down with the Communists!" and "Let us fight by peaceful means!"[231] In Wuhan the kung-tsei were able to take advantage of Hsiao Yao-nan's repression of the left-wing unions, and also benefited from the support of the Sunyatsenist Society.[232] They also found ready support among those peasants who were flocking into the city because of the recent floods,[233] and their activities seem to have caused the Communist militants serious concern. An article in *Hsiang-tao* mentions a number of attempts made by them, with the connivance of employers and of the police, to form unions and foment strikes at the cotton mill, among the rickshaw men and dyers, and on the northern section of the Yueh-Han line.[234]

Despite the counterattack, economic strikes came thick and fast throughout the fall, winter, and spring, an added stimulus being the renewed fighting between the warlords in the North and in the Yangtze valley,[235] with the usual sequel of requisitioning of labor, slowing down of business, and inflation.[236] In Chang Tso-lin's territory the feng-p'iao, which was theoretically at par with the yuan, stood at 200 to the yuan in January and 391 in May, with over 500 million in banknotes in circulation,[237] and this certainly had a good deal to do with the sudden outburst of strikes in the Northeast, where hitherto the development of the labor movement had lagged behind that in other regions. There were in all 36 strikes in the Northeast between October 1925 and June 1926,[238] mostly in Japanese concerns—the Penhsihi and Fushun mines, the Toa tobacco factory, the hemp factories in Mukden, the oil-pressing mills in Liaoyang, the cotton mills in Mukden—but also in the B.A.T. factory and the small Chinese workshops in Mukden. And these strikes, many of which obtained at least a nominal increase in wages, were no longer the spontaneous protests of the preceding period; it is apparent, even from the garbled accounts given by the Japanese-owned Dairen press, that behind many of them lay organizations and even embryonic unions supported by the left wing of the Kuomintang, particularly its student element.[239]

Another area where economic strikes were frequent during this period was the secondary textile center in the Lower Yangtze region, including the cities of Chinkiang, Soochow, Hangchow, Wusih, Nantung, and Shaohing. These were all cities where, in contrast to Shanghai, the modern cotton and silk industries were direct heirs to the old craft traditions of manufacture, and where the guilds still flourished and modern trade unionism had made scarcely any progress at all. Here the wave of economic strikes that began early in 1926 seems to have been activated by the Shanghai textile unions, which had been very active since the summer of 1925, rather than to have been the result of a crisis brought about by military operations.[240]

The only area where the Chinese labor movement was free to develop was still, as in the summer of 1925, the territory controlled by the Kuominchun. After the withdrawal of the Fengtien armies in December 1925, this territory included the industrial areas of Chihli and of western Shantung in addition to the parts of Honan and the northwestern plateaus already under Feng Yü-hsiang's control.[241]

The importance of Kuominchun support for the Nationalist revolution must not, of course, be exaggerated. Feng Yü-hsiang and his generals may have been on good terms with the Nationalist government in Canton,[242] and Hsü Ch'ien, a jurist and a Christian who was one of Feng's political advisers, may have had close ties with the left wing of the Kuomintang;[243] but after all the Kuominchun was a military organization that was recruited from a rather narrow section of society and that was only gradually coming under the influence of new ideas. Although Feng seems to have had ideas of reaching a military pact with the Soviet Union even before his visit to Moscow in January 1926, and although there was close collaboration between his armies and the Communists,[244] there was never any question of a real political alliance,[245] and the Communists themselves do not ever seem to have seriously considered one or to have regarded the Kuominchun as a genuinely revolutionary force.[246]

Nevertheless, during the short period when Feng's armies were in control of the whole of North China, they gave every support to the labor movement. Unions sprang up "like bamboo shoots after rain," as one conservative newspaper in Peking put it.[247] The Cheng-T'ai railwaymen's union was allowed to resume its activities,[248] and thanks to a subsidy of 500 yuan granted by the Kuominchun First Army, the Ching-Feng railwaymen's union reopened its library at the Tangshan depot and renewed its social and cultural services.[249] When the Kuominchun entered Tientsin, they released the K.M.A. union leaders who had been arrested by Li Ching-lin after the defeat of the strike in August 1925, and on January 18 the Tangshan miners' union was officially reinstated in the presence of officers of the Ninth Regiment.[250] The Kuominchun also gave official permission for the re-formation of the Tientsin General Union[251] and for the creation of a General Union in Peking with which printers', mechanics', and craftsmen's unions would be affiliated;[252] and it supported the Tangshan miners' strike in February, called to obtain a bonus from the British owners.[253] In exchange, the unions gave the Kuominchun active support when military operations began at the end of the winter, during which the Fengtien armies gradually reconquered the whole of Chihli. The railwaymen in particular declared their support for Feng's armies[254] and did their best to hinder the movements of enemy troops.[255]

It was probably also thanks to the power that the Kuominchun had over the Peking government, whose "executive head" Tuan Ch'i-jui was now a mere figurehead, that the Minister of Agriculture and Commerce took steps to implement the plans for labor legislation that had been discussed before May 30. A draft bill published in July 1925 had been severely criticized by the Shanghai General Union and by the All-China General Union. The new bill was more or less completed by the beginning of 1926. It permitted the formation of unions both on an industrial and on a trade basis, and while the draft bill had stipulated that there must be 50 foundation members who had been employed in the industry concerned for at least three years and who were over 30 years of age and could read and write, the new one merely stipulated that there must be a core of 30 adult workers who were actually employed in the industry concerned. It laid down procedures for arbitration, and prohibited strikes and lockouts while arbitration was in process; and it insisted on compulsory registration of unions in state-owned enterprises.[256] Several weeks later, however, the Kuominchun had to evacuate Peking owing to the advance of the Fengtien armies, and these comparatively liberal measures were never actually promulgated.

When the Kuominchun armies were chased out of Chihli and Honan in the spring of 1926, they took refuge in Shensi and Kansu, where they adopted the same liberal attitude toward labor problems. In the enterprises in Sian, Lanchow, and other urban centers in the region, hours of work were limited to nine or ten a day, child labor was controlled, and one day or a half-day off per week was granted.[257] At the beginning of 1927 this policy was given official expression in "Provisional Labor Legislation for the Northwestern Provinces," which went so far as to accept the principle of the minimum wage under a system of factory inspection, and the possibility of collective bargaining.[258] In this remote region, however, there were no big factories, but only small textile workshops employing a few dozen workers, so that only a very marginal section of the Chinese working class was affected.

It was in fact this marginal role of the Kuominchun that was its congenital weakness. No one has yet made a study of its contribution to the Chinese political scene and its unique attempt to combine Christianity and Sunyatsenism,[259] but one thing is certain: it was unable to create a stable counterpart in the North to the revolutionary Canton government in the South. When the Kuomintang launched its Northern Expedition in July 1926, the industrial areas in Chihli and Honan, which could have been of both economic and strategic importance, had already been evacuated by the Kuominchun. Feng's armies were not in control there long enough to enable the labor movement to recover from the setbacks due to the general policy of repression adopted by the warlords from 1923 on.

In Hupeh, held by the Chihli faction, and in the Northeast and in Shantung, controlled by the Fengtien faction, this policy of repression had operated almost continuously since the fall of 1925, and had added to the labor movement's difficulties stemming from the counterattack of the employers and the activities of the kung-tsei there. It is true that the railwaymen had succeeded in carrying out the task of restoring the unions, begun in 1924–25. When they held their Third National Congress in February 1926, they had unions on all of the 16 main railways in China,[260] including the provincially owned Nanchang-Kiukiang line[261] and the Chinese Eastern Railway.[262] But all these unions were more and more reduced to operating through clandestine activities, and were continually hunted down by the police of the various warlords, especially after the defeat of the Kuominchun in the spring.[263] Armed intervention on the part of the warlords was responsible also for the dissolution of the Anyuan miners' club in September 1925 and for the suppression of the K.M.A. miners' strike;[264] and in Wuhan the armed intervention of police had put a stop to attempts to organize a "Workers' Delegates' Conference" on the model of the one held in Canton.[265] In Harbin, the few unions that had recently been formed were banned in February 1926 by Chang Tso-lin,[266] in whose territory factory discipline was maintained "at the point of the sword," according to the expression used in a Japanese-owned Dairen newspaper.[267]

This "White Terror" became all the more acute when in the spring the undying hatred between the Fengtien and Chihli factions was suddenly ended by their coming to terms in order to consummate the defeat of the Kuominchun and prepare themselves for the threatened attack from Canton. Marshals Wu P'ei-fu (who reappeared after two years in retirement) and Chang Tso-lin solemnly agreed to forget their long-standing enmity, and declared that priority must be given to the fight against Communism and the labor movement.[268] Both of them issued strict instructions that all labor activities be suppressed, especially in Peking and Tientsin.[269] Thus the rivalries between the warlords, those so-to-speak medieval relics who dominated the Chinese political scene during the years after the First World War, were abruptly terminated when they sensed the pressure of the labor movement within the Nationalist movement as a whole; and the sudden realignment of the northern warlords was certainly not unconnected with the policies of the Canton government after the May Thirtieth Movement.

CHAPTER XII

The Canton–Hong Kong Strike

It was in South China that the Nanking Road incident had the most dramatic and longest-lasting effects. The direct result in this area was the Canton–Hong Kong strike, which lasted for sixteen months, ending in October 1926.

Before discussing this sudden resurgence of the labor movement in South China, however, a word must be said about the political situation that had developed there. To outward appearances at least, the Canton government remained firm after the death of Sun Yat-sen in March 1925, and still pursued the "three new policies" laid down at the beginning of 1924.[1] The electoral body for the appointment of a successor to the presidency was the Central Executive Committee of the Kuomintang that had been elected at the congress of January 1924, and it included the Communists Li Ta-chao, T'an P'ing-shan, and Yü Shu-te as well as powerful personalities, such as Liao Chung-k'ai and Wang Ching-wei, who belonged to the left wing of the Kuomintang. Members with more moderate views, such as Hu Han-min, Chiang Kai-shek, and General Hsü Ch'ung-chih, had not yet openly expressed any disagreement over the Soviet alliance and collaboration with the Communists. In February and March the "First Eastern Expedition," in which the Whampoa cadets played an active part, had driven Ch'en Chiung-ming's armies, which were still a potential threat, to the eastern borders of Kwangtung; at the same time the whole of Kwangsi had been brought under the control of the Canton government by the elimination of the local warlords who had formerly been Sun's allies. Finally, on June 13 Liu Chen-huan and Yang Hsi-min, two *condottieri* whom Sun Yat-sen had allowed to take control of the city of Canton itself in exchange for the support they had given him on his return in 1923, were removed after it was discovered that they had been in league with Ch'en Chiung-ming and also with T'ang Chi-yao of Yunnan, who was always up to some new intrigue. With the help of the Whampoa cadets, the troops of Hsü Ch'ung-chih and Chiang Kai-shek managed to disarm the mercenaries without firing a shot. On the same day an important meeting of the Central Executive Committee was held, at which the post of General-in-Chief (held temporarily by Hu Han-min, following the death of Sun Yat-sen) was abolished, and a "'Nationalist government" was officially established, accountable to the Kuomintang, with Wang Ching-wei as president. The Canton–Hong Kong strike was to provide this government with the opportunity for putting the third of Sun Yat-sen's "new policies," namely, support for the workers and peasants, into practice, and it gained in authority by doing so. The strike also increased the prestige of the labor organizations and of the Communist Party in the eyes of the government and of the bourgeoisie in the South, and in Cantonese public opinion as a whole.[2]

The idea of holding a strike was formed at the beginning of June, immediately after the Shanghai incident. Hong Kong, being Great Britain's main base in the Far East, was an obvious place to stage a demonstration of solidarity with the workers who had been killed by British bullets in Shanghai. The leaders of the All-China General Union[3] entered into negotiations with the two groups of moderate associations in the colony, the General Association of Chinese Workers and the General Association of Labor Organizations; but in view of the hesitations of both groups, they decided to start the strike in sectors of industry where their influence was strong enough to enable them to act alone—namely among the seamen, the telegraphers, the newspaper compositors, and the employees of foreign firms. All these came out on strike on June 19. They adopted the 17 demands of the Shanghai strikers and added others of a local nature: complete freedom of speech, association, and publication on the territory of the colony, equality of treatment for Chinese and foreigners, extension of the franchise to Chinese on the same terms as to foreigners, the introduction of labor legislation including the eight-hour day, the minimum wage, collective bargaining, the abolition of the pao-kung system, and workers' insurance, and assurances of the freedom to live in any district on the island and of a reduction in rents.[4] As in Shanghai, the platform of demands reflected both the needs of the working class and the wishes of the Chinese population of Hong Kong as a whole. The strikers departed immediately for Canton, taking with them a number of workers from other trades so as to "remove the ground from under the feet" of the leaders of the moderate organizations, as the strike organizers put it.

In Canton a big procession of all the strikers who had arrived there, joined by some of the Whampoa cadets, by students, and by craftsmen belonging to the Canton guilds, was held on June 23.[5] When, in the afternoon, the procession turned into Shakee Road, which is separated by only a narrow channel from the island of Shameen, where the foreign concessions had been heavily fortified several days before, a burst of gunfire killed 52 and wounded over a hundred of the marchers.[6] The official documents later published by the Powers accused the marchers of having fired first,[7] but the evidence collected by the Canton government's commission of inquiry[8] and by the American teaching staff at the Canton Christian College,[9] not to mention that provided by the left-wing unions,[10] indicates that it was the British and French sentries on Shameen that opened fire.

The All-China General Union immediately called a meeting of the union leaders of Canton and Hong Kong, including those whose unions were not its affiliates, and it was decided not only to intensify the strike in Hong Kong and extend it to all Chinese employed in Shameen, but also to put a stranglehold on Hong Kong by means of a total boycott of all ships and merchandise having Hong Kong as their destination.[11] By the end of June over fifty thousand workers had left the island, most of them dockers, factory workers, employees in public transport and public utilities, and craftsmen.[12] Even the Mechanics' Union, at first suspicious as usual of any initiative from the left, came out on strike on July 5.[13] The British authorities tried to break the strike by setting up a "Labor Maintenance Association" that tried to recruit coolies at 1.50 yuan a day plus two good square meals;[14] but by mid-July the number of strikers that had left Hong Kong had risen to over eighty thousand.[15] The boycott was just as successful. It was at first applied without distinction to all ships and merchandise going to or from Hong Kong, or to or from any port in Kwangtung. To obtain exemption, Chinese merchants had to get a special permit from the Strike Committee.[16] Traffic with the colony was practically at a standstill by the beginning of July.[17]

The Canton–Hong Kong strike had a powerful organization behind it. Central control was maintained not only by a Strike Committee consisting of 13 persons, but also by a "Strikers' Delegates' Congress" comprising over 800 delegates (one for every 50 strikers), which was a kind of workers' parliament. It met three times a week, thus ensuring constant contact with the rank and file.[18] The committee of 13, four members representing Shameen and nine Hong Kong, was presided over by Su Chao-cheng,[19] with Teng Chung-hsia as his chief adviser[20] and other Communists, such as Lo Teng-hsien and Ch'en Ch'üan, playing an important part; and the strike leaders worked in close collaboration with members of the All-China General Union such as Liu Shao-ch'i and Hsiang Ying.[21] Thus the strategy and organization of the strike were essentially in the hands of Communist cadres, and neither the Nationalist government nor the people of Canton had any illusions about this.

The Strike Committee was assisted by many special departments (administration, propaganda, recreation, communications, finance, and so on),[22] for the tasks it had to deal with were many and varied. The chief task was to provide for the subsistence and the social activities of the tens of thousands of strikers who had left Hong Kong.[23] Nine local offices, dispersed among the districts of Canton, dealt with feeding and housing problems. Use was made of requisitioned gambling houses, unused stationary railway coaches, and other improvised dormitories. In order to keep its troops united and to boost their morale, the Strike Committee published a weekly newspaper, *Kuangtung kung-jen chih lu* ("The Labor Way"), organized courses in political and general education, and got the strikers to start building a road from Canton to the new port planned for Whampoa; this was to be called the "Sun Yat-sen Road."[24] As the strike wore on, educational activities grew in importance, and in April 1926 the Strike Committee established an education committee, which opened a "Workers' College" for union cadres, eight extramural schools for adult workers, and eight primary schools for workers' children.[25]

The cost of these activities was met, according to a balance sheet published by the Strike Committee in July 1926, by contributions from various sources: 250,000 yuan collected in China, 1.13 million from overseas Chinese, 2.8 million advanced by the Canton government, 400,000 from the sale of merchandise seized by the union officials in control of the boycott, and 200,000 raised in fines imposed by them. Thus between June 1925 and July 1926 the funds administered by the Strike Committee amounted to nearly 5 million yuan.[26] This was a very large amount of money, equal to 15 million days' wages for a Chinese worker at that time.

The responsibilities of the Strike Committee went far beyond the normal field of activities of a union organization dealing with a work stoppage. During the summer of 1925 the committee became, in fact, a kind of workers' government—and indeed the name commonly applied to it at that time by both its friends and its enemies was "Government No. 2."[27] This quasi-governmental status of the Strike Committee was even more evident in its handling of the boycott against Hong Kong and the sanctions it imposed against its infringement. The committee had at its disposal an armed force of several thousand men, organized into units at various levels, from squads of twenty up to regiments; there were five regiments, each containing 540 men.[28] These strike pickets (or "corps of guards," *chiu-ch'a-tui*), dressed in blue with red armbands, examined the merchandise arriving at or departing from Canton by land or sea, and inspected the arrivals and departures of individual persons, in order to cut off all relations with Hong Kong.[29] Anyone infringing the regulations was brought before a court set up by the Strike Committee, which had appointed the judges; and this court imposed either fines or prison sentences that were served out in jails belonging to the committee.[30] Although a few of the strike pickets may have abused their powers for financial gain,[31] the strike seems on the whole to have been conducted with great integrity and efficiency. Lewis Gannett, the special correspondent of the American liberal weekly *The Nation,* was present at a trial of a peasant who had attempted to get his vegetables shipped on a British steamer. Three judges presided, with a jury of six strikers, and sentence was pronounced after the hearing of evidence provided by strike pickets. Gannett described the orderliness and seriousness of the proceedings of this court as "quite extraordinary," and declared that it was the only court in China where civil cases were properly tried.[32] The Strike Committee had established its headquarters in the Tung-yuan ("Eastern Gardens"), a former amusement park that had gone out of use, and the daily comings and goings there give a good idea of the committee's multiple activities. Three buildings, one of which had three stories, were entirely occupied by the various administrative services; an open space served as a training ground for the pickets; and in addition there were three prison cells, a canteen, several dormitories, a number of classrooms, and sheds for housing confiscated goods.[33]

The boycott of Hong Kong, to be effective, could not be confined to the city of Canton alone. The Strike Committee therefore had to extend its activities over the whole area actually under the control of the Southern government. In Swatow, the second largest port in Kwangtung, a sympathy strike was declared in mid-June in several British firms. Things had taken the same turn there after the Shakee Road affair as in Canton and Hong Kong. There was a complete stoppage of work among employees of Western firms and a boycott of all traffic with Hong Kong.[34] As in Canton, pickets were organized to keep watch over the Hong Kong traffic and impose fines when necessary.[35] When Ch'en Chiung-ming entered the city in September, these activities had to be suspended, but they were resumed again in December after the successful "Second Eastern Expedition" conducted by the Cantonese armies.[36] After the recapture of Swatow, the strike committee there held a general meeting of strikers to whom it explained its aims in detail: reduction of hours, a wage increase, reinstatement of strikers, strike pay, and union control over the engagement and dismissal of workers.[37] The southern peninsula of the province had been in the hands of local mercenaries since 1925, but after the successful "Southern Expedition" launched by the Canton government in January 1926,[38] the Strike Committee stationed pickets in Peihai (Pakhoi) in February in order to enforce the boycott there.[39] A whole network of pickets had already been established in the main maritime and riverine ports of Kwangtung at the beginning of the strike, and by the spring of 1926, when the Strike Committee was at the height of its power, it controlled the whole coast from Pakhoi to Swatow. The entire coastal area was divided into seven regions, the last to be incorporated being the district of Swatow, which came under the joint control of detachments of pickets from Canton and from Swatow itself.[40] Twelve gunboats manned by pickets were in operation on the high seas.[41]

This extension of the boycott to all the small ports and the coastal regions of the province raised the question of the relations between the Strike Committee and the peasants. There had been a great development of peasant unions in Kwangtung toward the end of 1925 and during the first part of 1926.[42] Their provincial federation was able to cooperate effectively with the strikers, and it joined in the activities of the Strike Aid Week in February, organized by various Cantonese associations. The peasants were kept informed about the strike by strikers who had returned to their villages as well as by the propagandists systematically sent out by the Strike Committee, and they gave active help in hunting out smugglers.[43]

The strike continued without faltering throughout the fall, winter, and spring of 1925-26; but at the beginning of July 1926, shipyard workers and domestic servants began to trickle back to work in Hong Kong, and the police were able to close the Labor Bureau that had been established early in the strike.[44] The seamen and dockers, however, stood firm and did not return from Canton; and in the docks, which were the crucial sector, attempts to break the strike by hiring hsin-kung (strikebreakers) through the "Labor Maintenance Association," which was subsidized by wealthy Chinese merchants and British firms in the colony, failed. In July one of its agents, who went around protected by an armed guard composed of former officers of no less a person than Wu P'ei-fu, was stoned in the middle of a main street.[45] In April 1926 there were still about thirty thousand strikers from the colony in Canton,[46] and the strike continued on the island of Shameen, access to which was blocked by armed pickets.[47] As for the boycott, it was being carried on with the same vigor and was now stricter than ever, for after the relaxations introduced in September at the request, and in the interests, of the Cantonese bourgeoisie, an embargo was now placed on the issue of permits for the loading and discharge of cargo.[48] The pickets were still systematically seizing all British goods and all foodstuffs destined for Hong Kong[49] and selling them by auction. These seizures brought them into conflict with Colonel Hayley Bell, the Customs Commissioner for the port of Canton, who threatened to close the port if the pickets went on examining the cargoes before the customs officials themselves had had a chance to do so. On the intervention of the Canton government it was agreed that in the future no goods would be seized until the customs formalities had been carried out.[50]

Throughout this whole period, despite a deterioration in the political situation in Canton and growing antagonism between the right and left wings of the Kuomintang, especially after the coup on March 20,[51] the Strike Committee carried on its activities and maintained its prestige. On March 30 it held a ceremony to mark its hundredth meeting, and distributed special allocations to the strikers on this occasion.[52] On June 19, 1926, the first anniversary of the strike was celebrated at the headquarters in the Tung-yuan.[53] It was not until July 1926, when the Cantonese armies were setting off on the Northern Expedition, that both the Cantonese working class and the Nationalist government began to feel that continuing the strike and the boycott would be an unnecessary waste of energy. After three months of negotiations,[54] both the strike and the boycott came to an end with the agreement of the Strike Committee and the Strikers' Delegates' Congress; this was on October 10, 1926, almost 16 months after the Shakee Road incident. This must undoubtedly be one of the longest strikes in the history of the international labor movement, or at least one of the longest on a large scale.

Growth of Union Organization in the South

The left wing of the labor movement in Canton, which, in this center of small-scale production with tenacious guild traditions, had been of small account until 1925, drew great strength from the strike and from the prestige of strike leaders such as Su Chao-cheng and Teng Chung-hsia.

The most active of these left-wing labor organizations was the Canton

Workers' Delegates' Conference, formed in 1924 by Liao Chung-k'ai and Sun Yat-sen as a counterweight to the conservative provincial federation of labor organizations and as a means of extending Kuomintang influence among the Cantonese workers. It was now completely separate from the party organization of the Kuomintang, and had become the regional federation of all unions supporting the line of the All-China General Union.[55] It held its first conference as a separate organization on April 1, 1926.[56] The conference was attended by 1,800 delegates representing 108 unions and 140,000 unionists,[57] including factory workers, railwaymen, printers, employees of foreign firms, and workers in oil-pressing mills, as well as a large number of craftsmen. The original purpose in convening it was to extend the scope of the organization. The Mechanics' Union and other right-wing organizations accepted the invitation to attend, but on the very first day their delegates quarreled with those of the other unions and withdrew.[58] The conference then had to confine itself to consolidating the organization of the left-wing unions and to defining its program. The economic demands laid down the year before by the All-China General Union were adopted: minimum wage, eight-hour day, limitation of night work, union control over employment, and prohibitions both against private profits made by foremen and against work done for them without pay. A special resolution on female and child labor (regarding age limits, wages, and time off) followed the lines of the programs elaborated several days earlier at a conference of young workers of Canton and a conference of women workers of Canton, both organized by the Workers' Delegates' Conference. These demands alone constituted a complete break with the guild traditions of the Cantonese trade associations, with their moderate attitude toward employers and management, their retention of the apprenticeship system, and their dislike of employing female labor. But the break became even sharper in the light of the resolution on organization passed by the conference, which explicitly defined unions as organizations designed to promote the class struggle, to put an end to political oppression, to awaken class consciousness, to further class unity, and to make an effective improvement in the lot of the workers by aiding the unemployed, controlling employment, promoting workers' education, and creating consumers' cooperatives. The resolution also stipulated that unions should refuse to admit employers or upper-rank employees (the admission of such employees was common practice among moderate unions such as the Mechanics' Union), should be organized on democratic lines, should hold proper meetings, should be controlled by a committee and not by a president, and should eliminate provincial rivalries.

Another sign of the progress made by the left-wing unions and the All-China General Union among the proletariat of South China was the creation in other centers of organizations similar to the Canton Workers' Delegates' Conference. Particularly important was the formation of a new Federation of Labor Organizations in Hong Kong in June 1925, which brought together all the unions that supported the strike and the boycott.[59] (Up to that time labor organizations there had been very demarcated, and had been grouped in two rival federations.) This organization was in turn replaced in December by the Hong Kong General Union, formed under the auspices of the All-China General Union and officially inaugurated at the latter's premises in Canton.[60] In the smaller industrial centers of Kwangtung (Shunteh, Chungshan, Kiangmen, Foshan, Swatow, etc.), general unions on similar lines were formed,[61] in which craftsmen no doubt outnumbered industrial workers but which nevertheless helped to extend left-wing influence over all of the territory that was under the control of the Nationalist government. After the Cantonese armies had expelled the followers of the Yunnan warlord, T'ang Chi-yao, from Kwangsi and established control over the province, a Workers' Delegates' Conference was set up in Nanning in June 1926. This group, which was obviously modeled on the organization of the same name in Canton, brought together 33 unions with 48,000 members, most of whom were craftsmen or transport workers.[62]

Belief in the superiority of industrial unionism over trade unionism, which had been upheld by the first two Labor Congresses (in 1922 and 1925) and before that by the Labor Secretariat in its inaugural manifesto, had made less headway in South China than elsewhere because of the persistence there of the old guild traditions. All the more remarkable, therefore, was the progress made in this direction as a result of the strike and the boycott. February 1926 saw the amalgamation of the five unions that had as their members the Chinese employed in the Shameen concessions, all of whom had been on strike for over eight months.[63] At the beginning of March the first National Conference of Seamen was held in Canton, attended by 102 delegates from Canton, 14 from Shanghai, and six from Swatow (those from Tientsin, Hupeh, and Shantung were prevented from attending); it was decided at this conference to strengthen the organization of the Seamen's Union, the earliest industrial union in China, by forming rank-and-file units on each ship in addition to the existing local branches in each port and the central committee. The conference condemned once again the regional mutual aid societies (the pang-k'ou), and stressed the need for committees at all levels of union organization. A decision was reached to join the transport section of the Red International.[64]

It was also in March 1926 that a Federation of Transport Workers' Unions was formed in Hong Kong, which had 17 different unions (of seamen, porters, public transport employees, dockers, and so on) affiliated with it, with a total membership of 200,000. This federation also joined the transport section of the Red International, and immediately declared its undying hatred of "British imperialism" and its desire to overthrow capitalism.[65] On April 11 a General Metallurgical Industries' Union was formed in Hong Kong, and on April 28 the Kwangtung Federation of Transport Workers' Unions was formed, including such worker groups as railwaymen, seamen, boathands, and porters.[66] In Canton, 23 unions amalgamated to form one organization in which the unions formed specialized branches.[67] In May 1926 the railwaymen on the three Kwangtung lines, who had for a long time been divided up into many small corporate groups affiliated with the Mechanics' Union, combined to form an industrial union affiliated with the Workers' Delegates' Conference.[68]

It should be noted that it was among the transport workers (seamen, railwaymen, dockers) that industrial unionism made most headway. They were in a better position than other workers to appreciate the prestige gained by the strike and the boycott; moreover, the success of the whole movement depended on their cooperation, and the importance that the leaders of the Strike Committee attached to this can be measured by the fact that Liu Shao-ch'i, Su Chao-cheng, Teng Chung-hsia, and Hsiang Ying all went in person to attend the inaugural meeting of the Transport Federation in Hong Kong.[69]

Hand in hand with this reorganization of existing unions on the twofold basis of local branches and industrial unions went the work of forming new unions. In Canton, between the start of the strike and boycott and the departure of the Northern Expedition, 80 new unions were formed, mainly among craftsmen, but also among postal workers, the customs staff, workers in match factories, and coal transport coolies on the docks.[70] The coal transport coolies' union, which covered the whole province, was inaugurated at the Strike Committee's premises in Hong Kong.[71] Because of this fever of organization, the Workers' Delegates' Conference was able to claim a membership of about 150,000 by the spring of 1926.[72] In Swatow, too, great activity went on during the summer of 1925, when the strike and the boycott were at their height. Unions were formed among the sailors on junks, the employees in foreign firms, the coolies, and the handicraft spinners. Ch'en Chiung-ming's recapture of the city interrupted these activities, but after his defeat they were resumed during the winter and spring among the tugboat seamen in the port, the weavers, the postal workers, the rickshaw men, and the masons. By the summer of 1926, 30 unions were functioning, with a total membership of 21,000, including craftsmen. Most of them had not been in existence before June 1925.[73] In Nanning, most of the thirty or so labor organizations that were federated in June 1926[74] had first appeared in 1925 and at the beginning of 1926, following upon the gradual consolidation of the Southern government's control over Kwangsi. As might be expected in an area where little economic development had taken place, the majority of these organizations were for craft workers, but some of them were for industrial workers, such as the unions for printing workers, mechanics, workers in clothing factories, deckhands on the West River steamers, and shipyard workers.[75]

It is easy enough to list all these new unions and federations, but to find out how they actually worked is a much more difficult matter. Were they all somewhat schematic, with membership figures expressing hopes rather than facts? And did they have any profound effect on the working class in the South? Certainly they seem to have made a real break with the old guild customs, especially in the matter of control. According to an inquiry conducted in 1926 by the Canton Municipal Council, 168 unions were controlled by an elected committee and only 12 by a president[76]—that is to say, the number of unions controlled by a committee greatly exceeded the number affiliated with the Workers' Delegates' Conference. Furthermore, entry fees and subscription rates in the left-wing unions seem to have been much lower than in the traditional associations,[77] and discipline much stricter. The pickets of the rickshaw men's union kept watch to make sure that coolies without union cards were prevented from working, and union members were given instruction in traffic regulations.[78] Another example of these new attitudes is an episode that took place in November 1925, when the union of employees in foreign firms decided that all workers in this category must register with the union; they then presented the employers with a demand for a 20 per cent wage increase in order to raise funds for the Canton–Hong Kong Strike Committee.[79] The main left-wing unions seem to have increasingly adopted the practice, during the winter of 1925–26, of forming "corps of guards" modeled on the pickets of the Strike Committee, just as the rickshaw men's, railwaymen's, and oil mill workers' unions had done.[80] Some of these bodies were armed, and others were not; but they were a concrete expression of the unions' capacity for action.

A further result of this renewal of activities in union organization was the appearance in Canton of a number of labor leaders of proletarian origin. Until 1925, most of the leaders of the Cantonese labor movement either belonged, like the leaders of the Mechanics' Union, to organizations strongly tinged with guild traditions and more or less under the control of the employers, or else were men employed by the right wing of the Kuomintang to organize unions, as in the case of Ch'en Ping-sheng and Hsieh Ying-po. Such left-wing leaders as there had been were almost all intellectuals such as Yuan Hsiao-hsien,[81] Ch'en Kung-po,[82] and Feng Chü-p'o;[83] the seamen Su Chao-cheng and Lin Wei-min, who were leaders of the Hong Kong strike in 1922 and who helped to organize the Second National Labor Congress, were the exceptions to the rule. But now, owing to the impetus given to the whole Cantonese labor movement by the Canton–Hong Kong strike, Su and Lin were joined by a number of other leaders of working-class origin. There was the seaman Ch'en Ch'üan, the seamen's delegate on the Strike Committee, who at the end of 1925 had helped to found the Hong Kong General Union and who in 1926 represented the Strike Committee at the International Congress in Brussels to ask for aid for China;[84] the seaman Teng Fa, a leader both of the seamen's strike and of the boycott;[85] the railwayman Liu Erh-sung, who helped to found the Canton Workers' Delegates' Conference,[86] organized

the Shameen strike in July 1924, and was a member of the executive committee of the All-China General Union in 1925 and 1926;[87] the mechanic Teng
Han-hsing, who was a delegate of the Shanghai Mechanics' Union at the
First Labor Congress in 1922,[88] and who in 1926 rejoined the All-China General Union and became a member of its executive committee;[89] Lo Teng-hsien,
a worker employed in the shipyards of Butterfield & Swire in Hong Kong,
who was a leader of the 1925 strike and was now president of the Hong Kong
General Union;[90] and Ma Ch'ao-fan, who organized the Canton printers'
union and engineered its affiliation with the Workers' Delegates' Conference.[91]

The growth in the number, importance, and internal strength of the unions,
and the increase in the number of working-class leaders, indicate the extent
to which the Canton–Hong Kong strike stimulated the development of the
labor movement in Canton and led to a new class consciousness among the
proletariat. Significant of this change was the request made by the workers
in the Canton electric power plant at the beginning of 1926 that the manager
address them by name instead of by the number marked on the badges they
wore, since, as they said, "a badge is a sign of servility."[92] The progress in
union organization was accompanied by a renewal of strike activities and of
public demonstrations organized by the labor movement insofar as it had any
energy left from the efforts made to sustain the main strike and boycott movement. Most of the strikes affected foreign enterprises, such as those on the
British section of the Canton-Kowloon railway in December 1925 and at the
American missionary hospital in Canton in March 1926; or else they affected
enterprises under foreign management, such as the Post Office.[93] The strike
at the hospital was firmly controlled by the pickets from the union of employees in foreign firms, and it led to a complete cessation of activities at the
hospital owing to the fact that the management preferred to suspend activities rather than recognize the union or consent to the wage increase it demanded.[94]

The large number of demonstrations held in Canton during the period of
the strike and the boycott is a further indication of the growing influence of
the working class in the social and political life of the city. On August 30,
ceremonies were held in honor of the Soviet trade union delegation,[95] and on
November 7 the anniversary of the Russian Revolution was celebrated by a
grand parade of all the unions, each one bearing the Red Flag.[96] A big public
meeting to protest Japanese infiltration of Manchuria—the Japanese wanted
to defend Chang Tso-lin against the revolt led by Kuo Sung-ling—[97] was held
in January 1926 at the Eastern Drill Ground, the center of which was marked
off for workers, strikers, and union representatives while the right side was
occupied by soldiers and the left by students and merchants.[98] On February 7,
approximately fifty thousand workers and students attended a meeting at the
University of Canton to commemorate the massacre of the Ching-Han railwaymen in 1923.[99] Many demonstrations were held during the first week of

May 1926, because in this one week came the May Day celebrations and the anniversaries of May 4, 1919, of May 5, 1921 (the reappointment of Sun Yat-sen as president of the Constitutional government), and of May 7, 1915 (the "Day of Humiliation," when Yuan Shih-k'ai was presented with the Twenty-one Demands), all of which were included in the Cantonese political calendar. To add to the complications, May 5 was also the anniversary of the birth of Karl Marx. On all four anniversaries large crowds of workers, students, and soldiers gathered; and 300,000 people attended the May Day celebrations and cheered the speakers, who included the Communist T'an P'ing-shan, speaking on behalf of the Kuomintang, and Ch'en Kung-po, a left-wing member of the Kuomintang, speaking on behalf of the government. A resolution was passed demanding an eight-hour day and the promulgation of labor legislation, and giving full support to the government and the party in power.[100]

May 1, 1926, was also the day on which the Third National Labor Congress was held, now convened by the All-China General Union, and not, as in 1922 and 1925, by less prestigious labor organizations. Like the two preceding ones, this congress was held in Canton, since the political situation there made it the only place where the congress could be held openly; but unlike the first two, the first of which was merely a tentative attempt to establish contacts and the second more in the nature of a council of war, the Third Congress took place in the midst of social and political struggles important to the Chinese working class. The Canton–Hong Kong strike and boycott were still in full swing, and although the May Thirtieth Movement in Shanghai had failed to achieve its political objectives, it was still being carried on in the economic field by means of the strike wave organized by the Shanghai General Union. In Hunan, the government of Chao Heng-t'i, the sworn enemy of the labor movement, was on the point of collapse;[101] in North China the recent defeat of the Kuominchun had not yet effaced the memory of the rapid progress made under its protection by the unions of Chihli and Honan; and there were stirrings of activity in the remote Northeast.

The Third Congress reflected the high degree of class consciousness attained by the Chinese working class during this period of struggle. The resolutions concerning workers' demands adopted by the delegates[102] included demands for the right of workers to belong to any union they chose, the right to strike and to hold meetings, liberty of association, freedom of the press, limitation of the working day to eight hours, paid days of rest on Sundays, holidays, and important anniversaries, double pay for extra hours of work, and limitations on female and child labor. Resolutions were also passed affirming the principle that wages must be high enough to give the workers a decent standard of living, that in cases of need the government should provide relief, and that wages should be paid in legal tender to the exclusion of all payments in kind or by vouchers, and demanding that unions have the right to conduct collective bargaining with employers, to have a say in the amount of extra hours worked, to take part in the management of employment bureaus and workers' insurance plans (the creation of which was also on the list of demands), and finally to be represented on the bodies appointed to work out the labor legislation demanded by the congress.

The congress also provided evidence of the leading position now held by the Communists in the Chinese labor movement. It was Liu Shao-ch'i who presented the general report on the activities of the All-China General Union since its foundation the year before; for particular unions, Chu Shao-lien reported on the activities of the Anyuan miners, Su Chao-cheng on the Seamen's Union, and Li Li-san on the Shanghai General Union.[103] The congress approved the establishment of relations effected the year before between the All-China General Union and the Red International;[104] and the 35 members and 17 deputy members elected to the Executive Committee included all the Communist cadres who, whether of working-class origin or not, had devoted themselves to trade union work during the past few years. These included Lin Wei-min, Su Chao-cheng, Li Li-san, Teng Chung-hsia, Liu Shao-ch'i, Hsiang Ying, Chu Shao-lien, Kuo Liang, Li Sen (the name adopted by Li Ch'i-han after coming out of prison in 1924), Liu Wen-sung, and Liu Erh-sung.[105] It was they who proposed the political resolutions that were adopted by the congress, the last of which stressed the need to give unfailing support to the Nationalist government and especially to the Northern Expedition, which was soon to set forth. This point will be taken up later.

To what extent did this congress and the All-China General Union behind it really represent the working masses? Did they not rather merely express the views of the more aware avant-garde? The congress was attended by 502 delegates, representing 699 labor organizations of various kinds: rank-and-file branches, trade and industrial unions, national industrial federations, and regional federations.[106] The total membership of all the organizations represented was said to be 1.2 million, which, even if account is taken of the large number of craftsmen and also of unemployed included in this figure,[107] probably comes to more than half the total number of industrial workers in China at that time. The sophisticated administrative arrangements of many unions (issue of union cards, collection of dues, and the like) indicate that they were fully in touch with their members, although many of the unions represented at the congress must have been unable to achieve such high standards, especially those operating in areas where only illegal or semi-legal activities could be conducted. But the real test of the support enjoyed was the extent to which unions were able to propel the working class into action. On this count, even if the mass uprising that later accompanied the Northern Expedition after it set forth in July 1926 is left out of consideration, it seems legitimate to regard the Third Congress and the All-China General Union as truly representative of the vast majority of the Chinese proletariat.

The vast majority, yes, but not the whole of the proletariat. For especially in Canton, despite the appreciable progress made by the left-wing unions there during 1925–26, there still remained a reformist section of the labor movement, imbued with the old guild traditions and influential enough to make the Third Congress consider it necessary to make a public gesture toward it. This consisted of an open letter composed just before the congress broke up and addressed to the two main moderate organizations in Canton: the Kwangtung provincial federation of unions, and the Mechanics' Union.[108] The letter urged these two organizations to enter into negotiations with their counterparts, the Hong Kong General Union and the Canton Workers' Delegates' Conference, in order to achieve unity in the labor movement. The year before, the Second Congress had merely enumerated 19 leaders of moderate unions whom they denounced as kung-tsei, among whom the leaders of the Mechanics' Union and of the provincial federation figured prominently.[109] But now it was clear from the activities conducted by these two right-wing organizations in Canton from the very beginning of the strike and the boycott that they still exerted considerable influence among certain important sections of the Cantonese proletariat.

Political Conflict in the Labor Movement

The Canton Mechanics' Union was the more active and vigorous of the two groups. Many of its members were the special type of worker found in Canton and the surrounding neighborhood, where small enterprises that were technologically modernized but that still retained something of the social relationships of the old craft workshops predominated; others were mechanics and electricians employed in various capacities in all the big industrial enterprises in Canton and Hong Kong. What we have here, in fact, is that rare thing in China, a labor aristocracy, as is indicated by the rather high entrance fee to the union (10 yuan).[110] The union openly proclaimed its adherence to guild traditions, and did not hesitate to place the interests of its members before, and apart from, the interests of the working class as a whole. It placed its hope for the future on the gradual modernization of Cantonese industry rather than on the general development of union organization and strike action. "The twentieth century is the age of mechanized industry, and machines are replacing men," it declared in a manifesto of January 1926, in which the emphasis lay on the comparative ease with which employers in mechanized industry could reduce production costs and raise wages.[111] The union was in fact placed in a favorable position by the mechanization of a number of craft industries in Canton such as flour milling, oil pressing, and weaving, with resulting appeals from employers to provide skilled labor to replace the craftsmen who had operated the discarded manually operated machinery.[112] In 1925 and 1926 there were a number of conflicts, sometimes leading to violent brawls, between the craftsmen's unions and the Mechanics' Union,[113] and there were frequent clashes between the "corps of guards" of the left-wing unions and the highly trained sports teams of the Mechanics' Union, which preferred recreational activities to political education.[114]

The opposition between the Mechanics' Union and the left-wing unions became more pronounced in 1925 and 1926 as the mechanics became less and less enthusiastic about the political tendencies and revolutionary aims of the Cantonese proletariat as a whole. The union was prevented by its long-standing ties with the Kuomintang from expressing open disapproval of the "three new policies" of 1924, but it adopted a very cautious attitude toward them. In 1924 it had declined to take part in the Canton Workers' Delegates' Conference convened by Liao Chung-k'ai, or in the suppression, led by that body, of the Merchant Volunteers' revolt. In May 1925 it stayed away from the Second National Labor Congress, although it had taken part in the first one. It was slow to join in the Canton–Hong Kong strike and boycott in 1925, and showed little enthusiasm when it did; and in July it cooperated with the big Chinese compradores of Hong Kong in forming the Labor Maintenance Society, which was in fact a center for recruitment of hsin-kung.[115] Its chief concern was to arrive at a rapid settlement of the dispute.[116]

As the strike wore on and the influence of the left wing was apparently increasing not only among the Cantonese working class but also within the Nationalist government itself,[117] the anti-Communist attitude of the mechanics hardened. In January 1926 they formed themselves into a properly constituted union, having until then been officially no more than a "Society for the Support of Mechanical Industry." They strengthened their internal organization by transforming the clubs in the various enterprises where members were employed into local branches, and by creating twenty different trade sections (for electrical workers, mechanized-loom operators, and so forth). The manifesto they published on this occasion reaffirmed their adherence to corporate principles and reformist policies and proclaimed their "undying hatred of Communism," while at the same time upholding the Three People's Principles and expressing their desire to improve the conditions of the working class.[118] Their hostility toward the left-wing unions was further increased during the winter of 1925–26 by the success of these unions in organizing the railwaymen on the three Kwangtung lines. The mechanics had always regarded these railwaymen as belonging to their union because of their qualifications as skilled workers; but at the beginning of 1926, the Kwangtung railwaymen formed an amalgamated union of their own, affiliated with the Workers' Delegates' Conference.[119] The rivalry between the Mechanics' Union and the Railwaymen's Union became very bitter toward the end of 1926, and sometimes resulted in pitched battles.[120]

The second of the organizations that supported the right wing of the Kuomintang, the provincial federation of Kwangtung unions (or, by its official title, the Kwangtung General Union), was a federation of about thirty unions, mostly for craft workers, with a total membership of around thirty thousand.[121] Its president was Ch'en Sen, founder of the union for restaurants that served bowls of noodles. He was well known to be closely associated with Cantonese employers, and he seems to have collaborated with them on several occasions by forming unions in one or two industries such as the match industry, the members of which would be rather more docile than those of the unions affiliated with the Workers' Delegates' Conference.[122]

The class basis of the provincial federation was quite different from that of the Mechanics' Union, but both organizations were equally hostile toward the left-wing unions. Antagonism between the right and left wings of the labor movement was already apparent when cooperation between the Kuomintang and the Communists was established in 1924, but it became more violent in 1925–26—not that union rivalries were anything new in Canton. Particularist trends and demarcation of trades had often led to conflict between the various porters' guilds, for instance, or between Hoifung and Cantonese rickshaw men, or between craftsmen and the mechanics who took their jobs as mechanization was introduced.[123] But in 1925–26 these customary disputes took on a specifically political aspect if one of the parties belonged to the left-wing unions and the other to the reformist organizations, each being given moral and practical support by the side to which it belonged. In August 1925 a brawl in which three people were killed occurred between members of the silk guild affiliated with the provincial federation and members of a silk-workers' union supported by the Workers' Delegates' Conference.[124] Similarly, one of the two dockers' associations that were frequently in conflict, with the support of the pickets of the Canton–Hong Kong Strike Committee, prevented members of the other from working.[125] The trouble in Swatow in January 1926 between seamen and hotel porters over which of them had the right to carry travelers' luggage was probably not unconnected with the political affiliations of the Seamen's Union, which was supported by the Strike Committee.[126] Political considerations also entered into the contentions between the railwaymen and the mechanics;[127] and the dispute between the latter and the workers in the unmechanized oil-pressing mills, which was primarily an economic dispute, ended by making the oil mill workers ardent supporters of the Workers' Delegates' Conference.[128]

The acute question of unemployment also intensified union rivalries. Each labor organization was primarily concerned to provide its members with the best opportunities of finding work, even if this was to the disadvantage of other organizations. An inquiry conducted by the Canton Municipal Council at the beginning of 1927 put the number of unemployed at about sixty thousand, and found that out of a total of 180 unions, 123 had unemployed members.[129] Of the approximately thirteen thousand members of the union for the unmechanized oil mills, about six thousand were unemployed in 1926. Teng Chung-hsia, in concluding his detailed analysis of the internal dissensions within the Cantonese labor movement, states that "the unemployed were prepared to support any politician, any employer, or any kung-tsei who enabled them to find a job."[130] Apparently the crisis of 1923-24 in China's national industry was still alive in Kwangtung in 1925-26, despite the trade revival brought about by the Hong Kong boycott.[131]

The left-wing unions were seriously disturbed by the dissensions within the labor movement. When the Workers' Delegates' Conference failed to get its opponents, the Mechanics' Union and the provincial federation, to join forces and attend its conference in April 1926,[132] all it could do was to pass a resolution[133] calling upon the workers of Canton to realize that in the atmosphere of comparative political freedom that existed in the South it was not surprising that employers should have recourse to "divide and rule" methods, since they were unable to attack the labor movement directly. To be sure, the resolution characterized these dissensions as a serious difficulty that must be remedied as soon as possible. Mere resolutions, however, were in themselves scarcely capable of mending the split within the Chinese proletariat, and the May Day celebrations of 1926 consisted of two separate processions: that of the Workers' Delegates' Conference, and that of the Mechanics' Union and the provincial federation.[134]

The split was to some extent the reflection of class differences within the Cantonese proletariat and of its acute economic difficulties, but it was also an aspect of the wider conflict that, since the death of Sun Yat-sen, had been developing more and more openly between the right and left wings of the Kuomintang. The Workers' Delegates' Conference had enjoyed the support of Liao Chung-k'ai until his death, but it then took up a position much closer to that of the Communists. On the other hand, the provincial federation maintained good relations with Hu Han-min and the right-wing elements.[135] The Mechanics' Union for its part had more than once demonstrated its antagonism to the left wing of the party, and with the help of supporters had tried during the summer of 1925 to organize a strike in Canton and Sanshui that was really a personal attack against Wang Ching-wei, one of the main left-wing leaders.[136] It also gave active support to Chiang Kai-shek in his dispute with the left during the political crisis in the spring of 1926.

Resurgence of Right-wing Elements in the KMT

The alliance between the Nationalist government and the labor movement remained unshaken throughout the period of the strike and the boycott, and officially the two parties to it were still on good terms, although the growing conflict between the right and the left within the government raised problems that had by no means been solved when the Northern Expedition set out in July 1926.

The left clearly had the upper hand both in the government and in the

Kuomintang until the beginning of 1926. The crisis caused in August by the assassination of Liao Chung-k'ai, one of its most determined and most popular leaders, ended to its advantage. Hu Han-min, whose brother was directly involved in the assassination, had to go into exile, and the Minister of War, Hsü Ch'ung-chih, was sent "on leave" to Shanghai. Wang Ching-wei and the other left-wing leaders were left in command of the situation.[137] The departure of Hsü Ch'ung-chih enabled them to put into effect the decisions on military affairs taken in June; thus, all the Cantonese armies were combined into one "Army of the Party," the various units of which were known simply by number.[138] At the Second National Congress of the Kuomintang held in January there were 98 left-wing delegates who were in favor of the alliance with the Soviet Union and with the Communist Party and of support for the labor movement, as against 65 from the center and three from the right.[139] They hesitated, however, to exploit their position to the full, and the new Central Executive Committee was made up of 14 left-wing members and seven Communists, as against 15 center and right-wing members.[140] But the congress reaffirmed its approval of the general line of the party and of the government's continued application of the "three new policies" of 1924, and it voted both to renew the contract with Borodin and the other Soviet advisers,[141] and to have Wang Ching-wei and his group continue as leaders.

At the time the congress was held, and until the end of the winter, the Cantonese labor movement and the Kuomintang leadership supported each other to the full. The right-wing intrigues that were to end in the assassination of Liao Chung-k'ai became more open at the beginning of the summer, and on August 11 the unions organized a big parade demanding the dismissal of both civilian and military right-wing figures.[142] The departure of Hu Han-min and Hsü Ch'ung-chih several weeks later helped to satisfy these demands. In November the Second Eastern Expedition, which finally got rid of Ch'en Chiung-ming and recaptured Swatow, was also supported by the labor organizations, which cooperated with the regular army and provided detachments for transport and for propaganda. The Seamen's Union provided an ambulance corps.[143] These auxiliary units were recruited from Hong Kong strikers who had withdrawn to Canton, and the government expressed its appreciation through Ch'en Kung-po, who was in charge of the Labor Department and who decorated 3,800 of them when the Expedition ended in victory.[144] The Cantonese troops and the strikers' detachments together made a triumphal entry into Swatow, which had been occupied by Ch'en Chiung-ming's army for two months. The president of the local branch of the Seamen's Union became chief of police,[145] and Chou En-lai, who was political adviser to the Expedition, celebrated the recapture of the city with a lengthy speech made on November 12 to an audience composed of the membership of all the Swatow unions.[146] The Canton government, for its part, was equally faithful in its support for the general activities of the labor movement in the territory under its control. As soon as the Shakee Road incident became known, it protested to the diplomatic corps in Peking.[147] It gave a large subsidy to the Strike Committee and provided it with all sorts of services, such as free travel permits on the section of the Canton-Kowloon railway that was under its control.[148] When Ch'en Kung-po became head of the Labor Department after the death of Liao Chung-k'ai, he continued to implement the policy of support for the labor movement,[149] and set up a commission (on which the unions were well represented) for drawing up labor legislation.[150] At the Second National Congress of the Kuomintang in January 1926, a number of resolutions on labor problems that were adopted were much more detailed than the decisions on matters of principle taken at the congress of 1924.[151] These resolutions recognized that the party had failed to carry out the 1924 decisions for improving the living standards of workers, and that the work of the Labor Departments that had been created at all party levels since 1924 had not been satisfactory. The congress then got down to working out a detailed program of social reform which included putting labor legislation into effect, establishing the eight-hour day, the minimum wage, workers' insurance, and measures for the protection of women and children, and abolishing the pao-kung system. This program was very similar to those of the Second and Third Labor Congresses of May 1925 and May 1926; but its implementation was deferred until after the completion of the Nationalist revolution. Another resolution adopted by the Kuomintang Congress of January 1926 was one declaring the need to respect the independence of the unions, which at the same time added that the party must retain the political leadership; and yet another urged that more importance be given to the activities of the Labor Departments of the Kuomintang.[152]

A contributory factor in the maintenance of good relations between the labor movement and the Nationalist government was the effect the strike and the boycott had on economic activities in Canton and in Kwangtung as a whole. The strike dealt a very hard blow to commercial and financial interests in Hong Kong. Port activities slowed down considerably,[153] the price of land on the island fell by half,[154] and the revenue of the Hong Kong government dwindled, while its expenditures mounted.[155] The boycott, during its first weeks in July and August, was extended to all ships and cargoes handled in the ports of Kwangtung, without exception. This meant that the whole province, and Canton in particular, suffered from a scarcity, and a rise in price, of imported commodities such as coal; and difficulties were also experienced in disposing of local products such as silk.[156] But at the beginning of September the Strike Committee and the Canton chambers of commerce met together and decided to allow non-British ships and cargoes to circulate freely, and the "special permits" that had until then been requisite were abolished.[157]

The decision to ease the boycott was a deliberate one on the part of the

leaders of the Strike Committee, and was made in order to encourage a revival of trade in Canton and to stimulate local capitalist enterprise. Slogans
such as "Long live the unity between workers and merchants"[158] and "Let us
strengthen the economic independence of Kwangtung"[159] figured frequently
at this time in the publications of the Strike Committee; and a letter to the
strikers sent by the Third Labor Congress in May 1926 stated: "Your struggle
has been of great benefit to the merchants and has strengthened the united
front of merchants and workers."[160] In point of fact, as soon as the boycott
was eased, the Hong Kong crisis brought substantial economic benefits to
Canton and the Canton bourgeoisie. Hitherto, Hong Kong had been able to
exercise control over Canton's trade through the warehouses it had there, and
also because its paper currency, used throughout the province, enjoyed greater
confidence than the banknotes issued by the Kwangtung provincial government. Now, however, this control was lost, and it was the provincial government's banknotes that soared in value.[161] Because of the boycott, trade
in Canton from July to September was appreciably below what it had been
in 1924; but from October it rose well above the 1924 figures. (See Fig. 1.)
The monthly returns of trade for the province of Kwangtung were at the low
figure of 830,000 yuan in 1922, and fell to 665,000 yuan in 1924, when Sun
Yat-sen was hardly able to maintain control over Canton alone. But in August
1925 the figure rose to 1.5 million yuan, and in November to 3.8 million yuan,[162]
as a result both of the trade revival brought about by the strike and of the
reconquest of the eastern areas of the province and the gradual elimination
of private armies.

   Thus, throughout the period of the strike and the boycott, the Cantonese
labor movement, under the aegis of the Nationalist government, faithfully
fulfilled its obligations to the alliance it had formed with the bourgeoisie of

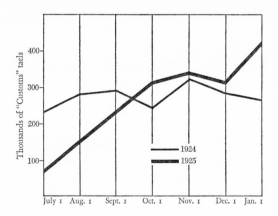

Fig. 1. Fluctuations in Canton trade, July through December, 1924 and 1925 (based on customs reports).

the South. But it got very little in return. The economic advantages accruing to right-wing elements in the Nationalist revolution from the strike did not in any way prevent them from being well aware of the political dangers the resurgence of the labor movement held for them. Already during the summer of 1925 these right-wing elements, and indeed all those who were opposed to the alliances made in 1924, were extremely active within the Kuomintang, and were steadily gaining influence right up until the departure of the Northern Expedition in July 1926.

During the second half of 1925 these right-wing elements began to reorganize themselves after the temporary setback they had suffered as a result of the assassination of Liao Chung-k'ai. In November they held a meeting in the vicinity of the tomb of Sun Yat-sen in the Western Hills near Peking in order to express their opposition to the line taken by the Kuomintang. Those who attended came to be known as the "Western Hills Group." Shortly afterward they set up a center in Shanghai for the purpose of contesting the Canton leadership of the Kuomintang, which they described as having been "bolshevized." Their many supporters in Canton formed a "Society for the Study of Sun-yatsenism," which was no less antagonistic than the Western Hills Group to the Communists and their left-wing allies. This society was supported by important figures among the Southern bourgeoisie such as Chien Chao-nan, a director of the Nanyang Brothers' Tobacco Company, and Chang Ching-chiang, who had made an enormous fortune on the Shanghai Stock Exchange; and, in a discreet sort of way, it was on friendly terms with the general in command of the Whampoa Military Academy, Chiang Kai-shek, who was Sun Yat-sen's brother-in-law and a personal friend of Chang Ching-chiang, whom he had come to know in stockbrokers' circles in Shanghai.[163]

At the Kuomintang Congress in January 1926 the left wing was greatly in the majority, but no attempt was made to break with the entire right wing. Only members of the Western Hills Group, which at the time was holding its own breakaway congress in Shanghai, were excluded from office. Sun K'o, Sun Yat-sen's son by his first marriage and the leader of the "prince's group," was elected to membership on the Central Committee, and Tai Chi-t'ao, the chief exponent of anti-Communist nationalism and a sponsor of the Western Hills meeting,[164] was reelected, despite the fact that both were notoriously hostile to collaboration with the Communists and support of the labor movement. It was also around this time that Chien Chao-nan was appointed chief adviser to the Canton government,[165] and Chang Ching-chiang returned to Canton from Shanghai.[166]

This attempt to arrive at a compromise with the right wing, together with the persistence of powerful right-wing influence in Canton, accounts for the deterioration of relations between the Cantonese labor movement and the Nationalist government just at a time—that is, during the fall and winter of 1925-26—when they appeared to be at their best. Several occurrences led to this deterioration of relations. In November the military commander in Canton, Wu T'ieh-ch'eng, who was a moderate, made an unsuccessful attempt to disarm the Strike Committee's pickets;[167] and in December the pickets were given the choice either of disbanding or of coming under government control, so that they were forced to become units attached to the regular army.[168] Wu T'ieh-ch'eng, as well as being military commander, was also head of the Labor Department of the Canton branch of the Kuomintang, and in March 1926 he set up a "Canton Municipal Council Labor Committee," formed expressly for the purpose of tightening his control over the unions.[169]

Further significant incidents occurred in Swatow during November. The provisional chairman of the Municipal Council, a man who belonged to the extreme left and who had been appointed by Chou En-lai, was replaced, on orders from the Canton government, by a man belonging to the center faction of the Kuomintang.[170]

So far, incidents of this kind were no more than cautious feelers; but with the coup of March 20, the counterattack of the moderates against the labor movement and the whole of the left wing reached a new intensity. On March 20, 1926, Chiang Kai-shek, the commanding general of the Nationalist government's army and since the January congress a member of the Central Committee of the Kuomintang, put Canton under military occupation on the pretext that he was defending it against a plot that was supposedly being prepared with the support of the gunboat *Chung-shan,* which was anchored off Canton and was commanded by a Communist. About fifty Communist militants were arrested, most of whom were political advisers to the Whampoa Military Academy or to the army; and the headquarters of the Canton–Hong Kong Strike Committee were searched by Chiang's troops.[171] This affair was afterwards officially regarded as a misunderstanding. Those who had been arrested were very soon released, the Strike Committee renewed its activities, and Chiang Kai-shek publicly reaffirmed his loyalty to the Communist alliance and his faith in the Soviet advisers.[172] Probably his intentions were confined to sounding out his opponents and discovering what sort of a fight they were able to put up. He undoubtedly realized that the moment had not yet come for a complete break with the Communist Party, whose skill in mobilizing the masses had been demonstrated by the success of the strike and the boycott, and whose support the bourgeois moderates were anxious to retain in view of the imminent departure of the Northern Expedition. A trial of strength with the vigorous left-wing organizations of Canton, which were reinforced by tens of thousands of Hong Kong strikers, was too risky, and in any case public opinion was not yet ready for it.

Nevertheless, even if Chiang had not carried his attempt through to its logical conclusion, he had still delivered a severe blow to the left wing, whose leader, Wang Ching-wei, hastened to stand down in favor of the man who was clearly becoming his direct rival.[173] On May 15 a meeting of the Central

Executive Committee of the Kuomintang was held that showed which way the wind was blowing in the matter of power.

At this meeting a number of decisions were taken concerning proposals put forward by Chiang Kai-shek under cover of putting party affairs in order, all of which revealed the decline of left-wing influence. They included decisions to forbid Kuomintang members from belonging to any other party, to make it compulsory for the Communist Party to provide a list of its members who had joined the Kuomintang, to make Communists ineligible for leading posts in the army and the government, to limit the proportion of Communist members of any unit of the Kuomintang at whatever level to 33 per cent, and to require that all directives issued by the Comintern be made known to a Committee to be appointed containing members of both parties.[174] The Kuomintang members of this committee all belonged to the right wing: Sun K'o, Chang Ching-chiang, and Chiang Kai-shek.[175] The new political line immediately became evident when, in June 1926, the southern section of the Canton-Hankow railway, which Sun Yat-sen had nationalized in 1923, was returned to the former shareholders,[176] and the oil monopoly that Liao Chung-k'ai had established in Kwangtung in 1925 in order to keep out British and American companies was abolished.[177]

The coup of March 20 and the decisions of May 15 meant an end, sooner or later, to the policy of mutual support that had been carried out for several years by the Nationalist government and the Cantonese labor movement. During the weeks following May 15 a number of measures were introduced that were disadvantageous to the strike and the boycott. The Strike Committee was told that it must not allow its pickets to enter the houses of foreigners; the gambling houses, which had been closed in June 1925 in order to house strikers, were reopened;[178] and the pickets were forbidden to make arrests without police permission.[179] Moreover it was now openly admitted in government circles that in order to get rid of these embarrassing partners, the dispute with Hong Kong must be settled as soon as possible. As early as April, Su Chao-cheng had been asked to put forward proposals for a settlement of the strike,[180] and the Canton government now took in hand the negotiations with Hong Kong, which hitherto had been conducted solely by the Strike Committee and the chambers of commerce.[181] A government decree of May 31 gave public notice of the need for a rapid settlement of the strike, and announced that the Minister of Foreign Affairs was going to take the necessary measures at once.

This withdrawal on the part of the Nationalist government was also evident in the labor policy it pursued during the four months between the March 20 incident and the departure of the Northern Expedition. At the meeting of the Central Executive Committee on May 15, when the party leadership passed to the right wing, a 54-hour week was decided on instead of the week of six eight-hour days laid down at the Second Kuomintang Congress in January.

This was merely a decision on principle;[182] but the decree of May 31, as well as urging a settlement of the strike and the boycott, also announced the creation of an Arbitration Bureau for labor disputes, to be composed of a government official as chairman and an equal number of employers' and workers' representatives as members; the decisions of this body were to be final. The decree also announced measures for strengthening the Cantonese police and for suppressing all "disorders" resulting from individual initiatives.[183] This was primarily aimed against the picket lines formed by many of the left-wing unions, on the model of those of the Strike Committee, during the past few months. Chiang Kai-shek began disarming the railwaymen's pickets as early as April and May.[184] Ch'en Kung-po, the weak and hesitant head of the Labor Department, who had taken over after the death of Liao Chung-k'ai, was hardly the type to stand up against the change in the government's policy. On the contrary, he fell in with it, and in June asked the unions to provide lists of the names of their members.[185] He also refused to support the demands of the employees of the hotels in Canton who went on strike at the end of May to protest the hotel owners' employment of men from Hong Kong.[186] On July 7 he resigned on the grounds that he found it impossible to settle the disputes between unions and employers or between the unions themselves.[187]

How did the labor organizations react to this return of the right wing to ascendancy in the Kuomintang and the Nationalist government? Neither the Strike Committee, nor the All-China General Union, nor the Canton Workers' Delegates' Conference made any protest about the compromise reached at the congress in January 1926 or took action against the March 20 coup and the measures introduced in May and June, which were the first real blows struck against the labor movement. This conciliatory attitude and absence of opposition were partly due to the astutely equivocal behavior of Chiang Kai-shek himself,[188] but they were rather surprising in view of the way in which, under other circumstances, the Cantonese proletariat and its organizations had actively intervened in order to tip the scales in favor of the left, as in September and October of 1924 in the Merchant Volunteers affair, or on August 11, 1925, when the mass demonstration against the army and compradore elements in the Canton government was held. Moreover, since the unions were now very much stronger than on these previous occasions, their cautious attitude during the winter and spring of 1926 seems all the stranger, and must surely have been deliberate.

Certainly the leaders of the big Chinese labor organizations and the Communist Party itself seem, perhaps for tactical reasons, to have been careful to play down the significance of the March 20 incident. This does not mean that they ignored or failed to denounce in general terms "the tendency on the part of the upper bourgeoisie to desert the united front because of class interests at a time when the working class is supporting and leading a genuine anti-imperialist movement," or the attempts of imperialists "to persuade the

Chinese capitalists to take sides with them."[189] But when it came to detailed criticism of "the reactionary activities of the upper bourgeoisie and their tendency to compromise," as contained in Liu Shao-ch'i's report to the Third Labor Congress, the only examples cited were taken from areas under the control of the warlords or the Western Powers: the dilatory attitude of the Shanghai Chamber of Commerce in May and June 1925, the collusion between the owners of the Chengchow cotton mill and the armed bands that attacked the union there in September 1925, the part played by the Hanyehping Company in closing down the Anyuan workers' club in September 1925, and the measures taken by the bourgeoisie of Wuhan and Peking to check the May Thirtieth Movement in the summer of 1925.[190] Nothing at all was said about the March 20 incident. At the Second Congress of the Kuomintang a special resolution was passed supporting the labor movement against the intrigues of the "warlords, the big compradores, and other tools of the imperialists,"[191] but no reference was made to the influence of these men in Canton and within the Nationalist government itself.

If anyone in the labor movement ventured to assess the strength of the right wing in the Kuomintang, a very narrow definition of what constituted the right wing was adopted. In the article in *Hsiang-tao* of December 1925 written by Ch'en Tu-hsiu in his capacity as General Secretary of the Communist Party, the right wing figured merely as the remnants of former ephemeral groups such as the "Political Science Group" formed by the Chinese conservative bourgeoisie between 1915 and 1920.[192] And in May 1926 Ch'en Tu-hsiu defined the right wing merely in terms of those in opposition to Chiang and Wang, and was quite satisfied that it was only the Western Hills Group who were expelled from the party at the Kuomintang Congress in January.[193]

It was on the question of the role of Chiang Kai-shek that this attitude, which was later condemned as opportunist, was most evident. Ch'en Tu-hsiu made every effort to avoid all criticism of him and to present the March 20 affair as an accident that would have no further consequences; in his account of the affair in *Hsiang-tao*, he was still referring to Chiang as a "pillar of the revolution."[194] He ended another article with the following ambiguous remarks: "We all have the duty to support the present Canton government. The Canton coup was potentially capable of overthrowing the Nationalist government. That is why whoever was responsible for it, whether it was a case of a Communist plot against Chiang or a right-wing plot against the Communists, should be punished by the nation and by the Nationalist government. No one, and no party, should try to shelter them."[195]

All Communist and labor movement texts of this period repeat over and over again that absolute priority must be given to the struggle against Wu P'ei-fu, Chang Tso-lin, and the other Northern warlords, and that the political alliance with the right wing of the Nationalist movement and with the Nationalist government must be retained at all costs. The resolution on "the rise of the labor movement and its role in the Nationalist revolution" adopted at the Third Labor Congress described the working class as the ruling class and called upon it to oppose the reactionary tendencies of the "big capitalists," but refrained from stating who these were.[196] The logical conclusion of all this was that the labor movement should continue to give unconditional support to the Canton government and its proposed Northern Expedition, and that no mention should be made of the March 20 crisis. This was implied in the resolutions on "the social and political situation" and on "the present situation of the Nationalist government" passed by the Third Labor Congress,[197] the second of which concluded by declaring: "The Nationalist government must be supported in their campaign against the Northern forces, which have regained strength following the defeat of the Kuominchun and of Kuo Sungling; the line adopted by this and the preceding Congress with regard to the role of the Nationalist government in the struggle against imperialism is entirely correct." The same line was adopted by various union conferences held in the spring, such as that of the Canton Workers' Delegates on April 1.[198]

An illustration of the uncertainty of attitude in the Cantonese labor movement just before the departure of the Northern Expedition is provided by the activities of a new organization known as "the Alliance of Workers, Merchants, Intellectuals, and Peasants of Kwangtung," formed immediately after the Third Labor Congress. It seems to have been in the nature of a top-level "get-together," and although it was jointly sponsored by the All-China General Union and by the Canton chambers of commerce,[199] it was thought to have close ties with Chiang Kai-shek;[200] and in fact it presented seven demands to the government on May 18, including demands for a settlement of the Hong Kong strike, the abolition of the government oil monopoly, the creation of an arbitration tribunal for labor disputes, the maintenance of public order, and the development of the port of Whampoa. Curiously enough, these demands corresponded point by point with the measures introduced by Chiang and announced in the decree of May 31.[201]

Altogether, it seems clear that the refusal to mount a counterattack against the new right-wing offensive was a tactical withdrawal on the part of the labor movement in the interest of maintaining a united front with the right wing because of the absolute priority given to the joint struggle against the Northern warlords, for which purpose it was essential that everything be done to make the Northern Expedition, now imminent, a success. To what extent was there opposition to this political line among the leaders of the left-wing unions and in the Chinese Communist Party? This is not the place in which to examine this problem in depth, since it concerns both the history of Chinese Communism and that of the international labor movement as a whole, and would involve a consideration of the role played by the Comintern and its representatives in China, and of the dissensions within the Chinese Communist Party. We are still far from knowing the full details about the failure of the Chinese revolutionaries to carry out their program in 1924-27, despite the many studies of this period made by distinguished writers. Nevertheless, it seems certain, for one thing, that the policy of compromise with the bourgeoisie advocated by Ch'en Tu-hsiu and the rest of the leadership of the Chinese Communist Party was supported by the Comintern, and, for another, that this policy met with vigorous opposition within the Communist Party and also within the Strike Committee, although party discipline prevented its being expressed openly. Some Communists, such as Chang Kuo-t'ao, advocated a policy of "splendid isolation," i.e. of having nothing more to do with the Kuomintang,[202] while militant trade unionists such as Su Chao-cheng, Teng Chung-hsia, and Hsiang Ying and leaders of the peasant movement such as Mao Tse-tung and P'eng P'ai, together with other leading Communist cadres such as Ts'ai Ho-sen and Chou En-lai, remained in favor of support for the Northern Expedition and for the alliance with the bourgeoisie, but maintained that action should be taken against the consequences of the March 20 coup.[203] Although they failed to win their case, they did at least succeed in postponing immediate settlement of the Hong Kong strike as demanded by Ch'en Tu-hsiu, who accused the Cantonese Communists of leftist tendencies that led them to ignore the difficulties and needs of the bourgeoisie.[204]

The radical tendencies within the Cantonese labor movement were expressed in a resolution adopted at the meeting of the Workers' Delegates' Conference on April 1, 1926, stressing the need to "take up a class attitude toward political events" and to give public demonstration of this attitude; this was a clear reference to the events of the preceding week and the labor movement's feeble response to them.[205] The members of the Strike Committee seem to have unanimously accepted the idea that it was possible to support the Kuomintang and the Nationalist government while at the same time opposing the influence within them of the upper bourgeoisie. In a pamphlet by Teng Chung-hsia published in Canton at this time he declared that "the capitalists and the proletariat are now struggling for the leadership of the revolution."[206] But these currents of opposition were not strong enough to prevent the majority of the Chinese Communists and the organizations that they controlled from following the "opportunist" line adopted by Ch'en Tu-hsiu.

The same hesitations were apparent in the attitude of the labor movement toward the poor and middle peasants, despite the emergence of a peasant movement during 1925-26 resulting in the existence of as many as 4,727 village peasant unions in Kwangtung by June 1926, with a total membership of 647,000. These unions, following the example of those founded in 1921 by the Communist P'eng P'ai in the Haifeng and Lufeng districts, were beginning to take a stand against the landowners and their tax collectors, to oppose arbitrary exactions, and to campaign for lower rents,[207] and at the provincial congress of peasant unions held in May 1926 it was decided to form defense corps that could put up a fight against the armed bands of the landowners and the rural gentry of Kwangtung.[208] The Canton government had given some support to the peasant movement. Although its "Workers' and Peasants' Department" was mainly concerned with the trade unions,[209] it also allocated a sum of 18,000 yuan per month to activities among the peasants[210] and sponsored a "School for the Chinese Peasant Movement," which functioned in Canton in 1925 and 1926 and was directed by Mao Tse-tung.[211] In return, the peasants had assisted the government at several moments of crisis, such as June 1925, when the mercenaries of Generals Liu and Yang were evicted, and during the Second Eastern Campaign against Ch'en Chiung-ming in October and November 1925. The latter expedition in particular had had the active cooperation of the Haifeng and Lufeng peasant unions, which supplied guides and scouts, provisions, and porters[212] and even took part in the fighting, although armed only with pikes and javelins.[213]

A resolution on cooperation between workers and peasants was passed at every Canton labor conference,[214] but prior to the Northern Expedition they had collaborated only occasionally. When the Expedition set forth, nothing had been done to implement decisions taken at the Workers' Delegates' meeting in April to form a workers' and peasants' club, publish a workers' and peasants' newspaper, or form a committee to coordinate the activities of Kwangtung workers' and peasants' unions. Yet, as we have seen, the peasant unions and the strike pickets did collaborate during the strike and the boycott.[215] The peasants supplied provisions and helped the pickets in hunting out smugglers; and in turn, the pickets stood with the peasants against the armed bands (*min-t'uan,* literally "people's corps") of landowners who kept trying to send their agricultural produce to Hong Kong.[216] The great success of the joint demonstration of delegates of the Third National Labor Congress and of the first provincial congress of peasant unions held in Canton in May 1926 was another indication that cooperation between workers and peasants was possible.

The failure to make full use of the peasants' potential capacity for cooperation was partly due to the inherent circumstances of the situation, but also to the attitude of the labor organizations. They still regarded the peasants simply as an auxiliary force. A special resolution passed at the Third Labor Congress explicitly referred to the supporting role of the peasants in relation to the regular army, pointing out that this accounted for the success of the Second Eastern Expedition as compared with the defeat of the Kuominchun in Honan.[217] The resolution on general policy was still more explicit. It maintained that, because the peasants were dispersed in small villages and small units of production, it was difficult for them to play an active part in political struggles and that for the time being their fate depended on the outcome of events in the big cities. Further, it described the peasants as the "rear guard" (*hou-tun*) of the labor movement.[218] This analysis of the respective roles of workers and peasants in the Chinese revolution was, however, soon to be proved incorrect in the course of the Cantonese army's march through the rural areas of the Lower Yangtze valley during the summer of 1926.

On July 7, the Central Executive Committee of the Kuomintang held a special meeting, and issued a manifesto announcing the long-awaited departure of the Northern Expedition and the appointment of Chiang Kai-shek as head of the party, the army, and the government.[219] The Chinese labor movement was now faced with new responsibilities and also with new dangers. It had acquired great prestige during the May Thirtieth Movement in Shanghai and in Central and North China and also during the strike and the boycott in Canton and Hong Kong, which had now been going for 13 months. It is true that in Central and North China all the labor organizations affiliated with the All-China General Union had had to work underground after the defeat of the Kuominchun at the beginning of 1926 and the subsequent consolidation of the forces of Wu P'ei-fu, Chang Tso-lin, and Sun Ch'uan-fang. The decline in the labor movement was particularly marked among the miners and railwaymen, and in the big cities such as Peking, Tientsin, and Hankow.[220] But the All-China General Union, despite this temporary setback, and despite certain weaknesses in its internal organization, was now by far the most powerful of the Chinese labor organizations. The left wing of the labor movement had almost completely eclipsed its former adversaries, the Canton guilds and the semi-working-class associations of Shanghai, and was now in a position to play an important part in helping the Canton armies to conquer the whole of China. With the victorious advance of these armies, leftists could take up posts in the big industrial centers as they became liberated and intervene actively in social and political affairs. On the other hand, the right-wing elements were merely biding their time to renounce the "three new policies" of 1924; and because the labor movement had decided not to put up any resistance to the right-wing counterattack during the spring of 1926, it now ran the risk of finding its difficulties increased by the very victories it was helping the Nationalist government to win.

CHAPTER XIII

The Labor Movement During the Northern Expedition

During the summer and fall of 1926 the Northern Expedition won some decisive victories. The Cantonese armies reached Changsha on July 17; and they took Yochow, the key to the Middle Yangtze valley, on August 22. By September 6 they had occupied Hankow and Hanyang, and early in October they took Wuchang, which was able to put up more resistance because of its fortified walls. An attack in Kiangsi was begun in September, but Sun Ch'uan-fang held out there more tenaciously than had Wu P'ei-fu in Hupeh. Kiukiang and Nanchang fell in November, after the defenders had beaten off the first attack in September. (The earlier attack had resulted in only a brief occupation of the provincial capital.) Other army divisions advancing up the coast gained control of Fukien during November and December, and reached Chekiang in February.[1] (See Map 10.)

These extensive victories were due partly to the superior organization of the Southern government armies, which had excellent leadership supplied by the Whampoa cadets, and partly to the lack of unity and coordination between the Northern warlords, particularly between Wu P'ei-fu and Sun Ch'uan-fang. This problem was aggravated by the desertion of many of their officers —especially in Central China—to the side of the revolutionary armies. Another factor of considerable importance was the "second front" in the Northwest and the diversion caused by remnants of the Kuominchun throughout the campaign. These remnants were still occupying Nankow, near Peking, when the Northern Expedition was launched, and were conducting a slow retreat along the Ching-Sui railway line. They had to abandon the siege of Tatung in August, and they evacuated Nankow in August, Suiyuan in September, and Paotow in December. But further south they succeeded in raising the siege of Sian, which had been beleaguered by Wu P'ei-fu's armies since April 1926, in November, and regained the offensive in Honan, where, in December, they occupied the Tungkwan Pass, the eastern gateway to the province; this brought them close to a link-up with the Cantonese armies, which had reached the Wushengkwan Pass on the borders of Hupeh and Honan in September. Their rearguard action in the North and their counteroffensive in Central China certainly diverted a considerable proportion of Wu P'ei-fu's forces at a decisive moment.[2] But in addition to these purely military con-

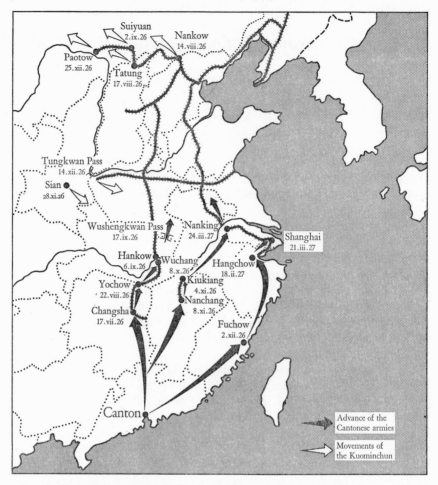

Map 10. Military Operations from the Summer of 1926 to the Spring of 1927.

siderations, political factors were of fundamental importance. The Southern government army was a revolutionary army, and was supported as such by the civilian population,[3] whereas its enemies, far from being able to count on the support of the people as a whole in the areas they still controlled, met continual opposition.

Our only concern here is with the role played by the labor movement in these military operations. The Canton–Hong Kong Strike Committee gave powerful support to the Northern Expedition as soon as it set forth from Canton, providing detachments of porters, stretcher-bearers, and propagandists, all recruited from among the strikers.[4] When the strike and boycott ended in October, the bands of pickets were integrated into the Nationalist army;[5] and during the army's march, many workers and coolies joined its ranks, especially in Hunan.[6] Anyuan miners joined the army and took part in the attack on Wuhan.[7] Many workers offered auxiliary services to the Cantonese forces. Thus, in Hunan the provincial federation of unions, which was re-formed as soon as the army entered the area, organized five corps of porters, each run by the union concerned—dockers, rickshaw men, and so on—who distributed leaflets as they transported supplies.[8] Similarly, Anyuan miners and Yueh-Han railwaymen worked as porters and scouts for the army.[9]

Workers also helped prepare the way for the entry of the revolutionary armies. In Changsha, as soon as it became known that the military commander of the Northern forces had fled after evacuating the city in order to avoid having to put up a fight,[10] the unions organized a militia that guarded the gates and the main thoroughfares of the city pending the arrival of the Southern troops.[11] The railwaymen on the Yueh-Han line got rid of the British Chief Engineer and themselves took control of the transportation of the Southern troops;[12] and in Hupeh, when Wu P'ei-fu still held the province, they sabotaged the running of the railway.[13] The workers of the Wuchang arsenal went on strike at the approach of the Nationalist army, thus holding up supplies of arms and ammunition for the Northern forces,[14] and Wu P'ei-fu failed to break the strike at the end of August even though he executed several Cantonese accused of fomenting trouble among the workers.[15] Similarly, in Nanchang it was the action taken by workers and students within the city that enabled the Southern troops to occupy it in September—only temporarily, as it happened.[16] The capture of Kiukiang in November was also accomplished with the help of supporters of the Nationalist government living in the city.[17] The importance of this cooperation between the labor organizations in the forward areas and the advancing Southern forces was again displayed by the Shanghai uprisings in February and March under the leadership of the General Union.

Union Development in Liberated Areas of Central China

In return, the labor movement benefited immediately from the victories of the Nationalist armies. As the autocratic rule of the warlords gave way in the newly conquered provinces to a form of government modeled on that of Canton,[18] unions began springing up everywhere.[19] It was in Hupeh, the center of heavy industry and of many different types of manufacture, where already in 1921 and 1922 the Labor Secretariat had succeeded in organizing large unions, that this new upsurge in the labor movement was most marked and most vigorous. A list of unions there published in November 1926[20] contains the names of 58 in Hankow, 11 in Wuchang, 4 in Hanyang, and 6 in Tayeh, with, respectively, 46,000, 21,000, 15,000, and 11,000 members. Most of them were formed in September and October, immediately after the arrival of the Cantonese army. On October 10 they combined to form a provincial federation,[21] and membership continued to rise during the fall and the winter. By the end of 1926, 200 unions with a total membership of 200,000 were registered with the authorities in the city of Wuhan alone,[22] and when the Hupeh provincial federation held its first congress in January 1927, it was attended by 580 delegates sent by 341 unions and representing 393,000 members.[23]

Union organizing went ahead in Hunan also. As soon as the Southern forces arrived, unions were formed or re-formed in 18 industrial or manufacturing centers, such as Changsha, Hengyang, Yochow, and Shuikowshan, and 32 hsien started making active preparations to do the same.[24] (See Map 11.) In Shuikowshan the miners' club that Chiang Hsien-yun and Liu Tung-hsuan had helped to found in 1922 was started up again by them.[25] A Hunan provincial federation was re-formed, and it held its first congress in December 1926.[26] In the spring of 1927 it had over 400,000 members, of which 90,000 were industrial workers.[27]

In Kiangsi there were similar activities from November on, when a general union was formed in Kiukiang.[28] In Nanchang the telephone workers', printers', and other unions set up a general union on January 1, to which 73 trade associations comprising a total of 40,000 members belonged.[29] In January, plans were made for forming a provincial federation based on the organizations already formed, or in process of formation, in Nanchang, Kiukiang, the Anyuan mines, and the potteries of Kingtehchen and among employees of the inland water transport system in Kanchow.[30] In Chekiang, unions of weavers, telephone workers, porters, postal workers, and railwaymen are mentioned at the beginning of 1927, and in February, after the area was firmly occupied by the Nationalist army, they formed a provincial federation.[31]

Of course these rapidly organized unions had not yet had time to exert any very profound influence, and the economic structure of the regions liberated by the Nationalist armies was such that the new provincial federations were by no means composed entirely of industrial workers. Apart from the transport and communications workers (railwaymen, postal workers, telephone workers, porters, rickshaw men) and the Changsha and Hangchow cotton workers, most of the members—in Kiangsi especially, and to a lesser extent in Hunan—were craftsmen, shop assistants, and workers in petty trades. Even in Hupeh, the center of heavy industry, where the Hanyang arsenal had a union with 13,500 members and the big cotton mills had unions with 9,000, 4,000, and 3,000 members,[32] the majority of the members of the provincial federation came from the ranks of those linked with small-scale production. Nevertheless, the very fact that all these unions and federations sprang up spontaneously, not to say in a quite haphazard way, is an indication of the vitality of the labor movement in the Lower Yangtze valley and of the

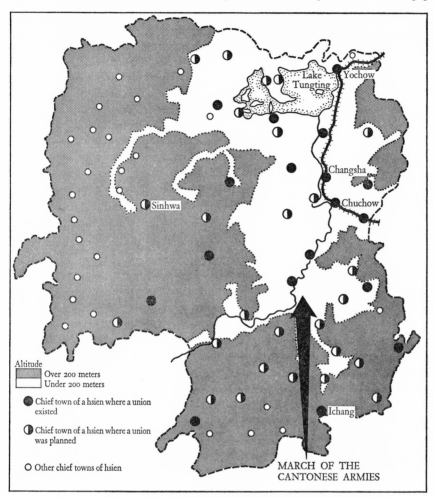

Map 11. The Development of Union Organization in Hunan in the Fall of 1926.

hopes aroused by the arrival of the Southern forces. Indeed, the Communist cadres who were working within the provincial federations—men such as Hsü Pai-hao and Liu Shao-ch'i in Hupeh,[33] and Kuo Liang in Hunan,[34]—apparently had to make great efforts to channel the movement during the following months. Judging from the rules drawn up and the resolutions adopted at the congress of the Hunan provincial federation in December and that of the Hupeh provincial federation in January, the main preoccupation seems to have been to coordinate and discipline these labor organizations that had "sprung up like mushrooms after rain." Thus at the Hupeh congress it was decided to combine all the various unions that had sprung up among the cottonworkers, the metalworkers (who had 19 unions), the employees in public utilities, the dockers (who had a separate union in each of the shipping companies),[35] and the coolies operating hand-drawn vehicles (who had a separate union for each type of vehicle), and to form a "General Industrial Union" for each of these branches of industry.[36] As at the Hunan congress held a month earlier, rules were drawn up for a highly centralized form of organization, in which each industry was to have its own union and each locality its own separate branch, while at the same time wide powers were to be given a Workers' Delegates' Conference in each industrial union. Both congresses further set up a strict hierarchy of organizations operating at both the local and industrial levels, whereby unions established in separate enterprises had to be affiliated both with the local general union and with the provincial industrial union, both of which organizations were in turn to be affiliated with the provincial federation. The Hupeh congress adopted a further resolution to the effect that in industries that had a national union, such as those of the railwaymen, the seamen, and, shortly afterwards, the postal workers, local union branches still had to belong to the provincial federation. It is difficult to assess the extent to which this rather cumbrous organizational structure was able to function effectively, but there seems little doubt that the provincial federations of Hupeh, Hunan, and later Kiangsi were based, at least as far as the main industrial centers and the main industries were concerned, on an organizational pattern similar to that laid down at these congresses. For instance, according to the reports of the delegation sent by the Red International,[37] a general union for the textile industry that was functioning in Wuhan in April 1927 was an amalgamation of the six unions formed independently in each of the cotton mills of the city during the preceding fall[38] together with the formerly separate weavers', dyers', linen-drapers', silk-spinners', and silk-weavers' unions. These eleven unions were now simply divided among various sections of the general union, each section having a branch in every enterprise where workers belonging to the category concerned were employed, and each branch having the right to elect a delegate to represent it at the higher organizational level.

The Middle Yangtze unions of 1926-27 were strictly working-class. The rules laid down by the Hunan provincial federation excluded employers, engineers, overseers, and labor contractors from membership,[39] and those laid down by the Hupeh federation contained stringent prohibitions against admitting foremen and high-ranking employees as members, and against their enjoying rights of any kind.[40] On the other hand, measures were taken to encourage female and child employees to take part in union activities, and even to become committee members.[41] At the Hupeh congress it was pointed out that if something was not done in this direction, female and child employees would tend to lose interest in the unions or would form their own.[42] The Hunan congress adopted two lengthy resolutions on the rights of women employees and on child labor, the second of which called for a reform of the apprenticeship system on the grounds that apprentices were not given any technical training but were simply used as domestic servants who had to perform all sorts of chores; it also demanded limitation of the period of apprenticeship to two years, a guarantee of employment after this period, the application of the "equal pay for equal work" principle, and a prohibition against ill-treatment.[43]

The unions of Hupeh and Hunan were, in fact, becoming a "workers' government" to an even greater extent than those of Canton had been during the Hong Kong strike and boycott. They controlled large funds obtained not only from dues, which varied from one grade of union hierarchy to another according to rates carefully fixed by the provincial congresses,[44] but also from contributions paid after successful settlement of a wage dispute, as a result either of a strike or of negotiations. (The increase on the first month's wages had to be handed over to the union.)[45] They also had armed and carefully trained bands of pickets similar to those the Canton unions began to form in 1925. This workers' militia was organized into units ranging from those at the rank-and-file factory-branch level, through those at the local and industrial union level, to those at the provincial level—or at least this was the ambitious plan outlined at the Hunan provincial congress, which requested from the authorities 1,000 rifles and 100,000 rounds of ammunition for its troops.[46] Certainly the militias seem to have been very active, at any rate in the big unions. In April 1927 the Wuhan Textile Union had a corps of 500 men, of whom 60 were always on duty on a three-month rotation; they were paid by the mills through the union intermediaries.[47] The militias intervened to ensure the success of strikes, especially in foreign-owned enterprises in the region.[48] They seem at times to have been over-zealous, and for this reason the Hupeh congress passed a resolution establishing central control of them and stipulating that their activities be confined to combating counterrevolutionary elements. This was in order to prevent their interfering with internal union matters, such as the collection of dues.[49] Altogether, the Hupeh and Hunan unions, and later those of Kiangsi, became powers in their own right. They insisted on the maintenance of strict discipline. When a worker in a Wuhan cotton mill was found to have stolen some cotton, he was expelled from the union after being paraded through the streets wearing a cap of shame.[50] According to an English observer, the executive committees of the large unions "were practically government departments with full administrative authority over their own people. They promulgated edicts and regulations, and used to arrest, try, and punish their members."[51]

The primary task of these unions, as we shall see later, was to formulate workers' demands and to see that economic disputes ended in satisfactory settlements with employers or local authorities. Here again strict discipline was maintained. It was laid down in the rules of the Hunan provincial federation that no rank-and-file unit could declare a strike without consulting the local branch of the general union.[52] The rules of the Wuhan printers' union forbade members to enter into relations with employers during a strike and stipulated that when a strike was successful they must pay a certain sum to the union; anyone contravening the rules would be expelled from the union and would be unable to find another job in Wuhan.[53] But the aims of the unions went far beyond the mere management of local disputes. The right to have a say in the engagement and dismissal of workers had been won by strike action in a number of cases, including the union branch of the railwaymen on the Nanchang-Kiukiang line[54] and those of seamen employed by British and Japanese shipping companies in Hunan and Hankow.[55] Some unions even demanded a share in the management of enterprises where their members were employed; thus the union in the Hankow cotton yarn factory demanded a 10 per cent share in the profits,[56] and several unions in foreign-owned factories insisted that their inspectors be allowed entry to the workshops.[57] At the Anyuan coal mines, where production was suspended when the Nationalist armies arrived, the union took over control and sold 300 tons of coal per day.[58]

Workers' welfare was another task assumed by the unions. The rules of the Hupeh provincial federation provided for the creation of cooperative banks, savings plans, producers' and consumers' cooperatives, insurance societies, and centers for education and training.[59] It is difficult to assess the extent to which this program was implemented, but despite the shortness of the period during which the unions were able to expand their activities, it appears that they had a number of achievements to their credit, especially in the educational field.[60]

All this upsurge of activity on the part of the left wing of the labor movement in Hunan and Hupeh more or less prevented the right wing from making any attempt to intervene. In Changsha one such attempt was opposed by the provincial government itself. This was the proposal to revive the "Hunan Workingmen's Association" made by Wang Kuang-hui and Shen Hsiao-ts'en, two former comrades of Huang and P'ang who were now in close touch with the anti-Communist circles of the Shanghai Federation of Labor Organizations.[61] Similar attempts among the Yueh-Han railwaymen and the Shui-kowshan miners were equally unsuccessful.[62] In Hupeh, Kuo P'in-po and Yuan Tzu-ying, two former militants of the Ching-Han railwaymen's union who had gone over to the kung-tsei after February 17, 1923, and had close ties with the Sunyatsenist society in Wuhan, were arrested by order of the political department of the army, which was directed by Teng Yen-ta, a leader of the left wing of the Kuomintang.[63]

As well as expanding their activities in the areas liberated by the Nationalist armies, to whose victories they owed their new-found vigor, the unions of Central China were also active on the second front of the revolutionary campaign, where they took up the fight against the big foreign interests in China. The fact that many of their members—seamen, factory workers in the Hankow concessions, porters and dockers—were employees of foreign firms strengthened their position, since the political struggle coincided with their own economic fight.

Between November and March about fifty big strikes were held in foreign-owned enterprises in the region, including strikes at the B.A.T. factory and the British-owned cotton yarn factories in Hankow, and strikes among the employees of the Hankow French Concession's Municipal Council, the employees at the warehouses of British shipping firms on the Yangtze, the Wuhan postal workers, the Kiukiang seamen and dockers, the seamen on foreign ships serving Changsha, the seamen of Ichang, the coolies employed by the British and American oil companies in Wuhan and the employees of Western banks and Western newspapers in Hankow.[64] All these strikes had a very strong anti-foreign tone. For instance, the B.A.T. workers went on strike because of several dismissals by a British overseer.[65] The Changsha postal workers, without actually going on strike, refused to take orders from the very unpopular provincial superintendent, a Frenchman named Jaurias, and recognized the authority only of his assistant, who was Chinese.[66] Most of the strikes were successful. The seamen employed by the Japanese shipping companies in Wuhan, after their strike in December, obtained a wage increase of 4 yuan per month (instead of the eight they had asked for), a December bonus equivalent to a fortnight's pay (instead of a month's), two paid Sundays off per month (instead of four), sickness benefits paid by the employers, and union control over the hiring of workers (but not, as demanded, over their dismissal).[67] The list of concessions won by the B.A.T. strike, which ended in December after lasting for nearly two months, is still more indicative of the progress made by the unions during the winter of 1926–27 and of their strengthened class consciousness.[68] Wages were raised by 3 yuan per month; paid time off was granted for women in childbirth, for sickness, for the lunar festivals, and for the main political anniversaries; shelters were to be constructed to protect workers from the cold and the rain at mealtimes; workers could be hired or dismissed only by agreement with the union; no new machines would henceforth be installed;[69] a bonus equivalent to two months' wages would be paid annually in December; and the company would contribute 1,500 yuan per month to the union's fund for educational activities.

This fight between the labor movement and the big foreign interests suddenly assumed dramatic proportions at the beginning of January, 1927, when something quite unprecedented since the time of the Opium Wars occurred: the British were forced by popular pressure to abandon their concessions in Hankow and Kiukiang. In Hankow[70] the trouble began with a big demonstration organized by the Hupeh unions, various students' associations, and the Hankow Chamber of Commerce, which was held on December 26 to protest the arrest of several Kuomintang militants by the authorities of the British Concession in Tientsin. The demonstrators demanded the release of the prisoners, the reopening of the Kuomintang offices in Tientsin, reprisals against British subjects taking part in counterrevolutionary activities on Nationalist government territory, and the severing of economic ties with Great Britain. Anti-British demonstrations continued into January. On January 3 a crowd of over 100,000 assembled around the British Concession in Hankow, and, in a clash with the police, several Chinese were killed and wounded. Eugene Ch'en, the Minister for Foreign Affairs in the Nationalist government, then demanded in the name of the government that the British immediately withdraw their marines from the concession. The next day the British complied with this demand, and the Chinese crowd swarmed into the concession; even those observers least inclined to be in favor of the labor movement were impressed by the strict order maintained by the militia of the provincial federation and by Nationalist troops.[71] A temporary administration for the area took the place of the British Municipal Council. This sudden and complete victory was in strong contrast to the timid efforts so far made by the successive conservative governments that had been in power since 1919, which had achieved nothing more than a breach here and there in the defenses of the Treaty Powers, such as the agreement of 1922 on the abolition of foreign control over the Post Office, or the reopening of negotiations on customs control and extraterritoriality in 1925. Now the pressure of the working masses, led by the unions and urged on by the personal efforts of such leaders of the All-China General Union as Li Li-san and Liu Shao-ch'i,[72] had for the first time forced the foremost of the Foreign Powers in China to withdraw without a fight.

In Kiukiang the local branch of the General Union launched a seamen's strike at the end of December which was a direct attack against foreign-owned companies, but which also demanded a raise in wages. The pickets kept the foreign ships anchored in the Yangtze immobilized, and the local union branch organized a procession in the city that ended with a collective recital of the last will and testament of Sun Yat-sen and with a call to fight against the military forces and the economic stranglehold of the Foreign Powers. Several people were wounded in a clash with the marines guarding the British Concession, and the Kiukiang General Union demanded indemnities, the return of the concession to China, and the restitution of the control of customs and of the Post Office, which had hitherto been in the hands of the British. On January 7 the crowd occupied the concession without a shot's being fired, and order was maintained by the union militia. The Wuhan government set up a commission of control headed by Teng Yen-ta.[73]

In the other big cities in the region the labor organizations were equally active in their display of hostility toward the Foreign Powers, particularly toward Great Britain. In Ichang, a strike of inland navigation employees in February led to a number of clashes with British sailors.[74] A similar strike in

Changsha in January was accompanied by a boycott of British and Japanese goods.[75] In Nanchang, when the press announced that the British were granting a large loan to Chang Tso-lin, a mass meeting was held with a union leader as chairman.[76]

By the end of the winter the situation was extremely tense throughout the whole of the Lower Yangtze region. Although London may have been considering a change of policy toward the Nationalist movement in China, based on hopes for a split in the movement,[77] local representatives of foreign (and especially British) interests, whether businessmen, administrators, or members of the armed forces, were coming into conflict more and more with the working population and with the unions. The British customs inspector in Changsha became alarmed at the way workers insulted foreigners and confiscated goods, and spoke of "mob rule" similar to that in Paris during the French Revolution;[78] and in January all the foreign firms there closed their offices.[79] Western economic activities gradually ceased in Wuhan. The B.A.T. factory closed at the beginning of February, throwing some three thousand workers out of jobs;[80] the banks also closed, refusing to meet the demands of the employees' union, which went so far as to ask for forty days' paid holiday a year, a year's wages in compensation if the bank closed down, three months' wages in compensation for dismissal after being employed for over a year, and a minimum wage of 15 yuan per month, plus 20 yuan extra for food.[81] In March the English-language newspapers of Wuhan—the *Central Post* (British) and the *Hankow Herald* (American)—suspended publication, the employees having stopped work on instructions from the provincial federation.[82]

While the strategy of strike action in foreign enterprises was a fairly simple issue, the questions of what strategy to adopt in Chinese-owned enterprises and what general economic policy to establish in the provinces of Central China liberated by the Nationalist armies raised more complex problems, not only for the labor movement but also for the Nationalist government.

From the fall on, the unions had acted in the interests of the proletariat as a class, which meant that Chinese and foreign enterprises in the liberated areas had been given the same treatment. The Hupeh provincial federation set up a committee for economic struggle, headed by Liu Shao-ch'i, in November.[83] At its January congress 13 yuan was fixed as the absolute minimum monthly wage, and a resolution was passed proposing a campaign for a wider distribution of the traditional annual bonuses but expressing disapproval in principle of this practice inherited from the former guilds.[84] A general wage increase had in fact been obtained during the fall in both Chinese and foreign enterprises, in some cases by strike action, in others by negotiation.[85] In Hunan, too, printers, weavers, dyers, and several other trades had obtained a considerable increase in wages.[86]

Stability of employment continued to be a matter of concern in the labor movement, and a number of unions succeeded in winning the right to have a say in the hiring and dismissal of workers.[87] But after the arrival of the Nationalist armies in Central China, unemployment seems to have been an even greater problem—a result of the fact that a number of foreign enterprises, especially in the ports, gradually slowed down production, and some Chinese enterprises did the same (including the Hunan mines, the owners of which had close ties with the conservative forces routed by the Nationalist armies).[88] The continuation of military operations in Central China during the fall and the winter further interfered with industry and commerce. It is therefore not surprising that the Hupeh congress passed a special resolution on unemployment,[89] and that the Hunan congress proposed the setting up of "national workshops" for the unemployed, to be run by local authorities and labor organizations.[90] Among the demands obtained by the printers of Chinese newspapers in Wuhan after their successful strike in November (which won them a raise in wages, a nine-hour day, and a maximum of 5,000 characters to manipulate) was the assurance that no apprentices would be engaged for the next 18 months, and that in general at least one adult worker would be employed for every two apprentices.[91]

The Nationalist government, which had transferred its seat to Wuhan at the end of 1926, and in which left-wing elements predominated,[92] could not but view with favor this renewal of labor activities; and with the transfer to Wuhan of the central committee of the All-China General Union, the presence there of Liu Shao-ch'i, Li Li-san, Su Chao-cheng, Chu Pao-t'ing, and other members of the general staff of Chinese trade unionism[93] gave additional prestige to the labor organizations in their dealings with the new government authorities in Central China. Indeed, from the very first the Wuhan government reaffirmed its support for the workers' demands for limitation of hours of work, a weekly day of rest, workers' insurance, and consumers' cooperatives.[94] On December 11, a big public meeting was held to celebrate the arrival in Wuhan of Sung Ch'ing-ling (the widow of Sun Yat-sen), Hsü Ch'ien, Eugene Ch'en, other Chinese left-wing leaders, and the chief Russian advisers. At this meeting Borodin stressed the point that the strengthening of the unions was all to the advantage of the Nationalist government.[95] The political parties supporting the Nationalist government adopted the same attitude. The second conference of the Hunan provincial branch of the Kuomintang, held in the fall of 1926, demanded the implementation of the decisions taken in January 1926 (on the eight-hour day, the minimum wage, paid holidays, workers' insurance, and so on), and proposed that 20 per cent of the party's expenditures be devoted to aid for the labor movement.[96] The sixth conference of the Hunan Communist Party, held during the same period, adopted a similar program, with additional proposals that workers be allowed to arm themselves in self-defense, that large-scale enterprises be owned by the state, and that the right-wing unions be eliminated.[97] All these resolutions were adopted by the Hunan provincial federation at its congress in December.[98]

One among many further indications of the predominance of left-wing influence in the Wuhan government and of the kind of support it enjoyed is provided by the official list of public holidays. Eleven of them were of a mainly Nationalist character, such as the anniversaries of the foundation of the Republic on October 10, of the death of Sun Yat-sen on March 12, of the movement that began on May 4, 1919, and of the humiliating treaty of September 7, 1901. Four were more directly concerned with the labor movement, namely the ceremonies held on February 7, May 1, May 30, and June 23. The remaining seven were holidays that primarily concerned the Communists and the extreme left: anniversaries such as that of the death of Lenin on January 21, of the proclamation of the Paris Commune on March 18, and of the birth of Karl Marx on May 5.[99]

Nevertheless the Wuhan government, and the unions as well, had to consider the moderate elements among the national bourgeoisie, and the new regime hastened to satisfy some of their demands, performing, for instance, the symbolic act of demolishing the walls of Wuchang[100] in order to provide the local businessmen with opportunities for expansion like those provided for Canton businessmen by Sun Yat-sen's first government in 1917-18. But the demands presented by strikers, particularly in the matter of wages, continued to cause anxiety to employers both in the big modern enterprises and in small factories and workshops.[101] At a meeting of the Hankow Chamber of Commerce on December 3 it was decided that the "excesses" of the union militias must be stopped, and that in the future only wage demands would be considered. A merchants' strike was threatened if the authorities did not do something immediately to improve relations between industrial and commercial employers and their employees.[102] The Wuhan government then agreed to set up an arbitration tribunal, and the unions had to comply.

On December 6, a commission was set up for the investigation of labor disputes, with quadripartite representation of the unions, the chamber of commerce, the Labor Department of the Kuomintang, and the Wuhan government.[103] On several occasions after the arrival of the Nationalist armies, government or Kuomintang organs had intervened to settle strikes in both Chinese and foreign-owned enterprises.[104] But the newly constituted commission had much more strictly defined powers, which were set forth in the provisional factory legislation promulgated in mid-December.[105] These laws met many of the demands presented by the unions: protection of women and children, collective bargaining, workers' insurance, consultation of the unions in the matter of the hiring and dismissal of workers. But to some extent they acted as a brake on the labor movement insofar as they required that all labor disputes be submitted to the newly formed commission for arbitration, and that no "hostile acts" be committed during the week allowed to the commission to reach its decisions, from which there was no appeal. A further point was that neither workers nor unions would be permitted to take part in the management of enterprises. Apparently both the unions and the Communist Party were in agreement with these measures,[106] which probably seemed reasonable to them so long as the left and the extreme left predominated in the Kuomintang and the government and so long as the unions and their militias continued to occupy a strong position in Central China.

New Restrictions on the Labor Movement in the South

The departure of the Northern Expedition left the Cantonese labor movement and the Strike Committee in an entirely new situation, and it was only after various complicated developments that a decision was finally reached in October 1926 to end the strike and the boycott unilaterally without demanding any concessions from the other side.

Many left-wing leaders and militants either left for the front in July or joined the campaign in Wuhan at the end of the summer, thus tipping the scales in the favor of the right wing in Canton. The Canton military authorities, now directly under Chiang Kai-shek, took full advantage of this, and on July 16 took over control of the labor organizations and published a list of those that were authorized. All strikes were prohibited in the "public interest," and an order was given for pickets to be disarmed, although this does not seem to have been carried out.[107] In August, arbitration procedures for labor disputes were introduced, to be carried out by a member of the government and representatives of both parties to the dispute.[108] The right wing also had in its favor the attitudes of men in moderate circles in Canton, who hoped for an end to the strike and the boycott because of the harm these actions were doing to Cantonese trade with Hong Kong and the opportunities for political agitation that they afforded the left.

For very different reasons, members of the Strike Committee too were beginning to be doubtful about prolonging the strike and boycott movement. It was certainly not that they had any reason to suppose that it was not still operating successfully, to judge from the small amount of maritime trade during the summer, or that it was likely to die out through lack of enthusiasm.[109] In July there were still tens of thousands of Hong Kong strikers in Canton, not to mention those who had returned to their villages.[110] It had, however, been impossible to prevent the gradual recruitment here and there of the 30,000 men required to carry on essential activities in Hong Kong, nor was it any longer possible to nourish illusions about making Canton into an effective trade rival of the British colony within a short period of time.[111] Moreover, relations between the Strike Committee and the peasants were beginning to deteriorate, especially in districts where agricultural products, such as silk or oil-bearing crops, used to be exported to Hong Kong.[112]

Thus the Strike Committee decided to consent to the opening of negotiations between the Nationalist government and the Hong Kong government in July, despite the fact that it was not allowed representation on the Chinese delegation.[113] But the delegation found that the British refused to acknowledge responsibility for the shootings on June 23, 1925, and to pay compensation to the victims or their families; nor would they advance the money required for the payment of compensation to Hong Kong workers who were not reinstated when the strike ended. All they were prepared to do was to provide a loan for the economic development of Kwangtung, to be administered under their control.[114] The talks broke down on July 23.[115]

Throughout these negotiations, the Strike Committee supported the government delegation and expressed satisfaction with its attitude.[116] Now it realized, along with the Nationalist government and on the recommendation of the Communist Party, that a tactical move for ending the strike would have to be made.[117] This position seems to have been arrived at as much because of the international situation that had arisen following the victorious entry of Cantonese armies into the traditional British sphere of influence in the Middle Yangtze region as because of the obvious unwillingness of the British to come to terms. Great Britain, which had lost millions of pounds through the strike,[118] was becoming more and more alarmed by the success of the Nationalists and the growth of the revolutionary movement in China. In July British gunboats went into action against pickets who were conducting operations against smugglers and killed 26 of them,[119] and in September British marines were landed right in the middle of the port of Canton, where they evicted the pickets stationed at the docks of Jardine, Matheson & Company.[120] The Wanhsien incident, in the Upper Yangtze region, when several hundred Chinese civilians fell under British artillery fire, confirmed anxieties about the possibility of British armed intervention in China. The British press both at home and in China openly called for it, and the Comintern stated that the risk of intervention had assumed alarming proportions.[121]

Since neither the Nationalist government nor the revolutionary movement as a whole wanted to run this risk, their views on the strike and the boycott changed accordingly. Now that the main theater of operations was in the Yangtze region, it seemed highly undesirable to keep a second front open in Canton, which had gone from being the area of advance attack against the foreign interests to one holding a strictly rearguard position.

The Strike Committee, fortified by the knowledge that it still enjoyed wide public support,[122] decided, after holding a conference of strikers' delegates,[123] to call off the strike and the boycott. It preferred to do this of its own accord so that it could maintain its prestige and its freedom of action, now that there was no further hope of coming to an agreement with the British. The decision was taken with the consent of the Nationalist government, which agreed to impose a surtax of 2.5 per cent on all foreign merchandise in order to provide funds for strikers who remained unemployed. This went into effect at the beginning of October.[124] The boycott ended at midday on October 10, the anniversary of the republican revolution, and the strike leaders explained the reasons for this at a big public meeting, the last to be held at the "Eastern Garden" (Tung-yuan), which had been the strike headquarters for the past 16 months. Two days later their arguments were repeated in two communiqués, one issued by the Kuomintang and the other by the Strike Committee. Both communiqués declared the need to give priority to the Northern Expedition and to adopt a new strategy in the fight against foreign interests. Kwangtung, they said, despite its successful struggle against the imperialists, must now withdraw in order to concentrate its efforts in new directions. The strikers' communiqué laid particular stress on the voluntary nature of the decision to withdraw the strike pickets: "We have taken this decision voluntarily. We have not reached any agreement with our enemies and have no obligations to them."[125] The Communist press also took up the argument that, with the victories of the Cantonese armies in Central China, the Nationalist struggle was now being fought on a different front, and the Canton–Hong Kong strike had ceased to be decisive.[126]

The Strike Committee continued in existence for some time after October 10 in order to look after the strikers who did not get reinstated, arranging for their lodging and finding employment for them or putting them on lists for work in government departments.[127] The prestige it had acquired during this historic 16-month strike remained intact, despite its relative failure to achieve its original objectives.[128] Moreover, the stimulus it had given to the Cantonese labor movement throughout the strike period enabled activities to continue unabated during the winter of 1926-27. Unions, such as those of the postal workers, the scavengers, the bank employees, and the oil mill workers,[129] continued to be formed or reorganized. The important survey carried out at the end of 1926 by the Canton Municipal Council listed 250 unions in the city, with a total membership of 290,620;[130] and according to what was probably a government source,[131] the number of unions in Kwangtung as a whole in February 1927 was 385, with a total membership of 511,850 (a figure that no doubt includes the rural handicraft workers in the silk-producing districts).

The Canton Workers' Delegates' Conference still remained in the forefront, although its rivals, the provincial federation and the Mechanics' Union, were still very active. It held a second conference in July 1926, and a third in December, which recorded the attendance of delegates of 203 unions with a total membership of 190,000, as against the 140 unions with a membership of 140,000 represented at the first conference held in April 1926;[132] and it maintained a firm hold on the main sectors of industry in Canton, with the exception of the mechanical workshops. Under its aegis the railwaymen formed an amalgamated union for all railways and tramways in the province.[133] This union was directed by a provincial committee of 19 members and backed by a union militia of 600 men. The printing workers, too, were solidly behind it, and in July they prevented the publication of all Cantonese newspapers, except for the two connected with the Kuomintang, because they carried attacks on the Workers' Delegates' Conference.[184] The newspaper proprietors appealed to the provincial federation to supply them with skilled labor, but the request was refused.[185] All the left-wing unions—and for that matter, the opposing unions as well—still had their militias, most of which were armed, if at times only with cudgels. This was in spite of the formal orders to disarm issued by Chiang Kai-shek in May and June, before the departure of the Northern Expedition, and again in July. These militias blockaded the store of the Commercial Press during the strike of its employees in September 1926,[186] and in December forced residents and passing travelers to leave the hotels where the staffs had gone on strike.[187] When a procession was organized to celebrate the success of the strike of the sewing machine factory workers, members of the union militias joined the line of march dressed in their uniforms and carrying cudgels,[138] and they also held up steamers of the C.M.S.N. Company suspected of being manned by hsin-kung hired during the strike and boycott.[139]

After the end of the strike and the boycott, a serious attempt seems to have been made by the unions affiliated with the Workers' Delegates' Conference to educate their members in political and ideological matters. The survey carried out by the Canton Municipal Council at the end of 1926 mentions 134 pamphlets then in circulation among the unions, 35 of which concerned labor and union problems while 53 were on Marxism and Communism, 19 on socialism, and 15 on cooperatives and corporatism.[140] Although the survey does not distinguish between unions affiliated with the Workers' Delegates' Conference and those affiliated with the moderate organizations, it seems likely that it was mainly among the left-wing unions that these pamphlets circulated, except perhaps for those in the last category.

Clashes between the left-wing unions and their rivals, the provincial federation and the Mechanics' Union, were now more frequent than ever, and often led to violence. As before, they often arose from demarcation disputes or regional rivalries. In August 1926, a brawl in which four men were killed occurred between members of two oil-pressers' unions, the one affiliated with the Workers' Delegates' Conference being exclusively for Cantonese, while the other, which was affiliated with the provincial federation, recruited its members from workers who came from the rural hsien of the region.[141] In November, dockers belonging to the union affiliated with the Workers' Delegates' Conference clashed with members of the old "Guild of Common Virtue," which was controlled by foremen and labor contractors.[142] A procession of the Canton unions was planned for January 1, 1927, to celebrate the victories of the Nationalist army in the Yangtze region, and the provincial federation claimed the right, on the grounds of seniority, to head the procession—a right that was disputed by the Workers' Delegates' Conference on the grounds that it had the larger membership. In the end the two groups marched side by side, and came to blows.[143]

The Mechanics' Union was an even tougher adversary than the provincial federation. Its "sports teams" were always liable to stir up trouble, as for instance at the employees' club of the Sincere & Co. department stores in September 1926,[144] or in February 1927, when they carried off a number of dock porters and kept them locked up in their headquarters.[145] At the beginning of 1927 it set up its own cooperative printing press because the printers refused to work for it.[146] The union's resentment against the railwaymen was particularly bitter, owing to the fact that they had gone over to the side of the Workers' Delegates; there were several clashes, the most serious of which occurred in January 1927 between some three hundred railwaymen on the Canton-Sanshui line and the mechanics employed at one of the stations, who were still members of the Mechanics' Union. The mechanics were armed with machine guns, and after a three-hour battle there were twenty dead and many wounded, whereupon the railwaymen's union sounded the alarm and called in its militia.[147] In the end the Canton government succeeded in getting both sides to accept its mediation.

This was only one of the instances that seemed to show that the Nationalist government (before its transfer to Wuhan), and afterward the provincial government left in charge of Kwangtung, still supported the policy of cooperation with the left wing of the labor movement laid down by the national congresses of the Kuomintang. In July and August 1926 several leaders of the provincial federation were arrested, including its president, Ch'en Sen, following the murder of two employees in a shop selling noodles by a gang employed by the federation;[148] and for a while government police cooperated with the left-wing union militiamen in keeping public order and preventing incidents between rival unions.[149] But when the attacks of the right-wing unions against those of the left increased in intensity during the winter, the Canton government ceased to do more than to attempt to mediate between the two parties without taking sides.

General Li Chi-shen and his colleagues in the provincial government inclined toward the policy of restricting the labor movement that had been outlined immediately after the March 20 coup; and in January 1927, Li himself replaced the ineffective Ch'en Shu-jen as head of the Labor Department of the Kwangtung branch of the Kuomintang.[150]

Soon after the departure of the Northern Expedition, the provincial government introduced a series of measures that hampered labor activities.[151] In January it promulgated regulations on labor disputes, including strict rules for the conduct of both parties to a dispute. Employers were not allowed to recruit strikebreakers or to form labor organizations to serve their own interests by counteracting the influence of existing labor organizations, nor were they to be allowed to be union leaders or to prevent their employees from belonging to unions. Much more severe restrictions were placed on the unions: their members were forbidden to arrest workers or managers of enterprises, or to interfere with other workers' freedom to work; during a strike, workers could not damage factory property or prevent employers from conducting operations they could carry out themselves; no labor organization could be formed without government permission, and until such permission was obtained it was illegal to collect dues or form picket lines; union members were not allowed to carry arms, even when taking part in demonstrations and processions, on penalty of having their union banned.[152] The lockout in November at the Canton arsenal and the replacement of the strikers by workers amenable to government regulations was a further move in the same direction.[153]

This deterioration in the relations between the labor movement in the South and the Canton government was part of the general trend within the Kuomintang after the departure of the Northern Expedition. The subsequent split and geographical separation between the left wing, in Wuhan, and the right, in Canton and Nanchang, will be discussed later;[154] but it should be said here that even at the time of the Expedition's departure, the Canton bourgeoisie was disturbed by the strength of the left wing of the labor movement, which had been steadily increasing since 1924, especially during the strike and the boycott.

After the more extreme right-wing leaders, such as Ch'en Lien-po, who was president of the Chamber of Commerce, had been ousted in October 1924, the Canton bourgeoisie appeared to accept the policy of the Nationalist government and to become temporarily resigned to the important position occupied by the labor movement in local affairs. But the costs of meeting union demands, especially the increase in wages that had been agreed to under pressure in 1926, were becoming steadily heavier.[155] The bank strike in December had shown how exorbitant the workers' demands were becoming: not only did the bank employees ask for higher wages, but they also demanded that only union members be employed and that dismissals be made only with the consent of the union, that the union be given the right to decide on the dates of (paid) holidays, and that commissions on loans, mortgages, and other business transactions be calculated every six months and divided among the employees.[156] These demands were postponed for further examination after a compromise had been reached between the union and the employers under Kuomintang arbitration,[157] but this did not lessen the anxieties of the bourgeoisie. Some firms chose to close down,[158] but others began to plan a counterattack they thought would meet with the approval of the provincial government. This was a campaign that was started in moderate circles to restrict the right to strike so as to prevent any weakening of the Nationalist movement and the united revolutionary front; the right-wing unions supported it in their own fashion, hailing the merchants as "revolutionaries" because of the funds they contributed to the Northern Expedition.[159] It is indicative of this trend that Teng Chung-hsia, in his study of the Cantonese labor movement published at the end of 1926, went to great lengths to defend the right to strike as being the main weapon of the working class.[160] The bourgeoisie intensified its attack in January 1927. A meeting of Canton merchants was held on the 15th, at which they called upon the government to protect local industries, to restore to their rightful owners the premises taken over by the unions during the strike and still occupied by them, and to uphold the traditional right of merchants and master craftsmen to dismiss their employees on the second day of the New Year festival (which was a few weeks ahead).[161]

The question of New Year dismissals—an old Cantonese custom that the Workers' Delegates' Conference had decided to oppose vigorously this year because of the rising unemployment—created a political crisis. The 72 traditional guilds and the four chambers of commerce called a meeting that was attended by 20,000 merchants, who declared their support for Li Chi-shen and demanded an assurance that the custom would be upheld. When the union pickets thereupon blockaded the shops, Li sent twelve companies of troops who made short shrift of them.[162] After lengthy negotiations, a tripartite arbitration commission was set up, charged with the task of drawing up strict regulations about rights of dismissal (giving previous notice, paying compensation, and so on).[163] This was only a partial victory for the unions.

As soon as the situation in Central China allowed, the provincial government and the Canton employers decided to step up their attack. The December regulations concerning the activities of the unions and their pickets were enforced more and more strictly,[164] and there was no longer any attempt to hide the growing hostility toward workers' demands. On March 2 the provincial civil commissioner stated roundly to the Red International delegation then visiting China: "The demands of the unions for higher wages and shorter hours have become incompatible with the present stage of development of Chinese industry.... This is why the Kwangtung government has changed its policy with regard to labor problems and disputes. The demands of the workers will not always be met...."[165] The same trend was apparent in other parts of Kwangtung.[166]

Despite these threats, the unions seem to have maintained the cautious and conciliatory attitude they had adopted toward the March 20 incident and the subsequent anti-labor measures of the spring of 1926. The counterattack policy advocated by Teng Chung-hsia in the book cited above does not ever seem to have been given serious consideration. Hopes were still placed in "collaboration between workers and merchants"[167] as the keystone of the united front against the Northern warlords and the Foreign Powers.[168]

The Increasing Influence of the Shanghai General Union

In Shanghai, the wave of economic strikes that had begun in the spring of 1926 was very little affected by the departure of the Northern Expedition, and was still in full swing during the summer and fall. In June there were 35 strikes affecting 107 enterprises and involving 65,000 strikers.[169] The figures were much the same in July (70,000 strikers in 105 enterprises),[170] and in August they stood at 37,000 strikers in 46 enterprises.[171] The strikes affected most of the big Japanese firms and several silk-reeling factories, but they occurred also in printing plants, tobacco factories, bookbinderies, and the Chinese tramways.[172] In December there was a tramways strike in the French Concession,[173] and in January a strike of workers in the big Chinese shops in Nanking Road.[174]

The main cause of these strikes was the rise in the cost of living, and in particular the rise in the price of rice and other articles of daily consumption. The price index of twenty varieties of foodstuffs rose from 141.2 in June 1926 to 163.1 in October, chiefly because of military operations in the Yangtze valley, and it remained above 140, taking 1925 as 100, until the beginning of 1927.[175] The wholesale price of rice ranged from 12.60 to 14.00 yuan per picul at the beginning of 1926, from 15.80 to 17.80 yuan at the beginning of July, and from 17.40 to 19.00 at the beginning of October.[176] But the vigor with which the strikes were conducted was an outcome of the political situation in Shanghai, where the memory of the great battles of the summer of 1925 was still fresh, and the successes of the Nationalist armies and their working-class allies in Central China gave a new stimulus.[177]

All this served, however, to harden the attitude of Chinese employers in Shanghai, as was indicated by the fines inflicted in June by printing employers on employees who had attended the ceremonies held to commemorate May 30.[178] The kung-tsei, including Mrs. Mu Chih-ying in the silk-reeling factories, resumed their activities. Sun Tsung-fang, the founder of an "Anti-Communist Workers' Alliance," formed a "Workers' and Merchants' Association" designed to counteract the influence of the unions in small-scale enterprises.[179] At the end of June, the Chinese authorities pronounced the General Union to be unlawful.[180] The decree was issued by Ting Wen-chiang, whom Sun Ch'uan-fang had appointed as Administrator-General of Shanghai, and whose international standing as a geologist gave him a certain amount of prestige.[181]

The General Union did not lose any of its authority by being forced once again to go underground, but rather continued to give vigorous leadership to the strikes that were held during the summer. Its central committee was divided into three separate departments (propaganda, administration, and organization), which were linked with the rank and file by the double network of local branches and industrial unions. It functioned effectively among the dockers, the printing workers, and the cotton workers,[182] and in July claimed a membership of 210,000.[183] This figure is more likely to have been that of the number of workers who came under its influence rather than of actual members, since the figures given at the Fourth Labor Congress in 1927 were much lower. They did, however, reflect the progress made since the departure of the Northern Expedition: 43,000 in June 1926, and 76,000 in January 1927.[184] In mid-July the General Union held a secret meeting attended by about a hundred union delegates to discuss the conduct of strikes then in progress.[185] It was probably behind the strike in the Japanese cotton mills in August, via the General Cotton Mills Union which was affiliated with it.[186] The need to operate clandestinely did not in any way interfere with its control over the conduct of strikes. Incidents of ta-ch'ang, formerly so frequent, especially in the textile industry, were now rare,[187] and so were regional rivalries. This was the result of the General Union's systematic efforts to promote the political education of workers.[188] Now the go-slow (tai-kung) form of strike was becoming accepted, which shows how the working class had achieved a self-control that was very different from their former proclivity to sudden outbursts of violence.[189]

The strikes during the summer and fall were remarkable not only for the way in which they were organized, but also because of the much wider demands that were presented. In August the General Union issued an eleven-point program: a minimum wage of 15 yuan a month; the introduction of a sliding scale of wages; a minimum ten-hour day; Sundays off with pay; the prohibition of corporal punishments and fines; no arbitrary dismissal by employers; regulations for workers' compensation; half-pay for periods of sickness; controls on female and child labor; freedom to hold meetings and freedom of association, of speech, and of the press; improvements in factory conditions (safety precautions, air supply, hygiene, and the like).[190] Most of the strikes during the summer presented some or all of these basic demands.[191] Sometimes preference was given to a demand for a separate allocation of wages for the purchase of rice instead of the establishment of a sliding scale of wages, this having been a practice adopted by Shanghai employers since the end of the First World War at times when the cost of living was high.[192] There were also occasional demands to have wages paid in a stable currency.[193] The question of identity checks by fingerprints or discs, although not expressly mentioned in the eleven-point program, was one that was raised by strikers in the cotton mills,[194] at the Franco-Chinese Machine Company in Nanshih,[195] and in the French-owned tramways.[196]

Although these strikes were mainly economic, nationalist questions were sometimes raised; for instance, the strikers in the Japanese cotton mills in August demanded not only a 20 per cent raise in wages, better treatment by management, and the reinstatement of workers recently dismissed, but also compensation from the Japanese consular authorities for the murder of the Chinese coolie Ch'en A-t'ang on board the *Manri-maru* when it was docked at Shanghai.[197] So great, however, was the determination of both Chinese and foreign employers not to yield an inch to the Shanghai proletariat—even on strictly economic matters—at a time when the Cantonese armies were winning victories in Hunan and Hupeh, that most of the strikes met with total or partial defeat. The above-mentioned strike at the Naigai cotton mills, which involved nearly twenty thousand workers and lasted over three weeks, obtained only an increased allocation of rice, a promise that the police would no longer be called in, and payment of 4 yuan in compensation;[198] moreover, 267 workers were dismissed. The strike at the printing plant of the American Presbyterian Mission in August, which lasted 13 days and presented bold demands for an eight-and-a-half-hour day, a wage increase of from 3 to 5 yuan, old-age pensions, compensation for accidents, prohibition of unjust dismissals, and a larger amount of food for the apprentices, obtained only a pay raise of from 1.5 to 2 yuan, reduction of hours to ten hours or to nine hours and forty minutes, and partial strike pay.[199] The combined efforts of the Settlement authorities and of Ting Wen-chiang's police did much to weaken the strike wave. Thirty-four leaders of the August cotton mill strike were arrested by the Chinese police, and at the end of the month martial law was declared in areas under police control.[200] The police of the International Settlement arrested seven leaders of the August China Bookshop strike;[201] the Mixed Court sentenced two workers to six weeks' imprisonment for distributing leaflets about the Ch'en A-t'ang affair; and six "agitators" involved in the strike at the Naigai No. 9 mill were given six months' imprisonment.[202]

At the beginning of the fall the Nationalist armies, having got rid of Wu P'ei-fu and gained control of Hupeh, entered Kiangsi and attacked Sun Ch'uan-fang, the warlord of the Lower Yangtze provinces. The Shanghai unions now reversed the process of the fall of 1925 and passed from economic to political struggle, all the keener to join in the fight against Sun because of their recent clashes with the authorities appointed by him. The first opportunity for them to do so came when Hsia Ch'ao, who was in command of Sun's forces in Chekiang, raised the banner of provincial autonomy and proclaimed his support for the Canton and Wuhan governments. Most of Sun Ch'uan-fang's forces were engaged in Kiangsi at the time, and only a few thousand troops were left in Shanghai. The leadership of the regional branch of the Communist Party, together with Chou En-lai and Lo I-nung, decided that the moment was ripe to organize an armed uprising in the Chinese districts of Shanghai, using the two thousand or so members of the various corps of pickets affiliated with the General Union, only 130 of which were armed. The uprising was planned in conjunction with Niu Yung-chien, special Kuomintang representative in Shanghai, who in turn made contact with Yü Hsia-ch'ing and the Chinese Chamber of Commerce, and thus had several thousand volunteers at his disposal. Leaflets were distributed calling upon the workers to overthrow Sun Ch'uan-fang, to transform Shanghai into a "special territory" controlled by the people, and to reestablish the General Union and restore civil liberties.[203] But just before October 24, the day fixed for the uprising, Niu received news that Hsia Ch'ao had been defeated by forces that had remained loyal to Sun, and he suspended taking action—without, however, warning the Communists and the General Union, who, left on their own, fought against hopeless odds in Nanshih and Pootung and were quickly dispersed. Over a hundred arrests were made, including that of T'ao Ching-hsuan, vice-president of the dockers' union and an old comrade of Liu Hua, who had been in command of the pickets. He and several of his companions were immediately court-martialled and shot.[204]

The General Union was not discouraged by this military defeat, and in November tried to form the widest possible political alliance against Sun Ch'uan-fang, based on the demand for "autonomy of the three provinces" (Kiangsu, Anhwei, and Kiangsi). This was a cry that had been raised for some time among the local bourgeoisie hostile to Sun, and one with which the General Union had been associated before the unsuccessful uprising on October 24. It renewed its old contacts with the students' and shopkeepers' associations, both of which had been allies of the General Union during the May Thirtieth Movement and several times since;[205] and contact was made with the Three Provinces Association recently formed by moderates such as Ts'ai Yuan-p'ei.[206] On November 30 the General Union, risking police prohibition, proclaimed that, of its own accord, it was resuming open activities; it called upon the workers to support the autonomist movement, the program of which had been enthusiastically accepted at a big public meeting held two days before that had been organized jointly by the students and the merchants.[207] It was decided that instead of simply re-forming the Workers', Merchants', and Students' Federation created in June 1925, a new organization should be formed for the purpose of directing the autonomist movement, to be called "The People's Municipal Congress of Shanghai." Although the big demonstration planned for December 5 by this new organization was prohibited by Sun,[208] and despite the fact that the General Union was closed down once again by the police on December 8,[209] agitation for the autonomy of the three provinces and for municipal autonomy in Shanghai continued through December and January, with the support of labor organizations;[210] and when Sun had to call upon the help of the Fengtien forces in North China after his defeats in Kiangsi and Fukien, the General Union launched a propaganda campaign against this new enemy.[211]

Thus, in January 1927 the Shanghai General Union, on the very eve of the great armed battles that were to put it in control of one of the biggest industrial centers in Asia while at the same time suddenly depriving it of the fruits of all its labors, was in full command of all its forces. Throughout 1926 it had directed all the economic struggles of the workers, as well as their political struggles against the anachronistic powers of the warlord Sun Ch'uan-fang; and after the July victories of the Northern Expedition in Central China, it had been unfailing in its support of the Nationalist government and in its sympathy with the contributions made by the labor movement toward these victories.[212] Its influence continued to spread in all directions. The French Tramways employees, who even in May 1925 had been unable to take strike action owing to the strict control kept over them, held a successful strike at the end of December;[213] and what was even more significant, labor organizations that had stuck to the old guild traditions, and indeed some that had belonged to the Anti-Communist Association, now came over to the General Union. In January, for example, the old Boatmen's and Warehousemen's Federation[214] and the workers' club at the Nanyang tobacco factory came under more militant leadership.[215] In December the General Union, despite the fact that it was still working underground, called a conference of delegates of all its rank-and-file unions; and at the beginning of January it conducted a survey of the unions, asking them to provide information about their rules, the number of members, the form of management, the monthly wages of members, and so on.[216] The survey listed 187 separate organizations divided between 20 industrial unions and six geographical areas.[217]

The Situation in the Northern Provinces

In North China, on the other hand, the workers' condition was worsening toward the end of 1926, and repression of the labor movement was intensified. Chang Tso-lin had associated himself once again with Wu P'ei-fu after the latter had been chased out of Hupeh by the Nationalist armies, and it was he who in December sent Chang Tsung-ch'ang, commander of the army in Shantung, to the rescue of Sun Ch'uan-fang when he found himself in difficulties against the winter offensive of the Nationalist armies. Chang Tso-lin was the last of the "strong men," in the tradition of Yuan Shih-k'ai and Ts'ao K'un, whom the conservatives and the Foreign Powers had so often trusted to check popular unrest. In December he assumed the title of Commander of the "National Pacification Armies" (*An-kuo-chün*), adopted a policy of extremely violent anti-Communism, and assured the Western Powers of his full support.[218] But the state of his currency, the feng-p'iao, was scarcely equal to his political ambitions, for its rate of exchange with the silver yuan, which at the beginning of 1926 was 260, fell to 480 at the end of the year and reached 1,170 in April 1927.[219] Stronghanded methods seemed to him, however, to be adequate for dealing with labor as well as with political problems, and when workers in the Northeast made the slightest attempts to take strike action, even if only because of the rise in the cost of living, they were ruthlessly put down, as in the lockout in the Mukden woolen factory in October 1926.[220]

The workers in North China, particularly the railwaymen, were also having a difficult time. Wages were often several months in arrears,[221] dismissals frequent, and repression so strong that not one of the unions formed in 1925 under the Kuominchun had survived to take the lead in presenting even elementary demands.[222]

The Foreign Powers were as suspicious as the warlords of any movement that seemed to support the Wuhan government, and were ready to clamp down on it immediately. In November the British police in Tientsin arrested

14 young Kuomintang militants accused of planning a strike in a cotton mill and handed them over to Chang Tso-lin's police; several were executed.[223] In Dairen the Japanese police likewise came down on anyone suspected of supporting the Southern cause.[224] A Comintern report reckons that several thousand persons were put to death without trial, condemned to death, or wounded in North China during the first few months of 1927.[225] Thus, although the success of the Northern Expedition gave a new stimulus to the labor movement in Hunan, Hupeh, and Kiangsi—and in Shanghai, too, even before the capture of the city—it was of little help to workers in the northern provinces.

CHAPTER XIV

The Shanghai Insurrection

Between mid-February and early April 1927 the struggle grew in intensity, and Shanghai replaced Wuhan as the storm center, just as Wuhan had replaced Canton during the summer of 1926. A new balance of forces began to appear toward the end of the winter, and since this largely explains the success of the Shanghai uprisings and of Chiang Kai-shek's coup, which put a sudden end to the unions' brief moment of power, something must first be said about it before discussing these events.

Less than two years after its formation in Canton in May 1925, and thanks to the victories of the Southern armies, the All-China General Union had by early 1927 achieved a cohesion and a strength it had never known before. It was now a mass organization with hundreds of thousands of industrial workers under its control, and over a million handicraft workers and shop employees.[1] As for its strength in industrial regions, it had lost the positions won in Chihli and Hunan in 1925–26 during the brief period the Kuominchun was in power, and it had never exercised much control in the Northeast; but it was firmly established in Kwangtung, Hupeh, and Kiangsi, where regional federations had been set up or re-formed as the Nationalist forces advanced. The Shanghai General Union had also gained in influence despite the semi-clandestine nature of its activities, and when the Nationalist armies occupied Chekiang in February[2] there was a new outburst of strikes and union organizing.[3] Further, there were now several well-organized national industrial unions upon whose support the All-China General Union could count. The earliest of these were the seamen's and railwaymen's unions (although the local branches of the latter that were situated within the warlords' sphere of influence had been closed down). To these was added, at the beginning of March, a national postal workers' union, formed after several months of discussion among the separate postal workers' unions in the main cities.[4] These discussions culminated in a conference held in Wuhan and attended by 54 delegates from ten provinces, some of whom came from North China;[5] and this broad participation helped to extend the influence of the All-China General Union, despite the restricted nature of the program adopted.[6] At the opening meeting the will of Sun Yat-sen was read aloud, three bows were made to his portrait, and the chairman called upon the delegates to support the Nationalist revolution and the Kuomintang.[7] At about the same time a committee was formed to plan a national industrial union of miners, the organization of which was entrusted by the All-China General Union to the miners' unions in Hunan and Hupeh. The committee held its first meeting in Wuhan on March 25, at which plans were made to launch the new industrial union on May 1, 1927.[8]

The various regional and industrial unions, like the General Union itself, extended their influence through the periodicals they published, some of which had quite a wide distribution. Five thousand copies of each issue of the All-China General Union's weekly, *Chung-kuo kung-jen,* were printed, 10,000 of the Canton General Union's weekly, *Kung-jen chih-lu,* 50,000 of the *Kung-jen hua-pao* ("Workers' Illustrated") published by the Hupeh provincial federation, and 50,000 of *Kung-jen chou-k'an* ("The Labor Weekly") of the National Railwaymen's Union. The National Postal Workers' Union distributed 20,000 copies of its *Chung-kuo yu-kung* ("Chinese Postal Worker"), and the Seamen's Union published a paper called *Chung-kuo hai-yuan* ("The Chinese Seaman").[9] It should be remembered that there were now almost no rival organizations, excepting the Mechanics' Union and the Kwangtung provincial federation, that were capable of effectively promoting reformist, corporate, or anti-Communist ideas.

In fact, by the spring of 1927 the patient efforts of the Communist militants during the six years since Teng Chung-hsia started working among the railwaymen of Changsintien and the Labor Secretariat was formed were now bearing fruit. The Chinese labor movement was now well organized and had close links with the Chinese Communist Party and, through it, with the whole international Communist movement. Most of its leaders were Communists, some of proletarian origin and some not: Liu Shao-ch'i, Li Li-san, Su Chao-cheng, and Teng Chung-hsia of the All-China General Union, Chu Pao-t'ing, Ch'en Ch'üan, and Teng Fa of the Seamen's Union, Kuo Liang, secretary of the Hunan provincial federation, Liu Erh-sung of the Canton Workers' Delegates' Conference, and Sun Liang-hui and Wang Shou-hua of the Shanghai General Union.[10] At all levels, the Communists were active in the unions, working through the "fractions" organized at the corresponding level of the party organization.[11] Signs of the close links with the international Communist movement were quite evident. The Shanghai General Union held its own commemorative ceremonies for the anniversary of the October Revolution in November 1926,[12] and of the death of Lenin in January 1927.[13] In the spring a delegation from the Red International visited China; it was composed of a Frenchman (Jacques Doriot), an Englishman (Tom Mann), and an American (Earl Browder), so as to symbolize the solidarity of the entire proletariat of the West with the Chinese revolutionary movement. The delegation arrived in Canton in February;[14] it went on to Kiangsi, and then, at the end of March, to Wuhan. It was greeted everywhere with mass welcoming demonstrations.[15]

The relations of the All-China General Union with the peasants were good, but not as close as might be expected. Nevertheless, the number of peasant unions had grown during the summer of 1926, especially on territory controlled by the Nationalist government, while the small peasants and the agricultural laborers were becoming bolder in pressing their demands; in Hunan particularly, they were putting up a stronger fight against exploitation by the landowners.[16] But despite the principles laid down at the Labor Congresses of 1925 and 1926, effective cooperation between the peasant unions and the trade unions does not seem to have developed with the same speed, and peasant support such as that given to the Canton railwaymen in November 1926 was a rare occurrence.[17] The Hunan congress of December 1926 called for vigorous measures against the *t'u-hao* and the *lieh-shen,* the two categories of the rural gentry most hostile to the peasant movement, and proposed setting up special courts for bringing them to trial, to be run with trade union support;[18] but the Hupeh congress in January 1927 paid little attention to the peasants' problems.[19] The explanation for this must be the attitude adopted by the Communist Party at that time toward "peasant excesses."[20]

The All-China General Union had also now become a truly national organization, with influence over the entire Chinese working class, and this gave it a position of primary importance in the social and political developments now taking place in China. It was of course hampered by difficulties of communication (a letter sometimes took as much as two months to reach its destination), and by the fact that the members of its central committee had their hands full with local commitments (Su Chao-cheng in Canton, where he presided over seven different unions, Li Li-san in Shanghai, and Liu Shao-ch'i in Wuhan).[21] However, an indication of the extent of its powers is seen in the fact that on February 28 it was able to organize a one-hour general strike in protest against the landing of Western and Japanese troops in China, in which two million workers in the seven provinces controlled by the Nationalist government took part.[22] The "general program for immediate working-class action throughout China," which the committee drew up in March 1927 and distributed throughout the country, is a much more sophisticated document than the manifesto of the Labor Secretariat in 1921, or the program for labor legislation in the summer of 1922, or even the resolutions of the Second Labor Congress. Both the extent of its demands and its realistic assessment of political and social problems show the way in which the Chinese labor movement had matured during these years of struggle. Among the 26 points of the program,[23] several concerned general political aims. The workers were called upon to oppose all attacks of the Treaty Powers, especially of Great Britain (point 1), to carry through the Nationalist revolution and refuse all compromise with the imperialists and the feudalists or with military dictators representing the feudal forces (points 2 and 3), and to help the Nationalist government to bring the Northern Expedition to a successful conclusion. Other points called for closer cooperation with the class allies of the proletariat, namely the peasants and the craft workers, and support for their economic struggles (points 5 and 12). Points 6 to 11 dealt with the main economic demands of the workers: the eight-hour day, Sundays off, a sliding scale of wages, equal pay for women and children, a prohibition against the employment of children under 13, and protection of women and children; and point 22 dealt with the abolition of the pao-kung system. Points 14 and 15 specified the need for closer links between the territorial and the industrial organizational networks, and point 18 the need to keep both on a strict class basis. Demands were also included for freedom to form labor organizations and to hold strikes, in both wartime and peacetime (points 13 and 17); point 19 urged refusal to comply with compulsory arbitration by government bodies, point 23 demanded unemployment insurance and aid for the unemployed with all costs borne by the state, and points 24 and 25 dealt with the rights of union representatives to take part in state organizations dealing with labor problems and in the management of state enterprises. Regarding employers, the program denounced reformist tendencies, capitalism, and procedures such as the distribution of shares to workers, demanded that unions be allowed to undertake collective bargaining and be consulted on the hiring of workers, and insisted that only the wealthy should be taxed (points 20, 21, and 26).

In the political field, the progress made by the workers' and peasants' movements in the provinces liberated by the Nationalist armies soon had the effect of bringing the left wing to the fore again in the Kuomintang. By the beginning of 1927 it had regained most of the ground lost after the March 20 incident in 1926. The quite remarkable support enjoyed by the Nationalist government and its armies since the departure of the Northern Expedition vindicated anew the policies pursued by the left wing, and another source of strength was the growing number of working-class members of the Kuomintang.[24] The official support given to the party by Feng Yü-hsiang in August 1926 had also helped to strengthen the left wing, and even constituted a threat to the personal prestige of Chiang Kai-shek as a political and military leader.[25] The moderates whom Chiang had left in charge of the party leadership in Canton when he departed for the North in July, including Chang Ching-chiang,[26] were gradually replaced during the summer, and this move toward the left was given further sanction when, at the plenary session of the Central Executive Committee on October 15, urgent demands were made for the return of Wang Ching-wei, who had gone into voluntary exile after the triumph of the right wing in the spring.[27] At this meeting the earlier party resolutions on the protection of labor, including the right to strike and to form unions, were readopted, and proposals were put forward for a 25 per cent reduction in land rents and for payment of rent in money to be limited to 20 per cent.[28] A further move toward the left took place when, in December, the Nationalist government was transferred to Wuhan. (Technically speaking, it was not a Nationalist government that was established there, but a "Mixed Council" composed of members of the Central Executive Committee and of the government.) The outstanding personalities in the Wuhan government were Hsü Ch'ien, Sung Ch'ing-ling, Teng Yen-ta, Eugene Ch'en, and M. M. Borodin, whose prestige and power seem to have reached their height at this time.[29]

There had also, however, been a strengthening of the forces opposed to the left wing of the Kuomintang, to Communism, and to the workers' and peasants' movements. It is true that at the beginning of 1927 the bourgeoisie gave more wholehearted support to the Nationalist government than it had done in 1925–26. The success of the Northern Expedition had made almost all those who had had hesitations rally to its support.[30] The president of the Alliance of Merchants, Peasants, Workers and Intellectuals of Kwangtung, who was one of the millionaire owners of the Nanyang tobacco company, organized the alliance's campaign in Canton for funds to support the Expedition;[31] and the Shanghai Chamber of Commerce, under its president Yü Hsia-ch'ing, took part in the fall of 1926 in the autonomist movement directed against Sun Ch'uan-fang. Nevertheless the ruling classes were far from giving unreserved support to the direction taken by the Chinese revolutionary movement during the summer of 1926. They were worried by the widening scope of the demands made not only in foreign enterprises, but also in their own mills and factories, and by the unions' increasingly active participation in political affairs. Those members of the bourgeoisie who still had ties with the rural gentry also felt threatened by the growth of the peasant unions; and this was especially disturbing to military men on the right wing of the Kuomintang who had joined the party after Sun Yat-sen's time, many of whom came from gentry circles. Even before the departure of the Expedition, Tai Chi-t'ao, one of the principal theorists of the Kuomintang right wing, had expressed the hostility felt by the bourgeoisie toward the socialist aspect of the Nationalist revolution; and this hostility grew during the winter of 1926–27 as the power of the trade unions in Central China and of the peasant unions in Hunan increased.

Another factor contributing to the split that was growing between the right wing of the Kuomintang and the forces of the left was the increasingly active intervention of the Foreign Powers, who in addition to exerting direct pressure by more or less disguised threats of armed intervention, were also putting out feelers to see if a compromise could be reached. They had been bringing in large military and naval reinforcements—especially British forces, and especially in the Lower Yangtze region—since the end of 1926 and even more since the sudden takeover of the British concessions in Hankow and Kiukiang. By April there were 22,400 foreign troops in Shanghai, 16,000 of which were British, 3,000 American, 2,000 Japanese, and 1,000 French;[32] and there were 42 warships in Shanghai waters, 14 of which were Japanese, 13 American, eight British, and three French, besides another 129 in other Chinese waters.[33]

It was these military preparations that drew the attention of both Chinese and international observers, that started the "Hands off China" campaign among Western members of the Comintern, and that aroused hopes within the Chinese labor movement that the foreign troops in China would fraternize with the Chinese revolutionaries;[34] but this was only one side of the picture. Diplomatic moves were afoot as well as preparations for armed intervention. It was Great Britain that first brought in troops, and Great Britain that was responsible for the Wanhsien affair; but it was also Great Britain that was the first of the Powers to establish relations with the Nationalist government when, in December, Sir Miles Lampson, the British minister in Peking, went to Wuhan after conferring with Chiang Kai-shek in Kiukiang.[35] An editorial in the December 23 issue of the *China Express and Telegraph,* the organ of British business circles in China, bore the significant title "The New Move in China," and declared that England was prepared "to assist Nationalist aspirations in so far as China shows she has mastered what is internationally required of all nations." On January 29 Sir Austen Chamberlain, the Secretary of State for Foreign Affairs, announced the intention of the British government gradually to give up British rights and privileges in China once order was restored there, and Frank Kellogg, the American Secretary of State, made a similar declaration.[36] The Municipal Council of the International Settlement of Shanghai had already agreed to admit Chinese members at the end of 1926,[37] and on January 1, 1927, the Mixed Court was restored to China in accordance with an agreement reached in August.[38] On February 19 a treaty was signed by Eugene Ch'en and Mr. O'Malley, the British diplomatic representative in Hankow, legalizing the transfer of the British concessions of Hankow and Kiukiang.[39] The Chinese bourgeoisie, and especially the compradores, who still maintained close ties with Western business interests, began to think that it might now be possible to dispense with the alliance with the popular forces and remove them from the political scene, and hoped for an amicable readjustment of relations with the Powers and of the unequal treaties.[40]

These considerations had made the Chinese bourgeoisie adopt a somewhat equivocal attitude toward the Nationalist revolution and the alliance with the popular forces during the previous few months or even years. It is enough to recall the events of March 20 in Canton and the measures that followed for restricting the activities of the Communists and the unions and for the abolition of the government oil monopoly. But now there was a complete change of attitude on the part of Chinese businessmen and of the politicians and military men of the Kuomintang right wing with whom they were closely linked, and above all on the part of Chiang Kai-shek and his entourage. Chiang was just the person to carry out such a switch in policy, since there were no doubts about his long-standing ties with business circles in Shanghai, whereas the position of special trust assigned him by Sun Yat-sen and his role since 1926 as leader of the Kuomintang and commander of the Nationalist army had always been slightly suspect. The first signs of a break with the Wuhan government came when he set up his headquarters at Nanchang at the end of 1926, and his intentions became still clearer during January and February of 1927.[41] Instead of pursuing the retreating warlord armies in the direction of the warlord capital, Peking, he had decided to make a "detour" to take in Shanghai, the main base of the foreigners and of the Chinese bourgeoisie. A foretaste of how bitter the "fight for Shanghai" between the right and left wings of the Nationalist alliance would be was provided by the scale of the unsuccessful uprising in February organized by the Shanghai General Union.[42] Chiang's choice of Nanchang was a good one for his purpose, for his position on the flank in Kiangsi enabled him to cut communications between the two main bases of the labor movement, Shanghai and Hupeh, while at the same time he was able to maintain contact with Canton, where Li Chi-shen and other right-wing figures had been in control since the departure of the left wing for Wuhan, and also with the petty local warlords of Fukien, Anhwei, and Chekiang who had come over to his side after the defeat of Sun Ch'uan-fang.[43]

From now on, every move made by the Wuhan government tended to be counteracted by "the Nanchang policy." The fact that the split within the Nationalist movement was now given geographical expression made it evident to all, and presaged the open break that was to take place in March and April. Chiang and the other right-wing leaders, many of whom had for several years been serving the interests of the Foreign Powers—Tai Chi-t'ao for Japan, Wu Chih-hui and Li Yü-ying for France, and Sung Tzu-wen (T. V. Soong) for the United States[44]—now went out of their way to placate the Powers. In an interview with an American journalist on November 19, Chiang was still declaring his intention to put an end to extraterritoriality, the concessions, and the unequal treaties, and vowing to conduct an all-out battle against imperialism; but on February 10 he was urging that respect be paid to the lives and property of foreigners, especially of missionaries.[45] In regard to internal affairs, he continued for the next few weeks to give an outward display of loyalty to the Wuhan government, while at the same time stepping up the attack against the Communists, who were after all one of the main supports of the Wuhan government.[46] At the end of 1926, Ch'en Kuo-fu, who was one of his advisers, organized an "Anti-Bolshevik League" in Kiangsi;[47] and in February 1927, Chiang himself chose a significant occasion—the fourteenth anniversary of the unification of North and South China by Yuan Shih-k'ai—to launch a direct attack on the "aggressive attitude" of the Communist Party and its allies in the Wuhan government, and to declare that he proposed "to put a stop to their activities."[48] In a speech he made in Nanchang on March 7, he again attacked "those insolent and violent people who claim to be in control of the party," while at the same time protesting his loyalty to the Soviet alliance "so long as Russia treats us as friends."[49]

The "Nanchang policy" implied an abrupt break with the policy of co-operation with the labor movement and the left-wing unions. It was no longer a question of making cautious attempts to put a brake on union activities, such as the regulations on labor disputes introduced in January 1927 by the Canton provincial government and adopted almost in their entirety by the Kiangsi provincial government on February 14.[50] Neither was it simply a matter of admitting the validity of the workers' demands and exhortations for a better understanding between workers and merchants, as Chiang did in his message to the merchants and workers of Wuhan on January 16, or in his speech at the banquet given in his honor by the Ningpo Guild of Wuhan on January 18.[51] Now a direct attack on the labor movement was being mounted by the right wing of the Kuomintang, and in carrying this out, they made good use of the anti-Communist kung-tsei. The kung-tsei were closely connected with the right wing, and the attempts made during the past few years to counteract the influence of the left-wing unions had depended upon their support.[52] In Hupeh and Hunan, all such attempts made after the liberation of the area by the Nationalist armies had failed because of the support given to the left-wing unions by the Wuhan government;[53] but Kiangsi offered better chances of success because it was a province where there was a low proportion of working-class population and which therefore provided no solid basis for left-wing union organization. In January the Anti-Bolshevik League organized a federation of shop assistants' unions, which had quite a large corps of armed pickets;[54] and at the beginning of March, right-wing elements in the Kuomintang instigated the assassination of the Communist president of the General Union of Kanchow, a center of inland navigation in southern Kiangsi.[55] Similar instances of violence occurred in the pottery district of Kingtehchen[56] and in other parts of the province, including Kiukiang, where, on March 17, the premises of the General Union were seized by a band of armed men who killed or wounded a number of people. The private armies of the local rural gentry took part in this operation, which, according to the report of a *North China Herald* correspondent, was personally directed by Chiang Kai-shek.[57] In Nanchang on the same day, Chiang used force to dissolve the committee of the city branch of the Kuomintang, and formed a new committee on which the former left-wing members were replaced by members of the Anti-Bolshevik League; he then dissolved the city's unions.[58] In Anking a similar operation was carried out under cover of an "Anhwei General Union" specially formed for the occasion.[59] In Fuchow the moderate unions, with the support of the local military authorities, held an anti-Communist demonstration at the beginning of March.[60] In Canton a member of the provincial government denounced the "tyranny" exercised by the unions, and the chambers of commerce launched the slogan: "No power on earth can ever make the workers into a privileged class."[61] Thus by the time when, on March 23, the Shanghai General Union gained control of the biggest city in China after an insurrection lasting two days, a policy of direct repression of the labor movement had already been put into effect, or had at least been tried out, throughout the area controlled by Chiang and his allies.

How did the Chinese Communist Party, the organized labor movement, and the left wing of the Kuomintang react to this right-wing counteroffensive? It would be an exaggeration to say that they remained indifferent to it. As early as January, the manifesto of the Hupeh provincial congress denounced the "handful of mill owners and shop owners who are against strike action and in league with the imperialists and the reactionaries," and declared that "whoever strikes against the labor movement not only hinders the progress of the revolution, but identifies himself with the imperialists, the militarists, and the reactionaries."[62] The program issued in March by the All-China General Union was still more explicit,[63] for its clauses warning against any kind of dictatorship representing the feudal forces, demanding the right to form unions and to strike even in wartime, and opposing all forms of compulsory arbitration, were scarcely veiled criticisms of the measures introduced at the beginning of 1927 by the Kwangtung provincial government and later adopted by that of Kiangsi.[64] The Central Executive Committee of the Kuomintang, on which there was still a left-wing majority, met in a third plenary session on March 11 and voted to abolish the posts of Military Adviser and Political Adviser to the Political Council—both of them held by Chiang, although the wealthy merchant Chang Ching-chiang had served in his place after the departure of the Northern Expedition.[65] A few days later, two Communists entered the Nationalist government—T'an P'ing-shan as Minister of Agriculture, and Su Chao-cheng as Minister of Labor.[66]

Nevertheless, the fact that Chiang still held a leading position in the government and in the party clearly shows that neither the left wing of the Kuomintang nor the Communist Party envisaged a complete break with the right wing; both still maintained illusions about the possibility of reaching a compromise. The main concern of Ch'en Tu-hsiu and his group[67] seems to have been to avoid antagonizing the bourgeoisie, or rather to avoid "entering into a struggle with it for leadership of the revolution."[68] This is shown by the timid tone of the attempts made in *Hsiang-tao* in January 1927 to justify the Wuhan strikes in reply to the accusations leveled by the *Shang-pao* ("Commercial News") of Shanghai.[69] CCP leaders doubted the ability of the masses to take part in the political struggle, and thus had underestimated the chances offered by the Northern Expedition, which they described as a merely "defensive move" on the part of the Southern government, devoid of "revolutionary significance."[70] Even in the accounts in *Hsiang-tao* of the victories gained in the summer and autumn, very little was said about the part played by the workers and peasants of Hunan and Hupeh.[71] Instead, warnings were given about "peasant excesses,"[72] and, as the biographies of Mao Tse-tung have often mentioned, Mao seems to have done little to support the peasant unions in his own province.[73] Ch'en Tu-hsiu also seems to have been extremely anxious not to offend Chiang Kai-shek even as late as March, and it was only against members of his group, chiefly Ch'en Kuo-fu and Chang Ching-chiang, that Communist Party criticism was directed.[74] It was not until March 18, that is, after the measures taken by the left wing at the meeting of the Central Executive Committee in Wuhan on March 11, that *Hsiang-tao* made a belated, and very moderate, reply to the speeches made by Chiang on February 21 and March 7.

There is little doubt that this very cautious line discouraged the labor movement from standing up to the attacks directed against it in Kiangsi during March, and more generally at the end of the month and at the beginning of April. Possibly the leaders of the All-China General Union tried to take a more positive attitude, as is indicated by its March program, but were inhibited by their close ties with the leaders of the Communist Party from adopting a different policy. Consequently the unions as a whole refrained from raising the question of political power and of the extent to which the working class should share in it.[75] The congresses of the Hunan and Hupeh unions went no further than demanding the convocation of people's provincial assemblies with merely consultative powers.[76] The attitude of the left-wing unions of Canton toward the affair of the New Year dismissals[77] was also modified by the desire to maintain good relations with the bourgeoisie at all costs, and it will be remembered that the affair ended in a compromise and an appeal for "cooperation between merchants and workers" without any conditions being attached.

Lessons Learned from the February Uprising

The success of the Shanghai insurrection at the end of March was an achievement of the Chinese labor movement that was of great importance both nationally and internationally; but it brought about an immediate reaction from members of the right wing of the revolutionary movement, who were greatly alarmed by the fact that China's main commercial center, which was also the principal base of the foreign interests in China, had fallen into the hands of their opponents.

The "second uprising" in mid-February enabled the Shanghai workers to express their active support for the Nationalist armies and to show their readiness to give assistance from behind the enemy lines. The Nationalist armies had taken Hangchow on February 17, and on the 18th were only about 45 miles from Shanghai. On the 19th, the General Union held a secret meeting attended by some five hundred delegates, and then declared a general strike.[78] The 17 demands presented included some political ones, such as demands for the eviction of Sun Ch'uan-fang, for solidarity with the revolutionary armies, for the formation of a People's Government in Shanghai, and for the preservation of civil liberties, but also the usual economic ones (for higher wages, recognition of unions, Sundays and holidays off with pay, workers' insurance, and the like).[79]

Shanghai was soon completely immobilized. Silence reigned everywhere—in the cotton mills and silk-reeling factories, in public transport and municipal services, in commercial firms big and small, on the docks—and the number of strikers must be reckoned at several hundred thousand.[80] The General Union and the organizations affiliated with it had taken great care, by means of leaflets, word of mouth, and communiqués, to explain the real nature of the strike both to the workers and to the general public,[81] and to ensure that public order was maintained. Instructions were given that no damage should be done to factory installations and no foreigners should be attacked,[82] and these were meticulously observed.[83]

Nevertheless General Li Pao-chang, in command of Sun Ch'uan-fang's troops in Shanghai, immediately used force to break the strike. Twenty strikers were publicly beheaded on its second day, and their heads displayed at the main crossroads.[84] The executioner drove in an automobile from district to district, while the troops dispersed all workers' gatherings[85] and arrested about three hundred strike leaders in five days.[86] It was not until February 22, after work had been resumed in the tobacco factories, in the silk factories, and by various craft workers' and other trade associations,[87] that the General Union gave the order for an armed uprising, in which several thousand union pickets took part.[88] The uprising failed, partly because of the delay in adopting force instead of strike action, and partly because the working class had lacked the support of the General Chamber of Commerce and of the shopkeepers' associations, who had refused to go on strike.[89] Moreover, on orders from Chiang, the Nationalist armies halted their advance on February 12, when they were only 25 miles from Shanghai, and this, to the great satisfaction of the right wing of the Kuomintang, gave Li Pao-chang the opportunity to intensify his reprisals against the leaders of the Shanghai labor movement.[90]

This second uprising did, however, provide useful experience for the successful insurrection of March 21. Meanwhile during March, the General Union and the unions affiliated with it made preparations for the final trial of strength, having decided to make still another effort to liquidate warlord rule in Shanghai. On March 6 they issued strict rules for union discipline, by which rank-and-file units were not allowed to stop or resume work except on instructions from the General Union, brawls between workers and resort to ta-ch'ang were prohibited, and regular payment of dues was demanded.[91] Strikes were continued in several important enterprises, and the extent of the demands presented by the seamen, the cotton workers, the Chinese Tramways employees, the dockers, and the telephone workers testify to the aggressive spirit and the high degree of class consciousness maintained by the Shanghai proletariat after the defeat of the February uprising.[92] Although in many cases the presentation of demands during mid-March was not accompanied by strike action, it was obviously a prelude to the mass action that was soon to contribute to the defeat of the Northern forces as well as to an improvement in the lot of the proletariat. In addition, there was continued action against the kung-tsei.[93] In the Chinese Tramway Company, the union merely demanded their dismissal;[94] but sometimes the unions took matters into their own hands and themselves dealt with these agents of the employers who had infiltrated their ranks, at times even conducting raids.[95] Special precautions were taken to ensure that the railwaymen in the area, whose ability to cut Sun's lines of communication at the crucial moment might be decisive, were mobilized for the uprising; and as early as March 12 the mechanics in the repair workshops of the Shanghai-Nanking line at Woosung went on strike, as did the engineers on the Shanghai-Hangchow line on March 15.[96]

At this time, the General Union had at its disposal approximately five thousand pickets, several hundred of whom were armed.[97] In preparation for the insurrection, it conducted a broad propaganda campaign, using leaflets and posters and extending the distribution of its illegal newspaper, *P'ing-min* ("The Common People").[98] The campaign raised the political issues involved: the eviction of the warlord forces, the formation of an autonomous People's Government, support for the Nationalist government, preservation of civil liberties, and tariff control in the concessions and on Chinese territory.[99] The manner in which this propaganda was formulated clearly reveals an anxiety to maintain the broad alliance of classes that had given strength to the May Thirtieth Movement and to the movement for the "autonomy of the three provinces" in the fall of 1926, the failure of which was largely responsible for the crushing of the February uprising. Contacts were established with the Chamber of Commerce and with the shopkeepers' associations in the hope of reestablishing the "Shanghai People's Municipal Congress" formed in December 1926. On March 20, three hundred delegates of various middle-class associations that supported the Nationalist government attended a meeting at which a provisional committee was formed consisting of 31 members, among whom were Lo I-nung, secretary of the local branch of the Communist Party, and Wang Shou-hua, president of the Shanghai General Union.[100] This committee became the Provisional Municipal Government of Shanghai after the insurrection had succeeded.

The propaganda put out by the General Union was not, however, confined to slogans for a united front with the bourgeoisie and the lower middle classes; it also dealt with matters that were the proper concern of the proletariat. On March 16 work was begun on a general program of strike demands. The program included economic demands similar to those presented on February 19: Sundays off with pay, workers' insurance, protection of women and children, and higher wages. It also affirmed the right of workers to receive proper training, and set forth large-scale proposals for canteens, dormitories, and consumers' cooperatives.[101]

The Short-Lived Victory of the March Insurrection

The repressive measures resorted to by Li Pao-chang and, after March 18, by his successor, the brother-in-law of Chang Tsung-ch'ang, far from damping the fighting spirit of the Shanghai proletariat, merely fed the fire. The same was true of the measures taken by the police of the International Settlement, who on March 6 arrested 24 leaders of the retail trade employees' union, and, on March 9, 78 postal workers—52 of them postmen in uniform—on the charge of discussing plans for a general strike.[102]

The general strike began on March 21, just as the advance guards of the Nationalist armies under Pai Ch'ung-hsi, who had been appointed by Chiang Kai-shek to lead the attack on Shanghai, arrived at Lunghwa, on the outskirts of the city.[103] The evening before, an emergency meeting had been held by the General Union, attended by 300 delegates, who had approved the plans for action proposed by Lo I-nung, Chou En-lai, Chao Shih-yen, and Wang Shou-hua.[104] These Communist militants themselves took charge of the situation,[105] and launched simultaneously a general strike and an armed insurrection, thus avoiding a repeat of the mistake made in February. The strike was declared at midday and took only a few hours to go into effect. Meanwhile the unions sent teams of propagandists all over the city to announce the arrival of Pai Ch'ung-hsi at Lunghwa (the Shanghai newspapers having been prohibited by the militarist authorities from publishing this news). According to the estimates of the General Union itself, there were 600,000 strikers,[106] while the figure given by the Shanghai press was 800,000.[107] There was a unanimous work stoppage throughout large-scale industry, in all the municipal services, in craft workshops, and in both wholesale and retail commercial concerns. At the same time, the various detachments of the union militias took up positions in different parts of the city and went into action against the 16 objectives singled out for attack. The electricity supply and the telephone and telegraph lines were cut; all the police stations, except the Chapei station, which was the headquarters of the Northern warlord forces, were taken by the evening of the first day of the insurrection; in the Nanshih district, the Kiangnan arsenal and the Chinese law courts were occupied, and the prisoners in the adjacent jail were released; the Southern Railway Station, which had been abandoned by the troops guarding it, was also taken. In the western districts of Shanghai—Pootung, Woosung, and Hongkew—success was just as rapid and as complete. It was only in Chapei that the battle was prolonged. Chang Tsung-ch'ang had not only the cream of his troops there, consisting of men from Shantung, but also an armored train manned by white mercenaries. It was there that most of the losses sustained by the union militias (approximately two hundred dead and thousands wounded) occurred.[108] There they had to take the last enemy strongholds one by one, by hard fighting: the Commercial Press building, the local police stations, the premises of the Huchow Guild, and finally the Northern Railway Station, where the defending troops held out until late afternoon on March 22. The end came when the First Division of Pai Ch'ung-hsi's army arrived. Its commander was in sympathy with the popular forces and had continued to advance against the orders of his commander-in-chief, who probably hoped that the forces of the unions would expend themselves in a lone fight against the Northern troops.[109]

This was, however, a self-defeating calculation, for it enabled the labor organizations and the Communist Party to play a decisive role in the Nationalist struggle and to take part in the joint administrative and military control of China's biggest industrial center. On March 22 the Executive Committee of the People's Municipal Congress became the Provisional Municipal Government of Shanghai, controlled by a committee of 19, on which Lo I-nung and the union leaders Wang Shou-hua, Li P'a-chih, and Wang Ching-yun sat side by side with representatives of the upper bourgeoisie.[110] This "people's government" immediately agreed to take into consideration the broad program of demands put forward on March 16 by the General Union in preparation for the strike, and the following day the General Union ordered a return to work on the grounds that its main political and economic objectives had been achieved. It issued a communiqué stating that "the strike declared by the workers of Shanghai for the purpose of welcoming the Southern army and eliminating the Northern militarists has been a resounding success, resulting in the establishment of the Provisional Government. We are happy to say that this success is due to the efforts of our workers."[111] At the same time the General Union reissued instructions to its members to maintain order and discipline, insisting that there be no looting, no attacks on foreigners or merchants, and, in fact, no illegal activity of any kind.[112] Its order to return to work was immediately complied with, and although one or two foreign enterprises, such as the French Tramway Company and the electric power plant of the International Settlement, at first refused to reinstate strikers, they finally gave in.[113]

Now, for the first time in the history of the Shanghai labor movement, leaving aside the brief period in 1912 during which labor organizations of uncertain character had flourished as a result of the republican revolution, the way was open for completely legal activities on the part of the unions. The General Union and the unions affiliated with it took full advantage of this. On March 24 the General Union announced the official resumption of its activities, and established its headquarters on the premises of the Huchow Guild. The following day it held a press conference at which its representatives described in detail the happenings of March 21 and 22.[114] A solemn inauguration ceremony was held on March 27 at the new headquarters, attended by approximately a thousand delegates representing some three hundred union branches. At this time an Executive Committee of 41, and a permanent Central Committee of five, were elected,[115] and Wang Shou-hua was made president.

Wang, a native of Chekiang who had spent some time in Vladivostok, had joined the Communist Party as a student, and had recently been doing work for the party as a union organizer in the Shanghai area.[116]

On March 31 the new Central Committee of the General Union issued very strict organizational regulations in order to reinforce discipline, clarify the hierarchy of the various unions and branches, and establish a standard nomenclature. Standard rules for rank-and-file unions were also issued, laying down in detail the functions and composition of the organs of control, specifying the occasions for the exercise of discipline by the Central Committee and for the exclusion of unions that failed to comply, and so on.[117] All the unions affiliated with the General Union were regrouped into eight union federations (*kung-hui lien-ho-hui,* or *kung-lien* for short), namely those of East Shanghai, West Shanghai, Chapei, Nanshih, Pootung, the French Concession, Hongkew, and Woosung, and into 16 general industrial unions (*ch'an-yeh tsung-kung-hui,* or *ch'an-tsung* for short). The intention was that the 16 industrial unions should contain all wage earners in Shanghai, whether industrial workers or not; hence industrial unions were formed for building workers, shop assistants, pharmacy and hospital employees, craftsmen, domestic servants, and theatrical and other performers. Other newly formed industrial unions represented merely a reorganization of unions that had been affiliated with the General Union since 1925, namely the seamen's, printers', and metalworkers' unions. The industrial unions set up for the textile industry (with three separate sections for the cotton, silk, and other textile industries), the municipal services (tramways, the electric power plants, etc.), and the local transport workers (dockers, stevedores, pullers of handcarts, etc.), were new creations, but contained unions that had been solidly established in Shanghai for some time. On the other hand, there was no firm organizational basis for the formation of industrial unions for the tobacco workers, the food factory employees, and workers in the chemical industries, or for the railwaymen on the Shanghai-Nanking, Shanghai-Woosung, and Shanghai-Hangchow lines.[118]

The reason the General Union made these efforts to control and normalize union organization was that since the time of the insurrection, innumerable rank-and-file unions had sprung up. Between March 21 and April 12, 75 new unions were formed, mainly in the smaller-scale industries such as oil-pressing mills, tobacco and match factories, and printing plants.[119] The Shanghai press devoted a lot of space during these days of rapid development within the labor movement to "news of various unions." For instance, half a page of the March 26 issue of *Shih-shih hsin-pao* was filled with union news.[120] According to the figures given by the Central Committee of the General Union, 499 unions with a total membership of 821,282 persons were affiliated with it at the end of March.[121] The increase in membership from the beginning of 1927, and still more from June 1926, just before the departure of the Northern Expedition, is most marked in the textile, metallurgical, and printing industries, and in the public utilities. (See Table 31.)

In view of the brief span of time during which the Shanghai unions' activities were legal, these figures probably indicate the number of workers influenced by the unions rather than the number of regular members taking active part in organized union activities.[122] Nevertheless the General Union had clearly attained a position of power never before equaled by a Chinese labor organization.

The upsurge of the Shanghai labor movement after the victory of March 22 also found expression in the scope of the demands now made. Many union branches and industrial unions now presented demands to employers, whether public bodies or private firms, Chinese or foreign, without going on strike. The employees at the Chinese-owned electric power plant, those of the stocking factory in Nanshih and the dyeworks in Chapei, the bookbinders, the newspaper workers, the Shanghai-Hangchow railwaymen, the workers at the Kiangnan arsenal and shipyards, the employees of the C.M.S.N. Company, the ironfounders,[123] and the printing workers[124] all presented demands during the last week in March, and apart from a few special matters such as the question of hygiene in the dyeworks, free passes on the railways, and permission to wear "Sun Yat-sen style" jackets at the electric power plant, the content of these demands was more or less the same in every case. At the top of the list was always the demand for recognition of the union as the representative organization of the employees, and sometimes there was an additional demand that the employer help subsidize its running costs. (The Kiangnan shipyard

TABLE 31

MEMBERSHIP INCREASE OF THE SHANGHAI GENERAL UNION, 1926–27

	Members of the Shanghai General Union			All Shanghai workers, end of March 1927
Industry	June 1926	Jan. 1927	End of March 1927	
Local transport	2,000[a] (6)	4,250 (6)	43,000 (8)	78,500
Public utilities	1,910 (3)	9,250 (8)	119,484 (40)	149,480
Railways	——	1,500 (1)	3,500 (1)	6,760
Textiles	27,280 (46)	25,640 (89)	175,280 (184)	241,390
Printing	5,880 (7)	4,793 (11)	36,445 (27)	36,445
Metalwork	420 (2)	2,406 (6)	21,100 (40)	39,600
Shipping (seamen).	1,200 (1)	4,500 (1)	6,800 (1)	6,800
Total (including other industries).	43,100 (75)	76,245 (187)	821,282 (499)	1,253,326

[a] The first figure in each of the first three columns represents the number of union members; the second, the number of unions.

workers and arsenal employees, for example, asked for 200 yuan a month.) Another item dealt with a raise in the basic wage, and often an additional demand for higher bonuses of the hua-li type and a wider distribution of them was presented (by the printing workers, the bookbinders, and the electricity workers). Further items concerned sick leave and sickness benefits, compensation for accidents, and prohibition of fines and corporal punishment. The eight-hour day and paid time off on Sundays and holidays figured on every list, and methods of labor recruitment were questioned by all workers and regarded as vitally important. All of them demanded that the unions be consulted on the engagement and dismissal of workers; and the stocking factory workers, the bookbinders, the newspaper workers, the railwaymen, the arsenal and shipyard employees, and the metalworkers all asked for the abolition of the pao-kung system. Several categories of workers asked for better pay and better treatment of apprentices, and a limitation on the number of apprentices employed in relation to adult workers. Among those who made this demand were the metalworkers (who specified that not more than four should be employed in a workshop with ten employees), the stocking factory employees, and the bookbinders.

It should be noted that these demands, although wide-ranging, were very moderate in tone. With a few exceptions, none of the unions questioned the capitalist system as a whole,[125] or the relations between capital and labor then existing in both Chinese and foreign enterprises. What British employers denounced as "ridiculous demands made by paid agitators and extremists attached to the General Labour Union"[126] were in fact demands that fell far short of what the workers themselves wished for. They were the result of the temporizing policy deliberately adopted by the leaders of the General Union, who after the insurrection had advised members to avoid all conflict with the merchant class.[127] It should also be noted that none of the above-mentioned demands was backed by strike action; instead, they were simply presented in the course of negotiations with employers or management.

The General Union was careful to adopt a similarly moderate policy toward the Foreign Powers. The "struggle against imperialism" and the abolition of the unequal treaties still figured in its "letter to the workers of the world" published on March 26,[128] and its call for a return to work on March 24 contained proposals that the foreign concessions in Shanghai should eventually be taken over and placed under Chinese control.[129] This issue was again raised at the public meeting held to celebrate the reopening of the General Union headquarters, and a demand for its implementation was addressed to Chiang Kai-shek.[130] All this, however, was merely a matter of laying down principles; as far as action was concerned, the General Union made it clear on several occasions that it would do nothing until the Nationalist government had entered into negotiations for the return of the concessions.[131]

Events Leading to the April 12 Coup

There were, however, two matters which, toward the end of March, caused conflict between the labor movement and Chiang Kai-shek's military authorities, who had taken over in Shanghai on March 22. The first of these was the question of the Provisional Municipal Government, in which the Communists were involved; this did not please Pai Ch'ung-hsi, despite the fact that Communists occupied only five out of the 19 seats on the provisional committee formed on the day when Shanghai was liberated. The General Union made no bones about its support for this democratic municipal government, and more than once demanded that it come into operation without further delay. It was in fact installed on March 29 in the presence of a large gathering; but most of the members, including Yü Hsia-ch'ing, Niu Yung-chien, head of the local branch of the Kuomintang, and Francis Hsia of the *China Courier,* obeyed the injunctions of Chiang Kai-shek and made various excuses for not attending.[132]

The second, and more serious, matter was the question of the workers' militias, which had played a decisive role in the insurrection and had thereby gained great prestige as well as having acquired a large quantity of arms and ammunition during the action (mainly from the various police stations).[133] The question of their continued existence was raised by their being specifically excluded from the order to return to work issued by the General Union on March 23.[134] A center for military training was set up in Chapei,[135] and on April 5 there was a grand parade of the militia to which each union was asked to send its own contingent.[136] The police of the International Settlement estimated their strength at around three thousand men.[137] Thus by the beginning of April there was open antagonism between the forces of the labor movement and the Nationalist right wing, and it was only a matter of days until the movement was crushed by the right-wing forces.

The awkward fact was that the Shanghai labor movement found itself placed in the very center of the right-wing sphere of influence, and over six hundred miles away from the left wing's stronghold in the Middle Yangtze provinces, with no hope of being able to establish communications with it. Since Shanghai was at once the main center both of the Chinese proletariat and of the Chinese commercial bourgeoisie, as well as the main economic and military base of the Western Powers in China, Chiang's detour on the northward march of his armies was made in order not only to link up with his Chinese and foreign friends but to keep an eye on their working-class opponents, with the hope of finally bringing them to their senses. The twenty days or so between the arrival of the Nationalist armies and the events of April 12, although they gave the Shanghai labor movement an opportunity to make further progress in matters of organization and the presentation of demands, were merely the time required by Chiang Kai-shek and Pai Ch'ung-hsi to obtain the necessary support for the coup they were planning.

Chiang Kai-shek, on his arrival in Shanghai on March 26, four days after the entry of Pai's army, immediately got in touch with the right-wing Kuomintang leaders who had gone there after being removed from office by the Wuhan government. These included the wealthy merchant Chang Ching-chiang, the former anarchist Wu Chih-hui, the prominent educator Ts'ai Yuan-p'ei, and the Nationalist doctrinaires Ch'en Kuo-fu and Tai Chi-t'ao. Pai had already received a visit from Fu Tsung-yao, a leading member of the General Chamber of Commerce, on March 23.[138] On March 29 a "Federation of Commerce and Industry" was formed, in which were associated the chambers of commerce and the associations of Chinese bankers and Chinese cotton mill owners, and at the head of which were big compradores like Yü Hsia-ch'ing. It immediately sent a delegation to Chiang, who received it very cordially,[139] and apparently they not only discussed a large loan, but actually negotiated one for the expenses of the April 12 coup.[140] Approaches were also made to the Western consular authorities, whom Pai assured on March 23 that "the armed civilians were not associated with the Nationalist army, and that he would do everything possible to suppress them."[141] Chiang for his part made contact, on arrival in Shanghai, with a representative of the police of the International Settlement, who issued him a special pass enabling him to circulate freely in the Settlement.[142] But in order to carry out a coup against the labor movement and the Communists, Chiang required reinforcements that would not offend Chinese patriotic feelings (as would armed intervention by the foreign troops stationed in Shanghai) and that would be more dependable than units of the regular army, who were still inclined to fraternize with the common people as they had done throughout the course of the Northern Expedition.[143] Here Chiang's long-standing contacts with the Shanghai underworld played a decisive part in the preparations for the coup, for it was only gangsters such as Huang Chin-jung, the redoubtable leader of the Green Gang, or Tu Yueh-sheng, who had close ties with the French consul general of Shanghai, who could provide the necessary reinforcements. Chiang had probably himself belonged to the Green Gang less than ten years before, when he was no more than a small broker of dubious reputation on the Shanghai Stock Exchange,[144] and on his arrival at Nanchang at the end of 1926 he had renewed contact with Huang and his associates.[145] Now it was through them that, at the end of March and the beginning of April, he recruited several hundred well-armed men[146] who were formed into a "Society for Common Progress" with temporary headquarters at Huang's house in the French Concession.[147] Chiang does not even seem to have bothered to keep these moves secret, at least so far as the police of the International Settlement were concerned, for their report for April 7 mentions the preparations being made by the Society for Common Progress for an attack on the headquarters of the General Union to be led by members of the Green Gang with the aid of soldiers dressed in civilian clothes.[148] In order to create a diversion on the trade union front, a General Federative Association of Industry was formed on April 2, with Chiang's approval;[149] it was led by several right-wing trade unionists such as T'ung Li-chang, who had been the leader of the Workers' and Merchants' Friendly Society from 1919 to 1924.[150]

At the same time these preparations were being made, Chiang and Pai in-introduced a series of measures that clearly showed their intentions concerning the Shanghai labor movement. On March 24 Pai held a press conference at which he announced the creation of an arbitration board for settling labor disputes and asked the unions to confine their demands to the question of wages.[151] At the beginning of April a Provisional Committee was appointed to replace the Provisional Municipal Government formed just after the insurrection; the unions had given up trying to keep the Provisional Municipal Government in existence after it had been boycotted by the bourgeoisie on Chiang's orders.[152] The right-wing leader Wu Chih-hui was placed at the head of it.[153] As we have seen, Pai had already publicly disowned any connection with the workers' militias and had vowed to suppress them,[154] and he several times ordered that they lay down their arms and become units of the regular army.[155] Since these orders were not obeyed, he sent his police to raid some of the union headquarters, and shots were exchanged on April 2 in Chapei[156] and on April 8 in Nanshih.[157]

In the other provinces under Chiang's control—Chekiang, Kiangsi, Fukien, and Kwangtung—the deterioration in the relations between the labor movement and the military authorities was just as pronounced except in Canton. The repressive measures introduced in Kiangsi during the month of March were applied even more ruthlessly in the other provinces, where Chiang and his generals were faced with unions that had been formed only recently and on an insecure industrial basis. (See Map 12.) In Nanchang the Anti-Bolshevik League conducted a further attack against the left-wing General Union of the city, which was countered by a big mass protest demonstration on April 3.[158] In Chekiang there was the same renewal of union activities after the arrival of the Southern armies in February as there had been in Hunan, Hupeh, and Kiangsi. The Chekiang General Union that had been formed at the end of 1926 and then reorganized during the winter[159] took a definite swing to the left in March, when it declared its intention to press workers' demands and elaborated a 39-point program for future action. The demands covered by this program included those for security of employment, recognition of unions, civil liberties, workers' insurance, and a weekly day of rest;[160] and a number of unions, including those of the mechanical loom operators and the textile workers, presented these demands to their employers.[161] At the end of March the General Union further announced that it intended to start a school for trade union leaders; and the program for this project clearly shows

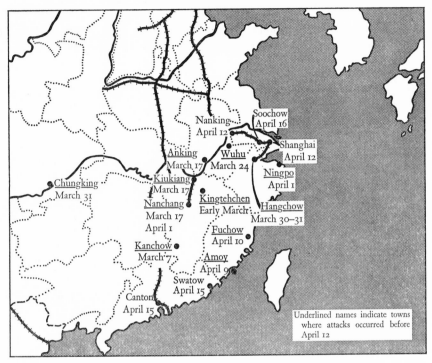

Map 12. Attacks on the Unions by the Kuomintang Right Wing, Spring 1927.

where its sympathies lay, for the subjects to be studied were problems of organization and discipline, the role of unions and of workers' militias, propaganda methods, analysis of the capitalist system, and the role of the Chinese working class in the Chinese and world revolutions.[162] The support that it could count upon consisted of 50 rank-and-file unions comprising a total of 100,000 members or sympathizers;[163] but most of these unions, because of the structure of local industry, were merely highly demarcated trade associations of craft workers. For instance, there were ten separate weavers' associations, differentiated according to the type of cloth woven.[164] The General Union was therefore adopting a line on political and organizational matters that was quite unrelated to its class basis.

As a counterweight to this organization, a "Federation of Workers and Employees" was formed at the end of March that enjoyed the support of the employers, the military authorities, and the committee of the Chekiang provincial branch of the Kuomintang. Typically enough, it exploited the regional rivalries that had always been rife between the weavers from various hsien in the province; for instance, a friendly society for workers who were natives of Tungyang, an important craft industry center, was affiliated with it.[165] On March 30 this federation, with the support of armed thugs, held a procession in Hangchow that threatened to attack the premises of the General Union, which in turn organized a big protest demonstration the following day, during which fighting broke out with its opponents. When the police intervened on the side of the federation, the unions suffered losses amounting to several dead and dozens wounded. When the military authorities thereupon ordered the disbandment of the workers' militias, a general strike was declared. The strikers demanded reparations, the dissolution of the federation, and the arrest of its leaders; but all they obtained was a vague promise that an inquiry would be held and compensation paid for damage to union headquarters.[166] Similar incidents took place in Ningpo on April 1, with similar losses suffered by the left-wing unions.[167]

In far-off Szechwan, where the local warlord, Yang Sen, had rallied to the Nationalist right wing at the end of 1926, the left-wing unions in Chungking also came into conflict with the authorities. On March 31 a mass demonstration was held in the district where the consulates were situated to protest the bombardment of Nanking by flotillas of the Foreign Powers.[168] The demonstrators came up against the police, who opened fire and killed or wounded a large number of them. The union leaders were arrested, and public gatherings prohibited.[169]

In Fukien, as in Chekiang, unions sprang up "like mushrooms after rain" upon the arrival of the Nationalist armies.[170] But here again the predominance of craft workers and of small-scale manufacturing meant that the "Fuchow General Union" formed in January was composed mainly of demarcated trade associations. About 75 unions were formed in the city during the first few months of 1927, most of which were craft unions;[171] and it is typical of the situation there that the thousand workers employed in a modern enterprise like the General Electricity Company of Fuchow were divided between five separate unions according to skills (mechanics, telegraphers, telephone workers, and so on).[172] This demarcation made it all the easier for the enemies of the labor movement to split it, and from the end of March splinter unions were formed in the main industries (among printing workers, mechanics, and dockers) with the support of the provincial committee of the Kuomintang. The purpose was to form opposition to the unions affiliated with the General Union.[173] In Shameen, too, an anti-labor offensive developed. On April 9 the commander of the garrison there, who was a naval officer, declared martial law, using as a pretext recent strikes by boatmen and postal workers. The unions were dissolved and their leaders arrested.[174]

In Canton, so long a stronghold of the labor movement, a similar offensive began early in April, despite the surviving strength of the Workers' Delegates' Conference, the Strike Committee, and the left-wing unions. The Mechanics' Union threw its whole weight into the fight, offering its members as replacements for the railwaymen who were gradually being laid off by the government,[175] and staging a big demonstration of right-wing unions to demand that repressive measures be taken against their opponents because of recent clashes between mechanics and railwaymen.[176] The railwaymen replied by declaring a general railway strike on April 8.[177] But the provincial government, now that it was in almost open revolt against the Wuhan government, clearly had every intention of making short shrift of the left-wing unions.[178] This change in the political situation in Canton did not go unperceived in Hong Kong. On March 31 the Hong Kong government closed down the General Association of Workers' Groups, an organization which it had allowed to function all through the 16 months of the strike and boycott.[179]

Thus the threats against the labor movement were mounting during the early days of April both in Shanghai and in all the rest of the territory held by the Nationalist armies (with the exception of Hupeh and Hunan), and the victories it had won since the departure of the Northern Expedition were in jeopardy. The Chinese conservative press joined in the attack, saluting the events in Hangchow and Ningpo as a "reawakening of the labor organizations,"[180] and announcing on March 31 the imminent disbandment of the Shanghai workers' militias.[181] In the political field, the Kuomintang right-wing leaders in Shanghai—Ch'en Kuo-fu, Wu Chih-hui, Ts'ai Yuan-p'ei, and Chang Ching-chiang—renewed their attacks on the Wuhan government and the Communists. On April 4 they addressed a note to Wang Ching-wei, who had just returned from his self-imposed exile in France, accusing their opponents of being unfaithful to the ideals of Sun Yat-sen and the decisions of the 1924 Congress, and of "everywhere creating unions for workers and peasants ... to which they give free rein."[182] The sudden attack carried out by Chang Tso-lin's police against the Peking Communists on April 6, which ended in the arrest of Li Ta-chao and 37 other party officials and which was accompanied by a raid on the Soviet embassy,[183] was perhaps no mere chance coincidence, for persistent rumors had been going around that Chang and Chiang had come to an agreement in order to weaken the left wing of the Nationalist movement.[184]

How did the left, and in particular the unions, react to these signs of mounting danger? It would be incorrect to say that an entirely passive attitude was adopted. The Wuhan government made an effort at the beginning of April to regain political control of the provinces occupied by Chiang's armies. A new provincial committee of the Kuomintang was appointed in Kwangtung and a new provincial government in Anhwei,[185] and cadres were even sent to Nanchang, Chiang's general headquarters, to reorganize the party there and get rid of the Anti-Bolshevik League elements.[186] The Communist Party for its part continued its campaign against "compradores, corrupt officials, militarists, traitorous members of the gentry, and other reactionaries," which drove the right wing of the Kuomintang further toward breaking completely with the left and attacking the labor movement directly. As part of this campaign it published a letter "to the whole of the Chinese working class," in which stress was laid on the fragile nature of the Shanghai proletariat's victory and the dangers of adopting a conciliatory policy toward the right wing.[187] In view of the growing activities of the gangsters of the "Society for Common Progress," the General Union forbade printing workers to handle their communiqués, and thus prevented them from appearing in the press.[188]

Nevertheless, the general mood was one of appeasement. Up to the very last moment, efforts were made to remain on friendly terms with the upper bourgeoisie of Shanghai and the civilian and military leaders connected with it, and especially to remain on good terms with Chiang Kai-shek. Chiang's name was never mentioned in the criticisms leveled against the right in various left-wing publications, despite the growing threats and attacks against the labor movement in the provinces under Chiang's control. The General Union went out of its way to be polite to Chiang, and frequently declared its continued support for him.[189] Chiang did everything to encourage this attitude, and was very astute at giving assurances of goodwill and at making ostentatious gestures of appreciation of the part played by the Shanghai unions in the capture of the city. In an interview given to the *North China Daily News* immediately after his arrival in Shanghai, he declared that he was concerned with military matters only, that he left questions of political control to the Wuhan government, and that there was no danger of a split in the revolutionary camp.[190] He repeated these assurances to Wang Ching-wei on his return.[191]

The General Union, judging from its public declarations, seems to have been above all anxious to avoid coming into conflict with the armies of Chiang and Pai, and on March 31 it solemnly denied any such possibility.[192] Like the Comintern and the whole international labor movement, it seems to have been moved chiefly by fear of armed intervention by the Foreign Powers.[193] On March 26 it published a "letter to the workers of the world," which was shortly followed by a "letter from the Communist Party to the workers of the world," in both of which an appeal was made for international solidarity.[194]

This conciliatory attitude had been displayed by the General Union when, immediately after its victory, it had agreed to a restraint being placed on workers' demands, had given up the attempt to keep the Provisional Municipal Government functioning, and had abandoned the political struggle for the retrocession of the Shanghai concessions.[195] It again became evident in the affair concerning the First Division of Pai Ch'ung-hsi's army. This division was known to be in sympathy with the labor movement, and the military command decided to remove it from Shanghai before the plans for the coup were put into effect. The General Union made several official requests to have it kept in the city, one of which was made during a big demonstration held in Chapei on March 27,[196] but made no attempt to prevent its departure at the beginning of April.[197] This was just at the time when Wang Ching-wei returned to Shanghai, after first visiting Wuhan, where he and Ch'en Tu-hsiu published a joint statement on April 5. The statement was so vaguely worded, so deliberately cautious regarding Chiang Kai-shek and the danger he constituted, that it was scarcely likely to rouse the Shanghai proletariat to rise in its own defense, or in defense of the fruits of the ephemeral victory it had won by the March insurrection;[198] in fact it left the Shanghai proletariat "morally disarmed."[199] Later, at the Fourth Labor Congress held in May 1927, the General Union confessed that it had not been sufficiently alarmed by the reactionary plans of the "new militarists," that it had placed too much confidence in them, and that it had failed to take adequate precautions against their plots.[200]

The April 12 Coup and Its Aftermath

As it finally happened, the concerted attack launched at 4 A.M. on April 12 against the headquarters of the main left-wing unions took them completely by surprise, and the 2,700 armed pickets answering to these unions were unable to put up a fight.[201] The operation was conducted by the armed bands of Huang Chin-jung and Tu Yueh-sheng, all of them wearing blue uniforms with armbands marked with the character *kung* ("labor").[202] In dozens, and at the more important points in hundreds, these men attacked the headquarters of the General Union on the former premises of the Huchow Guild in Chapei, the premises of the Commercial Press union and workers' club (which served as headquarters for the workers' militias), the premises of the Chinese Tramways in Nanshih, and about twenty more points in Chapei, Pootung, Nanshih, and the western districts of Shanghai.[203] Because of the element of surprise, and the support of units of the Nationalist army and the police, they succeeded within several hours in disarming all the pickets and in taking into custody a number of labor leaders, including Wang Shou-hua, the president of the General Union.[204]

On the afternoon of April 12, Pai tried to justify the coup by saying that the troubles during the night were the result of altercations between unions, and that both sides had had to be disarmed in the interests of maintaining public order. The bands of the Society for Common Progress, once they had played their part in the drama as planned, did in fact make a great show of handing over their arms to the army and the police. Although only a small proportion of workers, consisting of union officials and the pickets, had taken part in the battles, there was nevertheless a mass reaction on the part of the workers as a whole. Of their own accord they stopped work and assembled in small groups, and by the afternoon of April 12 a big outdoor meeting had gathered in Chapei. Speakers recalled the earlier services rendered by the pickets to the Nationalist armies and demanded that their arms be restored to them, the aggressors punished, the unions protected from attack, and sanctions taken against the officials who had ordered the militias to be disarmed. A similar meeting was held in Nanshih.[205] But in these first expressions of protest, the unions, as well as the students' associations and what remained of the Provisional Municipal Government, hesitated to place the responsibility for the recent events on persons of higher rank,[206] and the discreet silence maintained about Chiang's part in them shows that the illusions and hopes nurtured during the past weeks were not easily dispelled. It was not until the following day, when, after holding out all this time, the last defenders of the Commercial Press workers' club surrendered, that more vigorous action was taken. The committee of the General Union, which by now was illegal, gave orders to strike, and the orders were largely followed in the cotton mills, the docks, and the printing works.[207]

That same day—April 13—another protest demonstration was held in Chapei, attended by workers, students, and townspeople of all kinds, totaling more than 100,000.[208] But when the demonstrators decided to set out to present their grievances to the military commander of the northern zone of Shanghai, they were met with machine-gun fire, which ruthlessly mowed down unarmed men, women, and children. There were a hundred deaths and several hundred wounded to add to the three hundred workers who fell during the initial attacks on union headquarters and to the other casualties during the course of the 13th.[209] The authorities of the International Settlement and the French Concession gave their full support to the action taken on both days. Starting at midnight on the 12th, they had been kept informed of the carrying out of Chiang's and Pai's plans.[210] It was from the French Concession that the armed bands set forth to attack the union headquarters in Nanshih,[211] and there also that Wang Shou-hua was arrested after having been lured to the house of a leader of the Green Gang.[212] The police of the International Settlement had helped Pai's troops seek out and arrest the trade unionists who managed to escape in Chapei and Nanshih on the morning of the 12th.[213]

Faced with this display of force, the labor movement was not in a position to carry on the fight. It may have been numerically stronger, but it was confronted with not only the well-armed troops at Chiang's and Pai's disposal in Shanghai, but also the other army divisions in the Lower Yangtze region, as well as the large contingents of Western and Japanese forces that had been brought in during the past few months.[214] Despite the fact that the foreign troops had so far refrained from intervening, they nevertheless weighed strongly in the balance. The general strike gradually subsided. By May 13 there were 111,000 strikers, by the 15th 104,000, and by the 16th 63,000.[215] All the left-wing organizations were declared illegal during the days following the coup, including the students' associations and also the Provisional Municipal Government, the members of which were arrested and taken to Pai's general headquarters.[216] Already by the evening of April 13, the General Federation of Workers and Employees, created a few days before at Chiang's order, had established itself in the former headquarters of the General Union in Chapei[217] and assumed the name of "Committee for the Unification of the Trade Unions."[218] The General Union had no choice but to give the order to return to work, which it did on April 15. At the same time it sent a last desperate protest and appeal for help to the Wuhan government, in which for once it did not hesitate to name those responsible for its misfortunes.[219]

The defeat of the Shanghai General Union brought with it, during the days that followed, the downfall of the left-wing labor organizations in all the provinces controlled by the right wing of the Kuomintang. In the various centers in Kiangsu, such as Soochow[220] and Nanking,[221] the unions were put down by force. In Fukien, Kiangsi, and Chekiang, most of the unions had already been suppressed by the end of March or the beginning of April. In Canton, where only a year earlier the labor organizations had been in the lead of the whole Chinese labor movement, General Li Chi-shen finally disposed of them on April 15 with the active support of the Mechanics' Union and the provincial federation. He suddenly had union leaders and Communists such as Liu Erh-sung, Li Sen, and Ho Yao-ch'üan arrested, and saw to it that the pickets of the Workers' Delegates' Conference were disarmed. Any attempts at armed resistance, such as that made by the railwaymen, were soon broken. There were over two thousand people arrested, including leaders of women's, students', and peasants' associations, and at least one hundred summary executions, with Liu, Li, Ho, and other militant unionists among the victims. Over two thousand railwaymen were dismissed and replaced by members of the Mechanics' Union.[222] The police did not even attempt to provide any justification for the use of force as the Shanghai authorities had done; all they did was to call upon the workers to remain faithful to the Kuomintang as they denounced the "traitors and agitators."[223] The Canton labor organizations seem to have been just as much taken by surprise as the ones in Shanghai,[224] and owing to the much greater severity of the repressive measures taken against them, they were unable to stage strikes and demonstrations such as were held in Shanghai on April 13 and 14. A few groups of seamen, printing workers, and rickshaw men tried to start a protest strike on April 23, but it only lasted a few hours.[225] As in Shanghai, the headquarters of the unions that had been dissolved were taken over by a new organization, here called the "Revolutionary Labor Federation," in which of course the Mechanics' Union and the provincial federation took part.[226] In Swatow a similar attack was carried out on April 15 against the seamen's and dockers' unions; their headquarters were seized and their leaders arrested.[227] The page had been turned, and, except in Hupeh and Hunan, the suppression of the labor movement was now complete throughout the country.

CHAPTER XV

Eight Years of Labor Struggles

The armed attacks carried out in mid-April against the unions of Southeast and South China are regarded here as the closing episode in a period of intense open activities on the part of the Chinese labor movement that began in 1919, even though these activities continued for a while longer in the areas controlled by the Wuhan government, that is to say, in Hunan and Hupeh.[1] In the weeks following the coups in Shanghai and Canton the Wuhan branch of the Kuomintang still pursued the policy of support for the workers and peasants laid down at the party congresses in 1924 and 1926. The president of the All-China General Union, Su Chao-cheng, was Minister of Labor in the Wuhan government, and the Hunan and Hupeh federations affiliated with the General Union were still extremely active. In May a trade union Conference of the Pacific was held in Wuhan under the auspices of the Red International and in the presence of its leader, Lozovsky, and it was attended by delegates from nine countries.[2] In June the Fourth National Labor Congress was held there, called by the All-China General Union and attended by 300 delegates who claimed to represent 2,800,000 union members, most of whom, however, were in areas where the unions had now gone underground.[3]

It was not long, however, before the Wuhan government collapsed, and with it went the left-wing unions that had made such rapid progress, first in the South, and then in Central China, once they had the support of the Kuomintang and the Communist Party. The collapse was partly due to the economic crisis brought about by the blockade of the central provinces, the suspension of Western business activities, the scarcity of silver owing to hoarding by the bourgeoisie, and a rise in prices;[4] but it was also the result of the indecision of the left-wing group of the Kuomintang that remained in control of the party and the government following the break with Chiang Kai-shek. The group contained only a few outright supporters of the "three new policies" laid down by Sun Yat-sen, the chief ones being Sung Ch'ing-ling, Sun's widow, and Teng Yen-ta, head of the political branch of the Military Council.[5] Its most prominent members, such as Wang Ching-wei and Ch'en Kung-po, were merely professional politicians of uncertain allegiance, and most of their circle were opposed to Chiang Kai-shek only out of personal animosity; others, such as General T'ang Sheng-chih, Sun K'o, and Sung Tzu-wen (T. V. Soong), had just as close ties with the big Shanghai capitalists and the feudal gentry as their Nanchang opponents. All of them regarded the policy of support for the workers and peasants and the alliance with the Soviet Union and the Communist Party as unavoidable evils to be dispensed with as soon as possible. Their chief concern was to prevent any disturbance of the old social relations in the villages, and by early spring they were in a strong enough position to interfere considerably in the activities of the peasant unions in Central China.[6] The Communist Party, for its part, and with it the leaders of the All-China General Union and of its affiliated unions, does not seem to have learned the lesson of the events of mid-April. At the Fifth Communist Party Conference held at the end of April 1927, a call was made for an intensification of revolutionary activity, particularly within the peasant movement. This was all very well, but the fact was that the party was very much divided. Ch'en Tu-hsiu, who was re-elected Secretary-General, had not given up hope of coming to terms with the moderates in the Nationalist government and with the urban and rural upper bourgeoisie, and therefore continued his campaign against "peasant excesses" and against excessive workers' demands.[7] Communist union leaders—some perhaps from conviction, but all out of respect for party discipline—followed the same line; and all, for instance, accepted the disbandment of the workers' militias.[8]

Thus the Wuhan government, undermined within and deliberately refusing to seek the support of the masses despite the fact that this support had often shown itself to be decisive in the political struggles of the past eight years, found that the territory under its control was gradually shrinking. On May 21 a military commander who had nominally recognized its authority staged a coup in Changsha that resulted in the banning of the workers' and peasants' unions and of the Communist Party in Hunan; and by the end of June, Wang Ching-wei had little more than the city of Wuhan and its outskirts under his control. On July 15, after the Communist Party had decided to withdraw its support, the remaining left-wing members of the Nationalist government entered into an agreement to join forces with the Nanking government, which had been officially set up by Chiang in April.[9] This was the end for the labor movement in Central China, after the brief respite it had enjoyed during the prolonged struggle between the Wuhan and Nanking governments. The All-China General Union and the Hunan and Hupeh federations now had to go underground like the labor organizations of Canton and of Shanghai and its adjoining regions.

It was, however, in mid-April that the fate of the labor movement, and indeed of the Chinese revolution as a whole, had been decided. Once the labor movement had been suppressed in the main financial and industrial center of China, there was no going back and no further hope of re-cementing the alliance between the Kuomintang and the Communist Party, as had several times been tried at the end of 1926 and the beginning of 1927, or of renewing cooperation between the left-wing unions and the bourgeoisie for political ends. The reason April 12, 1927, is a date of cardinal importance is that Shanghai held a central position in Chinese social and political life while at the same time being of great strategic importance to the Foreign Powers; it is for this reason that I have chosen the date as the terminal point for this study. The remaining pages, then, will be devoted to a general assessment of the eight years of struggle between the big strikes and demonstrations of the May Fourth Movement and Chiang Kai-shek's April 12 coup.

Economic Gains Achieved by the Labor Movement

The most striking characteristic of this eight-year period was the intensity of the conflict over economic issues. Ch'en Ta's "Analysis of Strikes in China from 1918 to 1926,"[10] which more or less covers the whole period, shows this very clearly. (See Table 32.) Most of these economic strikes arose over the question of wages. Out of the 1,207 strikes listed by Ch'en Ta, 584 were held either for a wage increase, for payment of various bonuses and benefits, or else in protest against a reduction in wages; and according to figures published by the city government of Greater Shanghai in 1933,[11] 267 of the 469 strikes held there between 1919 and 1926 were concerned with wages, while the very detailed survey of strikes in Shanghai during 1926 carried out by the Bureau of Economic Information in Peking[12] shows that out of the 169 strikes held during that year, 146 were either entirely or partially concerned with wage demands. The same applies to 64 out of the 118 strikes that were held in Canton during the four-year period 1923–26;[13] and in the Japanese sphere of influence in the Northeast (in Kwantung and South Manchuria), the wage question accounted for 146 of the 206 strikes recorded for a period lasting from 1917 to 1925.[14]

In many cases—for example during the rice crisis in Shanghai, as well as on many later occasions—it was simply a question of an elementary demand for a raise in the basic wage rate. But in others, demands were presented for

TABLE 32
STRIKES DURING THE PERIOD 1919–26[a]

	Excluding May 30th Movement	During May 30th Movement	Total
Number of strikes	1,073	134	1,207
Strikes for which number of strikers is known	548	95	643
Number of strikers	1,425,349	381,487	1,806,836
Strikes of which duration is known	631	25	656
Number of days of strikes	4,273	1,746	6,019

[a] Figures supplied by Chen Ta [Ch'en Ta] for all of China.

regularity in the payment of wages, payment in a stable form of currency (especially during periods when there was monetary instability), the abolition or reduction of fines, or a raise in pay for dangerous or particularly exhausting work.[15] On the other hand, the concept of an inclusive wage does not ever seem to have been arrived at even as late as 1926–27, and demands continued to be presented for special food allocations, or for annual bonuses on the pattern of the hua-li of the old guild system, over and above the normal wage.[16] Yet the principle of the basic wage—the real sign of maturity of the proletariat —appeared as early as the summer of 1922 in the program for labor legislation worked out by the Labor Secretariat, and was again taken up at the National Labor Congresses of 1925 and 1926.[17] It also figured in the demands of the Hong Kong strikers in June 1925 and of the workers of Shanghai during the summer of 1926.[18] The principle of a sliding scale of wages first appeared in the "program for immediate action" issued by the All-China General Union in March 1927.[19]

Next in order of importance after the question of wages came that of working conditions. A very large number of strikes were called to protest hours of work, corporal punishment, violence on the part of foremen and overseers, and factory regulations or output norms, of which many examples have been given in the preceding chapters. Ch'en Ta lists 213 strikes of this kind out of his total of 1,207 for the 1919–26 period,[20] and the survey of strikes in Shanghai in 1926 gives 24 motivated by demands for a reduction in hours per day, per week, or per month, 13 by demands concerning factory installations, ten by indignation over ill-treatment, and nine by antipathy toward regulations.[21] We have seen that the demand for an eight-hour day was already being presented in the early days of the May Fourth Movement, this being a basic demand of all labor organizations.

Another question often raised was that of recruitment and employment of labor. Ch'en Ta mentions 36 strikes in protest against unjust dismissals,[22] and all those called to protest the pao-kung system can be included in this category, such as the railwaymen's strikes in Central China and the Anyuan miners' strike in 1922.[23]

Then there were a large number of strikes—particularly important in the development of the labor movement and the heightening of class consciousness—in which the demands presented went beyond the basic economic ones and were more concerned with obtaining some degree of security and of human dignity for the workers. Examples that might be mentioned are the request of the Changsintien railwaymen in the summer of 1922 to have rest rooms provided for them,[24] that of the Hong Kong strikers in June 1925 for sickness benefits and a scale of compensation for injuries,[25] and that of the Canton electric power plant workers to be known by name and not merely by number.[26] In nine of the 1926 strikes in Shanghai, demands for accident compensation were presented, and in eight, demands for sickness benefits; four were protests against the use of identity cards with photographs or other identity checks, which the workers regarded as humiliating.[27] Demands of this kind were made not only during strikes, but also in union manifestoes and in congress resolutions. We have seen how the questions of protection for women and children, workers' insurance, improvement of sanitary measures and safety precautions, and workers' training figured prominently in the resolutions of the first three National Labor Congresses, and also in the program for labor legislation drawn up by the Labor Secretariat in 1922, as well as in the "program for immediate action" of the All-China General Union in March 1927.

On the other hand, demands for workers' participation in the management of enterprises or for a right to share in the profits were rare—whether backed by strike action or not. It was only in Hunan and Hupeh, after the arrival of the Southern armies, that a few were put forward during the fall and winter of 1926–27.[28]

A review of the action taken by the Chinese proletariat during these eight years must take into consideration not only the demands presented, but also the strategies for waging the fight. Great progress was made in this respect between 1919 and 1927. Before the May Fourth Movement the Chinese working class had never done more than make sudden stands when conditions became unendurable, usually with aims limited to such things as obtaining a slight wage increase or the dismissal of a particularly unpopular foreman. The outbursts of rage, or ta-ch'ang, to which the Shanghai cotton workers were given, were typical of this stage. It is true that ta-ch'ang remained a traditional form of protest in Shanghai long after 1919. On the other hand, it was only on rare occasions that craft workers expressed their resentment of the competition of modern industry by resorting to ta-ch'ang; and only incidents such as the attacks made by the rickshaw men against the trolleybus or motor bus companies could be described as genuine Luddism.[29] Ta-ch'ang (of which Ch'en Ta reports thirteen outbreaks in 1926, eight of them in textile mills)[30] was much more the expression of the hatred of employers that was felt by a semi-peasant proletariat only recently settled in the cities.

From year to year, however, workers on strike showed a growing capacity for discipline. In Shanghai this was observable from the beginning of the May Thirtieth Movement, and in 1926 the Shanghai General Union, whose authority, as we have seen, then stood high, came out openly against the use of ta-ch'ang.[31] "Go slow" tactics (tai-kung) began to be adopted in 1926, which is another indication of a growth in maturity. Other indications were the way in which strikers and their leaders were able to withstand the pressures and repressive measures used against them by employers and government authorities, and their ability to compel acceptance, de facto if not de jure, as equal parties in labor negotiations with employers. The negotiations of the Seamen's Union with the government and business firms of Hong Kong in 1922, of Liu Hua with the Japanese cotton mill owners in the spring of 1925, and of Li Li-san with the Japanese consul general in Shanghai in the summer of 1925, are typical instances of the authority attained by the labor organizations in the course of the strikes they organized. The spontaneous economic battles fought by the Chinese proletariat before 1919 gradually gave way to well-organized strikes under the firm leadership of the unions, especially during the strike wave of 1922 and from 1925 on.

Yet another indication of the general progress made between 1919 and 1927 is the ever-widening scope of the demands presented, showing the growing capacity of the working class to deal with increasingly complex problems. Of course demands for higher wages continued to be made. A comparison of a graph showing monthly variations in the price of rice with one showing the monthly variations in number of strikes clearly indicates that a concern for sheer survival was still a motive for strike action. The strike graph shows that the months of May and June, being the "hinge" period before the harvest, were particularly critical, and were usually a seasonal high point for strikes, especially in 1920, 1922, 1924, and 1926. (See Fig. 2.) But the imposing lists of demands formulated in the summer of 1922 by the Anyuan miners and the Yueh-Han railwaymen, in August 1925 by the employees of the Commercial Press and of the Central Post Office in Shanghai, and during the summer of 1926 by the workers in the Japanese cotton mills in Shanghai show that workers had progressed far beyond a sole concern for having their "rice-bowls" filled, which was the motive rather contemptuously imputed to them by foreign employers.

Their growing maturity and capacity for self-discipline did not, however, prevent the young Chinese proletarians from displaying the aggressiveness they had shown earlier. Out of the 535 strikes that were listed by Ch'en Ta for all of China during the year 1926, armed intervention of the police was felt to be necessary in 44 of them, of the army in 15, and of foreign armed forces in 13.[32]

It might be useful to extend this analysis of strike action in China between 1919 and 1927 by taking several other factors into account. The chronological method adopted in the present study makes it unnecessary to discuss further the question of periodicity: it has already been shown that there was a strike wave in 1922 and a still more vigorous one in 1925–27, with a period in between when activity ebbed. (See Table 33.) But an analysis of strike action in terms

TABLE 33

ANNUAL NUMBER OF STRIKES, 1919–26[a]

Year	Strikes	Year	Strikes
1919	66	1923	47
1920	46	1924	56
1921	50	1925	318
1922	91	1926	535

[a] Figures taken from Chen Ta [Ch'en Ta], *CEJ*, Oct.–Dec. 1927.

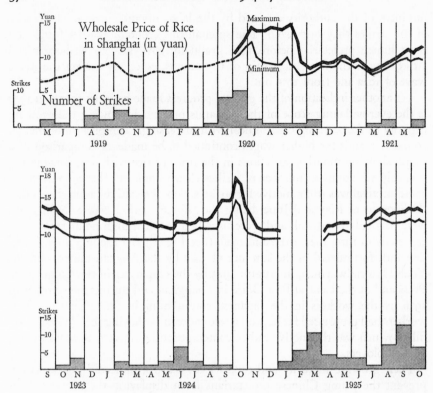

Fig. 2. Fluctuations in the Price of Rice and the Number of Strikes in Shanghai, 1919–27. The prices of rice for the period May 1919 to June 1920 are based on rough figures from contemporary press accounts, with no

of region, of industry, and of nationality of ownership of the enterprises concerned, has not yet been made, and I propose to deal with each of these factors now.

Shanghai, China's main industrial center, was by far the most important center of strike action. Ch'en Ta's list includes 374 strikes held there between 1918 and 1925,[33] and the later survey conducted by the city government of Greater Shanghai lists 469 strikes between 1919 and 1926.[34] These figures tally fairly well because of the large number of disputes during the spring and summer of 1926. But the various surveys available for the rest of the Lower Yangtze region and the other five industrial regions show that they, too, were powerfully affected by strike action. Ch'en Ta's assessment, although based on information derived from the Shanghai press and therefore obviously incomplete for the other regions, leads to the same conclusion. It is in

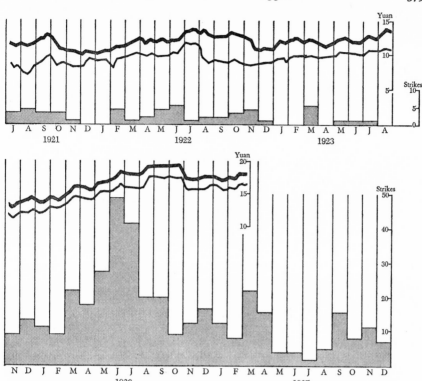

differentiation between maximum and minimum; the prices shown for
the period June 1920 to March 1927 are based on figures in *PDR*; and
the numbers of strikes shown are based on *Strikes and Lockouts* [18].

any case the only available source for Central China and Shantung. (See Table
34.) Thus solely on the basis of the available figures for the number of strikes
in the various regions, the Chinese proletariat seems everywhere to have shown
an equal, or at least a comparable, degree of ardor, and there is nothing here
to explain why it was that the northern regions fell so far behind those in the
South in matters of organization and participation in the political struggle.

Next comes the question of which sections of industry were the most active.
Here the available information gives only the number of strikes, with no indication of the duration of the strikes or the number of strikers involved. (See
Table 35.) It is interesting to see that the number of strikes in the textile industry is not only relatively, but also absolutely, greater than in any other industry, and that the next most important figures are those for the number of
strikes occurring in the transport industry (railways and shipping) and the

TABLE 34
REGIONAL DISTRIBUTION OF STRIKES, 1919–27

Region	Various surveys	Ch'en Ta's survey (1918–25)
Canton, Hong Kong, and surrounding region[a]	118 (1923–26)	32
Hupeh and Hunan (including the Anyuan coal mines)	—	64
Shanghai[b]	469 (1919–26)	374
Secondary textile center of the Lower Yangtze (Kiangsu and N. Chekiang)	—	110
Shantung	—	15
Chihli[c]	61 (1919–27)	46
The Northeast[d]	206 (1917–25)	3

[a] Yü Ch'i-chung [83], p. 13.   [b] Strikes and Lockouts [18], p. 63.   [c] Fong, CSPSR, April 1931.   [d] MDN, 21.vii.25.

TABLE 35
DISTRIBUTION OF STRIKES BY INDUSTRY, 1919–27

Region	Textile	Printing	Transport, municipal services	Mines, heavy industry	Metallurgy, heavy engineering	Light industries
All of China (1919–26)[a]	392	72	198	27	131	335
Shanghai (1919–26)[b]	204	36	51	26	9	114
All of China (1926)[c]	201	41	77	5	64	128
Shanghai (1926)[d]	96	20	8	—	18	23

[a] Chen Ta [Ch'en Ta], CEJ, Oct. 1927.   [b] Strikes and Lockouts [18], p. 64.   [c] Chen Ta [Ch'en Ta], CEJ, Dec. 1927.   [d] CEJ, March 1927.

municipal services. In relation to the total number of strikes, the number of those held in these sectors of industry is greater than the proportion of workers employed in them compared with the total number of workers. This would seem to indicate that, in general, it was in these industries that the most active workers were concentrated, both during the 1922 strike wave and in that of 1925–27. During 1921–22 action was taken mainly by the Hong Kong and Yangtze seamen, the railwaymen of North and Central China, and the Anyuan and Pingsiang miners; and in 1925–27 by the cotton workers of Shanghai, Tsingtao, and Tientsin, the postal workers, the workers in the B.A.T. factories in Shanghai and Wuhan, the Shanghai dockers, and the seamen and railwaymen in the South. The printing workers must also be included, because throughout these years of struggle, whether in Canton, Shanghai, or Changsha, and despite the fact that many of them were employed in small workshops, they displayed an aggressiveness and loyalty equal to that of printing workers in the West. And not to be forgotten is the valiant and enthusiastic company of rickshaw men, who, although by no means belonging to the vast new force of industrial workers in the strict sense of the term, were nevertheless in the forefront of the struggle throughout the period in question, especially in Shanghai and Wuhan.

With regard to nationality of ownership, it would seem that employees in foreign firms and enterprises were more active than others. In Shanghai, for instance, the number of strikers in the 180 strikes recorded for foreign-owned enterprises during 1919–26 was far greater than the number of strikers in the 272 strikes recorded for Chinese-owned enterprises,[35] many of which were no more than small workshops. In the cotton mills, where the enterprises were of comparable scale, there were 85 strikes during 1919–26 in the Japanese mills in Shanghai and 20 in the British, as against 34 in the Chinese mills, even though the Chinese mills outnumbered the others.[36] And leaving statistical data aside, we have seen how in the strike waves of 1921–22 and 1925–26 it was workers in foreign firms that led the way: the seamen and shipyard mechanics of Hong Kong, the K.M.A. and Peking Syndicate miners, the B.A.T. employees, the dockers employed by the big British and Japanese shipping companies, and the workers in the Japanese cotton mills of Shanghai, Tsingtao, Tientsin, and Wuhan.

To judge from the available surveys, most of the economic strikes during the period in question seem to have been at least partially successful. Out of the 691 strikes of which the result is known listed by Ch'en Ta for 1918–26, 448 were successful (meaning that at least 60 per cent of the strikers' demands were met), which comes to 64.83 per cent of the total; 129, or 18.68 per cent, were

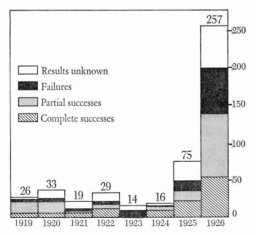

Fig. 3. Relative Effectiveness of Shanghai Strikes, 1919–27
(*Strikes and Lockouts* [18], p. 71).

partially successful; and 114, or 16.49 per cent, failed completely.[37] In Canton during 1923-26, that is, at a time and place particularly favorable for the labor movement, there were, according to one writer, 75 strikes of which the result is known, and of these, 63 were completely successful, 11 partially so, and only one a failure.[38] In Shanghai, where the social and political situation was much less favorable, the city government survey shows that successes outnumbered failures, especially during the strike waves of 1919-20, 1922, and 1925-26; only in 1923 did failures outnumber successes, which is further evidence of the setbacks in the labor movement at that time. (See Fig. 3.) Apparently successes were less frequent in foreign enterprises, especially Japanese ones, than in Chinese firms; at least this was so in Shanghai, if the figures for the years 1925 and 1926 are taken as a sample. In both these years the number of failures in Japanese enterprises was approximately double that in Chinese enterprises. (See Table 36.)

A more vital question, however, than the percentage of successes and failures, the way strikes were conducted, or the scope of the demands presented, is that of the extent to which the strikes of 1919-27 led to an improvement in the lot of the Chinese working class. Unfortunately it is not easy to assess this as far as wages are concerned. The considerable wage increases obtained quite often during the strike waves of 1921-22 and 1925-27 were probably never enough to compensate for the depreciation of copper currency and the rise in prices. We have seen how serious the rise in prices was in centers like Shanghai,[39] but it is seldom possible to make a statistical study of the relation between prices and wages. However, the Canton unions carried out a study of this kind in 1926 based on information received from 38 unions,[40] which shows a constant reduction in real wages since 1919 except for a period in 1919-20; it also shows that in every year except the first, the number of industries in which real wages had fallen was greater than the number in which they had risen. (See Table 37.)

TABLE 36

RESULTS OF STRIKES IN SHANGHAI, 1925-26[a]

Category and year	Total number of strikes	Complete successes	Partial successes	Failures
Strikes against Chinese enterprises:				
1925	29	13	10	6
1926	107	28	53	26
Strikes against Japanese enterprises:				
1925	16	5	6	5
1926	51	10	16	25

[a] Adapted from *Strikes and Lockouts* [18], p. 71.

TABLE 37

VARIATIONS IN REAL WAGES IN CANTON, 1919–27

Year	Number of cases in which real wages:			Average general variation in real wages
	Decreased	Increased	Did not change	
1919–20	3	8	27	+4.8
1920–21	27	10	1	−5.5
1921–22	29	8	1	−1.8
1922–23	25	10	3	−0.7
1923–24	32	4	2	−0.8
1924–25	27	9	2	−0.6
1925–26	22	14	2	−0.6

Improvements such as shorter hours of work and paid holidays—of which numerous examples have been given in the preceding chapters—are by their nature more stable than wage increases and payments of subsidiary benefits; and distinct, if limited, progress seems to have been made in securing these more stable benefits during the successive strike waves. In Shanghai in the early summer of 1926 the workers in the three Chinese printing plants there obtained Sundays off and a working day lasting from 8 A.M. to 6 P.M.,[41] and those in the American Presbyterian Press printing plant a day lasting from 10 A.M. to 9:40 P.M. with one hour off (but their demand for Sundays off was rejected).[42] But the twelve-hour day remained the general rule, as in the cotton mills; and all that the women employees in the silk-reeling factories were able to obtain after their strike in June 1926 was a reduction of hours from 13 or 14 to 12, with one hour off for the midday meal.[43]

The principle of the eight-hour day figured in the program of the Kuomintang and was reaffirmed at the Second Party Congress in January 1926; and in Canton, where the Nationalist government was in control for most of the period under review, a real effort was made to reduce hours of work. A survey conducted toward the end of 1927 by the Canton Municipal Council shows that out of the 71 factories investigated, 65 had regulations concerning hours of work, of which 33, or almost half, had established a working day of ten hours or less, 12 having a day of eight hours or less, 13 a nine-hour day, and 8 a ten-hour day; but 10 factories continued to have an eleven-hour day, 12 a twelve-hour day, and 10 a day of thirteen hours or more.[44] In Hupeh and Hunan, after the arrival of the Nationalist armies, it seems to have become fairly generally accepted that workers should have Sundays off, and some enterprises adopted a ten-hour day, which was upheld in principle by the labor legislation introduced by the provincial government in January 1927.[45] The Wuhan printing workers, after their strike in November, even managed to obtain a nine-hour day with Sundays off and twelve days' holiday at the lunar New Year;[46] and the Hunan railwaymen obtained an eight-hour day.[47] But many of the factories in the territory controlled by the Wuhan government in 1926-27 were still working an eleven-, twelve-, or thirteen-hour day, as in the Wuchang cotton mill and in most of the other textile factories.[48]

One great change brought about by the Chinese workers' eight years of struggle was the change in the relations between capital and labor. Employers had gradually been made to realize that the workers were not merely an anonymous mass ready to accept any kind of treatment in order to get their "bowl of rice," but human beings with the right to a better life. The vast program of demands elaborated by the unions was of course far from being achieved, but such gains as had been won here and there were enough to encourage the workers to fight for more, and made them better aware of their rights and their potentialities. In June 1926 the workers at the Naigai cotton mill in the northwest section of Shanghai were promised that an inquiry would be made concerning a particularly unpopular foreman,[49] and in the same month the workers in a Chinese printing plant in Shanghai were assured by the employer that there would be no more corporal punishment or unjust dismissals.[50] The women employees in the Chapei silk-reeling factories obtained permission to use the dispensaries run by the employers and hitherto reserved for the use of more privileged categories of employees.[51] In July 1926 the strike at the Nanyang Brothers' Pootung factories won for the workers paid holidays and sick leave;[52] and after the December strike of the French Tramways employees, the use of fingerprints was abolished and raincoats were provided by the company.[53] The year before, the settlement reached by the unions and the employers that ended the May Thirtieth Movement had included an assurance that foreign employees and foremen would no longer carry arms in the factories, a practice that had led to the killing of Ku Cheng-hung, which was the original cause of the trouble.[54] Important, too, was the fact that in several cases the pao-kung system had been abolished; this was done, for instance, after the Hong Kong seamen's strike in February 1922, and after that of the Anyuan miners in the fall of the same year.[55]

Finally, any survey of the economic struggles of the Chinese proletariat between 1919 and 1927 must point out the total ineffectiveness of all attempts at social reform from above. However meager the economic advantages gained by strike action may have been, they were still far in advance of the concessions voluntarily granted by either Chinese or foreign employers, who did little to improve the lot of the workers either during the first big strike wave of 1921-22 or in the lull of 1923-24, when the situation was much more in their favor.[56] The few efforts made during the strikes of 1925-27 did not amount to very much: the Commercial Press started a savings plan,[57] the S.M.R. a sickness insurance plan (with, however, all contributions paid by the workers);[58] the Shanghai cotton mills introduced a monthly incentive bonus, only half of which was paid out in cash while the other half was withheld until the worker left the factory;[59] and the B.A.T. Company installed dispensaries in its factories.[60] Nor were the official and unofficial efforts made by Protestant organizations to promote social reforms any more effective. Both Western and Chinese employers turned a deaf ear to the proposals made by the National Christian Council for Sabbath observance,[61] and even the Shanghai Presbyterian Press disregarded them. The movement to abolish the employment of children on night work, fervently supported by liberal-minded Protestants in Shanghai for several years, met with complete failure,[62] and the "Model Village Movement," launched in 1926, was another example of the futility of attempts to introduce reforms. All the efforts of the Shanghai Y.M.C.A. to improve workers' housing resulted in nothing more than one very small housing project in Pootung, consisting of 12 houses built in 1926, for which the required sum of 11,000 yuan was collected with the utmost difficulty. The purchase of the land alone came to 6,000 yuan, which goes to show how the economic situation in Shanghai in general, and in this specific case the speculation in land, made all attempts at social reform quite hopeless.[63]

I.L.O. activities relating to China during the 1919–27 period provide further proof of the impossibility of applying there the methods of collaboration between classes so dear to Western employers and to some sections of the trade union movement in the West from the late nineteenth century on. I.L.O. activities were confined to the exchange of a certain amount of correspondence, the publication of several articles in the *International Labour Review* and other publications of the I.L.O., and the dispatch in 1924 of a mission that had no mandate and no powers, and whose report the organization prudently refrained from publishing. The I.L.O. attitude toward China suffered, in fact, from the congenital defect of being meekly in line with the League of Nations attitude on colonial questions and of ignoring the whole issue of the dependent status of countries overseas and the effect this had on labor problems. At the inaugural conference of the I.L.O. in 1919 it was agreed to regard China as one of the "special cases" to which Western norms were not applicable,[64] and this position was maintained even during the vigorous expansion of the Nationalist movement between 1924 and 1927. It is typical that even in 1929 Albert Thomas, the Secretary-General of the I.L.O., wrote a letter to *The Times* denying categorically that he had made the remarks criticizing the Treaty Powers imputed to him by certain Chinese newspapers.[65] The I.L.O.'s attitude toward trade unionism, its sympathies with the Amsterdam International, and its basic disagreement with the methods and aims of the revolutionary unions of the Red International precluded its making contact with the really representative elements of the Chinese labor movement; and thus all its efforts were ineffectual.[66]

One of the axioms of the I.L.O. was that it was possible to induce governments, whatever the economic basis of the nation in question, gradually to introduce labor legislation. But no Chinese government during this period showed itself capable of carrying out any effective attempts in this direction. We have seen how feeble were the attempts to carry out the factory acts of 1923 and the measures introduced by several provincial governments at that time; and as for the authorities of the International Settlement, they were incapable even of promulgating a regulation to deal with so urgent a problem as the employment of children under 12 on night work. Only the Nationalist government, first at Canton and then at Wuhan, made a start at putting into effect the labor legislation it drafted during the first revolutionary civil war.

The Chinese workers conducted their economic struggles of 1919-27 in a very different historical context from that in which the British and French workers conducted theirs from the middle of the nineteenth century on. They fought against opponents, whether private employers or government authorities, Chinese or foreign, who, because of their class interests, the economic and financial structure of their enterprises, and their political views, were little disposed to make concessions or introduce reforms. Nor was there any kind of a labor aristocracy desirous of reform and prepared to take action to support it. In the semifeudal, semicolonial condition of China in 1919-27, economic struggles, however important, could never be an end in themselves. They were more in the nature of a preparatory stage for later action, during which class consciousness was awakened and forces were organized, than of a direct solution to the basic problems of the Chinese working class; and the labor movement was hardly ever deflected by these economic issues from taking part in the political struggle.

The Labor Movement's Role in Political Developments

The period extending from May 4, 1919, to April 12, 1927—from the strikes protesting the Treaty of Versailles to the attack conducted by the right wing of the Kuomintang against the workers' militias—is characterized primarily by the extent and the intensity of the political struggle waged by the working class. The bold and turbulent entry of the Chinese labor movement into the political arena radically altered the balance of forces in China and the course of political developments.

Throughout the period, the labor organizations played a leading part in the struggle against the conservative forces, whether warlords, civilian political factions, or other representatives of feudal and landowner interests. We have seen how the spontaneous strikes of the May Fourth Movement, directed against the Anfu faction then in power in Peking, already had this coloring; and the brutal attack of February 7, 1923, by a warlord government that until then had adroitly contrived to obscure its real intentions, raised the proletariat's battle against the warlords and their supporters to new heights. From that time on, the overthrow of the militarists and feudal forces became one of the main political objectives of the working class, as exemplified by resolutions adopted at Labor Congresses and by battles and demonstrations in the streets. In 1925–27 the Shanghai proletariat came into direct conflict with various military governments in control of the city—first, that of the Fengtien faction, then that of Sun Ch'uan-fang, and finally that of Chang Tsung-ch'ang; and Chang's overthrow resulted in the short-lived victory of March 22, 1927. Further blows struck by the Chinese labor movement against the medieval powers of the warlords were those of the Cantonese workers when they helped to expel the *condottieri* of Kwangtung, those of the Hunan workers directed against Chao Heng-t'i, and those of the Wuhan workers when the Southern armies were approaching.

The labor organizations also played an active part in the fight of the Nationalists against the rights enjoyed by the Foreign Powers and against the big foreign business interests in China. This was of course no new departure, for prior to 1919 the Chinese working class had been as deeply involved in the fight against the Treaty Powers as in the fight against the conservative forces. But here again a decisive step was taken during the 1919–27 period that amounted to a qualitative advance. The May Fourth Movement was still strongly tinged by the ideas of "national salvation" then upheld by the intelligentsia and the lower middle classes; but the participation of the workers produced a new and much broader threat to the Foreign Powers, who until then had been accustomed to the idea that they could have their own way in China. "Anti-imperialist" motives clearly lay behind the strikes held by employees of foreign enterprises in 1922–23, although no specific program of this kind was formulated; and these motives were even more evident in the Hong Kong seamen's strike of January–March 1922. The first time the labor movement really came to grips with the idea that imperialism was a system of international relations based on inequality was during the strikes held in the foreign enterprises of Wuhan during the winter of 1922–23, and after that it began to adopt a more conscious militance toward imperialism. The theme had already been sounded in the propaganda issued by the Chinese Communist Party and the Red International in 1922, some of which reached the Shanghai proletariat; and during the big wave of economic and political strikes in 1925–27 the fight against imperialism figured prominently, finding expression in the May Thirtieth Movement, the Canton–Hong Kong strike, and the takeover of the British concessions in Hankow and Kiukiang in January 1927. During this strike wave the economic strikes held in the Japanese cotton mills in Shanghai in February 1925 and the summer of 1926 had more prominent political overtones than ever before.

The ups and downs of the Chinese revolution and the misfortunes it had encountered from the time of the Taipings to the fall of the Manchu dynasty were largely responsible for the fact that, throughout that half century, the struggle against the conservative forces had remained separate from the struggle against the big foreign interests. Neither the peasantry nor the bourgeoisie had succeeded in combining these two historic missions—at least they had failed to do so on a national scale. In contrast, the May Fourth Movement, as already mentioned, joined these two basic objectives of the Chinese revolution for the first time; and this combination of antifeudalist and anti-imperialist struggles continued to characterize the political activities of the Chinese proletariat until 1927. For instance, the rising power of the trade unions in Central China at the end of 1922 constituted a threat both to the warlords and to the big foreign interests; and although the attack on February 7, 1923, was openly conducted by the former, it was prepared in close collaboration with the latter. It is true that, owing to circumstances, the May Thirtieth Movement in 1925 and the Canton–Hong Kong strike and boycott were mainly directed against the Foreign Powers; but the Northern Expedition made it possible for the labor movement to conduct a simultaneous campaign on both fronts in 1926-27, and the Labor Congresses of 1925 and 1926 continued to proclaim—as did the leadership of the Kuomintang and of the Communist Party—that the fight against the conservatives and that against the Foreign Powers were one and the same.

In examining the political struggles of the period, it is even more necessary to discuss separately the regions, the sectors of industry, and the nationality of ownership of the enterprises concerned, than in the case of the economic struggles waged at this time.

All the industrial regions were affected in one way or another by workers' strikes and demonstrations during the May Fourth Movement, but during the following years the workers' political struggles were marked by the polycentrism and the shifting of focus that were typical of the political struggles of the late nineteenth and early twentieth centuries. In 1920-22 it was the Cantonese working class that led the way in political action, supporting the efforts of Sun Yat-sen and taking part in his quarrels with the Southern warlords. During the winter of 1922–23 the focus shifted for a short time to Wuhan, and then, after the two-year lull, to Shanghai, with its May Thirtieth Movement, and again to Canton, with the Canton–Hong Kong strike. Then, apart from the brief Kuominchun episode in North China, Wuhan once again became the forward area of the fight during the winter of 1926–27, and finally the Shanghai proletariat was the advance guard for a very brief period in the spring of 1927.

This curious shifting of focus from one geographical area to another was in the first place a reflection of the instability of the political situation in China as a whole. The Cantonese proletariat was fortunate in being for most of the time under a government with a more liberal outlook and with closer links with the bourgeoisie and the people as a whole than any other government of the time; moreover, it was a government that knew how to enlist the support of the proletariat. The workers of Wuhan and of Shanghai were also fortunate to the extent that the advance of the Cantonese armies allowed them to join in the political struggle. On the other hand, the workers in the North and the Northeast were never able to achieve much in this respect, for this whole area remained the undisputed stronghold of the big warlords, and was also an area where the Powers, particularly Great Britain and Japan, held very strong positions.

The general political situation does not, however, provide a complete explanation for the varying degrees of political participation manifested by the working class in the various regions; another factor to be taken into account is the variation in proletarian class structure from one region to another. In Canton, the "working class" was still very largely composed of workers that might better be called artisans than industrial workers, and it was easily influenced by the political ideas of the middle and lower middle classes and ready to take joint action with them in support of Sun Yat-sen and the Kuomintang. In the regions where large-scale industry predominated, there were marked contrasts. Not surprisingly, the proletariat of Central China—because it was long-established, was engaged in heavy industry or in work on the railways, and had a high proportion of male workers and considerable experience in strike action—became involved in political action much sooner and much more energetically than did the proletariat of Tientsin, let alone that of the Northeast, both of which were hampered by their inexperience, their largely peasant origin, and their lack of opportunity to take a stand against their employers. In Shanghai itself the proletariat consisted mainly of villagers from the Kompo who had only recently been transplanted to the city, and contained a large proportion of women and children; and it was only after the May Thirtieth Movement and again in the spring of 1927 that it belatedly, and in a sudden outburst of feverish activity, was able to display its capacity for political protest.

The same variation can be discerned from one industry to another. Seamen, dockers, railwaymen, and rickshaw men were in the forefront of the political battles of the May Fourth Movement, and of many later battles as well. All of them in their daily work came into direct contact with both forces against which the Chinese revolution was directed: the advantageous position of the Foreign Powers in China's economy and the ruthless methods of the feudal forces in power were concrete realities for them. Moreover the transport and dock workers were able to interfere effectively with the movement of troops and of merchandise, and their contributions to the May Fourth Movement and to the political struggles of 1922–23 and 1925–27 were often considerable and sometimes decisive. To them must be added the printing workers, who were more interested in ideas and better informed about political questions in general than other workers, and who during the May Thirtieth Movement unhesitatingly gave up the guild traditions and the apolitical attitude that had sometimes characterized them. On the other hand, the part played by the miners in the political struggle, although by no means negligible, was never very great, probably because of the geographical situation of the mines, most of which were in North and Northeast China, areas that were more strongly dominated by warlords and the Foreign Powers and that were at some distance from the main industrial centers and from the Treaty Ports. The exception that proves the rule was provided by the miners of Hunan (at the Anyuan coalfields and the Shuikowshan tin mines), who were very active in 1922-23 and again in 1926 and 1927. Another factor accounting for the slowness of the miners to take political action was that they had not yet shaken themselves entirely free of their rural origins and were far less class-conscious than such sections of the proletariat as the transport and factory workers in the big cities. Their only contribution to the May Thirtieth Movement was the strike at the Peking Syndicate collieries in Honan and one or two minor protests elsewhere.

Of the large number of workers employed in light industry in the cities, the cotton workers (especially those employed in the Japanese mills) seem to have attained the highest degree of political awareness, at least from 1925 on. This is shown, for instance, by their response to the killing of Ch'en A-t'ang in August 1926.[67] On the other hand, the workers employed in the silk-reeling factories, the match and tobacco factories, and the plants manufacturing various kinds of food products very seldom engaged in political struggles, and then only during broad movements like the strike of March 20-22 in 1927. The abstention of the workers in the Shanghai silk factories from participation in the May Thirtieth Movement has already been mentioned.

As has frequently been shown in the course of this study, it was the workers employed in the big foreign enterprises who were in the forefront of the political fight—the seamen, the dockers, and the cotton workers, to whom may be added the railwaymen, including those employed on the state railways, since many foreigners were employed by them in various managerial capacities; and for the same reason, the postal workers should also be included. It was this section of the proletariat that, owing to the very nature of its class relations and its economic interests, became most directly involved in the fight against the Foreign Powers. It provided the most active of the working-class fighters in the combined struggle against the warlords and the Powers during the May Fourth Movement, again in 1922-23, and even more so in 1925-26 in Shanghai and Hong Kong and 1926-27 in Wuhan.

The wide variations among regions, industries, and types of enterprise in the degree to which workers took part in the political struggle must not, however, allow us to lose sight of the traits apparent in workers throughout the labor movement, above all the fighting spirit, the energy, and the courage displayed by strikers everywhere, whether in Hong Kong in February 1922, at the K.M.A. in October 1922, in the Ching-Han incident in February 1923, or in Shanghai in February and March 1927. These qualities doubtless reflected the youthfulness of the Chinese proletariat as a class and of many of its individual members. Their fighting spirit was particularly evident during the various "movements" (*yun-tung*) such as that of May and June 1919, and to a lesser extent those of the summer of 1922 for the promulgation of labor legislation, of the spring of 1925 for the convocation of a National Assembly, and of May 30, 1925, when 500,000 strikers were involved in Shanghai and throughout China. These yun-tung, which often suddenly became widespread after a period of apparent inactivity, and which, as will be discussed presently, gave vent to feelings shared by all classes, were a special feature of the "political style" of the Chinese labor movement during this period, and remained a characteristic of the Chinese revolution both before and after the Liberation (*chieh-fang*) in 1949.

Another special feature of the Chinese labor movement of the period was the importance attached to the formation of its own corps of pickets (chiu-ch'a-tui), which first appeared in the summer and fall of 1922. They were formed primarily to keep order during economic strikes such as those of the K.M.A. and Anyuan miners or of the Shanghai seamen, and also to make the hsin-kung and the agents prepared to supply them show a proper respect for the strikers. It was in Shanghai in June and July 1925 that these detachments, although not yet armed, began to fulfill more political functions, in that they provided a frontline corps for the working masses in their fight against the big foreign interests, and enabled them to sustain strike action in a way that was impossible for the more spontaneous protests of June 1919. In Canton, because of the political situation there, these detachments became armed union militias from the time when Sun Yat-sen and Liao Chung-k'ai fought the Merchant Volunteers in the summer of 1924, until finally the Canton–Hong Kong Strike Committee had its own armed forces as well as its own courts and prisons. After that it became common practice in 1926 for all left-wing unions to have their armed workers' militias, and the practice was adopted by their opponents, such as the Mechanics' Union. Following upon the victories of the Northern Expedition, the left-wing pickets assumed quite important functions, especially in Hunan and Hupeh; it was they, for example, who kept order in Hankow in January after the capture of the British Concession, and in Shanghai the workers' militias played a decisive role in the insurrection at the end of March, when the arms they seized from the Northern forces added considerably to their military strength. But even in the territory under the control of the Nationalist government certain restrictions were placed on this arming of the workers. The militias played a very subordinate role in the Northern Expedition, the military command of the Southern armies apparently deliberately employing them only as ambulance, propaganda, and transport corps, and not allowing them to take part in the fighting. And even in Hunan and Hupeh during the winter of 1926–27, the Nationalist government seems to have restricted their activities, as can be seen by a resolution passed at the Hupeh provincial congress of labor organizations.[68] The working masses themselves, however, expressed an open desire throughout the period, and especially after 1925, to have their own armed forces and to possess the military strength that would enable them to take part in the political struggle on equal terms with other social classes.[69]

The intervention of the working class did, in fact, prove to be decisive throughout the period. As early as May and June of 1919, the Shanghai strikes had far greater weight than the students' protests or even the agitation conducted by the merchants, and it was they who forced the Anfu government to make concessions such as the dismissal of the three pro-Japanese ministers. In 1922 the success of the Hong Kong seamen's strike was largely responsible for the new policies adopted by Sun Yat-sen and for his alliance with the Communists both at home and abroad. The May Thirtieth Movement, although it failed so far as its immediate objectives were concerned, considerably weakened the position and prestige of the Foreign Powers in China, and forced them, without further delay, to give at least formal promises that they would renounce extraterritoriality and customs control. The Canton–Hong Kong strike, apart from the fact that it lost Great Britain a great deal of money, gave the Southern revolutionary movement the stimulus required for undertaking and successfully carrying out the long-planned Northern Expedition, which overthrew the power of the warlords in the Middle Yangtze valley. In Shanghai in March 1927, it was the general strike and the insurrection organized by the unions that enabled the Nationalist armies to occupy the city without firing a shot. This intervention of the working class in China's political struggles was the outstanding new feature of the 1919–27 period.

Nevertheless, owing to its numerical weakness, the working class was never able to act on its own, but always had to form political alliances with other classes. Neither the choice nor the carrying out of these alliances was easy. Among possible partners, the poor and middle peasants offered the largest resources in manpower, but, as we have seen, except on one or two occasions cooperation between workers and peasants fell in practice very far short of some of the resolutions passed at labor congresses, and many of the resolutions expressed a very narrow view of such cooperation. The only times when workers and peasants together engaged in political struggle on a large scale were in 1926 and 1927, mainly in Kwangtung and Hunan. Alliances were more easily formed with the urban lower middle classes—petty traders, craftsmen, employees of various kinds—and especially with the intelligentsia. All of these often fought on the side of the working class, especially in Shanghai and Canton, against both the warlords and the foreign interests. But the alliance with the national bourgeoisie, although justified on political grounds, was complicated and weakened by the conflict of economic interests that inevitably arose within the system of capitalist production. Nevertheless the working class adopted the policy of an alliance with the bourgeoisie during the May Fourth Movement for the purposes of what was then called "national salvation," and persevered in it during the first revolutionary civil war, both in Shanghai during the May Thirtieth Movement and in the territories gradually brought under the control of the Nationalist government, often at great sacrifice to themselves. It was the members of the bourgeoisie who finally broke with this united front, because their satisfaction with the advantages it brought them was outweighed by their alarm at the aggressive spirit in which the proletariat fought for aims they had in common.[70]

Thus, except in 1921–23, the political activities of the Chinese proletariat and its labor organizations between 1919 and 1927 consisted of revolutionary action conducted in alliance with other social classes and other types of organization, and it was during this period that the proletariat came to realize both the need for such alliances and the difficulties they involved.[71]

Within the united front, however, the balance of forces changed greatly during these eight years. In 1919 the role of the working class, although decisive, was still a subsidiary one. Leadership was in the hands of the students and the merchants, and the working class was content to play the part of "rear guard" (hou-tun), to use the expression often applied to it. Six years later, however, the working class was in command of operations. It was the workers' battles in the Shanghai cotton mills that started the powerful movement that for three months paralyzed the biggest commercial and industrial center in China, brought about strikes and demonstrations of solidarity throughout the country, and produced further repercussions in the form of the Canton–Hong Kong strike and boycott. It is significant that in the title of the united front organization that led the strike action of June and July 1925, the character *kung* (labor) preceded the characters *shang* (commerce) and *hsueh* (learning), these being the three social groups that had combined to form this action committee. This rise in the standing of the working class, and the awakening of the proletariat's sense of class consciousness, were a direct result, as the study of the May Thirtieth Movement and of the Canton–Hong Kong strike and boycott has shown, of the organizational activities, the propaganda, and the leadership of the Communist Party.[72] It was a combination of the awakening of the working class and of Communist leadership that enabled the labor movement to assume a leading role in the revolutionary struggle in China.

Growth of Class Consciousness and Union Organization

In the course of its economic and political struggles between 1919 and 1927 the Chinese working class underwent profound internal changes. Conversely, it was its increasing class consciousness and the rapid development and strengthening of its organizations that enabled it to undertake these struggles.

It has already been noted, in assessing the nature of the strikes during this period, how demands concerning matters of human dignity and protests against corporal punishment, insults, and humiliating identification marks grew in importance, and how, year by year, economic demands and political aims became both more extensive and more specific. An indication of the progress made in this respect during these eight years is provided by a comparison between the letter written by the Shanghai metalworker Li Chung to the journal *Lao-tung-chieh* in the fall of 1920 and the "program for immediate action" formulated in March 1927 by the All-China General Union.[73] The first is simply an individual and somewhat confused attempt to formulate the role of the unions, whereas the second contains 25 detailed points based on an analysis in depth of the economic situation and the political problems of the Chinese proletariat at that time.

The growth in class consciousness also found expression in the protests on behalf of militant workers who had been punished, dismissed, or arrested for their participation in strike action. In Shanghai, 35 of the strikes held in 1926 were declared for the purpose of demanding the reinstatement of dismissed workers, and this demand was second in importance only to that for higher wages, which accounted for 72 out of the total of 169 strikes. In addition, ten strikes were held to demand the release of workers who had been arrested, and one to protest possible dismissal of strikers.[74]

Class consciousness was further enriched by the traditions that gradually grew up during the struggles of this period. In 1919 the only festivals celebrated by the industrial workers were those of the lunar calendar, which had always been celebrated by the craft workers and the peasants from whose ranks they had hardly yet emerged. Labor Day, on May 1, provided one of the first breaks with tradition, and except during the lull of 1923–24 it yearly became more widely celebrated throughout the country.[75] But soon many other days were added to the new calendar of traditional working-class celebrations, days commemorating victories achieved or martyrs who had fallen in the fight conducted in China since 1919; thus by 1928, when all such events were still fresh in people's memories, a private report made by the British police of the International Settlement of Shanghai listed 36 "dangerous days" during which troubles were likely to occur within Settlement territory. In addition to May 1, these included January 17 (anniversary of the execution of the anarchists Huang and P'ang in Changsha in 1922), February 7 (anniversary of the massacre of the Ching-Han railwaymen in 1923), May 4 (anniversary of the 1919 movement), May 30 (anniversary of the Nanking Road incident in 1925), July 15 (anniversary of the departure of the Northern Expedition in 1926), and December 17 (anniversary of the execution of the union leader Liu Hua in Shanghai in 1925).[76]

From 1925 on, this class consciousness and the traditions that enshrined it increasingly took on a national, and even international, character, as the regionalist tendencies still strong in 1919 began to disappear. The failure of the attempts made in Shanghai in 1922 to recruit Ningpo seamen in order to break the Hong Kong seamen's strike shows that even at that time regional rivalries were a thing of the past; another example is the decreasing frequency, if not the complete disappearance, of brawls between natives of the Kompo and those of Shantung in the Shanghai cotton mills. In the realm of labor organizations, the complete disappearance in 1925 of the regional friendly societies in which, during 1923–24, the right-wing Federation of Labor Organizations had placed all its hopes, provides further evidence of the decrease in regional loyalties. Meanwhile the working class increasingly displayed a sense of national unity. The fact that workers everywhere, from Peking to Canton, and from Shanghai to Wuhan and Chungking, took part in the May Fourth Movement, was one of its new features; and later the same solidarity was displayed in all the regions at every crisis of the labor movement: solidarity with the Hong Kong and K.M.A. strikers in 1922, with the campaign for labor legislation during the summer of 1922, and with the victims of the Ching-Han incident in February 1923. There was also coordination between regions regarding the declaration of strikes, especially when it was a question of strikes in factories belonging to the same firm.[77] National unity was finally achieved in 1925, when practically every one of the industrial regions of China contributed its quota to the 500,000 strikers that came out during the May Thirtieth Movement.[78]

This advance in class solidarity was not due solely to the growth of coordinated action in the labor movement. It was accelerated and amplified by the activities and the propaganda of the Communist militants and the organizations they sponsored, among which the Labor Secretariat seems to have been of particular importance. The advances in trade union organization made during these eight years were due also to this combination of a growing maturity on the part of the proletariat and of direct and systematic action on the part of the Communists.

In 1919 most labor organizations, except perhaps for the seamen's associations, either had scarcely emerged from the old guild traditions, or else had suddenly sprung up in connection with the efforts made by small-scale employers to promote "industrial advance," whereas eight years later modern trade unionism was firmly established and had become an independent force, because of both the scale of membership and the capacity for action it displayed. The All-China General Union claimed to have 540,000 members at the time when it was founded in May 1925, 1,240,000 members when its congress was held in May 1926, and 2,800,000 members at the time of the congress held in June 1927.[79] We have seen that after 1919 trade union organization was carried out mainly among the seamen, the railwaymen, and the postal workers, and that one after another they formed powerful national industrial federations, as did later the printing workers, the rickshaw men, and to some extent the miners and the dockers. In light industry, it was only in the cotton mills that genuine trade unions developed; and even in the mills unions developed slowly in Shanghai, and were formed in Wuhan only after the arrival of the Northern Expedition. In other sectors, such as the silk, tobacco, match, and flour-milling industries, the workers, despite their numbers, were not much involved in the trade union movement, except in the territories controlled by the Nationalist government.

With regard to regions, it was in Canton that the most progress was made, mainly because of the favorable political situation there and despite the fact that workers tended to be dispersed throughout the region rather than concentrated in big enterprises. Hardly a year, or even a few months, passed without the appearance of several new unions in the great Southern capital. But the trade union movement reached its height there in 1921–22, thanks to the particularly tolerant attitude of the Constitutionalist government then in power, and in 1925–26, during the wave of enthusiasm engendered by the strike and boycott. (See Fig. 4.) In Hupeh and Hunan, the existence of rela-

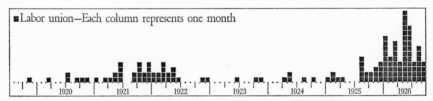

Fig. 4. Number of Labor Unions Founded in Canton, 1920–26
(*Nien-chien* [138] II, 73–79).

tively long-established industrial enterprises would lead one to expect that the proletariat there was better prepared than elsewhere for modern trade unionism; but it was only during the months preceding the incident of February 7, 1923, and again after the arrival of the Northern Expedition, that the unions made much headway. During these two short periods powerful provincial federations were formed, as well as the industrial union in the Hanyehping combine, which was unique of its kind. In Shanghai, the development of true industrial unionism was for a long time hampered by the presence of a large proportion of female and child labor, by the semi-peasant nature of the main body of the proletariat, and by the favorable climate the city provided for the kung-tsei and for union subversionists of all kinds. It was not until the great strike wave of the May Thirtieth Movement in 1925 that Shanghai's hotheaded and inexperienced proletariat began developing self-discipline and became organized into powerful unions that were federated in the Shanghai General Union. Thereafter, and especially during the summer of 1926, the General Union had full control of the economic struggle there, and after leading the rising in March 1927 it gained full political control, if only for a few days.[80] On the other hand, in Shantung, Chihli, and still more in the Northeast, union organization was very weak. This backwardness of the North was no doubt due in part to the lack of any political counterweight in this area to the power of the warlords, who had the support of the Foreign Powers. It was also due to the fact that the proletariat there had not been established for long and was still unstable.

The feature of all these unions, whether strong or weak, short-lived or enduring, was their novelty. There had never before been anything like them in Chinese society. They made a complete break with guild traditions, apart from a few survivals of these in Canton. Their class basis, the idea of industrial unionism that grew in strength after 1921, the rules laying down a three-level organizational structure, and of course their ideological outlook, were all things that were totally foreign to the old guilds. Also new was their ability to organize and take action at a national level, since the craft guilds had always been narrowly regional, reflecting the backward and restricted nature of the market system. Even the organizations of the most modern sectors of the bourgeoisie had scarcely managed to go beyond the local or regional level, and in 1920–23 dreams of forming a powerful national federation of chambers of commerce had never come to anything. The very existence of the "All-China" (*ch'üan-kuo*) General Union was enough to show that, of all classes, the working class was the one that was most detached from the old form of society and the furthest advanced along the path toward national unity, to which the bourgeoisie, the intelligentsia, and the urban middle classes all aspired but which they were unable to achieve because of the centrifugal tendencies of the warlords and the conservatives upon whose support they depended.

The working class also showed itself to be furthest advanced in the matter of international contacts and affiliations. The leading role played by the Communists in the labor organizations after 1920 naturally resulted in their turning toward the Red International of Labor Unions, with which they entered into relations in 1922 and with which the All-China General Union became affiliated when it was formed in 1925. The contemptuous tone adopted by the Amsterdam International Federation of Trade Unions toward the Chinese unions, especially during the strike wave of 1925–27,[81] only strengthened relations with the Red International. These relations were not merely a matter of form. The organizational structure adopted by the Chinese unions was clearly modeled on that of the revolutionary unions. Moreover, the Shanghai strikers obtained substantial financial aid from the Red International and from Soviet unions in the summer of 1925,[82] and a Soviet trade union delegation visited Shanghai and Canton at that time; and in the spring of 1927 a Red International delegation visited South and Central China. Both delegations were greeted with huge mass demonstrations.[83] It was during these years that the Chinese workers became aware of international proletarian solidarity, and their horizons were extended beyond the frontiers of the Middle Kingdom. It is interesting to find that during the summer of 1926 the Canton unions, apparently better informed about European affairs than the Amsterdam Federation was about China, collected over 10,000 yuan to send to the strikers in the General Strike in Great Britain.[84]

Throughout the period, the left-wing unions were concerned mainly with strike action and the political struggle; but they did not neglect cultural and social tasks when the political situation allowed, and organized many social services run by workers in their own interests. They were not, in principle, against such activities, and the only reason they quarreled with the reformist unions on this issue was that they insisted on the need for combining such activities with the mass struggle. Thus, between 1922 and 1925 the social work done by the Anyuan miners' club[85] rivaled that of the reformist Canton Mechanics' Union, of which it was so proud. Similarly the Canton–Hong Kong Strike Committee, from the time of its formation in the winter of 1925 until the winter of 1926-27, ran training and educational facilities of all kinds, as well as canteens and dispensaries, and it spent a lot of money on them. Of all such services, those that had the most permanent effect were the extramural schools, the evening classes, and the "schools for the common people" run by the Chinese labor movement. Such schools provided better opportunities for organizing the workers than larger-scale organizations. They were flexible and mobile, required very little investment of funds, and enjoyed greater security against police intervention at times when unions as such were banned. As we have seen, a workers' school or evening class often provided the nucleus from which a union could eventually be formed, as in Changsintien in 1920, in Tientsin in 1924, and in the Shanghai cotton mills during the winter of 1924-25. But it would be wrong to regard these schools simply as a cover for more militant activities. The desire to overcome illiteracy had always been and continued to be very strong among Chinese workers, and was probably all the greater because of the difficulties of the ideographic script and the prestige the educated man had always enjoyed in China. Whenever the unions were able to conduct their activities freely and openly, as in Canton, or in Wuhan after October 1926, educational activities, far from decreasing, expanded in all directions.

What was the real nature of the unions that sprang up in crowded ranks, "like mushrooms after rain," in Canton from 1920 on and especially after 1924, in North and Central China under the stimulus of the Labor Secretariat in 1921-23, in Shanghai as a result of the enthusiasm engendered by the May Thirtieth Movement, in the North during the brief period in 1925-26 when they had the protection of the Kuominchun, and in the Middle and Lower Yangtze regions after the arrival of the Northern Expedition? To what extent were they effectively organized and able to provide firm leadership? How much real support did they have from their members and how conscious was this support? It would, of course, be absurd to compare their internal organization with that of the British T.U.C. or the French G.C.T., for it is clear that during the period in question the Chinese labor movement was much weaker in this respect than in its capacity for action, as is shown, for instance, by the fact that after the big strike wave in 1925, the degree of union organization that remained when the lull came was far from commensurate with the action that had been taken. Nor should the membership figures as announced by the unions, or as given at the various National Labor Congresses, be taken at face value. Nevertheless, most of the left-wing unions can be regarded as having been truly representative of the working class; indeed, this was the difference between them and their right-wing opponents the "poster" unions, as they were contemptuously called, whose leaders, with the sole exception of those of the Canton Mechanics' Union, spoke only for themselves.

That the left-wing unions were held in high regard by the workers is shown by the number of strikes called to demand that the employers give official recognition to the unions, or to protest sanctions imposed on unions or union leaders. Demands of this kind were a feature of the 1921–23 strike wave in Central China and in that of 1926 in Shanghai.

Yet even if their internal organization was not always very strong, the unions were nevertheless able to influence the masses and organize them for action. The extent of the control they were able to exercise is shown by the discipline maintained during the economic strikes in Shanghai in 1925–26 and during the 1927 armed uprisings, and even more by the obstinate refusal of the railwaymen of the Ching-Han stations to go back to work in February 1923 unless the order was given by the union, "the second self of the workers."

The labor press, during both the times when the unions were prospering and those difficult times when they were reduced to conducting clandestine activities, helped greatly to keep the leadership in touch with the working masses. We have seen how helpful it was to the small Communist groups in 1920, and a little later to the Labor Secretariat; and how the journal *Lao-tung-chieh*,[86] to judge from the many letters from workers it published, had a wide circulation in the industrial enterprises of Shanghai and Central China. We know also how big the circulation figures of the labor press in Canton were after the left-wing unions were established there, and in Wuhan after the arrival of the Northern Expedition.[87]

The surest evidence of the extent to which the unions were representative of their members and able to speak with authority is, however, provided by the way in which employers and civilian or military government authorities, whether Chinese or foreign, accepted them as the parties with which to negotiate labor disputes. This happened even in areas where the right of workers to form trade unions was disputed—which is as much as to say, the whole of China except for the territory under the control of the Nationalist government. In November 1922, the strike in the British Cigarette Company's factory in Hankow was settled at a meeting between the manager, Mr. J. Gilliam, and two delegates of the factory union, presided over by the president of the Hupeh provincial federation;[88] and in Shanghai, the negotiations conducted between the Japanese cotton mill owners and Liu Hua in February 1925, and, even more, those conducted in the summer between the Japanese consul general and Li Li-san, implied de facto recognition of the unions involved. Many other examples of this kind could be cited.

It is true that the survival rate of all these unions that formed the backbone of the labor movement was not very high. In Shanghai, unions formed in 1922 simply disappeared during the repression that followed, and did not come into being again until the summer of 1925; and in Hunan there was a similar eclipse between the periods of intense activity in 1922–23 and 1926–27. The railwaymen of North China were the pioneers of the Chinese trade union movement in 1921–23, and after the lull following the incident of February 7, 1923, they tried to carry out an ambitious program of "restoration of the unions"; yet by the end of 1925 there was hardly a union left that was capable of taking action.[89] This failure to survive was due largely to the changing political situation from one year to the next and from one region to the next. Nevertheless during the years from 1919 to 1927 the Chinese working class learned the lesson that labor organizations enjoying mass support and determined to take revolutionary action were powerful weapons in both the economic and the political struggle, however short-lived or intermittent their power might be.

Sources of Union Leadership

The question of leadership was of vital importance during the initial stage of the labor movement, when experience in union organization was extremely limited; naturally leaders of nonproletarian origin were needed at first until genuine members of the proletariat could be promoted to positions of responsibility. But gradually the number of working-class union leaders increased during the period under review, and, although there is very little information on this point,[90] the outstanding ones all seem to have been recruited from the ranks of the skilled workers—the seamen, the mechanics, the railwaymen, and the printing workers—many of whom came to occupy responsible posts in the Labor Secretariat and, from 1925 on, in the All-China General Union and its affiliated unions. The seamen produced three important leaders: Lin Wei-min, a leader of the Hong Kong seamen's strike in 1922 and president of the All-China General Union in 1925;[91] Chu Pao-t'ing, who in 1922 organized the Shanghai movement of solidarity with the Hong Kong seamen, who was in command of the pickets during the May Thirtieth Movement,[92] and who was a deputy member of the Executive Committee of the All-China General Union in May 1926;[93] and most important of all, Su Chao-cheng, chief organizer of the 1922 strike, president of the All-China General Union in 1926, president of the Canton–Hong Kong Strike Committee in 1925–26, and Minister of Labor in the Wuhan government in April 1927.[94] Three prominent leaders from the mechanics were: Teng P'ei, a Cantonese who came to Tientsin as an apprentice in 1898 at the age of 14, entered the Tangshan mechanical workshops in 1901, organized working-class protests in that city during the May Fourth Movement, attended the Congress of Toilers of the Far East in Moscow at the beginning of 1922 as a delegate, organized the strikes in the fall of 1922 at the Tangshan railway workshops, the Tangshan cement works, and the K.M.A. mines, and later left for Canton, where he became a member of the Executive Committee of the All-China General Union in 1926;[95] Liu Tung-hsuan, a mechanic at the Shuikowshan mine, who founded the workers' club there in 1922 and took part in reorganizing it after the arrival of the Northern Expedition in 1926;[96] and Hsü Pai-hao, the delegate of the Canton Mechanics' Union at the First National Labor Congress in May 1922, who in 1924 took part in the movement for the restoration of the railwaymen's unions, and who was a member of the Executive Committee of the All-China General Union in 1925[97] and president of the Hupeh provincial federation in 1926–27.[98] The railwaymen produced at least two important leaders: Lin Hsiang-ch'ien, an apprentice in a Fuchow mechanical workshop who became a railwayman on the Ching-Han line,[99] who was a leader of the pang for natives of Fukien on that line,[100] secretary of its workers' club, and later secretary of the Kiangan union branch, and who was beheaded on the station platform at Kiangan in February 1923 for having refused to give the order to return to work;[101] and Liu Wen-sung, founder in 1922 of the Chengchow railwaymen's club,[102] vice-president of the All-China General Union in May 1925,[103] and founder of the Honan provincial federation in the summer of 1925.[104] And finally, among the leaders produced from the printing workers were two very active men: Liu Hua, a China Bookshop apprentice who got a job as a technician at the Shanghai University, where he became acquainted with some Communist intellectuals, and who later organized both the West Shanghai Workers' Club and the strike in the Shanghai cotton mills (February 1925), and directed the Shanghai General Union from the time it was founded on May 31, 1925, until he was arrested by the police of the International Settlement on September 18 and turned over by them to the Chinese authorities, who put him to death in November;[105] and Ma Ch'ao-fan, the son of a Kwangtung craftsman, whose classical education was broken off when his father's business failed, who then became an apprentice in a printing plant, and who later organized an industrial union for printing workers first in Hong Kong and then in Canton, where he became one of the leaders of the Canton Workers' Delegates' Conference.[106]

In addition to these union leaders from the ranks of the skilled workers, there were a few who had been unskilled workers: Hsiang Ying, a Wuhan cotton worker, who joined the Labor Secretariat in 1922 as a result of reading *Lao-tung chou-pao* and later became one of the outstanding leaders of the All-China General Union in 1925;[107] Hsiang Chung-fa, a coolie on the ore-barges of the Hanyehping Company, who became a leader of the industrial union formed in this enterprise, and then of the Hupeh provincial federation at the end of 1922 and again in 1926;[108] and the docker T'ao Ching-hsuan, who led the pickets of the Shanghai General Union during the May Thirtieth Movement.[109]

Nevertheless, the merest glance at the record of the activities of the Labor Secretariat in 1921–23 and of the All-China General Union from 1925 on is enough to show that leadership was mainly in the hands of the Communist intellectuals assigned by their party to the task of union organization. The careers of three of the most eminent among them—Teng Chung-hsia, Li Li-san, and Liu Shao-ch'i—are an illustration of the important part played by them, not only in the early stages of the Chinese labor movement, but also in all the later battles of the Chinese working class.

Teng Chung-hsia came of a rural gentry family in Honan, and was won over to Marxism through his contacts with Li Ta-chao's circle in Peking. At the beginning of 1921 he and Chang Kuo-t'ao started the Changsintien workers' club, and in May 1922 he attended the First Labor Congress, after which he was put in charge of the Labor Secretariat, with Chang Kuo-t'ao acting as an assistant. He took the lead in organizing the campaign for labor legislation in August 1922, and then in October he went to the K.M.A. mines in order to make sure that the strike about to be declared there was carried through. In 1923–24 he was one of the chief opponents of the "liquidation" policy then being advocated by some members of the Communist Party, and in October 1924 he and Chang Kuo-t'ao launched the review *Chung-kuo kung-jen*. In February 1925 the party sent him to take charge of the strike in the Shanghai cotton mills. When the All-China General Union was founded he was put in charge of propaganda, and in July 1925 he became chief adviser to the Canton–Hong Kong Strike Committee, serving as the direct representative of the Communist Party.[110]

Li Li-san, a Hunanese who, as a student, went to France on the "Work and Study" plan, helped to found the Anyuan miners' club in the spring of 1922. Later he went to Shanghai and helped Teng Chung-hsia in organizing the cotton workers' strike in February 1925. He remained there and led the Shanghai General Union all through the May Thirtieth Movement, conducting in its name the more or less official negotiations with the Chinese Chamber of Commerce and the Japanese and British mill owners.[111] In May 1926 he was put in charge of the organization department of the All-China General Union.[112]

Liu Shao-ch'i, another Hunanese, ran the Anyuan miners' club until the fall of 1923.[113] He worked with Li Li-san in running the Shanghai General Union during the May Thirtieth Movement,[114] and in May 1925 he became a vice-president of the All-China General Union. In May 1926 he was put in charge of its administration department.[115] In the fall he went to Wuhan along with all the other leaders of the All-China General Union. It was he who organized the mass demonstration that ended in the taking of the British Concession in Hankow in April 1927.[116]

These three men each played a particularly important role as leaders of the Chinese labor movement, filling many of the most responsible posts during its various phases. But on a lower level young Marxist intellectuals also played a decisive part in all the various industrial regions. In Shanghai, for instance, the Hunanese student Li Ch'i-han took part in starting the first evening classes in the cotton mill district at the end of 1920, in founding the Labor Secretariat in 1921, in arranging the May Day celebrations of 1921 and 1922, and in organizing the seamen's, postal workers', and Pootung textile workers' strikes in 1922.[117] In Wuhan, the lawyer Shih Yang established schools for workers in 1920, was in charge of the local office of the Labor Secretariat in 1921–22, helped to organize the strikes of the rickshaw men and of the Yueh-Han railwaymen, and acted as legal adviser to the newly formed unions in Hupeh; he was arrested and put to death at the time of the incident of February 7, 1923.[118] In Hunan, the student Kuo Liang organized the Changsha rickshaw men's strike in 1921, and in 1922 started workers' clubs and organized strikes in the main railway stations of Hunan. In November 1922 he became, along with Mao Tse-tung, one of the leading figures in the provincial federation of unions formed at that time, and he re-formed the federation after the arrival of the Northern Expedition in 1926.[119] Chao Hsing-nung, a Shanghai student who was sent to Nanchang in October 1922 for the purpose of forming youth and union organizations there, succeeded in founding several unions in 1924; but when Sun Ch'uan-fang's armies were defeated in August 1926, he was arrested and executed.[120] And in North China many of the students coming under the influence of Li Ta-chao, who enjoyed a great reputation as a university teacher and a leading intellectual, were persuaded to take up union work during 1921–22 and to offer their services to the Labor Secretariat.[121]

Many more examples of Marxist intellectuals who became leaders of the Chinese labor movement could be quoted; but very soon they merged with the leaders of working-class origin, and there seems to have been no antagonism between the two throughout the period under review. Difference of origin was of little account in carrying through the task at hand: both the mechanic Lin Hsiang-ch'ien and the lawyer Shih Yang were executed by Wu P'ei-fu when he broke the Ching-Han railwaymen's strike in February 1923.

The Labor Movement and the Communist Party

The preponderance of Marxist intellectuals among the leaders of the Chinese labor movement raises the question of its general ideological orientation and of the relations between the unions and the Chinese Communist Party. Relations with the Communist Party grew ever closer as one by one the other political and ideological currents that had at one time influenced, or tried to influence, the working class began to lose ground. The anarchists, who had got in ahead of the Marxists in their attempts to gain influence among the proletariat and had published their magazine *Lao-tung* in Shanghai as early as 1918, were very influential in Hunan, Canton, and other centers in 1920-21, but their numbers began to dwindle during the lull of 1923-24; after 1925 they disappeared altogether and seem to have played no part either in the May Thirtieth Movement or in the Canton–Hong Kong strike. Just as complete was the failure of the Shanghai reformist organizations, which in 1919-21 exerted considerable influence in certain sections of the proletariat there, especially among the skilled workers. Their ideas about "industrial advance" and their hopes of a type of economic collaboration between employers and workers that would be to the advantage of both gave way in 1922 to a deep hostility toward the Communists, with whom they had for a short time cooperated. The period of repression in 1923-24 enabled them to come to the fore temporarily, but as soon as the labor battles in Shanghai on both the economic and political fronts once again took on the nature of a mass movement, they met with total defeat. They reappeared in 1926 as direct agents of the employers, and again in April 1927, when Chiang Kai-shek sought allies for the "reorganization" of the unions after he had ruthlessly disposed of their Communist leaders. The defeat of the Christian reformers was still more rapid, as can be seen by what happened to the efforts of the Y.M.C.A. and the National Christian Council. Promoters of reform like Chu Yü-ts'ang, the industrial secretary of the Y.M.C.A. who was employed by the Commercial Press in 1927 to look into their labor problems,[122] do not seem to have even attempted to set up proper labor organizations, although the "industrial departments" of the Y.M.C.A. formed in 1920 did at one time propose to do so. Instead, they confined themselves to works of a charitable nature like the "Model Village" in Pootung, and to programs of reform which did little to disturb either Chinese or Western employers. The apolitical trade associations, despite their long-established guild traditions, also consistently lost ground between 1919 and 1927. It was only among the Canton mechanics that these traditions had what might be described as a mass following. This was because some of them were skilled workers employed in the modern enterprises of Canton and Hong Kong, who, because they were in short supply, formed a kind of labor aristocracy, while the rest were employers and employees in the many small, semi-craft mechanical workshops of the region. Their union (which did not call itself a union until 1926) succeeded in making its members agree to its conciliatory tactics in labor disputes,[123] and in maintaining its fierce hostility toward the political line of the Kuomintang and Communist Party left wings. This hostility led to pitched battles against left-wing unions, such as the Kwangtung railwaymen's union, in 1926. But elsewhere in China, in Shanghai or Hupeh for instance, the old guild outlook was no longer of any account. Finally, the Nationalist moderates, as represented by the right wing of the Kuomintang, never succeeded, despite repeated attempts, in winning over the workers to their views. During the 1921–23 strike wave they were quite unable, except in Canton, to compete seriously with the Communist militants of the Labor Secretariat. After 1924, when the anarchists, the promoters of industrial advance, and the Christian reformists had almost completely lost influence among the working class, the most strenuous opponents of the revolutionary labor movement were the trade unionists linked with the right wing of the Kuomintang and with the Sunyatsenist Society, who adroitly claimed to be carrying out the policy of "support for the workers" laid down by the Kuomintang Congress. Thus the fight against the kung-tsei, or "yellow" unions, which represented the interests of the employers, took on a special complexion in China: it became part of the struggle for leadership of the Nationalist movement between the proletariat and the bourgeoisie. But the kung-tsei did not succeed in subverting the mass following of the All-China General Union and the unions affiliated with it, and Ma Ch'ao-chün and his friends were unable to persuade the workers to pay much attention to the ideas of Tai Chi-t'ao, who denied the existence of the class struggle in order to safeguard the interests of intransigent and jingoistic employers.

Thus, except in Canton, ideological currents opposed to Marxism were of little account in the Chinese labor movement in 1919–27. The labor organizations and the movement as a whole developed in close collaboration with the Communist Party and followed the party's lead. The party concentrated its efforts almost entirely on advancing the labor movement, and its best cadres were assigned to the task of supporting and developing union organization and strike action, even if the strikes were purely economic ones. Despite the fact that the founders and early leaders of the party were intellectuals, it very soon took root among the working class. The militant trade unionists of working-class origin who emerged during the course of the struggles of 1921–22 and of 1925–27 were almost all members of the Communist Party. Some of them joined at the time when the Labor Secretariat was operating—for example, Hsiang Ying, who founded a number of unions in Wuhan,[124] or Teng P'ei, the Tangshan mechanic who at the end of 1921 became the first working-class member of the party in North China.[125] Others, such as the seamen Su Chao-cheng, Lin Wei-min, and Chu Pao-t'ing, became members during the revival of the labor movement in the spring of 1925.[126] Thus throughout the period the Communist Party was regarded as the one most closely linked with the working class.[127] It fulfilled the desire of the Chinese proletariat to have a party of its own—a desire that had been vaguely felt as long ago as 1911, when it had found expression in the Labor Party formed by Hsü Ch'i-wen. And indeed the political aims of the Communist Party and of the working class were much the same. The workers gave full support to the policy of cooperation with the Kuomintang, although before 1924 the Kuomintang had very little working-class support outside Canton and workers elsewhere in China did not join until after the reorganization congress.[128] Again, in the case of the events leading up to the May Thirtieth Movement in Shanghai, the initiative taken by the Communist Party leadership in organizing the Nanking Road demonstration was in close harmony with the actions taken by the mass of the workers, and particularly by those employed in the cotton mills. In 1926 the launching of the Northern Expedition was fully supported both by the unions and by the Communist Party; and during the armed uprisings in Shanghai in February and March 1927, the actions of the entire proletariat of the city were completely at one with those of the Communist Party as such and of its individual cadres.

The role of the Communist Party was, however, not always a positive one, at least as far as the immediate situation was concerned. The party had its weaknesses, both in its practical work and in the elaboration of its political strategy. These weaknesses were partly due to the inexperience of youth, but they also reflected the way in which the situation was understood at that time within the international labor movement. Marxism was introduced into the Chinese labor movement from outside, and external influences molded its development in the early stages. The opportunistic tendencies of the party leadership have already been mentioned.[129] They were particularly noticeable in the failure to make a determined stand against the coup of March 20, 1926, and in the conciliatory policy adopted in Shanghai toward Chiang Kai-shek at the beginning of 1927; and this attitude had direct repercussions in the political strategy of the unions and of the labor movement in general.

Thus, throughout the period the fusion between the Communists and the Chinese labor movement was almost complete, except among certain sections of skilled workers in Canton. It was so complete that in July 1924 the Executive Committee of the Kuomintang made the following statement: "The Chinese Communist Party is the result neither of speculation on the part of any individual nor of artificial transplantation from abroad to China. The Chinese Communist Party is a political organization that is crystallized out of the natural class struggle of the industrial proletariat that is just developing in China. ... Even were we able to dissolve the existing Chinese Communist Party by force, we could not destroy the Chinese proletariat, for they would organize again."[130]

It is, however, important to realize that although the progress of the Chinese labor movement was inseparably connected with the activities of the Chinese Communist Party, the Chinese labor organizations were in no way simply the creations of the party. The party was officially founded in July 1921 as a result of the merging of the small Communist groups which had at that time been in existence for only a few months at the most. At this time, the working class had already had considerable experience in labor struggles, including those of the May Fourth Movement, in which it had taken active part. Moreover, it already possessed a number of labor organizations:[131] some of these, it must be admitted, were under the control of employers or foremen, or were merely mutual benefit societies with no clear ideological outlook; yet others were solid working-class organizations, such as the seamen's associations in the South or the Shanghai mechanics' union. It was only because there already were genuine stirrings among the Chinese working class that the Communist Party was able to make rapid progress in providing vigorous leadership.

The Chinese Labor Movement in Perspective

Now finally we must relate these eight years of labor struggles to the development of the Chinese labor movement as a whole, and to the general history of modern China. The outstanding feature of the period here studied is the great widening of horizons that took place in comparison with former times. Prior to 1919, the Chinese proletariat had engaged in a great number of labor struggles: strikes had been held, labor organizations akin to modern trade unions had been formed, and attempts had been made in the political field to give support to the Republicans. But the feebleness of all these efforts only points up the tremendous advances made in 1919–27 on economic and political issues, in union organization, and in the awakening of class consciousness. We have here a classic case of the "acceleration of historical development," and this development must be placed in the context of the international labor movement as a whole. The Chinese labor movement was able to benefit from the experience gained in the extensive strike waves and labor struggles that occurred more or less throughout the world as an aftermath of the First World War. In particular, it benefited from the October Revolution in Russia and the birth of the Comintern, the rapid strides subsequently made being due largely to the introduction of Marxist ideas in their Leninist form.

These rapid strides made by the Chinese labor movement at this time were also due to the ever-increasing disintegration of the old forms of Chinese society and to the fact that, owing to the dominant position occupied by the Foreign Powers in China's political and economic life, the Chinese bourgeoisie was unable to take over governmental powers in the classic Western manner. The failure of the 1911 revolution and the comparative failure of the May Fourth Movement, or at least of the projects for industrial expansion cherished by the Chinese bourgeoisie at that time, are indications of China's state of political tutelage. Thus the internal situation was abnormally favorable for the development of the labor movement, and the suddenness with which it sprang into being had something premature about it. As a result, its successes won in 1921–23 and 1925–27 and the leading role it assumed as soon as it entered the political arena were not very securely based. Defeat, when it came in 1927, was sudden and severe.

The breakdown of the united front with the Kuomintang that occurred then and the break that soon followed between the labor movement and the Nationalist government, which was about to gain control of the whole of

China, were extremely serious defeats on a short-term view. For one thing, the labor movment was decimated; a large number of its leaders were put to death or exiled, and others had to go into hiding.[132] For another, apart from the few months' respite in Wuhan, the labor organizations in all the main industrial centers had to go underground, and did not emerge again until 1949. A Fifth National Labor Congress was held in Shanghai in November 1929,[133] but it was more concerned with the past than with plans for future action. It was 19 years before the Sixth Congress met in Harbin, in March 1948, by which time the civil war was in full swing—the People's Armies had gained control of vast "liberated areas," including important industrial regions, and victory was already in sight.[134] During all this time the Chinese proletariat did, it is true, continue to hold economic strikes—in Shanghai, for example, where they came into conflict first with the Kuomintang and then with the Japanese.[135] But for over twenty years after the defeat of 1927, labor struggles were no longer the main front or the main motive force of the Chinese revolution.

In examining the reasons for the defeat, it would be unwise to attribute it exclusively to sociological factors. It is true that the working class, as its leaders themselves admitted, was weak numerically and inexperienced, had many marginal elements in its lower ranks, and was still strongly tinged with guild traditions and regionalist attitudes.[136] But as has already been pointed out, its numerical weakness was more than compensated for by its high degree of concentration within certain regions and within certain industries; and although it may have been unstable and lacking in unity, it was no more so than the bourgeoisie or the militarist and feudal elements. Indeed it had far more homogeneity as a class than either, and hence a greater potential capacity for political action.

The real explanation of the 1927 defeat lies in the realm of political strategy. The defeat was brought about by the breakdown of the united front formed in conjunction with the bourgeoisie in 1924. Up to a point this political alliance during the three years it lasted had good results: the May Thirtieth Movement, the Canton–Hong Kong strike and boycott, the liquidation of warlord rule in Central China, and successful strike waves in Canton, Shanghai, and Wuhan. All these were truly proletarian victories, and were possible only because, on the Comintern's advice, the proletarian unions and political organizations had maintained their independent existence after the alliance with the Kuomintang.

Nevertheless, all in all the united front was a failure. The bourgeoisie made the break deliberately after the May Thirtieth Movement and the Canton–Hong Kong strike and boycott, when it found that the labor movement was no longer the docile partner it had been during the May Fourth Movement and that it would not, as the bourgeoisie had hoped in 1924, remain simply an auxiliary force in a subordinate role. In 1926-27 the defense of class interests and of the existing social order came first with the bourgeoisie, especially since its links with the rural gentry made it particularly sensitive to the threat constituted by the mass movement among the poor and middle peasants. These fears proved stronger than its anxieties about the disorders caused by the warlords and about foreign competition—the anxieties that had led to the alliance with the proletariat in 1924. The labor movement, for its part, was unable to prevent the united front from being deliberately broken by its bourgeois allies, and thus failed to maintain the revolutionary movement as a mass movement, as it had been at the beginning of the Northern Expedition. Because we lack detailed information, it is perhaps too soon to attempt to assess how far responsibility for the defeat lies with the international labor movement. But it is clear that the Chinese labor movement failed to arrive at a correct solution of the contradictions arising from the alliance with the bourgeoisie, and in particular of the contradiction between the alliance with the bourgeoisie and the alliance with the peasants. As for the attitude of the proletarian organizations toward the bourgeoisie, it would be an exaggeration to say that they simply gave in all along the line. The length of the Canton–Hong Kong strike and boycott, the sudden strike wave in Shanghai in 1925–27 (which included strikes in Chinese enterprises), the fight against the kung-tsei unions linked with the right wing of the Kuomintang, and the launching of the armed uprisings in Shanghai prior to the arrival of the Northern Expedition—all these show how hard the proletariat fought to gain control and consolidate its position in the Nationalist movement, refusing to be simply an auxiliary force for the bourgeoisie. But the fight for political control was not intransigent enough. The Communist Party leadership, and, because of party discipline, the Communists who were union leaders, did undoubtedly adopt a policy of appeasement toward the bourgeoisie from the time of the affair of March 20, 1926, on. Many examples of this policy have been mentioned in relation to political struggles and strike action in Canton, Wuhan, and Shanghai.[137]

Not only did this appeasement policy undermine the fighting spirit of the proletariat, but the alliance with the peasants had to be sacrificed to it: "peasant excesses" were blamed for the bourgeoisie's lack of revolutionary fervor and its eventual defection, and the political potentialities of the poor and middle peasants were consistently underestimated. This does not, however, seem to have been merely a by-product of the tactics of compromise with the bourgeoisie; it was also the result of a rather mechanical borrowing of theoretical concepts based on Western experience, according to which the big industrial cities provided the essential motivating force in the struggle and were therefore the main theater of events. But this hardly applied to China in 1919–27, for there the balance of forces was upset by the presence of the Western Powers in the main industrial centers, where they were able to use their administrative machinery and threats of armed intervention to repress union activity and to introduce corrupt practices into union organization through the compradores and the kung-tsei; and this unequal balance of forces was likely to remain so long as the social and political struggle was confined to the cities, while the peasants were looked upon as a mere "rear guard."

It was only after many hesitations and differences of opinion that the Communist Party leadership got rid of these theoretical concepts. In 1930–31 and again in 1934–35 it was still preaching Li Li-sanism, that is, giving priority to organizing uprisings in the towns, which from the outset were doomed to be defeated, just as in fact the short-lived Canton Commune was defeated in December 1927. But in the main the Chinese revolutionaries adopted an entirely new policy from 1927 on, one in which they concentrated their efforts on the rural districts. It was in 1927 that the Autumn Harvest peasant rebellion took place in Kiangsi; soon after this Mao Tse-tung and Chu Te formed the Red Army, and owing to its intervention, huge "soviet districts" were established south of the Yangtze. These districts were destroyed in 1934, but after the Long March, they survived in the form of the peasant guerrilla areas and the liberated areas which, as we know, played so great a part in preparing the Liberation of 1949.

However, even though the struggles conducted by the Chinese working class between 1919 and 1927 ended in temporary failure, they prepared the way for the crucial change in the center of gravity for the Chinese revolution from the cities to the countryside that occurred in 1927. It was these struggles that made the change possible, for they had awakened the poor and middle peasants—who had scarcely been touched by the republican revolution of 1911—to political awareness. The advance of the Nationalist armies in South China, and the tremendous response to it made by the labor movement in Shanghai, Canton, and Wuhan, started a ferment among the peasants of these regions which very soon gained in intensity. Furthermore, from 1927 on, the hard core of working-class militants and of intellectuals who had worked within the labor movement during these eight years of struggle, and who were by now seasoned veterans, provided the peasants with the leadership that they needed and that they would have been unable to supply themselves. The early career of Mao Tse-tung is typical of this sequence of events: in 1919 he was organizing groups of young radical intellectuals in Hunan; in 1922 he was secretary-general of the provincial federation of unions in that province; but after 1927 he was redirecting Communist Party activities to the rural areas. Thus in 1927 the political experience of the working class was handed on, through many of its leaders, to the poor and middle peasants,[138] who were later able to make their own breakthrough and to help bring about the final victory of the revolution.

Important as these eight years of struggle were in the history of the Chinese revolution, they are also not without interest insofar as they enable us to appreciate the role played by the Chinese labor movement in modern world history. In the first place, they show how similar the world over were the problems faced by the modern proletariat as a result of capitalist mechanized industry. Class barriers were more important than any imposed by time or by place, so that the historian of "classic" labor movements, such as those in France or in England, finds himself less at sea than he might have expected when he comes to study the labor movements that arose on the far side of the ancient Eurasian continent. He finds there the same conflict between old guild traditions and the new industrial unionism that threatened them; the same mutual benefit societies that were the precursors of modern trade unionism, although they did not make the same insistent demands; the same outstanding capacity for organization among railwaymen and printing workers; and the same tendencies toward social reform during periods of relative inactivity in the labor movement. In China as in the West, the working class proved itself to be a new force, capable of taking decisive action in the social and political struggle.

However, there were characteristics that differentiated the Chinese labor movement from those in the industrialized countries of the West, but that bear remarkable similarities to characteristics of labor movements in the underdeveloped or comparatively unindustrialized countries of the world. For instance, in the matter of social stratification, the Chinese proletariat was peculiar in that it lacked a labor aristocracy, while at the same time its lower ranks were swelled by elements that were not yet fully differentiated from the peasantry. Regarding ideology, it was the Leninist stage of Marxism that penetrated the Chinese labor movement, so that it did not suffer from the schism between Communism and Socialism that played so great a part in the development of the labor movement in the West. It was able to adopt Communism straightaway, without any internal divisions of this kind. As for political strategy, there is no further need to go into the problems that arose as a result of the alliances entered into with the national bourgeoisie and with the poor and middle peasants in order to conduct the fight against the big foreign interests and the feudal forces, except to emphasize the difference this made between the Chinese labor movement and labor movements in the West.

Finally, although this may seem to contradict the preceding remarks, the essential "Chineseness" of the Chinese labor movement during the 1919–27 period must be emphasized. It was influenced not only by events taking place on Chinese territory and within the Chinese society of that time, but also by the survivals of precapitalist Chinese traditions, numerous examples of which have already been noted with respect to the labor organizations and the general way of life of the Chinese proletariat. Another specifically Chinese trait was the differentiation between regions: the labor organizations of Shanghai and Canton, of Wuhan and North China, differed considerably in organizational structure and in tempo of development. This was partly simply a consequence of the vast geographical area of the country and of the difficulties of communication between regions, but it was a result also of the unequal economic development of the various regions. Regional differentiation was a feature of earlier stages of development in the history of modern China. It had characterized to some extent the political struggles at the end of the Manchu dynasty, and it was a factor again in the years between 1928 and 1949, with the appearance of "revolutionary bases" and "liberated areas" that enabled the revolution to take firm root in some regions before its final triumph in the country as a whole. By this time the Chinese labor movement had learned that in China political aims had to be backed by armed force, and this discovery links it with all the other social and political struggles in China from the end of the nineteenth century on, whether conducted by the revolutionaries of the T'ung-meng-hui, by the conservative forces of Yuan Shih-k'ai, or later by the peasants of the Chinese soviets and those engaged in guerrilla warfare against the Japanese. From this point of view, the union pickets and the workers' militias were of basic importance, and were not merely an episode in the development of the labor movement.

Thus the Chinese labor movement of 1919-27 belongs at one and the same time to the history of the Chinese revolution, to the history of the whole movement toward political emancipation in all the Afro-Asian countries during the twentieth century, and to the history of the fight against capitalism waged over the past century by the workers of the world.

Appendixes

Maps of the Main Industries around 1919

In the maps that follow, the first 16 (pp. 416–23) show the geographical distribution of the main industries over all of China, and the last six (pp. 424–26) show the main industries of each industrial region. The maps in the first group are based on the data cited in Chapter II. Only those concerned with the cotton and silk industries are based on actual statistics, and the statistics for the silk industry are only approximate. In most of the other maps in this first group, all that can be done is to show the number of enterprises, leaving their size out of account. Japanese and British enterprises are indicated by special symbols, but other foreign concerns, such as the Russian firms in the Northeast, are not distinguished from Chinese-owned enterprises. In the case of mines and railways, only the main centers have been indicated. In order to avoid cluttering up these maps with place-names, only those names not included in the maps of the industrial regions are given. In the industrial region maps, large and small symbols are used to distinguish between the main and subsidiary centers of each of the industries included. Because of regional variations in industrial concentration, the scales are not uniform in these maps. (See the scale provided for each map.)

Symbols used on the maps are as follows:

● Chinese enterprise ◉ Japanese enterprise ○ British enterprise

Basic industries: metallurgy, metal-works, cement works, fiber-baling factories

Food industry: flour mills, oil mills, canneries, distilleries, breweries, powdered-egg factories

Various light industries: chemical industries, brickworks, match and tobacco factories

Coal mines and metal ore mines

Textile industries: cotton, silk

Electric power plants

Railway workshops

Printing industry

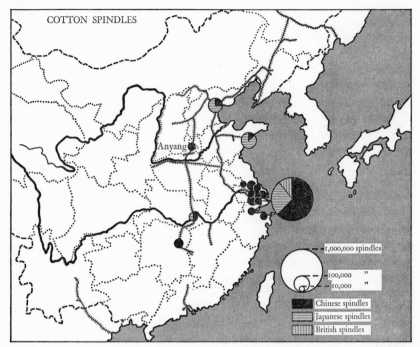

COTTON SPINDLES

Anyang

1,000,000 spindles
100,000 "
10,000 "

Chinese spindles
Japanese spindles
British spindles

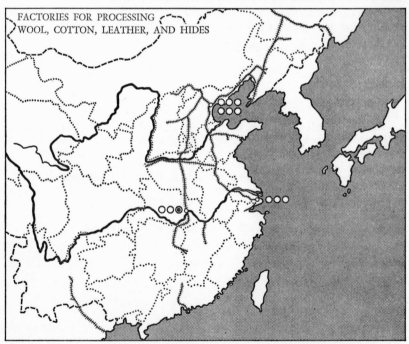

FACTORIES FOR PROCESSING
WOOL, COTTON, LEATHER, AND HIDES

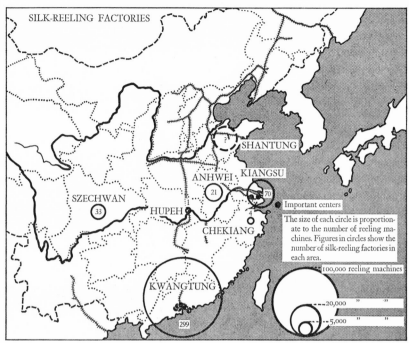

SILK-REELING FACTORIES

SHANTUNG

ANHWEI KIANGSU

SZECHWAN

HUPEH

CHEKIANG

KWANGTUNG

Important centers

The size of each circle is proportionate to the number of reeling machines. Figures in circles show the number of silk-reeling factories in each area.

100,000 reeling machines

20,000 " "

5,000 " "

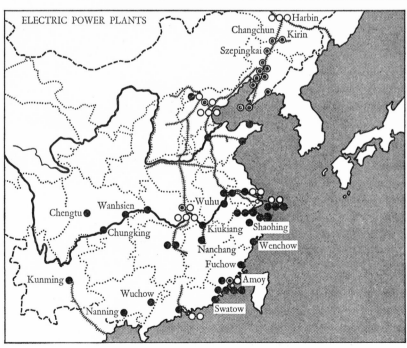

ELECTRIC POWER PLANTS

Harbin

Changchun Kirin

Szepingkai

Chengtu Wanhsien Wuhu

Chungking Kiukiang Shaohing

Nanchang Wenchow

Fuchow

Kunming Amoy

Wuchow

Nanning Swatow

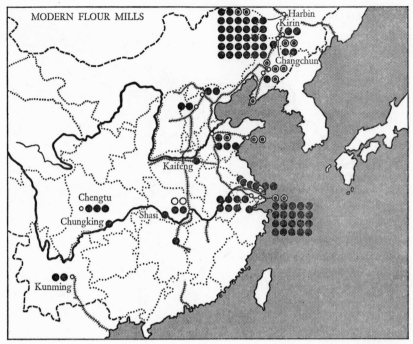

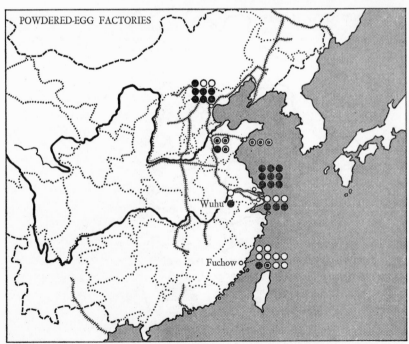

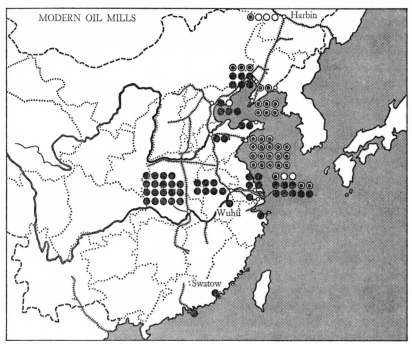

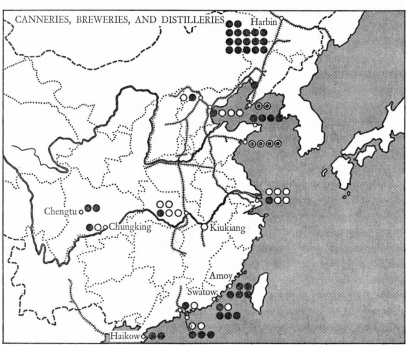

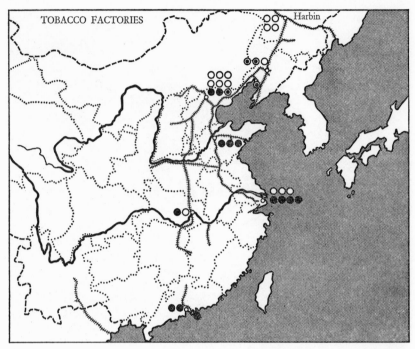

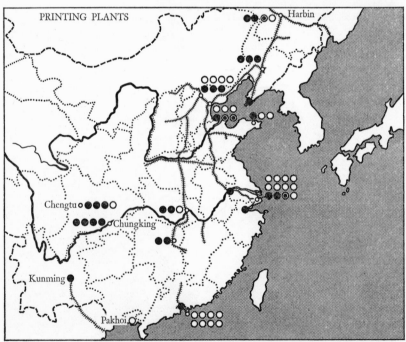

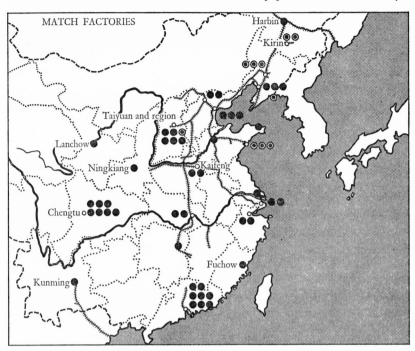

MATCH FACTORIES

Harbin
Kirin
Taiyuan and region
Lanchow
Ningkiang
Kaifeng
Chengtu
Fuchow
Kunming

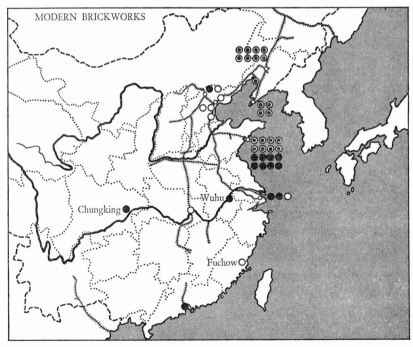

MODERN BRICKWORKS

Wuhu
Chungking
Fuchow

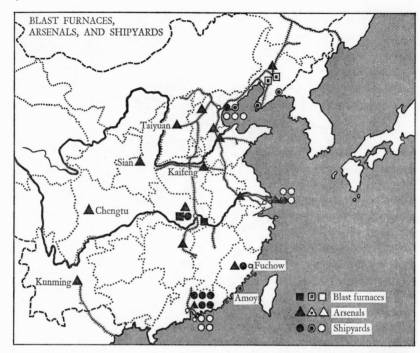

BLAST FURNACES,
ARSENALS, AND SHIPYARDS

Taiyuan

Sian

Kaifeng

Chengtu

Kunming

Fuchow

Amoy

Blast furnaces

Arsenals

Shipyards

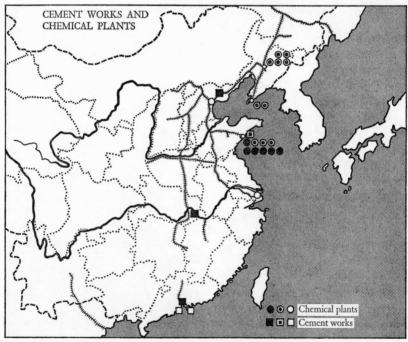

CEMENT WORKS AND
CHEMICAL PLANTS

Chemical plants

Cement works

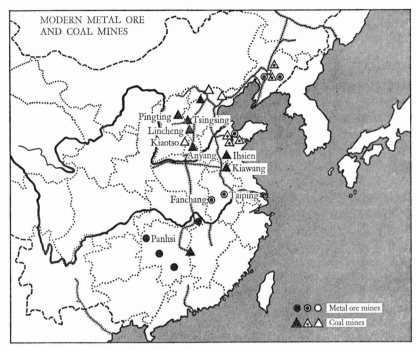

MODERN METAL ORE
AND COAL MINES

Pingting
Tsingsing
Lincheng
Kiaotso
Anyang
Ihsien
Kiawang

Fanchang
Taiping

Panhsi

Metal ore mines
Coal mines

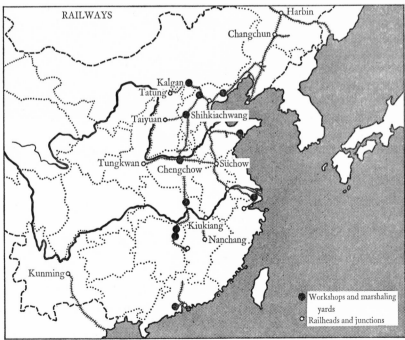

RAILWAYS

Harbin
Changchun

Kalgan
Tatung
Shihkiachwang
Taiyuan

Tungkwan
Chengchow
Süchow

Kiukiang
Nanchang

Kunming

Workshops and marshaling
yards
Railheads and junctions

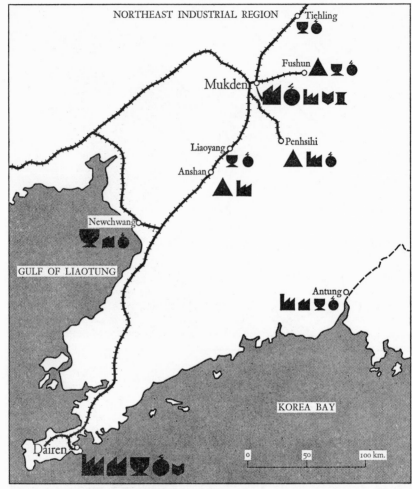

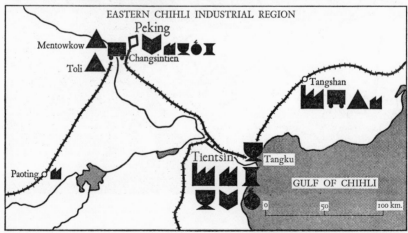

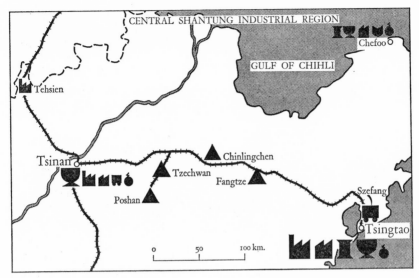

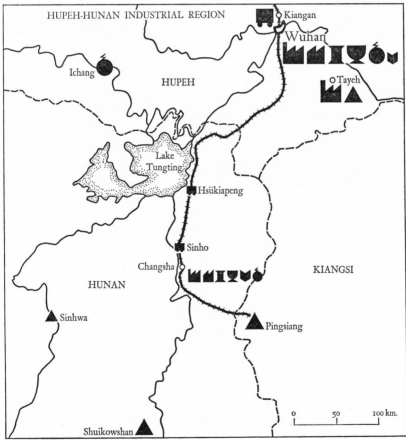

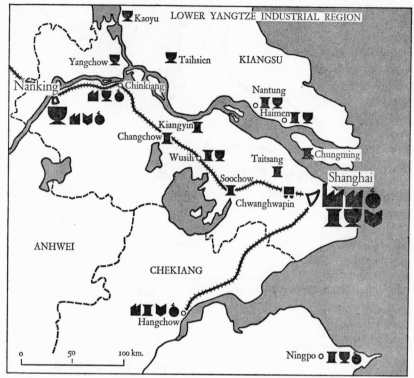

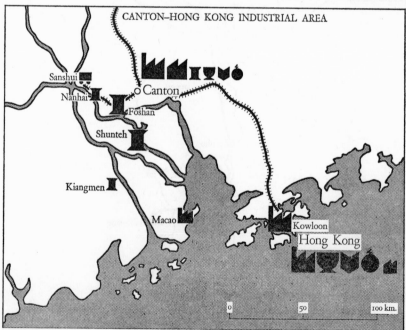

List of Workers Interviewed

See Appendix C for workers' names in Chinese characters

It must be understood that the interviews I had during the summer of 1957 with the following 32 elderly workers, kindly arranged by the Chinese People's Society for Foreign Cultural Relations, are in no sense to be regarded as forming part of a planned program of sociological or historical research. They were simply arranged when circumstances allowed, and no special selection was made of particular categories of workers or of particular industrial centers. Some of the workers interviewed gave a fairly full account, others quite a brief one; but all helped to clarify various historical details, and above all, their accounts of their own personal experiences enlivened the background of my research, besides giving corroborative evidence for the conclusions drawn from written sources.

Chao Chin-ying. Interviewed in Shanghai; b. 1907; daughter of a worker in the B.A.T. Pootung factory; entered this factory in 1918.

Chao Yin-ying. Interviewed in Shanghai; b. 1911; sister of the above; entered the B.A.T. Pootung factory in 1920.

Ch'en Kuo-hsiang. Interviewed in Tangshan; son of a Paoting peddler; worked in the Tangshan railway workshop, and then later at the K.M.A. mines.

Cheng Kuo-chün. Interviewed in Chengchow; b. 1900; son of a Hupeh peasant family; became a coal-transport coolie at Chengchow railway station in 1920.

Chiang Hai-sheng. Interviewed in Chengchow; son of a Hupeh peasant family; apprenticed as a youth in a copper foundry; became a Ching-Han railwayman in 1908.

Chou Kuo-ch'iang. Interviewed in Shanghai; b. 1908 in a small town in Kiangsu (social origin not specified); came to Shanghai in 1922 and became successively a boathand on the Whangpoo, a shop employee, a worker in the B.A.T. factory, and finally a tramway conductor in the French Concession.

Chung Sheng-fu. Interviewed in Shanghai; b. 1895; son of a Hupeh agricultural laborer; came to Shanghai in 1912 and became a docker.

Fang Lan-ying. Interviewed in Shanghai; b. 1915; daughter of a family of poor peasants in the Kompo; recruited in 1928 through the pao-kung system as a worker in a Japanese cotton mill in Shanghai.

Feng Jui. Interviewed in Canton; b. 1901; son of a poor peasant family (his father worked for a time as a coolie in a Malaysian tin mine); a seaman on the Hong Kong shipping lines beginning in 1914.

Jen Ch'i-hsiang. Interviewed in Shanghai; son of a small shop employee in Shanghai; worked at the Commercial Press from 1919 to 1927.

Li Chen-kang. Interviewed in Tientsin; son of a family of satin-workers in Honan; railwayman on the Ching-Han line, and then on the Lunghai line.

Li Ch'üan-te. Interviewed in Chengchow; son of a Wuhan cabinetmaker who became a carpenter on the Ching-Han line; was taken on as apprentice by the Ching-Han line in 1920.

Li Tien-ch'ing. Interviewed in Tientsin; son of a Tientsin carpenter; entered the Yü-yuan cotton mill in 1921.

Lin Mao-hsiang. Interviewed in Chengchow; son of a Fukien peasant family; served as an apprentice mechanic in the Fuchow arsenal, and later was employed by the Ching-Han line. His brother was Lin Hsiang-ch'ien, the leader of the Ching-Han Union, who was beheaded on 7.ii.23 by order of Wu P'ei-fu.

Liu Ch'ing-chou. Interviewed in Tientsin; son of a Chihli peasant family who escaped to Tientsin during the 1920 famine; entered the Yü-yuan cotton mill as an apprentice in 1921.

Liu Hsin-jung. Interviewed in Tientsin; son of a Tientsin coolie; entered the Yü-yuan cotton mill in 1918.

Liu Mo-kuang. Interviewed in Tientsin; son of a Chihli peasant family who escaped to Tientsin during the 1920 famine; entered the Yü-yuan cotton mill as an apprentice in 1921.

Liu T'ung. Interviewed in Chengchow; b. 1900; son of a Peking tinsmith; orphaned at the age of three; became a beggar; taken on as a coolie by the Ching-Han line in 1918.

Ma Te-liang. Interviewed in Tangshan; son of a poor Chihli peasant family; K.M.A. miner since 1922.

Miu Fu-ch'un. Interviewed in Tangshan; son of a poor Chihli peasant family; K.M.A. miner.

Shen Pao-hua. Interviewed in Changsintien; son of a Peking slippermaker; taken on in 1918 as a painter in the Changsintien workshop of the Ching-Han line.

Ssu Fu-te. Interviewed in Tangshan; son of a Chihli peasant family; housepainter, then K.M.A. miner.

Sun Fu-ch'un. Interviewed in Tangshan; son of a Chihli peasant family; K.M.A. miner.

Sun Mao-lin. Interviewed in Changsintien; b. 1899; son of a Ching-Han coolie; taken on as a coolie at the Changsintien depot in 1915.

Sun Yü-liang. Interviewed in Tangshan; son of a Chihli peasant family; K.M.A. miner since 1920.

T'a Jung. Interviewed in Canton; son of a Hong Kong joiner; seaman since his youth.

Ting Jui-sheng. Interviewed in Tangshan; son of a Tangshan craftsman; K.M.A. miner.

Ts'ao Chih-fang. Interviewed in Shanghai; b. 1897; son of a poor Ningpo peasant family; apprentice in a small metallurgical workshop in Shanghai, then, successively, a worker in the British-owned Ewo cotton mill, a coolie in the Bassorah Chinese coolies' camp during the First World War, and a worker in the Kiangnan shipyard, in a metallurgical workship in the French Concession of Shanghai, and from 1923, in the Yangtzepoo electric power plant.

Tso Chen-yun. Interviewed in Tientsin; son of a peasant family who escaped to Tientsin during the 1920 famine; entered a Japanese cotton mill in Tientsin in 1920.

Wang Ch'un-jung. Interviewed in Changsintien; b. 1898; son of a Chihli peasant family taken on as a carpenter in the Changsintien depot of the Ching-Han line in 1918, having learned his trade in a small workshop in the town.

Wang Jui-an. Interviewed in Shanghai; b. 1900; son of a peasant of Shasi (Hupeh), who was taken on as a scavenger by a school in Shanghai; entered a Japanese cotton mill in Shanghai in 1919.

Wu Sung-shou. Interviewed in Tangshan; b. 1903; son of a Chihli peasant family; at first earned his living by collecting firewood; then went to Tangshan, where his brother was employed in a cement works, and became a K.M.A. miner.

List of Chinese Characters

The names supplied in the following list include those of all Chinese authors of works in Chinese listed in the Bibliography, all workers interviewed, and all persons of any importance mentioned in the text. Most of the Chinese terms and the names of Chinese firms are included.

ch'a-t'ou (factory overseer) 查头

Chai Han-ch'i 翟汉奇

ch'an-yeh tsung-kung-hui 产业兒工會

Chang Ch'ien 張謇

Chang Chih-tung 張之洞

Chang Ching-chiang 張靜江

Chang Ching-lu 張靜盧

Chang Kuo-t'ao 張国濤

Chang Lien-kuang 張連光

Chang Te-hui 張德惠

Chang T'e-li 張恃立

Chang Tso-lin 張作霖

Chang Tsung-ch'ang 張宗昌

Chang Tsung-hsiang 張宗祥

Chang Wei-ying 張瑋瑛

ch'ang-kung (permanent employees) 常工

Chao Chin-ying 趙金英

Chao Ch'in 趙親

Chao Ch'uan-ch'iang 趙傳強

Chao Heng-t'i 趙恆惕

Chao Hsing-nung 趙醒儂

Chao shang-chü (the C.M.S.N. Co.) 招商局

Chao Shih-yen 趙世炎

Chao Yin-ying 趙銀英

ch'e (reeling machines) 車

Ch'en A-t'ang 陳阿堂

Ch'en Ch'i-mei 陳其美

Ch'en Chiung-ming 陳烔明

Ch'en Ch'üan 陳权

Ch'en Kuo-fu 陳国夫

Ch'en Kuo-hsiang 陳国祥

Ch'en Kuo-liang 陳国梁

Ch'en Kung-po 陳公博

Ch'en Kung-shou 陳恭受

Ch'en Lien-po 陳廉伯

Ch'en Ping-sheng 陳炳生

Ch'en Sen 陳森

Ch'en Shu-jen 陳樹人

Ch'en Ta 陳达

Ch'en T'ieh-ch'ing 陳鉄卿

Ch'en Tu-hsiu 陳独秀

Ch'en Yueh-fu 陳月夫

Cheng Kuo-chün 鄭国鈞

cheng-shih-kung (regular employees) 正式工

Cheng-T'ai (Shihkiachwang-Taiyuan railroad) 正太

Ch'i Hsieh-yuan 齊變元

ch'i-hsin-chiu (wine drunk in pledge in secret societies) 齐心酒

Ch'i-wu lao-jen 棲梧老人

Chia Chih 賈芝

chia-kung (Category A workers) 甲工

Chiang Chieh-shih (Chiang Kai-shek) 蔣介石

Chiang Hai-sheng　姜海生

Chiang Hsien-yun　蔣先云

Chiang K'ang-hu　蔣亢虎

Chien Chao-nan　簡照南

Ch'ien Hsiao-yü　錢孝栯

chih-ku-shu (letter from a guild authorizing a master to engage an apprentice) 志雇書

chih-nien (director of a guild)　值年

Chin-P'u (Tientsin-Pukow railroad) 津浦

Ching-Feng (Peking-Mukden railroad) 京奉

Ching-Han (Peking-Hankow railroad) 京漢

Ching-Sui (Peking-Suiyuan railroad) 京綏

Ching-yuan (Canton printers' guild) 景源

Ch'ing-pang (Green Gang)　青幫

chiu-ch'a-tui (pickets)　糾察队

Chiu-ta (salt refinery in Tangku)　久大

Ch'iu-shih　秋石

Chou En-lai　周恩來

Chou Fu-hai　周佛海

Chou Kuo-ch'iang　周国強

Chu Chih-yao　朱志尧

Chu Hsin-fan　朱新繁

Chu Pang-hsing　朱邦兴

Chu Pao-t'ing　朱宝庭

Chu Shao-lien　朱少蓮

Chu Te　朱德

Chu Yü-ts'ang　朱育滄

chü-lo-pu (club)　俱樂部

Ch'ü Ch'iu-pai　瞿秋白

Ch'ü Wei-t'o (pseudonym of Ch'ü Ch'iu-pai)　屈維它

Ch'üan Han-sheng　全汉昇

Chün-an (seamen's guild)　均安

chün-chu-kuan (seamen's employment agency)　君主館

Chung Sheng-fu　鍾生福

Chung-hsing (colliery)　中兴

Chung-hua (Tientsin match factory) 中华

Chung-hua shu-chu ("China Bookshop") 中兴書局

Chung-yuan (colliery)　中源

Fang Chiao-po　方椒伯

Fang Lan-ying　方蘭英

Feng Chü-p'o　馮菊坡

Feng Jui　馮藥

Feng Kuo-chang　馮国璋

feng-p'iao (Fengtien banknotes)　奉票

Feng Yü-hsiang　馮玉祥

Fu Tsung-yao　傅宗耀

hang 行

Han-yeh-p'ing (mining and heavy industry combine)　汉冶萍

Heng-feng (Shanghai cotton mill) 恆丰

Heng-ta (Shanghai cotton mill)　恆大

Ho Feng-lin　向丰林

Ho Shu-heng　向叔衡

Ho Yao-ch'üan　向耀全

Ho Ying-ch'in　向应欽

hou-tun (rearguard)　后盾

hsi-ma-sha (seamen's labor contractors) 洗馬沙

Hsia Ch'ao　夏超

Hsia Ch'i-feng　夏奇峯

Hsia Yen　夏衍

Hsiang-ching (Shanghai silk factory) 祥經

Hsiang Ching-yü　向警予

Hsiang Ying　項英

hsiao-yang ("small money")　小洋

Hsiao Yao-nan　蕭耀南

Hsieh Huai-te　謝怀德

Hsieh Ying-po　謝英伯

hsin-kung (strikebreakers)　新工

Hsiung-ti-kuan (seamen's cooperative employment agency)　兄弟館

Hsü Ch'i-wen　徐企文

Hsü Ch'ien　徐謙

Hsü Ch'ung-chih　許崇智

Hsü Hsi-lin　徐錫林

Hsü Hsieh-hua　徐协华

Hsü K'o-hsiang　許克祥

Hsü Lo-te　徐洛德

Hsü Pai-hao　許白昊

Hsü Shih-ch'ang　徐世昌

Hsü Shih-hua　許世華

Hsü Sung-ling　徐嵩齡

Hsü Wen-t'ien　許聞天

Hu Ch'iao-mu　胡喬木

Hu Han-min　胡汉民

Hu Hsin　胡信

Hu Hua　胡华

Hu I-sheng　胡一生

Hu Shih　胡适

hu-ch'ang (unionist subservient to employers)　虎伥

Hu-Ning (Shanghai-Nanking railroad)　沪宁

Hua Hung-t'u　华鸿图

Hua Kang　华崗

Hua-ch'ang (Hunan antimony foundry)　华昌

Hua-hsin (Shanghai cotton mill)　华新

Hua-hsing (Tientsin cotton mill)　华兴

hua-li (annual bonus)　花利

Huang Ai　黄愛

Huang Chieh-min　黄介民

Huang Chien-sheng　黄兼生

Huang Chin-jung　黄金荣

Huang Huan-t'ing　黄焕庭

Huang I-po　黄艺博

hui-kuan (regional friendly society)　会館

huo-kung (free labor)　活工

huo-yu (journeyman, shophand)　夥友

hung-li (annual bonus)　紅利

Hung-pang (Red Gang)　紅帮

I-ho (the Ewo Co.)　怡和

i-kung (Category B workers)　乙工

i-t'u (apprentice)　艺徒

i-t'u ho-t'ung (contract of apprenticeship)　艺徒合同

Jen Ch'i-hsiang　任其祥

Jen Shu-te　任樹德

Jih-hua (Japanese cotton mill in Pootung)　日华

Jui-chi (Shanghai cotton mill)　瑞記

K'ai-lan (K.M.A.)　开滦

K'ang Yu-wei　康有為

Ko ("ancestral master" of dyers etc.)　葛

Ku Cheng-hung　顧正紅

Ku Chia-hsi　顧家熙

ku-chu (master craftsman)　雇主

ku-kung (free labor)　雇工

kuan-tien (employment agency in Tientsin)　館店

Kuang-ming (Shanghai electrical equipment factory)　光明

Kuang-ta (Shanghai textile mill)　光达

Kung Chün　龔駿

kung-chieh (industrial world)　工界

kung-hui (trade union)　工会

kung-hui lien-ho-hui　工会联合会

kung-so (guild)　工所

kung-t'ou (foreman)　工头

kung-t'uan (workers' corps)　工团

kung-tsei ("yellow" unionists)　工贼

Kuo Chi-sheng　郭寄生

Kuo Liang　郭亮

Kuo P'in-po　郭聘帛

Kuo Sung-ling　郭松齡

Lai Hsin-hsia　來新夏

lao-pan (labor contractor)　老板

Lei Chia　雷加

Li Chen-kang　李宸剛

Li Chi-shen　李济琛

Li Ch'i-han (Li Sen)　李啓汉（森）

Li Chin-p'o　李金坡

Li Ching-lin　李景林

Li Ch'üan-te　李全德

Li Chung　李中

Li Fu-ch'un　李富春

Li Han-chün　李汉俊

Li Heng-lin　李恆林

Li Hung-chang　李鴻章

Li Jui　李鋭

Li Li-san 李立三

Li Lung-mu 李友枞

Li Ming-jen 李明仁

Li P'a-chih 李怕之

Li Pao-chang 李宝章

Li Shih-yueh 李时岳

Li Shu 李澍

Li Ta 李达

Li Ta-chao 李大釗

Li Tien-ch'ing 李殿清

Li Wei-nung 李慰农

Li Yü-ying 李煜瀛

Li Yuan-hung 李元洪

li-chin (the likin tax) 厘金

li-kung ("internal" labor) 裡工

Liang Ch'i-ch'ao 梁啓超

Liang Shih-i 梁士詒

Liang Yü-k'uei 梁玉魁

Liao Chung-k'ai 廖仲愷

lieh-shen (despotic landlords) 劣紳

Lin Hsiang-ch'ien 林祥謙

Lin Mao-hsiang 林茂湘

Lin Wei-min 林偉民

Lin Yü-nan 林育南

lin-shih-kung (temporary labor) 臨时工

Liu An-i 刘安益

Liu Chen-huan 刘震寰

Liu Chih-tan 刘志丹

Liu Ch'ing-chou 刘清洲

Liu Erh-sung 刘尔崧

Liu Hsin-jung 刘鑫荣

Liu Hua 刘华

Liu Kuan-chih 刘貫之

Liu Li-k'ai 刘立凯

Liu Mo-kuang 刘墨广

Liu Shao-ch'i 刘少奇

Liu Shih-fu 刘師復

Liu Tung-hsuan 刘東軒

Liu T'ung 刘桐

Liu Wen-sung 刘文松

Liu Yao-han 刘堯汉

liu-mang (gangsters) 流氓

Lo I-nung 罗亦农

Lo Teng-hsien 罗登賢

Lu Cheng-hsiang 陸徵祥

Lu Jung-t'ing 陸荣廷

Lu Wei-ch'ang 盧瑋昌

Lu Yung-hsiang 盧永祥

Lu-feng (Tsinan cotton mill) 魯丰

Lu-pan ("ancestral master" of carpenters etc.) 魯班

Lu-ta (Japanese mining co.) 魯大

Lun K'o-chung 倫克忠

Lung-hai (railroad) 泷海

Ma Ch'ao-chün 馬超俊

Ma Ch'ao-fan 馬超凡

Ma Ch'i 馬七

Ma Te-liang 馬德良

Mao Tse-tung 毛澤东

Miu Fu-ch'un 繆福春

Mo Jung-hsin 莫荣新

Mu Chih-ying 穆志英

Mu Ou-ch'u (H. Y. Moh) 穆藕初

Nan-yang hsiung-ti (Nanyang tobacco co.) 南洋兄弟

Nieh Ch'i-chieh (C. C. Nieh) 聶其杰

Niu Yung-chien 鈕永建

pa-t'ou (labor contractor) 把头

Pai Ch'ung-hsi 白崇禧

pan (shift) 班

pang (mutual aid association) 帮

pang-hui (mutual aid association) 帮会

pang-k'ou (mutual aid association) 帮口

P'ang Jen-ch'üan 龐人銓

Pao-ch'eng (Tientsin cotton mill) 宝成

Pao-chin (coal mine) 保晋

pao-fan-tso (labor contractor) 包飯作

pao-kung (contract labor) 包工

pao-jen (apprentice's guarantor) 保人

pao-tan (certificate of guarantee for an apprentice) 保單

pei-fa (Northern Expedition) 北伐

P'eng Chiang-liu 彭江流

P'eng Ming 彭明

P'eng P'ai 彭湃

P'eng Tse-i 彭澤益

Pien Hsiao-hsuan 卞孝萱

pu-lo-chia (women who refused to marry) 不罗嫁

San-hsin (Shanghai cotton mill) 三新

Shang-wu yin-shu-kuan (The Commercial Press) 商务印書館

Shao Hsün-cheng 邵循正

Shao Li-tzu 邵力子

Shao Ying 邵英

Shen Hsiao-ts'en 諶小岑

Shen Pao-hua 沈宝华

Shen Yai-fu 沈涯夫

shen-kung (incentive bonus) 伸工

shen-shih (gentry) 紳士

Sheng Hsuan-huai 盛宣怀

Shih Kuan-t'ao 史觀濤

Shih Yang 施洋

Ssu Fu-te 司福德

ssu-kung ("private work" done for foremen) 私工

Su Chao-cheng 苏兆徵

Sun Ch'uan-fang 孫傳芳

Sun Chung-shan (Sun Yat-sen) 孫中山

Sun Fu-ch'un 孫福春

Sun K'o (Sun Fo) 孫科

Sun Liang-hui 孫良惠

Sun Mao-lin 孫茂林

Sun Pin ("ancestral master" of shoemakers etc.) 孫賓

Sun Tsung-fang 孫宗昉

Sun Yü-liang 孫玉良

Sun Yü-t'ang 孫毓棠

Sung Chiao-jen 宋敎仁

Sung Ch'ing-ling 宋慶齡

Sung Han-chang 宋汉章

Sung Mei-ling 宋美齡

Sung Tzu-wen (T. V. Soong) 宋子文

ta-ch'ang (factory-wrecking) 打厂

Ta-k'ang (Tsingtao cotton mill) 大康

ta-pao (chief labor contractor) 大包

ta-shih-fu (master craftsman) 大師傅

ta-yang ("big money") 大洋

ta-yuan-shou ("boss"; leader of a right-wing union) 大元首

T'a Jung 禤荣

Tai Chi-t'ao 戴季陶

tai-kung ("go slow") 怠工

Tan-hua (Tientsin match factory) 丹华

T'an Jen-feng 譚人冈

T'an P'ing-shan 譚平山

T'an Yen-k'ai 譚延闓

T'ang Chi-yao 唐緓堯

T'ang Hai 唐海

T'ang Sheng-chih 唐生智

T'ao Ching-hsuan 陶靜軒

T'ao Chü-yin 陶菊隱

Teng Chung-hsia 邓中夏

Teng Fa 邓發

Teng Han-hsing 邓汉兴

Teng P'ei 邓陪

Teng Yen-ta 邓演达

Ting Jui-sheng 丁瑞生

Ting Wen-chiang 丁文江

Ting Yu 丁又

t'ou-mu (head of a mutual aid group) 头目

Ts'ai Ho-sen 蔡和森

Ts'ai Yuan-p'ei 蔡元培

Ts'ao Chih-fang 曹志芳

Ts'ao Ju-lin 曹汝霖

Ts'ao Jui 曹鋭

Ts'ao K'un 曹錕

Ts'ao Ya-po 曹亜伯

Tso Chen-yun 左振云

Tso Tsung-t'ang 左宗棠

tsou-kou ("running dogs") 走狗

tsu-chang (labor contractor) 組長

tsu-shih ("ancestral master" of a guild) 祖師

Tu Yueh-sheng 杜月笙

tu-chün (warlord) 督軍

tu-tu (provincial governor in 1912) 都督

t'u-fa (local customary methods) 土法

t'u-fei (outlaws) 徒匪

t'u-hao (despotic landlords) 土豪

t'u-ti (apprentice) 徒弟

Tuan Ch'i-jui 段祺瑞

Tung Ch'u-p'ing 董鋤平

Tung Pi-wu 董必武

Tung-hua (Chinese hospital in Canton) 东华

T'ung Li-chang 童理璋

T'ung-ch'ung-hai (group of cotton mills) 通崇海

T'ung-hsing (Shanghai cotton mill) 同兴

t'ung-hsiang-hui (regional friendly society) 同乡会

t'ung-i-hui (common association) 同一会

t'ung-jen ("common virtue") 同仁

wai-kung ("external" labor) 外工

Wang Cheng 王真

Wang Ching-wei 王精衞

Wang Ching-yü 王敬虞

Wang Ching-yun 王景雲

Wang Ch'ing-pin 王清彬

Wang Chung-hsiu 王中秀

Wang Ch'un-jung 王春荣

Wang Hsün 王洵

Wang Jui-an 王嵩安

Wang Kuang-hui 王光輝

Wang Lin 王林

Wang Shih 王裳

Wang Shou-hua 王寿华

Wen-ming (Shanghai publishing firm) 文明

Wu Chih-hui 吳稚暉

Wu Chü-t'ing 吳菊庭

Wu P'ei-fu 吳佩孚

Wu Sung-shou 吳松寿

Wu T'ieh-ch'eng 吳鉄城

Wu T'ing-fang 伍廷芳

Wu Ts'an-huang 吳燦煌

Yang Chih-hua 楊之华

Yang Hsi-min 楊希閔

Yang I-te 楊一德

Yang Ming-ch'ai 楊明齐

Yang Sen 楊森

Yang Shao-ying 楊紹英

Yang Te-fu 楊德甫

yang-ch'eng-kung (apprentices) 养成工

Yeh Kung-ch'o 葉恭綽

Yen Chung-p'ing 嚴中平

Yeng-ying (Shanghai seamen's guild) 焱盈

Yu T'ien-yang 游天洋

yu-lo-pu ("recreation section") 遊樂部

Yü Ch'i-chung 余啓中

Yü Hsia-ch'ing 俞冶卿

Yü Hsiu-sung 俞秀松

Yü Hui-min 俞惠民

Yü Jih-chang (David Yui) 余日章

Yü Shu-te 于樹德

Yü-feng (Chengchow cotton mill) 豫丰

Yü-ta (Tientsin cotton mill) 裕大

Yü-yuan (Tientsin cotton mill) 裕元

Yuan Cheng-tao 袁正道

Yuan Hsiang 阮湘

Yuan Hsiao-hsien 阮嘯仙

Yuan Shih-k'ai 袁世凱

Yuan Tzu-ying 袁子英

Yung-hua (Shantung match factory) 永华

Notes

In the notes beginning on the following page, books and articles are referred to by short titles. Full publication data are given in the Bibliography, pp. 541–62. For books, a bracketed number in the note refers to a particular Bibliography entry; for articles, an abbreviation of the periodical title is given in the note, and the bracketed numbers referring to Bibliography entries are supplied in the following list of abbreviations.

AAAPS *Annals of the American Academy of Political Science* [84]
CCCP *Cheng-chih chou-pao* [89]
CEB *Chinese Economic Bulletin* [94]
CEJ *Chinese Economic Journal* [95]
CEM *Chinese Economic Monthly* [96]
CF *Ch'ien-feng* [90]
CFJP *Chieh-fang jih-pao* [224]
CHHP *Ch'ing-hua hsüeh-pao* [87]
CJSA *China Journal of Science and Arts* [85]
CKKJ *Chung-kuo kung-jen* [53], [98] and [225]
CMMJ *China Medical Missionary Journal* [86]
CP *Ch'en-pao* [119]
CSPSR *Chinese Social and Political Science Review* [97]
CTSTL *Chin-tai-shih tzu-liao* [151]
CWR *China Weekly Review* [91]
CYB *China Year Book* [92]
ECB *Eastern and Colonial Bulletin* [100]
EE *Eastern Engineering* [99]
FER *Far Eastern Review* [101]
FTHP *Fu-tan hsüeh-pao* [226]
HC *Hsien-ch'ü* [103]
HCN *Hsin-ch'ing-nien* [104]
HCPP *Hung-ch'i p'iao-p'iao* [55]
HKC *Hsin-kuan-ch'a* [54]
HNLSTL *Hu-nan li-shih tzu-liao* [150]
HT *Hsiang-tao* [102]
HWP *Hsin-wen-pao* [122]

ILR *International Labour Review* [33]
IPC *International Press Correspondence* [106]
IS *Informations sociales* [30]
JWC *Japan Weekly Chronicle* [107]
KMJP *Kuang-ming jih-pao* [227]
LCT *London and China Telegraph* [110]
LSYC *Li-shih yen-chiu* [228]
LTC *Lao-tung-chieh* [109]
MDN *Manchuria Daily News* [111]
MKJP *Min-kuo jih-pao* [125]
MLR *Monthly Labor Review* [42]
NB *News Bulletin* [113]
NCH *North China Herald* [115]
NQ *Nankai Economic and Social Quarterly* [112]
PA *Pacific Affairs* [88]
PDR *Police Daily Reports* [12]
PP *Politique de Pékin* [117]
PPW *Pan-Pacific Worker* [116]
PV *Problemy Vostokovedeniya* [323]
RT *Returns of Trade* [27]
SCMP *South China Morning Post* [118]
SHSP *Shang-hai shih-pao* [128]
SK *Sovetskoe Kitaevedenie* [325]
SMCR *Shanghai Municipal Council Report* [37]
SP *Shen-pao* [129]
STSP *Shun-t'ien shih-pao* [132]
TIB *Trade Information Bulletin* [40]
TSTL *Tang-shih tzu-liao* [152]
VI *Voprosi Istorii* [326]

Chapter I

1. See Willoughby, *China at the Conference* [316], chap. 6.
2. Sun Yat-sen, trans. d'Elia [163], chaps. 1 and 2.
3. The concessions were in principle established by agreement with the local Chinese authorities, and the settlements by a unilateral decision on the part of the Powers. See Willoughby, *Foreign Rights* [315], chap. 19.
4. Complete list in *CYB*, 1921–22, pp. 221–22.
5. See Chapter VII below.
6. *SMCR*, 1920. (The figure given is 682,000.)
7. See the Feetham Report [38], Pt. II, for a detailed analysis of the status of the International Settlement. See also Kotenev, *Shanghai, Its Mixed Court and Council* [157].
8. Willoughby, *Foreign Rights* [315], chap. 17.
9. See Endacott, *A History of Hong Kong* [246], chaps. 5 and 6.
10. *Ibid.*, pp. 294–95. The total population of Hong Kong in 1921 was 625,166, of which 610,368 were Chinese (*ibid.*, p. 289).
11. Willoughby, *Foreign Rights* [315], p. 856.
12. *Ibid.*, pp. 156 and 226 (Manchurian lines); see also MacMurray, *Treaties and Agreements* [135], p. 457.
13. Willoughby, *Foreign Rights* [315], p. 227.
14. See Chapter VIII below on the K.M.A. miners' strike of 1922.
15. "Concessions," "leased territories," and "spheres of influence" are terms in general use, but "special status zones" is one I have coined myself in order to accentuate the variety of methods employed in the dismemberment of China.
16. Willoughby, *Foreign Rights* [315], p. 854.
17. *Ibid.* In 1903, after an American gunboat had been sent to the Upper Yangtze, the U.S. Secretary of State wrote: "Even if this right were not granted to us by treaty, Rear Admiral Evans is unquestionably right in using it when like ships of other Powers are constantly doing so."
18. These terms are used interchangeably by most writers.
19. Willoughby, *Foreign Rights* [315], chap. 22.
20. In 1920 there were 115 provincial postal superintendents, of whom 22 were French and 53 British (*CYB*, 1921–22, pp. 472–73). *Ibid.*, pp. 875–77, gives a list of the names of the provincial postal superintendents.
21. *CYB*, 1921–22, p. 479. In 1920 the number of foreign post offices was as follows: 13 French, 12 British, 124 Japanese, 1 American.
22. *Ibid.*, p. 506 (a list containing 10 Japanese, 1 American, 3 French radio stations in Shanghai, Kunming, and Kwangchowwan, and 3 British stations, two at Hong Kong and one in Kashgar).
23. *Ibid.*, pp. 869ff (a list giving the names of the customs inspectors at the main ports).
24. Willoughby, *Foreign Rights* [315], chap. 30.
25. *CYB*, 1921–22, pp. 248ff.
26. See the chapters on Finance in the various issues of *CYB*.
27. In 1919 the Chinese government estimated its debt to be about 1.2 billion yuan, and the repayments and payments of interest during that year to have been 114 million yuan (*CYB*, 1921–22, p. 237).
28. Remer, *Foreign Investment* [299], p. 76 and *passim*.
29. See Allen and Donnithorne, *Western Enterprise* [230], *passim*.
30. Remer [299] and Allen and Donnithorne [230]. Further discussion of the various foreign industrial enterprises in China will be found in Chapter II below.
31. Remer [299], p. 202.
32. They are listed in *CYB*, 1921–22, p. 94.

33. See [89].

34. A list of the more important of them is given in *CYB*, 1921–22, p. 559.

35. On this solidarity between the missions and the Powers, see for instance Leclerc [272], *passim,* and Varg [310], chaps. 3 and 4.

36. Since my study is confined to the labor movement between 1919 and 1927, there is no need to enter into the historical problems involved in this position of power. No attempt has been made, for example, to differentiate between treaty rights (e.g. extra-territoriality) and rights arrogated by means of a unilateral decision on the part of the Powers, nor to show how earlier rights were directed toward ensuring freedom of movement for trade and traders (concessions, extraterritoriality, limitation of tariffs), whereas after the breakup the rights demanded (control of finance, leased territories) reflected the anxiety of the Powers to safeguard their investments in China. It is the task of the historians of Western penetration of China to decide whether the unequal treaties were simply an extention of the relations between the Chinese on one side and the "barbarian" tributaries and the Arab merchants in the Middle Ages on the other, as maintained by Fairbank in *Trade and Diplomacy on the China Coast* [248], or whether they represented a complete reversal of relations between China and foreign countries, at China's expense. The history of the expression "unequal treaties" and its effect on Chinese attitudes has still to be written.

37. *CYB*, 1921–22, p. 622; Levi, *Modern China's Foreign Policy* [274], pp. 139 and 152.

38. *CYB*, 1921–22, p. 625. It was not until 1920, a year after the Soviet government's renunciation of the rights granted to the Tsarist government, that the Chinese government ceased to grant these rights to the White Russians and their organizations and representatives (*ibid.,* pp. 628–29).

39. Morse and McNair, *Far Eastern International Relations* [293], chap. 28.

40. *Ibid.*

41. *CYB*, 1921–22, pp. 683ff (text of the Twenty-one Demands).

42. In August 1920, for instance, the diplomatic corps released the sum of 4,280,000 yuan under the guise of "salt tax surplus," with detailed stipulations on how the money should be spent (for military and central government expenditure, etc.) (*CWR*, 21.viii.-20). In April 1926 it released 600,000 yuan of the customs surplus to pay the government police in Peking so as to maintain order there (*CWR*, 17.iv.26).

43. During this period the diplomatic corps granted the Constitutionalist government in Canton 13.7 per cent of the revenue collected by the Chinese Maritime Customs, this percentage corresponding to the volume of trade in ports effectively under the control of the Canton government (*CYB*, 1921–22, p. 247). But this allocation was suspended in the spring of 1920, when the Kwangsi militarists were in sole control of Canton; Sun Yat-sen and his successors in the Nationalist government never again obtained any part of the surplus.

44. Kung Chün, *Chung-kuo hsin-kung-yeh* [204], pp. 95 and 114. These figures given by the Nung-shang-pu, like those for the numbers of workers employed (see below, pp. 26–27), are not too reliable. After Yuan Shih-k'ai's death in 1916, an increasing number of provinces sent in incomplete statistics or sometimes none at all. This explains why the figures for 1916 are higher than those for 1918: 284 million yuan invested in banks, 132 million in industry, 20 and 23 million in commerce and transport. Yet China was in a period of expansion during the First World War.

45. See Chapter II below for a more detailed discussion of industrial enterprises owned by the Chinese bourgeoisie in 1919.

46. Chu Hsin-fan, *Chung-kuo tzu-pen-chu-i fa-chan* [193], pp. 93–100, includes a list of the chief industrial enterprises founded during this period, with the amounts of capital invested.

47. Yen Chung-p'ing, *T'ung-chi tzu-liao hsuan-chi* [141], pp. 108–9.

48. Chow Tse-tsung, *The May Fourth Movement* [242], p. 380, quotes figures from a report of the Nung-shang-pu. Probably the number of chambers of commerce continued to increase during the First World War, when Chinese capitalism was expanding; but as already mentioned, the Nung-shang-pu statistics are incomplete after 1916.

49. The term is of Portuguese origin (lit. "buyers"), and designates the Chinese managers of the big foreign banks and commercial firms in China.

50. On the respective roles of these three strata of the new bourgeoisie, see Levy and Shih Kuo-heng, *The Rise of the Modern Chinese Business Class* [276], and Feuerwerker, *China's Early Industrial Development* [251].

51. *CWR,* 5.viii.22.

52. *CWR,* 10.iii.23.

53. *Who's Who in China,* 1920 ed. [185], p. 155.

54. On these traditional merchant groups, see below, p. 113.

55. For a list of associations affiliated with the Chinese Chamber of Commerce in Shanghai, see *CEB,* 20.ix.24.

56. *CYB,* 1926, p. 1220. On the part Yü played in 1925–27, see Chapters XI and XIV below.

57. *CWR,* 8.x.21.

58. The grandson of Li Hung-chang was chairman of the C.M.S.N. Co. (*CWR,* 29.-xii.23), and the son of Sheng Hsuan-huai was managing director of the Anyuan mines (*HT,* 2.xii.25).

59. On Chang Ch'ien, see Levy and Shih Kuo-heng [276], p. 31.

60. Willoughby, *Foreign Rights* [315], pp. 748–57.

61. Lieu, *China's Industries and Finances* [278], pp. 129ff. This writer estimates that there were 790 likin stations in 1925.

62. See for example Lieu, *The Growth and Industrialisation of Shanghai* [280], pp. 91ff, and Fong, *Industrial Capital* [254].

63. According to Nung-shang-pu figures from a census of 956 Chinese enterprises carried out in 1918 (Kung Chün [204], p. 115), 378 of them, or 40 per cent, had a capital of under 10,000 yuan, 275, or 29 per cent, a capital of 10,000 to 50,000 yuan, 86, or 9 per cent, a capital of 50,000 to 100,000 yuan, 157, or 16 per cent, a capital of 100,000 to 500,000 yuan, 27 a capital of 500,000 to 1,000,000 yuan, and 33 a capital of over 1,000,000 yuan.

64. Thus the firm of Jardine, Matheson & Co., closely linked with the Hongkong and Shanghai Banking Corporation, controlled, in addition to its steamship lines, cotton mills and silk factories in Shanghai and Hongkong, and tramways and insurance companies in Hong Kong; it also had a share in the collieries of the Peking Syndicate in Honan (Yen Chung-p'ing [141], pp. 255–57).

65. See Chapter II below for details of Chinese energy sources in 1919.

66. In 1918 the number of Chinese merchant ships using Chinese ports was 43,638, with a tonnage of 17 million, as against 54,782 foreign ships with a tonnage of 57 million—that is, less than a quarter of the total tonnage (Yen Chung-p'ing [141], p. 221). On the Yangtze in the same year the C.M.S.N. Co. (the biggest Chinese shipping company) had only 8 ships in use, as against 17 belonging to the British firms of Jardine, Matheson & Co. and Butterfield & Swire, and 14 belonging to the main Japanese company (*ibid.,* p. 248).

67. *CYB,* 1921–22, chap. 20.

68. See, for instance, references in the "éphémérides" in Wieger, *La Chine moderne* [139].

69. *CYB,* 1921–22, pp. 95–130 (list established according to the registrations of periodicals at the Chinese Post Office). See also Lin Shu-shen, *Histoire du journalisme* [281].

70. Chow Tse-tsung, [242], p. 379.

71. No sociological study has been made of Chinese students during this period, nor of the intelligentsia in general. Cf. Kiang Wen-han, *The Chinese Student Movement*

[265] (mainly concerning the intellectual and political aspects), and Tretiakov, *A Chinese Testament* [49].

72. The 1912 census gives a figure of 361 million and the 1928 census 474 million (Nanming I Liu, *Contribution à l'étude de la population chinoise* [296], pp. 104 and 111). The Chinese Post Office estimated the population of China to be 427 million in 1921 (*CYB, 1921*, p. 3). These figures are presumably too low, since the 1953 census established the figure of 582 million for the population of mainland China (*JAS*, Aug. 1957, "The Chinese 1953 Census").

73. Yen Chung-p'ing [141], p. 123. There is no need to stress the unreliability of these figures.

74. See Lieu, *China's Industries* [278], pp. 115–20, on the Chinese system of weights and measures. There were wide variations between provinces. The *mou* in principle equals 6,000 square feet, but may equal as much as 17,000. The *tan* ("picul"), a measure of weight, was equal to 150 Chinese pounds (*chin*) or "catties" in Shanghai, but to 1,200 pounds in Yunnan. ("Picul" and "catty" are pidgin terms.) The equivalents adopted by Westerners in China during this period (1 mou = .15182 acre; 1 catty = 1⅓ lb.; 1 picul = 133⅓ lb.) were therefore no more than useful conventions. See *CYB*, 1919, pp. 86–87, for a table of equivalents.

75. The extreme confusion of the Chinese monetary system during this period was due not only to the localized nature of economic life, but also to the decay of the bureaucratic machinery after the fall of the Empire, as well as to the penetration of foreign business interests. Cf. Kann, *Currency in China* [264], *passim*; Lieu [278], pp. 37ff and pp. 120ff; *CYB, 1919*, pp. 360–64.

Chinese currency was traditionally based on the tael (*liang*), which was a weight of silver with wide provincial variations; for instance, 100 "Customs taels" equaled 101.75 Amoy taels, 104.77 Kiukiang taels, 111.40 Shanghai taels. The tael was only an accounting unit, not an actual coin; but coins were minted of its multiple, the "cash" (in theory, one thousandth of a tael), in the form of the "copper cash" with a value of ten "cash," and this coin was in wide circulation.

In addition, foreign silver coins (the Mexican dollar, the Hong Kong dollar, Spanish dollars from the Philippines) had been used in the Treaty Ports since the middle of the nineteenth century; and there was the *yuan,* or Chinese dollar, which Yuan Shih-k'ai tried to establish as the national currency in 1914, the paper money issued by provincial civil or military governments when short of funds, and foreign bank notes, such as those of the Hong Kong Bank, which were widely used in Kwangtung.

There was no fixed relationship between these currencies, either from one place or from one time to another. The rate of exchange for silver constantly varied, and so did that between the yuan and its subsidiary silver coins (of 10 and 20 *fen*—the *fen* being one hundredth of a yuan), and between the yuan and the copper "cash." The constant depreciation of the latter was of direct concern to the working class (see Chapter V below), as was the difference between being paid in *ta-yang* (big money) and being paid in *hsiaoyang* (small money). In the first case, wages were paid in pieces of one yuan, with coins of smaller denomination to make up the total; in the other, they were paid entirely in coins of smaller denomination, at their face value, with no account taken of their depreciation in terms of the yuan. (Gamble, *Peking: A Social Survey* [66], p. 215.)

76. See Chapter VI below on the decline of the traditional guilds at the beginning of the twentieth century.

77. *CWR*, 30.ix.22 (according to a study made by the Chinese bankers' association).

78. *CEB*, 16.i.25.

79. The phrase comes from Lattimore, *Inner Asian Frontiers* [271], p. 49. See also Fei Hsiao-tung, *China's Gentry* [250], which stresses the feudal nature of Chinese rural society right up until the twentieth century. There is of course another school of thought

which regards the traditional form of Chinese society as fundamentally "bureaucratic," membership in the bureaucracy being the economic basis of the ruling class. (Cf. Chang Chung-li, *The Chinese Gentry* [236].)

80. Cf. Mao Tse-tung on the Chinese revolution and the CCP (*Works* [161] II, 305–14). Cf. also Ch'en Po-ta, *A Study of Land Rent* [237].

81. See Buck, *The Chinese Farm Economy* [57], pp. 46 and 231–37. This survey, carried out around 1928, gives an average of 2.3 crop hectares per farm; four-fifths of the farms were worked by the peasant proprietor, sometimes with the help of other members of his family. See also Tawney, *Land and Labour in China* [78], p. 41n.

82. In 1917 the Nung-shang-pu figures give a total of 49 million farmers, of which 24.5 million were owners, 14 million part-tenants, and 10.5 million tenants (Lamb, *Agrarian Movement* [267], p. 19). These figures approximate those issued by the Peasant Department of the Central Committee of the Kuomintang in 1927, which give 150 million small owners, 136 million part-tenants and tenants, and 30 million agricultural laborers (*ibid.*, p. 14).

83. See Ch'en Po-ta [237], chap. 2; also *Nien-chien* [138] I, 451 (various types of rent in Kiangsu).

84. *CWR*, 21.xi.25, "Unfavorable Conditions in Northern Kiangsu."

85. Cf. for instance the childhood memories of Chu Te (Agnes Smedley, *The Great Road* [48], pp. 16–18) on the tyranny exercised by the Ting family, the big landowners in the district, over the peasants of his native village at the end of the nineteenth century. On usury, see examples given in *Agrarian China* [148], pp. 188–204.

86. Cf. the description of the armies of the shen-shih in Hunan in the report on the peasant movement in that province made by Mao Tse-tung in 1926 (*Works* [161] I, 41–42).

87. Cf. *PA*, Oct. 1929 ("The Burdens of the Chinese Peasantry"). Government military expenditure alone had risen from 25 million yuan (or the equivalent) in 1895 to 203 million yuan in 1918.

88. Ch'en Po-ta [237], p. 62.

89. In the *hsien* (districts) of Kunshan and Nantung in Kiangsu, the price index of polished rice had risen, taking 1905 as 100, to 157 and 140 in 1914, and to 296 and 228 in 1924 (*Nien-chien* [138] I, 450). See Table 1.

90. Cf. the figures given for the hsien of Kunshan and Nantung (*Nien-chien* [138] I, 449). Taking 1905 as 100, the price index of medium quality land had risen to 189 and 140 in 1914, and to 369 and 242 in 1924. Poor quality land rose even more: 213 and 147 in 1914, 464 and 255 in 1924. See Table 1.

91. At the end of the nineteenth century local combustible oils began having to compete with American kerosene in the villages of Szechwan (Smedley [48], p. 53). On the crisis in rural industry, see also the examples quoted by Fong, *Rural Industries* [255], and in *Agrarian China* [148], pp. 224–27 (pottery in Shantung, brasswork in Kiangsu, silk spinning and weaving in the Wusih region).

92. *Agrarian China* [148], pp. 94–101.

93. Figures given by the International Famine Relief Commission, formed in 1920–21 by Protestant missionaries in Peking (*CWR*, 25.x.24).

94. Figures given (for a slightly later date) by the Peasant Union of Kwangtung province in 1926 (Lamb [267], p. 21).

95. Figures given in *Nien-chien* [138] I, 447ff. All the figures on peasant ownership that I have quoted from various sources in this chapter are mentioned only as examples; I have not attempted to make a systematic survey, or to comment on such questions as the comparatively stable position of the part-owners or the rapid decrease in the size of farms belonging to small peasant proprietors.

96. See Mallory, *China, Land of Famine* [287], and McNair, *With the White Cross*

[46]. It would be interesting to compare the social crisis in the early twentieth century with China's other periodic agrarian crises, and especially with the one that occurred around 1850, just before the Taiping Revolution and the accompanying Nien and Mohammedan revolts.

97. On the recruitment of peasants as industrial workers, see below, pp. 48ff.

98. See Purcell, *The Chinese in South-East Asia* [298]; around 1920 there were 260,000 Chinese emigrants in Siam, 200,000 in French Indochina, over a million in Malaysia, and 800,000 in Indonesia.

99. F. L. Ho, "Population Movement to the Northeastern Provinces," *CSPSR*, Oct. 1931.

100. *RT*, 1921, Wanhsien, p. 9.

101. *CWR*, 18.vi.21.

102. Cf. the Chinese Post Office report for 1918 [35], *passim*, for incidents of attacks by outlaws on post offices and postal services.

103. See Eberhard, *Chinese Festivals* [245].

104. See Lang, *Chinese Family and Society* [270], especially chaps. 3, 6, and 10, where family relations, social relations, and nepotism are discussed.

105. Cf. for instance the young intellectuals that figure in the novels of Lu Hsün and, a little later, of Pa Chin (see Schyns, *1,500 Chinese Novels and Plays* [4]).

106. For a list of the ministries, see *CYB*, 1919, p. 304.

107. *Ibid.*, pp. 306–8. See also *Chung-kuo nien-chien* [169], 1924, pp. 224–25. There were, for instance, five "circuits" in Kiangsu (*Nien-chien* [138] I, 2).

108. Houn, *Central Government in China* [261], p. 142.

109. Li Chien-nung, *Political History* [277], chaps. 11 and 12, *passim*.

110. *Ibid.*, chap. 12.   111. *Ibid.*, pp. 383–84.

112. Wieger, *La Chine moderne* [139] IV, 21.   113. See Chapter XV below.

114. This title derives from a combination of the title of *tu-tu*, borne by the provincial governors at the time of the Revolution of 1911, and that of *chiang-chün* ("General"); it was conferred on the provincial governors by Yuan Shih-k'ai in 1914 (*CYB*, 1919, pp. 306–7).

115. For instance in November 1921, Wu P'ei-fu, a leader of the Chihli faction, demanded 3 million yuan from the Wuhan Chambers of Commerce to meet his military expenses (*CWR*, 19.xi.21).

116. In Yunnan the price of opium rose from 8 yuan per ounce in 1916 to 80 yuan in 1920 (*CWR*, 3.iv.20). Cf. the examples quoted in *Agrarian China* [148], pp. 118–31, of the cultivation of opium demanded by the warlords in Kansu, Fukien, and Yunnan.

117. For example in April 1919 the press revealed that there was a big trade in French and American arms in the direction of Hunan and Kweichow (*JWC*, 24.iv.19). In the same year, the Italian Legation in Peking was said to have a large stock of arms obtained from surplus stocks left over from the First World War (*CWR*, 18.iv.24, "Who Sells Guns to China's War Leaders?").

118. *CWR*, 24.ii.23 ("Mutiny Cases in China Since the Revolution").

119. Cf. the Who's Who sections of the various editions of *CYB* for many examples of official careers of the gentry.

120. For instance, Wu P'ei-fu, a leader of the Chihli faction, obtained the First Degree in the Confucian literary examinations before taking up an army career (*CYB*, 1923, p. 877). On the other hand, Chang Tso-lin was a former brigand chief, and Feng Kuo-chang began life as an itinerant musician (Kotenev, *New Lamps for Old* [266], p. 102).

121. Cf. for instance Sun Yat-sen (*Hsuan-chi* [163], p. 442), in a letter of 18.viii.22 to members of the Kuomintang, in which he condemned provincialist tendencies.

122. *CYB*, 1919, pp. 306–7. The lack of monographs on any of the provincial assemblies makes it impossible to give details concerning their social basis; but as far as can be as-

certained, the influence of the rural gentry was preponderant. The preponderance was almost certainly not that of the new bourgeoisie, contrary to the too hasty conclusions drawn in my article in *Annales* [319], July 1954.

123. For example, early in 1921 the Provincial Assembly of Shansi objected to a decree placing all the unexploited mines in the province under the central government, declaring that they belonged to the people of Shansi (*CWR*, 25.vi.21). Regional tendencies had also been strong during the summer of 1911 among the gentry of the Middle Yangtze region (E-tu Zen Sun, *Chinese Railways* [305], pp. 117–19).

124. Founded in 1912 (Yen Chung-p'ing [141], p. 167).

125. Both these cotton mills were founded in 1920 (Chu Hsin-fan, *Chung-kuo tzu-pen-chu-i fa-chan* [193], p. 96).

126. Hu Sheng, *Imperialism and Chinese Politics* [262], chap. 5.

127. *Ibid.*, p. 230.

128. Nothing has been written on the Chinese secret societies in the twentieth century—not even a chapter or a short account. See Chapter VI below for comments on their relations with the labor organizations, and for other references.

129. Mao Tse-tung, *Selected Works* [161] I, 19. See also Li Ta-chao, *Hsuan-chi* [159], pp. 564ff, on the Red Swords and on secret societies in general among the peasants north of the Yangtze.

130. Ma Ch'ao-chün, *Chung-kuo lao-tung yun-tung shih* [209], pp. 76–77.

131. Teng and Fairbank, *China's Response to the West* [307], pp. 239–54.

132. Li Jui, *Mao Tse-tung* [206], pp. 53–82.

133. Teng and Fairbank [307], pp. 239–54.

134. *CYB*, 1923, p. 883.

135. This disappointment is reflected in several short stories by Lu Hsün written about this time, such as "In the Wine Shop" and "The Misanthrope" (Lu Hsün, *Selected Works* [286], pp. 174ff and 212ff).

136. See Chapter VI below.

137. Cf. *AAPS* (1930), "China's Use of the Boycott as a Political Weapon."

138. Chow Tse-tsung [242], p. 24.

139. The Provincial Assembly of Hupeh suspended its regular meeting on May 7, 1920, as a sign of mourning (*CWR*, 15.v.20).

140. Hu Sheng [262], p. 242.

141. *CYB*, 1921–22, pp. 719–38.

142. On the Y.M.C.A. and on relations in general between Protestantism and the national awakening in China, see Varg, *Missionaries, Chinese, and Diplomats* [310], chap. 4.

143. See Bibliography, entries [91] and [97].

144. Hu Sheng [262], pp. 190–92.

145. A special study should be made of the activities of the Commercial Press, the biggest Chinese publishing firm at this time. See *Ch'u-pan shih-liao* [134], Supplementary Vol., pp. 557ff, for a chronology of the firm's development since its foundation in 1897.

146. *Who's Who in China*, 1920 ed. [185], pp. 5 and 108.

147. On Sun Yat-sen's activities around 1919 see Chesneaux, *Sun Yat-sen* [239], pp. 171ff.

148. See *CYB*, 1923, *Who's Who*.

149. In 1922 the *CWR* organized a referendum among its readers, who mainly belonged to the new Chinese bourgeoisie, on "the twelve greatest living Chinese." The results were published in the issue of 6.i.23: Sun Yat-sen took first place, in preference to Feng Yü-hsiang, the "Christian General," and Wellington Koo, the Chinese negotiator at the Washington Conference.

150. See Sun Yat-sen, *Hsuan-chi* [163], p. 339.

151. "The first thing to do is to restore to Parliament its rights," he declared in February 1919 (*ibid.*, p. 420).

152. *Ibid.*, pp. 186ff.

153. By July 1917, 305 former members of parliament had arrived in Canton (*SCMP*, 3.viii.17).

154. The work of demolition started in December 1918 (*FER*, Feb. 1920).

155. Li Chien-nung, *Political History* [277], p. 387.

156. Kotenev [266], p. 102.

157. Li Chien-nung [277], p. 387.

158. *Ibid.*, pp. 390–93.

159. Sun Yat-sen, trans. d'Elia [163], p. 12.

160. This type of literature, very critical of China, flourished among Western residents in China just after the First World War. See Bibliography, entries [273], [231], and [257].

161. See Li Chien-nung [277], *passim.*

162. On the various Chinese dialects, see Forrest, *The Chinese Language* [256], pp. 194ff.

163. These associations had already arranged for a "National Peace Conference" to be held in Peking in December 1918 (Wieger, *La Chine moderne* [139] VII, 22).

Chapter II

1. The statistics of the Nung-shang-pu cover enterprises employing more than seven workers (*Nien-chien* [138], I); those of the Nanking government after 1928 cover enterprises employing more than 30 workers (Fang Fu-an, *Chinese Labor* [249], chap. 2). Surveys conducted by the Japanese S.M.R. Co. were restricted to enterprises employing over 50 workers (*CEB*, 22.xi.24).

2. In Tsinan, according to figures given for 1925, 70,000 women and children did work at home, as against 10,000 employed in modern enterprises and 30,000 in craft workshops (*CEB*, 22.viii.25).

3. Simine, *Le travail des femmes* [313], pp. 61, 63, 65, 89.

4. In the hsien of P'ing-hu in Chekiang, for instance, a rural stocking-manufacture industry was established in 1910, which in 1925 employed up to 10,000 workers (Kung Chün, *Chung-kuo hsin-kung-yeh* [204]). The merchant-manufacturers distributed the machines and the raw material and paid at piecework rates, but demanded rent for the machines and a cash deposit; a machine valued at 20 yuan was hired out at one yuan per month. No workers who owned their own machines were employed (Simine [313], pp. 89–90).

Before the republican revolution Tientsin merchants had begun to hire out weaving looms throughout the nearby rural hsien of Kao-yang, also supplying the cotton yarn; by 1926 90 per cent of the rural population were thus employed (Kung Chün [204], p. 100).

Around 1925 a French firm in Ningpo employed thousands of women in the neighboring villages who worked at home making hats of a type in demand in London and in Paris, where the hats were finished off. (*CWR*, 31.vi.26.) A Cantonese merchant established a match factory at Wuchow in 1922 that employed 260 workers in the factory and over a thousand women in the countryside (*RT*, 1922, Wuchow, p. 15).

5. *Nien-chien* [138] I, 9–141.

6. *Ibid.*, p. 15.

7. Quoted in *La Revue du Pacifique*, Sept. 1925 ("Le prolétariat industriel en Chine"), from the Bulletin of the Red International of Labor Unions of Dec. 1924 [187].

8. Wales, *The Chinese Labor Movement* [312], p. 9.

9. *MLR*, Sept. 1923.

10. See Chapter X below.

11. Figures published in the *Manchuria and Mongolia Handbook* and quoted in *CWR,* 6.vi.30.

12. See Chapter III below.

13. See Lieu, *The Silk Reeling Industry* [279].

14. This brief introductory description shows how greatly a thorough history of modern industrial development in China is needed. For brief accounts, see Kung Chün [204], Chu Hsin-fan [193], Fong and Ho [260], Nagano [295], and Mitchell [230].

15. See Allen and Donnithorne, *Western Enterprise* [230], p. 166.

16. Fong, *Cotton Industry* [252], p. 114.

17. *Ibid.,* p. 8 (4 million spindles and 29,000 looms in 1925, 1.8 million spindles and 16,000 looms in 1919).

18. In 1925, about 133,000 workers were employed in the Chinese mills, 60,000 in the Japanese, and 16,500 in the British (*ibid.,* p. 13). In 1919 the Chinese mills had about half the number of spindles as in 1925, the Japanese two-thirds, and the British the same number (*ibid.,* p. 8).

19. Precise figures for the geographical distribution of spindles exist for Chinese mills only (*ibid.,* p. 16): 80 per cent in Kiangsu (Yangtze estuary), 10 per cent in Central China (Hankow and Changsha), 5 per cent in the northern ports (Tientsin and Tsingtao), 5 per cent in Chekiang (Hangchow and Ningpo). At the beginning of 1921 about 60 per cent of the Japanese spindles were in Shanghai, 20 per cent in Tientsin, and 20 per cent in Tsingtao (*CEB,* 17.vi.21). All the British spindles were in Shanghai (*CYB,* 1921, p. 762).

20. *CYB,* 1919, p. 90.

21. *CEB,* 17.vi.21.

22. On the development of the silk industry in China, see Kung Chün [204], pp. 27ff, 150ff; Howard and Buswell, [68]; Tsing Tung-chun, *La production et le commerce de la soie en Chine* [309]; and Lieu [279].

23. At Wusih in 1925, 14,000 workers were employed on 6,000 ch'e (Stewart and Fang Fu-an, "A Statistical Study of Industry and Labor in China," *CEJ,* Oct. 1930). At Shanghai in 1927, 60,000 workers were employed on 22,000 ch'e (Kung Chün [204], p. 159). But in the Shunteh district near Canton only 65,000 workers were employed on 55,000 ch'e (Howard and Buswell [68], p. 25).

24. Kung Chün [204], p. 152.

25. The estimated figure for Kwangtung corresponds with the figure of 140,000 silk workers in Kwangtung given by Ho and Fong [260], p. 19.

26. According to *CEJ,* June 1929, "Labor Conditions in Canton," the majority of the silk-reeling plants in the Canton region were craft workshops.

27. A British consular report mentions 20,000 to 30,000 workers in 42 silk-reeling factories (mostly modern) in this province in 1924 (*Labour Conditions* [20], p. 34).

28. The Nishikawa survey (see Table 3) has only 130,000 silk workers for 1923, but there had just been a crisis in the silk industry at that time (see Chapter XIII below).

29. Kung Chün [204], pp. 164–67, gives the figures of about 2,000 modern looms in Chekiang, several hundred in Shanghai, and the same in Nanking, Soochow, and Chengtu. At Hangchow in 1922 7,000 workers were employed in 10 silk-weaving factories (*CEB,* 29.v.22).

30. A list of Shanghai mills and factories made by the Child Labor Commission set up by the Shanghai Municipal Council in 1923 includes 27 foreign silk-reeling factories (6 Italian, 5 French, 9 British, 5 American), employing 23,000 workers (Kotenev [156], pp. 306–10). Between 1919 and 1923 there was scarcely any difference in the number of ch'e in the silk factories (Lieu [279], p. 5); but because several Chinese factories came under Western ownership during the crisis of 1922–24, the number of workers employed in foreign silk factories in 1919 must have been less.

31. On the carpet industry in China, see Fong, *The Tientsin Carpet Industry* [65], and Chu and Blaisdell, *Peking Rugs* [59].

32. Fong [65], p. 7, estimates that the average number of workers employed on each loom was 4.2.

33. Chu and Blaisdell [59], pp. 22ff.

34. See *CEB*, 21.x.21.

35. Kung Chün [204], pp. 168–76. In 1926, 450 workers were employed in the Mukden factory (*MDN*, 13.x.26).

36. Fong, *Hosiery Knitting* [63], stresses the large amount of work done in the home in Tientsin.

37. Kung Chün [204], p. 178, gives a list of factories making stockings, nets, etc., in which 1,735 machines were in use. Simine [313], p. 82, quotes a figure of 15,000 women employees in the hosiery industry in Shanghai, taken from statistics drawn up by employers at a slightly later date. According to the list quoted by Kotenev [156], pp. 306ff, some of them worked in Japanese factories. In Hangchow, in 1923, there were three hosiery factories employing 500 workers (*CEB*, 21.vi.24), and in Hankow, in 1925, there were 53 factories in which 1,167 machines were in use (*CEB*, 16.i.25).

38. *Nien-chien* [138] I, 196.

39. See *CEJ*, June 1928, "Flour Mills in China," and July 1933, "Flour Industry in Kiangsu"; see also Kung Chün [204], pp. 183ff.

40. *CEJ*, June 1928, "Flour Mills in China."

41. In Wusih in 1925 there were 30 flour mills employing 2,000 workers—an average of 66 workers per mill (*CEB*, 19.ix.25). In Shanghai in 1926 there were 20 flour mills employing 3,000 workers, an average of 150 per mill (*CEB*, 1.iv.26). In Tsinan in 1925 an average of 80 to 100 workers were employed in each flour mill (*CWR*, 1.xi.25).

42. A figure near the one given by Nishikawa Kiishi for 1923 (see Table 3).

43. *CEJ*, June 1928.

44. Fong, *Grain Trade* [62].

45. See Dyson, "The Oil-mill Outlook in China" (*CWR*, 15.x.21). See also Kung Chün [204], pp. 227ff.

46. There were 60 Japanese oil mills in Dairen in 1919 (Kung Chün [204], p. 230), and 17 (also Japanese) in Tsingtao in 1921 (*CWR*, 2.x.21). An incomplete list of oil mills for 1920 includes six other Japanese mills situated in other towns, and several established by Italian, American, and British firms (*CYB*, 1921, pp. 777–78).

47. In 1921, 1,650 workers were employed in 15 of the 17 Tsingtao oil mills (*CWR*, 2.x.21). In Wuhan in 1925 the average number of workers per mill was 200 (*CEB*, 26.iv.25).

48. *CWR*, 15.x.21.

49. Kung Chün [204], p. 146.

50. Exports of albumen from China in 1913 came to the value of 2.7 million taels (*CYB*, 1919, p. 178) and 24 million taels in 1920 (*CYB*, 1921, p. 1108).

51. *CYB*, 1921, p. 760.

52. This applies in particular to the factories of the British firm International Export Co. at Nanking (*CYB*, 1921, p. 760). Other factories were smaller, such as the two Japanese ones in Tsingtao, which in 1921 employed 200 workers each (*FER*, March 1921).

53. *CEJ*, Oct. 1927, "A Study of the Sugar Industry in China," lists the principal refineries and gives a figure of about 3,000 workers for 1927. The figure for 1919 must have been much the same, for the list of sugar refineries published in *CYB*, 1921, p. 786, is very close to the 1927 list.

54. See Lin Sung-ho, *Factory Workers in Tangku* [74], p. 16.

55. There were 41 modern rice-husking works in Shanghai in 1919 (*CEB*, 20.v.21) and 11 in Wusih (*CWR*, 17.vii.20). In 1921 the *CYB* (pp. 781 and 786) names 60 modern

rice-husking works and six modern tea factories. These figures cast some doubts on the Nung-shang-pu figures quoted in Table 2, where the figure for workers in the tea industry seems too high and that for workers in the rice-husking industry too low.

56. *CYB*, 1921, pp. 761 and 766.

57. One brewery in Shanghai, for instance, employed 50 workers in 1925 (see Kotenev [156], list on pp. 306ff).

58. Kung Chün [204], pp. 222–23. See also the *Record in China of the B.A.T.* [182].

59. Kung Chün [204], p. 222.

60. *CYB*, 1921, p. 787.

61. *Record of the B.A.T.* [182], p. 10.

62. The survey published in the special May 1920 number of *HCN* devoted to labor problems gives the figure of 20,000 tobacco workers in Shanghai.

63. On the match industry see Kung Chün [204], pp. 198–205. Incomplete lists of factories are published in *CYB*, 1921, pp. 776–77 (61 factories, ten of them Japanese), and in *CEJ*, July 1928, "Match Factories in China" (63 factories in 1919).

64. Some examples of exact figures available for this period are as follows: in Shanghai, four match factories employing in all 2,900 workers (Kung Chün [204], p. 204), and another employing 2,400 (Henry report [10] on Shanghai); in Hangchow in 1925, one factory employing 1,000 workers (*CEB*, 17.iv.26), and for the same year another factory employing the same number (*RT*, 1926, Suchow, p. 2); in Tsinan in 1925 two factories employing in all 1,500 workers (*CWR*, 1.xi.25).

65. *CYB*, 1921, pp. 773–74, gives an incomplete list of 23 glass and ceramic works; only five are mentioned in the *CYB* of 1912 (p. 5). These factories did not employ large numbers of workers: 320 in all for seven glass works in Tientsin in 1925 (*Nien-chien* [138] I, 190); 20 to 250 per factory in four "fairly large" glass works in Shanghai in 1926 (*CEB*, 12.vi.26).

66. An incomplete list in *CYB*, 1921, p. 785.

67. Four hundred workers in one factory in Shanghai in 1925 (Kotenev [156], p. 306), 200 in one factory in Tientsin (*CEM*, Oct. 1926, "Wages in Tientsin Industries"), 140 in four factories in Hangchow in 1923 (*CEB*, 21.vi.24).

68. *CYB*, 1921, pp. 775 and 779.

69. In Chekiang in 1925 one paper works employed 300 workers (*CEB*, 12.ix.25); four in Shanghai each employed about 170 (*CEJ*, June 1928, "Paper Manufacturing in China").

70. In 1925, 6,000 were employed at Anshan and 3,000 at Penhsihi (Torgasheff, "Mining Labor in China," *CEJ*, June 1930). In 1919 the output at Penhsihi was more or less the same as in 1925, whereas that at Anshan was three times less (Hsüeh, "Iron and Steel Industry in China," *CEJ*, Jan. 1928), hence the estimate of 2,000 workers for Anshan in 1919.

71. In 1916 the number of workers in the Hanyehping blast furnaces was 20,000 (Torgasheff, *CEJ*, June 1930), and in 1914 the number employed in the Yangtze Engineering Works blast furnaces was 3,000 (*Chung-kuo chin-tai kung-yeh* [137] II, 1187). There was very little increase in the iron output of these two centers in 1919 (Hsüeh, *CEJ*, Jan. 1928).

72. *Nien-chien* [138] I, 188 (for 1926).

73. *Ibid.* (for 1926).

74. *Ibid.*, p. 186 (for 1924).

75. See Lowe Chuan-hua, *Facing Labor Issues* [284], p. 57.

76. The Fuchow, Kiangnan, and Hanyang arsenals were founded between 1870 and 1890 by the viceroys Tso Tsung-t'ang, Li Hung-chang, and Chang Chih-tung as part of the *tzu-ch'iang* or "self-strengthening" policy (see Teng and Fairbank [307], pp. 79 and 111).

77. An official list (*Nien-chien* [138] I, 196) gives 5,000 workers in the army arsenals

and 3,000 in the shipyards for the year 1924; but these figures are far too low because the list does not include the arsenals at Tsinan, Kaifeng, Taiyuan, and Changsha, which together employed about 2,000 workers in 1922 (*CYB*, 1923, pp. 592–94), or the Canton arsenal, which in 1922 had 1,800 employees (*HT*, 15.x.21). Moreover the list gives the figure of 2,335 for the number of employees at the Hanyang arsenal, whereas *CYB*, 1923, gives 5,000. Further arsenals not included in it are those at Mukden, Paoting, Sian, Nanking, Chengtu, and Kunming, which together must have employed about 3,000 workers if their output was comparable to that of the arsenals mentioned above. Thus the total number of workers employed in arsenals and shipyards comes to about 15,000. To these must be added the 5,500 workers in the two Chinese-owned shipyards in Shanghai (*Nien-chien* [138] I, 188).

78. *CYB*, 1921, p. 767, lists three Japanese and 11 British shipyards. Two British shipyards in Shanghai employed 2,500 workers in 1920 (*HCN* survey, May 1920), and in 1924 the docks of Butterfield & Swire at Hong Kong employed 4,000 workers (Henry report [10]).

79. Kung Chün [204], pp. 218ff.

80. Two thousand workers were employed at the Tangshan cement works (Yeh Kung-cho, *Industrial Tour* [82], p. 77), and 350 at the Canton cement works (Clements, "The Cement Industry in China," *CWR*, 20.v.22). According to the latter survey, these two cement works produced respectively 3,000 and 550 barrels of cement per day, whereas the total production of all the other works came to about 4,000 barrels a day, so that the number of workers employed in them must have been around 3,000.

81. *CYB*, 1921, pp. 768ff, lists them by name.

82. The power plant in the International Settlement of Shanghai had 2,312 employees in 1920 (*SMCR*, 1921, p. 20); the Mukden power plant, which was only one among several in the region controlled by the S.M.R., had 400 (*CEJ*, March 1928, "Industrial Works in Mukden").

83. *China: A Commercial and Industrial Handbook* [41], p. 420.

84. Tayler, "Hopei Pottery Industry," *CSPSR*, April 1930.

85. Cf. the list of 44 modern brickworks in *CYB*, 1921, p. 762, of which 21 were Japanese, 8 French or British, etc.

86. A Japanese brickwork at Newchwang employed 350 workers (Yeh Kung-cho [82], p. 79). Eight Japanese brickworks in Tsingtao each employed about 150 workers (*FER*, March 1921), and five in Mukden employed in all 1,000 in 1926 (*MDN*, 17.vi.26).

87. *CYB*, 1921, p. 763, lists 18 factories (10 of them Japanese).

88. *CYB*, 1921, p. 779, lists 36 Japanese and Western printing works.

89. According to figures given by the Nung-shang-pu, in 1921 the Commercial Press had a capital of two million yuan, and the China Bookshop a capital of one million yuan; other printing presses in Shanghai and the provinces had a capital investment not exceeding several tens of thousands of yuan (*FER*, Oct. 1921).

90. Around 1925, the Commercial Press had 5,000 employees (Malone, *New China* [45], Part II, p. 7), and in 1924 the state printing press in Peking had 1,700 (*Nien-chien* [138] I, 196). According to the list in Kotenev [156], pp. 306ff, one Japanese printing plant in Shanghai had 150 employees, and one British printing plant 360.

91. *CYB*, 1921, p. 788, lists 12 of the principal factories, 11 of which were British and one Japanese.

92. In 1925 the four Hankow factories employed 9,000 workers (*CEB*, 9.i.25).

93. *Nien-chien* [138] I, 196.

94. *CEB*, 22.xi.24.

95. See Carson, *The Kailan Mines* [235]; Collins, *Mineral Enterprise in China* [243].

96. *CYB*, 1923, pp. 115ff.

97. Figures are available for a seventh group of collieries (those belonging to the K.M.A.) for around 1920, but they are much less reliable. The figure of 50,000 employees given by Teng Chung-hsia at the time of the 1922 strike (*Chien-shih* [163], p. 79) approximately corresponds with the known output figure for the other six mines (100,000 tons per 1,100 workers); but that of 25,000 employees in 1920 given by *CEB*, 7.i.22, is much too low, since it corresponds to an output of 100,000 per 570 workers. In any case it is a much less reliable figure than that given by Teng Chung-hsia, who was actually present at the time; it perhaps represents the number of miners signed on directly by the K.M.A., omitting those recruited on the pao-kung system.

98. Torgasheff ("Mining Labor in China," *CEJ*, June 1930) estimates the number of miners in the iron mines of Anshan and Penhsihi in 1925 to have been 2,350, and at Tayeh 2,500. In 1919 output at Tayeh was 33 per cent higher than in 1925, whereas that of the two Fengtien mines was approximately the same (Hsüeh, "Iron and Steel Industry in China," *CEJ*, Jan. 1928).

99. Their output in 1919 (340,000 tons) was well below that of Anshan, Penhsihi, and Tayeh, which came to a total of one million tons (*ibid.*).

100. *Nien-chien* [138] I, 206.

101. Torgasheff (*CEJ*, June 1930) estimates the number of miners in the old-style metal ore mines at 120,000, and in the small coal mines at 650,000.

102. *Statistics of Government Railways* [36], Section XL: "Employees." The only figure given is that for 1922, but the 1919 figure was probably the same, since there was no extension of the railways in the interval.

103. The area was at that time occupied by the allied troops engaged in the "intervention" against the Soviet Union.

104. Teng Chung-hsia, who himself took part in organizing the unions in these workshops, considers the figures given in official statistics much too low. In an article written in 1924 ("Wo-men-ti li-liang" [Our Forces]) he gives a figure, based on his own personal knowledge, of 3,000 employees in the Changsintien workshop, and not 700 as given by the Chiao-t'ung-pu; similarly, he reports 2,000 at Tangshan and not 370, etc. (The article is republished in *Kung-jen yun-tung* [146], p. 4.)

105. The isolation of the miners, mentioned earlier, was thus partially diminished, and cooperation between the miners and the railwaymen grew during the big strike waves of 1922, 1925, and 1927.

106. *Report on the Chinese Post Office* [35].

107. See Table 3.

108. In the article "Wo-men-ti li-liang" (see note 104 above).

109. In 1920 it amounted to 104 million tons, 27 million of which were Chinese vessels (*CYB*, 1921, p. 1030). The figure for 1924 is 141 million tons (*CYB*, 1926, p. 822).

110. *Nien-chien* [138] I, 625–26.

111. *HCN*, May 1920.

112. According to *HT*, 4.vi.24, there were 40,000 dockers in Dairen in 1924, whereas *Nien-chien* [138] I, 625–26, gives 12,800 for 1925.

113. Interview with an old Shanghai docker, Chung Sheng-fu. See also *EE*, 24.ii.27 (a study of the different categories of street-porters in Southwest China).

114. *Nien-chien* [138] I, 614, gives the figure of 500,000 rickshaw men in Shanghai, which is obviously a misprint.

115. *CYB*, 1921, p. 788.

116. The Public Works Department of the Shanghai Municipal Council employed 526 craftsmen, 238 foremen, 3,456 unskilled laborers, and 159 scavengers in April 1919. April was the main month for signing on labor. (*SMCR*, 1919, p. 168.)

117. Lack of space prevents any thorough comparison here of the figures given in

Table 5 and those provided by the Nung-shang-pu or by the sources used in Table 3. The Nung-shang-pu figures seem fairly reliable, but their usefulness is reduced because of the exclusion of foreign enterprises and the inclusion of craft industries. The figures of Nishikawa Kiishi and Su Chao-cheng are on the whole reliable, but occasionally much too high (e.g. for metalworkers, electrical workers, and tobacco workers).

118. These percentages are very approximate, since they are almost all based on the lists (themselves incomplete) given by the *CYB*, in which no distinction as to size of factories is made. Only the percentages for cotton, silk, blast furnaces, cement, and mines have been established on the basis of output or of production potential.

119. On the development of Shanghai and the various industrial districts see Murphey, *Shanghai: Key to Modern China* [294], which includes a large Chinese and English bibliography. See also endpaper map.

120. *HCN,* May 1920.

121. In 1920 Wusih had 14 modern silk-reeling factories, 11 mechanized rice-husking factories, five modern flour mills, three cotton mills, two oil mills, a brewery, and an electric power plant, all employing a total of 30,000 workers (*CWR,* 17.vii.20 and 4.ix.20).

122. In 1921 Chinkiang had one flour mill, one match factory, one silk factory, five soap factories, two large oil mills, etc. (*CWR,* 4.vi.21).

123. In 1921 Nantung had eight factories (cotton mills, flour mills, oil mills), and the price of land rose from 100 yuan in 1910 to 1,000 taels in 1921 (*RT,* 1921, Shanghai, p. 43).

124. Teng Chung-hsia, *Kuang-chou kung-ch'ao* [153], pp. 55–56: 17,000 industrial workers, 25,000 handicraft workers, 13,000 dockers.

125. Teng Chung-hsia, *Chien-shih* [165], p. 38.

126. No contemporary figures are available—not even approximate ones—for the number of workers in Central China, Shantung, Chihli, and the Northeast. I have not attempted to supply any by applying to these regions estimates based on the already somewhat unreliable figures given above for each branch of industry. All that can be said is that the Northeast probably had the largest number, followed by Hupeh-Hunan, Chihli, and Shantung in that order.

127. A figure of over 10,000 workers has been given for the modern enterprises in Tangshan in 1926 (*CEJ,* Oct. 1927, "Tangshan, an Industrial Town").

128. See Young, "Chinese Labor Migration to Manchuria," *CEJ,* July 1927.

129. See *North Manchuria and the C.E.R.* [180], and *Report on Progress in Manchuria* [184].

130. Since I have been unable to consult local sources in Russian, it is difficult to know what happened to the numerous oil mills, flour mills, distilleries, etc. in Harbin and other centers in North Manchuria listed by the pre-1914 volumes of *CYB*. Probably some of them remained in the control of White Russians, while others came under Chinese ownership.

131. On the population of China in 1919, see p. 11 above.

132. *CYB,* 1921, p. 21.

Chapter III

1. In this and the following two chapters it has been necessary to overstep the limits set for the period studied here (1919–27) owing to gaps in the available documentation, and to make frequent use of data from a slightly later period. The composite picture that unavoidably results means that no study can be made of variations in labor conditions during the set period. It must be emphasized that in these three chapters all I have tried to do is to provide such data concerning the Chinese proletariat as are essential for understanding the history of the labor movement, and no attempt has been made to present a systematic study in industrial sociology.

2. Fong, *Tientsin Carpet Industry* [65], p. 44.

3. Lamson, in "The Effect of Industrialization upon Village Livelihood" (*CEJ*, Oct. 1931), quotes from an interview with an old peasant in a village near Shanghai, who said that only the old people were left, the young men and women having been recruited as workers in the mills.

4. Kyong Pae-tsong, *Industrial Women in Wusih* [70], p. 6.

5. *SCMP*, 13.i.22.   6. *Hu-nan lieh-shih-chuan* [223], p. 109.

7. Wales, *Red Dust* [50], p. 10.   8. Strong, *China's Millions* [304], p. 100.

9. *Ibid.*, p. 89.   10. Su Chao-cheng [222], p. 27.

11. *Ko-ming chan-shih-chi* [178], p. 43.

12. These examples are quoted simply to indicate the peasant origin of many workers; see Chapter XV below for a more detailed analysis of the social origins of trade union leaders.

13. Out of 985 *li-kung* employed by the Chunghsing mine interviewed in 1931, 197 had been small peasant proprietors, of whom 158 had owned less than ten *mou* (Lin Hsiu-chuan, *Labor Conditions* [73]).

14. *CWR*, 21.xi.25 ("Unfavorable Conditions in Northern Kiangsu").

15. In one Shanghai cotton mill, 579 of the 861 men employed (or 65 per cent) in 1925 came from the Kompo as did 798 of the 1,336 women employed (or 59 per cent) (*Nien-chien* [138] I, 360–62). Sixty per cent of the women employed in the silk-reeling factories also came from the Kompo (Kung Chün [204], p. 166).

16. The *Municipal Gazette* [39], 13.ii.34, comments that most of the Shanghai rickshaw men were peasants from the Kompo who could no longer make a living there.

17. *Nien-chien* [138] I, 365.

18. See Mallory, *China, Land of Famine* [287].

19. Interviews with the workers Liu Mo-kuang, Liu Ch'ing-chou, Li Tien-ch'ing, and Tso Chen-yun, who all became employees of the Yü-yuan cotton mill in Tientsin after they and their families were hit by the famine and came to the city.

20. Young, "Chinese Labor Migration to Manchuria," (*CEJ*, July 1927).

21. *Labor Conditions* [20], pp. 43ff, report of Consul Clenwell. The influx of peasants caused a crisis in Fuchow in 1925, when there were more rickshaw men than rickshaws (*CEB*, 2.v.25).

22. Lin Sung-ho, *Factory Workers in Tangku* [74], p. 53.

23. See Chapter V below.   24. Fong, *Cotton Industry* [252], p. 126.

25. *Municipal Gazette* [39], 13.ii.34.   26. *RT*, 1926, Changsha, p. 3.

27. *MDN*, 10.x.18.   28. *CEB*, 5.ii.27.

29. *CEB*, 12.vii.24.

30. Yeh Kung-cho, *An Industrial Tour* [82], p. 27.

31. Chu and Blaisdell, *Peking Rugs* [59], p. 21.

32. Tchou, *Report on Industrial and Social Survey* [80], p. 15.

33. See p. 105 below.

34. Lin Sung-ho [74], p. 61. The traveling expenses of Chiu-ta workers earning 115 to 140 yuan per month amounted to 6.6 per cent of their budget (8 yuan per year), and came third in the list of items after food and clothing (these were resident workers); the portion fell to 3.6 per cent (4.80 yuan per year) for those earning from 165 to 190 yuan per month.

35. Lou Yee-wen, *Les oeuvres sociales dans les chemins de fer chinois* [283], p. 88.

36. Teng Chung-hsia, *Chien-shih* [165], p. 168.

37. Lin Sung-ho [74], p. 21.   38. *NCH*, 1.vi.20.

39. *NCH*, 25.ii.22.   40. *Chien-shih* [165], p. 146.

41. Lou Yee-wen [283], p. 88.

42. Cf. Fei Hsiao-tung, *China's Gentry* [250], chap. 6.

43. Of the 32 old workers I interviewed in 1957, six were the sons of craftsmen. One

of the six was a Cantonese seaman, son of a Hong Kong joiner; one a Lunghai railway-man, son of a Honan satin-weaver; one a Kailan miner, son of a Tangshan craftsman; and the other three were Ching-Han railwaymen whose respective fathers were a car-penter, a tinsmith, and a shoemaker in Peking. Thus all except one were in transport work that required a high degree of skill, and their places of work were close to centers of traditional craft industries. But 17 of the workers interviewed were of peasant origin: six of the eight miners, five of the twelve factory workers, four of the nine railwaymen, one docker, and one seaman.

44. Lin Sung-ho [74], p. 18.　　　　　45. Henry report [10], Tsingtao.

46. *IS*, 1924, III, 494.　　　　　　　47. *CEB*, 7.viii.26.

48. The Kaiping mines, which formed the central core of the Sino-British K.M.A. collieries, were founded by a Cantonese merchant (Carlson [235], pp. 4–5).

49. Simine, *Le travail des femmes* [313], p. 83.

50. *MDN*, 10.xi.22.

51. *Chin-tai kung-yeh* [137] II, 1174 and 1176.

52. *CEM*, Nov. 1926, "Industrial Nantungchow."

53. Interview with the Ching-Han railwayman Lin Mao-hsiang, himself a native of Fukien. The list of names of the 55 workers killed in February 1923 contains 12 from Fuchow (*CTSTL*, 1955, No. 1).

54. Fong, *Cotton Industry* [252], p. 118.

55. Murphey, *Shanghai* [294], p. 20.

56. Of the 32 old workers interviewed in 1957, four belonged to this category: a worker in a Shanghai cotton mill, son of a scavenger employed by a school; a Tangshan miner, son of a Paoting peddler; a printer at the Commercial Press, son of a shophand; and a worker in a Tientsin cotton mill, son of a Tientsin coolie.

57. See Chapter VI below.

58. This question will be discussed in Chapter VI in connection with the part played by the guilds in the traditions of organization among the proletariat in 1919.

59. Tayler and Zung, "Labour and Industry in China," *ILR*, July 1923.

60. On the carpet and knitting factories in Tientsin, see Simine [313], pp. 74–85.

61. See *Nien-chien* [138] I, 582 (a table showing conditions of apprenticeship in 40 workshops in Tientsin).

62. Fong, *Rayon and Cotton Weaving* [64], p. 33.

63. *CEJ*, Feb. 1927, "Labor Conditions in Chekiang."

64. Interviews with the old workers Liu Ch'ing-chou and Tso Chen-yun, who worked in the Yü-yuan cotton mill in Tientsin.

65. Fong, *Cotton Industry* [252], p. 118. In 1926, the six cotton mills of Tientsin em-ployed 3,500 "apprentices," the total number of employees being 13,100 (*Nien-chien* [138] I, 570).

66. *Ibid.*, p. 118.

67. *CEJ*, Oct. 1927, "Tangshan: An Industrial Town."

68. In 1926, 500 of the 1,000 workers employed in one of the two match factories of the Chinese-owned Tan-hua company were "apprentices," as were 500 out of the 800 workers employed in the other factory (*Nien-chien* [138] I, 572).

69. Henry report [10], Hong Kong and Peking.

70. Interview with the worker Li Ch'üan-te, a carpenter on the Ching-Han line.

71. Simine [313], p. 54.　　　　　　72. *Chin-tai kung-yeh* [137] I, 1194.

73. *Nien-chien* [138] I, 570.　　　　　74. *Ibid.*, I, 583.

75. Interview with the worker Jen Ch'i-hsiang. Around 1920 the apprentices at the Commercial Press no longer signed a contract; they were paid (at a low rate), but given neither board nor lodging; they also no longer had to do services for their employer as in the old system, yet received proper training in technical skills.

76. Interview with Mrs. Fang Lan-ying, who in 1928 entered Factory No. 3 of the Naigai Wata Kaisha in Shanghai.

77. See the descriptions in Simine [313], pp. 16–18, and Lowe Chuan-hua [284], p. 19, which agree in the main with the foregoing testimony.

78. An example is provided by the following contract (trans. from Simine [313], p. 17): "The undersigned X., because of economic difficulties, wishes to hire out her daughter Y ... to the recruiting agent, who will take her with him to work in the cotton factory in Shanghai; the hiring payment will be thirty dollars for a period of three years; the money will be paid in three annual installments of ten dollars each. The girl when at work in the factory will owe obedience to the recruiting agent. In the case of her abscondence or death, the undersigned takes full responsibility; but if she should fall ill, the recruiting agent will be responsible for medical expenses. Throughout the contracted period, the girl will be clothed and fed by the recruiting agent. If any working time is lost for one reason or another, the girl will have to make it up."

The hardships undergone by the women and girl employees in the Shanghai cotton mills are often featured in the writings of the realist novelists of the "left-wing school" in the 1930's; cf. the short story by Hsia Yen, *Pao-shen-kung* ("Contract Labor"), trans. into English in *Chinese Literature,* 1960, No. 8.

79. *Tsu-chang* was the term employed in the Hanyehping mines (Fairbank and Banno [2], No. 7.11.18, quoting a Japanese worker on the *pao-kung* system in the mines of Central China). In North China the terms *pao-kung-t'ou, pao-t'ou-jen,* and *Pa-t'ou* were used (Torgasheff, "Mining Labor in China," *CEJ,* May 1930).

80. Torgasheff, *ibid.*

81. Lin Hsiu-chuan [73].

82. I.L.O. Archives C/1802/3 and C/1802/1 (reports on the K.M.A. mines) [11]. See also Lowe Chuan-hua [284], pp. 21–22, and Teng Chung-hsia, *Chien-shih* [165], pp. 80 and 111.

83. Ting, "Coal Industry in China," *NQ,* July 1937.

84. I.L.O. Archives C/1802/3 [11]. See also Teng Chung-hsia, *Chien-shih* [165], p. 80 (on the K.M.A. mines).

85. The terms *wai-kung* and *li-kung* were those most commonly used (*Nien-chien* [138], *passim*).

86. Torgasheff, "Mining Labor in China," *CEJ,* April 1930.

87. 55 per cent in the K.M.A. mines, 66 per cent in the Anshan mines, 80 per cent in the Tzechwan and Tsingsing mines (*ibid.*).

88. See Chapter IV below.

89. Teng Chung-hsia, *Chien-shih* [165], pp. 44–45; interview with the seaman Feng Jui.

90. I.L.O. Archives C/1803/1930 (report dated Nov. 1930 on the work of the dockers); interview with the Shanghai docker Chung Sheng-fu.

91. I.L.O. Archives, *ibid.* 92. *CEB,* 7.xi.25.

93. *SCMP,* 25.v.21. 94. *SMCR,* 1921, pp. 1B and 15B.

95. Interview with the worker Chou Kuo-ch'iang.

96. Interviews with the workers Chao Chin-ying and Chao Yin-ying, who worked at the B.A.T.

97. Interview with Lin Mao-hsiang, a Ching-Han railwayman.

98. E.g. in the British Jui-chi cotton mill in Shanghai (*Chin-tai kung-yeh* [137] II, 1236), and also in the big British shipping companies of Shanghai around 1930 (I.L.O. Archives C/1803/20). In Hong Kong around 1920 the *hsi-ma-sha* were often compradores attached to the shipping companies (*SCMP,* 25.i.22).

99. Fong, "Grain Trade and Milling in Tientsin," *CSPSR,* Oct. 1933.

100. *CEB,* 12.xii.25.

101. *CEM*, April 1926, "The Yunnan Tin Industry." See also Shih Kuo-heng, "Social Implications of the Tin-Mining Industry in Yunnan," *PA*, March 1947.

102. Ting, "The Coal Industry in China," *NQ*, April 1937.

103. *CEB*, 9.x.26. See also *CWR*, 30.iv.21.

104. On building workers in Changsha, see *CEB*, 12.xii.25; on workers in the tobacco craft industry in Kiangsi, see *PPW*, 15.x.27. Hsia Yen, in the story mentioned in note 78, p. 453, points out that the labor contractor usually recruited workers from his own district.

105. The manager of the British Ewo cotton mill (a subsidiary of Jardine, Matheson & Co.) told the Child Labor Commission in 1923 that workers used to be paid direct, but now the mill used as much contract labor as possible (Minutes of the meeting held 22.vi.23) [17].

106. This was the case in 1930 in big foreign-owned mines such as the K.M.A. and the Fushun colliery (Lowe Chuan-hua [284], p. 22).

107. The *cai* ("Corporal") system in the mines of North Vietnam and the rubber plantations of South Vietnam during the colonial period was almost identical with the *pao-kung* system (see Thompson, *Labor Problems in South-East Asia* [308], p. 201). In Japan, women employees in the silk factories were also recruited by agents who later deducted a regular amount from their wages (Saito [299], p. 46). Industrialized countries in the West had similar methods of recruitment in the nineteenth century, e.g. the *marchandeurs* in France.

108. Fong, *Cotton Industry* [252], p. 118.

109. Chen Ta, "Labor Unrest in China" (*MLR*, Aug. 1921), p. 22. The appearance of these advertisements in the Hunan newspapers started a violent press campaign of a regionalist character, protesting against these "maneuvers" to entice the Hunanese away from home.

110. *NCH*, 9.vii.21.   111. *MDN*, 27.iii.24.

112. *MDN*, 2.iii.25.

113. Ho, "Population Movement to the Northeastern Provinces of China," *CSPSR*, Oct. 1931.

114. See, for instance, Tayler and Zung (*ILR*, July 1923); Lamson, *Social Pathology in China* [269], p. 120; Lowe Chuan-hua [284], p. 115.

115. Fong, *Cotton Industry* [252], p. 118.

116. Fong, *Tientsin Carpet Industry* [65], p. 73.

117. *Chien-shih* [165], pp. 44–45.

118. In Hong Kong in 1921 this subscription was 1.50 yuan, or about 7 per cent of the wages (*SCMP*, 2.xii.21).

119. This commission was one month's wages in the French Tramway Co. (information given by the worker Chou Kuo-ch'iang), and a fortnight's wages at the B.A.T. factory at Pootung (according to the worker Chao Chin-ying). In Tientsin, the worker Liu Ch'ing-chou said he had paid a foreman four yuan in order to obtain employment.

120. Interview with the worker Chou Kuo-ch'iang.

121. *NCH*, 19.iv.24.

122. See below, pp. 73 and 94.

123. Wagner, *Labor Legislation in China* [311], p. 53.

124. Simine [313], pp. 48–49.

125. Information obtained from the workers Chou Kuo-ch'iang (for the French Tramway Co. in Shanghai) and Shen Pao-hua (for the railway workshops on the Ching-Han line).

126. Ting, "Coal Industry in China," *NQ*, July 1937.

127. It was the subject of acute conflict between the merchants and the trade unions of Canton during the winter of 1927 (see Chapter XIII below).

128. *Nien-chien* [138] I, 5 (figures taken from the Kiangsu Province Year Book for 1924).

129. Yang and Tao, *Standard of Living of Working Families in Shanghai* [81], p. 26.

Chapter IV

1. *CEB*, 1.vii.21; Malone, *New China* [45], Part II, pp. 5–6.

2. *Nien-chien* [138] I, 309–11.

3. For example, the Kuang-ta weaving mill in Shanghai in 1926 (*Nien-chien* [138] I, 307), or a Japanese silk-reeling factory in Tsingtao in 1924 (Henry report [10], Tsingtao).

4. For example, those of Shanghai (*Nien-chien* [138] I, 326), of Wuhu (*CEB*, 9.i.25), and of Tsangchow in Chihli (*CEJ*, Nov. 1927, "Three Towns in South Chihli").

5. For example, in a powdered-egg factory in northern Kiangsu in 1925, or the Tientsin oil mills (*Nien-chien* [138] I, 325).

6. *Ibid.*, p. 316.
7. *Ibid.*, p. 312.
8. *Ibid.*, pp. 321–22.
9. *Ibid.*, p. 315.

10. Bulletin of the Chinese Y.M.C.A. No. 62 (April 1923), quoted in Wieger, *La Chine moderne* [139], p. 435.

11. *Nien-chien* [138] I, 318.

12. *CEB*, 9.v.25 (slippers) and 24.i.25 (coal depots).

13. On the Shantung electric power plants, see *Nien-chien* I, 319.

14. *Ibid.* (on the Peking waterworks).

15. For example, a glassworks in Chinghwangtao (*Nien-chien* I, 315), or an electric bulb factory in Peking in 1925 (*ibid.*, p. 317).

16. *Ibid.*, p. 320.

17. *CEJ*, April 1930, "Manufacturing Industries in Northern Manchuria."

18. Paul Henry reports in his travel notes [10] that when he visited a Chinese flour mill the manager told him that the mill employees only worked an eight-hour day, but when Henry discovered that there were in fact two twelve-hour shifts, the manager finally confessed that the visit had been "prepared" according to telephoned instructions from the Ministry. (Peking document.)

19. Malone [45], Part II, p. 6.

20. Minutes of the Child Labor Commission [17], meeting of 6.vii.23.

21. *Nien-chien* [138] I, 308.
22. *Ibid.*, pp. 310–11.
23. *Ibid.*, pp. 314–15.
24. Chu and Blaisdell [59], p. 22.

25. Chen Ta, "Labor Unrest in China," *MLR*, Aug. 1921.

26. *Nien-chien* [138] I, 317–18.
27. *Ibid.*
28. *Ibid.*, pp. 312–13.

29. *MLR*, March 1924 (for Shanghai). In Hong Kong the "Taikoo" shipyards of Butterfield & Swire worked from 7 A.M. to 12 noon, and from 1 P.M. to 5 P.M. (Henry report [10], Hong Kong).

30. *Nien-chien* [138] I, 326.

31. Lin Sung-ho, *Factory Workers in Tangku* [74], p. 22.

32. For example, in Peking (*CEB*, 11.iv.23).

33. *CEJ*, July 1928, "Shanghai Silk Filatures."

34. Henry report [10], Shanghai.
35. *Labour Conditions* [20], p. 24.
36. Malone [45], Part II, p. 5.
37. *Labour Conditions* [20], p. 19.
38. See above, p. 72.
39. *CEB*, 12.vii.24.
40. See Eberhard, *Chinese Festivals* [245].
41. *Nien-chien* [138] I, 229.
42. Lin Sung-ho [74], p. 24.
43. Chu and Blaisdell [59], p. 22.
44. *Nien-chien* [138] I, 334.

45. Chen Ta, "Labor Unrest in China," *MLR*, Aug. 1921.

46. Henry report [10], Shanghai.

47. Chen Ta, *MLR*, Aug. 1921. Cf. a list of 23 enterprises giving a weekly day of rest in *Nien-chien* [138] I, 327.

48. *CEJ*, July 1928, "Shanghai Silk Filatures."

49. Most of them worked 330 to 340 days per year (*Nien-chien* I, 334). Cf. a list of 20 enterprises observing a day of rest every two months in *Nien-chien* I, 327–28.

50. Malone [45], Part II, p. 6.

51. See below, p. 94.   52. See for instance Chapter VIII below.

53. Kotenev, *Shanghai, Its Municipality and the Chinese* [156], pp. 306–10.

54. In 1924 the British Minister in Peking, on instructions from the Foreign Office, asked all the British consuls in China to supply him with information on child labor in foreign enterprises in China, especially the British ones. These consular reports [20] detail many examples of the unwillingness of employers to discuss this subject. The big British tobacco and cotton-baling firms in Hankow failed to reply to the request for information (p. 67), as did the B.A.T. in Mukden (p. 74).

55. See Chapter IX below.

56. Minutes of the Child Labor Commission [17], 16.x.23 (visit to three silk factories and a cotton mill).

57. Malone [45], Part II, p. 6.

58. *Chin-tai kung-yeh* [137] II, 1195.

59. *CEJ*, June 1927, "Women's Work in Kwangtung Province."

60. *CEB*, 29.iii.24. Only 13 per cent of the workers were adult men.

61. *CEJ*, Oct. 1928, "Industrial Works of Wuhan." The three cotton mills employed 5,700 women and 1,100 children out of a total of 7,647 employees.

62. See Simine [313], pp. 80–98. (These pages concern, among others, knitters in Shanghai, Tientsin, and Chekiang; embroiderers in Ningpo; lace makers in Shanghai; and embroiderers in Kwangtung and Chefoo.)

63. Kotenev [156], pp. 306–10. Of the 5,301 workers employed in the Chinese-owned factories, 3,664 were women, and of the 7,647 workers employed by foreign factories, 4,727 were women and 565 children.

64. Information obtained from Mrs. Chao Chin-ying.

65. *Nien-chien* [138] I, 560. The terms *wai-kung* and *li-kung* do not have quite the same meaning here as in the mines. Around 1927, the biggest match factory in Tientsin employed over 2,000 women and many children out of a total of 3,600 employees (*CWR*, 28.iv.28).

66. Kotenev [156], pp. 306–10.   67. *CEB*, 9.i.25.

68. *Nien-chien* [138] I, 549.

69. It would be interesting to know the differences between provinces in the percentage of women and children employed, because this would enable us to assess the part played by local customs and social habits in addition to purely economic factors; but the data are insufficient, and sometimes contradictory. According to the careful investigation of the cotton industry made by H. D. Fong in 1930 ([252], p. 148), the percentage of women and children employed in Shanghai was 78.6, in Wuhan 47, and in Tsingtao only 6.4, which shows considerable variation within this one industry. But these figures do not agree with those given by the Nung-shang-pu for 1920 (*Nien-chien* I, 549), which are supposed to cover all Chinese-owned enterprises (factories and workshops). The Nung-shang-pu lists 73 per cent women employees in Kiangsu and 34 per cent in Hupeh, both of which seem reasonable; but 35 per cent for Shantung seems too high, and 1.6 per cent for Chihli is quite incompatible with the large number of women and children known to have been employed in Tientsin and its surrounding districts.

70. *Nien-chien* [138] I, 565 (Tientsin cotton mills); Malone [45] Part II, p. 6 (Shanghai cotton mills).

71. Simine [313], *passim.*

72. *MLR*, Dec. 1920. On the lack of social welfare provided by employers and the failure of reforms, see Chapter IX below.

73. See Chapter IX below.

74. *Chin-tai kung-yeh* [137] II, 1208.

75. *LCT*, 22.i.17.

76. *Nien-chien* [138] I, 353–54.

77. *Ibid.*

78. *JWC*, 15.iii.19.

79. *CWR*, 30.x.20. See a detailed account of the Tangshan disaster in *LTC*, Nos. 11 and 12 (17.x.20 and 24.x.20).

80. *NCH*, 29.iii.24; *Chien-shih* [165], p. 122.

81. Ting, "Coal Industry in China," *NQ*, July 1937.

82. *Chien-shih* [165], p. 122.

83. See *Nien-chien* [138] III, 13–28, for the regulations of the Japanese mines at Pen-hsihi and Fushun, and of the Chinese mine at Pingting.

84. Lamson, "Industrial Accidents in China" (*CWR*, 1.ii.30 to 8.v.30).

85. *Chien-shih* [165], p. 122.

86. Decker, "Industrial Hospital, Shanghai," *CMMJ*, March 1924.

87. *NCH*, 19.xi.21.

88. *CWR*, 15.ii.30.

89. Hinder, *Social and Industrial Problems of Shanghai* [258], p. 15.

90. Minutes of the Child Labor Commission, meeting of 3.vi.23, deposition of Dr. Decker [17].

91. Lamson, "The Effect of Industrialization upon Village Livelihood," *CEJ*, Oct. 1931.

92. *CWR*, 30.x.20.

93. *FER*, Feb. 1920.

94. *Nien-chien* [138] III, 31.

95. *Ibid.*, p. 29.

96. See the texts of these regulations in *Nien-chien* III, 29.

97. See Maitland, "Phosphorus Poisoning in Match Factories in China," *CJSA*, Nos. 2 and 3, 1925.

98. Out of the 3,612 surgical cases treated in the hospital for these two factories between October 1924 (when the hospital was founded) and September 1925, 2,271 were cases of inflammation of the tissues (the total number of employees in the two factories being about 900). (Lin Sung-ho [74], p. 118.)

99. Out of the 999 workers in one of these factories examined at a missionary hospital in Peking, 922 (39.7 per cent of the total number employed) were suffering from trachoma (Yao Hsun-yuan, "Industrial Health in the Peiping Special Health Area," *CMMJ*, April 1929).

100. Gear, *Industrial Health in Shanghai*. Vol. I, *An Investigation of Printing* [67]. Out of 89 workers examined, 27 were found to be suffering from lead poisoning.

101. *Labour Conditions* [20], p. 30.

102. Simine [313], p. 23.

103. The bad ventilation struck all visitors. Cf. Malone [45] Part II, p. 6; Henry report [10], *passim.*

104. Decker, *CMMJ*, March 1924.

105. *CEB*, 5.xii.25.

106. Henry report [10], Chefoo.

107. Out of 999 medical cases examined in a Peking carpet factory in 1928, 291 were suffering from gastrointestinal complaints (*CMMJ*, April 1929). At the Chiu-ta salt refinery, out of the 4,080 medical cases treated in 1924–25, 1,021 were suffering from gastrointestinal complaints and 1,194 from "systemic and blood diseases"; in addition there were 683 cases of dermatitis (Lin Sung-ho [74], pp. 117 and 119).

108. At the Fushun mines in 1921, the management staff consisted of 653 Japanese and two Chinese, and the workers comprised 2,515 Japanese and 4,199 Chinese (Yeh Kung-cho [82], p. 23).

109. For example, a Japanese cotton mill in Yangtzepoo (*NCH*, 2.x.22), and a Chinese cotton mill in Shanghai (*NCH*, 19.vi.20).

110. *NCH, passim.*

111. On the nationality of the engineers on each line, see for instance *CYB*, 1921–22, pp. 441ff.

112. See the annual reports of the Chinese Post Office [35].

113. On the better hours of work for foreign employees in industrial enterprises see for instance *Nien-chien* [138] I, 306. The Chinese seamen, whose quarters were in the hold, were envious of the better pay and treatment given to foreign seamen and quartermasters for the same work (*Chien-shih* [165], p. 45). On the scornful attitude of management toward workers, information was obtained from the Ching-Han railwaymen Shen Pao-hua, Wang Ch'ün-jung, and Sun Mao-lin, who in 1957 could still quote from memory the French swearwords flung at them by the engineers; similar testimony was given by Chao Chin-ying and Chao Yin-ying, women workers at the B.A.T. Pootung factory.

114. For example, a Sikh night watchman at the docks was murdered by a worker whom he had prevented from sleeping there at night (*NCH*, 6.vi.21). Another example is a brawl in Harbin between some workers and six Sikh overseers of the Ice Storage Co., in which two of the Sikhs were killed (*LCT*, 1.i.17).

115. For example, the strike in a Japanese printing works in Shanghai in 1922 over the workers' insistence on the dismissal of a Sikh. Among other demands made was one for the workers' right to choose their foreign overseers (*NCH*, 21.x.22).

116. For example, the strikes of October 1921 (*CWR*, 22.x.21) and April 1925 (*SCMP*, 10.iv.25) on the British section of the Canton-Kowloon line, in protest against various decisions made by the British engineers; or the strike in 1915 in the Pingsiang mines in protest against a German engineer accused of encouraging brutality among the foremen (*Chien-shih* [165], p. 4).

117. See the large number of corporal punishments listed in *Chin-tai kung-yeh* [137] II, 1216–20.

118. Quoted by Wieger [139] IV, 446.	119. *NCH*, 19.iv.24.
120. *NCH*, 3.vii.26.	121. *CEB*, 2.x.26.
122. *SCMP*, 7.ii.27.	123. *MDN*, 28.viii.19.

124. This was the case, for instance, with the scale of fines used in the Kwangtung silk factories (see Chapter V below).

125. The introduction of a regulation of this kind caused a strike in a Shanghai cotton mill in March 1920 (*Municipal Gazette* [39], 17.iv.20, report of the Police Superintendent).

126. This prohibition caused a strike in a Shanghai cotton mill in February 1922 (*Chien-shih* [165], p. 35).

127. In June 1920 a case came up before the British Police Court in Shanghai in which a worker accused a Sikh overseer of striking him while searching his clothing; other workers and passersby had taken the side of the victim and seriously wounded the Sikh and two of his companions (*NCH*, 20.vi.20).

128. As in the French Tramways in Shanghai in 1926 (*NCH*, 31.xii.26) and the Fushun mines in 1927 (*MDN*, 16.iii.27).

129. As in cotton mills Nos. 3 and 4 of the Naigai Wata Kaisha in Shanghai (*NCH*, 3.vii.26) or the Société Franco-Chinoise de Construction Métallique in Shanghai (*CEB*, 21.viii.26).

130. As in several Japanese cotton mills in Shanghai (information supplied by the worker Wang Jui-an).

131. As in the B.A.T. (information supplied by the woman worker Chao Chin-ying).

132. *MDN*, 16.iii.27.

133. In a report presented by the management of the Ewo cotton mill to the British Con-

sul in Shanghai in 1925 it was stated that the average output of the Chinese cotton spinners, working 11¾ hours per day, was only 25 per cent of the average output of Lancashire spinners, working an eight-hour day, owing to a much lower degree of skill (*Labour Conditions* [21], p. 19).

134. *CEM,* Oct. 1926, "Wages in Tientsin Industries."

135. Lieu, *Silk Industry* [279], p. 69. The percentages he arrived at were the result of an investigation of 66 silk factories in 1930, and of 45 silk factories in 1931.

136. Lin Hsiu-chuan [73].

137. In the Fushun mines the free labor consisted of carpenters, mechanics, and pit workers, whereas the 30,000 or 40,000 workers recruited by the *pao-kung* were unskilled workers (Ch'en Ta, *Lao-tung wen-t'i* [190], pp. 65–68).

138. T'ang Hai (*Lao-tung wen-t'i* [164], pp. 271–72) distinguishes eleven causes of the low degree of skill of Chinese workers: the low level of wages, the lack of interest in work done merely to earn the bare means of livelihood, bad working conditions, too long hours, hostility toward employers, the fact that demands were never met, the bad health and undernourishment of workers, poor quality of raw materials, the bad layout of factories, the difficult climatic conditions in China, and lack of technical training.

139. Wou Monpeng, *L'évolution des corporations* [317], p. 69.

140. *Nien-chien* [138] I, 387.

141. *Chin-tai kung-yeh* [137] II, 1184–92.

142. Kotenev, *Shanghai, Its Municipality and the Chinese* [156], pp. 306–10.

143. In Shanghai, according to the 1923 list, there were only 14 foreign enterprises employing less than 100 workers.

144. See above, p. 43. 145. See above, p. 44.

146. *CYB,* 1928, p. 969.

147. Strong, *China's Millions* [304], pp. 92–93.

148. The worker Chou Kuo-ch'iang (interviewed in Shanghai in 1957), before joining the French Tramway Co. in 1925, had been successively a seaman on the Whangpoo, a shop hand in Shanghai, a B.A.T. worker in Pootung, and a worker in a hosiery factory in Shanghai. The worker Ts'ao Chih-fang, after serving as an apprentice in a small machine shop in Shanghai, had worked in the Ewo cotton mill, then in the British camps at Bassorah, then in the Kiangnan shipyards, then in a French machine shop in the Nanshih district, and then in the electric power plant of the International Settlement in Yangtzepoo.

149. Teng Chung-hsia, for instance, directed the railwaymen's club in Changsintien in May 1921, then the K.M.A. miners' strike in October 1922, then the Shanghai cotton mills strike in February 1925, and later the Canton–Hong Kong strike in June 1925 (*Chien-shih* [165], *passim*).

150. *Nien-chien* [138] I, 370. This investigation does not mention the average number of workers employed in the mill during this period.

151. *Nien-chien* I, 367. 152. *Ibid.,* p. 371.

153. Henry report [10], Part II, p. 3. 154. Chu and Blaisdell [59], p. 19.

155. Ting, "Coal Industry in China," *NQ,* April 1937.

156. Henry report [10], Part II, p. 3.

Chapter V

1. On the beginnings of a labor market in China at the end of the Ming and the beginning of the Ch'ing dynasties (17th to 18th century), and the appearance of a wage-earning class, see *Chin-tai shou-kung-yeh* [136], especially Vol. I, Part I.

2. Piece rates were paid in the Tientsin B.A.T. factory (*CEM,* Oct. 1926, "Wages in

Tientsin Industries"), in the match factories in Shanghai (*MLR,* Aug. 1921), and in Hangchow (*CEB,* 17.iv.26).

3. According to the survey conducted by T. Y. Tsha (*NQ,* Oct. 1926, "Wage Rates in Shanghai"), 80 per cent of the 60,406 cases investigated in the cotton mills, 78 per cent (out of 7,895 cases) in the hosiery workshops, and 71.5 per cent (out of 7,562 cases) in the silk-weaving industry, were paid at piece rates.

4. In 1925, 87.2 per cent of workers in mechanical workshops were paid time rates, 100 per cent in the shipyards, oil mills, and flour mills, and 56 per cent in the printing works (Tsha, *ibid.*).

5. Lieu, *Silk Industry* [279], pp. 69ff.

6. Ch'en Ta, *Lao-tung wen-t'i* [190], pp. 65–68.

7. These brief remarks on the subject of piece-rate and time-rate wages merely show the need for a more systematic study of the question based on the archives of business firms and on information supplied by the Chinese newspapers subsidized by employers. Account would have to be taken of customs inherited from the guilds (in which both types of payment were used) and of policies adopted by managements for increasing productivity, as well as of the mere factor of skill. It would also be necessary to ascertain whether the tendency to change from time rates to piece rates, as reflected in some of the strikes that were held, was general in the large new industrial enterprises. Simine ([313], pp. 21–22) reports, for instance, that around 1930 the older Chinese-owned cotton mills in Shanghai still paid time rates, whereas the more recently established ones paid piece rates.

8. Lieu [279], pp. 84–85.

9. *Nien-chien* [138] I, 318.

10. They amounted to as much as half the sum of wages in the K.M.A. mines (*Chien-shih* [165], p. 80). According to Ting (*NQ,* July 1937), a contractor in these mines received 237.60 yuan from the company for each 2,400 tons extracted, but paid out only 151.7 yuan in wages, despite the fact that all the material equipment was supplied by the K.M.A. Similarly, it is reported in *CEB,* 1.v.26, that hotel porters in Kiukiang at this time received 12 copper cash for each piece of luggage, although the customers paid the hotel 50 cash per piece; the remainder was shared with the labor contractor.

11. According to a survey carried out by the I.L.O. in 1932 (Archives C/1803/20 [11]), the Shanghai dockers received no more than 40 per cent and sometimes as little as 20 per cent of the wages paid out by the shipping firms.

12. In Hong Kong, for instance, the pao-t'ou, who were often synonymous with the compradores in the big foreign firms, charged an interest of 10 per cent on advances on wages; they then deducted this from wage payments (*SCMP,* 25.i.22).

13. Liu Shao-ch'i, in his memoirs as a militant trade unionist in the Anyuan and Ping-siang mines ([160], p. 2), reports that the company paid 27 silver cents (*ta-yang* or "big money") per miner, but that the middlemen gave the miners only 27 cents in copper, which came to about half as much since at that time and in that area the silver yuan was worth about 210 copper cents.

14. See Ting, "Coal Industry in China," *NQ,* July 1937. Teng Chung-hsia, who was in the K.M.A. mines in 1922 when the big October strike took place, gives other examples of the way the contractors manipulated the exchange rates between silver and copper currency for their own advantage (*Chien-shih* [165], p. 80).

15. See for example an I.L.O. report on the K.M.A. mines made in 1935 (Archives C/1802/3 [11]).

16. Teng Chung-hsia (*Chien-shih* [165], p. 110) gives a vivid description of fraudulent practices indulged in by the contractors in the Pingsiang mines: *ch'ih-tien* ("eat the morsel") consisted in declaring a larger number of miners than those actually employed; *mai-k'ung* ("buying emptiness") was the term for fraud practiced regarding the amount

of coal extracted and supplied; and *tso-lung* ("making holes") designated a fraudulent declaration of the amount of equipment and labor required for digging out galleries. Other types of fraud concerned the quality of the coal extracted. Sometimes foremen bribed the company chemists to accept coal containing more than the allowed amount of waste, an operation described by the workers as *mai-hui* ("buying cinders"). It was always the miners, if only indirectly, who bore the brunt of these practices, which increased the profits of the contractors and the foremen without adding anything to the wage rates of the miners.

17. On the Tientsin-Pukow line, for example, there was a ruling that the pao-t'ou should pay 60 per cent of the compensation payments for workers under their control ([32], p. 3).

18. Lieu, *Silk Industry* [279], pp. 69ff.   19. *Municipal Gazette* [39], 13.ii.34.

20. *FER*, Feb. 1920.

21. Ch'en Ta, *Lao-tung wen-t'i* [190], pp. 65–68.

22. Lieu [279], pp. 69ff.   23. *CEB*, 23.i.26.

24. *CEJ*, Nov. 1927, "Three Towns in South Chihli."

25. *CEJ*, July 1928, "Match Factories in China."

26. *CEB*, 13.vi.25.

27. *TIB*, No. 7, 27.iii.22, "Cement Industry in China."

28. *CEB*, 12.vii.24.   29. Lieu [279], p. 84.

30. *Nien-chien* [138] II, 159.   31. Lin Sung-ho [74], p. 33.

32. Lieu [279], p. 84.

33. This was the practice in the Yung-hua match factory in Shantung (*CEJ*, Nov. 1927, "Three Towns in Chihli"), and in the Chiu-ta salt refinery (Lin Sung-ho [74], pp. 26 and 32), where a third stage was reached with the issue of meal tickets with which food could be bought at the canteen; the value of the tickets was deducted from wages.

34. *CEB*, 14.ii.25.

35. *Nien-chien* [138] I, 223.

36. Lin Sung-ho [74], p. 26. The frequent references to this monograph are simply due to its reliability; there is no reason to suppose that the Chiu-ta factory was in any way exceptional.

37. Interview with the worker Jen Ch'i-hsiang. See also Wou Monpeng [317], p. 118.

38. *CEJ*, April 1928, "Manufacturing Industries in Northern Manchuria."

39. *Labour Conditions* [20], p. 34 (report of J. W. Nipps, industrial secretary of the Y.M.C.A. in Chefoo).

40. Lin Sung-ho [74], p. 28.

41. *CEJ*, Feb. 1927, "Labor Conditions in Chekiang." For other scales of efficiency bonuses, see *Nien-chien* [138] I, 223–24.

42. *NCH*, 18.ix.20.

43. For example, one Japanese cotton mill in Shanghai gave a bonus of one yuan for every 15 yuan earned by workers who had reached a daily output of thread worth at least 7 yuan above the norm, a bonus of 0.60 yuan for an output of 4 yuan above the norm, etc. (*Nien-chien* [138] I, 225).

44. *CEM*, Oct. 1926, "Wages in Tientsin Industries."

45. Simine [313], pp. 62 and 86.

46. In 1924 the Commercial Press gave workers earning less than 15 yuan a month a monthly bonus of 2, 3, and 5 yuan as the price of one *tou* (bushel) of rice rose to 9, 11, and 14 yuan; the higher the wage rate, the lower the bonus, until at a certain level no bonus at all was given (Wou Monpeng [317], p. 27).

47. Chen Ta, "Labor Unrest in China," *MLR*, Aug. 1921.

48. Lin Sung-ho [74], p. 29.

49. In *FER*, Nov. 1919, an account is given, supplied by a man formerly employed with the Shanghai Municipal Police, concerning a worker who was trying to support a family

of six on a monthly wage of 25 yuan. Every night the worker would steal a basket of coal worth about 50 cents, but one night he was killed by a policeman who surprised him in the act. The narrator of the incident concluded his story with a firm declaration that foreigners were gravely mistaken if they thought that the Chinese were dishonest by nature.

50. Fong, *Industrial Organisation* [253], p. 57.

51. *Chien-shih* [165], p. 44. 52. Fong [253], p. 57.

53. Interview with the worker Shen Pao-hua.

54. It was the introduction of a rule of this kind that caused a strike by all the workers in the "Shanghai No. 2" Chinese-owned cotton mill in February 1922 (*Chien-shih* [165], p. 35).

55. *CEB*, 18.iv.25.

56. The case of a woman employee who was fined 20 per cent of her daily wage for this offense is described in *NCH*, 29.v.20.

57. In the Kwangtung silk-reeling factories, breaking the thread cost 5 cents silver, and spinning a thread that was too thick or too thin brought a fine of anything from a half-day's pay to ten days' pay, according to the gravity of the offense (Howard and Buswell [68], p. 130).

58. This resulted in a 20-cent fine in the Tientsin tramways (*CEM*, Oct. 1926, "Wages in Tientsin Industries").

59. *NCH*, 29.iv.22.

60. Wou Monpeng [317], p. 20.

61. *CEM*, Oct. 1926, "Wages in Tientsin Industries."

62. Quoted by Wieger [139] IV, 446. 63. See above, p. 73.

64. Interviews with the worker Wang Jui-an and the railwayman Shen Pao-hua.

65. Interviews with the worker Wang Jui-an and the woman employee Fan Lan-ying, both of whom were employed during this period in the Shanghai cotton mills. See also Lieu, *The Growth and Industrialisation of Shanghai* [280], pp. 169–70, for articles from the Chinese press describing how young women workers were drafted into brothels.

66. See Lowe Chuan-hua, *Facing Labor Issues* [284], p. 28.

67. Information on these two ways of reckoning wages obtained from interviews with the worker Wang Jui-an. See also Gamble and Burgess [66], pp. 215–16.

68. Thomas Tchou, an expert employed by the Chinese Y.M.C.A., in his report on an industrial and social survey ([80], p. 19), estimated that the average wage of unskilled workers in the silk factories was 8.50 yuan per month for men and 7.50 yuan for women, and that the equivalent wage rates in the cotton mills were 9 yuan for men and 7.50 for women, as contrasted with the 14-yuan wage rate for workers in the mines, and the 15-yuan wage rate for metalworkers. Owing to the regional differences in wage rates already mentioned, these figures may not be of much value, but they would seem to confirm the conclusions drawn above.

69. *NB*, 24.v.27. 70. Lieu [279], p. 86.

71. *CEJ*, Nov. 1927, "Three Towns in Chihli."

72. *MDN*, 15.iii.21. 73. *TIB*, No. 61 (18.ix.22).

74. Survey conducted by *Shih-shih hsin-pao* [130], quoted in *Nien-chien* [138] I, 532.

75. Fang Fu-an, "Shanghai Labor," *CEJ*, Sept. 1930.

76. Fang Fu-an, "Shanghai Labor," *CEJ*, Aug. 1930.

77. Yang and Tao [81], pp. 46 and 76. 78. *CWR*, 30.ix.22.

79. Lin Sung-ho [74], p. 86. 80. Tchou, *Report* [80].

81. *FER*, Nov. 1919. 82. Chu and Blaisdell [59], p. 21.

83. Lin Sung-ho [74], p. 62. 84. Yang and Tao [81], pp. 48–50.

85. Lee Wei-yung and others, *Industrial Health in Shanghai* [71], III.

86. Frequently mentioned in *Minutes* [17] and in L'Estrange Malone [45].

87. There was a canteen at the Chiu-ta salt refinery (Lin Sung-ho [74], p. 32).

88. The apprentices in the Tientsin match factories, for example, did this (Simine [313], p. 62).

89. Kelsey, "China's Industrial Workers," *NCH*, 17.iii.23 to 14.iv.23.

90. *Ibid.*

91. *FER*, Nov. 1919, "The Cost of Living to Chinese in Shanghai."

92. See the survey conducted by T. Tchou in Shanghai in 1926 on behalf of the Y.M.C.A. [79] (English text). Lengthy excerpts from the original Chinese text are printed in *Nien-chien* [138] I, 392ff.

93. Eddy, *The New World of Labor* [61], p. 23.

94. Fang Fu-an, "Shanghai Labor," *CEJ*, Aug. 1930.

95. Yang and Tao [81], p. 60. 96. Lin Sung-ho [74], p. 81.

97. Yang and Tao, p. 61. 98. Tchou [79], *passim.*

99. Kelsey, *NCH*.

100. Lamson, "The Problem of Housing for Workers in China," *CEJ*, Aug. 1932.

101. Kyong Pae-tsung [70], p. 10.

102. Torgasheff, "Mining Labor in China," *CEJ*, Aug. 1930.

103. *Ibid.* 104. *MDN*, 9.x.24.

105. Henry report [10], Tsingtao. 106. *FER*, Oct. 1922.

107. Lamson, *CEJ*, Aug. 1932. 108. Henry report, Hong Kong.

109. Lamson, *CEJ*, Aug. 1932.

110. Only a thorough examination of the archives of firms that provided workers' housing would enable a study to be made of how, and also why, this policy was gradually adopted by many firms, especially the larger enterprises. The motives were undoubtedly political as much as economic. The available data are neither sufficient in quantity nor uniform enough to make such a study feasible.

111. Henry report [10], *passim.*

112. Chu and Blaisdell [59], pp. 20 and 31.

113. *CEM*, June 1926, "Economic Study of Peking Rickshaw-Pullers."

114. On these dwellings see Tchou, *Housing* [79]; Lamson, *Social Pathology* [269], p. 165; Kelsey, *NCH*; "Squatters' Huts in Shanghai" [14].

115. "Squatters' Huts" [14]. 116. Tchou [79].

117. Lamson, *CEJ*, Aug. 1932.

118. See *SMCR*, annual report of the Fire Department; fires were particularly frequent in the districts occupied by these huts.

119. On speculation in land in Shanghai around 1925, see *CWR*, 4.xii.26 (special number on Greater Shanghai).

120. Chung and Baywell [60], p. 10.

121. *CEB*, 9.x.26.

122. Ling and Johnson, "A Study of Women and Girls in Tientsin Industries," *CEJ*, June 1928.

123. Kelsey, *NCH*.

124. Figures given by a survey of Shanghai workers made in 1925 and quoted in "1919 nien chih 1927 nien Chung-kuo kung-jen yun-tung kai-kuang" (General survey of the Chinese labor movement from 1919 to 1927), *CTSTL*, 1954, No. 4.

125. Lieu, "China's Industrial Development," *CEJ*, July 1927.

126. Ling and Johnson, *CEJ*, June 1928.

127. *CEJ*, April 1928, "Manufacturing Industries in Northern Manchuria."

128. On Chinese folk traditions, see for instance H. Doré, *Recherches sur les supersti-tions* [244].

129. The decrease in the number of workers employed and in the number of arrivals and departures in the Northeast during peak periods in agricultural work is another indi-

cation of the close links maintained between industrial workers and their home villages (see Chapter III above).

130. Kelsey, *NCH.* See also the photograph of a family altar in a worker's home in Lin Sung-ho [74], facing p. 69.

131. Lin Sung-ho [74], p. 34. See also the photograph facing p. 33 of workers dressed up as traditional characters in Chinese opera.

132. The data on this point provided by various surveys of the 1930's are brought together in Lamson [269], pp. 63–64.

133. Lin Sung-ho [74], p. 34.

134. See for instance the excellent monograph by Gamble and Burgess, *Peking: A Social Survey* [66], chap. 8.

135. *Nien-chien* [138] I, 385.
136. Yang and Tao [81], p. 73.
137. Lin Sung-ho [74], p. 74.
138. See above, p. 18.

139. On changes in the extended family during this period, see Lamson [269], chap. 17, and Levy, *The Family Revolution* [275].

140. Lamson, *CEJ*, Oct. 1931.

141. On unmarried workers in Kwangtung, see Howard and Buswell [68], p. 139. See also Simine [313], p. 51.

142. Lang, *Chinese Family and Society* [270], p. 203.

143. *Ibid.*, p. 206.

144. Lin Sung-ho [74], p. 49 (figures from the factory archives).

145. *Ibid.*, pp. 19–20.

146. Interview with Wang Jui-an, who worked in the Shanghai cotton mills.

Chapter VI

1. *Report on British Trade with China* (1919) [19], p. 50. On the actual relations between China and the I.L.O. at this time, see Chapter VII below.

2. There is no detailed study of the Chinese guilds of former times or of their development in modern times, but only brief accounts or else a chapter in books on broader subjects. Cf. Ma Ch'ao-chün, *Lao-tung yun-tung* [209], chap. 2, pp. 63–85; Ch'üan Han-sheng, *Hang-hui chih-tu shih* [195]; Ch'en Ta, *Lao-tung wen-t'i* [190], pp. 84–96; Burgess, *The Guilds of Peking* [58]; Gamble, *Peking: A Social Survey* [66], chap. 7; Morse, *The Guilds of China* [292]. See also *Nien-chien* [138] II, chap. 1.

3. See Gamble [66], p. 436.

4. See Ma Ch'ao-chün [209], pp. 66–67.

5. See, for example, the rules of the Barbers' Guild, quoted by Gamble [66], pp. 188–89.

6. See Gamble [66], pp. 195–96.

7. In 1918 the annual expenditure of the Boot Guild of Peking amounted to nearly 230,000 cash (approximately 170 yuan), devoted almost exclusively to the maintenance of the guild temple and to the annual ceremony held there (Gamble [66], pp. 439–40).

8. The Barbers' Guild of Peking, for instance, was completely reorganized in 1914, after the fall of the Empire and the abolition of the compulsory wearing of the pigtail. The new rules are quoted in Gamble [66], pp. 433–38.

9. See *Nien-chien* [138] II, 10–20, for the rules of the guilds of masons, carpenters, manufacturers of bamboo articles, stonecarvers, goldsmiths, coppersmiths, tinsmiths, hatters, tailors, and dyers.

10. Chen Ta, "Labor Unrest in China," *MLR*, Aug. 1921.

11. Burgess [58], p. 119.

12. See *Labour Conditions* [20], p. 26 (report of Consul General Jamieson).

13. Among the craft associations legally registered in Hong Kong in 1917, there were seven separate guilds of tinsmiths and six guilds of masons (*Government Gazette* [24], 27.iv.17).

14. *IS,* 1924, III, 494.

15. Henry report [10], Peking.

16. *Nien-chien* [138] I, 611.

17. *Chin-tai kung-yeh* [137] II, 1266ff.

18. *Ibid.*

19. *CEB,* 26.vi.24. The Shanghai guild to which incense manufacturers from other parts of the country belonged declared a strike at this time that was not supported by the local manufacturers' guild.

20. Gamble [66], p. 178.

21. *Nien-chien* [138] I, 609.

22. On the regional friendly societies or "guilds," see *Chien-shih* [165], pp. 2–3, and Ch'en Ta, *Lao-tung wen-t'i* [190], p. 93. Some confusion has been caused by applying the term "guild" to these societies as well as to the trade corporations.

23. Thus Liao Chung-k'ai, who was a native of Hweichow in Kwangtung province and one of the leading figures in the friendly society for natives of that town residing in Canton, was able to put the premises of the Hui-chou hui-kuan at the disposal of the All-China General Union when it was formed in Canton in May 1925 (see Chapter X below).

24. Some writers fail to distinguish between the hui-kuan and the pang-hui, probably because in both the basis of recruitment was the local origin of members. Sometimes, of course, contacts were established between the two types of associations, either because a coolies' pang might ask for help from the wealthy merchants of the hui-kuan, or because the latter might seek to extend their influence among the pang-hui. But it seems clear that a definite distinction must be made between the two types of organization, as is done by Teng Chung-hsia (*Chien-shih* [165], pp. 2–3).

25. For example, the coolies in the Japanese sphere of influence in the Northeast formed pang for natives of Shantung, Fukien, the "North," and the "South" (*Nien-chien* [138] II, 2).

26. Maybon and Fredet, *Histoire de la concession française de Changhai* [289], pp. 63–64.

27. On this strike in 1884, see below, p. 132.

28. On these two secret societies, see Ma Ch'ao-chün [209], pp. 74–77.

29. Gangs were active in the miners' strike in Kiangsi in 1915, and that of the Shanghai carpenters in 1918 (see below, p. 127).

30. See *Chien-shih* [165], pp. 3–4.

31. The workers in the Yangtzepoo cotton mills, for instance, frequently were pressured to donate "gifts" to these gangs (see p. 93 above). See also Isaacs, *The Tragedy of the Chinese Revolution* [263], p. 142.

32. See Burgess [58], chap. 13.

33. *Nien-chien* [138] I, 608–11. Around 1919 the dyers formed an employees' association (*t'ung-i-hui,* a "common" society) which was quite separate from the traditional guild, although it continued to worship the same ancestral master, Ko.

34. *Nien-chien* I, 612. Independent workers' associations were formed in all three of these trades in 1917.

35. A list of Chinese guilds exempted from the formalities of registration, published in 1917 by the Hong Kong government (*Government Gazette* [24], 27.iv.17), consists of 31 guilds for employers only (in trades such as silk, sandalwood, copper, and wicker furniture), 35 skilled craftsmen's guilds (tinsmiths, masons, sandalwood workers, etc.), and only five guilds with mixed membership.

36. Burgess [58], chap. 13.

37. Burgess, *ibid.,* lists 40 that were still active in Peking when he made his survey in 1927, some of which (for silk-weavers, tailors, manufacturers of decorative papers, etc.) had a membership of several thousand.

38. A list published in 1922 by the Economic Information Bureau in Peking includes mixed guilds of barbers, tailors, manufacturers of silk crepe, etc. (*CEB,* 11.iii.22).

39. This was true, at least, in the big urban centers, where all the main trades already had their guilds before the appearance of modern factories; but it was not so in villages such as Changsintien, where there was no local guild to which skilled workers employed in the big Ching-Han depot there could belong. (Interview with the worker Wang Ch'un-jung.)

40. *CEJ*, Feb. 1927, "Labor Conditions in Chekiang."

41. As already mentioned, the carpenters employed in the British shipyards belonged to the various provincial carpenters' guilds in the town (*Chin-tai kung-yeh* [137] II, 1266 and 1269), as did those employed in the Chinese-owned Kiangnan shipyard (*PDR*, 17.ix.20).

42. *Wu-ssu yun-tung* [144], pp. 466ff. This guild declared the strike of the mechanics employed in modern enterprises in June 1919. See also *HCN*, 1.v.20, where it is reported that according to the survey carried out by this newspaper in 1920, the Metalworkers' Guild of Shanghai then had a membership of 40,000, including both craftsmen and industrial workers.

43. In 1878 the Shanghai Cantonese Carpenters' Guild fought a lengthy court case against three Cantonese carpenters employed by an American firm in Hongkew because they refused to pay the guild the percentage of their wages laid down by the guild rules (*Chin-tai kung-yeh* [137] I, 1246–47). In 1880, six Ningpo carpenters employed in a British shipyard in Shanghai were involved in an affray with their foreman because he had taken on workers who were not members of their guild (*ibid.*, I, 1247–48).

44. On the origins of the Canton Mechanics' Union, see Lowe Chuan-hua [284], pp. 56ff (based on documents supplied by the union). See also Ma Ch'ao-chün [209], pp. 81–82; I.L.O. Archives C/1802/3 [11]; *Chien-shih* [165], p. 10.

45. See *LSYC*, 1959, No. 2. See also Li Shih-yueh, *Hsin-hai ko-ming kung-jen yun-tung* [207].

46. *HWP*, 1.iii.20. Teng Chung-hsia [165], p. 9, accuses it of having "deceived the workers" by adopting slogans in favor of capitalism when it was founded in February 1919. It gave active support to the strikes in June 1919, and in 1920 sponsored the first May Day celebration in Shanghai (see Chapter VII below).

47. One of its founders was the electrical worker Li Heng-lin, who was a Christian and who, in the name of this association, helped to instigate the strikes of June 1919 (*Wu-ssu yun-tung* [144], p. 701). The *kung-chieh lien-ho-hui* in its official Chinese title literally means "federation of industrial circles." This ambiguous term includes employers, overseers, technicians, and skilled workers, and emphasizes the atmosphere of class collaboration which characterized these associations.

48. This association also supported the strikes in June 1919 (*Wu-ssu yun-tung* [144], p. 568), and it was still included in the official list of Shanghai labor organizations drawn up in 1922 (*CEB*, 11.iii.22).

49. *HWP*, 19.i.20.

50. Interview with the worker Jen Ch'i-hsiang. Lowe Chuan-hua [284], p. 63, also gives 1917 as the year in which this association was founded. *SP*, 26.ii.19, mentions that the Commercial Press also had a "Commercial Press Association for Industrial Advance," which was said to have been founded in 1911 and to have had a membership of over 1,000 at the beginning of 1919. According to *MKJP*, 24.vii.24, an "Association for the Advance of Young Industrial Workers" was founded during the same period. Probably both refer to the same association. The expression "industrial advance" (*kung-chieh li-chih*) indicates that it was not a militant organization.

51. *NCH*, 15.iii.19. A mixed association for the rickshaw trade also existed at this time in Hangchow (*CEJ*, Feb. 1927, "Labor Conditions in Chekiang").

52. Ma Ch'ao-chün [209], p. 81.

53. *LSYC*, 1959, No. 2.

54. *CEB*, 5.xii.25. This association was called a *kung-hui,* but the character used for *kung* was the character meaning "public," whereas the term *kung-hui* that was subsequently adopted for "trade union" was written with the character *kung* meaning "work," which has exactly the same pronunciation.

55. Ma Ch'ao-chün [209], p. 84.

56. Chen Ta, *MLR*, Aug. 1921. The break-away Cantonese group very soon became involved in political action (see below, pp. 135–36).

57. *LSYC*, 1959, No. 2.   58. *SP*, 11.iv.12.

59. Lin Sung-ho [74], p. 42.

60. See Lowe Chuan-hua [284], pp. 51ff. (This writer consulted the original documents belonging to the Seamen's Union in 1930.)

61. *LSYC*, 1959, No. 2.

62. See Lei Chia, *Chu Pao-t'ing* [205], p. 18.

63. Ma Ch'ao-chün [209], p. 84.

64. Interview with the worker Wang Jui-an.

65. *Shang-hai ch'an-yeh* [194], p. 133.

66. Interview with the railwayman Lin Mao-hsiang.

67. Liu Shao-ch'i, *An-yuan chü-lo-pu* [160], p. 4.

68. Interviews with the women workers Chao Chin-ying and Chao Yin-ying.

69. *CEB*, 20.ii.20.   70. *Chien-shih* [165], p. 4.

71. *Ko-ming chan-shih-chi* [178], p. 8.

72. *Ibid.*, p. 31. Also from information obtained from an interview with the railwayman Li Ch'en-kang.

73. Li Shih-yueh [207], p. 10.

74. On the political repression at the end of the Ch'ing, see for instance Li Chien-nung [277], *passim.*

75. *CYB*, 1916, p. 312.

76. *1919–27 kung-jen yun-tung* [208], p. 13, has a rule that, in the case of workers in the same firm going on strike, the maximum sentence for the strike leader is fourth degree imprisonment or a fine of 300 yuan, and for the rest, a fine of 30 yuan or the equivalent term of imprisonment.

77. For excerpts from this law see Lowe Chuan-hua [284], p. 83, and for a summary of it, see *Min-kuo fa-ling ta-ch'üan* [149], p. 485.

78. See *LSYC*, 1959, No. 2. The friendly society for women silk workers, for instance, was dissolved in September 1912 (*SHSP*, 22.ix.12).

79. See below, p. 129.

80. *Min-kuo fa-ling ta-ch'üan* [149], p. 1197, gives a summary of the text. Excerpts are given by Lamb, *Origin and Development of Social Legislation* [268], p. 23.

81. *Chien-shih* [165], p. 10.

82. See *Treaties and Agreements* [135], p. 456: "With a view to preventing agitators from making their way into the province, the Chinese laborers coming from other provinces, as well as those recruited in Yunnan, must present themselves to the local authorities to be matriculated." Also *ibid.*, p. 913: ". . . in order to ensure peace and tranquillity and to prevent complications, the Syndicat du Yunnan Ltd. may, on giving notice to the local authorities, recruit near its mines native soldiers, who shall be placed under the command of an officer chosen for that purpose, [and] who shall reside with his men near the workings."

83. *Ibid.*, pp. 25 and 133.

84. See Chapter VIII below.

85. See the Feetham Report [38] I, 222–23.

86. *Municipal Gazette* [39], 17.iv.20, in which warning is given that all attempts at intimidation by any type of union or association will be severely punished.

87. *NCH*, 20.iv.17.

88. Twenty-five yuan a day was charged for a white mounted policeman, 16 yuan for a white policeman on foot, 8 yuan for a Japanese, 6 for a Sikh, and 3 for a Chinese policeman (*Municipal Gazette* [39], 25.x.17).

89. Feetham Report [38] I, 173. On the Mixed Court in general, see Kotenev, *Shanghai, Its Mixed Court and Council* [157].

90. The Mixed Court was, for instance, applying the laws of 1912 and 1914 when, in February 1925, it sentenced several newspapers with Nationalist tendencies to pay heavy fines for publishing communiqués of the strike committees in the Japanese cotton mills in Shanghai (see Kotenev, *Shanghai, Its Municipality* [156], p. 196).

91. For example, the CCP was founded in the French Concession of Shanghai in July 1921. The Labor Secretariat chose to have its headquarters in the territory of the International Settlement, and stayed there from the time it was formed until its premises in Chengtu Road were closed down by the Shanghai municipal police (see Chapter VIII below).

92. This happened to Li Ch'i-han in 1922, and Liu Hua in 1925 (see Chapters VIII and IX below).

93. See, for instance, the list in *Government Gazette* [24], 27.iv.17.

94. Several of the seamen's unions were banned for this reason at the end of 1922 (*Orders in Council* [25], 13.x.22).

95. In August 1922, 27 rickshaw men in the "Peak" residential district of Hong Kong were given prison sentences for refusing to work during heavy rain (*CWR*, 30.ix.22).

96. See Chapters VII and VIII below.

97. See *Chin-tai kung-yeh* [137] II, 1299–1301, for lists concerning the 1895–1913 period, and *LSYC*, 1959, No. 2, for an estimate of the number of strikes between 1914 and 1917. For 1918, see Chen Ta, "Analysis of Strikes in China," *CEJ*, Oct. 1927.

98. *Chin-tai kung-yeh, ibid.*

99. *MKJP*, 22.vii.17.

100. *Chin-tai kung-yeh* [137] I, 1250.

101. *Ibid.*, II, 1259.

102. *SHSP*, 15.viii.18.

103. *Chin-tai kung-yeh* [137] II, 1299.

104. *Ibid.*, I, 1249.

105. *Chien-shih* [165], p. 4.

106. Li Shih-yueh [207], p. 5.

107. *Chien-shih* [165], p. 4.

108. *Ibid.*

109. *Shih-shih hsin-pao* [130], 14.v.18, where it is reported that the strikers drank a "purification toast" (*ch'i-hsin-chiu*).

110. *Chin-tai kung-yeh* [137] II, 1263.

111. *Ibid.*, II, 1263–64.

112. *Ibid.*, II, 1263.

113. *Shih-shih hua-pao* [131], 1905, No. 7, and 1906, No. 29.

114. *Chin-tai kung-yeh* [137] II, 1264 and 1286–87.

115. *Shih-shih hsin-pao* [130], 19.iv.18.

116. *Chin-tai kung-yeh* [137] II, 1289.

117. *Ibid.*, II, 1269.

118. See *Min-sheng tsa-chih* [126], No. 21. See also *1919–27 kung-jen yun-tung* [208], p. 14.

119. *Chin-tai kung-yeh* [137] II, 1299–1301.

120. *Ibid.*

121. On these three strikes, see *Chien-shih* [165], p. 4, and *LSYC*, 1959, No. 2. The Peking postal workers' strike was caused by the introduction of a regulation raising the number of daily deliveries to eight.

122. In the absence of any detailed study of the Chinese labor movement before 1919, these remarks are based on the lists and studies of strikes referred to in note 97 above.

123. Two of the strikes took place in both Chinese and foreign-owned enterprises, which accounts for the total with regard to nationality of employers coming to 74 instead of 72. A further point: 39 of the strikes were in the textile industry, twelve in the metal-

lurgical and shipbuilding industries, four in printing and paper works, and eight in various other industries.

124. See *LSYC*, 1959, No. 2, for numerous examples of this.

125. See p. 12 above. 126. *SCMP*, 29.vii.19.

127. *CEB*, 4.vii.25.

128. Kann, *Currency in China* [264], p. 537.

129. *CEB*, 24.iv.25. 130. *CWR*, 28.i.28.

131. *FER*, Jan. 1920.

132. Chen Ta, "Analysis of Strikes in China," *CEJ*, Oct. 1927.

133. *Nien-chien* [138] II, 154. 134. *SCMP*, 31.xii.18.

135. *SCMP*, 24.iv.18.

136. *MDN*, 14.i.18. As soon as the strike was declared, a raise in wages was granted "because of the distress caused to the workers by the abnormal rise in prices."

137. *Nien-chien* [138] II, 154.

138. *Chien-shih* [165], p. 6.

139. *Nien-chien* [138] II, 154.

140. *NCH*, 11.v.18. The men distributed leaflets against the high cost of living and declared: "Whoever refuses to stop work or to attend the Guild meeting [held at the Lu-pan temple] will have the sun and moon shine on his back" (*i.e.*, is no more than a beast).

141. These are Chen Ta's figures, in *CEJ*, Oct. 1927.

142. *Strikes and Lockouts* [18], p. 65.

143. *NCH*, 7.ii.20 (Report of the Board of the British-owned Yangtzepoo Cotton Mill).

144. On the strike in Hong Kong in 1884, see Marlat, "Les émeutes de Ouentcheou et de Hong-kong," *Revue Historique* [324].

145. See *CTSTL*, 1958, No. 5. On the boycotts during this period, see Shigeharu, *The Historical Development of Chinese Boycotts* [288], and *AAAPS*, Vol. 152 (1930), "China's Use of the Boycott as a Political Weapon."

146. *LSYC*, 1959, No. 2. 147. *Ibid.*

148. On this strike see *LSYC*, 1954, No. 2.

149. *CTSTL*, 1958, No. 5.

150. See Chesneaux, *Sun Yat-sen* [239], p. 72.

151. *LSYC*, 1955, No. 1.

152. A case in point is the seaman Su Chao-cheng, who from 1920 to 1927 was one of the principal promoters of trade unionism among the seamen (*Ko-ming lieh-shih-chuan* [221], pp. 133ff).

153. *LSYC*, 1959, No. 2.

154. Ch'en Ta, *Lao-tung wen-t'i* [190], p. 102.

155. Lei Chia, *Chu Pao-t'ing* [205], p. 13.

156. Li Shih-yueh, *Hsin-hai ko-ming kung-jen yun-tung* [207], p. 6.

157. See Lowe Chuan-hua [284], p. 52. 158. See p. 122 above.

159. British Consul Moss, in a report on trade unionism in Shanghai made in 1924 (*Labour Conditions* [20], p. 84), states that a new electricians' union had been founded by a certain Han-Hwe [*sic*], a Kuomintang militant.

160. *LSYC*, 1959, No. 2.

161. On the many political parties and cliques in China after the revolution, see for instance Li Chien-nung, *Political History* [277], pp. 275ff.

162. *LSYC*, 1959, No. 2. 163. Lowe Chuan-hua [284], p. 31.

164. *Chien-shih* [165], p. 5. 165. See *FTHP*, 1952, No. 2.

166. Ch'en Ta, *Lao-tung wen-t'i* [190], p. 102. It is, however, difficult to believe the tradition, reported here, that the student in question had "returned from Moscow," since this was a year before the Bolshevik revolution.

167. *Chien-shih* [165], p. 5.

168. See the interview given to *SCMP*, 10.iii.22.

169. *SCMP*, 15.iv.19 and 3.v.19.

170. On the *Kung-tang,* see Li Shih-yueh [156], pp. 13–25, and also *Chin-tai kung-yeh* [137] II, 1273ff, and *LSYC,* 1959, No. 6. The last presents a different view from that of Li Shih-yueh, and tends to regard the Kung-tang as a bourgeois party devoid of any working-class character.

171. "All workers over 16, whether male or female, rich or poor, and practicing whatever trade, can, if they are earning their living, belong to the party" (*Chin-tai kung-yeh,* II, 1273).

172. Li Shih-yueh, p. 21.

173. On the Tangshan branch, see *HCN*, 1.v.20; see also Ch'en Ta, *Lao-tung wen-t'i* [190], p. 100.

174. After 1916, apparently a certain number of Kung-tang militants became active again. In 1917 they are mentioned as supporting the Pootung and Commercial Press strikes (*MKJP*, 21.vii.17, and *SHSP*, 28.iii.17). The name "Kung-tang" reappears at the time of the May Fourth Movement (see below), but I have been unable to ascertain whether this was the same organization.

175. *FTHP*, 1952, No. 2.

176. *Ibid.*

177. See *Wu-ssu ch'i-k'an* [145] II, 167–78 (description of *Lao-tung*); p. 546 (text of the manifesto published in the first number); and p. 679 (detailed table of contents of all five issues).

178. Snow, *Red Star over China* [302], pp. 146 and 149 (notes taken during the course of a conversation with Mao Tse-tung in 1937).

179. *Chien-shih* [165], p. 5.   180. *Ibid.*

181. *LSYC*, 1957, No. 5.

182. These three articles by Li Ta-chao are included in the *Selected Works* (Hsuan-chi [159], pp. 138, 153, 171).

183. The slogan "Work is sacred" (*lao-kung shen-sheng*) was much in use in these circles at this time (*Chien-shih* [165], p. 9). It figured, for instance, in a speech given by Ts'ai Yuan-p'ei, the Chancellor of Peking University, at the ceremony held to celebrate the end of World War I (*HCN*, Nov. 1918).

184. *LSYC*, 1958, No. 2, gives no concrete example of any such influence during the period preceding May 4.

185. This information was passed on to me by M. Haupt, who examined the archives at the offices of the Socialist International in Brussels while working on his forthcoming book on the Second International.

186. There were 40,000 such workers, according to *NCH*, 15.xi.19, most of whom were employed in the Don coal basin.

187. See P'eng Ming, *Chung-Su yu-i-shih* [211], pp. 81–82.

188. See Whiting, *Soviet Policies in China* [314], p. 36 (based on information taken from the Soviet daily press).

189. *Ibid.*

190. *Ibid.*

191. See *SCMP*, 18.iv.19, announcing the imminent arrival in Canton of 2,000 Chinese Bolsheviks, and *NCH*, 12.iv.19, reporting a special meeting of the cabinet in Peking to discuss special security measures to be taken concerning the coolies repatriated from Russia.

192. Whiting [314], p. 293 (from *Izvestia*, 22.vi.20).

193. This was so among the seamen in Shanghai (Lei Chia [205], p. 17).

194. Ch'i-wu lao-jen, *HKC*, 1.vii.57.

195. *MDN*, 16.v.18.   196. *MDN*, 5–7.ix.18.

197. *MDN*, 26.viii.19.

198. A worker named Chao Chuan-ch'iang, who had been formerly employed on the railways in Eastern Siberia and who spoke Russian, was an assistant to the Communist Li Ch'i-han at the Shanghai offices of the Labor Secretariat in 1922 (see Chapter VIII below), and helped him to prevent the recruitment of strikebreakers during the Hong Kong strike (*PDR*, 31.i.22).

199. See Chen Ta, *Chinese Migrations* [238], chapter 9. See also Blick, "The Chinese Labor Corps" [232].

200. Chen Ta [238], p. 151.

201. See *Current History Magazine*, Dec. 1919, "Managing 200,000 Coolies in France."

202. *NCH*, 15.iii.19.

203. Tyau, *China Awakened* [166], p. 237.

204. Isaacs, *Tragedy* [263], p. 55.

205. The workers employed in French enterprises had about 2 francs a day left after deductions for living expenses. The British labor contracts allowed 1 franc for coolies and 2 francs for skilled workers, plus 10 yuan a month for family remittances (Chen Ta, *Chinese Migrations* [238]). In 1918 the British government sent 3.5 million yuan in postal orders to Shantung (Post Office report [35], 1918, p. 11).

206. Out of the 323 workers brought back in October 1921 on the *André Lebon* (*PDR*, 24.xii.21), 307 immediately left Shanghai by train.

207. These workers who returned from France were reduced to becoming coolies, beggars, or rickshaw men, even in the cases of those who had received a good technical training in France (*NCH*, 24.xii.21). This is confirmed by a statement made in September 1920 by the Association of Returned Workers (*LTC*, No. 6, 19.ix.20).

208. See below, p. 160.

209. The engineer Demaret, reporting on the causes of the Tangshan colliery strike in June 1921, writes that one of the causes was the influence of workers recently returned from France and Russia (K.M.A. Archives [15], document 14/2/9).

210. Chow Tse-tsung, *The May Fourth Movement* [242], pp. 36–39.

211. On the beginnings of the "work and study" movement in Hunan, see Li Jui, *Mao Tse-tung* [206], pp. 83–91.

212. Several Chinese trade unions are said to have been formed in Dairen around 1920 under the influence of Japanese trade unionism (*CEB*, 22.xi.24). Account should also be taken of the contacts between Chinese students in Japan and the Japanese Socialist movement from the beginning of the twentieth century; for instance, it was during his time as a student in Japan that Chiang K'ang-hu, who founded the Chinese Socialist Party in 1912, was introduced to socialist ideas (Chow Tse-tsung [242], p. 33).

213. Teng Chung-hsia (*Chien-shih* [165], p. 10) considers that the splitting up of the Cantonese guilds into employers' and workers' associations was part of the process of "Europeanization" stimulated by the proximity of Hong Kong and by contacts with British trade unionism; but he gives no concrete examples.

214. In 1918 they began publication of a *Chinese Student Monthly*, which very soon devoted a great deal of space to labor problems. In a private interview, Mr. George Hardy, formerly Secretary General of the I.W.W., told me that around 1918–19 Chinese students often came to his office in Chicago to buy pamphlets and other documents on Syndicalism, which they mailed to China. Hsieh Ying-po cannot have been the only Chinese studying in the U.S.A. around 1914 to become a member of the American Socialist Party (see above, p. 134).

215. Out of the 32 old workers interviewed in 1957, only four had working-class fathers: the two women workers in the B.A.T. Pootung factory were the daughters of a worker in that factory; a Changsintien railwayman was the son of a coal porter on the Ching-Han line; and a Chengchow railwayman was the son of a carpenter on the same line.

216. *CWR*, 22.iii.24, comments on the scandalously low wages of Chinese workers compared with workers in other countries.

217. An editorial in *NCH*, 15.x.21, suggests that the betterment of workers' living conditions might be "a paying proposition."

218. Remarks made by the Shanghai managing director of Jardine, Matheson & Co. in an interview with an I.L.O. envoy in 1924 (Henry report [10], Part II).

219. The Hunan provincial government was in direct control of the Changsha cotton mill, the mint, and the Shuikowshan and Sinhwa mines, as well as the foundries supplied by them (*RT*, 1922, Changsha, pp. 13–14, and *CEB*, 22.xi.24).

220. The term "rearguard" was used in this sense at the Third National Labor Congress (see Chapter XII below).

221. In August 1920 they organized a Labor Information Bureau, which in February 1922 took the name of the Employers' Federation (I.L.O. Archives 206/1/13/1). I have failed to discover any mention of this organization in the various sources consulted—not even in *NCH*, although it was directly linked with foreign business interests in Shanghai. It must, however, have played an active part during periods of crisis in Shanghai, as for instance in 1925, but only when access to the archives of foreign firms in China is granted will more be known about it.

222. For instance, the British marines were brought in against the K.M.A. miners' strike in October 1922 (see Chapter VIII below); and the Japanese consul general negotiated a settlement of the strike in the Japanese cotton mills in Shanghai in August 1925 (see Chapter IX below).

223. This happened in February 1923 during the repression of the general strike held by the Ching-Han railwaymen (see Chapter VIII below).

224. During February and March 1922, for instance, the chambers of commerce collected funds for the strikers employed by foreign shipping firms in Hong Kong. From 1924 on, there was large-scale cooperation between the labor movement and the bourgeoisie (see Part II below).

Chapter VII

1. On the May Fourth Movement, see Hua Kang, *Wu-ssu yun-tung shih* [201]; *Kuang-hui-ti Wu-ssu* [219]; *Wu-ssu yun-tung* [144]; see also the very detailed account by Chow Tse-tsung, *The May Fourth Movement* [242].

2. *Shih-shih hsin-pao* [130], 8.v.19.

3. On the anti-Japanese boycott of 1919, see Shigeharu, *The Historical Development of Chinese Boycotts* [288].

4. These "Groups of Ten" consisted of a chairman, an inspector (who inventoried Japanese goods in shops), an editor, a disciplinarian (to impose and collect fines), a treasurer, and five orators (to exhort people to "buy Chinese"). See Chow Tse-tsung [242], p. 141.

5. *Wu-ssu yun-tung* [144], p. 133.   6. *CTSTL*, 1957, No. 4.

7. *Wu-ssu yun-tung* [144], p. 133.   8. *Ibid.*, p. 808.

9. Interview with the worker Wang Ch'un-jung.

10. Li Jui, *Mao Tse-tung* [206], pp. 97–98.

11. Teng Chung-hsia (*Chien-shih* [165], p. 8) gives the number of workers on strike in Shanghai at the beginning of June as 60,000. According to the report of the Commissioner of Police of the Shanghai International Settlement, the number of strikers in the International Settlement alone was 24,000, which more or less tallies with the foregoing estimate covering the whole of the city (*Municipal Gazette* [39], 26.vii.19).

12. *Wu-ssu yun-tung* [144], pp. 831–48.   13. *PDR*, 6–12.vi.19.

14. *Wu-ssu yun-tung*, p. 130.   15. *Ibid.*, p. 460.

16. This applies to the guilds of the wood-engravers and the soapmakers (*ibid.*, p. 130), and to the tea guild (*ibid.*, p. 462).

17. *Ibid.*, p. 466.

18. *Ibid.*, p. 461.

19. *Ibid.*, p. 496.

20. *SHSP*, 8.vi.19.

21. *Wu-ssu yun-tung* [144], p. 568.

22. *Ibid.*, p. 701.

23. *Ibid.*, p. 701.

24. Chow Tse-tsung [242], p. 154.

25. *Wu-ssu yun-tung*, p. 472.

26. This term was used, for instance, at the meeting of workers held by the Industrial Federation on June 11 (*ibid.*, p. 472).

27. *Ibid.*, p. 464.

28. Cf. the seamen's strike declaration (*ibid.*, p. 460), or the resolutions adopted at the meeting on June 11 (*ibid.*, p. 472).

29. Matters were very different during the big tripartite strike in June 1925, when it was the unions that initiated the strikes, and the demands presented included items (such as the demand for the eight-hour day) that were in the interests of the workers as such (see Chapter IX below).

30. *Chien-shih* [165], p. 8.

31. *Wu-ssu yun-tung* [144], p. 826.

32. *SCMP*, 12.vi.19.

33. *Wu-ssu yun-tung*, pp. 828, 842, 843, 851.

34. *Ibid.*, pp. 847 and 851.

35. *Ibid.*, p. 853.

36. *Ibid.*

37. Fifty-four strikes between July 1919 and July 1921 are mentioned in *Strikes and Lockouts* [18], p. 61. Chen Ta ("Analysis of Strikes in China," *CEJ*, Oct. 1927) reckons that in 1920 alone there were 46 strikes in the whole of China, for 19 of which the number of strikers is known and comes to a total of 46,000. According to the 1920 annual report of the Commissioner of Police of the Shanghai International Settlement, the number of strikers in Shanghai during that year was just over 57,000 (Kotenev, *Shanghai, Its Municipality* [156], p. 9).

38. The list of strikes given in *Nien-chien* [138] II, 155–57, is very incomplete, as has been proved by systematic perusal of *CWR, NCH, SCMP*, and *MDN*. But the information supplied by these newspapers is also far from being complete, so that it has not been possible, on the basis of these sources alone, to establish a detailed list of strikes. All that can be done is to note the general trend, and to examine a few concrete examples.

39. Chen Ta, *CEJ*, Oct. 1927.

40. *Nien-chien* [138] II, 157. Chen Ta (*CEJ*, Oct. 1927) reckons that in 1920 seven strikes were held because of ill-treatment by overseers and foremen or dislike of factory regulations.

41. *SHSP*, 21.vii.21.

42. *MKJP*, 18.vi.20.

43. *SCMP*, March 1921, *passim*.

44. *Ibid.*

45. *NCH*, 7.ii.20.

46. Lowe Chuan-hua, *Facing Labor Issues* [284], p. 60.

47. *NCH*, March 1921, *passim*.

48. *SMCR*, 1920, p. 67A.

49. *Municipal Gazette* [39], 21.viii.20.

50. *NCH*, 31.vii.20.

51. *Ibid.*

52. Chen Ta, "Labor Unrest in China," *MLR*, Aug. 1921.

53. *EE*, 18.v.22.

54. *NCH*, 26.vii.19. Similar sentiments were expressed in *FER*, Jan. 1920, in a statement made by Brooke Smith, the chairman of the Ewo firm, and also in *NCH*, 7.ii.20 (report of complaints made by the share holders of the British-owned Yangtzepoo cotton mill regarding the shortage of labor) and in *LCT*, 7.iii.21 (reported discussion between various foreign firms in Shanghai on the shortage of labor).

55. *NCH*, 5.iii.21 and 12.iii.21.

56. *Nien-chien* [138] II, 156.
57. K.M.A. Archives [15], document 14/2/9 (a letter from the managing director dated 28.vi.20, and the report of Demaret, the chief engineer).
58. *NCH*, 10.vii.20. See also *PDR*, 11.vii.20.
59. *NCH*, 29.v.20.
60. *SCMP*, 2.vii.20.
61. *NCH*, 30.vii.21. On 2.vii.21, for instance, a coolie employed at the waterworks was sentenced to a fine of 3 yuan or three days' imprisonment for hitting a nonstriker.
62. Teng Chung-hsia (*Chien-shih* [165], p. 19) says that this strike occurred in March 1921, whereas May is the month given in *CWR*, 14.v.21.
63. *SHSP*, 21.vii.21. 64. *PDR*, 17.ix.20.
65. *SCMP*, April 1920, *passim*. 66. See p. 164 below.
67. The text of this manifesto is in Lowe Chuan-hua [284], p. 59.
68. *Ibid.*, p. 61.
69. Between April and August 1920, 26 craftsmen's strikes are reported in *SCMP*, including strikes by carpenters and bricklayers in Hong Kong, of workers in the oil-presses in Kiangmen, of goldbeaters in Canton and Foshan, weavers in Canton, and cabinetmakers in Hong Kong; almost all resulted in a 20 to 35 per cent rise in wages.
70. *SCMP*, March 1921, *passim*.
71. *SHSP*, 7.vii.19. 72. *SP*, 1.vii.19.
73. *SP*, 5.viii.19. According to *MKJP*, 24.vii.24, this association was formed in 1917 by members of the Canton hui-kuan in Shanghai.
74. Ma Ch'ao-chün, *Lao-tung yun-tung* [210], p. 98.
75. *SHSP*, 9.i.20. 76. *MKJP*, 4.viii.20.
77. *MKJP*, 20.vii.24. 78. *Wu-ssu yun-tung* [144], p. 701.
79. *MKJP*, 24.vii.24.
80. *Chien-shih* [165], p. 9. Huang Chieh-min was also one of the leaders of the Society for Industrial Advance (Ma Ch'ao-chün [210], p. 97). There were many such cases of plural board membership.
81. *FTHP*, 1952, No. 2. 82. *CWR*, 1.i.21.
83. *SP*, 1.i.19. 84. *SP*, 28.vii.19.
85. *SP*, 7.vii.19. 86. *CWR*, 20.iii.20.
87. *SP*, 1.vii.19 and 10.viii.19.
88. *SP*, 5.viii.19. A similar slogan, "Virtue and skill" (*tao-te kung-i*), was taken up in February 1919 at a meeting held to celebrate the eighth anniversary of the Society for the Advance of Young Workers, to which young workers in the Commercial Press belonged (*SP*, 26.ii.19).
89. The Y.M.C.A. was to be in charge of the above-mentioned Hankow factory (*CWR*, 20.iii.20). Hsia Ch'i-feng, the president of the Returned Laborers' Association, was a member of the managing committee of the Y.M.C.A. (*CWR*, 1.i.21).
90. Chen Ta, "Labor Unrest in China," *MLR*, Aug. 1921.
91. *SP*, 15.ix.19 (letter to the Returned Laborers' Association from the Industrial Society).
92. *SP*, 15.ix.19 (on the club for workers and employees).
93. Chen Ta, *MLR*, Aug. 1921.
94. In 1920, the Returned Laborers' Association announced that it was in direct touch with the American A.F.L. (*NCH*, 17.i.20).
95. *MKJP*, 2.xii.19.
96. *SHSP*, 22.xi.19. In 1919 the I.L.O. scarcely had any relations with China. At its inaugural conference in Washington, the delegates from countries enjoying extraterritoriality in China requested that China be classed as one of the "special countries" to which the resolutions adopted at the conference regarding such matters as the eight-hour

day were not applicable. There was no Chinese delegate either at this conference or at the one held in Geneva the following year. It was not until 1921 that a Chinese delegation attended the I.L.O. annual conference, and even then it lacked the threefold representation (of government, employers, and wage earners) required by I.L.O. rules, and consisted merely of two diplomats from Berne.

97. *SHSP,* 9.i.20.

98. *SP,* 8.viii.19 (concerning a meeting of the Society for Industrial Advance).

99. *SHSP,* 7.ix.19 (concerning a meeting of the Industrial Society).

100. This was the case with the General Trade Union Society and with the Returned Laborers' Association.

101. *SP,* 7.vii.19. 102. *MKJP,* 3.iv.19.

103. *SP,* 7.vii.19. 104. *MKJP,* 24.vii.24.

105. The first Secretary General of the Electrical Industries Federation was Ch'en Yueh-fu, who was manager of a firm in Nanking Road dealing in electrical equipment (*MKJP,* 2.v.20). In September 1920, a meeting of this association was held at which a collection was made for the victims of the increase in the price of rice. The contributions were of a size no worker could afford: two people gave 10 yuan, and four contributed 5 yuan (*LTC,* No. 7, 26.ix.20).

106. *MKJP,* 3.iv.20.

107. In a French stocking factory, for instance, an association of women employees was formed in May 1920 that announced its intention to promote peaceful negotiations instead of strikes; it was handsomely subsidized by "a wealthy foundress" (*SP,* 29.v.20).

108. In September 1920 a manifesto of the Electrical Industries Federation set forth a program for workers' training, appealed to the good will of employers, and requested that parks and gardens in the Settlement be open to Chinese workers (*LTC,* 3.x.20).

109. *SP,* 20.iv.20 (on a meeting of the Electrical Industries Federation).

110. Teng Chung-hsia, himself a militant Communist, described them as "poster unions" (*chao-p'ai kung-hui*)—that is, more interested in self-advertisement than in taking action for the workers (*Chien-shih* [165], pp. 20–21).

111. *SHSP,* 14.iv.20, and *SP,* 1.i.20. 112. *MKJP,* 24.vii.24.

113. *SHSP,* 2.v.20.

114. Li Heng-lin, the first president of the Electrical Industries Federation, was active in the Industrial Federation around the time of May 4, 1919 (*SP,* 7.vii.19).

115. Concerning May Day in Shanghai in 1920, see *MKJP* and *SP,* April and May, *passim.*

116. See Tyau, *China Awakened* [166], p. 227. See also the Commercial Press propaganda pamphlet [183].

117. *NCH,* 5.iii.21 and 12.iii.21. 118. *LTC,* No. 9, 10.x.20.

119. *LTC,* No. 19, 19.xii.20.

120. *SHSP,* 2.vii.21, and *LTC,* No. 18, 12.xii.20.

121. *Nien-chien* [138] II, 6.

122. Hong Kong Government, *Ordinances* [26], 1920, No. 8.

123. Hong Kong Government, *Administrative Reports* [23], 1920, p. C.14.

124. See Huang I-po, *Kuang-tung chi-ch'i kung-jen* [202], pp. 8–9. See also Ma Ch'ao-chün, *Lao-tung yun-tung* [210], pp. 162–65.

125. For instance, already in December 1920 the Shanghai Mechanics' Union was quoting the illustrious example of the Canton mechanics (*LTC,* No. 19, 19.xii.20).

126. *SCMP,* 5.v.21. 127. Huang I-po [202], p. 11.

128. Lowe Chuan-hua [284], p. 53.

129. *Chien-shih* [165], p. 46. Teng Chung-hsia comments that the seamen, by the nature of their occupation, were in a better position to know about the great strike wave in Europe in 1919–20.

130. *SCMP*, 24.i.21.

131. Cf. comments by Ch'en Tu-hsiu in *LTC*, 5.ix.20, paying homage to the maturity of the Cantonese workers and to their class-consciousness.

132. The printers and the mechanics, for example, made this demand in the spring of 1921. The latter, in the manifesto they sent to the employers before the strike, referred explicitly to the resolutions recently adopted at the International Trade Union Conference in Amsterdam (Lowe Chuan-hua [284], p. 59).

133. *Chien-shih* [165], p. 45.

134. Union members in the Hong Kong tea factories went on strike in February 1921 in protest against nonmembers' receiving the annual bonus (*SCMP*, 18.ii.21). In September 1921, several hundred union members in a tea factory in Honam, a suburb of Canton, stoned nonmembers and told them to leave the factory (*SCMP*, 6.ix.21).

135. On the political situation in the South in 1919, and on the affair concerning the appointment of the civilian provincial governor, see Li Chien-nung, *Political History* [277], p. 397.

136. *SCMP*, 15.vii.19 and 16.vii.19, and *NCH*, 19.vii.19.

137. Ma Ch'ao-chün [210], pp. 133–35.   138. *CWR*, 30.x.20.

139. *CWR*, 6.xi.20.   140. *SCMP*, 6.v.21 and 7.v.21.

141. *CWR*, 29.i.21. The other members of the municipal advisory council were either appointed by the government, introduced by merchant organizations, or elected.

142. *CWR*, 19.ii.21.   143. *SCMP*, 19.iv.21.

144. *SCMP*, 4.v.20.   145. *SCMP*, 4.v.21.

146. Lowe Chuan-hua [284], p. 60.   147. Ma Ch'ao-chün [210], p. 158.

148. *Ibid.*, pp. 153–54.   149. *Ibid.*, p. 174.

150. *LTC*, No. 16, 28.xi.20.

151. *LTC*, No. 19, 19.xii.20 published a letter from a worker in the Hua-ch'ang antimony foundry stating that all the genuine working-class employees in the arsenal, the mines, and the factories belonged to this association. But another correspondent from Changsha, in the same number, wrote that the Mechanics Society was simply an offshoot of the Chinese Union of Hunan, which was merely the tool of a politician named Ch'en. He went on to report that at the inaugural meeting of the Chinese Union of Hunan not a single worker was present, but only people who came in their sedan chairs to support their "boss" (*ta-yuan-shou*); and he maintained that the Mechanics Society was run on the same lines.

152. *Nien-chien* [138] II, 94; *Chien-shih* [165], p. 33; Li Jui, *Mao Tse-tung* [206], p. 161. But Edgar Snow reports that Mao Tse-tung, in personal conversation with him, described the leaders of the Hunan Workingmen's Association as "right-wing elements" recruited from among the students, some of whom were under anarchist influence (*Red Star over China* [302], p. 156).

153. Ma Ch'ao-chün [210], pp. 151–53.

154. *LTC*, No. 17, 5.xii.20

155. *LTC*, No. 19, 19.xii.20. The writer of this letter reports that after making inquiries, the workers in the foundry discovered that the Workingmen's Association had only a few hundred members, mostly students and merchants, and that it was simply "an association of workingmen for the benefit of the capitalists," whereas genuine workers belonged to the Mechanics Society (see note 151 above). This account not only contradicts what the correspondent referred to in note 151 wrote about the Mechanics Society, but also does not tally with the later activities of the Workingmen's Association, when it had known links with the labor movement. Possibly it was inspired by employers who wanted to maintain their control in the area.

156. For the affair of the Changsha cotton mill, see *RT*, 1921, Changsha, p. 15, and *CWR*, 30.iv.21 and 21.v.21.

157. See *Huang-P'ang chou-nien chi-nien-ts'e* [175], p. 13. According to this source, the big demonstration took place on April 13 and not on March 21 as stated in *CWR*. Perhaps there were two separate occasions.

158. *CWR*, 14.v.21.

159. Li Jui, *Mao Tse-tung* [206], p. 122. On the autonomist movement in Hunan in general, see Li Chien-nung [277], pp. 404–5. In October 1920 the Changsha students' association had launched the slogan "A Monroe doctrine for Hunan" (*CWR*, 6.xi.20).

160. *LTC*, No. 18, 12.xii.20.

161. *Labour Conditions* [20], p. 39 (report of Consul Ogden, mentioning a "Society for Workers' Self-government" in Chengtu, founded in 1920 and supported by employees of Western firms).

162. In December 1919 a "Printing Workers' Mutual Aid Association" was formed here, which, as in Changsha the year before, and like the Ching-yuan guild in Hong Kong, included in its membership lithographers, letterpress printers, and compositors, and aimed to "eliminate divisions and form a single organization that will be strong and enduring" (*Kuang-hui-ti wu-ssu* [219], p. 174).

163. In 1920 a "Mutual Aid Association for the Printing Companies of Chekiang" was formed here, run by young intellectuals who published a journal named "The Labor Wave in Chekiang" (*Wu-ssu ch'i-k'an* [145] II, 465–66).

164. *CWR*, 7.v.21.　165. Li Chien-nung [277], pp. 394–96.

166. *LCT*, 28.xii.20.

167. *CWR*, 7.v.21. It is well known that the militarists of the Chihli faction, to which Yang I-te belonged, had close links with the British interests in China.

168. See Ch'en Ta, *Lao-tung wen-t'i* [190], p. 217; also *Chien-shih* [165], p. 24.

169. On the rise of Marxism in China before 1921, see Hu Hua, *Chung-kuo ko-ming-shih* [200]; Wang Shih, *Kung-ch'an-tang li-shih chien-pien* [214]; also Schwartz, *Chinese Communism* [301].

170. Wang Shih [214], p. 17.

171. Cf. Schwartz [301], chap. 1 (where perhaps too negative a view is taken).

172. On this dispute, see Li Ta-chao, *Hsuan-chi* [159], pp. 228–34.

173. Cf. *Chien-shih* [165], p. 20.　174. See Wang Shih [214], pp. 17 and 18.

175. See *KMJP*, 12.v.55.

176. Li Jui, *Mao Tse-tung* [206], pp. 133–44.

177. See P'eng Ming, *Chung-Su yu-i-shih* [211], pp. 60–61. The interest aroused throughout China in the Soviet Union is exemplified by the fact that the seven organizations that sponsored the first Labor Day celebrations held in Shanghai in May 1920 (all of which represented conservative or reformist views) sent a telegram on this occasion to the Soviet government (*SHSP*, 2.v.20).

178. The text is in Whiting, *Soviet Policies in China* [314], p. 269.

179. See Wang Shih [214], p. 20, and Hu Hua [200], p. 40.

180. See Hu Hua [200], p. 40. On Voitinsky's mission, see the recollections of an old militant that appeared in *HKC*, 1.vii.57.

181. Li Jui [206], p. 146.　182. Hu Hua [200], p. 40.

183. See *HKC*, 1.vii.57.

184. See, in No. 1, the article on the principles of organization in Communist parties; in No. 4, a detailed critical analysis of Western anarchism (which, however, makes no mention of anarchist currents in China); and in No. 3, an article on the Second and Third Internationals.

185. See Chow Tse-tsung [242], p. 250.

186. On the anti-Japanese demonstrations in the spring of 1920, see for instance *SMCR*, 1920, p. 69A, or *CWR*, 29.v.20 (Changsha) and 8.v.20 (Wuhan). On the anti-Japanese boycott, see *CTSTL*, 1957, No. 4, concerning Nanchang, and Li Jui [206], p. 115, con-

cerning Hunan, where in December 1919 the workers in the foundries and the cotton mill took part in a demonstration organized by students to protest the importation of Japanese goods.

187. On these teachers' strikes see for instance *NCH*, 27.xii.19, 26.iii.21, and especially 11.vi.21, where it is reported that during a strike provoked by a three months' delay in the payment of salaries, several teachers were wounded in a clash with the police.

188. Li Ta-chao, *Hsuan-chi* [159], pp. 311–27.

189. *MKJP*, 3.v.23.   190. *HKC*, 1.vii.57.

191. Between 1919 and 1921 the Criminal Investigation Department of the International Settlement seized 27 "Bolshevik" journals and pamphlets (*SCMR*, 1921, p. 61A). In 1920 it was reported that in Shanghai Bolshevik propaganda was being disseminated among the rickshaw coolies and people of that kind, and that there was talk of a marvelous new doctrine from Russia that would put an end to the miseries of poor people (*PP*, 15.ii.20).

192. *Chien-shih* [165], p. 17.

193. Ch'i-wu lao-jen, *Erh-ch'i pa-kung hui-i* (*HKC*, 15.i.57, 1.ii.57, 15.ii.57), p. 32.

194. *Wu-ssu ch'i-k'an* [145] II, 61–70.   195. *LTC*, No. 7 and No. 2.

196. *LTC*, No. 8.   197. *LTC*, Nos. 6, 11, 12.

198. *Wu-ssu ch'i-k'an* [145] II, 71.   199. *Ibid.*, pp. 75 and 80–85.

200. *Ibid.*, pp. 644 and 645.

201. On the educational activities of Peking students, see *CTSTL*, 1955, No. 2, "Pei-ching ta-hsueh p'ing-min chiao-yü," which consists of daily notes made by a student who took part in the Changsintien project, which had difficulty getting started: only five to ten people, including some children, attended the first meeting on April 13, 1920.

202. *Chien-shih* [165], p. 16.

203. It is best to follow the example of Chinese historians and regard these collieries as forming part of the Hunan region, although in fact they are on the far side of the border with Kiangsi.

204. Li Jui, *Mao Tse-tung* [206], p. 148.

205. *LTC*, Nos. 10 and 17.

206. Wilbur and How, *Documents* [140], p. 53. This attitude also appears in the articles written by Li Han-chün for *LTC*, of which he was probably editor; see for instance his article in No. 8 on the rise of the price of rice, or the publicity he gave in No. 6 to a workers' savings bank in Yangtzepoo.

207. See his articles in *Chieh-fang yü kai-tsao* [120], the organ of the moderates who were followers of Liang Ch'i-ch'ao (Jan. and April 1920).

208. Chow Tse-tsung [242], p. 248.

209. Mif, *Pour une Chine forte et libre* [290], p. 14.

210. *Wu-ssu ch'i-k'an* [145] II, 75.

211. For instance, in No. 4 there is a lengthy theoretical analysis of anarchism, very dogmatic in tone, which makes no mention of anarchist currents in China, although these had great influence among intellectuals and even among the working class (cf. *Chien-shih* [165], p. 20). No. 4, dated 7.v.21 (i.e. five months after the first appearance of the journal), was the first number to contain a regular column on "News of the Chinese Labor Movement." The journal does not mention May Day celebrations, to which *HCN* had devoted an entire number the year before. There is no doubt that *Kung-ch'an-tang* was much less in touch with the Chinese labor movement, and seemed less interested in it, than *LTC* had been.

212. "The workers are higher than emperors because they have created all the values," declared Ch'en Tu-hsiu at the inaugural meeting of the Boatmen's and Warehousemen's Federation (*MKJP*, 3.iv.20).

213. *SHSP*, 12.vii.20 (Ch'en Tu-hsiu's speech to the Electrical Industries Federation).

214. In March 1920 Chang Kuo-t'ao was one of the leaders of the Industrial Society (*MKJP*, 11.iii.20), and he put Ch'en Tu-hsiu in charge of education (*MKJP*, 19.v.20).

215. On this weekly, which ceased publication in December 1920 because of lack of funds, see *TSTL*, 1955, No. 3.

216. *PDR*, 21.iv.21, 25.iv.21, 2.v.21.

217. Ch'i-wu lao-jen, *HKC*, 1.vii.57. On the part played by Li Ch'i-han in the May Day preparations, see *CKKJ*, 27.iv.57, "Wei Chung-kuo kung-jen yun-tung tsao-lao-ti."

218. *SP*, 8.viii.19.

219. *MKJP*, 3.iv.20.

220. *HWP*, 1.iii.20. The 18.i.20 issue of this journal contains a letter from Ts'ao Ya-po making a plea for banks, training workshops, and schools for workers.

221. *LTC*, No. 1, 15.viii.20.   222. *LTC*, No. 2, 22.viii.20.

223. *LTC*, No. 7, 26.ix.20.   224. See pp. 163–64 above.

225. *LTC*, No. 9. The same applies to the printers' union formed in March 1921 (Hu Hua [200], p. 42).

226. *Chien-shih* [165], p. 19.

227. Li Jui, *Mao Tse-tung* [206], pp. 148–49.

228. *Ibid.*, pp. 104 and 161.

229. An example of this is Ch'en Kung-po, who left the CP soon after it was founded, and whom Teng Chung-hsia (*Chien-shih*, p. 37) accuses of "opportunist" tendencies.

230. Ma Ch'ao-chün [210], p. 158.

231. See Teng's own detailed account (*Chien-shih*, pp. 15–16).

232. *Ibid.*

233. See Chen Ta, *Chinese Migrations* [238], p. 150.

234. The rules of this Chinese union formed in France are given in Ch'en Ta, *Lao-tung wen-t'i* [190], pp. 112–16.

235. See *Hu-nan ko-ming lieh-shih-chuan* [223], pp. 13–14 (biography of Ts'ai Ho-sen).

236. On the activities of Chinese Communists in France and their difficulties, see *CTSTL*, 1955, No. 2.

237. See p. 174 above.

238. This letter is given in *Hsien-tai ch'u-pan shih-liao* [134] I, 435–40.

Chapter VIII

1. On the foundation of the CCP, see Hu Ch'iao-mu, *Chung-kuo kung-ch'an-tang ti san-shih-nien* [199], p. 7, and Hu Hua, *Chung-kuo ko-ming shih chiang-i* [200], pp. 52–56. Both these are official publications, and do not give details supplied by such contemporary observers as the writer of the article in *HKC*, 1.vii.57. See also Brandt and others, *Documentary History* [133], pp. 30ff. The official chronology of the CCP was only gradually established, especially as regards the distinction between the "small Communist groups" and the party proper. Teng Chung-hsia, for instance, writing in 1930 (*Chien-shih* [165], p. 13), gave 1920 as the year in which the party was founded; but today the group that was founded in Shanghai in that year is regarded merely as a precursor group.

2. These were supposed to consist of two delegates each from Peking, Tsinan, Hankow, Changsha, and Shanghai, and one each from Tokyo and Canton. (Paris was not represented.) According to *HKC*, 1.vii.57, Tokyo sent two delegates, hence the total of 13.

3. *HKC*, 1.vii.57. The writer of this article hid his identity by adopting the pseudonym Ch'i-wu lao-jen ("Old Ch'i-wu").

4. See Hu Hua [200], p. 53, and the *HKC* article. Possibly the Labor Secretariat was founded slightly earlier than the CCP. No. 6 of *KCT*, published in July by the small Com-

munist group of Shanghai, mentions the founding of the Labor Secretariat but does not mention the founding of the party.

5. On the other hand, in 1921 the founders of the CCP paid little attention to the peasants. They were not much interested in the revolutionary potentialities of the peasantry, and were more or less cut off from the Chinese tradition of peasant risings, although these had been very important in earlier times and also at the beginning of the modern period. In contrast to the Kuomintang and its predecessor the T'ung-meng-hui, the CCP when it was founded does not seem to have had any relations with the rural secret societies. It was only from 1926–27 on that Chinese Communism linked up with the Chinese tradition of peasant revolution (see Chapter XIV below).

6. *KCT*, No. 6, 7.vii.21.

7. *Chien-shih* [165], p. 17.

8. *Ibid.*, p. 15.

9. See p. 171 above.

10. See *CFJP*, 9.x.56.

11. *PDR*, 16.i.22.

12. *Ibid.*, 9.ii.22.

13. *Chien-shih* [165], p. 19. A further rise in the price of rice, from 8.80 yuan per picul in April 1921 to 10.80 in June, and again to 12.50 in October (*PDR, passim*), led to a series of strikes in Shanghai at the end of the summer.

14. See *KMJP*, 28.x.54, "Shih Yang lieh-shih."

15. *Chien-shih* [165], p. 19. For an account of this strike, see *Nien-chien* [138] II, 311–14. The demand for higher wages was met.

16. Yang Shao-ying, *Chung-kuo kung-jen ti pa-kung tou-cheng* [215], pp. 7–10.

17. *Ibid.*, p. 9.

18. See the biography of the student Yu T'ien-yang, who was sent by the Labor Secretariat to organize workers on the Lunghai line in 1921 (*Ko-ming chan-shih-chi* [178], pp. 8–9).

19. *MKJP*, 26.xi.21 and 2.xii.21. The strikers obtained the dismissal of a much hated Belgian engineer.

20. See the biography of Yu T'ien-yang ([178], pp. 8–9).

21. *Chien-shih* [165], p. 40.

22. Li Jui, *Mao Tse-tung* [206], pp. 168–69.

23. *Ibid.*, pp. 167–68. The textbooks used in these schools contained passages on the rights of workers, the role of unions, and the like.

24. *Ibid.*, p. 181.

25. See the biography of Kuo Liang in *Hu-nan ko-ming lieh-shih-chuan* [223], p. 21.

26. Yang Shao-ying [215], pp. 10–12. This strike won a raise in wages and a reduction in hours.

27. Li Jui, *Mao Tse-tung* [206], p. 176.   28. *Chien-shih* [165], p. 33.

29. Li Jui, *Mao Tse-tung* [206], p. 179.

30. *Wu-ssu ch'i-k'an* [145] II, 121–34 and 667ff.

31. On this strike and the repression that followed, see Wieger, *La Chine moderne* [139] IV, 441–42, and *Chien-shih* [165], p. 33.

32. On these manifestations of solidarity, see *World Tomorrow* [188].

33. See p. 131 above. The price of polished rice in Hong Kong rose by 155 per cent between 1914 and the beginning of 1922 (*MLR*, May 1922, "The Shipping Strike in Hong Kong").

34. *NCH*, 7.i.22.

35. See p. 164 above.

36. See p. 166 above. He was formerly a steward, and belonged to the T'ung-meng-hui before joining the Kuomintang (*NCH*, 29.iv.22).

37. See I Pin, *Hsiang-kang hai-yuan ta-pa-kung* [203], p. 16.

38. *Chien-shih* [165], p. 47.

39. *SCMP*, 2.xii.21 (containing the text of the letter sent by the union).

40. *SCMP*, 14.i.22.   41. *Chien-shih* [165], p. 47.
42. *Ibid.*, p. 50.   43. *SCMP*, 28.i.22.
44. *SCMP*, 21.i.22. In Hong Kong the price of rice rose by 69 per cent between January 10 and 24, the price of beef by 50 per cent, and the price of fish by 146 per cent (*Chien-shih* [165], pp. 49–50).
45. On the details of these negotiations, see *SCMP, passim, Chien-shih*, pp. 48–49, and Hong Kong Government, *Gazette* [24], 10.iii.22 (giving a complete account of the strike).
46. *SCMP*, 31.i.22 and 3.ii.22.
47. *Chien-shih* [165], p. 48.
48. *NCH*, 4.ii.22. See also Hong Kong Government, *Orders in Council* [25] and *Gazette*, 1.ii.22.
49. Hong Kong Government, *Orders in Council* [25], 8.ii.22.
50. Hong Kong Government, *Ordinances* [26], 1922, No. 4.
51. On these negotiations, see *Chien-shih* [165], pp. 51–52, and *SCMP*, Feb., *passim*.
52. *SCMP*, 7.ii.22, and *Chien-shih*, p. 55.   53. *NCH*, 18.ii.22.
54. *MLR*, May 1922, "The Shipping Strike in Hong Kong."
55. *Chien-shih* [165], pp. 48 and 60.   56. *SCMP*, 20.i.22.
57. *Chien-shih* [165], p. 59.
58. *SCMP*, 14.i.22. The shelter offered was often rather makeshift—in junks and sampans, for instance (*SCMP*, 17.i.22).
59. *SCMP*, 26.i.22 and 9.ii.22.   60. *SCMP*, 26.i.22 and 27.i.22.
61. *MKJP*, 31.i.22.
62. On these events, see *PDR*, 30.i.22 and 9.ii.22, and *Chien-shih* [165], p. 55.
63. On their arrival in Canton the strikers were greeted by 200 delegates of 38 unions and guilds who had come to make arrangements for lodging them (*SCMP*, 19.i.22).
64. *CWR*, 25.ii.22.
65. *Chien-shih* [165], p. 61.
66. Cf. for instance a letter from Eugene Chen, adviser to the Southern government, in the *North China Daily News* of Shanghai (quoted in *SCMP*, 6.ii.22).
67. On January 19, for instance, a meeting between seamen and British officials was held at the house of the provincial governor, Ch'en Chiung-ming (*SCMP*, 21.i.22).
68. On January 18, seven thousand seamen marched in procession shouting "Long live Governor Ch'en! Long live President Sun!" and were received at the premises of the Kuomintang (*SCMP*, 19.i.22 and 20.i.22).
69. He gave a tea in honor of the strikers (*SCMP*, 19.i.22).
70. See *SCMP*, 8.ii.21 (subscription fund organized by the Cantonese unions in support of the war against the Kwangsi clique). See also *SCMP*, Nov. 1921, *passim* (celebrations organized by the Cantonese unions for Ch'en Chiung-ming's victories in Kwangsi).
71. On the ties between Ch'en Chiung-ming and Chinese conservative circles, see p. 202 below.
72. It made a first attempt through the mediation of the Canton Mechanics' Union—further evidence of its moderate outlook (Hong Kong Government, *Gazette* [24], 10.iii.22)—and a second one on February 26 (*NCH*, 4.iii.22).
73. *SCMP*, 28.ii.22.
74. See the list given in *SCMP*, 10.iii.22.
75. *SCMP*, 3.iii.22.
76. 30 per cent on river steamers, 20 per cent on ships sailing between Chinese ports and along the coast, and 15 per cent on liners to Japan and the East Indies and on oceangoing liners.
77. *NCH*, 11.iii.22. The *SCMP* did not appear because its staff was on strike.
78. According to *NCH*, 1.i.22, this amounted to £93,912; but according to official

sources, the figure was £59,394 (Hong Kong Government, *Administrative Reports* [23], 1922, A-1, A-2).

79. Shanghai Municipal Council Archives [13]. This letter of March 26, 1922, written less than a month after the end of the strike, points out the lessons to be drawn from the strike. It urges employers to treat workers' demands, however unreasonable they might at first appear to be, seriously, sympathetically, and in a businesslike manner. It also expresses some astonishment at the way workers were prepared to make sacrifices in support of sympathy strikes, and at the unexpected efficiency of the strike leaders.

80. Among the strikes were those of the Hong Kong barbers and carpenters, the Canton saltworkers, masons, and butchers (*SCMP, passim*), and the Yangtze seamen (see p. 194 below).

81. *Novyi Vostok* [127], No. 2, p. 344.

82. *Lao-tung ta-hui* [142], p. 2; *Chien-shih* [165], p. 68.

83. Cf. for instance the communication to the Shanghai newspaper *Shen-pao* (*Lao-tung ta-hui*, p. 2).

84. *Chien-shih* [165], p. 67. According to *NCH*, 11.iii.22, this was done on the initiative of Hsü Ch'ien, the president of the Courts of Justice in Canton and a personal friend of Sun Yat-sen. He was one of the more progressive members of the Kuomintang. It must be remembered, however, that in contrast to these liberal measures, the Canton government insisted on compulsory registration of unions with the Municipal Council at the end of March (*SCMP*, 23.iii.22).

85. Cf. an interview with Frank Li, Commissioner for Foreign Affairs in the Canton government, in which he expressed his support for the labor organizations (*SCMP*, 23.iii.22).

86. These are the figures given by Teng Chung-hsia (*Chien-shih* [165], p. 69), who was present at the Congress. They agree with those of a Y.M.C.A. report (*IS*, 1922, III, 187).

87. A list is given in *MKJP*, 8.v.22.

88. These documents were lost (*Chien-shih* [165], p. 70), and the only available sources are some press cuttings (*Lao-tung ta-hui* [142], pp. 3–6) and the notes included in Teng's *Chien-shih*.

89. *Chien-shih*, pp. 69–70. This was a compromise reached between the Labor Secretariat group and the moderates, despite the opposition of the anarchists.

90. Teng Chung-hsia (*Chien-shih*, pp. 72–73) mentions nine resolutions. The reporter of *Hsin-shen-pao* (*Lao-tung ta-hui* [142], pp. 5–6) mentions ten; with two important exceptions, these ten are the same as the resolutions mentioned by Teng.

91. The resolution uses the term *hu-ch'ang* ("tiger ghost") to describe those who had strayed from the path of trade unionism. According to legend, the ghosts (*ch'ang*) of men eaten by tigers have to go on helping the tiger to find further prey. The expression as used here indicates those who help the employers.

92. Teng Chung-hsia does not mention this resolution, although the Hankow rickshaw men's union was in close touch with the Secretariat. Nothing seems to have come of the idea.

93. This resolution is reported in *Hsin-shen-pao* but is not mentioned by Teng Chung-hsia.

94. Li Ta, in order to emphasize the strength and the dangers of regionalism among Chinese workers, gave a new twist to Marx's famous phrase by saying: "The workers have no country, not even a province."

95. Some indication of this is given by the extent of May Day activities in 1922, when a large meeting attended by workers' associations of all kinds was held in Shanghai (*PDR*, 2.v.22), a big workers' club was inaugurated at the Anyuan collieries (see p. 189

below), a mass meeting was held in Changsha, and there were demonstrations by rickshaw men in Hankow (*CWR*, 20.v.22), a meeting of students and workers in Nanchang (*CTSTL*, 1957, No. 4), and public meetings in Tsinan, Changsintien, Peking, and Tangshan (*MKJP*, 3.iv.22).

96. Some unions that were very hostile to the Communists, such as the Canton Mechanics' Union, withdrew from the Congress before it ended and later contested the validity of its decisions (Ma Ch'ao-chün, *Lao-tung yun-tung* [210], p. 201).

97. Chu represented the Chün-an Seamen's Guild at the Congress (Lei Chia [205], p. 31). It should be noted that the Labor Secretariat leaders in Hunan, Li Li-san, Mao Tse-tung, Liu Shao-ch'i, and Kuo Liang, seem to have taken very little interest in the Congress.

98. See p. 195 below.

99. *Chien-shih* [165], pp. 38–39.

100. In 1921–22 the Secretariat published *Lao-tung chou-k'an* ("Labor Weekly"), of which 18 numbers appeared (*Wu-ssu ch'i-k'an* [145] II, 92–98). *Kung-jen chou-k'an* ("Workers' Weekly"), founded at the beginning of 1922, was at first the organ of the Peking office of the Secretariat, and then became the main organ when the central office was transferred to Peking in June; it lasted until 1925 (*ibid.,* pp. 99–110). The Tsinan office published *Shan-tung lao-tung chou-k'an* ("The Shantung Labor Weekly") in 1922 (*ibid.,* pp. 111–16).

101. See Liu Shao-ch'i, *An-yuan chü-lo-pu* [160], p. 20.

102. *KMJP*, 28.x.54 (biography of Shih Yang).

103. Biography of Kuo Liang (*Hu-nan lieh-shih-chuan* [223], p. 42).

104. Li Jui, *Mao Tse-tung* [206], p. 206.

105. *Ibid.,* p. 208. For the rules of this union, see *Nien-chien* [138] II, 108.

106. *Chien-shih* [165], p. 39.

107. Li Jui, *Mao Tse-tung* [206], p. 212.

108. Among whom unions were formed in October 1922 (*CF*, 1.vii.23).

109. *Chien-shih* [165], p. 39.   110. *Ibid.,* pp. 15–16.

111. Liu Shao-ch'i [160], pp. 20–21.   112. Li Jui, *Mao Tse-tung* [206], p. 205.

113. This was why the railwaymen who were natives of Tientsin refused to take part in the general strike held throughout the network in the fall (*Nien-chien* [138] II, 313).

114. *CWR*, 12.viii.22, and *IS*, 1924, III, 394. See also *Chien-shih* [165], p. 39.

115. *CWR*, 21.x.22.

116. See Li Jui, *Mao Tse-tung* [206], p. 163.

117. *Chien-shih* [165], p. 40.

118. On this wave of strikes, see *Chien-shih*, pp. 24–32, and also *CWR*, *passim*. (The Hankow correspondent of this journal sent a great deal of information to Shanghai about the strikes.)

119. *CWR*, 14.x.22.

120. Li Jui, *Mao Tse-tung* [206], p. 184. According to Liu Shao-ch'i [160], p. 6, the Anyuan strike was also linked with the Hanyang steelworks strike.

121. On the demands presented during these various strikes, see Liu Shao-ch'i [160] for Anyuan; *HNLSTL*, 1958, No. 2, for Shuikowshan; *CWR*, 14.x.22, for the Yangtze Engineering Works; *RT*, 1922, Hankow, for the Hanyang arsenal and other factories in Wuhan; *Nien-chien* [138] II, 311–14, for the Yueh-Han line.

122. Sometimes it was the club or union in the enterprise concerned that negotiated a settlement; at other times, as with the strike of the B.A.T. Company's workers, it was the Provincial Federation.

123. This was the case at Anyuan, at the Hankow waterworks and electric power plant, and at Shuikowshan.

124. The strikes at the Hanyang steelworks and the Yangtze Engineering Works were in reply to attempts to close down the unions in these two works.

125. This was the demand of the Shuikowshan strikers.

126. *CWR*, 25.ix.22.   127. *CWR*, 9.xi.22.

128. Liu Shao-ch'i [160], p. 14.

129. See the biography of Kuo Liang [223], p. 43.

130. See Li Jui, *Mao Tse-tung* [206], p. 213.

131. On the question of the relations between the working class and the peasants, see Chapter X below.

132. As was mentioned above (p. 179), the strike on the Lunghai line at the end of 1921 was declared and led by the foremen, who were in conflict with the Franco-Belgian owners of the line (see *Chien-shih* [165], p. 40). *CWR*, 19.viii.22, reports a strike on the southern section of the Ching-Han line in August 1922, which was held in order to have three foremen reinstalled after their dismissal by a Belgian railway official.

133. On the political crisis of 1922 and the triumph of the Chihli faction, see Li Chien-nung, *Political History* [277], pp. 408–14.

134. See *CKKJ*, 27.iv.57, "Ko-ming lieh-shih Li Ta-chao."

135. According to Teng Chung-hsia (*Chien-shih* [165], p. 25), he had medals struck with his head on them, which he distributed to the railwaymen.

136. During the preceding years it had organized a number of training schools and mutual aid societies for the railwaymen, particularly on the Ching-Han line, which was the most important one from the political and military point of view. See Ch'i-wu lao-jen, *Erh-ch'i hui-i-lu* [51], p. 49.

137. *Ibid.*, p. 71, where the names of the secret inspectors and of the lines on which they operated are given. They were apparently students of Li Ta-chao. For the dealings between Li Ta-chao and Wu P'ei-fu, see also *CKKJ*, 27.iv.57, "Ko-ming lieh-shih Li Ta-chao."

138. *Chien-shih* [165], p. 107.

139. The cadres of the Labor Secretariat were prompt to make use both of the clubs controlled by foremen and of the pang-k'ou (the regional friendly societies) in order to make contact with the railwaymen. (See for instance Ch'i-wu lao-jen, "Erh-ch'i pa-kung hui-i," *HKC*, 1957, No. 3.) For example, they made their first contacts with the railwaymen of the stations on the central section of the Ching-Han line through a Kaifeng club controlled by foremen and through the pang-k'ou in the station at Chengchow.

140. *Chien-shih* [165], p. 40.

141. During the summer and fall of 1922 the Peking government (now in the hands of the Chihli faction) several times arrested members of the Communications Clique on the charge of having fomented strikes on the Ching-Han or Ching-Sui lines (*NCH*, 16.vii.22; *SCMP*, 17.xi.22).

142. *Chien-shih* [165], pp. 24–29. On these strikes, see also *Nien-chien* [138] II, 315 (the Shanhaikwan strike), p. 305 (the Ching-Sui strike), pp. 317–18 (the Tangshan strike).

143. *Chien-shih*, p. 41.

144. *CKKJ*, Nov. 1924, "Wo-men-ti li-liang."

145. On this strike, see *Nien-chien* [138] II, 302–4, and *Chien-shih* [165], pp. 81–83. See also K.M.A. Archives [15], document 14/2/13.

146. *Nien-chien*, II, 303. *MDN*, 10.xi.22, describes the K.M.A. Cantonese mechanics as being the most enlightened and progressive. Of the eight delegates who presented the demands at the beginning of the strike, four were turners and one was a smelter (K.M.A. Archives 14/2/13, report of the chief engineer dated 27.xi.22).

147. See K.M.A. Archives [15] 14/2/13, No. 229 (a letter from the Chihli police to the

company). The strikers, after their defeat, accused Yang I-te of having been given money by the K.M.A. to put down the strike (*JWC*, 9.xi.22).

148. The year 1922 was marked by the eviction of the Japanese from Shantung following upon British pressure brought to bear at the Washington Conference, and also by the eviction of the pro-Japanese Fengtien faction from Peking as a result of Wu P'ei-fu's spring offensive. See p. 191 above.

149. *Chien-shih* [165], p. 84.

150. Help came from the workers of Tangshan, in particular.

151. The students of the "University of Communications" in Tangshan made great efforts to collect and administer funds in aid of the strikers.

152. The Tangshan Chamber of Commerce contributed 50 yuan a day. See also *HT*, 15.xi.22, for the text of a declaration of solidarity with the strikers made by the Tangshan students.

153. Twenty thousand yuan were collected in Shanghai, 10,000 in Canton, 9,000 in Singapore, 16,000 in Peking and Tientsin (*Nien-chien* [138] II, 303). But the strike cost 5,000 yuan per day (*Chien-shih* [165], p. 83).

154. *Chien-shih*, pp. 23–24.

155. See Lei Chia, *Chu Pao-t'ing* [205]. Lin Wei-min became secretary-general of the branch (*SMCR*, 1922, p. 246A). See *Nien-chien* [138] II, 116–17, for the branch rules, which expressly stated that the Shanghai branch was under the control of the Hong Kong Federation, thereby reflecting the progress made in the idea of a labor organization on a national rather than on a local scale.

156. *NCH*, 12.viii.22 and 2.ix.22. The strike lasted 21 days, and won a raise in wages of 20 to 30 per cent and the right of the union to have a say in dismissals.

157. *PDR*, 22.v.22. Li Ch'i-han had been one of the organizers of the postal workers' strike in April (see the commemorative article on Li in *CKKJ*, 27.iv.57).

158. *PDR*, 20.iii.22. Li Ch'i-han was personally responsible for the formation of the Cotton Mills Union, and was present, together with Ch'en Tu-hsiu, at its inauguration. The Communist Tung Ch'u-p'ing was one of its main leaders.

159. *PDR*, 21.iv.22 (on the committee to aid the Pootung strikers).

160. During the summer and fall, the Shanghai Municipal Council formed an emergency plan in case a general strike similar to the Hong Kong strike in March should take place in Shanghai. A meeting was held on September 13, 1922, to discuss the arrangements that had been made for taking over essential services, arresting workers' leaders, prohibiting public meetings, and the like (Shanghai Municipal Council Archives [13], Nos. 28–79).

161. Ho Feng-lin was subordinate to Lu Yung-hsiang, the governor of Chekiang, who was one of the last members of the Anfu faction to hold power in the provinces after the fall of the Anfu government in Peking in 1920 (see Li Chien-nung, *Political History* [277], p. 424).

162. *PDR, passim.*

163. *SMCR*, 1922, p. 77A. See also *Chien-shih* [165], p. 36.

164. *CKKJ*, 27.iv.57 (commemorative article on Li Ch'i-han).

165. It was, for instance, the owners of the Japanese cotton mill in Pootung, where a strike was declared on May 20, who arranged for the leading union organizer in the mill to be arrested and brought before a Chinese court (*NCH*, 27.iii.22). See also the correspondence in July between Mackay, representing the big Western employers in Shanghai, and Liddell, the secretary of the Shanghai Municipal Council (Shanghai Municipal Council Archives [13]). Mackay complained that the strikes on Settlement territory were organized by troublemakers. Liddell agreed that the Pootung textile workers' union and the Chün-an Seamen's Guild contained troublemakers of this kind, but assured

him that the police of the International Settlement, the French Concession, and the Chinese city government had all cooperated in putting down the strikes at the Pootung cotton mills in April. See also Shanghai Municipal Council Archives, document 3192 (correspondence between the Naigai Wata Kaisha and the Shanghai Municipal Police concerning additional police protection in Hongkew on territory which the company was offering to cede). In 1922 the Mixed Court tried 64 persons for strike offenses, and sentenced 59 of them (*SMCR*, 1922, p. 77A).

166. *NCH*, 12.viii.22.

167. *NCH*, 7.x.22 and 25.xi.22. Recourse to ta-ch'ang was had again in December in another Pootung cotton mill, where several hundred women, protesting against fines that had been imposed, attacked an inspector and an engineer. Although they were held back for a while by water-hoses turned on them, the women finally wrecked the plant, the electric light bulbs, and the furnishings (*NCH*, 30.xii.22).

168. Cf. the letter of 2.v.22 sent by Lozovsky, the president of the Red International, to the workers of China: "The echoes of your recent struggles have reached our ears.... The Chinese and foreign capitalists work hand in hand against you.... The Red International urges all you Chinese workers to join the international family of the revolutionary proletariat." This letter was distributed in China by the Labor Secretariat (*PDR*, 7.vii.22).

169. The guilds had no intermediate body between the general membership and the managing committee (which was usually composed of twelve persons so as to facilitate monthly rotations in duty). See p. 114 above.

170. Neither in the old-style guilds nor in the pang was there any organization of the rank and file.

171. For examples of union rules, see *HNSTL*, 1958, No. 2, containing the rules of the Shuikowshan workers' club dealing with the formalities of becoming a member, the powers of the general assembly and of various committees, discipline, financial resources, and the internal functioning of various special departments (for education, training, pickets, mutual aid, recreation, and so on); and *Nien-chien* [138] II, 106, for the rules of the Yueh-Han club. See also *Chien-shih* [165], p. 41, for general remarks about the rather artificial nature of these rules, and the proposed rules for the amalgamated Ching-Han union (pp. 86ff).

172. See p. 189 above.　　　　　　　　　173. *Rabochii Kitai* [181], p. 105.

174. *Chien-shih* [165], pp. 41–42.

175. *Hu-nan lieh-shih-chuan* [223], pp. 113–14.

176. Li Jui, *Mao Tse-tung* [206], pp. 212–15.

177. See p. 194 above.

178. Ch'i-wu lao-jen, "Erh-ch'i pa-kung," *HKC*, 1957, No. 3.

179. See p. 188 above.

180. Lin Yü-nan, who was secretary of the amalgamated Ching-Han union at the time of the February 7 incident, had earlier belonged to the anarchist "Communal Life Society" in Wuhan (Ch'i-wu lao-jen, "Erh-ch'i pa-kung," p. 9).

181. See the remarks of T. C. Woo, who was a member of the left wing of the Kuomintang, on the ardor and devotion shown by these young Communist students (*The Kuomintang and the Future of the Chinese Revolution* [168], pp. 142–44). The various collections of biographies show that in fact many of them died young from illness of some kind—probably tuberculosis.

182. A rare exception was a worker in the Hankow cotton mills named Hsiang Ying, who had been at school until the age of 15, and who became secretary of the Kiangan railwaymen's club in 1922 at the suggestion of the Secretariat (*HKC*, 1957, No. 3).

183. *Chien-shih* [165], p. 42.

184. Teng Chung-hsia ("Wo-men-ti li-liang," *CKKJ*, 1924, No. 2) estimates that 270,000 workers belonged to unions, but he includes moderate unions such as the corporate associations of Canton and Hong Kong (with 50,000 members), seamen's associations (45,000 members), and various "miscellaneous" associations (30,000 members).

185. See p. 186 above on the May 1 number of *HC*. The second CCP conference, in June 1922, also planned a campaign for labor legislation (see Brandt and others, *Documentary History* [133], pp. 63ff, and Hu Hua, *Chung-kuo ko-ming shih chiang-i* [200], p. 67).

186. On the return to Peking of the former president and of the Old Parliament, see Li Chien-nung, *Political History* [277], p. 420.

187. As already mentioned (p. 192 above), his "four points" included "the protection of labor."

188. See *Nien-chien* [138] II, 436–38, for the text of this program.

189. Wieger, *La Chine moderne* [139] II, 438.

190. *Nien-chien* [138] II, 438.　　　191. *Chien-shih* [165], p. 78.

192. Wieger [139], p. 438.　　　193. *Chien-shih* [165], p. 78.

194. *CWR*, 21.x.22.　　　195. *NCH*, 16.ix.22.

196. Kotenev, *Shanghai, Its Municipality* [156], p. 10.

197. *NCH*, 19.viii.22.

198. Teng Chung-hsia (*Chien-shih* [165], p. 78) mentions contacts between the Secretariat and certain "politicians." In September several members of the Peking parliament brought in a bill for the protection of workers, which included some of the proposals of the Secretariat. This bill, which was never passed, may well have been the outcome of the contacts mentioned by Teng. (See *IS*, 24.xi.22, quoting a Japanese journal.)

199. *Chien-shih*, p. 78.

200. As does, for instance, Ma Ch'ao-chün, the former leader of the Canton Mechanics' Union, who does not even mention Teng Chung-hsia when describing the founding of the Changsintien railwaymen's club, and makes no reference to the clubs and unions organized by the Secretariat in Central China in 1922 (*Lao-tung yun-tung* [210], pp. 170 and 208–39).

201. Ch'ü Ch'iu-pai, "Pei-ching cheng-pien hou ti chieh-chi," *CKKJ*, April 1925.

202. See the list of 47 "unions," most of which were semi-working-class associations, in *CEB*, 11.iii.22. Also included are mixed guilds such as the Sugar Guild and the Rickshaw Guild, trade associations (for tailors, laundrymen, tinsmiths), and a very small number of labor organizations for industrial workers, such as the Pootung textile workers' union (which was not yet dissolved) and the printers' and mechanics' unions (formed in 1920).

203. *PDR*, 2.ii.22.　　　204. *PDR*, 20.iv.22 and the following days.

205. *MKJP*, 2.v.22.　　　206. *PDR*, 2.viii.22.

207. *PDR*, 11.ix.22.

208. The postal worker Hsü Hsi-lin, who played an active part in these associations, was reported in June to be one of the leaders of the Pootung textile workers' union (*PDR*, 3.vi.22).

209. *PDR*, 6.x.22 and 6.xi.22.

210. *PDR*, 1.xii.22.

211. When this society was first formed, it organized the strike in the silk-reeling factories in August (*IS*, 6.x.22). Later, after being dissolved by the police, it came under the control of Mrs. Mu Chih-ying, one of the leading moderates (*PDR*, 11.x.22).

212. *PDR*, 11.ix.22. An association with a similar name is mentioned in a report of the May Day celebrations (*MKJP*, 2.v.22).

213. *PDR*, 4.x.22.

214. It took part in the May Day celebrations (*MKJP*, 2.v.22), and in those held on October 10 (*PDR*, 11.x.22).

215. *PDR*, 1922, *passim*.

216. *MKJP*, 24.vii.24.

217. *PDR*, 1922, *passim*.

218. See p. 173 above.

219. *PDR*, 1922, *passim*.

220. I have had to use the transcription of this name as it appears in the *PDR*, because I have been unable to identify the person referred to in any Chinese sources.

221. See Willoughby, *China at the Conference* [316]. On the feelings aroused in China at this time, see *CWR*, 1921, *passim*, and Wieger, *La Chine moderne* [139] IV, 375.

222. See Wieger, *ibid.*, and *CWR*, 24.xii.21 (on a procession of workers and students).

223. At one Peking meeting, held on December 27, 1921, by 37 associations of the city, a Ching-Feng railwayman proposed placing mourning flags and banners on railway engines (*CWR*, 7.i.22).

224. The Hunan Workingmen's Association, shortly before its dissolution, organized a big procession on December 25, in which 10,000 took part, to demand the return of Shantung (*CWR*, 14.i.22).

225. The coolies of Chungking boycotted Japanese goods (*RT*, 1922, Chungking, p. 9), as did those of Chengtu (Hewlett, *Forty Years in China* [44], p. 132).

226. This lack of enthusiasm on the part of the Secretariat cannot, it seems to me, be entirely explained by the inadequate means at its disposal or the restricted number of its correspondents. The fact is that the Chinese Communists, like the Soviet Union, did not expect very much from a conference dominated by "bourgeois" Powers. Cf. the article on the conference in the sixth and last number of *KCT*, the organ of the Shanghai Communist group before the party was founded, which ends: "Chinese brothers, do not let us hope for too much from the Conference on Pacific Affairs; long live the social revolution!"

227. *SP*, 9.xii.21.

228. Wieger, *La Chine moderne* [139] IV, 368. See also *PDR*, 9.viii.22, which reports that the demonstration was a failure.

229. *PDR*, 5.v.22 and 19–26.vi.22. On the Macao affair, see pp. 203–4 below.

230. *PDR*, 22.ix.22.

231. *PDR*, 11.x.22.

232. The Cantonese correspondent of the Communist journal *HT* (1.xii.22) distinguished five groups (*p'ai*) at this time in the Cantonese labor movement: the mechanics, the conservative provincial federation, the mutual benefit society run by the politician Hsieh Ying-po, the Workers' Cooperative Society, and the anarchists. The fourth of these was of no importance, but the first and the third had close links with Sun Yat-sen and the Kuomintang.

233. *SCMP*, 16.xii.22.

234. See *Nien-chien* [138] II, 73–79, for a list of the most important of these associations.

235. *Ibid.* (where the distinction is made between teahouses proper, teahouses where wine was served, and those where noodles were served).

236. *NCH*, 29.iv.22 (building carpenters, furniture makers, and woodcarvers).

237. *Nien-chien* [138] II, 73–79.

238. *SCMP*, 27.iii.22.

239. This federation was formed in spring 1922 (Ma Ch'ao-chün [209], p. 95).

240. *SCMP*, 22.i.23.

241. *SCMP*, 5.v.23. About 40 craft guilds belonged to this federation (*Chien-shih* [165], p. 223).

242. *SCMP*, 3.vii.23. This guild included both journeymen and entrepreneurs in its membership.

243. This was the aim of the strike held by the tramway conductors of Hong Kong (*SCMP*, 30.iii.22), and of the tugboat seamen's strike (*ibid.*, 23.v.22).

244. In September 1922 the Mechanics' Union settled a dispute with a British firm in Hong Kong concerning the reinstatement of a dismissed worker, without going on strike, and also put a stop to "unofficial" sympathy strikes (*SCMP*, 8.ix.21). The provincial federation often played the role of mediator, for instance in the tugboat-men's strike in April 1922 (*SCMP*, 13.iv.22).

245. *SCMP*, 22.iv.21. The book-trade union had plans for creating a printing cooperative, and bought machines for this purpose.

246. *SCMP*, 20.x.22 (on restaurants), and 2.xi.22 (on watchmakers). Attempts of this kind were seldom made in the centers of heavy industry, but during the "three-cornered" strike in October 1922 (see p. 195 above) the Shanghai jewelers and goldsmiths tried out a plan for setting up a cooperative workshop with the modest capital of 2,000 ten-yuan shares (*NCH*, 21.x.22).

247. See p. 186 above.

248. Hsieh Ying-po, in an interview given to the *SCMP* (10.iii.22), posed as a revolutionary trade unionist; he had portraits of Liebknecht and Rosa Luxemburg in his office and spoke of the imminence of a world proletarian revolution. In fact, the activities of his mutual benefit society were of a very moderate kind; its 50,000 members each paid 30 cents per month into a fund for sickness benefits for workers and their families.

249. On these events see Li Chien-nung, *Political History* [277], p. 418.

250. Ch'en's choice for the post of provincial governor after the eviction of the Kuomintang shows how close his ties were with the moderate bourgeoisie in the South. The man he appointed was described in *SCMP*, 30.viii.22, as "a Chinese merchant prince," and was the brother of the head compradore of the British Douglas Steamship Co. in Hong Kong. Ch'en received a large loan from Hong Kong after his coup (*CWR*, 28.x.22, "The British Loan to Canton").

251. *SCMP*, 24.vii.22.

252. They protested, for instance, against the projected British loan to Ch'en Chiung-ming (*ibid.*, 2.x.22) and against various restrictions on civil liberties (*ibid.*, 21.x.22).

253. *SCMP*, 20.vi.23 and 15.vii.22. The federation declared that the guilds under its control would not become involved in politics.

254. *SCMP*, 11.x.22.

255. *Chien-shih* [165], p. 37.

256. For instance, when the nightsoil-collectors' union went on strike in December 1922 Ch'en had its leaders arrested (*SCMP*, 8.xii.22). Actually repression of strikes had already begun in Canton shortly before the fall of Sun Yat-sen in June. When the salt workers went on strike in May, Wu T'ing-fang, the civil governor of Kwangtung, used force to close down their union and ordered many of them to leave the city (*SCMP*, 21–29.v.22; *Chien-shih*, p. 37). Apparently the conservative forces that were to bring Ch'en to power were already in control in Canton when Sun was at the northern front, and the eighty-year-old Wu T'ing-fang's position was a purely nominal one.

257. See *HT*, 23.xii.22, and *SCMP*, 6.xi.22.

258. *Chien-shih* [165], p. 38.

259. Ma Ch'ao-chün [210], pp. 198–99.

260. *Ibid.*, pp. 200–201. See also *Chien-shih* [165], p. 41.

261. *Ko-ming chan-shih-chi* [178], p. 233.

262. *SCMP*, 31.v.22 to 15.vi.22, *passim*; *Chien-shih* [165], p. 37.

263. *SCMP*, 10.ii.23. Much to the annoyance of the other guilds, the powerful Mechanics' Union negotiated a separate settlement with the Portuguese a few days earlier on behalf of members that were involved in the affair (*SCMP*, 1.ii.23).

264. *CWR*, 11.iii.22.
265. See note 160, p. 485.
266. On anti-Christian propaganda in China in 1920–21, see Wieger, *La Chine moderne* [139] III, items 1 to 33.
267. See *CWR*, 6.v.22 (report of the missionary C. F. Remer to the National Christian Council, in which he warned against the danger that the Chinese labor movement might follow the same path as that taken in the West, and maintained that owing to the ignorance of the Chinese workers, this would have far more serious effects).
268. The supercilious and uncharitable tone adopted by Father Wieger in *La Chine moderne* [139] is typical (e.g., III, 438–39 on the K.M.A. strike in October 1922, or IV, 441–43, on the January 17 incident and the execution of Huang and P'ang). See also the Henry report [10], Part IV, Appendix 1, containing a recorded conversation between Paul Henry, sent by the I.L.O. to China in 1924, and Father Robert, procurator for the Foreign Missions and the chief financial expert among the Catholic missionaries. Henry reports: "We had a long talk about Chinese workers. He [i.e. Father Robert] thinks that they are much lazier than they used to be, and puts a large part of the blame on the foreigners who have tried so hard to introduce trade unionism. With the old guilds everything went quite smoothly. The workers were members of the guilds, but only the employers had a say."
269. See Porter, *China's Challenge to Christianity* [162], pp. 57ff. I was unable to find any documentary material sent in by these "industrial secretaries" at the international headquarters of the Y.M.C.A. in Geneva. Their surveys would be of great value, judging from the survey made by the industrial secretary in Chefoo that was incorporated in the British consular reports of 1924 [20], pp. 34–39.
270. On the formation of this organization and its political context, see Varg, *Missionaries* [310], chaps. 11 and 12.
271. *CWR*, 6.v.22, gives a summary of this report.
272. For instance, in December 1922 Dr. Eddy spoke before the Chinese Chamber of Commerce of Shanghai, informing them of the three points adopted in May by the National Christian Council (*NCH*, 2.xii.22). See also Wieger, *La Chine moderne* [139] IV, 434–38 (Dr. Eddy's account of his visits to factories). Dr. Eddy devotes a chapter to China in his *The New World of Labor* [61].
273. Porter, *China's Challenge to Christianity* [162].
274. *CWR*, 22.x.21 and 2.ii.22.
275. *Chien-shih* [165], p. 19. The Y.M.C.A. in Canton also tried to be accepted as mediator in the Hong Kong seamen's strike (*SCMP*, 6.ii.22).
276. Chen Ta, "Labor Unrest in China," *MLR*, Aug. 1921.
277. Decker, "Industrial Hospital, Shanghai," *CMMJ*, March 1924.
278. Henry report [10], Part IV, Appendix 1.
279. *Modern Industry in China* [179].
280. This hospital was opened in 1922. See Ch'en Ta, *Lao-tung wen-t'i* [190], p. 49.
281. *NCH*, 18.xi.22. See also the B.A.T. record [182].
282. Hong Kong Government, *Ordinances* [26], 1922, No. 22. Text given in Anderson, *Humanity and Labour* [56], pp. 267–71.
283. See Hong Kong Government, *Administrative Reports* [23], 1923, C 13, in which it is announced that measures had been taken to control and regulate the employment of children for work (such as garbage disposal and carrying bricks up to the Peak district) that was open to view and liable to cause concern among residents and visitors.
284. *Chien-shih* [165], p. 91. Teng Chung-hsia estimates that the raise in wages obtained by the railwaymen as a result of this strike cost the mine seven or eight thousand yuan extra per annum.

285. *Chien-shih*, p. 91.

286. The military government of Hupeh (which had links with the Chihli faction) had already brought in troops against the Yueh-Han strikers (see pp. 190–91 above).

287. *FER*, Feb. 1923, "Labor Unrest in China"; *NCH*, 13.i.23.

288. *SCMP*, 12.i.23.

289. *CWR*, 20.i.23.

290. *JWC*, 1.ii.23, and *CWR*, 3.ii.23.

291. See *FER*, Feb. 1923, for the settlement of the British Cigarette Co. strike, and *JWC*, 8.ii.23, for the Mackenzie & Co. strike.

292. Quoted by *JWC*, 8.ii.23.

293. For the Ching-Han affair as a whole, see *Chien-shih* [165], pp. 85–107; *CTSTL*, 1955, No. 1; and *HKC*, 1957, Nos. 2, 3 and 4. The author of the last, whose pseudonym is Ch'i-wu lao-jen, has published his recollections in a more extended form [51]. See also *Ching-Han kung-jen liu-hsüeh-chi* [173]. The accounts given by the Western press (e.g., *SCMP*, 19.ii.23) more or less tally with those given by the various Chinese sources.

294. Text in *Chien-shih*, pp. 86–90.

295. Mif, *Pour une Chine forte et libre* [290], p. 20. It would be interesting to know whether only local questions were discussed at this meeting, as seems to be indicated by the people who attended it, or whether it decided upon the general line to be taken toward the Ching-Han strike as a whole, in which case the decisions taken must have been communicated to Wu P'ei-fu.

296. On these sympathy strikes, see in particular *CTSTL*, 1955, No. 1.

297. *PDR*, 12.ii.23. 298. *Chien-shih* [165], p. 104.

299. *PDR*, 13.ii.23 and 22.ii.23. 300. Text of the message in *HT*, 27.ii.23.

301. See *CTSTL*, 1955, No. 1, for texts of various messages and protests.

302. *NCH*, 13.ii.23.

303. These feelings were even echoed in the Peking Parliament, despite its close ties with the Chihli faction. On February 12 a group of members tabled a motion asking the government to forbid the use of troops in labor conflicts, to recognize the rights of trade unions, to compensate the families of the victims, and so on (*NCH*, 17.ii.23).

304. On this attempt at self-criticism see *Chien-shih* [165], pp. 104–5.

Chapter IX

1. No general study has yet been made of Chinese warlordism at this time and of its social and political significance. For some introductory remarks on the subject, see Chesneaux, *Le phénomène du militarisme chinois* [240]. For a chronological account of events, see Li Chien-nung, *Political History* [277], and T'ao Chü-yin, *Pei-yang chün-fa* [212]. See also Wieger, *La Chine moderne* [139], "éphémérides" (especially Vols. IV and V).

2. *MDN*, 5.v.23 and 24.viii.24.

3. *CWR*, 7.iv.23, and *Nien-chien* [138] II, 197.

4. *Nien-chien*, II, 197.

5. *IS*, 1924, III, 193, and *CEB*, 1.xi.24 (following these two strikes respectively 9 and 18 "ringleaders" were imprisoned).

6. *CWR*, 22.viii.23. 7. *NCH*, 11.vii.24.

8. *CEB*, 30.viii.24.

9. *CWR*, 24.iii.23 (arrest of a worker who had distributed leaflets at the Hanyang steelworks). See also *CWR*, 7.vi.24 (arrest of six "agitators" who were deported to Loyang).

10. *CWR*, 8.xi.24. Because the seamen were particularly affected by this measure, their union protested in a communication to the press.

11. On the policy of Chao Heng-t'i, see *Chien-shih* [165], p. 109.

12. *NCH*, 30.vi.23; *Chien-shih*, p. 109. The lease of the two above-mentioned Japanese Treaty Ports was due to expire in 1923, and demonstrations of all kinds were being held in China to pressure the Chinese government into refusing to renew the lease.

13. *CWR*, 12.vii.24. Repressive measures had already been taken against this club at the end of 1923 (*HT*, 29.xii.23).

14. See *CKKJ*, Oct. 1924, "Chao Heng-t'i." For comments on this trade union law see *CKKJ*, Nov. 1924, "Fan-tui kao-kung-hsi pao-pan kung-hui."

15. *Ibid*. Several former comrades of Huang and P'ang assisted Chao in re-forming the association.

16. See Chapter X below.   17. See p. 221 below.

18. See Chapter X below.

19. Ts'ao K'un's brother Ts'ao Jui, the governor of Chihli, became the owner of a cotton mill in Tientsin in 1921 (*FER*, Oct. 1921). Wu P'ei-fu acquired the four textile mills in Wuchang as a personal investment in 1922 (*CWR*, 8.vii.22). Chang Tso-lin and his group owned oil mills in Yingkow (*MDN*, 6.v.23), wool and cotton factories in Mukden (*MDN*, 13.v.25), and so on.

20. During the war between Hupeh and Hunan in 1920 the railwaymen on the Yueh-Han line fled, leaving the soldiers to run the trains themselves, to the great detriment of the rolling stock (*CWR*, 17.vii.20).

21. See the account given by the British consul in Chungking of the requisitioning of coolies; the coolies were marched through the city roped together (*Labour Conditions* [20], p. 42).

22. *MDN*, 15.viii.23, and *CWR*, 12.iv.24 (on the embargo placed by Wu P'ei-fu on travel by coolies between Shantung and Dairen); *CEB*, 7.ii.25 (an account of some workers from Nanking who were requisitioned during the Chekiang-Kiangsu war in 1924 and who lost their jobs on their return).

23. See *RT*, 1921, Shasi, p. 9, and Ichang, p. 11 (on the scarcity of labor in the Upper Yangtze valley during the war between Wu P'ei-fu and the petty warlords of Szechwan); *RT*, 1924, Newchwang, p. 1 (on the scarcity of labor in Yingkow during the second Chihli-Fengtien war); *SCMP*, 4.ii.25 (concerning the protest of the Shanghai Chinese Chamber of Commerce against militarist requisitioning of labor).

24. Such a shortage hit the Hankow metalworkers in 1924 (*CEB*, 13.xii.24).

25. The Tientsin cotton mills were affected during the second Fengtien-Chihli war in 1924, when the Ching-Han line, by which coal from the K.M.A. was transported, was cut (*CKKJ*, Nov. 1924, "Chan chih hou-tz'u").

26. This happened in the flour mills in the Lower Yangtze valley in 1924 (*RT*, 1924, Chenkiang, p. 1), and the Shanghai silk-reeling factories (*CKKJ*, *ibid*.).

27. *CKKJ*, *ibid*.

28. There is no good general study of the crisis in Chinese industry during the years 1922–25.

29. See Chesneaux, *Aspects économiques* [241]. See also *CWR*, 23.xii.22, "The Cause for the High Price of Cotton"; in 1923 the Chinese-owned cotton mills in Shanghai were operating at a loss; the price of cotton rose from 24 to 28 taels a picul between 1922 and 1923, and the price of yarn fell from 153 to 127 taels between July 1921 and October 1922.

30. In 1919 China exported wheat and imported only 272,000 tons of flour; but in 1923 it imported 2.225 million tons of wheat, and in 1922, 3.6 million tons of flour (*CEB*, 15.iii.24).

31. The Hanyehping Co. lost 3.5 million yuan in 1922 and three million in 1923 (*CEB*, 17.i.25); because of the 1913 contract it was obliged to sell below cost (*CWR*, 10.iv.23).

32. *CWR*, 16.xii.22.

33. *CEB*, 14.iv.23.

34. *CWR*, 16.v.25 (Hankow); *RT*, 1924, Hangchow, p. 3 (1,200 workers laid off in a mill employing 2,600); *CEB*, 22.xi.24 (in Chengchow 4,000 out of 5,000 workers laid off); *CEB*, 27.ix.24 (Changsha).

35. *RT*, 1923, Wuhu, p. 4; *RT*, 1923, Ningpo, p. 3; *CEB*, 19.vii.24 (Wuhan).

36. The mill at Soochow (*RT*, 1923, Soochow), one at Wuhan (*CEB*, 25.x.24), one at Nantung (*CEB*, 24.i.25), one at Hangchow (*RT*, 1924, Hangchow, p. 3), the mill at Chengchow (*CEB*, 9.v.24), and the mill at Changsha (*CEB*, 24.i.25). During the summer of 1924 almost a million spindles in China were idle—i.e. about a third of the total number (*CEB*, 4.x.24).

37. *Foreign Trade of China* [28], 1924, p. 3. In 1923, 43 of the 61 Chinese-owned oil mills in Dairen were closed (*MDN*, 30.vi.23).

38. *RT*, 1922, Kiukiang, p. 12; *CEB*, 8.iii.24 (Wusih); *CEB*, 28.iii.24 (Soochow).

39. There were 20,000 to 30,000 unemployed in the silk-producing area of Shunteh (*SCMP*, 23.iv.24).

40. *CWR*, 10.iv.23 (Hanyang), and 16.v.25 (Yangtze Engineering Works).

41. *CEB*, 26.vii.24 (the wages were reduced from 45 cents a day in 1923 to 38 cents in 1924).

42. *PDR*, 13.ii.24.

43. *SCMP*, 12.iii.25 (Shunteh), and Ch'en Ta, *Lao-tung wen-t'i* [190], p. 177. In February 1925 the wages of the Hangchow weavers fell from 0.9 yuan a day to 0.7 yuan. See also *CEB*, 7.iii.25 (concerning the Hangchow silk weavers).

44. *NCH*, 23.vi.23.

45. *CWR*, 12.vii.24. The percentage of pure metal, on which the rate paid for a basket of ore was based, was raised.

46. *Nien-chien* [138] II, 161 (the Jih-hua cotton mill in Pootung).

47. The silk weavers of Nanking went on strike in May 1922 in order to obtain payment of wages in silver cents instead of copper cash (*RT*, 1922, Nanking, p. 9).

48. See Henry report [10], *passim*. In Shansi in 1923 a one-yuan piece was worth 2,052 cash, but one yuan in silver cents was worth only 1,786 cash.

49. In 1925 a silver yuan was worth 3,000 cash in Hupeh paper money (*RT*, 1925, Shasi, p. 3).

50. The amount circulating in notes in the Northeast was 17 million in 1917, 36 million in 1922, 51 million in March 1924, and 223 million in November 1924 after the war with the Chihli faction (*CEJ*, March 1927). The Fengtien paper yuan, known as the *feng-p'iao*, was theoretically at par with the Chinese silver yuan, but in 1924, 100 silver yuan were worth 194 to 305 feng-p'iao (*RT*, 1925, Mukden, p. 1), and this depreciation increased during 1925–26.

51. *CWR*, 28.i.28 (Canton government statistics).

52. Hwang, "Coal Mining in China," *CEJ*, April 1933.

53. *Nien-chien* [138] I, 216 (for 1920), and *CEB*, 18.iv.25 (for 1925).

54. *CEB*, 30.v.25.

55. The part played by factors such as warlordism and foreign dominance in the realignment of social and political forces in China in 1924–25 will be examined in greater detail in Chapter X below.

56. See Lin Sung-ho, *Factory Workers in Tangku* [74], p. 20. The number of workers there who sent for their families increased from 70 to 136 (out of a total of over 500) during the winter of 1926 alone, a trend that had begun in 1923. The author concludes that this was not a sign of prosperity.

57. On these three disasters, see the commemorative editorial in *HT*, 26.iii.24.

58. *Nien-chien* [138] II, 154–282. The Northeast region is not included in the list given here, but there were not many strikes in foreign enterprises there either.

59. *Ibid., passim*.

60. Disputes arose in a Hankow cotton-baling factory in October 1924, between natives of Hupeh and natives of Hunan (*Nien-chien*, II, 162), and in a Shanghai cotton mill in April 1923 between natives of Shanghai and natives of Canton (*NCH*, 25.iv.23).

61. For example, the Hankow rickshaw men protested in September 1924 against the opening of a bus route (*Nien-chien*, II, 197).

62. The positions won in the matter of recruitment were lost again. Among the seamen the hsi-ma-sha recruiting agents, whose power had been undermined by the 1922 strike, now regained it (I Pin, *Hsiang-kang hai-yuan ta-pa-kung* [203], p. 42).

63. This occurred in a Shanghai silk factory (*NCH*, 23.vi.23), in the Hunan manganese mines (*CWR*, 12.vii.24), and in the Nanyang factory in Pootung in September 1924 (*HT*, 17 and 24.ix.24).

64. The workers in the Tunghsing cotton mill asked for a hua-li in March 1923, the Soochow silk weavers in June 1923 (*Nien-chien* [138] II, 154–282, *passim*), the workers in the Yingkow oil mills in April 1923, and the workers in various Japanese factories in Mukden in June 1923 and May 1924 (*MDN, passim*).

65. *Nien-chien, ibid.* On the Nanyang strike see also *CKKJ*, Nov. 1924, "Nan-yang yen-ts'ao pa-kung," and *Nan-yang hsiung-ti shih-liao* [143], pp. 328–47.

66. *MDN*, 1.vi.23.   67. *MDN*, 26.vi.23.

68. *MDN*, May–June 1924, *passim*.   69. *Chien-shih* [165], p. 106.

70. It was probably the Labor Secretariat that in the spring of 1923 published in Peking the anonymous work commemorating the massacre (*Ching-Han kung-jen liu-hsüeh-chi* [173]).

71. See for instance the editorial of *HT*, 20.xi.22, entitled "The Awakening of the Chinese Working-Class Masses," which declared: "The workers in our modern industries are already awakened; they are no longer the passive slaves they used to be. . . . The workers are a new force in Chinese society, and will have a very important position in it in the future."

72. *HT*, 11.vi.24.

73. *CF*, 1.xii.23, "Chung-kuo kuo-min ko-ming."

74. *Chien-shih* [165], pp. 112–13.

75. On the formation of the alliance between the Communists and the Kuomintang, see Chapter X below.

76. *Ching-Han kung-jen* [173], pp. 185–88: "The workers need a political party."

77. See Chapter X below.   78. *Chien-shih* [165], p. 121.

79. *HT*, 17.x.23.   80. On this incident see p. 213 above.

81. According to *CKKJ*, Oct. 1924 ("Chao Heng-t'i"), 29,000 of the members belonged to industrial workers' unions and 22,000 to craft unions.

82. See a list of these unions in *CF*, 1.vii.23 ("Sheng-hsien-hsia-ti Hu-nan").

83. *CEB*, 1.vii.23.

84. See *Chien-shih* [165], pp. 109–11. See also Liu Shao-ch'i, *An-yuan chü-lo-pu* [160], pp. 23–24, and *Hung-se-ti An-yuan* [52], *passim*. The last work contains many old workers' recollections of the period.

85. The fact that in 1923–24 the Hanyehping Company was in serious economic difficulties may have had something to do with the success of the Anyuan workers' club during this period.

86. *Chien-shih* [165], p. 116.   87. Text in *Nien-chien* [138] II, 102–6.

88. *Chien-shih* [165], pp. 117–19.   89. *Ibid.*, p. 67.

90. *PDR*, 14.v.24.

91. See a discussion between Teng Chung-hsia and Lin Wei-min on the situation in the Seamen's Union and the possibilities of improving it, in *CKKJ*, Oct. 1924 ("Hai-yuan hsuan-ch'uan wen-t'i").

92. *Chien-shih* [165], p. 121.

93. *Ibid.*, p. 136.

94. See Li Li-san, "Tao Hsiang Ching-yü t'ung-chih" (*HCPP*, 15.xii.57).

95. See *CKKJ*, Oct. 1924 ("Shan-tung Lu-ta"). According to the correspondent of this journal, the miners of Tzechwan tried to form a society for technical studies for workers (from which foremen were excluded) in April 1924. The society soon found it necessary to make certain demands, whereupon the Lu-ta Company that owned the mine quickly had it dissolved by the police.

96. *Labour Conditions* [20], p. 42. The union referred to in this report is probably the one that was banned by Yang Sen in the summer of 1924 (*CEB*, 30.viii.24).

97. *CTSTL*, 1957, No. 4, "Nan-ch'ang ta-shih-chi."

98. On these associations see pp. 159–62 above.

99. Founded in spring 1920 (*MKJP*, 7.iv.20).

100. These included groups such as the workers' clubs of the Commercial Press, the China Bookshop, and the Wen-ming Publishing Company (*MKJP*, 24.vii.24).

101. See *MKJP*, 15–24.vii.24 (reports on various workers' groups).

102. Ma Ch'ao-chün, *Lao-tung yun-tung* [209], p. 98.

103. *MKJP*, 24.vii.24.

104. *Shang-hai ch'an-yeh* [194], p. 482.

105. For examples of plural officeholding, see notes 80 and 114, pp. 474 and 475 above.

106. On these early efforts, see Ma Ch'ao-chün [209], p. 98.

107. *PDR*, 2.iv.23.

108. *PDR*, 11.iv.24. Ma Ch'ao-chün [209], p. 98, places its official foundation in August.

109. *MKJP*, 19.vii.24. The last resulted from a split in the former Electrical Industries Federation, founded in 1920. Some of its members who did not wish to remain in the same association as their employers formed their own "Association of Comrades for the Promotion of Electricity."

110. See Henry report [10], Part III, Appendix 3, for Henry's account of the first anniversary of this club in November 1924, which he attended. The club's meeting place was provided by the factory, which also gave a subsidy of 300 yuan per month; a further 300 yuan per month came from a monthly deduction of 10 cents from the wages of the club's members (numbering 3,000 out of a total of 6,000 workers employed).

111. The meeting place of this "Association for the Moral Improvement of the Workmen of the China Bookshop" was in the firm's offices (*MKJP*, 24.vii.24), and this was also the case with the Commercial Press club.

112. *MKJP*, 2.v.24.

113. See for example the rules of the Electrical Workers' Union (*Labour Conditions* [20], p. 92), the Mechanics' Union (*Nien-chien* [138] II, 53–56), and the Boatmen's and Warehousemen's Federation (*ibid.*, pp. 57–60). It should be remembered that the Labor Congress of May 1922 passed a special resolution on the need for organizing sympathetic strikes.

114. *Nien-chien*, II, 8.

115. *HCPP*, No. 8 ("I Ch'iu Pai").

116. *HT*, 1.x.24. Before the strike, however, certain elements among the membership had managed to get rid of the former leaders, who consisted of cadres and skilled workers (see *CKKJ*, Nov. 1924, "Nan-yang yen-ts'ao pa-kung"). The president of the club whom P. Henry met in November 1924 had just taken up office, his predecessor having been dismissed after the strike.

117. See a letter signed by 17 leaders of the rickshaw men's union (Shanghai Municipal Council Archives, document 1484, Part III).

118. *PDR*, 31.iii.24. A little later the Ningpo Guild also created a workers' savings bank (*CEB*, 24.i.25).

119. *Nien-chien* [138] II, 57–60. The Nanyang club also ran a life insurance plan (Henry report [10], Part III, Appendix 3).

120. *MKJP*, 27.vii.24. 121. *Nien-chien*, II, 53–56.

122. *Labour Conditions* [20], p. 92.

123. *PDR*, 28.i.24. The Kuomintang Congress of 1924 did the same (see p. 245 below).

124. *HT*, 31.xii.24, accused Chang Te-hui and Yuan Cheng-hao, former leaders of the Ching-Han union who had gone over to the moderates after February 7, of denouncing the Communists to the French police in Tientsin.

125. The militant Communist Hsiang Ching-yü was trying to fight the influence of Mrs. Mu Chih-ying in Chapei (*HCPP*, No. 8).

126. *MKJP*, 2.v.24.

127. *Nien-chien* [138] II, 8.

128. In 1923–24 Sun Yat-sen and the Kuomintang maintained good relations with the remaining members of the Anfu faction (still in control of Chekiang), and with Chang Tso-lin, in their common enmity toward the Chihli group (see p. 253 below).

129. *PDR*, 26.vi.23, 6.x.23, 11.v.23 (concerning demonstrations of the moderate associations of Shanghai against the election of Ts'ao K'un as President of the Republic).

130. *PDR*, 2.v.23.

131. *PDR*, 2.v.24. See also Anderson, *Humanity and Labour* [56], pp. 177ff. On the failure of Dame Adelaide Anderson's mission to China see p. 229 below.

132. On the crisis in the leadership of the Seamen's Union in 1923–24 see pp. 221–22 above.

133. The printing workers' associations, in many of which the old guild attitudes persisted, made an important advance in the fall of 1924 with the formation of the Shanghai Printing Workers' Federation, which included in its membership all categories of printing workers employed in all the leading firms. At first it was affiliated with the Federation, but it became very active during the big strikes in the summer of 1925 (*Shang-hai ch'an-yeh* [194], p. 482).

134. Ma Ch'ao-chün [209], pp. 98–99.

135. See *CKKJ*, 12.v.57 ("Hui-i Li Ta-chao t'ung-chih"), where it is stated that Chang Te-hui and Chang Lien-kuang, two of the Ching-Han trade unionists who had been given the task of collecting funds for the victims of February 7, made off with the money in order to rally a following of *kung-tsei* ("union brigands") in Shanghai.

136. In August 1923 several Cantonese, including Ch'en Ping-sheng, former president of the seamen's union, were expelled from the Federation for being in sympathy with two fellow Cantonese accused of corruption (*PDR*, 15.viii.23). In April 1924 another crisis arose over disputes between the leadership of the Federation and groups under Cantonese influence, such as the Nanyang club, the Canton Friendly Society, and the Mechanics' Union (*PDR*, 21.iv.24).

137. *PDR*, 18.i.24.

138. See for instance the rules of the Mechanics' Union or those of the Boatmen's and Warehousemen's Federation (*Nien-chien* [138] II, 53–60).

139. Units of this kind existed in the Electrical Workers' Union (*Labour Conditions* [20], p. 92).

140. See *IPC*, 19.iii.25 (supply of strikebreakers by the secret societies), and *IPC*, 23.vi.27 (influence of the Green Gang among the Shanghai proletariat until the formation of the big industrial unions in 1925). On the Shanghai underworld, see also Isaacs, *Tragedy* [263], p. 131, and Tayler and Zung, *ILR*, July 1923.

141. Regarding the situation in Canton in 1923–24 see pp. 245–46 below.

142. Chen Ta, "Analysis of Strikes in China," *CEJ*, Nov. 1927.

143. See d'Elia, *Le triple démisme* [163], p. 233.

144. *HT*, 4.vi.24.

145. *HT*, 20.vi.23. This was merely a trade association of railwaymen formed under the direction of the governor of Heilungkiang in order to stimulate rivalry with the Russian railwaymen, who enjoyed better pay and conditions.

146. *Chien-shih* [165], p. 151. See also p. 259 below.

147. Chen Ta, "Analysis of Strikes," *CEJ*, Nov. 1927.

148. Chinese text in *Nien-chien* [138] III, 183–85; trans. in I.L.O. *Legislative Series* [34], China, No. 1.

149. Regulations for treatment of workers in mines (12.v.23), for safety precautions in mines (5.v.23), for the prevention of anchylosis (15.v.23), for the prevention of explosions (17.v.23). Texts published in I.L.O. *Legislative Series*, China, Nos. 2, 3, 4, 5.

150. *Modern Industry in China* [179].

151. *IS*, 1924, I, 38.   152. *NCH*, 21.vii.23.

153. *NCH*, 14.vi.23.

154. Formed in December 1922 (*IS*, 1923, II, 143).

155. Formed in October 1923 (*CEB*, 20.x.23).

156. Formed in August 1923 (*CEB*, 11.viii.23).

157. *NCH*, 21.vii.23.

158. These reports are all in *Labour Conditions* [20]. On the failure to apply the 1923 regulations see for instance the report of Lancelot Giles, Consul at Changsha (p. 29), or that of Consul-General Jamieson from Canton (p. 27).

159. The 1923 and 1924 Conferences were attended by Lu Cheng-hsiang, the Chinese minister in Berne, and one of his assistants (I.L.O. Annual Conference reports [29]).

160. I.L.O. Archives 200/1/13 [11], Note of 9.ii.25.

161. *IS*, 1923, II, 268. This resolution was applicable beginning January 1, 1925.

162. The Chinese Communist press conducted a vigorous attack against Paul Henry, who during his visit to Shanghai made contacts only with the moderate circles connected with the Federation of Labor Organizations. See *CKKJ*, Nov. 1924, "Kuo-chi lao-tung-chü chih chen-hsiang," and *HT*, 10.x.24. Father Wieger once again demonstrates his aversion for all labor activities by merely making a passing reference in the "éphémérides" in *La Chine moderne* [139] IV, 13, to "un camarade qui se dit délégué par le comité du travail de la Société des Nations" [*sic*] ("a comrade who claims to be a delegate of the Labor Committee of the League of Nations").

163. I.L.O. Archives 200/1/13 [11], Note of 9.ii.23.

164. See Anderson, *Humanity and Labour* [56], pp. 125–63.

165. The text of the report is in *Labour Conditions* [20], pp. 113–63.

166. These minutes have never been published. Miss Harrison, shortly before her death, was kind enough to give me permission to consult them.

167. There were massive abstentions among the Japanese (out of a total of 509, only 79 voted), and among "various nationalities" (188 out of a total of 1,402 voted). Even among the British voters, despite the fact that the British consul, J. T. Pratt, was backing the bylaw, only 355 out of 832 attended (I.L.O. Archives, P.L. 13/5/1).

168. On the political situation in Shanghai in the spring of 1925 see Chapter XI below.

169. See, for instance, *SCMP*, 8.i.24, for an account of the incidents in Hankow in January 1924, when the rickshaw men's union decided to refuse to transport Japanese nationals or to allow any of its members to enter the Japanese Concession until the affair of the murder of a Chinese by a Japanese was settled. See also *SCMP*, 21.v.24, concerning a brawl that broke out in Tientsin in May 1924 after a Japanese seaman refused to pay the rickshaw man he had hired.

Chapter X

1. See Whiting, *Soviet Policies in China* [314], pp. 30ff.
2. See Bloch, *German Interests and Policies* [233], chap. 1.
3. See Willoughby, *China at the Conference* [316], Appendix II.
4. On this incident, see for instance *NCH*, May 1923, *passim*. According to the accounts of old China hands, the attack against the train was an act of reprisal on the part of a bandit leader who had failed to get delivery of a consignment of arms from an Italian supplier despite the fact that payment had been made.
5. See *CWR*, 2.vi.23 and 7.vii.23 (discussions of the foreign General Chamber of Commerce of Shanghai, and a speech by John Harold Dollar).
6. See p. 211 below.
7. See the statement of Wu P'ei-fu's collaborator, Yang I-te, urging the K.M.A. miners to return to work in 1921, and explaining that British activities in China were beneficial to the country (*CWR*, 13.xi.21). Another point to notice is the caution displayed by the Chinese delegations at Versailles in 1919, and at Washington in 1922, on the subject of China's international status; the first delegation represented the Anfu faction, and the second the Chihli faction. On the collusion between the warlords and the Powers, see also Hu Sheng, *Imperialism and Chinese Politics* [262], chap. 6.
8. *Statistics of Government Railways* [36], 1924.
9. *Report of the Chinese Post Office* [35], 1924.
10. Fong, *Cotton Industry* [252], p. 8.
11. It seemed unnecessary to attempt to draw up a detailed table of the number of workers employed in 1924–25, since it would be just as unreliable as the one already attempted for 1919.
12. See Vinogradov (*Voprosi Istorii*, 1952, No. 10 [326]).
13. See pp. 214–15 below.
14. At the beginning of 1925, the Changsha cotton mill had to pay the warlord government five years' taxes in advance (*CEB*, 5.v.25). On the summary methods adopted by Wu P'ei-fu with regard to the Wuhan merchants from 1921 to 1925, see *CWR*, *passim*. In April 1922, for instance, he demanded 300,000 yuan from the Hankow Chamber of Commerce and 100,000 yuan from the association of Chinese bankers in the city in order to pay his troops (*CWR*, 6.v.22).
15. See pp. 214–15 below.
16. The Chengchow cotton mill was up for sale in 1924 (*CEB*, 12.vii.24), that of Wuchang was in debt to a foreign bank (*CWR*, 11.x.24), and two Shanghai cotton mills were bought by a Japanese firm at the beginning of 1925 (*CEB*, 7.ii.25).
17. As in Hupeh (*CWR*, 8.iv.22, 15.iv.22, and 22.iv.22).
18. The chambers of commerce held national conferences in October 1921 in Shanghai (*CWR*, 8.x.21), and in November 1922 in Hankow (*CWR*, 16.xii.22); a National Industrial Conference was held in Peking in September 1924 (*CEB*, 18.x.24).
19. *CWR*, 8.iv.22.   20. *CWR*, 2.xii.22.
21. See *CEB*, 18.x.24 (the conference in Peking in September 1924).
22. At the end of 1921 Yeh Kung-ch'o, one of the leaders of the "Communications Clique," wrote an article entitled "Salvaging China Industrially" (*CWR*, 8.x.21), in which he demanded the abolition of the likin and all internal customs, and proposed instead an average 12 per cent tariff on foreign goods. In 1925 the commission for the study of the revision of tariffs proposed by the Washington Conference had not yet met (see Wright, *China's Struggle for Tariff Autonomy* [318]).
23. For example the chambers of commerce protested in April 1923 against the plans

for a Japanese monopoly of telecommunications in China (*CWR*, 12.v.23). Demands were made at the conference in Peking in September 1924 for the protection of Chinese flour mills against the imports of foreign flour (*CEB*, 18.x.24).

24. In 1925 foreign residents paid 1,763,385 taels in rates as against 2,021,702 taels paid by Chinese residents (*SMCR*, 1926, p. 405).

25. See Kotenev, *Shanghai, Its Municipality* [156], pp. 164–68. This Advisory Committee seems to have had purely nominal powers; according to the Feetham report [38] (Part II, chap. 6, p. 128), "it did not play a very prominent part."

26. These shopkeepers' associations, which were formed during the May Fourth Movement, continued to support Chinese representation on the Municipal Council and to protest against the payment of rates and the like. Their attitude was much more radical than that of the Ratepayers' Association (*SMCR*, 1920, p. 66A).

27. *Chien-shih* [165], p. 182.

28. *CWR*, 23.xii.22, "The Causes for the High Price of Cotton."

29. The concern to keep the working class down and to prevent it from making economic demands upon Chinese employers was shown very clearly in a speech made by Sun Yat-sen on May 1, 1924, to the workers of Canton on the theme of "hardships suffered by Chinese workers as a result of the unequal treaties" (*Hsuan-chi* [163], pp. 839–46). See p. 246 below.

30. See Wieger, *La Chine moderne* [139] III and IV, *passim* (numerous documents on student activities during this period).

31. See *CEB*, 25.iv.25 (night work in Peking oil mills); *CEB*, 9.v.25 (night work in Peking footwear factories); *Nien-chien* [138] I, 311 (a 15-hour day in the Yingkow silk factories to keep up with Japanese competition).

32. Several craftsmen's strikes were declared demanding payment of wages in silver instead of copper currency; see *CEB*, 1.xi.24 (Hankow indigo dyeworks), *CEB*, 10.i.25 (Peking mat manufacturers and Pootung tailors).

33. A typical case was that of the Peking house painters, whose leaders were arrested by the police in April 1924 (*CEB*, 19.iv.24).

34. The many journeymen's guilds that had been formed in an effort to break away from the old mixed guilds still tried to use the old methods for controlling the labor market. Thus the Tientsin guild for barbers' employees handed out certificates to its qualified members (*CEB*, 12.vii.24); the Fuchow guild for shophands in the silk shops demanded that employers must not engage more than one apprentice in each shop (*CEB*, 28.ii.25); and the Changsha mat weavers' guild demanded a payment of 8 yuan from journeymen from other towns who tried to get work there (*CEB*, 2.ii.24).

35. See Hu Sheng, *Imperialism and Chinese Politics* [262], p. 286.

36. On the forced cultivation of opium and the warlords' traffic in it, see *NCH*, 31.v.24, which reports the survey conducted by the International Anti-Opium Association. In Fukien the peasants had to buy licenses for cultivating opium, and then had to pay for rights to sell the crop.

37. When Wu P'ei-fu attacked Hunan in 1921 he ordered embankments in Hupeh to be cut, an action that ruined whole stretches of rural areas (*CWR*, 14.i.22).

38. See the account of a British correspondent in Fukien (*NCH*, 16.ii.24).

39. See Chen Han-seng, "The Burdens of the Chinese Peasantry," *PA*, Oct. 1929, where reference is made to a district in Chihli, to another in Shantung where the nominal tax rate rose by 53 and 47 per cent between 1911 and 1928, and to a district in Hunan where taxes for the period up to 1930 were levied in 1924, and another in Szechwan, where taxes for the period up to 1957 were levied in 1926.

40. See for example *CEB*, 20.ii.26 (emigration from Amoy).

41. These tu-fei ("brigands") began to cause much concern among Western press

circles in China at this time. Cf. *CWR*, 6.i.26, "The Real Significance of Banditry in China," and 1.ix.25, "Agricultural Unrest May Lead to Bolshevism in China."

42. This was true of the Red Swords Society in Honan (see Li Ta-chao, *Hsuan-chi* [159], pp. 564–70), and the Taoist sects in Szechwan (*NCH*, 26.iv.24), Shansi (*NCH*, 26.i.24), and western Hupeh (*CWR*, 14.v.21); there was also a resurgence of Taiping ideas about the Heavenly Kingdom in Szechwan (*RT*, Wanhsien, 1921, p. 9) and in Hupeh (*CWR*, 18.v.22), and a reemergence of the Boxer Movement in Honan (*CWR*, 20.i.23).

43. See Lamb, *Agrarian Movement in China* [267], pp. 22–24. See also *Nung-min yun-tung* [147], pp. 6–17.

44. Ho Kan-chih, *Modern Revolution* [259], p. 83.

45. See p. 191 below.

46. Mif [290], p. 24, reproaches the CCP for having neglected the advice of the Comintern on the peasant question at the time of the Third Annual Conference in June 1923.

47. It must be understood that the present study concerns the Chinese labor movement only, and wherever mention is made of the parts played by the CCP or the Comintern, important as they were, no systematic use has been made of primary sources. All that has been attempted is to present the essential facts concerning the matters dealt with here, many of which have been derived from secondary sources.

48. Hu Hua, *Ko-ming-shih* [200], pp. 64–65.

49. *Ibid.*, p. 63.

50. Whiting, *Soviet Policies in China* [314], p. 79.

51. Hu Hua [200], p. 68. Cf. Brandt and others, *Documentary History* [133], pp. 52–53.

52. Whiting [314], p. 240, and Hu Hua [200], p. 75.

53. See the editorial in *HT*, 1.viii.23, on the shutdown of a Chinese cotton mill in Shanghai and the crisis of Chinese capitalist enterprise. See also the important article by Ch'ü Ch'iu-pai (under the pseudonym of Ch'ü Wei-t'o) in *CF*, 1.vii.23, in which he stresses the importance of the contradictions between the Chinese bourgeoisie and the combined forces of the militarists and the imperialists, and calls for an alliance between the labor movement and the bourgeoisie ("the bourgeois Nationalist movement cannot succeed without the revolutionary vigor of the working class").

54. Hu Hua, *Ko-ming-shih* [200], p. 74.

55. *Ibid.*, p. 76. The controversies within the CCP at this time to a large extent reflected those that were dividing the Comintern. Lack of space prevents detailed discussion here.

56. Teng Chung-hsia wrote that at this time the Kuomintang barely existed—there was only Sun Yat-sen (*Chien-shih* [165], p. 114).

57. See Chesneaux, *Sun Yat-sen* [239], chap. 7. On Ch'en Chiung-ming's links with Hong Kong see p. 202 above.

58. During a reception given for the delegates of the Labor Congress in May 1922, Sun Yat-sen urged them to "do all they could to further the interests of the state and of society as a whole" (*MKJP*, 8.v.22).

59. In an interview given to the *Japan Chronicle* on 9.xi.22, he stated that his aim was to obtain recognition of the workers as people of importance in the community. Hitherto, he said, they had had no say in Chinese political life, and were regarded as menials unworthy to express their opinions. But now they would make an important contribution to the life of the country as a whole.

60. *CWR*, 3.xi.23.

61. A leader of the Mechanics' Union presided at a workers' meeting on December 16 (*SCMP*, 18.xii.23). The Canton unions joined the "Citizens' Diplomatic Support Association," which was formed to support Sun Yat-sen (*SCMP*, 18.xii.23), and addressed

a solemn appeal to the workers of the U.S., Great Britain, France, Japan, and Italy concerning the question of the "customs surplus" (*NCH*, 12.i.24, and *HT*, 9.i.24).

62. Hu Sheng, *Imperialism and Chinese Politics* [262], p. 290.

63. Woo, *The Future of the Chinese Revolution* [168], p. 151.

64. Sun Yat-sen, *Hsuan-chi* [163] I, 434.

65. Hu Hua, *Ko-ming-shih* [200], p. 78.   66. *Ibid.*, p. 62.

67. Li Chien-nung, *Political History* [277], p. 443.

68. On the 1924 Congress, see Woo [168], chaps. 2 and 6; Hu Hua [200], pp. 88–90; and Li Chien-nung [277], pp. 444–58.

69. It also sent a telegram of congratulations to Ramsay MacDonald on becoming Prime Minister. The Russians replied, but not the British (Tang Leang-li, *Inner History* [306], p. 180).

70. Among the main workers' strikes declared during 1923 in order to obtain higher wages and the abolition of the pao-kung system, *SCMP* (*passim*) mentions one by the mechanics in a British sugar refinery in Hong Kong in March, one by the mechanics employed by Butterfield & Swire in Hong Kong in April, one by the tinsmiths in the same firm in November, and one by the mechanics of the Canton electric power plant.

71. *CWR*, 7.iv.23.   72. *HT*, 15.x.24.

73. *SCMP*, 3.ix.24.

74. Ma Ch'ao-chün, *Lao-tung yun-tung shih* [210], p. 287.

75. In 1923, May 5, the anniversary of Sun Yat-sen's becoming President of the Southern Constitutionalist Government in 1921, was given precedence over May 1 (*SCMP*, 7.v.23).

76. *MLR*, Aug. 1924.

77. See Sun Yat-sen, *Hsuan-chi* [163], pp. 839–46.

78. See Chen Ta, *ILR*, March 1927, and Lowe Chuan-hua, *Facing Labor Issues* [284], p. 148.

79. *SCMP*, 27.ii.23. Sun Yat-sen suggested that the organization be called the Chinese General Union.

80. On October 10, 1924, this federation held a public meeting and adopted Sun Yat-sen's slogan urging the fight against militarism and imperialism (*NCH*, 4.x.24).

81. See Voitinskii, *Chto proishodit v Kitae* [167], p. 56.

82. There were a great many of these trade associations at this time (list in *Nien-chien* [138] II, 73).

83. Voitinskii [167].

84. *HT*, 15.x.24 (a violent attack against Ma Ch'ao-chün by a worker at the arsenal, accusing him of favoritism, of collusion with the pao-kung-t'ou, of playing tricks with the workers' club and the workers' consumers' cooperative, and of paying too low wages and demanding too long hours).

85. In August 1924 there was a clash between members of a tavern union and members of a mixed association called the Workers' and Merchants' Friendly Society (it is not known if it had any connection with the Shanghai association of the same name), each of which was trying to get hold of the other's members (*HT*, 27.viii.24).

86. *SCMP*, 31.i.24.

87. *SCMP*, 3.vii.24.

88. On this affair see *SCMP*, July–Aug. 1924, *passim*.

89. Hu Hua, *Ko-ming-shih* [200], p. 95.

90. The consuls at first refused to reinstate the policemen. When they finally agreed, it was arranged, in exchange for this concession, that the men would resign as soon as the strike ended (*SCMP*, 14.viii.24).

91. See *SCMP*, *passim*, regarding taxes on silks in December, on rickshaws and matches in January, on junks and banquets in April, and on cold drinks and medicines in May.

92. In November 1923 the Canton Chamber of Commerce and about a dozen other bourgeois organizations protested against the taxes and against the exactions of the mercenaries (*SCMP*, 3.xi.23).

93. *SCMP*, 16.vii.22.   94. *CWR*, 12.vii.24.

95. *SCMP*, 28.viii.24. See also *Chien-shih* [165], p. 123.

96. *CWR*, 21.vi.24.

97. During the May Day procession in Kiangmen, clashes occurred between the unions and the Volunteers in which several workers were killed (*SCMP*, 9.v.24). Already in January the Volunteers had tried to break the strike of the rice-transport coolies (*SCMP*, 30.i.24).

98. Voitinskii, *Chto proishodit v Kitae* [167], p. 29.

99. See *SCMP* and *HT*, *passim*. See also *Chien-shih* [165], p. 123, and *LSYC*, 1956, No. 3.

100. *SCMP*, 29.viii.24; Hu Hua, *Ko-ming-shih* [200], p. 195.

101. See *Chien-shih* [165], pp. 105–7.

102. See Chapter VII above.   103. *SCMP*, 9–17.x.24.

104. *HT*, 15.x.24. The printers, having won the second point, decided to leave the question of their wages to Liao Chung-k'ai.

105. Within the government itself, men like Hu Han-min tried all through August and September to reach a compromise satisfactory to both parties; they persuaded Sun Yat-sen to offer to surrender the arms on August 29 and again on September 13 in exchange for a promise that the Volunteers would be reorganized (*SCMP*, 16.ix.24). It was the intransigence of the latter that led to the break in October.

106. These assemblies, which were still operating in 1919, had never been formally dissolved. The Canton Assembly gradually ceased to function in 1923, but its members still had a certain prestige, and its president called for foreign intervention against Sun Yat-sen's government at the beginning of September 1924 on the grounds that it was improperly constituted and had never been officially recognized either at home or abroad (*SCMP*, 9.ix.24).

107. One of the points raised by the Volunteers when the general strike of merchants was held on October 11 was that the Communists should be eliminated (*SCMP*, 12.x.24); on the same day the United Chamber of Commerce of Kwangtung accused Sun Yat-sen of being dominated by mercenaries and Communists, and of doing as much harm as the Northern government that he criticized so strongly (*SCMP*, 14.x.24).

108. In eastern Kwangtung the local branches of the Volunteers fraternized with Ch'en's troops (*SCMP*, 9.x.24).

109. *SCMP*, 5.ix.24 (text of the consul general's note).

110. *CWR*, 27.ix.24.

111. Text of Sun Yat-sen's reply in *SCMP*, 5.ix.24. See also *ibid.* for Sun's telegram to MacDonald, in which he said that in view of the aid constantly given by successive British governments to the counterrevolution in China, and of the fact that his government was the only center of resistance to the counterrevolution, he was forced to assume that the real aim of the ultimatum was the destruction of his government. After his defeat, Ch'en Lien-po took refuge in the British consulate in Shameen, and the consul refused the Canton government's request for his extradition on the grounds that he knew Ch'en only as the compradore of the Hongkong and Shanghai Banking Corporation (*SCMP*, 28.x.24).

112. *PP*, 30.xi.24.

113. *CWR*, 22.xi.24. See also Wieger, *La Chine moderne* [139] VI, 110 (text of the speech given on this occasion by Sun Yat-sen).

114. The full Chinese text is in *Nien-chien* [138] II, 218–21; summary in Lowe Chuan-hua, *Facing Labor Issues* [284], p. 42.

115. On the boycott of the Nanyang products, see *HT*, 24.xii.24, and *SCMP*, 14.i.25, 22.i.25. According to the latter, it was a reprisal against the Nanyang Company for having recently refused a loan to the Canton government.

116. Full text in *CYB*, 1924, pp. 1192ff.

117. *HT*, 18.vi.24, "Kuo-min-tang yü lao-tung yun-tung." This article emphasizes that it was a question of cooperation and not of amalgamation.

118. Hu Hua, *Ko-ming-shih* [200], p. 104. The CP had about a thousand members at this time, and the Chinese Socialist Youth Corps nine thousand (Mif [209], p. 24).

119. These passages are from the article in *CF*, 1.xii.23, which expresses an attitude that seems to have been very general in 1924 and 1925.

120. *Hu-nan lieh-shih-chuan* [223], p. 22 (biography of Teng Chung-hsia).

121. In the first number of *CKKJ* (Oct. 1924), the important article by Chao Shih-yen makes no mention of the question of alliances, but merely urges action for the right to strike and to form unions, and for the achievement of other strictly labor movement objectives. (Chao was a student who, after spending some time in France, lived in Moscow from 1920 to 1924. See his biography in *HCPP*, 15.xii.57.)

122. Teng Chung-hsia, in his article on the Northern Expedition in *CKKJ*, Oct. 1924, wrote that the Expedition had no connection with the real revolution of national liberation, and that workers' and peasants' unions should have nothing to do with it. These doubts and hesitations were not felt by Chinese Communists alone, but also by the Comintern and its various members in other countries. But here again I have not attempted to follow out the possible connection between the controversies within the CCP and those at the International level.

123. *Nien-chien* [138] II, 8.

124. See the manifesto they sent to the Soviet government in March 1924 (*NCH*, 15.iii.24).

125. See p. 225 below.

126. *HT*, 17.ix.24 and 24.ix.24; *CKKJ*, Oct. 1924, "Nan-yang yen-ch'ang pa-kung."

127. See p. 247 below.

128. See Ma Ch'ao-chün, *Lao-tung yun-tung shih* [210], pp. 300, 330, 349.

129. *Chien-shih* [165], pp. 115, 116; the secretaries and executive members of these labor departments were usually Communists.

130. *CTSTL*, 1957, No. 4, "Nan-ch'ang ta-shih-chi."

131. See Li Chien-nung, *Political History* [277], pp. 467–73, for the political events in the fall of 1924; also Kotenev, *New Lamps for Old* [266], pp. 116–21.

132. During Sun Yat-sen's stay in Shanghai in 1922 he made contacts with delegates of Tuan and of the Fengtien faction (*Chien-shih* [165], p. 125). He maintained cordial relations with them after his return to Canton (*SCMP*, 27.iii.24).

133. In November the new Northern government introduced better conditions for railwaymen—higher wages, regular promotion, restriction of fines, etc. (*CEB*, 22.xi.24).

134. See Hsü Hsieh-hua, *T'ieh-lu lao-kung wen-t'i* [196], p. 177. These leaders were imprisoned after a strike in May 1924, even though the strike was successful.

135. *Chien-shih* [165], p. 126.

136. New unions were formed on the Chiao-Chi in February 1925 (*CKKJ*, April 1925, "Ch'üan-kuo t'ieh-lu tsung-kung-hui"), and on the Ching-Feng in April 1925 (*Nien-chien* [138] II, 108, including the text of the union rules).

137. On this congress, see the above article in *CKKJ*, April 1925, and *Nien-chien*, II, 377–92.

138. *Chien-shih* [165], pp. 126–27.

139. According to the reports on the various railway lines presented at the congress (*Nien-chien* [138] II, 378–86), the Communications Clique still had influence on the Ching-Sui and Chin-P'u lines, and among the foremen on the Lunghai line; the workshop

employees, gangers, and train crews still had disagreements on the Ching-Feng line, and formed three rival clubs on the Canton-Sanshui line.

140. One of the chief of these deserters was Yang Te-fu, a leader of the Ching-Han union before February 7, 1923, who fled to Shanghai, where he became connected with the Federation. In February 1924 he again collaborated with the Communists in forming a clandestine National Railwaymen's Union, but then finally broke with them. In 1925 the National Union accused him of having been a secret agent of the Communications Clique in 1923, and in 1924 of having denounced his comrades (*HT*, 26.iv.25).

141. *HT*, 28.iii.25.

142. The seamen gave financial support to the Shanghai cotton mill strike in February 1925 (see p. 254 below), which the Federation said was the result of Communist intrigues (*PDR*, 16.ii.25).

143. Most of the Tientsin factories dated from the time of the First World War, and the proletariat there was less homogeneous and less firmly established than in Hupeh-Hunan or even Shanghai; there was great use made of child labor, seasonal female labor, and temporary migrants. In 1919 Tientsin had almost no tradition of strikes or labor organizations.

144. See Wang Lin, *Po-chung* [213], pp. 2–6.

145. Kotenev, *New Lamps for Old* [266], pp. 120–21. Troops of the Chihli faction remained in control of the Shanghai area after the defeat of the faction in the fall of 1924, but were removed by the Fengtien armies the following spring.

146. See *Chien-shih* [165], pp. 132–40; *PDR, passim*; *NCH*, 14.ii.25, 21.ii.25, and 28.ii.25; see also *CKKJ*, April 1925, "Shang-hai Jih-pen sha-ch'ang pa-kung."

147. Liu Hua, a proofreader at China Bookshop, was subsequently employed by Shanghai University, an independent establishment where Communist intellectuals such as Ch'ü Ch'iu-pai, Teng Chung-hsia, and Ch'en Tu-hsiu were teaching toward the end of 1923. It was through this university that Communist influence on the youth of Shanghai was maintained during the period of setbacks in the labor movement. For Liu Hua's biography, see *Ko-ming lieh-shih-chuan* [221], pp. 189ff.

148. *PDR*, 11.ii.25 (on the role of Li Li-san); *Hu-nan lieh-shih-chuan* [223], p. 22 (on Teng Chung-hsia's role).

149. *PDR*, 16.ii.25, 18.ii.25, 28.ii.25.   150. *PDR*, 23.ii.25.

151. *PDR*, 24.ii.25 and 27.ii.25.

152. *IPC*, 12.iii.25; also 5.iii.25 (account of an appeal launched by the Red International for international solidarity with the strikers).

153. *PDR*, 16.ii.25 and 24.ii.25.

154. According to *IPC*, 19.iii.25, the Japanese government presented Tuan Ch'i-jui with what was virtually an ultimatum demanding that the strike be put down by the use of force. Tuan confined himself to making several arrests of individuals, who were shortly released (*Chien-shih* [165], p. 139).

155. *PDR*, 19.iii.25, and *Chien-shih*, pp. 141–42.

156. See *CKKJ*, 27.iii.57, "Liu Hua lieh-shih"; in *PDR*, March and April, *passim*, there is frequent mention of discussions between Liu Hua and Japanese firms concerning individual cases.

157. *NCH*, 16.v.25.

158. *PDR*, 2.v.25. The Federation held a meeting in Chapei and distributed photographs of Chiang and Socialist Party leaflets.

159. The railwaymen objected to the appointment of a man who was not a native of Shantung as head of the network there (*NCH*, 21.ii.25). The Tsingtao Chamber of Commerce supported the strike, which succeeded in having a change made in the appointment by Peking; the strikers also obtained recognition of the union and a raise in wages.

160. The fall in the price of silk had resulted in a lowering of wages in the factories in both these regions. In Kwangtung the women workers, with the support of the Kuomintang labor department, formed unions of a sort, and in reply to a lockout even wrecked one of the reeling factories (*SCMP*, 4.iv.25). A 20 per cent raise in wages was finally obtained (*CEB*, 14.iii.25, 11.iv.25, and 6.vi.25).

161. *CWR*, 14.iii.25.

162. *SCMP*, 10.iv.25.

163. *MDN*, 1925, *passim* (strikes in the Japanese hemp and wool factories in Mukden).

164. *MDN*, 27.v.25.

165. *Chien-shih* [165], pp. 144–45; also *HT*, 24.v.25.

166. Two killed and twenty wounded according to *NCH*, 6.viii.25; eight killed and ten wounded according to *HT*, 6.vi.25.

167. See Li Chien-nung, *Political History* [277], pp. 475–79. See also Wieger, *La Chine moderne* [139] VI, 130 (text of the CP proposals for the National Convention).

168. Wieger, VI, 120–21 (Sun Yat-sen's statement listing the groups that ought to be invited to take part).

169. *HT*, 10.xii.24, "Mu-ch'ien cheng-chü."

170. *SCMP*, 23.xii.25 (on a workers' meeting in Canton).

171. *PDR*, 2.i.25. See also Wieger, *La Chine moderne* [139] VI, 136–37 (attendance of workers at a meeting of delegates from 143 Shanghai associations).

172. Wieger, VI, 105 (resolution of the Kwangsi General Union).

173. *Chien-shih* [165], p. 129. Also *Nien-chien* [138] II, 377ff. (a resolution at the Railwaymen's Congress in February 1925).

174. Wieger, VI, 27. Su Chao-cheng was one of the delegates, representing the Canton seamen's union there; he stayed on in the North to make preparations for the Second National Labor Congress (*Su Chao-cheng* [222], p. 10).

175. Wieger, VI, 31.

176. *CKKJ*, April 1925, "Pei-ching cheng-pien."

177. *CKKJ*, April 1925, "Chih-kung yun-tung." The cry for the "fight for civil liberties" had already been raised at the Second National Railwaymen's Congress in February 1925 (*Nien-chien* [138] II, 377).

178. *Lao-tung ta-hui* [142], p. 8.

179. It is hardly ever mentioned in the Communist press of 1924–25 (*HT*, *CKKJ*, and so on) although there are many reports of activities in Hunan.

180. *Lao-tung ta-hui*, p. 8, note 1.

181. *Chien-shih* [165], p. 151. Teng Chung-hsia indicates that the CP decided to give up operating through the Labor Secretariat and instead to give priority to the big industrial unions it was organizing.

182. These are the figures given by Teng Chung-hsia, who was present at the congress (*Chien-shih*, p. 153). The invitation sent out by the four unions that convoked the congress suggested that every group of 100 to 1,000 members be represented by one delegate, with an extra delegate for every additional thousand members. This was in order to eliminate very small groups, and to limit the representation of very large unions (*Lao-tung ta-hui* [142], pp. 8–9). Teng's figures suggest that not all the unions represented made full use of their quota.

183. *PDR*, 17.iv.25, 24.iv.25. There were seven delegates of this union, including Sun Liang-hui and Liu Kuan-chih, who were leaders of the February strike.

184. *PDR*, 24.iv.25.

185. *Chien-shih* [165], p. 154.

186. The program of demands and of union organization had already been put forward in an article by Teng Chung-hsia in *CKKJ*, May 1925 ("Lao-tung yun-tung").

187. The text of these resolutions is in *Lao-tung ta-hui* [142], pp. 12–35.
188. See p. 252 above.
189. Ma Ch'ao-chün, *Lao-tung yun-tung shih* [210], pp. 344–45.
190. Those who were denounced included Yang Te-fu and Chang Te-hui, deserters from the Ching-Han General Union; Wang Kuang-hui, a former associate of Huang and P'ang in Changsha; T'ung Li-chang, a leader of the Shanghai Federation; Ma Ch'ao-chün and Huang Huan-t'ing, leaders of the Canton Mechanics' Union.
191. See, for instance, in *CKKJ*, No. 1 (Oct. 1924), the translation of a report by Lozovsky, the president of the Red International, on strike strategy. No. 3 was devoted entirely to the activities of the Red International and affiliated organizations. In reply to the decision of the All-China General Union to become an affiliate, the R.I. sent a message to the workers of China assuring them of its support (*IPC*, 21.v.25).
192. *Lao-tung ta-hui* [142], p. 21.
193. *Chien-shih* [165], pp. 152–54.
194. *CWR*, 16.v.25.
195. In Hong Kong, for instance, the unions organized a big procession preceded by decorated automobiles in which union leaders were seated (*SCMP*, 2.v.25). In Tientsin, a workers' meeting was held in one of the main squares, where the union flags were hoisted (Wang Lin, *Po-chung* [213], p. 10).
196. The content of the resolutions passed corresponded, in the main, with the proposals outlined by Chang Kuo-t'ao and Teng Chung-hsia in their articles published in *CKKJ*, No. 5 (May 1925), just before the congress.

Chapter XI

1. *PDR*, 30.v.25. It will be remembered that the bylaw on child labor came up at the same meeting of the Municipal Council as these other bylaws, either through inadvertence or possibly with intent, and that the failure to vote it through was largely due to the dislike that the Chinese population of the International Settlement had for the other bylaws. See Chapter IX above.
2. Kotenev, *New Lamps for Old* [266], pp. 117–21. The Fengtien armies had been occupying the Shanghai area since January 1925.
3. It fell from 195–209 cents to the yuan in January to 226–30 cents to the yuan in May (*CEB*, 8.viii.25).
4. *PDR, passim*. During the same period in 1923 and 1924, prices had remained almost stationary.
5. *Chien-shih* [165], p. 181; Kotenev [266], pp. 121ff.
6. *PDR*, 21–23.v.25.
7. *PDR*, 25–28.v.25.
8. The students, having been forbidden by the Minister of Education to celebrate May 7 (a "Day of National Humiliation"), proceeded to attack his house; 17 of them were arrested and three were killed (Kotenev [266], pp. 121ff).
9. *Hu-nan lieh-shih-chuan* [223], p. 15 (biography of Ts'ai Ho-sen). Ch'en Tu-hsiu seems to have thought that no more than three to five hundred people would take part in the demonstration.
10. *Wu-sa yun-tung chung ti Shang-hai kung-jen* [220], p. 11.
11. A complete list of the victims was published in *Wu-sa yun-tung* [197], p. 31; they include cotton workers, stokers, telephone workers, tramwaymen, and B.A.T. workers.
Ma Ch'ao-chün [210], p. 387, gives a rather different account of these events, and himself assumes responsibility for the demonstration on May 30. He was in Shanghai at the time trying to gain support among the Kuomintang right wing for the Sunyatsenist Society he and his political associates had recently founded in Canton. He claims to have

arranged the demonstration in association with students' groups and people like Tu Yueh-sheng, whom he describes as a "notable" (*shen*), although it is difficult to believe that he was unaware of the fact that Tu was head of the Green Gang and engaged in the drug traffic in the French Concession (see Chapter XIV below). Actually Ma Ch'ao-chün's role must have been a very minor one, and even a non-Communist account such as Chang Wei-ying's [189] makes no mention of him.

12. Kotenev, *New Lamps for Old* [266], p. 132.

13. *PDR*, 1.vi.25. Yü Hsia-ch'ing, the president of the chamber, was in Peking at the time (*Chien-shih* [165], p. 195).

14. *NCH*, 6.vi.25. See also *SMCR*, 1925, p. 67.

15. *PDR*, 1.vi.25.

16. *Chien-shih* [165], p. 185. It had been decided at the Second National Labor Congress to form a general union in Shanghai, and preparations had already been made. On the activities of the General Union at this time, see Kartunova, *PV*, 1960, No. 2. This article is based on *Je-hsüeh jih-pao* ("The Bloodshed Journal"), published by the Workers', Merchants', and Students' Federation.

17. Examples are the meeting on June 1 of 200 employees of the Chinese Tramways, and another on June 2 of 250 telephone workers and 200 employees of the electric power plant (*PDR*, 2.vi.25 and 3.vi.25).

18. *SMCR*, 1925, p. 68; *Wu-sa yun-tung* [197], pp. 60–77.

19. *Wu-sa yun-tung, ibid.*

20. *CWR*, 25.vii.25.

21. *SMCR*, 1925, pp. 29–31.

22. *Chien-shih* [165], pp. 185–86. On June 6, 1,337 marines of various nationalities were landed (Shanghai Municipal Council Archives, document 4207, Part I, a letter from the commander of the American flotilla in Shanghai).

23. *Chien-shih* [165], p. 187 (according to an inquiry made by the Peking government).

24. *Ibid.*, p. 188.   25. *PDR*, 12.vi.25.

26. *Chien-shih* [165], pp. 197–98.

27. Heller, *Die Arbeiterklasse und die Nationalbewegung* [170].

28. *PDR*, 12.vi.25.

29. *Wu-sa yun-tung chung ti Shang-hai kung-jen* [220], p. 16.

30. *PDR*, 10.vi.25.

31. Throughout the Movement the Municipal Council published a large number of leaflets and pamphlets in Chinese, under the general title of "The Truth." In July, for instance, 731,000 leaflets on "The Soviet Danger," "What Is Extraterritoriality?" and "The Facts of May 30" were distributed, and over 8,000 yuan was spent on propaganda (Shanghai Municipal Council Archives, document 4207, Part I).

32. *Ch'u-pan shih-liao* [134], Supplementary volume, pp. 263–64; the bulletin appeared every three or five days.

33. *HCPP*, No. 8, "I Ch'iu Pai." Ch'iu Pai was the editor of this paper, of which 24 issues appeared in all.

34. *PDR*, 15.vi.25, 26.vi.25, and 7.vii.25. Also from information obtained in interviews with Wang Jui-an (who in 1925 was a member of the Chapei picket corps), and with Chao Chin-ying and Chao Yin-ying, who in 1925 belonged to the pickets in the B.A.T. factory in Pootung.

35. See for instance *PDR*, 4.vi.25, which reports that on June 3 Liu Hua held four meetings of cotton workers, each attended by several hundred people; and *PDR*, 10.vi.25, which reports that 7,000 strikers registered at the Chapei center and that a meeting of 5,000 strikers was held in Yangtzepoo.

36. The dockers and coolies received 20 cents a day (*PDR*, 26.vi.25; also information

obtained from the former docker Chung Sheng-fu). According to *PDR,* 11.vi.25, 15.vi.25, 21.vi.25, the Pootung and Yangtzepoo cotton workers received one yuan a day, but this seems much too high. According to Communist sources (*IPC,* 6.viii.25) the rates of payment were 6 yuan a month for coolies, 8 yuan for factory workers, and 20 yuan for skilled workers.

37. *IPC,* 6.viii.25.

38. At a meeting of the Action Committee on July 15, it was announced that 165,000 yuan had been collected in ten-cent silver coins, and 93,000 yuan in copper cash (*NCH,* 18.vii.25).

39. *IPC,* 25.vi.25. See also Mandalyan, *Das Internationale Proletariat* [170].

40. *PPW,* No. 7, 1.x.27, "Amsterdam and China."

41. See P'eng Ming, *Chung-Su yu-i shih* [211], p. 122.

42. Tuan Ch'i-jui sent 100,000 yuan in the name of the Peking government (*NCH,* 4.vii.25), and Generals Feng Yü-hsiang and Chang Tsung-ch'ang sent respectively 5,000 and 2,000 yuan as personal contributions (*NCH,* 13.vi.25).

43. The Nanyang tobacco company, for example, is said to have contributed 100,000 yuan (*PDR,* 18.vi.25).

44. *IPC,* 6.viii.25.

45. *PDR,* 3.vii.25.

46. *Municipal Gazette* [39], 6.viii.25 (the report of the Commissioner of Police). The leaflet was distributed in the name of the Kuomintang, but it reads as if it had been written by the Communist militants who were members of the Shanghai committee of the KMT.

47. Interviews with Chao Chin-ying and Chao Yin-ying.

48. *CWR,* 25.vii.25.

49. *PDR,* 1.vi.25.

50. *Chien-shih* [165], p. 196; at a meeting of merchants on June 18 it was proposed that the boycott be limited to British goods (*IPC,* 27.viii.25).

51. *Chien-shih,* pp. 197–98.

52. Ho Kan-chih, *Modern Revolution* [259], p. 94. A conference on tariff revision was held in Peking in October 1925 (*CYB,* 1926, pp. 1106ff).

53. *HT* was highly critical of the tendency to compromise displayed by the upper bourgeoisie, e.g., in an editorial of June 6 or an article by Ch'en Tu-hsiu on June 20, in which he proposed that a national congress of workers, merchants, students, and soldiers be held in Shanghai for the purpose of getting the unequal treaties abolished. On June 22 Ch'ü Ch'iu-pai lashed out at the Chamber of Commerce, accusing it of abandoning the struggle for national liberation and being interested only in local problems and the attack against British interests. See *Wu-sa yun-tung chung ti Shang-hai kung-jen* [220], p. 19.

54. The decision was taken by Yü Hsia-ch'ing on June 20, despite efforts to prevent it by Li Li-san, accompanied by the presidents of the students' and the shopkeepers' associations (*PDR,* 21.vi.25); it was ratified on June 24 by 18 votes to 7, with 4 abstentions, at a combined meeting of the Chamber of Commerce and the shopkeepers' associations (*PDR,* 26.vi.25). The General Union began distributing leaflets on June 20, accusing Yü Hsia-ch'ing of receiving a large sum of money from the Western interests (*PDR,* 21.vi.25).

55. *PV,* 1960, No. 2.

56. *NCH,* 11.vii.25. It was the manager of the Arnhold & Company cotton mill who made the suggestion on June 27 (Shanghai Municipal Council Archives 4207, Part I).

57. *Municipal Gazette* [39], 6.viii.25 (the report of the Commissioner of Police).

58. *IPC,* 6.viii.25.

59. *NCH,* 25.vii.25.   60. *PDR,* 15.vii.25.

61. *SCMP,* 30.vii.25.

62. Lo Ren-yen, *China's Revolution* [282], p. 90.

63. *Chien-shih* [165], p. 200. (No actual examples are given.)

64. *CYB*, 1926, p. 929.

65. *PDR*, 14.viii.25.

66. *SMCR*, 1925, p. 62.

67. *NCH*, 18.vii.25; *PDR*, 9.vii.25.

68. *PDR*, 24.vii.25.

69. *PDR*, 26.vii.25 and 28.vii.25.

70. *PDR*, 3.viii.25 (a report on efforts made by tramwaymen and dockers to obtain an increase in strike payments from the General Union).

71. *PDR*, 28.vii.25, describes a leaflet attacking Li Li-san signed by associations that seem to have had no real existence, such as the "Association of Comrades of May 30 for National Salvation," or the "Shanghai Labor Protection Corps." It was rumored that they represented the "yellow" unions affiliated with the Federation. See also *NCH*, 22.viii.25 (concerning leaflets attacking the leaders of the General Union).

72. *NCH*, 15.viii.25. *HT*, 18.viii.25, accuses the instigators of this demonstration of being in league with the authorities of the International Settlement. See also Lei Chia, *Chu Pao-t'ing* [205], p. 79, where the blame is laid on the Federation and in particular on the Chün-an Seamen's Guild, a mutual aid society that had become very hostile to the labor movement.

73. *NCH*, 29.viii.25; *PDR*, 23.viii.25.

74. *PDR*, 24.viii.25. See the communiqué issued by the General Union (*NCH*, 29.viii.25) in which these accusations are made, and the Chinese police are reproached for having witnessed the incident without intervening.

75. *PDR*, 7.viii.25. See *Nien-chien* [138] II, 63–65, for a complete list of the unions, including membership figures. The same list is included in T'ang Hai, *Chung-kuo lao-tung wen-t'i* [164], pp. 510–20, where the names and the districts of origin of the union presidents are also given.

76. *CEB*, 18.vii.25.

77. *Nien-chien*, II, 46–48 (which contains the text of its rules).

78. *Shang-hai ch'an-yeh* [194], p. 483. See *Nien-chien* [138] II, 49–52, for the text of the rules of the China Bookshop and the bookbinders' unions.

79. See Chapter XIII below.

80. See *Nien-chien* [138] II, 46–48, 49–50, 51–52, 118–20, for the rules of unions in the cotton mills, the China Bookshop, the bookbinding industry, and the Post Office.

81. *PDR*, 8.vii.25 (on the struggle against strikebreakers); *PDR*, 1.vii.25 (on the management of strike funds and the like).

82. *PDR*, 3.viii.25. See *Die Arbeiter Chinas im Kampf gegen Imperialismus* [171], the report on the visit of this delegation. The visit lasted from July to October 1925, and was spent mainly in Shanghai and Canton.

83. Chen Ta, *ILR*, March 1927. On July 10 the General Union published a severe criticism of the government's proposals, objecting, for instance, to the insistence that union funds be deposited in a government bank, and to the limitations imposed regarding the type of group considered to be capable of founding a union. The ministry concerned took account of some of these criticisms.

84. *PDR*, 7.viii.25; see also *Chien-shih* [165], pp. 211–12.

85. *PDR*, 12.viii.25.

86. *PDR*, 13.viii.25. This agreement was made public on August 14 (*PDR*, 16.viii.25).

87. *PDR*, 19.viii.25.

88. *PDR*, 25.viii.25.

89. *NCH*, 12.ix.25.

90. *Chien-shih* [165], p. 112.

91. On these negotiations, see *Die Arbeiter Chinas im Kampf gegen Imperialismus* [171], pp. 22–29.

92. *NCH*, 22.viii.25; *HT*, 30.viii.25; T'ang Hai, *Chung-kuo lao-tung wen-t'i* [164],

pp. 468–72. See also *Shang-hai ch'an-yeh* [194], p. 421, for the manifesto of the Post Office strikers.

93. T'ang Hai [164], pp. 73–86. See also *Ch'u-pan shih-liao* [134] I, 445–46, for the manifesto of the Commercial Press strikers; also *NCH*, 29.viii.25.

94. *NCH*, 5.ix.25.

95. This is the theory propounded by Brandt, *Stalin's Failure in China* [234], pp. 54–55.

96. The decisions adopted at the Washington Conference were only very gradually implemented, and in 1925 a number of important positions in the Chinese postal service were still held by foreigners (*CYB*, 1925, p. 394). The postal workers' manifesto simply complained about the control exercised by "foreigners," and did not mention the word "imperialists."

97. T'ang Hai, *Chung-kuo lao-tung wen-t'i* [164], p. 479.

98. The Commercial Press reserved its recognition of the union until such time as the Peking government had promulgated trade union laws (*NCH*, 29.viii.25); Chinese firms, in their negotiations during August with the General Union, maintained the same reservation (*Die Arbeiter Chinas* [171], pp. 22–25). It was these difficulties that made Li Li-san go to Peking on August 29 in order to urge the promulgation of trade union legislation (*PDR*, 21.viii.25).

99. *NCH*, 5.ix.25, 12.ix.25. A union was formed on this line as a result of this success (Hsü Hsieh-hua, *T'ieh-lu lao-kung wen-t'i* [196], p. 176).

100. *Chien-shih* [165], p. 214.

101. *NCH*, 12.ix.25. Work was resumed after there had been a well-disciplined procession conducted by the leaders of the union, arranged in agreement with the General Union, and on the understanding that the cotton mill owners and the Chinese Chamber of Commerce would contribute 90,000 yuan toward the expenses of the strike.

102. *NCH*, 26.ix.25.

103. *NCH*, 26.ix.25 and 3.x.25 (concerning the cotton mills), and 17.x.25 (concerning the Commercial Press).

104. *PDR*, 24.ix.25.　　　　　　　　　　105. *NCH*, 3.x.25.

106. See *Wu-sa yun-tung* [197] and *Wu-sa t'ung-shih* [186]; see also Chang Wei-ying [189]. Nothing is said in this chapter about the repercussions of May 30 in Canton and South China, which will be discussed in the following chapter.

107. *HT*, 2.vii.25.　　　　　　　　　　108. *Nien-chien* [138] II, 457.

109. *HT*, 26.vii.25.　　　　　　　　　　110. *PP*, 14.vi.25.

111. *MDN*, 17.vi.25.

112. *NCH*, 27.vi.25. According to *Chien-shih* [165], p. 121, this meeting was held on June 2.

113. *Wu-sa yun-tung* [197], p. 21.

114. Hewlett, *Forty Years in China* [44], p. 154.

115. *PP*, 14.vi.25; see also *Wu-sa yun-tung* [197], p. 78.

116. *Wu-sa yun-tung* [197], pp. 125 and 134.

117. *HT*, 15.viii.25.　　　　　　　　　　118. *MDN*, 17.vi.25.

119. *Wu-sa t'ung-shih* [186], p. 50.　　　120. *CWR*, 17.x.25.

121. *Wu-sa t'ung-shih* [186], p. 51.

122. Hewlett, *Forty Years in China* [44], p. 154.

123. Chang Wei-ying [189], p. 84.　　　　124. *Nien-chien* [138] II, 457.

125. *Wu-sa t'ung-shih* [186], p. 50.　　　126. Chang Wei-ying [189], p. 84.

127. *Ibid.*, p. 85.

128. *Chien-shih* [165], p. 190. See also *Nien-chien* [138] II, 456 (a detailed analysis of the strikers' demands).

129. *NCH*, 8.viii.25; *Chien-shih* [165], p. 209.

130. See pp. 207–8 above.

131. *Chien-shih* [165], p. 191; *HT*, 2.vii.25; *PP*, 21.vi.25.

132. There were said to be 100,000 unemployed in Wuhan alone, without counting those who came there from other parts of the province (*STSP*, 24.viii.25).

133. *HT*, 1.v.26, article by Ch'en Tu-hsiu, dealing with the negative factors (political repression, influx of unemployed, etc.) which in his opinion had retarded the labor movement in Wuhan during the May Thirtieth Movement. His pessimistic outlook concerning the potentialities of the proletariat in this region is interesting in view of the big upsurge in the labor movement there five months later, after the arrival of the Nationalist armies.

134. *Wu-sa yun-tung* [197], pp. 128–32, contains a list of the names of the victims.

135. Chang Wei-ying [189], p. 89; *Wu-sa yun-tung* [197], p. 184.

136. *NCH*, 15.viii.25 (report of J. P. Kenrick, general manager of the Kiaotso mines).

137. *NCH*, 1.viii.25; *Chien-shih* [165], p. 209. Chang Wei-ying ([189], p. 90) reports that Chang Tsung-ch'ang was paid 300,000 yuan by the Japanese for carrying out this operation.

138. Wang Lin, *Po-chung* [213], pp. 13–26; *NCH*, 15.viii.25 and 22.viii.25.

139. *PP*, 16.viii.25.   140. Wang Lin [213].

141. *MDN*, 23.vi.25 and 30.vi.25.

142. K.M.A. Archives [15], 14/2/21, No. 46 A (report of the managing director on the September strike), and No. 71 (manifesto and rules of the Chaokochwang union).

143. *Ibid.*   144. *CEB*, 31.vii.26.

145. *Nien-chien* [138] II, 10. See also Hsü Hsieh-hua, *T'ieh-lu lao-kung wen-t'i* [196], pp. 174–78.

146. *Nien-chien*, II, 115.

147. In Tsinan a General Union was formed on July 28, initiated by the local branch of the Chin-P'u railwaymen's union, the cotton workers' union, and the rickshaw men's union (*Nien-chien*, II, 97).

148. *Nien-chien*, II, 97.

149. *Ibid.*, p. 99; but this union was dissolved several weeks later by Li Ching-lin, after the Yü-ta cotton mill strike.

150. *Ibid.*, p. 98.

151. See *IPC*, June, July, and Aug. 1925, *passim*.

152. See p. 270 above.

153. See Wieger, *La Chine moderne* [139] VI, 196–98.

154. *Wu-sa t'ung-shih* [186], pp. 113ff.

155. *Wu-sa yun-tung* [197], p. 37.   156. *Ibid.*, p. 41.

157. See for instance how the peasants took part in the fight of the Canton government against the petty warlords of Kwangtung (pp. 316–17 below).

158. *HT*, 26.vii.25.   159. Chang Wei-ying [189], p. 86.

160. *MDN*, 25.vi.25.

161. Hewlett, *Forty Years in China* [44], p. 154. See also *SCMP*, 30.vii.25, on the efforts of the Amoy compradores and their staffs to hinder the boycott.

162. *NCH*, 13.vi.25.   163. *HT*, 15.viii.25.

164. *MDN*, 17.vi.25.

165. Li Chien-nung, *Political History* [277], pp. 482–84.

166. Wieger, *La Chine moderne* [139] VI, 205.

167. *NCH*, 11.vii.25.

168. The mill belonged to the big industrialist Mu Ou-ch'u (H. Y. Moh); the Communist paper *HT* (31.viii.25) accused him of having arranged the attack.

169. *HWP*, 20.viii.25; *I-shih-pao* [123], 23.viii.25; *I-shih-pao* [124], 30.viii.25.

170. Interview with the railwayman Li Ch'en-kang.

171. *I-shih-pao* [123], 21.ix.25; see also *Nien-chien* [138] II, 97, on the founding of this union.

172. *CWR*, 3.x.25.   173. *I-shih-pao* [123], 21.ix.25.
174. *CP*, 13.ix.25.

175. See *Ko-ming chan-shih-chi* [178], pp. 28ff (a biography of the student Wang Chung-hsiu, secretary of the Lunghai union, who cooperated with the Kuominchun against Wu P'ei-fu during the summer of 1925).

176. See Chapter XII below.

177. According to lists in *Nien-chien* [138] II, 154–282.

178. The price rose from 11 yuan the picul in spring 1925 to 16 yuan in April 1926 and 18 yuan in June 1926, owing to rumors of a bad harvest which reached Shanghai, and also to the warlords' taxes (*CEB*, 21.viii.26).

179. These figures are from *HT*, 7.vii.26 (which lists 35 strikes, most of which affected several firms at once). The report of the Commissioner of Police of the International Settlement lists 40 strikes for the month of June, with over 50,000 strikers; *Nien-chien*, II, 154–282, lists 49 strikes for this month.

180. See pp. 283–84 below.

181. *Nien-chien*, II, 63–65, gives a detailed list of all the unions, including membership figures, that were affiliated with the Shanghai General Union in July 1925; *HT*, 7.vii.26, gives a similar list for June 1926.

182. See *Nien-chien*, II, 63–65, and *HT*, 7.vii.26.

183. *HT*, 23.vi.26.   184. *NCH*, 12.vi.26.
185. *CEB*, 31.vii.26.

186. This demand was made in the strike of the telegraphers (*NCH*, 10.x.25), and in the one at the No. 3 mill of the Naigai Wata Kaisha (*NCH*, 19.vi.26).

187. A right demanded in the British "Oriental Cotton Mill" (*NCH*, 19.xii.25). This right was granted (*CEB*, 23.i.26).

188. Demand made in the British Ewo cotton mill (*NCH*, 12.xii.25).

189. Demanded by the strikers at the Japanese Jih-hua cotton mill, held to protest the arrest of a worker by the Chinese police of Pootung (*NCH*, 21.xi.25), and by the Commercial Press strikers who were protesting the dismissal of the leaders of the strike held in August 1925 (*NCH*, 2.i.26).

190. *NCH*, 26.vi.26.   191. *NCH*, 20.iii.26.
192. *CEB*, 16.x.26.

193. *CEM*, Oct. 1926 ("Strikes in Shanghai").

194. *HT*, 23.vi.26. Already in March the General Union frowned on the use of ta-ch'ang by strikers in a Yangtzepoo cotton mill (*NCH*, 13.iii.26).

195. *NCH*, 26.vi.26.

196. *HT*, 23.vi.26.

197. *Huang P'ang ssu-chou-nien* [176], pp. 30, 49, 88. The ceremonies took place on the premises of the club run by the management of the Nanyang Company and were attended by about twenty right-wing associations, including the Hunan and Canton regional guilds and some craft guilds, and also by some members of the Central Committee of the Kuomintang (no doubt members of the dissident right wing; see p. 310 below).

198. See *HT*, 23.vii.26, *NCH*, 3.vii.26, and *NCH*, 10.vii.26, where Mrs. Mu is described as "a social worker ... who was employed by some of the silk filature proprietors to keep conditions smooth in the filatures."

199. Ma Ch'ao-chün [210] says nothing at all about any activities of the Federation during the May Thirtieth Movement; he admits (p. 486) that very few of the members were industrial workers, and that such as there were were all employed in small workshops.

200. See *Nien-chien* [138] II, 154–282, for a chronology of strikes during this period.

201. *PDR*, Nov. 1925, *passim*.

202. *CEM*, Oct. 1926 ("Strikes in Shanghai").

203. For instance, a system of identity discs in the Société Franco-Chinoise de Construction Métallique was protested (*CEB*, 21.viii.26). After the May Thirtieth Movement, each worker in the Japanese cotton mills was compelled to wear a numbered disc and to carry identity papers with a photograph (interview with the worker Wang Jui-an). The French Tramways took the fingerprints of their workers (*NCH*, 31.xii.26).

204. This was protested in an embroidery factory in April (*CEM*, Oct. 1926).

205. Protested in a British cotton mill in May (*ibid.*).

206. Protested in the Naigai cotton mill No. 3 in March (*ibid.*).

207. One example is the strike in the Naigai cotton mills Nos. 2 and 3 in June 1926, demanding the dismissal of four "armed bullies" recently engaged by the factory (*NCH*, 19.vi.26).

208. *CEM*, Oct. 1926.   209. *Nien-chien* [138] II, 154–282.

210. Li Chien-nung, *Political History* [277], p. 487.

211. *NCH*, 7.xi.25; *PDR*, 21.x.25.

212. *PDR*, Nov.–Dec. 1925, *passim*.

213. Isaacs, *Tragedy* [263], pp. 78–79.

214. *Ko-ming lieh-shih-chuan* [221], pp. 189ff (biography of Liu Hua).

215. *PDR*, 10.iv.26.   216. *NCH*, 23.i.26.

217. *NCH*, 27.ii.26.   218. *PDR*, 3.v.26.

219. *PDR*, 27.v.26, 31.v.26, 1.vi.26.

220. *PDR*, 28.vi.26; *HT*, 30.vi.26.

221. *Nien-chien* [138] II, 396–97.

222. *CP*, 12.xii.25 (report of a strike against the dismissal of 100 women by the B.A.T.); *MKJP*, 23.ii.26 (report of a strike against the dismissal of 700 older workers in a hemp factory).

223. *HT*, 6.viii.26; *CWR*, 12.vi.26.

224. *MDN*, 6.iv.26.

225. *MDN*, 16.iii.27. (This Japanese-owned paper explicitly stated that it was a question of getting rid of workers with "unwholesome ideas.")

226. *MKJP*, 23.ix.25 and 24.ix.25; *HT*, 3.xii.25.

227. According to *HT*, 5,000 were laid off; the figure was 8,000 according to *MKJP*, 24.ix.25 and 10,000 according to *CP*, 2.x.25.

228. *HT*, 30.xii.25; *NCH*, 28.xi.25.

229. On the split in the Kuomintang see pp. 310–11 below.

230. *STSP*, 24.xii.25; *Shih-shih hsin-pao* [130], 3.i.26.

231. *STSP*, 8.ii.26.

232. *Lao-tung ta-hui* [142], p. 78 (report of the Wuhan unions to the Third Labor Congress).

233. During the winter of 1925–26 the number of unemployed persons in Wuhan is said to have been double that of workers employed (*HT*, 3.iv.26).

234. *HT*, 3.iv.26.

235. For details concerning these wars see Wieger, *La Chine moderne* [139] VI, 33–76.

236. In Hupeh the provincial paper money depreciated rapidly during 1926, falling as low as 20 per cent below nominal value; the exchange rate with the silver yuan changed from 3,000 to 11,000 paper cash (*RT*, Shasi, 1926, p. 3).

237. *MDN*, 23.ii.26 and *passim*. The yuan was worth 500 feng-p'iao at the beginning of August and 850 in March 1927.

238. This figure is arrived at by combining the chronology in the *Nien-chien* and reports in *MDN*.

239. One example was a strike in a Dairen machine shop demanding recognition of the local union (*MDN*, 26.xii.25, 29.xii.25). There was also a strike in the Dairen textile factories in April, when the strikers sent representatives to Shanghai and other industrial centers (*MKJP*, 13.vii.26).

240. *CEJ*, Feb. 1927, "Labor Conditions in Chekiang."

241. See Wieger, *La Chine moderne* [139] VI, 58ff.

242. *PP*, 17.i.26 (exchange of messages between Feng and the Central Executive Committee of the Kuomintang).

243. Hsü Ch'ien, surrounded by officers of the 2nd Kuominchun, made a speech at the funeral service held in Peking on January 27 for Kuo Sung-ling (*JWC*, 4.i.26), who had just been killed in battle in his abortive revolt against his chief, Chang Tso-lin; he wanted to join forces with the Kuominchun (Wieger [139] VI, 64–68).

244. For example, the student Li Chih-tan was assigned by the CP to be political adviser to the 2nd Kuominchun (*Ko-ming lieh-shih-chuan* [221], p. 68).

245. *PP*, 21.i.26 (on a circular in which the 1st Kuominchun denied that it was Bolshevist. "Since our country is based on agriculture, there are neither very rich nor very poor people.")

246. *HT*, Dec. 1925–Jan. 1926, *passim.*   247. *I-shih-pao* [123], 3.i.26.

248. *Nien-chien* [138] II, 115.   249. *I-shih-pao* [123], 19.i.26.

250. *Ibid.*, 26.i.26.

251. *HT*, 1.v.26. Before the retreat of the Kuominchun, this union is said to have had 50,000 members.

252. *Nien-chien* [138], 98–99; *I-shih-pao* [123], 4.i.26.

253. *STSP*, 8.ii.26. On this occasion the Kuominchun called upon workers' groups in Tangshan to support the strikers "against British imperialism."

254. *CP*, 15.xii.25. In Nankow two thousand railwaymen held a meeting to express their hostility toward the Fengtien faction and their support for the Kuominchun, and they called for a national association for the abolition of the unequal treaties and the introduction of civil liberties.

255. Interview with the railwayman Li Ch'en-kang, who took part in the actions of the "special groups" of railwaymen on the Lunghai line, operating in liaison with the Kuominchun. See also *Ko-ming chan-shih-chi* [178], p. 34 (biography of the Communist railwayman Ma Ch'i, who collaborated with the Kuominchun on the Ching-Sui line and was killed in a battle against the Fengtien faction).

256. *IS*, 1926, III, 18; Chen Ta, *ILR*, March 1927.

257. *CEM*, No. 1926 ("Factories in Shensi and Kansu"). The "model cotton mill" in Sian employed 85 workers on a nine-hour day (seven hours for apprentices); the 50 workers employed by a Lanchow wool factory worked a seven-hour day, and the 125 workers in a match factory worked a nine-and-a-half-hour day. In all three cases Sunday was a day of rest.

258. Lamb, *Social Legislation* [268], appendix; see also *Nien-chien* [138] III, 191–95.

259. But see Sheridan, *Chinese Warlord* [301a]. This study of Feng Yü-hsiang was published in 1966, after the original edition of the present work came out.

260. *HT*, 10.ii.26.   261. *I-shih-pao* [123], 25.xi.25.

262. *CP*, 19.i.26. In giving this information, this conservative paper denounced the "red influence" in the C.E.R. union.

263. *PP*, 9.v.25 (instructions given by Wu P'ei-fu to the management of the Ching-Han for the repression of union activities).

264. See pp. 276 and 285 above.

265. *HT*, 3.iv.26. See also *Lao-tung ta-hui* [142], pp. 72ff (report of the Wuhan delegates to the Third Congress).

266. *NCH*, 26.ii.26.

267. *MDN*, 15.iii.26.

268. See for instance an interview with a representative of Wu P'ei-fu in *PP*, 2.v.26, who said that Wu was prepared to fight to the end in order to crush Bolshevism in China, and that this was why he had formed an alliance with Marshal Chang. See also a statement made by Chang Tso-lin to foreign journalists in Mukden (*PP*, 19.iv.26), in which he declared that his sole aim was to exterminate Bolshevism, after which he would withdraw north of the Great Wall and devote himself to the reconstruction of Manchuria.

269. *PP*, 9.v.26 (an account of large-scale arrests in Peking by order of the commander of the Fengtien garrison).

Chapter XII

1. On the political situation in Canton in the spring of 1925, see Li Chien-nung, *Political History* [277], pp. 495–98, and Hu Hua, *Ko-ming shih* [200], pp. 120–22.

2. On the Canton–Hong Kong strike as a whole, see Akatova, *S'angan-Guanchzhou-skaya zabastovka* [229].

3. *Chien-shih* [165], p. 224.

4. *Ibid.*, p. 225; Chen Ta, "Analysis of Strikes," *CEJ*, Nov. 1927. The demands concerning reduction of rents and rights of residence are mentioned only by Teng Chung-hsia (in *Chien-shih*).

5. There were 100,000 participants according to Teng Chung-hsia, 10,000 according to Chen Ta (*CEJ, ibid.*).

6. See *June Twenty-third* [177], Appendix B, which lists the names of the 52 killed and 117 wounded.

7. *The Shameen Affair* [22].

8. This commission, set up by Hu Han-min immediately after the incident, was composed mainly of leaders of moderate organizations such as the chamber of commerce, the Y.M.C.A., and teachers' associations; the only trade unionist was Ch'en Sen, a leader of the right wing of the Canton labor movement. Its report states that the first shots were fired from Shameen and were shortly followed by machine-gun fire (*June Twenty-third* [177], p. 8).

9. *SCMP*, 27.vi.25 (text of a resolution adopted unanimously by 17 American teachers of the Canton Christian College, dated June 24).

10. *Chien-shih* [165], p. 227.   11. *Ibid.*, pp. 227–28.

12. Hong Kong Government Administrative Report [23], 1925 (which lists 28 trades on strike).

13. *Ibid.*   14. *Ibid.*

15. *SCMP*, 15.vii.25.

16. *CTSTL*, 1958, No. 5, "Sheng-Kang pa-kung."

17. *SCMP, passim.*

18. *Chien-shih* [165], p. 227; see also Teng Chung-hsia, *Sheng-Kang pa-kung kai-kuan* [154], p. 7.

19. *Chien-shih*, p. 227.

20. *Hu-nan lieh-shih-chuan* [223], p. 22 (biography of Teng Chung-hsia).

21. Akatova [229], pp. 110 and 124.

22. There were 19 according to Teng Chung-hsia, 30 according to a report in *SCMP*, 31.xii.25.

23. In view of the fact that there was one delegate for every 50 workers in the Workers' Delegates' Conference, and that the total number of delegates was 800, it may be assumed

that there were about 40,000 strikers who remained in Canton, the rest having gone to their villages. According to the count made by the Strike Committee in September, there were then 51,858 strikers in Canton (*CWR*, 19.ix.25). Sokolsky (*NCH*, 24.iv.26 and 8.v.26) reckoned the total number of strikers at 100,000, which more or less accords with the above figures.

24. *CWR*, 19.ix.25, 16.i.26, 22.v.26, 12.vi.26; *SCMP*, 4.viii.25, 25.viii.25.

25. Teng Chung-hsia [154], p. 28.

26. Ch'en Ta, *Lao-tung wen-t'i* [190], p. 213.

27. *ECB*, II, No. 4 (April 1929).

28. Teng Chung-hsia [154], p. 28.

29. On the activities of the pickets, see the account by Sokolsky of his visits to Canton and Hong Kong in *NCH*, 24.iv.26 and 8.v.26; see also *Chien-shih* [165], p. 230.

30. Teng Chung-hsia [154], p. 13; *SCMP*, 19.xii.25. In December 1925, the "workers' prison" contained 300 prisoners.

31. *SCMP*, 29.xi.25 (arrest of a strike leader accused of corruption and of collusion with the troops of Ch'en Chiung-ming). Forty-six cases of corruption were examined by the Workers' Delegates' Conference in the course of its first hundred meetings (*CTSTL*, 1958, No. 5, "Sheng-Kang pa-kung").

32. Gannett's articles in *The Nation* were printed in *CWR*, 12.vi.26.

33. *SCMP*, 8.xi.26.

34. *SCMP*, July 1925, *passim*.

35. For example, a Norwegian ship had to pay a fine of 2,000 yuan (*SCMP*, 31.vii.25).

36. See p. 307 below.   37. *SCMP*, 20.xii.25.

38. See Ho Kan-chih, *Modern Revolution* [259], p. 99.

39. *RT*, 1925, Pakhoi, p. 1.

40. Teng Chung-hsia [154], p. 28 (containing the precise delimitation of these districts). In December 1925 the pickets were in control of 19 Kwangtung ports (*CWR*, 12.xii.25).

41. Teng Chung-hsia [154], p. 28.

42. See p. 316 below.

43. See Akatova [229], pp. 119–20 (largely based on the *Min-kuo jih-pao* of Canton).

44. *SCMP*, 27.vii.25.   45. *SCMP*, 1.viii.25.

46. *SCMP*, 16.iv.26.

47. Sokolsky's account in *NCH*, 24.iv.26 and 8.v.26.

48. *CTSTL*, 1958, No. 5, "Sheng-Kang pa-kung."

49. For example, in February 1926 goods to the value of 100,000 yuan were seized on a boat destined for Macao (*SCMP*, 11.ii.26). When Sokolsky visited Canton in April 1926 (see note 47 above), the boycott was still in full swing there.

50. *SCMP*, 26.ii.26, 27.ii.26. This incident demonstrates the extremely moderate attitude of the Nationalist government. Although it had called for the abolition of the unequal treaties and had broken off all relations with the Northern government, it nevertheless refrained from interfering with the local Inspectorate of Customs, nominally under Peking but traditionally under the control of a British inspector.

51. See p. 311 below.

52. *SCMP*, 31.v.26; see also *CTSTL*, 1958, No. 5, "Sheng-Kang pa-kung," containing the text of the resolutions and reports at this hundredth meeting.

53. *SCMP*, 21.vi.26.

54. See Chapter XIII below.

55. In May 1925 it was one of the four labor organizations that convened the Second National Labor Congress, after which the All-China General Union was formed (see p. 258 above).

56. On this conference, see *Kung-jen yun-tung* [146], pp. 199–218 (full text of the resolutions adopted); see also *PPW*, Nos. 6 and 7 (15.ix.27 and 1.x.27), Stoler, "The Trade Union Movement in Canton" (an account of a visit to South China by a trade unionist of the Red International in February 1927).

57. There were 2,500 delegates from 140 unions, according to the Kuomintang publication *CCCP*, May 1926 (*Kung-jen yun-tung* [146], p. 191).

58. Teng Chung-hsia, *Kuang-chou kung-ch'ao* [153], p. 65. See also Ma Ch'ao-chün [210], pp. 517–20.

59. Teng Chung-hsia [154], p. 57.

60. *Nien-chien* [138] II, 80, gives a long list of the guilds and unions affiliated with this organization; Teng Chung-hsia [154], p. 57, gives May 15, 1926, as the date of its foundation.

61. *Kung-jen yun-tung* [146], p. 188 (according to the *CCCP* survey referred to in note 57 above).

62. *CEB*, 21.viii.26 (list of the Nanning unions).

63. *CWR*, 20.ii.26.

64. *Kung-jen yun-tung* [146], pp. 170–86 (resolutions of the seamen's conference, taken from the journal *Chung-kuo hai-yuan*).

65. Stoler, *PPW*, Nos. 6 and 7; see also Akatova [229], p. 113.

66. *Kung-jen yun-tung* [146], pp. 189–90.

67. Teng Chung-hsia, *Kuang-chou kung-ch'ao* [153], p. 63.

68. *SCMP*, 17.v.26.

69. Akatova [229], p. 13 (based on *Min-kuo jih-pao* of Canton).

70. *Nien-chien* [138] II, 73–79. (This list of the Canton unions, taken from a survey made by the municipality at the end of 1926, gives for each the date of foundation and the number of members.)

71. *SCMP*, 17.x.25.

72. There were 140,000 according to *PPW*, 15.ix.27; 160,000 according to Teng Chung-hsia, *Kuang-chou kung-ch'ao* [153], p. 59.

73. *CEB*, 14.viii.26 (a detailed list of the Swatow unions, with dates of foundation and number of members).

74. See p. 297 above.

75. *CEB*, 21.viii.26 (list of the Nanning unions).

76. *CYB*, 1928, pp. 1028–29.

77. In April 1926 the Workers' Delegates' Conference fixed a 5 yuan maximum entry fee for the unions affiliated with it. But according to the survey conducted by the municipality of Canton (*Nien-chien* [138] II, 73–79), fees were much higher in some of the conservative unions: 15 yuan for the autobus union, 14 for the dockhands' Guild of Common Virtue, 20 for the sewing machine factory union, and 48 for the fiber-balers' union.

78. *SCMP*, 7.i.26.

79. *SCMP*, 1.xi.26.

80. *CWR*, 10.iv.26; Stoler, *PPW*, Nos. 6 and 7; the latter report estimates that in early 1927—that is, slightly later—the left-wing unions in Canton had 2,000 pickets.

81. In 1920 he edited the Canton journal *Lao-tung-che*, which had an anarchist flavor (see pp. 171–72 above).

82. He was a leader of the small Communist group in Canton in 1920–21; in 1923 he was thrown out of the CP for "opportunism" (*Chien-shih* [165], p. 37), and then joined the left wing of the Kuomintang; he was appointed head of the Labor Department of the Kuomintang in place of Liao Chung-k'ai after the latter was assassinated (*SCMP*, 9.i.26).

83. In 1922 he was in charge of the local branch of the Labor Secretariat (*Chien-shih*, p. 38); he was one of the founders of the Workers' Delegates' Conference in 1924 (Huang

I-po, *Kuang-tung chi-ch'i kung-jen* [202], p. 44). Liao Chung-k'ai appointed him secretary of the Labor Department of the Kuomintang Central Committee, which Liao headed (see p. 246 above).

84. *Su Chao-cheng* [222], p. 27.

85. *Ko-ming lieh-shih-chuan* [221], p. 144.

86. Huang I-po [202], p. 44.　　　　　87. *Lao-tung ta-hui* [142], pp. 31 and 125.

88. *Ibid.*, p. 6.　　　　　　　　　　89. *Ibid.*, p. 125.

90. *Ko-ming lieh-shih-chuan* [221], p. 152.　　91. Strong, *China's Millions* [304], p. 96.

92. *SCMP*, 18.i.26.

93. *CEB*, 29.v.26 (list of strikes in Canton 1925-26).

94. See the pamphlet published by the hospital management concerning the strike, *Chinese Communists and Christian Properties* [172].

95. *SCMP*, 4.ix.25.　　　　　　　　96. *SCMP*, 13.xi.25.

97. See note 243, p. 514.　　　　　　98. *SCMP*, 23.i.26.

99. *SCMP*, 11.ii.26.　　　　　　　　100. *CCCP*, 17.v.26.

101. Li Chien-nung, *Political History* [277], p. 503.

102. *Lao-tung ta-hui* [142], pp. 96–116. See also *IS*, III, 178–79 (taken from the Chinese press in Canton).

103. *Lao-tung ta-hui* [142], pp. 49, 60, 82, and 86.

104. *Ibid.*, p. 124.　　　　　　　　105. *Ibid.*, p. 125.

106. *Ibid.*, p. 127 (manifesto of the Third Congress).

107. On the question of unemployment, see pp. 305–6 below.

108. *Lao-tung ta-hui* [142], p. 137.　　109. *Ibid.*, p. 23; see p. 259 above.

110. Stoler, *PPW*, Nos. 6 and 7.

111. Huang I-po, *Kuang-tung chi-ch'i kung-jen* [202], p. 22.

112. *Ibid.*, p. 45.　　　　　　　113. *CWR*, 11.iv.25; *SCMP*, 6.viii.25.

114. Stoler, *PPW*, Nos. 6 and 7.　　　115. *SCMP*, 20.vii.25.

116. For example, on August 15 it attended a meeting at the Hong Kong Chamber of Commerce, along with several craft unions, for the launching of an appeal to put an end to the strike (*SCMP*, 17.viii.25).

117. See pp. 306–7 below.

118. Huang I-po, *Kuang-tung chi-ch'i kung-jen* [202], pp. 25-26; Ma Ch'ao-chün, *Lao-tung yun-tung shih* [210], pp. 537–41 (a list of the local branches).

119. See p. 298 above.　　　　　　120. See Chapter XIII below.

121. Stoler, *PPW*, Nos. 6 and 7.

122. On the collusion between Ch'en Sen and Cantonese employers see *HT*, 29.viii.26.

123. Examples quoted by Teng Chung-hsia, *Kuang-chou kung-ch'ao* [153], pp. 27-31.

124. *SCMP*, 14.viii.25.　　　　　　125. *SCMP*, 23.x.25.

126. *SCMP*, 22.i.26.

127. See the Mechanics' manifesto of January 1926 (Huang I-po, *Kuang-tung chi-ch'i kung-jen* [202], p. 25), which accuses an "ill-intentioned party" of having incited the railwaymen against them.

128. *Ibid.*, pp. 44–45.　　　　　　129. *CWR*, 28.i.28.

130. Teng Chung-hsia [153], p. 31.　　131. See pp. 308–9 below.

132. See p. 296 above.　　　　　　133. *Kung-jen yun-tung* [146], pp. 214–15.

134. *SCMP*, 19.v.26.

135. The president of the provincial federation was Ch'en Sen, who in June 1925 was the only trade unionist on the commission of inquiry into the Shakee Road incident (see note 8, above).

136. The managing director of the line was a relation of Wang Ching-wei (*SCMP*, 14.viii.25).

137. Ho Kan-chih, *Modern Revolution* [259], p. 99; Wieger, *La Chine moderne* [139] VII, 13–14.

138. *SCMP*, 27.x.25. T'an Yen-k'ai's Hunanese army, for instance, became the 2nd Army Corps.

139. *Gomindan* [174], p. 51.

140. Ho Kan-chih [259], p. 93.

141. *SCMP*, 27.i.26.

142. Ho Kan-chih [259], p. 99.

143. *Chien-shih* [165], pp. 234–35.

144. *SCMP*, 3.xi.25.

145. *SCMP*, 16.xi.25 and 26.i.26.

146. *Chinese Bulletin* [93], No. 3.

147. *SCMP*, 27.vi.25 (telegram sent to Karakhan, the Soviet ambassador in Peking, who had retained the position of doyen of the diplomatic corps held by his Tsarist predecessor).

148. *SCMP*, 8.xii.25.

149. *SCMP*, 9.i.26.

150. *IS*, 1926, II, 391.

151. See p. 245 above.

152. *Kung-jen yun-tung* [217], pp. 31–40 (text of these resolutions).

153. In 1924 there were usually 210 ships a day using the port of Hong Kong, but only 34 in July and August 1925 (Teng Chung-hsia [154], p. 69).

154. *Chien-shih* [165], p. 232.

155. The revenue from taxes on imports in the fall of 1925 was half that of autumn 1924 (Teng Chung-hsia [154], p. 69). British commercial firms in Hong Kong were saved from bankruptcy only by large government subsidies, and the official estimate of the cost of the strike to the Hong Kong government was £198,106 (Administrative Report [23], 1925, p. 4).

156. *SCMP*, 7.viii.25.

157. *SCMP*, 10.ix.25. Teng Chung-hsia dwells at length (*Chien-shih* [165], pp. 235–36, and *Sheng-Kang pa-kung kai-kuan* [154], pp. 20–25) on the relaxation of the boycott in September, and it may be supposed that as adviser to the Strike Committee and unofficial representative of the CCP, he was to some extent responsible for the introduction of these measures.

158. Teng Chung-hsia [154], pp. 19–20.

159. *Ibid.*, p. 83.

160. *Lao-tung ta-hui* [142], p. 135.

161. Teng Chung-hsia [154], p. 72.

162. *Chien-shih* [165], pp. 240–41.

163. Ho Kan-chih, *Modern Revolution* [259], pp. 110–12. All that can be done here is to indicate the stresses and strains within the Kuomintang so as to throw some light on the attitude of the labor movement toward it.

164. Ho Kan-chih, *ibid.*

165. *SCMP*, 19.xii.25.

166. Isaacs, *Tragedy* [263], p. 92.

167. *SCMP*, 25.xi.25.

168. *SCMP*, 10.xii.25.

169. Ma Ch'ao-chün, *Lao-tung yun-tung shih* [210], pp. 513–14.

170. *SCMP*, 18.xi.25.

171. Ho Kan-chih, *Modern Revolution* [259], pp. 112–13; *SCMP*, 20–25.iii.26.

172. Wieger, *La Chine moderne* [139] VII, 21.

173. *Ibid.*

174. *SCMP*, 17.v.26; Hu Hua, *Ko-ming shih* [200], p. 134.

175. *SCMP*, 22.v.26.

176. *CWR*, 13.v.26.

177. *SCMP*, 5.vi.26; the monopoly was instituted when the Asiatic Petroleum Co., Standard Oil, and others refused to pay Sun Yat-sen the tax on oil.

178. *SCMP*, 28.v.26.

179. *CWR*, 12.vi.26.

180. *CWR*, 24.iv.26.

181. Akatova [229], chap. 4.

182. Stoler, *PPW*, No. 7.

183. *CWR*, 13.vi.26.

184. *SCMP*, 27.iv.26 and 15.v.26.

185. *SCMP*, 9.vi.26.

186. *SCMP*, 28.v.26. At the end of March, Ch'en supported the seamen employed on

the junks plying the rivers when they threatened to go on strike for higher wages (*CWR*, 10.iv.26).

187. *SCMP*, 8.vii.26.   188. See p. 311 above.

189. *Lao-tung ta-hui* [142], p. 127 (manifesto of the Third Labor Congress).

190. *Ibid.*, pp. 49–61.   191. *Kung-jen yun-tung* [217], p. 40.

192. "Kuo-min-tang tso-yu-p'ai," *HT*, 3.xii.25.

193. "Nan-fang ching-shih," *HT*, 15.v.26.

194. *HT*, 3.iv.26.   195. *Ibid.*

196. *Lao-tung ta-hui* [142], p. 116.   197. *Ibid.*, pp. 118–19.

198. *Kung-jen yun-tung* [146], p. 199.   199. Teng Chung-hsia [154], p. 50.

200. *SCMP*, 16.vi.26.

201. *SCMP*, 20.v.26. On the day after the promulgation of the May 31 decree the "alliance" organized a big procession to celebrate this success (*SCMP*, 2.vi.26).

202. Hu Hua, *Ko-ming shih* [200], pp. 131–33.

203. Akatova [229], p. 124.

204. *Chien-shih* [165], p. 298; Akatova, *ibid.* (quoting from a study of the history of opportunism in the CCP by Ts'ai Ho-sen).

205. *Kung-jen yun-tung* [146], p. 206.

206. Teng Chung-hsia, *Kuang-chou kung-ch'ao* [153], pp. 90–94.

207. *Nung-min yun-tung* [147], p. 17.

208. Ho Kan-chih, *Modern Revolution* [259], p. 100.

209. In 1926 this department was split into two, which suggests a desire to do more for the peasants (*Nung-min yun-tung* [147], p. 8).

210. *Ibid.*

211. Hu Hua, *Ko-ming shih* [200], p. 138.

212. Ho Kan-chih, *Modern Revolution* [259], p. 101; *Nung-min yun-tung*, pp. 40ff.

213. *SCMP*, 1.x.25.

214. Such resolutions were passed, for example, at the Canton Workers' Delegates' Conference in April 1926 (*Kung-jen yun-tung* [146], p. 213) and at the Third Labor Congress in 1926 (*Lao-tung ta-hui* [142], p. 120).

215. See p. 294 above.

216. Teng Chung-hsia [154], p. 29; *HT*, 18.ix.25.

217. *Lao-tung ta-hui* [142], p. 120.

218. *Ibid.*, p. 96. These limitations on the alliance between the peasants and the working class sprang from the concept of a restricted role of peasants in the Chinese revolution. In 1925–26 the CP leadership began to warn against "peasant excesses;" it did so still more after the transfer of the Nationalist government to Wuhan, when peasant unions began springing up in Central China (see Wilbur, *Documents* [140], p. 277). It was this that to a large extent accounted for the accusations of "opportunism" later leveled against Ch'en Tu-hsiu (Hu Hua, *Ko-ming shih* [200], pp. 159–61).

219. *SCMP*, 9.vii.26.

220. *Lao-tung ta-hui* [142], p. 94 (views on the general situation in China expressed at the Third Congress). See also pp. 288–89 above.

Chapter XIII

1. On these military operations, see Wieger, *La Chine moderne* [139] VII, "éphémérides." See also Tang Leang-li, *Inner History* [306], pp. 255–56.

2. On the operations of the Kuominchun armies, see Wieger, *ibid.*, and *HT*, 4.xi.26.

3. Cf. the eyewitness account by Chapman (*The Chinese Revolution* [43], p. 20): ". . . it was found that the Nationalist soldiers never looted, and broadly speaking paid

for everything they wanted at market rate, and that only in urgent necessity did they impress the labour of carrying coolies, and even in such a case usually paid for it. The villagers and townspeople rubbed their eyes in amazement: the propaganda was true after all that these men were 'one with the common people.' The people reciprocated this attitude with open cordiality, and it was not uncommon to see, a few hours after the occupation of a town or a village, the soldiers fraternising and chatting in a most friendly way with the shopkeepers and their families on the street front. An indigenous intelligence service was thus ready [and] waiting to assist the incoming army. Reliable guides were available to serve whenever wanted, [and] in some cases, days before the army arrived, towns and cities were taken possession of by little groups of enthusiasts, perhaps with the aid of a handful of local militia, in the name of the Nationalist Government."

4. Hu Hua, *Ko-ming shih* [200], p. 150; *SCMP*, 2.vii.26. The total number of strikers attached to the Nationalist army when it arrived in Wuhan was around 20,000 (*PP*, 3.iv.27).

5. *SCMP*, 15.x.26.

6. *SCMP*, 30.ix.26, reports some scarcity of labor in Changsha, and notes that the laboring classes there were awaiting the arrival of the Southern army as a "boon" for them.

7. Wales, *Red Dust* [50], p. 83 (autobiography of the miner Ts'ai Shu-fan).

8. *Kung-jen yun-tung* [146], pp. 319–28.

9. *Ibid.*; see also Strong, *China's Millions* [304], p. 100 (recollections of the miner T'ang Shou-i).

10. Chao Heng-t'i's government had been overthrown in the spring by a popular uprising combined with militarist intrigues; but his adversary, T'ang Sheng-chih, who was an ally of Canton, was able to maintain control over only the south of the province, and the rest had fallen into the hands of supporters of Wu P'ei-fu (see Li Chien-nung, *Political History* [277], p. 503).

11. Ho Kan-chih, *Modern Revolution* [259], p. 124.

12. Wales, *Red Dust* [50], p. 90 (autobiography of the railwayman Wang Cheng).

13. *Kung-jen yun-tung* [146], pp. 319–28.   14. Hu Hua, *Ko-ming shih* [200], p. 151.

15. *PP*, 5.ix.26.

16. See Wieger, *La Chine moderne* [139] VII, 41.

17. *Ibid.*, p. 48.

18. At a meeting of the Central Committee of the Kuomintang on October 15, 1926, it was decided to organize provincial governments in the liberated territories on the lines of the Kwangtung provincial government (Tang Leang-li, *Inner History* [306], p. 260).

19. The *Han-k'ou shang-pao* of 14.ix.26 reported that unions in Hankow were "rising like the wind and multiplying like clouds."

20. *CEB*, 27.xi.26.   21. *Kung-jen yun-tung* [146], p. 399.

22. Chen Ta, "Analysis of Strikes," *CEJ*, Nov. 1927.

23. *SCMP*, 7.i.27.

24. *Kung-jen yun-tung* [146], p. 320.

25. Li Jui, *Mao Tse-tung* [206], p. 226.

26. *NCH*, 11.xii.26; see *Kung-jen yun-tung* [146], pp. 331–72 (text of the resolutions passed at this congress).

27. Stoler, "A Visit to Hunan Province," *PPW*, No. 4.

28. *NCH*, 31.xii.26.

29. *CTSTL*, 1957, No. 4, "Nan-ch'ang ta-shih-chi."

30. *Ibid.*

31. *Nien-chien* [138] II, 88–89. See p. 355 below.

32. *CEB*, 27.xi.26.

33. *Kung-jen yun-tung* [146], pp. 399ff. Hsü, a former leader of the railwaymen's union (*Chien-shih* [165], p. 118), was president of the Hupeh federation, and Liu was secretary of the committee for economic demands.

34. *Kung-jen yun-tung* [146], *ibid.* Kuo Liang was president of the Hunan federation; in 1922 he had helped Mao Tse-tung in running the earlier provincial federation (see p. 191 above).

35. They are listed in *CEB*, 27.xi.26.

36. *Kung-jen yun-tung* [146], pp. 425–32.

37. *IPC*, 2.vi.27.

38. *CEB*, 27.xi.26.

39. *Kung-jen yun-tung* [146], p. 335.

40. *Ibid.*, p. 407.

41. In April 1927 it was compulsory for every branch of the Wuhan general textile union to have at least one woman and one young worker on its executive committee (*IPC*, 2.vi.27).

42. *Kung-jen yun-tung* [146], p. 417.

43. *Ibid.*, pp. 338ff.

44. *Ibid.*, p. 407.

45. *NCH*, 24.xii.26.

46. *Kung-jen yun-tung* [146], pp. 345–49.

47. *IPC*, 2.vi.27.

48. *SCMP*, 19.xi.26. The union militias occupied the offices of the B.A.T. Hankow factory until the demands presented by the union were accepted. See also *NCH*, 15.i.27, which reported that the Kiukiang militias blockaded shipping until the strike of the dock coolies was settled.

49. *Kung-jen yun-tung* [146], pp. 420–21.

50. *NCH*, 18.xii.26.

51. Chapman, *The Chinese Revolution* [43], p. 91. See also *NCH*, 12.ii.27, which reports that the union to which domestic servants employed by foreigners belonged tried its members at its own courts and no longer brought them before the civil courts.

52. *Kung-jen yun-tung* [146], p. 335.

53. Chen Ta, "Analysis of Strikes," *CEJ*, Nov. 1927.

54. *NCH*, 15.i.27.

55. *Kung-jen yun-tung* [146], pp. 375–77.

56. *SCMP*, 25.i.27.

57. *NCH*, 24.xii.26.

58. *NCH*, 12.ii.27.

59. *Kung-jen yun-tung* [146], p. 402.

60. See for instance *STSP*, 25.xi.26, which reports a large number of workers' schools instituted by the Hupeh provincial federation and subsidized, by agreement, by the employers. See also *IPC*, 2.vi.27 (the report of the Red International delegation, according to which the General Textile Union of Wuhan stipulated, in their agreement with the employers, that there be an education fund to which the employers would contribute 4,000 yuan monthly). According to Li Li-san (*TSTL*, 1954, No. 4), there were 70 workers' schools, with 9,000 pupils, in Wuhan in the fall of 1926.

61. Hsü Wen-t'ien, *Kung-jen yun-tung shih ch'u-kao* [198], p. 123. On Wang Kuang-hui and Shen Hsiao-ts'en, see p. 225 above.

62. Kuo Liang, *Hu-nan kung-jen yun-tung* [158], p. 2.

63. Ma Ch'ao-chün, *Lao-tung yun-tung shih* [210], p. 578.

64. See the chronology of strikes in *Nien-chien* [138] II, 154–282; see also *NCH*, *passim*.

65. *Nien-chien*, II, 290.

66. *PP*, 16.i.27.

67. *Kung-jen yun-tung* [146], pp. 375–77.

68. *Nien-chien* [138] II, 290–92.

69. The threat of unemployment resulting from the introduction of new machines had been one of the main anxieties of the workers in the B.A.T. Hankow factory for several years. See p. 285 above.

70. On the takeover of the British Concession in Hankow, see, on the Chinese side, *Kung-jen yun-tung* [146], pp. 383–98, and on the Western side, *NCH*, 8.i.27, *PP*, 9.i.27, *SCMP*, 15.i.27. The last is based on the account of an inspector of the Asiatic Petroleum Company. See also the account of Chapman, *The Chinese Revolution* [43], pp. 33–35.

71. Chapman, pp. 34–35.

72. Li Li-san organized the big demonstration of December 26 against the Tientsin arrests, and Liu Shao-ch'i encouraged the crowd to occupy the concession on January 4 (*Kung-jen yun-tung* [146], p. 383).

73. *Kung-jen yun-tung* [146], pp. 389ff, and *NCH*, 15.i.27 and 22.i.27.

74. *NCH*, 26.ii.27, and *SCMP*, 8.iii.27.

75. *RT*, 1927, Changsha, p. 1.

76. *CTSTL*, 1957, No. 4, "Nan-ch'ang ta-shih-chi."

77. See p. 350 below. 78. *RT*, 1927, Changsha, p. 1.

79. *SCMP*, 22.i.27. 80. *NCH*, 12.ii.27.

81. *Ibid.* It was probably demands of this kind that Liu Shao-ch'i had in mind when he said, in an interview with Nym Wales (*Chinese Labor Movement* [312], p. 48): "At first the strikes were very Leftist in tendency.... Sometimes the workers' demands were too high."

82. *CWR*, 2.iv.27. 83. *CP*, 21.xi.26.

84. *Kung-jen yun-tung* [146], p. 415.

85. The increase was often nearly as much as 50 per cent (*PP*, 10.iv.27). The Wuhan printers obtained a raise of 7 yuan a month (Chen Ta, "Analysis of Strikes," *CEJ*, Nov. 1927), which is probably less than the average amount obtained.

86. *Kung-jen yun-tung* [146], p. 326 (a list of the categories of workers that obtained higher wages).

87. See p. 326 above. In Nanchang the employees in Chinese shops went on strike in January to protest the custom of dismissing all employees at the lunar New Year, which gave the employers the opportunity of taking on whatever workers they chose. The strikers' demand was met (*CTSTL*, 1957, No. 4).

88. *RT*, 1927, Changsha, p. 3.

89. *Kung-jen yun-tung* [146], p. 422.

90. *Ibid.*, p. 362.

91. Ch'en Ta, *Lao-tung wen-t'i* [190], p. 225.

92. See Tang Leang-li, *Inner History* [306], p. 260. In actual fact, what is generally known as the "Wuhan government" was at this time no more than a "Mixed Council" composed partly of members of the Central Executive Committee of the Kuomintang and partly of members of the Nationalist government who were residing temporarily in Wuhan (*Kung-jen yun-tung* [146], p. 359). On the general development of relations between the left and right wings of the Kuomintang and the reascendance of the left wing during the winter of 1926–27, see p. 348 below.

93. *Lao-tung ta-hui* [142], p. 166 (Liu Shao-ch'i's report to the Fourth Congress).

94. *Kung-jen yun-tung* [146], p. 359. 95. *PP*, 10.iv.27.

96. *Kung-jen yun-tung* [146], p. 362. 97. *Ibid.*, p. 363.

98. *Ibid.*

99. Holcombe, *The Chinese Revolution* [260a], p. 206.

100. *SCMP*, 27.x.26.

101. These anxieties were reflected in articles that appeared in Shanghai commercial newspapers such as *Shang-pao*, which urged that labor activities in Wuhan be confined to the fight against the warlords and the big foreign interests (*HT*, 6.i.27).

102. Ch'en Ta, *Lao-tung wen-t'i* [190], p. 225.

103. Chen Ta, "Analysis of Strikes," *CEJ*, Nov. 1927.

104. The postal workers' strike was settled by government representatives in the presence of Liu Shao-ch'i, representing the All-China General Union (*Kung-jen yun-tung* [146], p. 378). The strikes of the Changsha rickshaw men and lithographers were settled through the mediation of the government in the first case, and of the labor department of the Kuomintang in the second (*Kung-jen yun-tung* [146], p. 326).

105. *Nien-chien* [138] III, 186-87; see also *IS*, 1927, II, 575.

106. The Hunan provincial trade union congress had already given its approval on December 1 to the labor program outlined at the second conference of the provincial branch of the Kuomintang, which included arbitration procedures (*Kung-jen yun-tung* [146], p. 360). Similarly, an editorial on the Wuhan strikes in *HT*, 6.i.27, replying to the employers' campaign for the limitation of labor activities and the introduction of compulsory arbitration, merely stated: "We are not 100 per cent opposed to arbitration, although we do not think that this will resolve all disputes."

107. *CWR*, 14.viii.26, 21.viii.26. (The authorities declared that any "further attempt during the period of war against the North to make trouble at home will be considered an act of counterrevolution and treason against the Kuomintang in Canton.")

108. *Nien-chien* [138] III, 252 (text of the Canton regulations for the arbitration commissions).

109. Teng Chung-hsia, *Sheng-Kang pa-kung chung chih Chung-Ying t'an-p'an* [155], p. 3.

110. *Ibid.*, pp. 1-2.

111. This argument was put forward in an editorial in *HT*, 19.x.26, which explained the reasons for ending the strike.

112. *Chien-shih* [165], pp. 298-99; *HT*, 19.x.26.

113. *CWR*, 17.vii.26 and 24.vii.26.

114. Teng Chung-hsia [155], pp. 35-39; see also *CYB*, 1926, pp. 926-28.

115. Teng Chung-hsia [155], pp. 39-41.

116. See *Kuang-tung kung-jen pa-kung* [218], especially documents Nos. 8 and 9, entitled "Criticism of the Strike Negotiations," which probably date from the end of August, and which end by declaring that "in principle we are satisfied with the attitude of the Chinese representatives during these negotiations."

117. See an article by T'an P'ing-shan in *HT*, 6.viii.26, in which he insists on an immediate end to the strike, and a letter from the CP leadership to the strikers (*HT*, 15.viii.26) assuring them that the strike was reaching a "satisfactory" conclusion, and that it was necessary to avoid suffering "excessively."

118. Mif, *Pour une Chine forte et libre* [290], p. 35.

119. Akatova, *S'angan-Guanchzhouskaya zabastovka* [229], p. 135 (based on the *Min-kuo jih-pao* of Canton).

120. *CYB*, 1928, p. 976.

121. Akatova [229], p. 139, quoting Soviet sources illustrating the propaganda campaign launched by the Comintern at this time.

122. After the July negotiations broke down, the Strike Committee received letters of encouragement from all over China. It held meetings in Canton which were attended by large numbers of the population (Akatova [229], p. 137, based on accounts in the Cantonese press).

123. *SCMP*, 4.x.26. The conference was held on September 12.

124. *SCMP*, 9.x.26.

125. *CYB*, 1928, pp. 977-78.

126. The editorial of *HT*, 19.x.26, entitled "The Hong Kong Strike Has Ended," declared that "victory in China's struggles can no longer be obtained as the result of one single strike or boycott."

127. In November 1926 a communiqué of the Canton government announced that 10,000 of the workers who had lost their jobs because of the strike were employed by government departments and another 10,000 by the Strike Committee and its pickets, while 8,000 were unemployed (*CWR*, 27.xi.26). In January 1927 there were still 1,300 houses requisitioned for lodging strikers (*SCMP*, 19.i.27).

128. In November 1926 the premises of the Strike Committee in the Tung-yuan, which it had occupied since June 1925, were destroyed by a fire in which large stocks of confiscated goods that had not yet been disposed of and all the Committee's archives perished (*SCMP*, 8.xi.26). Wieger (*La Chine moderne* [139] VII, 48) suggests that the fire was the result of foul play; this is not impossible, for even though the strike was over, the Committee still had a lot of power and doubtless many enemies.

129. *SCMP*, 4.viii.26, 26.xi.26, and 11.xii.26.

130. *CWR*, 28.i.28. The preceding chapter (p. 299 above) made use of the fragmentary extracts from the survey contained in *Nien-chien* [138] and in *CYB*, 1928.

131. *SCMP*, 18.ii.27.

132. Stoler, "The Trade-union Movement in Canton," *PPW*, Nos. 6 and 7.

133. *IPC*, 7.iv.27.   134. *SCMP*, 28.vii.26 and 21.viii.26.

135. *Ibid.*   136. *SCMP*, 25.ix.26.

137. *SCMP*, 28.xii.26.   138. *SCMP*, 7.x.26.

139. *CWR*, 11.xii.26.   140. *CWR*, 28.i.28.

141. *SCMP*, 9.viii.26.   142. *RT*, 1926, Kongmoon, p. 1.

143. *SCMP*, 4.i.27. Among the members of the Workers' Delegates' Conference who were most active on these occasions were the actors who performed the popular "lion dance," accomplished acrobats whose union was affiliated with the Conference (*SCMP*, 11.i.27).

144. *SCMP*, 23.ix.26.   145. *SCMP*, 15.ii.27.

146. *CWR*, 15.i.26.

147. *SCMP*, 4.i.27, 7.i.27. The same week, the mechanics also attacked the railwaymen on the Yueh-Han and Canton-Kowloon lines (*CP*, 18.i.27).

148. *SCMP*, 13.vii.26 and 13.viii.26; see also *HT*, 29.viii.26.

149. *SCMP*, 16.xi.26.   150. *HWP*, 4.i.27.

151. See p. 332 above.

152. *Nien-chien* [138] III, 254–56. The summary of the text in *CYB* 1928 is erroneously dated January 1926.

153. *SCMP*, 16.xi.26.

154. See p. 351 below.

155. During the second part of 1926, strikes followed by a wage increase are reported to have occurred in the newspaper offices, the big stores, the match factories, the rice shops, and the banks, as well as in the arsenal, the Post Office, and the provincial railways (*SCMP, passim*).

156. *SCMP*, 7.xii.26.   157. *SCMP*, 10.xii.26.

158. The match factories announced that they would move from Canton because of the "workers' tyranny" there (*CWR*, 22.i.27).

159. Stoler, "The Trade-union Movement in Canton," *PPW*, Nos. 6 and 7.

160. Teng Chung-hsia, *Kuang-chou kung-ch'ao* [153], p. 24.

161. *CWR*, 22.i.27.   162. *SCMP*, 12.ii.27 and 18.ii.27.

163. *HT*, 6.iii.27; *SCMP*, 26.iii.27.

164. Stoler, *PPW*, Nos. 6 and 7; *SCMP*, 4.iii.27.

165. Stoler, *ibid.*

166. In Swatow, Ho Ying-ch'in, the commander of the garrison, had had all the leaders of the left-wing unions deported during the summer of 1926; in doing this, he had the support of one moderate union and the White Lotus and Green Lotus secret societies (*SCMP*, 21.viii.26).

167. The article in *HT*, 6.iii.27, on the affair of the New Year dismissals dwells at length on the need for collaboration between workers and merchants.

168. Stoler, who was a member of the Red International delegation, was already criti-

cal of this overly timid policy when he wrote his articles (*PPW*, Nos. 6 and 7) in the summer of 1927.

169. *HT*, 7.vii.26 (statistics supplied by the Shanghai General Union).

170. *HT*, 15.viii.26 (from the same statistics).

171. *HT*, 25.ix.26.

172. *CEB, passim.*

173. Archives of the French Concession of Shanghai [16], HS 1019.

174. *NCH,* 22.i.27, 29.i.27. According to the Commissioner of Police of the International Settlement, there were 14 strikes in December and 20,000 strikers. These figures are not comparable with those given by the Shanghai General Union, because the police reports give them for the territory of the International Settlement only. Thus they give the figures of 35,000 and 25,000 strikers for July and August, whereas the General Union gives 70,000 and 37,000.

175. Lieu, *China's Industries and Finances* [278], p. 109 (based on statistics given by the Chinese authorities in Shanghai).

176. *PDR, passim.*

177. For instance at a meeting of the unemployed in October 1926, a leader of the Shanghai General Union spoke enthusiastically about the victories of the Nationalist armies and the benefit this would bring to the workers of Hupeh (*CWR*, 23.x.26).

178. *HT*, 23.vi.26.   179. *Ibid.*

180. *HT*, 7.vii.26.

181. He had studied in Cambridge and in Glasgow, and in 1913 was put in charge of the newly created Chinese Geological Survey (*CYB*, 1926, p. 1200).

182. *Lao-tung ta-hui* [142], pp. 190ff (report of the General Union to the Fourth Congress).

183. *HT*, 7.vii.26.   184. *Lao-tung ta-hui* [142], pp. 192–93.

185. According to the report of the General Union to the Fourth Congress (*Lao-tung ta-hui*, p. 172), this meeting was held on 23.vii.26, but according to other sources (*Nien-chien* [138] II, 22) the meeting was on July 11.

186. *Lao-tung ta-hui*, p. 172.

187. In September 1926, when it was announced at the Nanyang factory in Yangtzepoo that new machines would be installed, the women employees, armed with iron bars and sticks, wrecked several of the workshops (*NCH*, 25.ix.26), and the damage was estimated at 500,000 yuan (*NCH*, 23.x.26).

188. In July 1926, a leader of the General Cotton Mills Union held a meeting of workers in the Naigai No. 3 mill, where there had recently been fighting between workers from the Kompo and workers from Shantung, at which he stated that "any person among us who attempts to stir up trouble amongst the workers shall be severely dealt with by his colleagues" (*NCH,* 10.vii.26).

189. *HT*, 23.vi.26.   190. *HT*, 15.viii.26.

191. *CEB* and *NCH*, June–Sept. 1926, *passim.*

192. This demand was presented by, among others, the printing workers (*CEB,* 7.viii.26), the workers in the carpet factories (*CEB,* 4.ix.26), and the employees of the Chinese Tramways in Nanshih (*CEB,* 18.ix.26).

193. Thus the postal workers succeeded in July in obtaining payment on the basis of the silver tael instead of on that of the Mexican dollar (*CEB,* 7.viii.26), and the teahouse employees in having their wages paid at a rate of exchange of copper currency that was higher than the current rate (*CEB,* 31.vii.26).

194. *Lao-tung ta-hui* [142], p. 172.

195. *CEB,* 21.viii.26.

196. Archives of the French Concession of Shanghai [16], HS 1019.

197. *Lao-tung ta-hui* [142], p. 172; *NCH*, 21.viii.26.

198. *Lao-tung ta-hui*, p. 172.   199. *CEB*, 21.viii.26 and 4.ix.26.

200. *NCH*, 4.ix.26.   201. *NCH*, 21.viii.26.

202. *NCH*, 28.viii.26.

203. *NCH*, 30.x.26 (containing a translation of one of these leaflets).

204. *NCH*, 30.x.26; *Kung-jen yun-tung* [146], pp. 447–48 (Ch'ü Ch'iu-pai's account of the rising). See also *CFJP*, 21.iii.57.

205. They had come together for the celebration of the anniversary of May 30 (see p. 284 above), for the Ch'en A-t'ang affair (*CEB*, 18.ix.26), and for the National Day of Humiliation on September 7 (*NCH*, 11.ix.26).

206. *NCH*, 18.xii.26; *Lao-tung ta-hui* [142], p. 177.

207. *Nien-chien* [138] II, 23; *CFJP*, 22.iii.57.

208. *NCH*, 11.xii.26.   209. *Nien-chien*, II, 23.

210. At a meeting of printers on December 17 in commemoration of Liu Hua, a motion of this kind was passed (*Shih-shih hsin-pao* [130], 18.xii.26).

211. In December, the union's posters were stuck up in Chapei and Nanshih calling on workers to persist in their support for the autonomy of Shanghai, to put up resistance to the Fengtien troops when they arrived in the city, and to boycott the Fengtien bank notes (*NCH*, 18.xii.26).

212. For instance, in January 1927, after the British Concessions in Hankow and Kiukiang had been taken over, the General Union launched a propaganda campaign against Great Britain, and together with the students' associations formed a committee for the breaking off of relations (*Lao-tung ta-hui* [142], p. 175).

213. Archives of the French Concession of Shanghai [16], HS 1019. This strike resulted from the formation of an employee's union that had been organized shortly before by the General Union.

214. *Shih-shih hsin-pao* [130], 18.xii.26.

215. *Nan-yang shih-liao* [143], pp. 348–51.

216. *Nien-chien* [138] II, 24.

217. *Lao-tung ta-hui* [142], pp. 190–93.

218. See Wieger, *La Chine moderne* [139] VII, 52–54, quoting Chang Tso-lin's proclamation of 6.xii.26, in which he declared that he would show no mercy to the Bolshevists but that he would extend protection to foreigners of all nationalities, and that he counted on their cooperation since he and they had common cause against Bolshevism.

219. *RT,* 1926, Mukden, p. 4, and 1927, p. 1.

220. *MDN*, 21.x.26.

221. *HT*, 28.vii.26 and 6.viii.26 (reports of 700 recent dismissals on the Chiao-Chi line, and three months' arrears in wages on the Ching-Han line).

222. *HT*, 6.viii.26. On the Lunghai line and in the Chengchow cotton mill the only unions that remained were those run by the employers.

223. *PP,* 28.xi.26. These arrests were the cause of the trouble that led to the taking over of the British concessions in Hankow and Kiukiang.

224. *MDN*, 3.ii.27.

225. *IPC*, 18.viii.27, gives the figures of 1,174 put to death without trial, 2,286 condemned to death, and 2,219 wounded.

Chapter XIV

1. Because there is no census of membership for this particular time, the figures for a slightly later date, given by the All-China General Union at the pan-Pacific trade union conference held in Wuhan in May, must be used. (See Stewart and Fang, "A Statistical

Study of Industry and Labor in China," *CEJ*, Oct. 1930.) The total membership figure then given was 3,065,000: 180,000 cotton workers, 160,000 seamen, 35,000 railwaymen, 50,000 printing workers, 60,000 miners, 150,000 coolies and porters, 120,000 silk workers, 60,000 rickshaw men, and in addition 2,000,000 craftsmen and shophands. As for regions, the highest membership figures were those for Shanghai (800,000), Hong Kong (250,-000), Hunan (250,000), Kwangtung (400,000), Wusih (120,000), Hupeh (400,000), Kiangsi (200,000), and Chekiang (300,000). These figures merely indicate the number of workers influenced by the General Union, and should not be taken literally. Moreover, the Union had considerably less influence in February, especially in Shanghai, Wusih, and Chekiang, where warlords were still in control at that time. But it would be impossible to estimate accurately the number of actual members of the All-China General Union throughout China at the end of the winter.

2. Wieger, *La Chine moderne* [139] VII, 66.

3. In Hangchow in December, when the Southern armies were already at the gates of the city, a general union was formed on the initiative of the printers', porters', telephone workers', and railwaymen's unions (*HWP*, 21.xii.26). In February new unions were formed, e.g., among the postal workers and the rickshaw men (*I-shih-pao* [123], 1.iii.27), while the silk workers of Hangchow, Shaohing, and Huchow went on strike for higher wages (*CEJ*, Feb. 1927, "Labor Conditions in Chekiang").

4. *CEB*, 4.ix.26.

5. *Shih-shih hsin-pao* [130], 15.iii.27.

6. *Nien-chien* [138] II, 392–93. The demands concerned compensation for accidents and illness, an eight-hour day, a limit of 60 *li* a day for postmen's rounds and of 50 catties for the weight of mail to be carried, and the abolition of the compulsory savings plan then in operation. The conference also demanded that the Minister grant leave for attending union meetings, that he not reassign union leaders without their consent, and that union leaders be appointed to the examining board for the recruitment of postal workers.

7. *Shih-shih hsin-pao* [130], 15.iii.27.

8. *Nien-chien* [138] II, 99–100.

9. Information given by Li Li-san in *TSTL*, 1954, No. 4.

10. On these leaders see Chapter XV below.

11. See the resolution on the labor movement voted at the plenary session of the CP in Shanghai in July 1926 (Wilbur, *Documents* [140], pp. 288–95), in which it was stated that "we should be able to progress from the former monopoly of union work by our Party fractions to a labor movement in which the masses of our Party members exert an influence over the workers."

12. *PDR*, 8.xi.26.

13. *NCH*, 29.i.27. Leaflets distributed on this occasion urged the study and adoption of Leninism and energetic support for the Chinese and world revolutions.

14. *SCMP*, 22.ii.27.

15. See Mann, *What I Saw in China* [47], *passim*.

16. In spring 1927, according to figures given by the Wuhan government, the peasant unions had nearly 10,000,000 members: 4,517,000 in Hunan, 2,502,000 in Hupeh, 705,000 in Shensi, 700,000 in Kwangtung, 382,000 in Kiangsi, and 245,000 in Honan (*Kung-jen yun-tung* [146], pp. 18–19). On the fight of these unions against the landowners, see the classic report of Mao Tse-tung on the peasant movement in Hunan (*Selected Works* [161] I, 23–59).

17. *SCMP*, 19.xi.26.

18. *Kung-jen yung-tung* [146], p. 366.

19. *Ibid.*, pp. 399–435.

20. See p. 353 below.

21. Examples are given in Liu Shao-ch'i's report to the Fourth Congress on the management of the General Union (*Lao-tung ta-hui* [142], p. 165).

22. *CP*, 2.iii.27; *Lao-tung ta-hui* [142], p. 167.

23. *TSTL*, 1954, No. 4.

24. At the end of 1926, 29 per cent of Kuomintang members were workers and 7.5 per cent peasants (Woo, *The Kuomintang* [168], p. 207).

25. Wieger, *La Chine moderne* [139] VII, 35.

26. *Ibid.*, p. 29.

27. Tang Leang-li, *Inner History* [306], pp. 260–61.

28. *Ibid.*

29. Wilbur, *Documents* [140], p. 381; Tang Leang-li, pp. 260–62.

30. The only exception seems to be the C.M.S.N. Company, which in November was still letting Sun Ch'uan-fang use its boats for the transport of his troops on the Yangtze. This policy, which caused a strike of its employees organized by the seamen's union (*NCH*, 20.xi.26), was even further evidence of the conservative outlook of this company, which was founded by Li Hung-chang and still had close ties with the upper ranks of the gentry.

31. *SCMP*, 28.vii.26.

32. *MDN*, 9.iv.27.

33. Chapman, *The Chinese Revolution* [43], pp. 124–25.

34. A leaflet, printed in English, was distributed among the British members of the Shanghai Defense Force. Its text included the following words: "Don't think about us, the Chinese toiling masses, as about the 'Chinks' whom you can slaughter like cattle. These times have passed for ever. Don't interfere in our REVOLUTION. This is our own affair." (*NCH*, 26.ii.27.) In the West, the "anti-imperialist" conference held in Brussels in February 1927, which was attended by Henri Barbusse, Félicien Challaye, Jawaharlal Nehru, Léopold Senghor, Mohammed Hatta, and, from China, Sung Ch'ing-ling, Shao Li-tzu (editor of a Kuomintang journal in Shanghai), and Ch'en Ch'üan of the Canton–Hong Kong Strike Committee, launched an appeal against intervention in China (*l'Humanité* [105], 4.iii.27). The campaign waged by *l'Humanité* during February and March of 1927 for fraternization between Western troops in China and the revolutionaries there, on the pattern of the Black Sea sailors, brought action against it by the French government (*l'Humanité*, 30.iii.27). Apparently foreign supporters of the Chinese revolution were much more afraid of armed intervention by the West than of an about-face by the Chinese bourgeoisie.

35. *LCT*, 16.xii.26.

36. Wieger, *La Chine moderne* [139] VII, 62–63.

37. Feetham report [38], Part II, p. 129.

38. Wieger, VII, 31, 58.   39. *SCMP*, 22.ii.27.

40. How far was this new attitude politically motivated, with fear of the workers' and peasants' movement resulting in a desire to reach a compromise with the Powers? And how far was it economically motivated? It has been seen that the crisis in Chinese-owned industries in 1923–24 contributed largely to the formation of an alliance between the bourgeoisie and the labor movement against "imperialism." But in 1926–27 there were signs of recovery, at least in some sectors, such as the Shanghai cotton industry (*RT*, 1926, Shanghai, p. 2). This was, however, far from being a general recovery, so that it seems to have been primarily political motives that made the bourgeoisie cut its links with the mass movement, *in spite* of the foreign economic competition it was still up against.

41. He made Nanchang his headquarters on November 11 (Wieger, *La Chine moderne* [139] VII, 50).

42. On the February uprising, see pp. 353–55 below.

43. The warlords of Fukien, of Anhwei, and also of Yunnan rallied to Chiang's side in

October 1926 (*SCMP*, 20.x.26). Their incorporation in the Nationalist armies strengthen-ed the opposition to the mass movement, especially to the activities of the peasant unions.

44. Ho Kan-chih, *Modern Revolution* [259], p. 146.
45. Wieger, *La Chine moderne* [139] VII, 51, 66.
46. Tang Leang-li, *Inner History* [306], p. 263.
47. *CTSTL*, 1957, No. 4, "Nan-ch'ang ta-shih-chi."
48. *SCMP*, 16.iii.27.   49. Wieger, VII, 133.
50. *Nien-chien* [138] II, 274–76.

51. Chiang told the merchants of Wuhan that the Kuomintang was a party that repre-sented the interests of the whole people, and that it respected the merchant class; but that they must cooperate with the workers if they wanted to survive and to get rid of the militarists and imperialists (*PP*, 9.i.27). His message to the workers was that they must on no account regard the merchants as their enemies, but must cooperate with them (*ibid*.). In his speech at the Ningpo Guild banquet he said that the merchants must be sympathetic toward the workers because of their ignorance, and that it must be remem-bered that the aim of the revolution was to put an end to suffering and unhappiness (*PP*, 6.ii.27).

52. See p. 259 above (Sun K'o's attendance at the inaugural meeting of the "All-China Federation"); note 11, p. 506 (Ma Ch'ao-chün's connection with the Sunyatsenist So-ciety); and pp. 285–86 (support given by the Kuomintang right wing to anti-Communist workers' groups).

53. See p. 326 above.   54. *CTSTL*, 1957, No. 4.
55. *Ibid.*   56. *Ibid.*
57. *NCH*, 2.iv.27.   58. *CTSTL*, 1957, No. 4.
59. Isaacs, *Tragedy* [263], p. 144.   60. *NCH*, 12.iii.27.
61. *PP*, 3.iv.27.   62. *Kung-jen yun-tung* [146], p. 400.
63. See pp. 347–48 above.   64. See pp. 331 and 352 above.

65. *SCMP*, 15.iii.27; Ho Kan-chih, *Modern Revolution* [259], p. 132.
66. *SCMP*, 18.iii.27; Tang Leang-li, *Inner History* [306], pp. 264–65. It is surprising to find Su described in Tang's book as having been a butcher in Hong Kong.

67. No attempt is made here to decide the extent to which either the CCP or the Comintern and the Soviet advisers in China were responsible for the line taken.

68. *HT*, 25.ix.26.   69. *HT*, 6.i.27.
70. *HT*, 7.vii.26.   71. See, for instance, *HT*, 10.ix.26.

72. Ho Kan-chih [259], pp. 131–32.

73. See Mao Tse-tung's own account as told to Edgar Snow (*Red Star over China* [302], p. 158).

74. Wilbur, *Documents* [140], p. 375.

75. Later Liu Shao-ch'i, in a conversation with Nym Wales, admitted that this was one of the chief mistakes made at the time (*Chinese Labor Movement* [312], p. 49).

76. *Kung-jen yun-tung* [146], pp. 364 and 424.

77. See p. 338 above.

78. *Nien-chien* [138] II, 457.

79. *Ibid.*, II, 457–58. It is therefore incorrect to say, as Isaacs does (*Tragedy* [263], p. 133), that the strike "had no goals of its own" and was confined to support of Chiang's armies.

80. *Nien-chien*, II, 458. Estimates vary because some workers, for instance those in the silk-reeling factories, did not come out until the third day, when craftsmen and cotton workers had already resumed work. A detailed chronological account of the strike is given in *HT*, 28.ii.27. The figure of 106,000 strikers given by the International Settlement police (*CYB*, 1928, p. 996) is certainly too low. The report of the Shanghai General

Union to the Fourth Congress (*Lao-tung ta-hui* [142], pp. 200–201) gives the figure of 250,000 strikers on the second day of the strike (Feb. 20), which is when the largest number were on strike.

81. See the letter sent by the Seamen's Union to *NCH* (26.ii.27), in which it was declared that the union "has the same aim as China's folk[:] to sweep obstacles that stand in the way of China's National Revolution." The union of the French Tramways employees published a manifesto requesting the company not to take action against the strike, since the strike was a political move against Sun Ch'uan-fang (French Concession Archives [16], MS 1019).

82. *Nien-chien* [138] II, 458.

83. *NCH*, 26.ii.27.   84. *Ibid.*

85. *PP*, 6.iii.27; eleven union militants of the Commercial Press were arrested and immediately executed.

86. *Lao-tung ta-hui* [142], p. 201.   87. *NCH*, 26.ii.27.

88. *CFJP*, 22.iii.57 (an article in commemoration of the three armed uprisings).

89. *Ibid.*

90. *NCH*, 12.iii.27; Isaacs, *Tragedy* [263], p. 135.

91. *Nien-chien* [138] II, 24.

92. See *NCH*, 19.iii.27 (demands of the cotton workers and the seamen); *Nien-chien*, II, 399, 400, 404 (demands of the Chinese Tramways employees, the telephone workers, and the dockers). These demands concerned not only wages, hours, paid holidays, and workers' insurance, but also recognition of the unions and their right to have a say in hiring and dismissal of labor, abolition of the pao-kung system and of industrial apprenticeship, reinstatement of all workers dismissed after May 30, 1925, and subsidies from the factory owners for workers' schools and hospitals.

93. See p. 339 above regarding the renewal of activity by the kung-tsei in Shanghai in 1926–27. In January 1927 employers in the metallurgical industry founded a "General Union of Capitalists and Workingmen in the Metallurgical Industry," of which the banker Fu Tsung-yao was president (*SCMP*, 11.i.27).

94. *Nien-chien* [138] II, 399.   95. *NCH*, 19.iii.27; *CFJP*, 23.iii.57.

96. *NCH*, 19.iii.27.   97. *CFJP*, 23.iii.57.

98. *NCH*, 19.iii.27.

99. These were the points raised in a leaflet distributed on March 7 in the big shops on Nanking Road (*NCH*, 12.iii.27).

100. *CFJP*, 23.iii.57.   101. *Nien-chien* [138] II, 31–33.

102. *NCH*, 12.iii.27 and 19.iii.27.

103. On the third uprising, see *HT*, 6.iv.27 (a detailed account of operations in each sector); *Lao-tung ta-hui* [142], pp. 179–80 (report of the Shanghai General Union to the Fourth Congress); *CFJP*, 24.iii.57; Chou Kuo-ch'iang, *Shang-hai ch'i-i* [192]. See also *SK*, 1958, No. 3.

104. *Nien-chien* [138] II, 460.

105. *Ko-ming lieh-shih-chuan* [221], pp. 223ff (biography of Lo I-nung).

106. *Lao-tung ta-hui* [142], p. 202.   107. *SP*, 22.iii.27.

108. *CFJP*, 24.iii.57.

109. Liu Li-k'ai, *1919–27 kung-jen yun-tung* [208], p. 56.

110. *Lao-tung ta-hui* [142], p. 180.

111. *NCH*, 26.iii.27.   112. *Ibid.*

113. French Concession Archives [16]. The Shanghai Provisional Government gave its written support to the protest made by the union to the company over its refusal to reinstate strikers.

114. *Nien-chien* [138] II, 25.   115. *NCH*, 2.iv.27.

116. *IPC*, 7.iv.27.   117. *Nien-chien* [138] II, 36–39.

118. *Lao-tung ta-hui* [142], pp. 191–92 and 195–96 (report of the General Union to the Fourth Congress).

119. List in *Nien-chien* [138] II, 67–69.

120. It included reports of new unions among employees in the vegetable, sugar, and fruit trades, in the Chinese Tramways, and among launderers, and items about a general union in the silk-reeling factories, a union in the Woosung sugar refinery, one in the Kiangnan shipyards, and so on.

121. *Lao-tung ta-hui* [142], pp. 192–93.

122. This is implied in the report of the General Union to the Fourth Congress (*Lao-tung ta-hui*, pp. 195–96).

123. *Nien-chien* [138] II, 399, 409, 410, 415, 416, 419–20, 421, 422, 423, 426.

124. *NCH*, 9.iv.27.

125. Exceptions included the demand of the printers to be given 40 per cent of the profits (*NCH*, 9.iv.27), and that of the telephone workers (addressed to the military commander) that they be put in permanent charge of the telegraph service, the manager of which had fled with Sun Ch'uan-fang (*NCH*, 2.iv.27).

126. *NCH*, 9.iv.27.   127. *NCH*, 26.iii.27.
128. *HT*, 6.iv.27.   129. *NCH*, 26.iii.27.
130. *NCH*, 2.iv.27.   131. *HWP*, 2.iv.27; *NCH*, 2.iv.27.
132. *NCH*, 2.iv.27.

133. When they were disarmed on April 12, a search of their headquarters in Chapei turned up 20 machine guns, 3,000 rifles, 200 Mauser pistols, 1,000,000 cartridges, and 2,000 lances (*SMCR*, 1927, p. 53).

134. *NCH*, 26.iii.27.

135. *Lao-tung ta-hui* [142], p. 182.

136. *Shih-shih hsin-pao* [130], 31.iii.27; *Nien-chien* [138] II, 25.

137. *PDR*, 28.iii.27.

138. *PDR*, 23.iii.27.

139. *NCH*, 30.iii.27.

140. The amount of the loan was given as 15 million yuan at the Fourth Labor Congress (*Lao-tung ta-hui* [142], p. 183). *PP*, 10.iv.27, gives no figures but reports that the bankers were eager to contribute funds toward the anti-Communist campaign. *CWR*, 9.iv.27, and *The New York Times*, 15.iv.27, report that two loans were negotiated at the beginning of April, one for 7 million and the other for 3 million yuan.

141. *NCH*, 26.iii.27 (report of a reception given by Pai for the French, Japanese, and British consuls and the Customs Commissioner).

142. Isaacs, *Tragedy* [263], p. 145, which does not give a source for this information. Probably it was a current rumor.

143. The First Division of Pai's army was known to be in sympathy with the left-wing forces (see Isaacs, pp. 170–71).

144. Isaacs, p. 143. See also *CYB*, 1928, p. 1361, where vague reference is made to Chiang's contacts with the Shanghai secret societies.

145. Isaacs, p. 143.

146. *Kung-jen yun-tung* [146], p. 142 (report of the General Union on the events of April 12).

147. *PDR*, 3.iv.27.   148. *PDR*, 7.iv.27.
149. *Nien-chien* [138] II, 41–42 (the rules of this association); *PDR*, 4.iv.27.
150. *Lao-tung ta-hui* [142], p. 182.   151. *CWR*, 2.iv.27.
152. *SK*, 1958, No. 3.   153. Isaacs, *Tragedy* [263], p. 173.
154. *NCH*, 26.iii.27.
155. *NCH*, 26.iii.27 and 9.iv.27; *HWP*, 6.iv.27.

156. *NCH*, 9.iv.27.

157. *PDR*, 8.iv.27. Chiang's police arrested 19 Communists on this occasion.

158. *CTSTL*, 1957, No. 4.   159. See note 3, p. 528.

160. *Nien-chien* [138] II, 398–99.   161. *Ibid.*, pp. 411 and 413–14.

162. *Ibid.*, p. 88.   163. *Ibid.*, p. 487.

164. *Ibid.*, p. 88.   165. *Ibid.*

166. *CWR*, 9.iv.27; *SCMP*, 11.iv.27; *Nien-chien* [138] II, 487.

167. *SCMP*, 2.iv.27.

168. Shortly after the capture of Nanking by the Nationalist armies, and in obscure circumstances, the Western flotillas opened fire on the Chinese quarters of Nanking, alleging that hostile acts had been committed against foreigners; see Ho Kan-chih, *Modern Revolution* [259], p. 145.

169. *RT*, 1927, Chungking, p. 1; *IPC*, 23.vi.27 (which reports 200 killed and 800 wounded).

170. *Nien-chien* [138] II, 91.

171. *Ibid.*, pp. 92–93 (a list of these unions).

172. *Ibid.*, p. 404.   173. *Ibid.*, pp. 489–90.

174. *SCMP*, 14.iv.27.   175. *CWR*, 30.iv.27.

176. *SCMP*, 7.iv.27.   177. *SCMP*, 9.iv.27.

178. *SCMP*, 9.iv.27 and 11.iv.27.

179. Hong Kong Government, *Gazette* [24], 1.iv.27.

180. *STSP*, 3.iv.27.   181. *I-shih-pao* [123], 31.iii.27.

182. Wieger [139] VII, 134.

183. *PP*, 10.iv.27. This raid resulted in the seizure of a large number of documents, the authenticity of which has been a matter of controversy (see Wilbur, *Documents* [140], Introduction).

184. *HT*, *passim*. See, for instance, the protest of the left-wing organizations in Canton (including the CP, the Workers' Delegates' Conference, the Hong Kong–Canton Strike Committee, the Seamen's Federation, and the Provincial Congress of Peasant Unions) against the announced agreement between Chiang and Chang (*SCMP*, 30.iii.27). See also *HT*, 6.iv.27, which pronounces against any compromise with the Northern forces.

185. *SCMP*, 2.iv.27 and 6.iv.27.   186. *CTSTL*, 1957, No. 4.

187. *HT*, 6.iv.27.   188. *PDR*, 11.iv.27.

189. See, for instance, *NCH*, 26.iii.27, and *Nien-chien* [138] II, 25 (mass demonstrations organized by the General Union to provide a triumphal welcome to Chiang and his army).

190. *NCH*, 2.iv.27.

191. Wieger, *La Chine moderne* [139] VII, 134.

192. *North China Daily News* (see *NCH*, 1.iv.27).

193. Because the present study purposely leaves aside the question of the role of the Comintern in the conduct of the Chinese revolution of 1924–27, all that need be done here is to note that in April 1927 the danger of foreign intervention tended to be regarded as primary by the Comintern, whereas it was hopeful about the alliance between the proletariat and the bourgeoisie. See, for instance, *l'Humanité*, 27.iii.27, which gives the translation of an article in *Pravda* on the successes achieved by the Chinese workers and peasants working within the right wing of the Kuomintang against imperialist intrigues. See also *ibid.*, 12.iv.27 (an article by Semard on the "Unity of the Chinese Revolutionary Front," in which it is stated that "the Kuomintang is strong enough to surmount these difficulties and to persevere in the struggle for liberation until victory is achieved").

194. *Kung-jen yun-tung* [146], pp. 482 and 485.

195. *SK*, 1958, No. 3. This study, based on the writings of Mao Tse-tung and Ts'ai Ho-sen, strongly criticizes the attitude of Ch'en Tu-hsiu and his group, and regards them as

responsible for the temporizing tactics of the Shanghai General Union on these various occasions.

196. *NCH*, 2.iv.27.

197. *SK*, 1958, No. 3.

198. The text of this statement is in *HWP*, 5.iv.27; Wieger [139] VII, 135 (containing a summary); and *l'Humanité*, 8.iv.27 (according to a report by its Shanghai correspondent). The statement, regarding the current rumors of a Communist coup against the concessions and of a Kuomintang coup against the unions, declared that for the time being it was impossible to go into the question of these ill-intentioned rumors and that it was enough to realize that the military government in Shanghai had declared its loyalty to the central government.

199. *SK*, 1958, No. 3.   200. *Lao-tung ta-hui* [142], p. 182.

201. *Kung-jen yun-tung* [146], p. 294.   202. *NCH*, 16.iv.27.

203. *PDR*, 14.iv.27.

204. See the detailed account in *Kung-jen yun-tung* [146], pp. 494-98.

205. *Ibid.*, pp. 507-9.

206. *Ibid.*, pp. 513-15.

207. *NCH*, 21.v.27.

208. *Kung-jen yun-tung* [146], pp. 516-17.

209. *Lao-tung ta-hui* [142], pp. 184-95. The number of deaths was given as 400 in the report made by the police of the International Settlement on the events of April (*NCH*, 21.v.27).

210. *NCH*, 16.iv.27.   211. *Kung-jen yun-tung* [146], p. 498.

212. *PDR*, 16.iv.27; *IPC*, 23.vi.27.   213. *Kung-jen yun-tung* [146], p. 498.

214. See p. 349 above. The "leftist" views of Harold Isaacs [263], which led him to reproach the General Union for having retreated in a fight in which it had military superiority, cannot be accepted here.

215. *NCH*, 21.v.27.   216. *Kung-jen yun-tung* [146], p. 525.

217. *Ibid.*, p. 523.

218. Its rules are given in *Nien-chien* [138] II, 42.

219. *Kung-jen yun-tung* [146], pp. 530-33.

220. *CWR*, 23.iv.27.   221. *NCH*, 16.iv.27.

222. *Kung-jen yun-tung* [146], pp. 535-36; see also *SCMP*, 18.iv.27.

223. Lozowski, *Revolution und Konterrevolution in China* [285], p. 68 (containing text of the police report).

224. *Ibid.*, pp. 66-67 (account of a Soviet trade unionist who was in Canton at the time).

225. *Kung-jen yun-tung* [146], p. 535.   226. *Ibid.*, p. 536.

227. *SCMP*, 18.iv.27.

Chapter XV

1. On the political situation in China during the months following the coup of April 12, see Ho Kan-chih, *Modern Revolution* [259], pp. 153ff; Isaacs, *Tragedy* [263], chaps. 13-16; Wieger, *La Chine moderne* [139] VII, 78-84.

2. *Lao-tung ta-hui* [142], p. 170.

3. *Ibid.*

4. Isaacs [263], p. 208; Ho Kan-chih [259], p. 159.

5. Sung Ch'ing-ling continued her active opposition to Chiang Kai-shek, and today still holds an important position in the Chinese People's Government (see *The Struggle for New China* [303], containing a collection of her political writings since 1927). Teng

Yen-ta, who escaped with her to Moscow after the debacle in July, returned to China to attempt to organize opposition to Chiang, and was executed by the police in 1931 (Perleberg, *Who's Who in Modern China* [297], p. 208).

6. Ho Kan-chih, *Modern Revolution* [259], p. 162.

7. *Ibid.*, pp. 155 and 162–64.

8. Isaacs, *Tragedy* [263], pp. 210–12; Ho Kan-chih, p. 165.

9. Ho Kan-chih, pp. 166–67; Wieger [139] VII, 78–84.

10. Chen Ta [Ch'en Ta], "Analysis of Strikes," *CEJ*, Oct.–Dec. 1927. I arrived at the figures in Table 32 by subtracting Ch'en's figures for 1918 from his totals for the period. The figures in his survey for the breakdown of strikes by year, by industry, and by region indicate only the number of strikes and not the number of strikers. The same is true of the other surveys used below, and one has to be content to use them on the supposition that the variations between them are more or less uniform.

11. *Strikes and Lockouts* [18], p. 63. (The figures of the above survey have also been taken into account.)

12. *CEJ*, March 1927, "Strikes in Shanghai in 1926."

13. Yü Ch'i-chung, *Kuang-chou cheng-i ti fen-hsi* [83], p. 13.

14. *MDN*, 21.vii.25.

15. In Shanghai three of the 1926 strikes were concerned with the currency in which wages were paid, five with the time and the regularity of payment of wages, eight with fines, and four with double rates for certain kinds of work (e.g. night work); see *CEJ*, March 1927, "Strikes in Shanghai."

16. *Ibid.* Nineteen of the 1926 strikes in Shanghai were for extra food allocations, and 13 for annual bonuses.

17. See p. 197 above.   18. See p. 340 above.

19. See p. 348 above.

20. Chen Ta, "Analysis of Strikes," *CEJ*, Oct.–Nov. 1927.

21. *CEJ*, March 1927.   22. Chen Ta, *CEJ*, Oct.–Dec. 1927.

23. See p. 190 above.   24. See p. 193 above.

25. See p. 291 above.   26. See p. 300 above.

27. *CEJ*, March 1927.   28. See p. 326 above.

29. In Hankow in September 1924 thousands of rickshaw men wrecked the premises and vehicles of a motor bus company that had just been established (Chen Ta, *CEJ*, Oct. 1927); in Swatow in 1926 rickshaw men wrecked the vehicles of a trolleybus line the day it was opened (*SCMP*, 15.xii.26). The action of the Peking water-carriers in doing battle against the workers laying new pipes for the water company was of the same nature (*CEB*, 3.vii.26).

30. Chen Ta, *CEJ*, Dec. 1927. See also p. 340 above.

31. See p. 340 above.   32. Chen Ta, *CEJ*, Dec. 1927.

33. Ch'en Ta, *CHHP*, June 1926; this regional study is not included in the wider survey published in English the following year.

34. *Strikes and Lockouts* [18], p. 61.

35. *Ibid.*, p. 70. The survey also mentions 17 strikes in enterprises where the nationality of the owners was uncertain.

36. Fong, *Cotton Industry* [252], p. 164.   37. Chen Ta, *CEJ*, Oct.–Dec. 1927.

38. Yü Ch'i-chung, *Kuang-chou lao-tzu cheng-i* [83], p. 19.

39. See pp. 157 and 262 above.

40. Teng Chung-hsia, *Kuang-chou kung-ch'ao* [153], p. 4.

41. *CEB*, 7.viii.26.   42. *CEB*, 4.ix.26.

43. "Strikes in Shanghai," *CEM*, Oct. 1926.

44. *CWR*, 28.i.28.

45. *IPC*, 14.vii.27; "With the Chinese Trade Unions," *PPW*, No. 4 (accounts by two Western trade unionists, one of whom had visited Hupeh and the other Hunan).

46. Chen Ta, *CEJ*, Nov. 1927.

47. *IPC*, 14.vii.27.

48. "The Wages of the Wuhan Workers," *PPW*, No. 7 (based on data collected by the unions and presented to the pan-Pacific trade union conference in May 1927).

49. "Strikes in Shanghai," *CEM*, Oct. 1926.

50. *Ibid.*

51. *Ibid.*

52. *CEB*, 31.vii.26.

53. *NCH*, 31.xii.25.

54. *NCH*, 3.x.25.

55. See pp. 184 and 190 above.

56. See pp. 204 and 228 above.

57. *Nien-chien* [138] III, 64–66.

58. *MDN*, 3.x.25. Each worker had to pay 40 sen a month, and was entitled to free medical care, a 25-sen sickness payment, and a pension for his family if he died. On leaving, a worker did not get the amount he had paid out refunded unless he had been employed for three years.

59. Chu Hsin-fan, *Chung-kuo tzu-pen-chu-i* [193], p. 62. The average monthly bonus was 1 or 2 yuan.

60. *Record of the B.A.T.* [182], p. 37.

61. See p. 206 above.

62. See p. 229 above.

63. Lamson, *Social Pathology* [269], p. 179. The Shanghai Y.M.C.A. had a folder advertising the Pootung "Model Village."

64. See note 96, p. 474.

65. I.L.O. Archives, No. 206/1/13/1.

66. It is also typical that Paul Henry, the I.L.O. emissary to China, mentions in his report only moderate unionists such as those in the Federation or in clubs run by employers ([10], *passim*). When in 1925 the Director of the I.L.O. asked, for purposes of documentation, what were the labor organizations that supported the May Thirtieth Movement, he was told that in the treaty ports there were only loosely organized groups stuffed full of Communist propaganda and that there was no properly organized trade union with which Amsterdam was in touch (I.L.O. Archives, 1925, Minute sheet No. 200/1/23).

67. See p. 340 above.

68. See p. 325 above. See also Mann, *What I Saw in China* [47], p. 24.

69. A passage from Mao Tse-tung that is often quoted points out that from the time of Yuan Shih-k'ai only parties and organizations backed by armed force had been able to intervene successfully in Chinese political struggles (*Selected Works* [161] II, 219–35).

70. See pp. 407–8 below on the significance of this rupture.

71. This realization is given expression in a little-known work written by Teng Chung-hsia in 1926 (*Kuang-chou kung-ch'ao* [153], pp. 93–94), in a passage that foreshadows the theory of New Democracy formulated in 1940. After condemning the tendency to be hostile toward the Kuomintang, he stresses the importance of carrying on the political struggle within its ranks in order to win over the "intermediate" classes—the peasants and the petty bourgeoisie—since it was problematic whether they would join forces with the proletariat or with the capitalists. He concludes: "The Chinese revolution will follow a path that is neither purely capitalist nor purely proletarian; it will take on a 'third form.' To achieve success, it will be necessary to found a united democratic dictatorship of the working class, the peasants, and the petty bourgeoisie—a revolutionary government of the united anti-imperialist front. . . . If this is done, the revolution cannot fall into the hands of the capitalists."

72. See pp. 403–7 below.

73. See pp. 174 and 347–48 above.

74. *CEJ*, March 1927, "Strikes in Shanghai."
75. See, for instance, pp. 186 and 260 above.
76. Shanghai Publicity Bureau, *News Bulletin* [114], Aug. 1928, p. 21.
77. In 1923, for instance, the workers in the Nanyang factory in Hong Kong demanded benefits like those granted earlier to the workers in the Shanghai factory. The Hong Kong workers had received a delegation of Shanghai workers and had read press accounts of their successes (*SCMP*, 9.i.23).
78. See Map 9.
79. Wales, *Chinese Labor Movement* [312], p. 164.
80. See Ch'iu-shih, *Shang-hai kung-jen* [191].
81. See "Amsterdam and China," *PPW*, No. 7. In August 1925, for instance, the Amsterdam Federation turned down the proposal of the Red International that it give joint aid to the Chinese strikers, on the grounds that it could not finance a movement about which it had no satisfactory information. In April 1927 the opinion was expressed in its official journal that European workers could not come to the aid of a country of over 300 million (*sic*) inhabitants that was unable to help itself.

82. See p. 266 above.
83. See Mann, *What I Saw in China* [47].
84. *SCMP*, 11.ix.26.
85. See p. 188 above.
86. See p. 172 above.
87. See p. 346 above.
88. *CWR*, 11.xi.22.
89. See p. 343 above.

90. There is no reliable information on the social origin of the members of the Executive Committee of the All-China General Union, and it was only possible to find this out about a few of them.
91. *Chien-shih* [165], pp. 23 and 170.
92. Lei Chia, *Chu Pao-t'ing* [205], pp. 77 and 215.
93. *Lao-tung ta-hui* [142], p. 125.
94. See *Su Chao-cheng* [222], and Wales [312], pp. 208–11.
95. See *Ho-pei ko-ming lieh-shih* [216], pp. 61–62.
96. Li Jui, *Mao Tse-tung* [206], pp. 212–16.
97. *Chien-shih* [165], pp. 73, 118, 170.
98. *Kung-jen yun-tung* [146], p. 406.
99. Interview with the worker Lin Mao-hsiang, brother of Lin Hsiang-ch'ien.

100. *HKC*, 1957, No. 3.
101. *Chien-shih* [165], p. 101.
102. *HKC, ibid.*
103. *Chien-shih*, p. 170.
104. *MKJP*, 21.ix.25.
105. See *CKKJ*, 27.iii.57.
106. Strong, *China's Millions* [304], p. 96.
107. Wales, *Chinese Labor Movement* [312], pp. 212ff.
108. *IPC*, 1.viii.31.
109. *CFJP*, 21.iii.57.
110. *Hu-nan lieh-shih-chuan* [223], pp. 20–26.
111. *Chien-shih* [165], pp. 30, 136, 218ff. See also *PDR*, June–Sept. 1925, *passim*.
112. *Lao-tung ta-hui* [142], p. 125.
113. *HNLSTL*, 1958, No. 2.
114. *PDR*, June–Aug. 1925, *passim*.
115. *Chien-shih* [165], p. 120; *Lao-tung ta-hui*, p. 125.
116. *Kung-jen yun-tung* [146], p. 383.
117. *CKKJ*, 27.iv.57. Li Ch'i-han was arrested by the police of the International Settlement in June 1922 and then handed over by them to the Chinese police in September. He remained in prison in Shanghai until the fall of the Chihli faction in 1924, and then went to Canton, where he became a union leader under the name of Li Sen (*Chien-shih* [165], p. 170).
118. See his biography in *KMJP*, 18.x.54.
119. *Hu-nan lieh-shih-chuan* [223], p. 22.

120. *CTSTL*, 1957, No. 4. See also *HT*, 16.x.26 (obituary).

121. *CKKJ*, 27.iv.57 (Li Ta-chao).

122. *CYB*, 1929, *Who's Who*.

123. In June 1924, for instance, the union leadership succeeded in stopping a strike that had been planned by the workers in the Butterfield & Swire shipyards in Hong Kong (*SCMP*, 30.v.24).

124. Wales, *Chinese Labor Movement* [312], pp. 212ff.

125. *Ho-pei ko-ming lieh-shih* [216], pp. 61–62.

126. *Chien-shih* [165], p. 151. Su Chao-cheng described himself as a Marxist in an interview given to a Hong Kong journalist in March 1922 (*SCMP*, 10.iii.22).

127. See Woo, *The Kuomintang* [168], p. 140.

128. *Ibid.*, pp. 196ff. Figures regarding the class composition of the KMT at this time are too contradictory to be usable. According to the *Canton Gazette* (quoted by *IPC*, 31.xii.26), in 1926 the number of KMT members in the province of Kwangtung was 158,085, 20 per cent of whom (about 31,500) were workers. But according to a survey carried out by the municipality of Canton on the unions in the city in 1926, 78,000 union members (out of a total of 290,000) declared themselves to be members of the KMT (*CYB*, 1928, pp. 1028ff).

129. See Chapters X and XIV above.

130. Woo, *The Kuomintang* [168], p. 166.

131. See Chapter VI above.

132. In the report of the Shanghai General Union presented to the Fourth Congress it was estimated that the losses sustained by union members in April and May of 1927 came to 200 dead, 500 wounded, 1,200 arrested, 5,000 dismissed (*Lao-tung ta-hui* [142], p. 189).

133. *Lao-tung ta-hui*, pp. 238–58.

134. *Ibid.*, pp. 360–436.

135. Wales, *Chinese Labor Movement* [312], chaps. 5 and 6; Epstein, *Labor Problems* [247] (covering the period of the war against Japan).

136. The unionist Hsü T'e-li reported to the Fourth Labor Congress in June 1927 that the guild system and the guild psychology were still very strong and deeply rooted, and that trades and regions were still very prejudiced against each other; he said also that the dispersion and demarcation of craft guilds made organization difficult, and that the difficulty was compounded by the fact that millions of workers were temporary migrants (*PPW*, No. 2).

137. These "opportunist" errors, which Mao Tse-tung was later to criticize so severely (*Selected Works* [161] III, 177–225), were commented on at the end of the summer of 1927 by the Red International delegation to China. (See Stoler, *PPW*, No. 7.)

138. On the part played by working-class militants who managed to escape from the repression of 1927 in the Soviet districts in Kiangsi and later in Yenan, see for instance Smedley, *The Great Road* [48], and Snow, *Red Star over China* [302], *passim*.

Bibliography

Bibliography

The Bibliography contains only the primary and secondary source material referred to in the text. It is arranged under headings according to the type of material, and within each section the entries are arranged in alphabetical order, first of authors, then of collections and so forth edited by an institute or other body, and finally of periodicals containing articles referred to. Brief abstracts are given of a few of the most important sources. The characters for the names of Chinese authors of works in Chinese are given on pp. 430–35.

CONTENTS

Bibliographies

[1] J. K. Fairbank and Kwang-ching Liu. Modern China: A Bibliographical Guide to Chinese Works, 1898–1937. Cambridge, Mass., 1950.

[2] J. K. Fairbank and Matasaka Banno. Japanese Studies of Modern China. Tokyo, 1955.

[3] Robert J. Kerner. Northeast Asia: A Bibliography. 2 vols. Berkeley, Calif., 1939.

[4] J. Schyns. 1,500 Chinese Modern Novels and Plays. Peiping, 1948.

[5] P. E. Skachkov. Bibliografiya kitaya. Moscow, 1932. New ed., Moscow, 1932.

[6] Tung-li Yuan. China in Western Literature: A Continuation of Cordier's Bibliotheca Sinica. New Haven, 1958.

[7] Tung-li Yuan. Economic and Social Development of Modern China: A Bibliographical Guide. New Haven, 1956.

[8] Chung-kuo k'o-hsüeh-yuan and other institutions. Chung-kuo shi-

hsüeh lun-wen so-yin (A guide to articles on Chinese history). 2 vols. Peking, 1957.

[9] Publications on Economic and Social China of the Nankai University. Tientsin, 1936.

Archives

Archives of the International Labor Office, Geneva. In particular:

[10] ——. Dossier G 900–28 (in French). I, 2 (Notes made by P. Henry during his visit to China, Sept.–Dec. 1924). Part 1: general account of the visit (Appendix 1, press cuttings; App. 2, list of people met; App. 3, notes on the political situation). Part 2: working conditions (App. 1, opinions expressed; App. 2, visits to factories; App. 3, a visit to workers' dwellings; App. 4, some statistics). Part 3: trade organizations (App. 1, guilds; App. 2, chambers of commerce; App. 3, labor organizations; App. 4, cooperatives). Part 4: social activities (App. 1, charities; App. 2, workers' education; App. 3, universities).

Owing to the outlook of the I.L.O. at this time, this voluminous report does not throw much light on the political problems of the Chinese proletariat. Its author does not even seem to have been aware of the effects of the Kuomintang Congress of 1924 on the progress of labor struggles, and the only union leaders he seems to have troubled to meet were those of the "yellow" Shanghai Federation. But this is an invaluable source of information concerning labor conditions, wages, and workers' housing in the main industrial centers of China.

[11] ——. (1) Dossier C/1802: correspondence with the I.L.O. office in Shanghai in 1934–36 and reports on the situation of the workers in various industrial centers. (2) Dossier 200/1/13: correspondence between the I.L.O. and the Chinese Government in 1925.

Archives of the Secretariat of the Municipal Council of the International Settlement of Shanghai (consulted in 1957 by permission of the People's City Government of Shanghai). In particular:

[12] ——. Police Daily Reports (from 1919 to 1927).

These reports were submitted daily by the Commissioner of Police of the International Settlement to the Secretary of the Municipal Council. They are a valuable source of information about the public activities of the labor movement (strikes, demonstrations, etc.), and also about the internal affairs of the right-wing unions, with which the police informants seem to have been in close touch. The informants seem to have found it more difficult to obtain information about the unions connected with the Communist Party.

[13] ——. Dossier 2514: correspondence concerning the threat of a general strike in 1922.

[14] ——. Dossier 2879: "Squatters' Huts."

[15] Archives of the Kailan Mining Administration (consulted only partially in 1957, by permission of the Tangshan Municipal Police). (1) Dossier 14/2/9: the 1920 strike. (2) Dossier 14/2/13: the 1922 strike. (3) Dossier 14/2/21: the 1925 strike.

[16] Archives of the French Concession of Shanghai (consulted only par-

tially in 1957 by permission of the People's City Government of Shanghai). In particular: Dossier 23, the French Tramways strike in Dec. 1926.

[17] Minutes of the Child Labor Commission, a body set up in 1923 by the Municipal Council of the International Settlement of Shanghai. A mimeographed copy of these Minutes was consulted in London in 1952 at the home of Miss Agatha Harrison, who sat on the Commission as representative of the Y.W.C.A.

Official Publications

[18] Bureau of Social Affairs, City Government of Greater Shanghai. Strikes and Lockouts in Shanghai since 1918. Shanghai, 1933. Text in both English and Chinese; the Chinese title is *Chin-shih-wu-nien-lai Shang-hai chih pa-kung t'ing-yeh.*
This survey, which was carried out in 1932 by the Kuomintang city government, contains a complete chronology of the strikes and many statistical tables showing their duration, their outcome, their distribution according to months and industries, the nationality of the employers, etc.

[19] Department of Oversea Trade, London. Report on the Commercial, Industrial, and Economic Situation in China. Published annually, beginning in 1919. In 1919–21 it was entitled *Report on the Conditions and Prospects of the British Trade with China.*

[20] Foreign Office, London. Papers Respecting Labour Conditions in China. London, 1925. (Cmd. 2442).
These are reports made by various British consuls in China at the request of the Government following a press campaign in Great Britain concerning labor conditions in British factories in China. Some of them are brief, but others contain a great deal of information.

[21] ——. Memorandum on Labour Conditions in China. London, 1927. (Cmd. 2846).

[22] ——. Papers Respecting the First Firing in the Shameen Affair of June 1925. London, 1926. (Cmd. 2636).

[23] Hong Kong Government. Administrative Reports. Annual.

[24] ——. Government Gazette.

[25] ——. Orders in Council.

[26] ——. Ordinances.

[27] Inspectorate General of Customs. Returns of Trade.
These are quarterly reports arranged according to district; an annual report on the economic situation in each port is appended to each final quarterly report. These reports vary in value according to the customs inspector's interest in Chinese social and economic affairs. Some are simply brief comments on the balance of trade in the port concerned; others contain detailed information about local affairs year by year.

[28] ——. Foreign Trade of China. An annual volume of statistics, with an introductory survey of the economic situation in China during the year, entitled *Report on Trade.*

[29] International Labor Office, Geneva. Reports of the Annual Conferences.

[30] ——. *Informations sociales.* Fortnightly, 1920– . In 1920 it was entitled *Revue quotidienne de presse,* and in 1921 *Informations quotidiennes.*

[31] ——. Annual Report of the Director. 1920– .

[32] ——. Report presented by the Chinese Government to the 1925 Annual Conference.

[33] ——. *International Labour Review.* Monthly 1920– . In particular: July 1923, J. B. Taylor and W. T. Zung, "Labour and Industry in China"; and Mar. 1927, Chen Ta, "The Labour Movement in China."

[34] ——. Legislative Series. Annual.

[35] Ministry of Communications, Peking. Report on the Working of the Chinese Post Office. Annual; text in both English and Chinese until 1920, subsequently only in English.

[36] ——. Statistics of Government Railways. Annual; in English until 1925, subsequently in both English and Chinese.

[37] Shanghai Municipal Council (International Settlement). Annual Report.

[38] ——. Report of the Hon. Mr. Justice Feetham. 2 vols. 1931.

[39] ——. Municipal Gazette. (Incorporated each month in the *North China Herald* [115]. In particular: 13.ii.34, "Report of the Rickshaw Committee."

[40] U.S. Department of Commerce, Washington. *Trade Information Bulletin.* In particular: No. 7, 27.iii.22, J. Clements, "Cement Industry in China"; and No. 75, 30.x.22, J. Arnold, "Labor and Industrial conditions in China."

[41] ——. China: A Commercial and industrial Handbook. Washington, 1926.

[42] U.S. Department of Labor, Bureau of Labor Statistics, Washington. *Monthy Labor Review.* In particular: Aug. 1921, Chen Ta [Ch'en Ta], "Labor Unrest in China"; and May 1922, "The Shipping Strike in Hong Kong."

Memoirs and Eyewitness Accounts

[43] H. O. Chapman. The Chinese Revolution, 1926–27: A Record of the Period under Communist Control as Seen from the Nationalist Capital, Hankow. London, 1928.

[44] M. Hewlett. Forty Years in China. London, 1943.

[45] Colonel C. L'Estrange Malone. New China: Report of an Investigation. Part I, "The Political Situation"; Part II, "Labour Conditions and Labour Organisations." London, 1926.

[46] H. F. McNair. With the White Cross in China: The Journal of a Famine Relief Worker. Peiping, 1939.

[47] T. Mann. What I Saw in China. London, [1927].

[48] A. Smedley. The Great Road: The Life and Times of Chu Teh. New York, 1956.

[49] S. Tretiakov. Chinese Testament: The Autobiography of Tan Shih-hua. London, 1934.

[50] N. Wales. Red Dust: Autobiographies of Chinese Communists as Told to Nym Wales. Stanford, Calif., 1952.

[51] Ch'i-wu Lao-jen. Erh-ch'i hui-i-lu (Memories of February 7). Peking, 1957.

[52] [Chung-kung P'ing-hsiang Mei-k'uang Wei-yuan-hui.] Hung-se-ti An-yuan (Red Anyuan). Nanchang, 1959.

[53] *Chung-kuo kung-jen* (The Chinese Worker). 12.v.57, Ch'i-wu Lao-jen, "Hui-i Li Ta-chao t'ung-chih" (Memories of Comrade Li Ta-chao).

[54] *Hsin-kuan-ch'a* (The New Observer), Peking. Fortnightly. 15.i.57, 1.ii.57 and 15.ii.57, Ch'i-wu lao-jen, "Erh-ch'i pa-kung hui-i" (Memories of the February 7 strike); and 1.vii.57, Ch'i-wu lao-jen, "Chung-kuo kung-ch'an-tang ch'eng-li ch'ien-hou ti chien-wen" (Memories of the times when the Chinese Communist Party was founded).

[55] *Hung-ch'i p'iao-p'iao* (The Unfurling of the Red Flag), Peking. 1957– . Collections of biographies and memoirs of revolutionary militants; appears at irregular intervals. In particular: No. 5, 15.xii.57, "I Chao Shih-yen" (Memories of Chao Shih-yen); *ibid.*, Li Li-san, "Tao Hsiang Ching-yü t'ung-chih" (Lament for Comrade Hsiang Ching-yü); and No. 8, July 1958, "I Ch'iu-pai" (In memory of Ch'ü Ch'iu-pai).

Surveys and Monographs

[56] A. Anderson. Humanity and Labour in China: An Industrial Visit and Its Sequel (1923 to 1926). London, 1928.

[57] J. L. Buck. Chinese Farm Economy: A Study of 2,866 Farms in Seventeen Localities and Seven Provinces in China. Chicago, 1930.

[58] J. S. Burgess. The Guilds of Peking. New York, 1928.

[59] C. C. Chu and T. C. Blaisdell. Peking Boys and Peking Rugs. Peking, 1924.

[60] H. Chung and M. Baywell. Women in Industry in Chapei, Hongkew, and Pootung. Shanghai, 1931. A Y.W.C.A. pamphlet.

[61] G. S. Eddy. The New World of Labor. New York, 1923.

[62] Fong, H. D. [Feng Hsien-ting]. Grain Trade and Milling in Tientsin. Tientsin, 1934. Nankai University Industry Series No. 6.

[63] ——. Hosiery Knitting in Tientsin. Tientsin, 1930. Nankai University Industry Series No. 3.

[64] ——. Rayon and Cotton Weaving in Tientsin. Tientsin, 1930. Nankai University Industry Series No. 2.

[65] ——. Tientsin Carpet Industry. Tientsin, 1929. Nankai University Industry Series No. 1.

[66] S. D. Gamble, with the assistance of J. S. Burgess. Peking: A Social Survey. New York, 1921. Conducted under the auspices of the Princeton University Center in China and the Peking Y.W.C.A.

[67] H. S. Gear and others. Industrial Health in Shanghai. Vol. I: An In-

vestigation of Printing Works. Shanghai, 1935. Chinese Medical Association Special Reports Series, No. 4.

[68] C. W. Howard and K. P. Buswell. A Survey of the Silk Industry in South China. Canton, 1925. Lingnan Agricultural College, Agricultural Bulletin No. 12.

[69] Hsia Yen. "Pao-shen-kung" (Contract labor), a short story in the collection *Yao-yuan ti feng-sha* (Sand blown from afar). Shanghai, 1947. English trans. in *Chinese Literature,* No. 8 (Peking, 1960). This short story is based on the author's experience as a worker in the Japanese cotton mills of Shanghai.

[70] Kyong Pae-tsung. Industrial Women in Wusih. Shanghai, 1929. Issued by the National Committee of the Y.W.C.A. in China.

[71] Lee Wei-yung and others. Industrial Health in Shanghai. Vol. III: Shanghai Diets Compared with Those of Institutional workers. Shanghai, 1936. Sponsored by the Henry Lester Institute for Medical Research. Chinese Medical Association Special Reports Series, No. 7.

[72] Li Chin-p'o. Wu-sa ts'an-an tiao-ch'a-chi (Report on the massacre of May 30). Peking, 1925.

[73] Lin Hsiu-chuan. Labor Conditions in the Chunghsing Coal Mine (Shantung). Peiping, 1933.

[74] Lin Sung-ho. Factory Workers in Tangku. Peking, 1928.
This excellent monograph presents the results of a survey conducted in May–July 1926 at the Chiu-ta salt refinery, on the outskirts of Tientsin. Eighty-six of the 556 workers employed there were interviewed, and detailed information is given about almost every aspect of working-class life: hours of work, sickness, food, housing, family life, wages, finances, recreation, etc.

[75] Meng T'ien-pei and S. D. Gamble. Prices, wages, and the Standard of Living in Peking, 1900–1924. Peking, 1926.

[76] Tao Li-kung. *Livelihood in Peking.* Peking, 1928.

[77] ——. The Standard of Living among Chinese Workers. Shanghai, 1931.

[78] R. Tawney. Land and Labour in China. London, 1932.

[79] T. Tchou. Housing and Social Conditions among Industrial Workers in Shanghai. Shanghai, 1926. Issued by the Industrial Department of the National Committee of the Y.M.C.A. in China.

[80] ——. Report on Industrial and Social Survey. Shanghai, 1922. Issued by the Y.M.C.A. Committee on Labor Problems. Consulted at the offices of the International Y.W.C.A. at Geneva. Mimeo.

[81] S. Yang and L. K. Tao. A Study of the Standard of Living of Working Families in Shanghai. Peiping, 1931.
This survey is based on the housekeeping accounts or records of expenditure and income of 230 working-class families in the Tsaokiatu district of Shanghai. The husband in each family was a worker in a cotton mill in the district. The information is very detailed.

[82] Yeh Kung-cho. An Industrial Tour around Manchuria. Peking, 1921. Issued by the Office of the High Industrial Commissioner.

[83] Yü Ch'i-chung. Kuang-chou lao-tzu cheng-i ti fen-hsi Min-kuo shih-

erh-nien erh-shih-erh-nien (Analysis of the conflicts between capital and labor in Canton from 1923 to 1933). Canton, 1934.

[84] *Annals of the American Academy of Political Science.* Nov. 1930, S. D. Gamble, "Peiping Family Budgets."

[85] *China Journal of Science and Arts.* Feb. 1925, C. T. Maitland, "Phosphorus Poisoning in Match Factories in China." (A report to the industrial committee of the National Christian Council of China.)

[86] *China Medical Missionary Journal.* Mar. 1924, H. W. Decker, "Industrial Hospital, Shanghai: Review of 880 Cases from the Cotton Mills"; and Apr. 1929, Yao Hsun-yuan, "Industrial Health in the Peiping Special Health Area."

[87] *Ch'ing-hua hsüeh-pao* (Journal of Ch'ing-hua University). June 1926, Ch'en Ta, "Chin-pa-nien-lai kuo-nei pa-kung ti fen-hsi" (Analysis of strikes in the country during the past eight years).

This survey is based on information given by the Shanghai daily newspaper *Shen-pao* [129] until 1924, and on information selected from eleven newspapers from various areas for 1925.

[88] *Pacific Affairs.* Mar. 1947, Shih Kuo-heng, "Social Implications of the Tin-mining Industry in Yunnan."

Periodicals

Periodicals Read Through Systematically for the 1919–27 Period

[89] *Cheng-chih chou-pao* (Political Weekly), Canton. Published by the Communist Party and the left wing of the Kuomintang in 1926. In particular: 17.v.26, Ch'iu-jen, "Kuo-min-tang hsia ti wu-yueh wu-i, wu-ssu, wu-wu, wu-ch'i chi-nien" (The anniversaries of May 1, May 4, May 5, and May 7 under the Kuomintang).

[90] *Ch'ien-feng* (The Advance Guard), Canton. Published monthly from 1923 by the Chinese Communist Party and intended for a wider public than *HT* [102]. In particular: 1.vii.23, Shih-shan, "Sheng-hsien hsia ti Hu-nan" (Hunan under the provincial constitution); *ibid.*, Ch'ü Wei-t'o (pseudonym of Ch'ü Ch'iu-pai), "Chung-kuo chih tzu-ch'an chieh-chi ti fa-chan" (The development of the capitalist class in China); and 1.xii.23, Tu-hsiu, "Chung-kuo kuo-min ko-ming yü she-hui ko chieh-chi" (The Chinese nationalist revolution and various social classes).

[91] *China Weekly Review,* Shanghai. At first called *Millard's Review of the Far East,* and then from 1921 *Weekly Review of the Far East.*

This weekly, edited by the American journalist J. B. Powell, conducted several campaigns against British and Japanese penetration of China. It had a wide readership among the Chinese bourgeoisie of Shanghai, and occasionally printed articles by well-known members of this class. Its provincial correspondents, who were Chinese, regularly contributed information about Chinese social and political affairs in the provinces, especially as regards Central China.

See in particular: 8.x.21, Yeh Kung-ch'o, "Salvaging China Industrially"; 15.x.21, V. Dyson, "The Oil Mill Outlook in China"; 20.v.22, J. Clements, "The

Cement Industry in China"; 28.x.22, "The British Loan to Canton"; 23.xii.22, H. Y. Moh, "The Causes for the High Prices of Cotton and the Low Prices of Yarn"; 6.vi.23, "The Real Significance of Banditry in China"; 24.ii.23, "Mutiny Cases in China since the Revolution"; 1.ix.23, "Agricultural Unrest May Lead to Bolshevism in China"; 10.iv.24, "Who Sells Guns to China's War Leaders?"; 21.xi.25, Shen Tsen-kwan, "Unfavorable Conditions in Northern Kiangsu"; and 1, 15, 22.ii.30 and 8.iii.30, H. D. Lamson, "Industrial Accidents in China."

[92] *China Year Book*, London. Annual.

[93] *Chinese Bulletin*, London. Mimeo. Published at irregular intervals from Dec. 1925 to Sept. 1927 by the Chinese Information Bureau, which had Nationalist sympathies.

[94] *Chinese Economic Bulletin*, Peking. Published weekly beginning in 1919 by the Chinese Government Bureau of Economic Information.

The Information Bureau that published this bulletin was nominally under the central government, but its director was an American named Donald, who carefully avoided becoming involved in the quarrels between the various militarist factions. The bulletin contains brief notes on Chinese social and economic matters in all the provinces, probably extracted from the press.

[95] *Chinese Economic Journal*, Peking, then Shanghai. Published monthly from 1927; formerly *Chinese Economic Monthly* [96]. In particular: Feb. 1927, "Labor Conditions in Chekiang"; Mar. 1927, "Strikes in Shanghai in 1926"; June 1927, "Women's Work in Kwangtung Province"; July 1927, W. Young, "Chinese Labor Migration to Manchuria"; July 1927, D. K. Lieu, "China's Industrial Development"; Oct.–Nov. 1927, "A Study of the Sugar Industry in China"; Oct., Nov., Dec. 1927, Chen Ta [Ch'en Ta], "Analysis of Strikes in China from 1918 to 1926" (based on the *CHHP* survey [87]); Oct. 1927, "Tangshan, an Industrial Town on the Peking-Mukden Railway"; Nov. 1927, "Three Towns in S.E. Chihli"; Jan. 1928, K. L. Hsueh, "Iron and Steel Industry in China"; Mar. 1928, "Industrial Works in Mukden"; Apr., May, June 1928, "Manufacturing Industries in Northern Manchuria"; June 1928, T'ao Ling and L. Johnson, "A Study of Women and Girls in Tientsin Industries"; June 1928, "Flour Mills in China"; June 1928, "Paper Manufacturing in China"; July 1928, "Shanghai Silk Filatures"; July 1928, "Match Factories in China"; Oct. 1928, "Industrial Works in Wuhan"; June 1929, "Labor Conditions in Canton"; Apr. through Aug. 1930, B. Torgasheff, "Mining Labor in China"; Aug.–Sept. 1930, Fang Fu-an, "Shanghai Labor"; Oct. 1930, M. Stewart and Fang Fu-an, "A Statistical Study of Industry and Labor in China"; Mar. 1931, "A Study of 262 Laborers in Hangchow"; Oct. 1931, H. D. Lamson, "The Effect of Industrialization upon Village Livelihood"; Aug. 1932, H. D. Lamson, "The Problems of Housing for Workers in China"; Apr. 1933, T. H. Hwang, "Coal Mining in China"; and July 1933, "Flour Industry in Kiangsu."

[96] *Chinese Economic Monthly*, Peking. 1924–26. In particular: Apr. 1926, "The Yunnan Tin Industry"; June 1926, "Economic Study of Peking Rickshaw-pullers"; Oct. 1926, "Strikes in Shanghai"; Oct. 1926, "Wages in Tientsin Industries"; and Nov. 1926, "Industrial Nantungchow."

[97] *Chinese Social and Political Science Review*, Peking. Published quar-

terly beginning in 1915 by the Chinese Social and Political Science Association. In particular: Apr. 1930, J. B. Taylor, "Hopei Pottery Industry and the Problem of its Modernisation"; Apr. 1931, H. D. Fong, "Industrialisation and Labour in Hopei with Special Reference to Tientsin"; Oct. 1931, F. L. Ho, "Population Movement to the Northeastern Provinces in China"; and Oct. 1933, H. D. Fong, "Grain Trade and Milling in Tientsin."

[98] *Chung-kuo kung-jen* (The Chinese Worker), Shanghai. Published by the Chinese Communist Party; five numbers were issued between October 1924 and May 1925. See in particular: Oct. 1924, [Teng?] Chung-hsia, "Kung-nung-chün yü Pei-fa" (The workers' and peasants' army and the Northern Expedition); *ibid.*, Shih-yen, "Ti-kuo-chu-i chih chin-kung yü Chung-kuo lao-tung yun-tung" (The imperialist attack and the Chinese labor movement); *ibid.,* Te-lung, "Nan-yang yen-ch'ang pa-kung shih-pai ti yuan-yin yü so-te ti chiao-hsün" (The causes of the defeat of the Nanyang tobacco factory strike and the lessons to be drawn); *ibid.*, Chung-yuan, "Chao Heng-t'i ts'ui-ts'an kung-jen chih yu-i fang-shih" (Yet another method employed by Chao Heng-t'i for oppression of the workers); *ibid.*, Chou-chang, "Shan-tung Lu-ta kung-ssu ya-p'o kung-jen" (The oppression of the workers by the Lu-ta company in Shantung); Nov. 1924, Hu-nan kung-jen (A Hunan worker), "Fan-tui kao-kung-hsi chia-kung-hsi pao-pan kung-hui ya-p'o kung-jen" (Against the seizure of union control and the oppression of workers by higher-ranking employees); *ibid.*, Chung-yuan, "Chan-chih hou-tz'u" (The benefits resulting from the war); *ibid.*, Chung-hsia, "Wo-men-ti li-liang" (Our forces); *ibid.*, Te-lung, "Kuo-chi lao-tung chü-chih chen-hsiang yü p'ai-jen lai Hua" (The real facts concerning the I.L.O. and the visit to China of its delegate); *ibid.*, Neng-chih, "Nan-yang yen-ts'ao pa-kung ti ching-kuo" (The events during the strike at the Nanyang tobacco factory); *ibid.*, Chung-hsia, "Hai-yuan hsüan-ch'uan wen-t'i" (Questions of propaganda among the seamen); Apr. 1925, Chang T'e-li, "Chih-kung yun-tung fu-shing chi ch'i ying-ch'ü chih fang-chen" (The restoration of the unions and the line to follow); *ibid.*, Ch'ü Ch'iu-pai, "Pei-ching cheng-pien hou ti cheng-chü yü kung-jen chieh-chi" (The working class and the political situation after the Peking coup); *ibid.*, Chung-hsia, "Shang-hai Jih-pen sha-ch'ang pa-kung so-te-lai ti ching-yen" (Experiences gained during the strike in the Japanese cotton mills of Shanghai); *ibid.*, Chang-T'e-li, "Ch'üan-kuo t'ieh-lu tsung-kung-hui ti-erh-tz'u tai-piao ta-hui chih shih-mo" (Complete account of the Second Congress of the General Railwaymen's Union); May 1925, Chung-hsia, "Lao-tung yun-tung fu-hsing ch'i-chung ti chi-ko chung-yao wen-t'i" (Some important questions concerning the revival of the labor movement); and *ibid.*, Chang T'e-li, "Ching-chu ti-erh-tz'u ch'üan-kuo lao-tung ta-hui" (Greetings to the Second National Labor Congress).

[99] *Eastern Engineering,* London. Monthly.

[100] *Eastern and Colonial Bulletin.* Moscow. Fortnightly, 1928–29. Mimeo.

[101] *Far Eastern Review,* Shanghai. Monthly. In particular: Nov. 1919, "The Cost of Living to Chinese in Shanghai"; and Feb. 1923, "Labor Unrest in China."

[102] *Hsiang-tao* (The Guide), Shanghai. English subtitle: *The Guide Weekly*. Published by the Central Committee of the Chinese Communist Party, beginning in 1922, sometimes at irregular intervals.

This periodical was mainly under the influence of Ch'en Tu-hsiu and his friend P'eng Shu-chih, although its editor-in-chief was Ts'ai Ho-sen, who probably did not always agree with their views. It therefore tends to play down the importance of the labor movement, especially in 1926–27; but it is nevertheless a source of primary importance.

See in particular: 20.xi.22, Sun-to, "Chung-kuo lao-tung-chieh ch'ün-chung ti chüeh-hsing" (The awakening of the working masses in China); 18.vi.24, [Ch'en] Tu-hsiu, "Kuo-min-tang yü lao-tung yun-tung" (The Kuomintang and the labor movement); 3.xii.25, Ch'en Tu-hsiu, "Shih-ma shih Kuo-min-tang tso-yu-p'ai?" (Who are the right and the left in the Kuomintang?); 10.xii.24, [P'eng] Shu-chih, "Mu-ch'ien cheng-chü yü kung-jen chieh-chi" (The present political situation and the working class); 1.v.26, Ch'en Tu-hsiu, "Ti-erh-tz'u ho ti-san-tz'u lao-tung ta-hui chih-chien ti Chung-kuo lao-tung yun-tung" (The Chinese labor movement between the Second and Third Labor Congresses); and 15.v.26, Ch'en Tu-hsiu, "Nan-fang ching-shih yü Kuo-min-tang" (The situation in the South and the Kuomintang).

[103] *Hsien-ch'ü* (The Pioneer), Shanghai. Published fortnightly but at irregular intervals by the Socialist Youth Corps of China, from Jan. 1922 to Aug. 1923. In particular: 1.v.22, a special number with articles by Ch'en Tu-hsiu, Li Ta, and Ts'ai Ho-sen.

[104] *Hsin-ch'ing-nien* (New Youth), Peking. French subtitle: *La Jeunesse*. Monthly except for a period in 1923 when publication was suspended. In particular: 1.v.26, special number on labor problems, with contributions by special correspondents in the main cities of China.

[105] *L'Humanité*, Paris. Daily.

[106] *International Press Correspondence*, Moscow and Berlin. Published twice weekly by the Comintern.

This periodical contains a great deal of information about the political activities and the strike action of the Chinese labor movement, especially after 1925. I have used the English edition, which sometimes differs from the German and French editions.

[107] *Japan Weekly Chronicle*, Kobe. A weekly supplement of the *Japan Chronicle*.

[108] *Kung-ch'an-tang* (The Communist Party), Shanghai. Published monthly; a total of six issues appeared, between Dec. 1920 and July 1921. In particular: July 1921, "T'ai-p'ing-yang hui-i chi wo-men ying-ch'ü ti t'ai-tu" (The attitude we ought to adopt toward the Pacific Conference).

[109] *Lao-tung-chieh* (The World of Labor), Shanghai. This weekly, published by the Shanghai "small Communist group," appeared during the summer and fall of 1920.

[110] *The London and China Telegraph*, London. In 1922 this weekly merged with the *London and China Express* and became the *China Express and Telegraph*.

[111] *Manchuria Daily News,* Dairen. Despite the name, publication was irregular during 1921–23.

This newspaper had close connections with the South Manchuria Railway Co. Because of its strongly conservative political views and its full support for Chang Tso-lin, it gave very little space to labor activities until after 1925.

[112] *Nankai Economic and Social Quarterly,* Tientsin. 1935– . In particular: Apr. and July 1937, L. G. Ting, "Coal Industry in China"; and Oct. 1935, T. Y. Tsha, "Study of Wage Rates in Shanghai."

[113] *News Bulletin,* Canton. Published at irregular intervals by the Chinese News Service from Dec. 1926 to the spring of 1927. Mimeo.

[114] [Shanghai Publicity Bureau.] *News Bulletin,* No. 1 (Aug. 1928).

[115] *North China Herald,* Shanghai. A weekly supplement of the *North China Daily News.*

This weekly was the official organ of the Municipal Council of the International Settlement of Shanghai and of the big British interests there. Its political outlook with regard to China was much more conservative than that of the *China Weekly Review* [91], and it hardly ever opened its columns to Chinese contributors. But it faithfully reflects the growing anxieties of foreign employers in Shanghai with regard to the labor movement. It published the *Municipal Gazette* [39] as a monthly supplement.

In particular: Mar. 17, 24, 31, Apr. 14, 1923, V. Kelsey, "China's Industrial Workers"; and Apr. 24, May 1 and 8, 1926, G. Sokolsky, "A Visit to Canton and Hong Kong."

[116] *The Pan-Pacific Worker,* Hankow, then Shanghai. Published fortnightly, 1927–28; the official organ of the Pan-Pacific Trade Union Secretariat, established in May 1927 by the Red International of Trade Unions after the Pan-Pacific Conference in Hankow. In particular: No. 2 (15.vii.27), S. Stoler, "A Visit to Hunan Province"; No. 4 (Aug. 1927), M. Apletin, "With the Chinese Trade Unions: A Visit to the Wuchang Textile Workers"; Nos. 6 and 7 (15.ix.27 and 1.x.27), S. Stoler, "The Trade Union Movement in Canton"; No. 7 (1.x.27), Lieu Men-tah, "Amsterdam and China"; and *ibid.,* M. Apletin, "The Wages of the Wuhan Workers."

[117] *La Politique de Pékin,* Peking. Weekly.

[118] *South China Morning Post,* Hong Kong. Daily.

Of the various British daily newspapers of Hong Kong, this one took the greatest interest in Chinese affairs, especially in social and political affairs in Canton. It often contained lengthy extracts from the *Canton Times,* an English-language Chinese newspaper that supported the Kuomintang.

Periodicals Occasionally Consulted

Most of the periodicals listed in this subsection were consulted in the collection of press cuttings for 1920–27 made by Ch'en Ta, which he deposited at the Institute for Labor Movement Studies of the All-China General Union in Peking.

[119] *Ch'en-pao* (The Morning Paper), Peking. Daily.

[120] *Chieh-fang yü kai-tsao* (Liberation and Reconstruction), Shanghai. Monthly (1920).

[121] *Han-k'ou shang-pao* (Hankow Commercial Paper).

[122] *Hsin-wen-pao* (News), Shanghai. Daily.

[123] *I-shih-pao* (Public Welfare), Peking. Daily.

[124] *I-shih-pao* (Public Welfare), Tientsin. Daily.

[125] *Min-kuo jih-pao* (Nationalist Daily), Shanghai.

[126] *Min-sheng tsa-chih* (Voice of the People Magazine), Shanghai.

[127] *Novii Vostok,* Leningrad.

[128] *Shang-hai shih-pao* (The Shanghai Times). Daily.

[129] *Shen-pao* (The Whangpoo Daily), Shanghai.

[130] *Shih-shih hsin-pao* (New Times), Shanghai. Daily.

[131] *Shih-shih hua-pao* (The Times Illustrated), Shanghai.

[132] *Shun-t'ien shih-pao* (Celestial Times), Peking. Daily.

Collections of Contemporary Source Material

[133] C. Brandt, B. Schwartz, and J. K. Fairbank. A Documentary History of Chinese Communism. London, 1952.

[134] Chang Ching-lu and others. Chung-kuo hsien-tai ch'u-pan shih-liao (Materials on recent Chinese publications). Vol. I (1919–27), Peking, 1954. Supplementary vol., Peking, 1957.

[135] J. V. A. MacMurray, ed. Treaties and Agreements With and Concerning China, 1894–1921. 2 vols. New York, 1921.

[136] P'eng Tse-i and others. Chung-kuo chin-tai shou-kung-yeh shih tzu-liao (Materials for the history of handicrafts in modern China [1840–1949]). 4 vols. Peking, 1957.

[137] Sun Yü-t'ang, Wang Ching-yü, and others. Chung-kuo chin-tai kung-yeh shih tzu-liao (Materials for the history of modern Chinese industry). Peking, 1957. Vol. I (1840–95) in 2 vols. Vol. II (1895–1914) in 2 vols.

[138] Wang Ch'ing-pin and others. Ti-i-tz'u Chung-kuo lao-tung nien-chien (The First Chinese Labor Yearbook). Peking, 1928.

This important compilation is valuable for both the quality and the quantity of its contents. The first part deals with labor conditions, the second with strikes and labor organizations, the third with social welfare. The authors have collected all available material concerning these three questions (press extracts, official or private surveys, statistics of all kinds, special studies), and have even added materials translated from Japanese and English.

[139] L. Wieger. La Chine moderne. 10 vols. Hsien-hsien, 1920–32.

This work may often raise a smile, since the author, to put it mildly, has neither sympathy with nor serious interest in the Chinese Nationalist movement. But he has brought together a large number of extracts from the Chinese press, for some of which the Chinese characters are given. The *éphémérides* (calendars of events) included in Vols. IV-X give a very complete, if not always reliable, chronology of political events year by year.

[140] C. M. Wilbur and J. Lien-ying How. Documents on Communism, Nationalism, and Soviet Advisers in China: Papers seized in the 1927 Peking Raid. New York, 1956.

The papers concerning Sino-Soviet military and political relations must be treated with the utmost caution, but those concerning Chinese internal affairs provide some useful information.

[141] Yen Chung-p'ing and others. Chung-kuo chin-tai ching-chi shih tung-chi tzu-liao hsüan-chi (A selection of statistics of modern Chinese economic history). Peking, 1955.

[142] [Ch'üan-kuo tsung-kung-hui.] Chung-kuo li-tz'u ch'üan-kuo lao-tung ta-hui wen-hsien (Texts of the various All-China Labor Congresses). Peking, 1957.

[143] [K'o-hsüeh-yuan ching-chi yen-chiu-so.] Nan-yang hsiung-ti yen-ts'ao kung-ssu shih-liao (Historical material on the Nanyang Brothers' Tobacco Company). Shanghai, 1960.

[144] [K'o-hsüeh-yuan li-shih yen-chiu ti-san-so.] Wu-ssu ai-kuo yun-tung tzu-liao (Materials on the patriotic movement of May 4th). Peking, 1959.

This collection contains numerous extracts from the Chinese and the Western press in Shanghai, besides many of the pamphlets and leaflets distributed at the time.

[145] [Chung-kung chung-yang Ma-k'o-ssu En-ko-ssu Lieh-ning Ssu-ta-lin chu-tso pien-i-chu yen-chiu-so.] Wu-ssu shih-ch'i ch'i-k'an chieh-shao (Introduction to the periodicals of the May 4th period). 2 vols. Peking, 1958 .

These volumes contain a very complete list of periodicals of all kinds published in China from 1919 to about 1922, the texts of the most important manifestos and editorials contained in them, a detailed table of contents for each issue, and finally a lengthy note on each periodical and its general trend. Considerable space is devoted to the labor press.

[146] Ti-i-tz'u kuo-nei ko-ming chan-cheng shih-ch'i ti kung-jen yun-tung (The labor movement during the first revolutionary civil war). Peking, 1953.

This collection is composed of extracts from the Chinese press of the period (including newspapers and union publications), and contains a large number of manifestos, union resolutions, and analyses of strikes. It was compiled by responsible union leaders, among them Teng Chung-hsia and Hsiang Ying.

[147] Ti-i-tz'u kuo-nei ko-ming chan-cheng shih-ch'i ti nung-min yun-tung (The peasant movement during the first revolutionary civil war). Peking, 1953.

[148] [Institute of Pacific Relations.] Agrarian China. Chicago, 1938. Intro. by R. Tawney.

[149] Min-kuo fa-ling ta-ch'üan (Summary of Nationalist legislation). Shanghai, 1924.

[150] *Hu-nan li-shih tzu-liao* (Materials on the History of Hunan), Changsha. Bimonthly. In particular: 1958, No. 2, Liu Shao-ch'i, "Tui chü-lo-pu kuo-ch'ü ti p'i-p'ing ho chiang-lai ti chi-hua" (Criticism of the past of the club and plans for the future); and *ibid.*, "Shui-k'ou-shan kung-jen chü-lo-pu chi-shih" (Facts concerning the Shuikoushan workers' club).

[151] [K'o-hsüeh-yuan li-shih yen-chiu ti-san-so.] *Chin-tai-shih tzu-liao* (Materials on Modern History), Peking. Bimonthly, 1954–58. In particular: 1955, No. 1, "Erh-ch'i kung-ch'ou" (Revenge against the workers on February 7); 1955, No. 2, "Pei-ching ta-hsüeh p'ing-min chiao-yü chiang-yen-t'uan" (The

Peking University group of teachers for the education of the common people); *ibid.*, Pien Hsiao-hsuan, "Liu-fa ch'in-kung chien-hsüeh tzu-liao" (Materials on the "work-study" groups of Chinese living in France); 1956, No. 1, "1905 nien fan-Mei ai-kuo yun-tung" (The patriotic anti-American movement of 1905); 1957, No. 4, "Nan-ch'ang ta-shih-chi" (Chronicle of Nanchang); 1958, No. 5, Ch'en T'ieh-ch'ing, "T'ien-chin fan-k'ang Fa-ti ch'iang-chan Lao-hsi-k'ai tzu-liao" (Materials on the resistance of Tientsin against the French imperialists' forcible occupation of Laohsikai); *ibid.*, Ting Yu, "1905 nien Kuang-tung fan-Mei yun-tung" (The anti-American movement in Kwangtung in 1905); and *ibid.*, "Sheng-Kang pa-kung kung-jen tai-piao ta-hui ti-i-pai-tz'u chi-nien-k'an" (Publication commemorating the hundredth meeting of the Canton–Hong Kong strikers' congress).

[152] Tang-shih tzu-liao (Materials on the history of the Party). Peking, 1953–55. In particular: 1953, No. 3, P'eng Chiang-liu, "An-yuan lu-k'uang kung-jen chü-lo-pu ti li-shih" (History of the Anyuan miners' and railwaymen's club); 1954, No. 4, Li Li-san, "1919 nien chih 1927 nien Chung-kuo kung-jen yun-tung kai-k'uang" (General account of the Chinese labor movement from 1919 to 1927); 1955, No. 3, Ku Chia-hsi, "Chieh-shao 'Lao-tung chieh' ho 'Shang-hai huo-yu'" (Introducing "The World of Labor" and "The Shanghai Shophand").

Contemporary Writings and Studies

[153] 1926 nien chih Kuang-chou kung-ch'ao (The strike wave in Canton in 1926). Canton, 1927.

[154] Sheng-Kang pa-kung kai-kuan (Short account of the Canton–Hong Kong strike). Canton, 1926.

[155] Sheng-Kang pa-kung chung chih Chung-Ying t'an-p'an (The negotiations between China and Great Britain during the Canton–Hong Kong strike). Canton, 1926.

[156] A. Kotenev. Shanghai, Its Municipality and the Chinese. Shanghai, 1927.

[157] ———. Shanghai, Its Mixed Court and Council. Shanghai, 1927.

[158] Kuo Liang. Hu-nan kung-jen yun-tung kuo-ch'ü yü hsien-tsai (The Hunan labor movement past and present). Changsha, 1927.

[159] Li Ta-chao. Hsüan-chi (Selected works). Peking, 1959.

[160] Liu Shao-ch'i and Chu Shao-lien. An-yuan lu-k'uang kung-jen chü-lo-pu lüeh-shih (Short history of the Anyuan miners' and railwaymen's club). Anyuan, 1923.

[161] Mao Tse-tung. Selected Works. 4 vols. Peking, 1964.

[162] L. Porter. China's Challenge to Christianity. New York, 1924.

[163] Sun Chung-shan (Sun Yat-sen). Hsüan-chi (Selected works). 2 vols. Peking, 1956. A translation of Sun's treatise on the "Three People's Principles," by d'Elia, appeared under the title *Le triple démisme* (Shanghai, 1930).

[164] T'ang Hai. Chung-kuo lao-tung wen-t'i (Labor problems in China). Shanghai, 1926.

[165] Teng Chung-hsia. Chung-kuo chih-kung yun-tung chien-shih (Short history of the Chinese labor movement). Peking, 1949. (Many other editions.) This study written in the Soviet Union in 1928–30, was incomplete when the author returned to China in 1930 and was never completed. He ultimately decided to publish the completed part, on the period 1916–26, by itself. There were to have been three introductory chapters, and a further fourteen chapters on the 1926–30 period. The book in its present incomplete form was first published in Moscow; the first Chinese edition appeared in 1943. The central part played by Teng Chung-hsia in the events of the period makes this work an authoritative source of fundamental importance.

[166] M. T. Z. Tyau. China Awakened. New York, 1922.

[167] G. Voitinskii. Chto proishodit v Kitae (What is happening in China?). Moscow, 1924.

[168] T. C. Woo. The Kuomintang and the Future of the Chinese Revolution. London, 1928.

[169] Yuan Hsiang. Chung-kuo nien-chien (The China yearbook). Shanghai, 1924 (the only year in which it appeared).

[170] [Red International of Trade Unions.] Arbeiterbewegung und Revolution in China. Berlin, 1925. This contains articles by various writers. In particular: L. Heller, "Die Arbeiterklasse und die Revolution in China"; XXX, "Die Gesetzgebung in China"; T. Mandalyan, "Das Internationale Proletariat und die Ereignisse in China."

[171] Die Arbeiter Chinas im Kampf gegen Imperialismus. Berlin and Moscow, 1927.

[172] Chinese Communists and Mission Properties. Hong Kong, 1926.

[173] Ching-Han kung-jen liu-hsüeh-chi (In memory of the blood shed by the Peking–Hankow railwaymen). [Peking, 1923.]

[174] Gomindan (Kuomintang). Moscow, 1926. (In Russian.)

[175] [Hu-nan lao-kung-hui.] Huang P'ang chou-nien chi-nien-ts'e (Commemorative volume for the anniversary of Huang and P'ang). Shanghai, 1923.

[176] [——.] Huang P'ang ssu-chou-nien chi-nien-ts'e (Commemorative volume for the fourth anniversary of Huang and P'ang). Shanghai and Changsha, 1926.

[177] June Twenty-third. Canton, 1925.

[178] [Ch'üan-kuo tsung-kung-hui.] Ko-ming chan-shih-chi ti-i ts'e (First collection of biographies of revolutionaries). Canton, 1926.

[179] [National Christian Council of China.] Modern Industry in China. Industrial Reconstruction Series No. 4. N.p., n.d.

[180] [Chinese Eastern Railway.] North Manchuria and the C.E.R. Harbin, 1922.

[181] Rabochii Kitai (Workers of China). Moscow, 1926. (In Russian.)

[182] [B.A.T.] The Record in China of the British-American Tobacco Company Ltd. N.p., [1925?]. (In English and Chinese.)

[183] [Commercial Press.] Regulations for the Welfare Work for the Commercial Press Employees. N.p., n.d.

[184] [S.M.R.] Report on Progress in Manchuria, 1907–1928. Dairen, 1929.

[185] [*Millard's Review.*] Who's Who in China. Shanghai, 1920.

[186] Wu-sa t'ung-shih (The painful history of May 30). Peking, 1925.

[187] *Revue du Pacifique,* Paris. Sept. 1925, "Le prolétariat en Chine."

[188] *World Tomorrow,* New York. Nov. 1923, a special number entitled "Capital and Labor Relations in China."

Books and Articles in Chinese

[189] Chang Wei-ying. "Wu-sa yun-tung chung ch'üan-kuo jen-min fan-ti tou-cheng ti kai-k'uang" (A sketch of the anti-imperialist struggle of the people throughout the country during the May 30th movement), in Ti-i-tz'u kuo-nei ko-ming chan-cheng shih-lun-chi (Collection of articles on the history of the first revolutionary civil war), ed. Lai Hsin-hsia. (Peking, 1957.)

[190] Ch'en Ta. Chung-kuo lao-tung wen-t'i (Chinese labor problems). Shanghai, 1929.

[191] Ch'iu-shih. Shang-hai kung-jen tsai chi-ko li-shih shih-ch'i chung ti ko-ming tou-cheng (The revolutionary struggles of the workers of Shanghai during several historical periods). Shanghai, 1956.

[192] Chou Kuo-ch'iang. Hui-i Shang-hai kung-jen ti san-tz'u wu-chuang ch'i-i (Memories of the three armed risings of the workers of Shanghai). Shanghai, 1957.

[193] Chu Hsin-fan. Chung-kuo tzu-pen-chu-i chih fa-chan (The rise of capitalism in China). Shanghai, 1929.

[194] Chu Pang-hsing and others. Shang-hai ch'an-yeh yü Shang-hai chih-kung (The industries of Shanghai and Shanghai's workers). Shanghai, 1939.

[195] Ch'üan Han-sheng. Chung-kuo hang-hui chih-tu shih (History of the guild system in China). Shanghai, 1934.

[196] Hsü Hsieh-hua. T'ieh-lu lao-kung wen-t'i (Labor problems on the railways). Peking, 1931.

[197] Hsü Shih-hua and others. Wu-sa yun-tung (The May 30th Movement). Peking, 1956.

[198] Hsü Wen-t'ien. Chung-kuo kung-jen yun-tung shih ch'u-kao (Preliminary outline of the history of the Chinese labor movement). Chungking, 1940.

[199] Hu Ch'iao-mu. Chung-kuo kung-ch'an-tang ti san-shih-nien (Thirty years of the Chinese Communist Party). Peking, 1951.

[200] Hu Hua. Chung-kuo ko-ming shih chiang-i (Explanation of the history of the Chinese revolution). Peking, 1959.

[201] Hua Kang. Wu-ssu yun-tung shih (History of the May 4th Movement). Peking, 1954.

[202] Huang I-po. Kuang-tung chi-ch'i kung-jen (The Kwangtung mechanics). Canton, 1928.

[203] I Pin. Hsiang-kang hai-yuan ta-pa-kung (The great strike of the Hong Kong seamen). Shanghai, 1955.

[204] Kung Chün. Chung-kuo hsin-kung-yeh fa-chan shih ta-kang (Short account of the development of modern industry in China). Shanghai, 1933.

[205] Lei Chia. Hai-yuan Chu Pao-t'ing (The seaman Chu Pao-t'ing). Peking, 1955.

[206] Li Jui. Mao Tse-tung t'ung-chih ti ch'u-ch'i ko-ming huo-tung (The early revolutionary activities of Comrade Mao Tse-tung). Peking, 1957.

[207] Li Shih-yueh. Hsin-hai ko-ming ch'ien-hou ti Chung-kuo kung-jen yun-tung ho Chung-hua min-kuo kung-tang (The Chinese labor movement at the time of the Revolution of 1911 and the Chinese Nationalist Labor Party). Shenyang, 1957.

[208] Liu Li-k'ai and Wang Cheng. 1919 chih 1927 nien ti Chung-kuo kung-jen yun-tung (The Chinese labor movement from 1919 to 1927). Peking, 1953.

[209] Ma Ch'ao-chün. Chung-kuo lao-tung yun-tung shih (History of the Chinese labor movement). Chungking, 1942.

[210] ——. *Chung-kuo lao-tung yun-tung shih* (History of the Chinese labor movement). 5 vols. Taipei, 1959.

[211] P'eng Ming. Chung-Su yu-i shih (History of Sino-Soviet friendship). Peking, 1957.

[212] T'ao Chü-yin. Pei-yang chün-fa t'ung-chih shih-ch'i shih-hua (History of the period of the Peiyang warlord government). 6 vols. Peking, 1958–59.

[213] Wang Lin. Po-chung: T'ien-chin kung-yun shih-hua (Seedtime: History of the labor movement in Tientsin). Tientsin, 1953.

[214] Wang Shih. Chung-kuo kung-ch'an-tang li-shih chien-pien (Short history of the Chinese Communist Party). Shanghai, 1959.

[215] Yang Shao-ying. Chung-kuo kung-jen ti pa-kung tou-cheng (Strikes and struggles of Chinese workers). Shanghai, 1957.

[216] [Ho-pei sheng min-cheng-t'ing.] Ho-pei ko-ming lieh-shih shih-liao (Historical material on the revolutionary martyrs of Hopeh). Vol. I: Paoting, 1959.

[217] Kung-jen yun-tung (The labor movement). Shanghai, 1927.

[218] [K'o-hsüeh-yuan li-shih yen-chiu ti-san-so.] Kuang-tung kung-jen pa-kung tou-cheng tzu-liao (Materials on the workers' strikes and struggles in Kwangtung). Peking, 1957.

[219] Kuang-hui-ti wu-ssu (The dazzling Fourth of May). Peking, 1959.

[220] Wu-sa yun-tung chung ti Shang-hai kung-jen (The workers of Shanghai during the May 30th Movement). Shanghai, 1957. Produced by the Committee for the Labor History of Shanghai. Mimeo.

[221] Chung-kuo ko-ming lieh-shih-chuan. (Chinese revolutionary martyrs). Hong Kong, 1948. (Many other editions.)

[222] [Ch'üan-kuo tsung-kung-hui.] Su Chao-cheng. N.p., 1930.

[223] [Chung-kung Hu-nan i-ch'uan-pu.] Hu-nan ko-ming lieh-shih-chuan (Revolutionary martyrs of Hunan). Changsha, 1952.

[224] *Chieh-fang jih-pao* (Liberation Daily), Shanghai. 9.x.56, Shen Yai-fu, "Lao-tung tsu-ho shu-chi-pu" (The Labor Secretariat); and 21–25.iii.57, "Shang-hai kung-jen san-tz'u wu-chuang ch'i-i ti chih-hui-pu: Shang-hai tsung-kung-hui" (The organization in control of the three armed risings of workers in Shanghai: the Shanghai General Union).

[225] *Chung-kuo kung-jen* (The Chinese Worker), Peking. 27.iii.57, Hsü Lo-te, "Liu Hua lieh-shih erh-san shih" (Some notes on the martyr Liu Hua); 27.iv.57, "Wei Chung-kuo kung-jen yun-tung tsao-lao ti ti-i-ko kung-ch'an-tang yuan" (The first member of the Communist Party to go to prison for the Chinese labor movement); and *ibid.*, Chia Chih, "Ko-ming lieh-shih Li Ta-chao chi-ko ku-shih" (Some anecdotes about the revolutionary martyr Li Ta-chao).

[226] *Fu-tan hsüeh-pao* (Journal of Futan University), Shanghai. 1952, No. 2, "Chung-kuo kung-jen chieh-chi pao-k'an ti ch'an-sheng ho ch'u-pu fa-chan" (the rise and early development of the Chinese labor press).

[227] *Kuang-ming jih-pao* (The Bright Daily), Peking. 18.x.54, Shao Ying, "Shih Yang lieh-shih yü Chung-kuo kung-jen yun-tung" (The martyr Shih Yang and the Chinese labor movement); and 12.v.55, Wang Hsün, "Wu-ssu yun-tung shen-ma-yang wei Chung-kuo kung-ch'an-tang ti ch'eng-li tso-le tsun-pei?" (How did the May Fourth Movement prepare the way for the founding of the Chinese Communist Party?).

[228] *Li-shih yen-chiu* (Historical Research), Peking. 1954, No. 2, Shao Hsün-cheng, "1905 nien ssu-yueh Chung-kuo kung-jen fan-k'ang ti-kuo-chu-i tzu-pen-chia ti tou-cheng" (The Chinese workers' struggle against imperialism and capitalism in April 1905); *ibid.*, Liu Yao-han, "E-kuo 1905 nien ko-ming tui Chung-kuo ti ying-hsiang" (The influence of the 1905 Russian revolution on China); 1955, No. 1, Li Shu, "1905 nien E-kuo ko-ming ho Chung-kuo" (The 1905 Russian revolution and China); 1956, No. 3, Hsü Sung-ling, "1924 nien Sun Chung-shan ti pei-fa yü Kuang-chou shang-t'uan shih-pien" (Sun Yat-sen's Northern Expedition of 1924 and the affair of the Kwangchow merchant guards); 1957, No. 5, Li Lung-mu, "Li Ta-chao t'ung-chih ho wu-ssu shih-ch'i Ma-k'o-ssu-chu-i ssu-hsiang ti hsüan-ch'uan" (Comrade Li Ta-chao and the propagation of Marxist ideas during the May 4th period); 1958, No. 2, Li Shu, "Shih-yueh ko-ming ho Chung-kuo kung-jen yun-tung" (The October Revolution and the Chinese labor movement); 1958, No. 3, Li Ming-jen, "1884 nien Hsiang-kang pa-kung yun-tung" (The Hong Kong strike of 1884); 1959, No. 2, Chao Ch'in, "Hsin-hai ko-ming ch'ien-hou ti Chung-kuo kung-jen yun-tung" (The Chinese labor movement at the time of the Revolution of 1911); 1959, No. 6, Liang Yü-k'uei, "Kuan-yü Chung-hua min-kuo kung-tang ti hsing-chih wen-t'i" (Concerning the character of the Chinese Nationalist Labor Party).

Books and Articles in Western Languages

[229] T. N. Akatova. S'angan-Guanchzhouskaya (Gonkong-kantonskaya) zabastovka (The Canton–Hong Kong strike). Moscow, 1959.

[230] G. C. Allen and A. Donnithorne. Western Enterprise in Far Eastern Economic Development. London, 1954.

[231] J. O. P. Bland. China; The Pity of It. London, 1932.

[232] Judith Blick. "The Chinese Labor Corps in World War I," in Papers on China. Issued by the East Asia Regional Studies Seminar, Harvard Univ. Vol. 9 (1955), 111–46.

[233] K. Bloch. German Interests and Policies in the Far East. New York, 1939.

[234] C. Brandt. Stalin's Failure in China. Cambridge, Mass., 1958.

[235] E. Carlson. The Kailan Mines, 1878–1912. Cambridge, Mass., 1957.

[236] Chang Chung-li. The Chinese Gentry. Seattle, 1955.

[237] Ch'en Po-ta. A Study of Land Rent in Pre-liberation China. Peking, 1958.

[238] Ch'en Ta. Chinese Migrations with Special Reference to Labor Conditions. Washington, D.C., 1923.

[239] J. Chesneaux. Sun Yat-sen. Paris, 1959.

[240] ———. "Le phénomène du militarisme chinois en Chine au lendemain de la Grande Guerre." Contribution to the Eighth Annual Conference of Junior Sinologues, Leiden, 1955. Unpublished.

[241] ———. "Aspects économiques et politiques de la crise de l'industrie cotonnière chinoise au lendemain de la Grande Guerre." Contribution to the Congrès des Sciences Historiques, Rome, 1955. Unpublished.

[242] Chow Tse-tsung. The May Fourth Movement. Cambridge, Mass., 1960.

[243] W. Collins. Mineral Enterprise in China. London, 1918.

[244] H. Doré. Recherches sur les superstitions populaires en Chine. 15 vols. Peking, 1911.

[245] W. Eberhard. Chinese Festivals. London, 1958.

[246] G. B. Endacott. A History of Hong-kong. London, 1958.

[247] I. Epstein. Labor Problems in Nationalist China. New York, 1949.

[248] J. K. Fairbank. Trade and Diplomacy on the China Coast. Cambridge, Mass., 1953.

[249] Fang Fu-an. Chinese Labor. London, 1931.

[250] Fei Hsiao-tung. China's Gentry. Chicago, 1955.

[251] A. Feuerwerker. China's Early Industrialization: Sheng Hsuan-huai and Mandarin Enterprise. Cambridge, Mass., 1958.

[252] H. D. Fong. Cotton Industry and Trade in China. 2 vols. Tientsin, 1932. Nankai University Industry Series No. 4.

[253] ———. Industrial Organisation in China. Tientsin, 1937. Nankai University Industry Series No. 10.

[254] ———. Industrial Capital in China. Tientsin, 1956. Nankai University Industry Series No. 9.

[255] ———. Rural Industries in China. Tientsin, 1933. Nankai University Industry Series No. 5.

[256] R. A. D. Forrest. The Chinese Language. London, 1926.

[257] R. Gilbert. What is Wrong with China? London, 1926.

[258] E. Hinder. Social and Industrial Problems of Shanghai. New York, 1942. Mimeo.

[259] Ho Kan-chih. A History of the Chinese Modern Revolution. Peking, 1959. Trans. from the Chinese.

[260] F. Ho and H. D. Fong. Extent and Effects of Industrialization in China. Tientsin, 1929.

[260a] Arthur N. Holcombe. The Chinese Revolution: A Phase in the Regeneration of a World Power. Cambridge, Mass., 1930.

[261] F. Houn. Central Government in China: An Institutional Study. Madison, Wisc., 1957.

[262] Hu Sheng. Imperialism and Chinese Politics, Peking, 1952. Trans. from the Chinese.

[263] H. Isaacs. The Tragedy of the Chinese Revolution. Rev. ed., Stanford, Calif., 1951.

[264] E. Kann. Currency in China. Shanghai, 1926.

[265] Kiang Wen-han. The Chinese Student Movement. New York, 1948.

[266] A. Kotenev. New Lamps for Old. Shanghai, 1931.

[267] J. D. H. Lamb. Development of the Agrarian Movement and Agrarian Legislation in China, 1912–1930. Peking, 1931.

[268] ——. Origin and Development of Social Legislation in China. Peking, 1930.

[269] H. D. Lamson. Social Pathology in China. Shanghai, 1935.

[270] O. Lang. Chinese Family and Society. New Haven, 1946.

[271] O. Lattimore. Inner Asian Frontiers of China. New York, 1940. American Geographical Society Research Series No. 21.

[272] J. Leclerc. Vie du Père Lebbe. Paris, 1955.

[273] A. F. Legendre. La civilisation chinoise moderne. Paris, 1926.

[274] W. Levi. Modern China's Foreign Policy. Minneapolis, 1954.

[275] M. J. Levy. The Family Revolution in Modern China. Cambridge, Mass., 1949.

[276] M. J. Levy and Shih Kuo-heng. The Rise of the Chinese Modern Business Class. New York, 1949. Mimeo.

[277] Li Chien-nung. The Political History of China, 1840–1928. Trans. from the Chinese by Ssu-yü Teng and Jeremy Ingalls. Princeton, N.J., 1956.

[278] D. K. Lieu. China's Industries and Finances. Peking, 1927.

[279] ——. (Lieou Ta-kiun). The Silk Reeling Industry in Shanghai. Shanghai, 1933.

[280] ——. The Growth and Industrialisation of Shanghai. Shanghai, 1936.

[281] Lin Shu-shen. Histoire du journalisme en Chine. Avesnes, 1937.

[282] Lo Ren-yen. China's Revolution from the Inside. New York, 1930.

[283] Lou Yee-wen. Les oeuvres sociales dans les chemins de fer chinois. Paris, 1937.

[284] Lowe Chuan-hua. Facing Labor Issues in China. Shanghai, 1933.

[285] A. Lozowski [A. Lozovsky]. Revolution und Konterrevolution in China. Berlin, 1928. Issued by the Red International of Trade Unions.

[286] Lu Hsün. Selected Works. Peking, 1956– .

[287] W. H. Mallory. China, Land of Famine. New York, 1926.

[288] Shigeharu Matsumoto. The Historical Development of Chinese Boycotts, 1834–1925. Tokyo, 1933.

[289] C. B. Maybon and J. Fredet. Histoire de la concession française de Changhai. Paris, 1929.

[290] P. Mif. Pour une Chine forte et libre. Paris, 1936.

[291] K. Mitchell. Industrialization of the Western Pacific. New York, 1942.

[292] H. B. Morse. The Guilds of China. London, 1932.

[293] H. B. Morse and H. F. McNair. Far Eastern International Relations. Boston, 1931.

[294] R. Murphey. Shanghai: Key to Modern China. Cambridge, Mass., 1953.

[295] A. Nagano. Development of Capitalism in China. Tokyo, 1931.

[296] Nanming I Liu. La population chinoise. Geneva, 1935.

[297] M. Perleberg. Who's Who in Modern China. Hong Kong, 1954.

[298] V. Purcell. The Chinese in South-East Asia. London, 1951.

[299] C. F. Remer. Foreign Investment in China. New York, 1933.

[300] K. Saito. La protection ouvrière au Japon. Paris, 1900.

[301] B. Schwartz. Chinese Communism and the Rise of Mao. Cambridge, Mass., 1952.

[301a] J. Sheridan. Chinese Warlord: The Career of Feng Yü-hsiang. Stanford, Calif., 1966.

[302] E. Snow. Red Star over China. London, 1942. (Many other editions.)

[303] Soong Ching-ling. The Struggle for New China. Peking, 1952.

[304] A. L. Strong. China's Millions. New York, 1928.

[305] E-tu Zen Sun. Chinese Railways and British Interests. New York, 1954.

[306] Tang Leang-li. Inner History of the Chinese Revolution. London, 1930.

[307] S. Y. Teng and J. K. Fairbank. China's Response to the West. Cambridge, Mass., 1954.

[308] V. Thompson. Labor Problems in South-East Asia. New Haven, 1947.

[309] Tsing Tung-chun. La production et le commerce de la soie en Chine. Lyon, 1928.

[310] P. A. Varg. Missionaries, Chinese, and Diplomats: The American Protestant Missionary Movement in China, 1890–1952. Princeton, N.J., 1958.

[311] A. Wagner. Labor Legislation in China. Peiping, 1938.

[312] N. Wales. The Chinese Labor Movement. New York, 1945.

[313] Wang Simine. Le travail des femmes et des enfants en Chine. Paris, 1933.

[314] A. S. Whiting. Soviet Policies in China, 1917–1924. New York, 1954.

[315] W. W. Willoughby. *Foreign Rights and Interests in China.* 2 vols. Baltimore, 1927.

[316] ——. China at the Conference. Baltimore, 1922.

[317] Wou Monpeng [Wu Meng-pen]. L'évolution des corporations ouvrières en Chine. Paris, 1931.

[318] S. Wright. *China's Struggle for Tariff Autonomy.* Shanghai, 1938.

[319] *Annales: Economie, Sociétés, Civilisations,* Paris. July 1954, J. Ches-

neaux, "Les transformations de la société urbaine chinoise au lendemain de la Grande Guerre."

[320] *Annals of the American Academy of Political Science,* New York. Vol. 152 (1930), D. Orchard, "China's Use of the Boycott as a Political Weapon."

[321] *Journal of Asian Studies,* New York. Aug. 1957, L. Orléans, "The Chinese 1953 Census."

[322] *Pacific Affairs,* New York. Oct. 1929, Chen Han-seng, "The Burdens of the Chinese Peasantry."

[323] *Problemy Vostokovedeniya,* Moscow. 1960, No. 2, A. T. Kartunova, "Deiatel'nost' shankhaiskogo soveta profsoiuzov v iiune-avguste 1925 g." (The activity of the Shanghai General Union in June–August 1925).

[324] *Revue Historique,* Paris. Oct. 1956, O. Merlat, "En marge de l'expédition du Tonkin: les émeutes de Ouen-tcheou et de Hong-kong" (The Wenchow and Hong Kong riots at the time of the Tonkin expedition).

[325] *Sovetskoe Kitaevedenie,* Moscow. 1958, No. 3, L. A. Bereznii, "Geroicheskoe vostanie shankhaiskogo proletaryata v marte 1927 g." (The heroic rising of the Shanghai proletariat in March 1927).

[326] *Voprosi Istorii,* Moscow. 1952, No. 10, N. P. Vinogradov, "Rabochie dvizhenie v Kitae nakanune obrazovaniya edinogo natsional'nogo antiimperialisticheskogo fronta, 1922–1923" (The Chinese working class just before the formation of the united national anti-imperialist front of 1922–23).

Index

Index

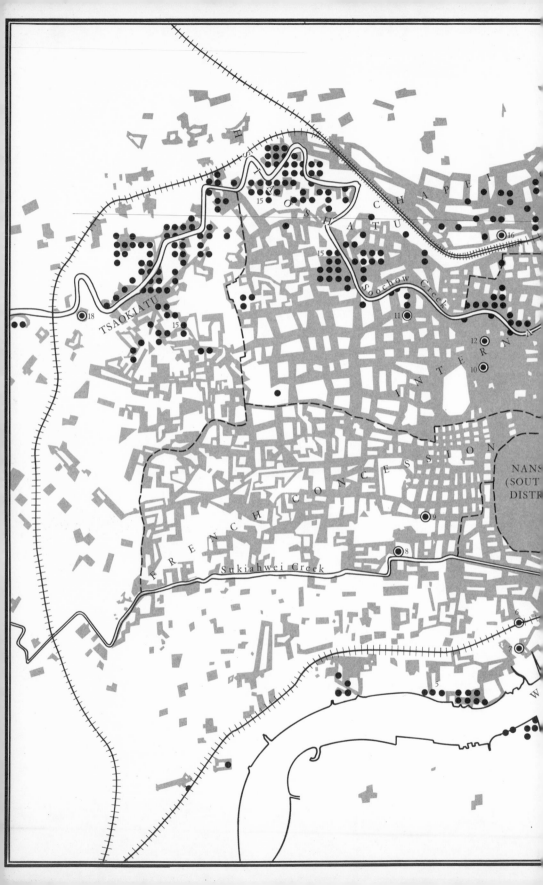